PREFACE

Owners and managers of hospitality operations of every type and size must secure a wide range of quality products and services to meet the needs of their customers. This requires the use of a broad array of procurement principles that begins with determining customer needs and continues through product acquisition, product use, the conclusion of a contracted service, or the end of the useful life of an equipment item. It's very easy to state the primary objectives of the process required to obtain these products and services: "Purchase the *right* products and services at the *right* price, in the *right* amount, and at the *right* quantity and *right* time, from the *right* supplier or service provider." It is, however, much more difficult to attain these objectives, especially because they must be accomplished simultaneously with multiple vendors providing numerous products and services.

This book, *Procurement of Hospitality Resources*, presented an exceptional planning challenge in its early developmental stages because the authors recognized that the subject matter required to address all aspects of the topic was so extensive. This book considers basic topics important to understanding the management of the purchasing process, and it presents information helpful in developing quality descriptions (specifications) for commonly purchased resources. However, it also addresses the broader topic of procurement (the entire process of acquiring and evaluating goods and services). Its scope identifies information important in the purchase of products and services used by foodservice and lodging properties, and global procurement concerns, among other specialized topics.

The premise of this book rests on the concept that hospitality buyers must work closely with their suppliers to enable both parties to obtain added value in their relationship. This is significantly different from a historical (traditional) perspective that focuses on the buyer "winning" (obtaining the lowest possible price) to the detriment of the seller (who must "lose" a financial incentive to participate in the relationship).

Price is, of course, an important factor in any procurement decision. However, so is quality. Therefore, value (the relationship between price and quality) is typically a better focus during purchase decision-making tasks than is price or quality alone. The concept of value is an integral element in discussions throughout the book, as is the service and information that buyers must consider as purchase decisions are made.

Technology has evolved to the point that many aspects of the procurement process can be, and increasingly are, automated. Details about procurement technology are discussed throughout the book. However, purchasers still require a foundation of knowledge along with experience and decision-making skills because the entire procurement task simply cannot be "delegated" to automated alternatives. This book addresses the concepts required for this critical hospitality-specific knowledge base.

FOCUS ON THE READERS

This book has been carefully written for the students and faculty in postsecondary hospitality management programs and for practicing hospitality managers. Fortunately, basic procurement principles remain the same in all types of hospitality operations such as hotels and restaurants in the commercial segment and non-commercial operations including private clubs, and healthcare and educational facilities.

HOSPITALITY STUDENTS

The information in this book is important to students interested in specific types of hospitality operations and for their counterparts who may be less certain about where their career paths will lead. As a result, examples of major concepts presented throughout the text address a variety of hospitality settings. This helps maintain the interest of readers with specific career goals and allows readers to learn how specific concepts apply to their areas of interest.

Today's students will be tomorrow's managers. The careers of some readers may lead to full-time procurement-related positions. However, it is much more likely that those working in various management positions will be required to purchase products as one responsibility of their job, or that they will interact with a purchaser who completes the procurement task. In both situations, it is necessary to ensure that the "right" objectives posed above are attained. This book clearly explains how this can be done.

HOSPITALITY FACULTY

Instructors want their students to have access to the very best learning resources. Their definition of "best" relates to contemporary and accurate content, use of relevant examples and anecdotes, chapter elements that help to maintain their students' interests, and a focused attention on what students must learn to have a practical foundation of procurement knowledge. This book addresses all of these concerns.

SUPPLEMENTAL MATERIALS FOR STUDENTS AND FACULTY

Instructors and students will find that a variety of supplemental materials are available to assist in learning the concepts discussed throughout this text and are available on our Instructor's Resource Center at URL www.pearsonhighered.com

HOSPITALITY MANAGERS

Many hospitality industry professionals are involved in ongoing professional development programs because they understand that they don't stop learning when they complete their formal education. Those interested in updates about hospitality procurement can obtain current information from this reference. A review of this information can have a twofold purpose:

- To provide general information helpful in career advancement and professional development programs.
- To help resolve specific procurement challenges as they arise. Review of this book's content may present unconsidered alternatives to existing procedures that may better address specific purchasing concerns within an operation.

ORGANIZATION OF THE BOOK

There are three basic ways to organize a hospitality procurement text: emphasis on basic procurement management procedures, focus on details about the products and services that are purchased, or information about both of these dimensions. This book uses the last alternative. It becomes increasingly easy to defend this approach given (1) that basic purchasing procedures are all that are really necessary for many hospitality operations, and they are a prerequisite for the more sophisticated procedures used by (almost exclusively) large and multi-unit organizations, and (2) the extensive amount of information about specific products and services available on the Web sites of applicable manufacturers, growers, producers, and service providers.

PROCUREMENT OF HOSPITALITY RESOURCES

Jack D. Ninemeier
The School of Hospitality Management
Michigan State University

David K. Hayes
Panda Pros Hospitality Management and Training
Okemos, Michigan

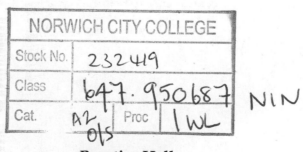
Prentice Hall
Upper Saddle River, New Jersey 07458

Library of Congress Cataloging-in-Publication Data

Ninemeier, Jack D.
  Procurement of hospitality resources / Jack D. Ninemeier, David K. Hayes.
    p. cm.
  ISBN-13: 978-0-13-514841-9
  ISBN-10: 0-13-514841-3
  1. Hospitality industry—Purchasing.   2. Hospitality industry—Management.
  3. Food service purchasing—United States. I. Hayes, David K. II. Title.
  TX911.3.P8N56 2009
  647.94'068—dc22

                                                          2008055776

Editor in Chief: Vernon Anthony
Acquisitions Editor: William Lawrensen
Editorial Assistant: Lara Dimmick
Production Manager: Wanda Rockwell
Creative Director: Jayne Conte
Cover Designer: Bruce Kenselaar
Cover photo: Getty Images Inc.
Director, Image Resource Center: Melinda Patelli
Manager, Rights and Permissions: Zina Arabia
Manager Visual Research: Beth Brenzel
Manager, Cover Visual Research and Permissions: Karen Sanatar
Image Permission Coordinator: Ang'John Ferreri
Director of Marketing: David Gesell
Campaign Marketing Manager: Leigh Ann Sims
Curriculum Marketing Manager: Thomas Hayward
Marketing Assistant: Les Roberts

This book was set in Palatino by Aptara®, Inc. and was printed and bound by Bindrite Graphics. The cover was printed by Demand Production Center.

Pearson Education Ltd., London
Pearson Education Singapore Pte. Ltd.
Pearson Education Canada, Inc.
Pearson Education—Japan

Pearson Education Australia Pty. Limited
Pearson Education North Asia Ltd., Hong Kong
Pearson Educación de Mexico, S.A. de C.V.
Pearson Education Malaysia Pte. Ltd

Prentice Hall
is an imprint of

PEARSON

www.pearsonhighered.com

10 9 8 7 6 5 4 3 2
ISBN-13: 978-0-13-514841-9
ISBN-10:   0-13-514841-3

The book is divided into five major parts. *Part One: Foundations of Procurement* provides background information about the scope and organization of procurement, as well as the flow of products through various distribution channels. This part also examines legal and ethical concerns applicable to procurement.

Part Two: Management of the Procurement Process addresses the management of purchasing using a procurement model (process). It begins with a definition of product or service needs and a consideration about whether they should be supplied by the organization's own employees or, alternatively, whether they should be outsourced. Successive chapters in this section address other components of the procurement process, including how to determine quality requirements (specifications), decision making regarding quantities needed, and essential cost/price issues. Other chapters in this part of the book address negotiation, supplier selection and relations, ordering tasks, receiving/storing, accounting, bill payment, and follow-up.

Part Three: Quality Considerations in Food and Beverage Product Purchasing contains five chapters that detail quality considerations for many of the products and services typically purchased for use in food and beverage operations. Web site addresses that provide additional, and in many cases even more detailed, information about these hospitality-industry-specific products are also provided in this important part of the book.

Part Four: Quality Considerations in Other Hospitality Purchases presents chapters applicable to the purchase of other industry products and services, including hotel supplies, services, capital equipment, and technology products and services. This section makes the book unique because traditional hospitality purchasing texts do not include specific and detailed information related to purchasing for the lodging segment of the hospitality industry.

Part Five: Global Procurement and Procurement System Evaluation concludes the book as it examines global aspects of purchasing (how do managers in international locations obtain the products and services they require?) and presents key principles of procurement system evaluation and improvement.

Taken together, the information presented in this book provides a background of critical information that can be modified as necessary to enable hospitality students to learn about procurement activities and to give hospitality managers the tools they need to develop specific procurement procedures for use in their own operations.

ORGANIZATION OF CHAPTERS

Each chapter includes several basic elements to keep readers interested:

- *Overview ("In This Chapter").*   An executive summary providing a concise preview of each chapter's contents.
- *Chapter Outline.*   Details about the breadth and depth of topic coverage within the chapter that shows the context within which specific information is presented and makes finding key information easy.
- *Key Purchasing Terms.*   Definitions of hospitality- and procurement-related terms that add to the readers' vocabulary skills, and allow them to understand the "jargon" of the industry and thus become more effective communicators.
- *Figures.*   Graphics, charts, and data sets that expand on topic details, and/or show relationships between important concepts.
- *Internet Purchasing Assistant.*   Web sites that provide additional information about specific topics presented throughout the chapter.
- *Purchasing Pros Need to Know.*   Complementary and anecdotal topical information applicable to chapter content.
- *The Supplier's Side.*   A close look at selected chapter topics from a supplier's perspective. This insight allows readers to learn supplier viewpoints that can be useful in understanding and improving the buyer–supplier "partnership."

- *On-the-Job Challenges in Purchasing.* "Mini-case" studies that review common situations hospitality buyers will likely encounter at work. Each case study poses questions that allow readers to apply information learned in the chapter to "real-world" work situations.
- *Photos.* Illustrations directly applicable to chapter contents. These are placed to help retain readers' interest in the topic, and to provide complements to the verbal discussions.
- *High-Tech Purchasing.* Specific information about advanced technology and its application to one or more specific aspects of the chapter. This detailed discussion is in addition to other information about technology presented throughout the text.
- *Purchasing Resources on the Internet.* Numerous Web site addresses that enable readers to learn even more about each chapter's topics.
- *Key Terms.* Chronological list of key purchasing terms defined throughout the chapter.
- *Think It Through.* Questions about important chapter concepts that allow readers to consider the "best" approaches from management's perspective as well as to critically consider their own values, beliefs, and attitudes about what they have learned.
- *Team Fun.* Mini-case projects that can be addressed by teams of class members.

NOTES OF APPRECIATION AND SOME FINAL THOUGHTS

The authors wish to thank Vernon Anthony, editor in chief, and William Lawrensen, senior editor, for their assistance with developmental aspects of this project. We would also like to acknowledge and genuinely thank the following persons for their assistance as a draft manuscript was turned into a professional document to which we are proud to attach our names: Linda Cupp, Lara Dimmick, Kris Roach, Wanda Rockwell, and Alex Wolf.

We would also like to extend a special "Thank You" to the following talented individuals who provided input to those experts by reviewing draft versions of the chapters of this book: Julie A. Doyle, Ferris State University; Elizabeth F. Reutter, University of Illinois at Urbana; and Kevin R. Roberts, Kansas State University.

Dr. A. J. Singh, Associate Professor, The School of Hospitality Business at Michigan State University, authored Chapter 22 (Purchasing in the Global Marketplace), and we thank him for his insightful efforts. His extensive international hospitality experience brings a dimension to the discussion of global procurement concerns that is unavailable elsewhere. This chapter should be of interest to all hospitality students beginning careers in an industry that, literally, serves the entire world.

The authors also sought the advice of several procurement professionals as they researched the content for this book. Mr. Steve Handy, Subway Restaurants franchisee in Hilo, Hawaii, made significant contributions to Chapter 2 (Product Flow through the Marketplace), and Mr. Stephen Marquard, account manager, American Restaurant Supply, Kailua-Kona, Hawaii, provided wise counsel for numerous "Supplier's Side" elements and served as a contributing author for Chapter 8 (Supplier Sourcing and Relations). Also, thanks go to Dave Segoula, Michigan regional director, Clark Foodservice, and to Allisha Miller, Panda Pros Hospitality Management and Training, for her insight and review of Chapter 18 (Procurement for Lodging Facilities) and Chapter 21 (Procurement of Technology-Related Products and Services).

A very special thanks for their contributions, including complimentary use of one-of-a-kind photos and insightful guidance, go to the gracious and generous professionals at Real Resorts, especially Beat Müller, gerente general (general manager) of The Royal Playa Del Carmen; Monica Roberts, corporate operations manager; and Fernando Garcia, president of Real Resorts & Best Day Travel. One of their many beautiful Mexican resorts is the setting for several of the unique photos presented in this text.

As always, our wives, Peggy Hayes and Leilani Sill Ninemeier, helped us at every stage of the planning for and writing of this book, and it could not have been published without their assistance. We also thank other family members and friends for their encouragement along the way.

DEDICATION

This book is dedicated to Lendal H. Kotschevar, Ph.D.

Professor Kotschevar's name would be included on anyone's list of the all-time most influential persons in the hospitality management academy. He may be the most prolific of all hospitality textbook authors over a career that extended throughout many decades. In fact, he authored the purchasing text used by both of the present authors many years ago when they were undergraduates embarking on their own study of hospitality management. Professor Kotschevar passed away in January 2007, at 98 years of age. Interestingly (but not surprisingly!), he authored several books while in his 90s, each of which is in use in hospitality programs around the world today. It is to his memory and lifelong commitment to hospitality education that we dedicate this text.

CONTENTS

1

The Scope of Procurement

In This Chapter

A significant percentage of the total revenue generated by hospitality organizations is used to procure the products, supplies, services, and equipment required to prepare the menu items and provide the services that customers desire. What exactly must be purchased? How, if at all, can purchasing costs be minimized while still providing consumer value? Addressing these two questions is at the center of the purchasing challenge for hospitality buyers. Some managers with purchasing responsibilities try to identify and work with the "cheapest" suppliers, and they encourage employees to reduce costs without all-inclusive concerns about customer satisfaction. Professional purchasers, however, use a much more comprehensive, planned, and coordinated approach to determine their purchasing needs as dictated by customer satisfaction concerns. These buyers identify and purchase needed items from the best sources using methods that ensure costs are minimized without sacrificing their customer-driven focus. To do so requires an extensive knowledge about a wide array of topics, all of which are the subjects of this book.

This chapter begins our study of procurement by reviewing the broadly diverse hospitality industry, and the many types of organizations that are part of it, to set the context for our study of the topic. Then we'll address basic concerns: What is procurement? Why is it important? What are the objectives of an effective procurement process? As these and related questions are answered, a foundation for detailed explanations of the many topics discussed in this book will be better established.

Next, you'll learn about the basic steps in the procurement process. This discussion will provide a preview of later chapters in this book that detail policies and procedures for each purchasing step.

Numerous internal factors affect procurement needs and procedures. Many of these factors are within the control of proactive purchasing managers, and will be explored. Other, external factors are beyond the ability of the purchasers to control but certainly within their responsibility to address. This chapter reviews some of the most important factors.

Who performs purchasing tasks in hospitality operations, and what must they do as they perform their duties? We'll examine the roles, responsibilities, and specific tasks of those at different organizational levels with purchasing responsibilities.

Purchasing, like all other hospitality management and operational functions, is in the process of change. What are the current and likely future roles of purchasing managers as they work to meet the needs of hospitality organizations and those whom they serve? This chapter concludes with a discussion of this topic.

■ ■ ■

Outline

Hospitality Industry Overview
What Is Procurement?
    Definitions
    Importance of Procurement

HOSPITALITY INDUSTRY OVERVIEW

Hospitality organizations provide specialized products and services that are desired by some, and required by other, segments of the markets they serve. They are part of the broad **travel and tourism industry**, which is described in Figure 1.1.

Our study relates to one dimension of this industry, the **hospitality industry**. A wide range of organizations comprise it, and Figure 1.2 provides an overview of many of them.

Basic management principles and procedures, including those for purchasing, remain constant in all types of travel, tourism, and hospitality organizations (and, for that matter, in most other types of businesses). This book addresses this broad "how to purchase" overview. However, purchasing policies and procedures are influenced by several factors, including:

- *Ownership (independent operator or chain).*   **Independent operators** who own their own restaurant or hotel, for example, can elect to purchase (or not purchase) any product or service they wish because they determine the business needs of their organization. By contrast, **chain** organizations typically want to offer many of the same products and services in each property. These items must, therefore, be available to ensure the consistency that many

---

Key Terms

Travel and tourism industry   All businesses that cater to the needs of the traveling public.

Hospitality industry   Organizations that provide lodging, foodservices, and/or other accommodations for people away from their homes.

Independent operator   An entrepreneur who owns or operates one or a very few hospitality properties.

Chain   A multi-unit hospitality organization.

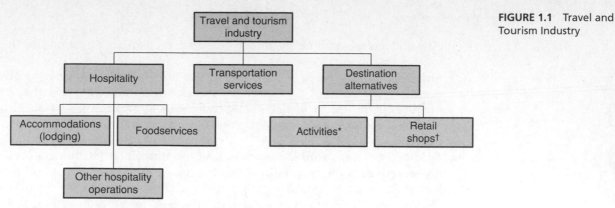

FIGURE 1.1 Travel and Tourism Industry

*Including sporting and cultural events, recreation, and geographic tours
†Including stores, markets, and shopping malls

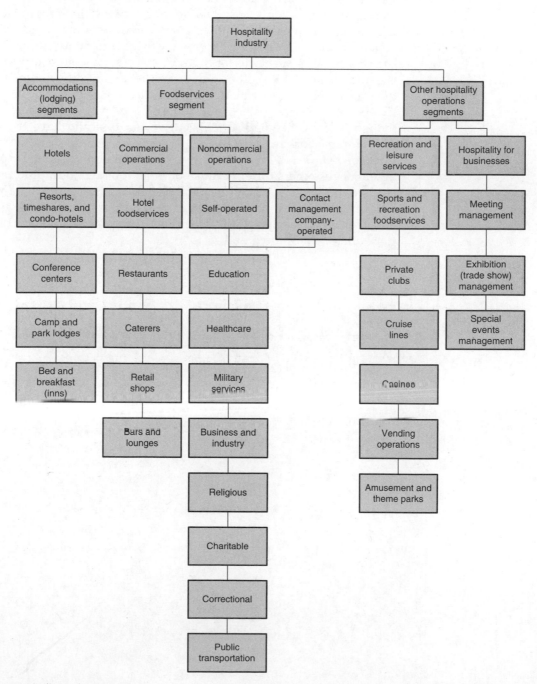

FIGURE 1.2 Hospitality Industry

customers want (and the reason why they select chain organizations for their lodging or foodservice visits).

- *Franchise affiliation, if any.*   **Franchisees** are typically required to offer products and services that meet the **franchisor's** standards, and they are often not permitted to offer customer choices not approved by the franchisor. For these reasons, many products and services represent nondiscretionary purchases.

- *Volume of organization's business.*   As the number of customers served and **revenues** of the hospitality operation increase, more products and services must be purchased. Larger quantity needs permit a wider variety of purchasing options because of increased suppliers' interests in selling to the organization.

- *Public sector* or *private sector.*   Organizations operated by the government, including schools, hospitals, and military installations, must typically follow rigid purchasing requirements. These are very standardized and "open" for public inspection and review by governmental authorities to ensure that monies spent are for society's benefit. By contrast, purchasers in restaurants, hotels, and other properties that are privately owned (those in the private sector) are primarily accountable to their organization's owners. Except in the largest of hospitality businesses, purchasing procedures, although business-like and formalized, do not typically have the extensive control framework required by their public-sector counterparts.

- *Consumer market.*   Products and services desired or needed by present or potential customers differ because of numerous **demographic factors,** including income, age, and education. Factors such as purpose of visit (to a hotel or restaurant) and frequency of visit (such as by students at a dining hall in an educational facility) also influence the variety of items or services to be offered (and purchased).

Key Terms

Franchise   An arrangement in which one party (the franchisor) allows another party (owners of the hospitality organization) to use its logo, common name, systems, and resources in exchange for a fee.

Franchisee   Those who own (or lease) the property and building and buy the right to use a franchisor's brand name for a fixed period of time and at an agreed-upon price; they typically pay royalties and contribute to regional and/or national advertising programs.

Franchisor   One who owns and manages the brand and sells the right to use it to franchisees.

Revenue   The amount of money generated from the sale of products and services to the customers of a hospitality organization.

Public sector   Hospitality services operated by government entities such as schools, hospitals, and military installations.

Private sector   Organizations with private ownership that are not controlled by the government.

Consumer market   The specific group of consumers for whom the products and services of the hospitality organization are provided.

Demographic factors   Factors such as age, marital status, gender, ethnicity, and occupation that can help to describe a person.

Internet Purchasing Assistant (1.1)

Because purchasing is an important topic, it enjoys significant coverage in hospitality literature. To review current articles about numerous aspects of purchasing, including technology applications in the hotel industry, go to Hotel-Online: www.hotel-online.com

At the home page, type "hotel purchasing" in the site's search box.

WHAT IS PROCUREMENT?

This book presents a comprehensive study of **procurement,** and a good starting place is at the beginning: What is procurement, and why is it important?

Definitions

Many hospitality managers use the terms *procurement* and **purchasing** interchangeably, and we will also do so throughout this book. However, technically, the terms have different meanings. Procurement involves a much more comprehensive scope of activities than does **purchasing** because it relates to the entire process of acquiring and evaluating goods and services needed by the organization. It begins as the buyer initially determines needs, and the process doesn't end until after products are used or contracted services have been rendered, or until the useful life of a **capital equipment** item has ended. There is also a significant emphasis on supplier involvement and interaction in efforts to provide greater value. By contrast, purchasing relates to the more repetitive, procedural, and clerical aspects of buying. These are the aspects of procurement that include determining purchase quantities or service requirements, placing an order, and paying a supplier after an order or service is received. Hospitality managers and readers of this book should consider the broad spectrum of procurement tasks regardless of the name that they attach to it, and this book will do so as it explains the many dimensions of the discipline.

Importance of Procurement

Those with procurement responsibilities have two primary concerns: identify and secure the products and services that best allow the organization to meet the wants and needs of its customers, and obtain them at a fair price. Effective procurement is critical for the success of any hospitality organization.

The purchasing process is never-ending. Identification of products and services for customers is ongoing because customer preferences change, and new

Key Terms

Procurement   The process of acquiring and evaluating goods and services, beginning with determining needs through product use and until the end of the contracted service or useful life of a capital equipment item.

Purchasing   The process of buying: placing an order, receiving a product or service, and paying the supplier.

Capital equipment   Equipment of material value with a life-expectancy of more than one year which is depreciated in the organization's accounting system.

Ingredients for all the menu items on this buffet line must be purchased.

Courtesy of Real Resorts

product and service alternatives are continually introduced in the marketplace. The management of prices paid for products and services received requires ongoing attention, and purchasers must continually research the marketplace and its suppliers, revise purchasing tools and procedures, and evaluate the success of their procurement efforts. As will be seen later in this chapter, purchasing personnel play an expanded role in some organizations because they provide input to

---

PURCHASING PROS NEED TO KNOW (1.1)

How important is effective purchasing? Although this question can be answered from several perspectives, let's think about money! Here are some industry statistics that quantify the economic affect of purchasing on a hospitality operation:

- Total food and beverage costs in a **full-service hotel**[*]   25.1% of total food and beverage revenues
- Total food and beverage costs in a 250-seat restaurant[**]   34.7% of total restaurant revenues

As seen above, 25.1% and 34.7%, respectively, of the total revenues generated by a hotel's food and beverage operation and by a restaurant are used to purchase the food and beverage products required to generate that revenue. In addition, linens, table service items, dishwashing and other cleaning chemicals, disposable goods, small wares and capital equipment items, uniforms, services, and numerous other items and services are required to enable the hotel or restaurant to meet the foodservice needs of the customers. In addition, hotels must purchase a wide range of guest room **FF&E,** supplies, services, and other needs as well as numerous capital equipment items for public and nonpublic areas throughout the property. The ability of purchasers to obtain the products and services needed by their organizations at costs representing a value to their employers has a significant financial affect on the hospitality operation!

[*]*Source: Trends*. 2006. San Francisco, CA: PKF Consulting.

[**]*Source: Restaurant Industry Operations Report 2006/2007*. Washington, DC: National Restaurant Association.

Key Terms

Full-service hotel   A hotel that provides guests with extensive food and beverage products and services.

FF&E   Abbreviation for "Furniture, Fixtures, and Equipment."

Internet Purchasing Assistant (1.2)

Many organizations offer purchasing and inventory management technology alternatives for hospitality operations. To view the Web site of one of these companies, and to learn about the systems that it makes available, go to the Eatec Web site: www.eatec.com.

When you reach the site, click on the hospitality market in which you are interested: restaurant chains, hotels, resorts, casinos, cruise lines, stadiums, arenas, convention centers, racetracks, foodservice management, theme parks and attractions, universities and K–12 schools, and/or airline catering.

strategic planning and to the organization's staffing needs as outsourcing decisions are made.

OBJECTIVES OF EFFECTIVE PROCUREMENT

The primary objectives of effective procurement are simple to state and shown in Figure 1.3: Obtain the *right* product or service at the *right* price from the *right* source in the *right* quantity at the *right* time. Unfortunately, the attainment of these objectives is much more difficult to accomplish than it is to simply write them down or read them.

As you review Figure 1.3, note that each of the procurement objectives noted earlier (right product, source, price, quantity, and time) is identified. Benefits accrue to both the customers and hospitality operation as each objective is achieved. Interactions between the organization and its customers help to identify changes needed in the products or services offered. Modifications to internal operating procedures may also influence how products and services are offered. These changes can lead to revised purchasing objectives, and the process is cyclical.

Purchasing objectives are important business considerations. They provide the foundation for our discussion of the purchasing process that will evolve throughout this book. However, these objectives are also important in daily operations because they establish expectations (what should purchasing staff do?). They also provide the framework within which the success of purchasing can be evaluated. Evaluation of the extent to which purchasing objectives are attained is the topic of Chapter 23.

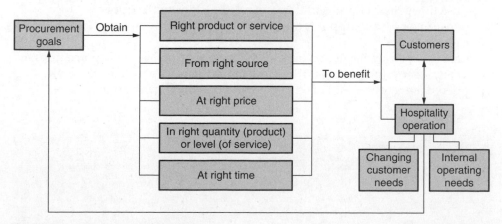

FIGURE 1.3 Procurement Objectives

Purchasers must ensure that cleaning supplies and tools are available to keep the hotel cleaned.

Shannon Fagan/Getty Images, Inc.-Taxi

Examples of activities that relate to attaining broader procurement objectives can include:

- Analyzing the organization's specific needs for products and services, and researching the marketplace to identify the best sources for them.
- Participating in decisions relating to products that should be produced and services that should be provided by the organization's employees versus those that should be secured from external suppliers.
- Determining ways that suppliers can provide increased value in the products and services they sell to the organization.
- Researching nontraditional purchasing methodologies to minimize organizational investments and maximize product availability when they are needed.
- Considering how technology can improve the organization's purchasing processes.

Other statements of objectives may include those that relate to routine and procedural aspects of purchasing of concern to buyers as they fulfill their day-to-day responsibilities. To address these objectives, purchasers must:

- manage the flow of incoming products and services to meet the organization's needs.
- develop policies and procedures to guide and define purchasing procedures.
- use efficient and effective purchasing practices to receive the best **value** for the purchasing dollars that are spent.
- use the highest ethical standards in relationships with suppliers.
- ensure on-time supplier payments and maintain appropriate supplier relationships.
- control the purchasing process by assuring that policies and procedures are consistently followed, and by confirming that all products or services ordered are received and used to the benefit of the organization.

Key Term

Value   The relationship between the prices paid to a supplier and what is received in return: product or service of required quality, helpful supplier information, and appropriate service.

On-the-Job Challenges in Purchasing (1.1)

"I've got some bad news," said Roberto, the general manager, as he addressed the department heads at the South Point Hotel. "Our financial statements aren't looking good, we're really over budget in almost every category of our expenses, and we've got to cut costs. We can't do much about our mortgage and other fixed expenses, but we sure can reduce the costs of the items we purchase. Everyone needs to consider how to 'do more with less,' and I think we should begin by figuring out how to reduce our purchasing costs.

"I hope each of you will be creative as you consider this issue," he continued. "However, you might want to begin by considering the use of less expensive items, and I've asked Joe to try to get 'better deals' from our suppliers. I know that, working together, we can figure ways to get out of this financial dilemma."

After the meeting, Lucy, the executive housekeeper, walked up to Joe, the hotel's purchasing manager, and a brief conversation ensued.

"Joe, there's really a lot of pressure on you to get us out of this financial mess by saving money on purchasing costs, isn't there?"

"Yes, there is, Lucy, and I'll do everything that I can. However, I hope it occurs to Roberto, to you, and to the other department heads, that purchase costs are only one aspect of cost. I can buy products at a very reasonable price. However, if the items are not used correctly in the departments, these inexpensive products can quickly become very costly. Resolving our financial problems must be a team effort, and I can't do it all by myself."

Case Study Questions

1. How, if at all, should a product's quality concerns be factored into purchasing decisions when there is an emphasis on purchase cost?
2. How can Joe work with each department head to best determine what products are required, ensure that correct quantities are purchased, and control purchase costs?
3. Assume that the hotel's expenses remain high. As Roberto and the department heads analyze them, how can they determine whether the "problem" rests with the purchasing department, the user department, or both?

OVERVIEW OF PROCUREMENT PROCESS

Several steps, each preceded by a significant amount of analysis and planning effort, are involved in the procurement process. Figure 1.4 provides an overview of these steps, and each will be discussed in depth in this book.

Let's review the procurement steps outlined above. You'll note that the process is straightforward; it is not difficult to understand because it is sequential. Remember that the procedures used to accomplish each step vary depending upon numerous factors including the specific requirements and needs of the organization.

- *Step 1: Identify Need for Product or Service*—The need for any product or service is driven by what the organization's customers want. For example, the menu of a foodservice operation is planned with the consumer in mind. If ground beef is a necessary ingredient for a required menu item (one that is desired by the customer), it must be purchased to prepare the item. If numerous guests visiting a hotel's bar prefer a particular **"call brand" of liquor,** it

Key Term

Call brand (of liquor)   A specific brand of liquor requested by a guest. Typically, these brands are more expensive and of higher quality than other brands offered by the operation. For example, a guest ordering a "Stoli and tonic" would be served Stolichnaya vodka in the drink rather than a lesser-quality (and lower-priced) brand.

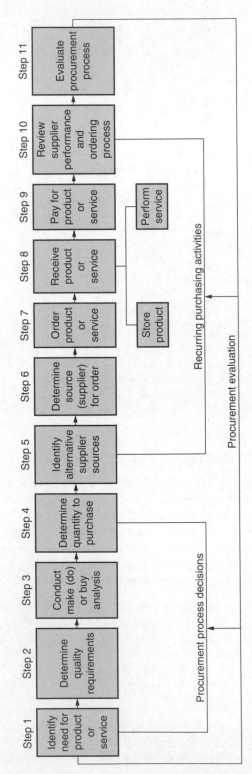

FIGURE 1.4 Steps in Procurement Process

must be purchased. If the owner of a small lodging property has landscaping that must be attended to, this service must be purchased unless he or she decides that the property's employees can perform these tasks at the required level of quality and at a more appropriate cost (see Step 3). The process to identify product or service need is described in Chapter 4.

- *Step 2: Determine Quality Requirements*—The term *quality* relates to how suitable a product or service is for its intended purpose. The ground beef ingredient referred to in Step 1 can be purchased with different percentages of fat content, and it can be purchased fresh or frozen. These and other purchase factors may affect its taste and will affect its cost. The quality of the liquor noted in Step 1 was specified by its brand, which is a description of quality. The lodging property's owner can pay for a landscaping service that provides all or part of his or her total landscaping needs, and these services can be provided as often as the owner wishes to pay for them.

   A direct relationship typically exists between the quality of a product or service and the price that the organization will pay for it. These purchase costs must, then, be passed on to customers who must generally pay more for a product or service with a higher-quality than for its lower-quality counterpart. The determination of quality drives the remaining steps in the purchasing process. It is also integral to the evaluation process that should then occur to assess whether the "right" products or services (those of the appropriate quality) that were ordered were, in fact, received (see Step 8). We will discuss quality aspects of purchase decisions in Chapter 4.

- *Step 3: Conduct Make (Do) or Buy Analysis*—Often, products of a specified quality that are needed can be prepared on-site or, alternatively, purchased partially or completely prepared. Assume the ground beef in Step 1 is required for a hamburger patty. Should the product be purchased in bulk and weighed and shaped into patties by the organization's cooks, or should the product be purchased in a patty of specified weight? Some or all of the landscaping services can be provided by the employees of the small lodging property or, alternatively, they can be "contracted out." Which is best? These decisions must be made on the basis of availability of alternatives (first), quality considerations (second), and, finally, on the basis of costs.

   Some purchasers refer to considerations about on-site preparation or purchase of needed products as "make or buy analysis," and they refer to making decisions about use of employees or suppliers to perform services as "do or buy analysis." Other hospitality professionals do not make this distinction and, instead, use the term "make or buy analysis" as they refer to their deliberations about both product and service alternatives. You will learn about make (do) or buy analysis in Chapter 5.

- *Step 4: Determine Quantity to Purchase*—Products can be purchased in large or small volumes, and services can be purchased for short or lengthy time periods. Factors such as available space and the possibility of theft (for products) and an interest in evaluating the quality of contractual compliance

---

Key Terms

Quality   Suitability for intended use or purpose; the closer that an item comes to being suitable for its intended use, or that a service fulfills its intended purpose, the more appropriate is the quality of the product or service.

Make (do) or buy analysis   A systematic process to determine whether products should be prepared on-site or purchased from an external supply source. Sometimes called "do/buy analysis" when on-site versus supplier-provided services are analyzed.

Is this person a hotel employee, or has a window cleaning service been purchased?
Howard Shooter © Dorling Kindersley

(of services) are important considerations, as are **cash flow** concerns when both products and services are purchased. We will review procedures to determine purchase quantities in Chapter 6.

- *Step 5: Identify Alternative Supplier Sources*—Hospitality operators in many areas of the country have numerous suppliers available that can provide needed products and services. One's experience, supplier references, and "trial orders" with potential suppliers are among the factors that can be used to determine a "short list" of the suppliers who will be considered when orders are placed by the organization. Information about supplier sourcing decisions is found in Chapter 8.

- *Step 6: Determine Source (Supplier) for Order*—Which of the alternate suppliers (Step 5) should be selected to provide the necessary products/services when they are needed? The answer depends, in part, upon the type of purchasing system used. Alternatives range from soliciting **price quotations** for items to be purchased for a specific order to long-term contracts that enable a supplier to provide agreed-upon products or services for many months (or longer) if all contractual terms are complied with. You will learn procedures to select suppliers for specific orders in Chapter 10.

Careful readers may wonder why determining purchase price is not identified as a separate step in Figure 1.4. In fact, as just noted, pricing agreements may be made when a long-term contract for agreed-upon quantities is negotiated (Step 4). If so, specific quantities required during the contractual period will then be received from that supplier at the agreed-upon price. Alternatively, prices for each order may be determined when suppliers are identified for each order. Further information about pricing considerations is presented in Chapter 7.

Key Terms

Cash flow   The ability of a business to pay its outstanding debts as they become due.

Price quotation   A request made by a purchaser to a supplier for the current price of a product or service that meets the property's quality requirements.

- *Step 7: Order Product or Service*—Products or services can be ordered after the proper quality and quantity are known (Steps 2 and 4), and after the appropriate supplier has been selected (Step 6). **Expediting** to ensure on-time delivery of products, and to confirm that services meet the buyer's expectations, may be necessary. Information about ordering procedures is reviewed in Chapter 10.

- *Step 8: Receive Product or Service*—Products that have been ordered must be delivered, and services that have been agreed upon must be rendered. Procedures are needed to ensure that the quality and quantity of products and services ordered are those that have been delivered. Products must be properly stored after delivery to best ensure that no quality deterioration or theft occurs. Record-keeping tasks applicable to product storage are also necessary. Services that have been agreed to must be provided, and purchasing staff help to confirm this occurs as they interact with user departments and supplier personnel. We will review procedures for receiving and storing products and for accepting services in Chapter 11.

- *Step 9: Pay for Product or Service*—The purchaser's financial obligations incurred when products and services are ordered (Step 7) must be satisfied. The timing of payments, concerns about fraud as payments are processed, and accounting concerns to identify and assign costs to the operating departments that incurred them are examples of issues that are important when payments are made. Payment and accounting-related issues are addressed in Chapter 12.

- *Step 10: Review Supplier Performance and Ordering Process*—Hospitality managers and employees who have participated in the procurement process, including purchasers, department managers, user personnel, and receiving/storing staff, among others, should provide input to help answer the question, "How can our purchasing process be improved?" As noted in Figure 1.4, these decision-making and problem-solving issues should be routinely addressed for each of the recurring activities (Steps 5–10) in the purchasing process. Recurring purchasing activities are explained in Chapter 23.

- *Step 11: Evaluate Procurement Process*—Basic concerns to be addressed when procurement systems are evaluated include: research about what customers want and need, the best products and services to address these needs, and the applicability of new purchasing methods. Additional procurement assessment factors are ways to improve buyer–supplier relationships, updating purchasing-related policies and procedures, and ways, if any, to better use technology. As noted in Figure 1.4, evaluation is useful for each step in the procurement process, and is cyclical: Evaluation results can affect the ways that emerging or changing product and service needs are identified. Details about the evaluation of the overall procurement process are presented in Chapter 23.

Figure 1.4 also helps to clarify the definitions of *procurement* and *purchasing* noted at the beginning of this chapter. Procurement involves each of the eleven steps in the process; purchasing typically involves only Steps 5–10. Figure 1.4 also indicates that several procurement activities (Steps 1–4) involve decisions that affect subsequent purchasing activities that are needed whenever a product or service is purchased.

Key Term

Expedite   The act of facilitating the delivery of products previously ordered or compliance with contracts for services that have been negotiated with suppliers.

HIGH-TECH PURCHASING (1.1)

In the not-too-distant past, the basic purchasing process involved a manual system with lots of paperwork. When additional products were needed to replenish inventory quantities, storeroom personnel sent a purchase requisition (paper) to alert the purchasing department that more products were required. Purchasing staff, in turn, sent a Request for Price Quotation (paper) to eligible suppliers who responded (on paper) with their "best" price. A purchase order (on paper) was issued, and the supplier subsequently delivered products along with a delivery invoice (paper). It was routed from receiving or storeroom personnel to the purchasing and/or accounting department with copies (paper) perhaps going to other personnel including those in the user's department. Purchase orders (paper) were then matched with delivery invoices (paper), and the payment (paper check) was prepared and mailed to the supplier.

As you'll learn throughout this book, all the above and other tasks in the purchasing process can be, and increasingly are, automated. It is no longer even necessary for storeroom personnel to prepare a list (paper) of items to be placed on carts or dollies for transport to user department locations at time of issue. Instead, the use of notebook computers and/or other technologies allow this physical task to be automated.

The purpose of the increased use of technology should be to reduce errors and increase the amount of time available for purchasers to assume other tasks, which then allow them to provide greater value to their employer.

FACTORS AFFECTING PROCUREMENT

A wide range of factors affect the specific policies and procedures used to manage each procurement step described in Figure 1.4. Some that have been identified relate to ownership, affiliation with a multi-unit hospitality organization including franchise arrangements, whether the organization operates in the public or private sector, and the specific consumer market served by the organization. However, additional factors can significantly affect the purchasing process of a specific organization.

Internal Factors

It is relatively easy to imagine the affect of internal factors on the purchasing needs and procedures of an organization. Hospitality purchasers must consider the skills and abilities of their staff members as make (do) or buy analyses are undertaken. Anticipated business volume, available storage space for products, and timing requirements for service deliveries are important. The property's ability to pay for the products and services it purchases on a timely basis, and the interest of owners and managers to participate in nontraditional purchasing methods (see Chapter 6), are additional factors.

Additional examples of internal influences on the purchasing process and its effectiveness include: opportunities, if any, for individuals in user departments to purchase some or all of the items and services needed; organizational structures that influence the reporting relationships of those with purchasing responsibilities; and the extent to which technology is used for recurring purchasing activities. Each of these should be considered in a procurement system designed to be most effective for the organization's use.

External Factors

Several factors external to the organization affect purchase decisions, and these are identified in Figure 1.5.

Our review of Figure 1.5 can begin by considering the consumers: hotel or restaurant guests, patients or residents in hospitals or long-term care facilities, private club members, cruise ship passengers, and others who affect the actions and/or choices of hospitality organizations. The concern about meeting the customers'

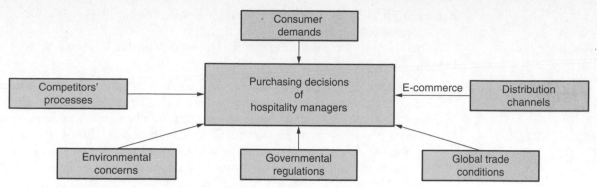

FIGURE 1.5 External Factors Impacting Purchasing Decisions

wants and needs applies to all aspects of the operation. Can the services of a musical band be purchased for the restaurant lounge? Should limousine service be available for the hotel's air travelers? Will our customers appreciate (and purchase) unique desserts flown in from a faraway city? Each of these is an example of a consumer-related demand that may be a priority in a purchase decision.

Suppliers, manufacturers, and others in **distribution channels** also influence purchasing decisions. They interact with hospitality organizations in an increasing number of **e-commerce** applications that, for example, provide information about brands and products carried (or represented) and can provide a wide range of helpful information to purchasers. Suppliers also increasingly participate in nontraditional purchasing arrangements with hospitality organizations. (These are discussed in detail in Chapter 6.) Many organizations in hospitality distribution channels become larger by mergers and acquisitions, and can offer **one-stop shopping** methods that reduce the number of necessary supply sources. This, in turn, makes it possible to reduce the labor costs otherwise associated with

This limousine might be owned or leased by the hotel; with either option, purchasing personnel may have been involved in its procurement.

Dorling Kindersley © Paul Wilkinson

Key Terms

Distribution channel   The organizations and/or individuals involved in the process of making a product or service available for use by a hospitality organization.

e-commerce   The process of conducting business and sharing information by using the computer and telecommunication networks, including the Internet.

One-stop shopping   Purchasing a wide range of products or services from a single supplier.

determining order quantities, assessing supplier prices, placing orders, and receiving products and making payments.

Let's briefly note the other external factors identified in Figure 1.5 that affect the purchasing process:

- *Global trade conditions*—We live and work in an ever-increasing global society that conducts business across international borders. Many manufacturers are becoming global organizations, and improved transportation systems make products from almost anywhere available at almost anytime. The global economy affects product availability and prices paid by all organizations, including those in the hospitality industry. We'll discuss more about global trade conditions in Chapter 22.

- *Governmental regulations*—Federal laws in the United States regulate the interstate (between-state) transportation of some products, and control the inspection of many food items. State laws directly affect how alcoholic beverages may be purchased and sold. Other laws impose sales and other taxes on the purchase of products and services, and affect the purchase, storage, and handling of many items, including cleaning chemicals and pesticides.

- *Environmental concerns*—Consumers' demands for, and the interests of hospitality organizations in, being "good community citizens" influence many **green purchasing** decisions. Examples are recycling of packaging materials, purchase of "environmentally friendly" cleaning and other chemicals, and concerns about the purchase and disposal of nonreusable foodservice items and other supplies.

- *Competitors' processes*—**Benchmarking** is increasingly used to study and learn about the functions of competitors in efforts to improve an organization's own processes, including those related to purchasing. Efforts to improve upon the products and services offered by one's competitors also affect the actual products and services that must be purchased when an organization reacts to competitive actions.

ROLES OF PROCUREMENT TEAM MEMBERS

Figure 1.4 identified eleven steps in the procurement process, each of which is important for effective purchasing. When products or services are purchased by large hospitality organizations, one or more persons with a relatively narrow range of job duties (**purchasing director, purchasing agent,** and/or other members of a purchasing department) are needed. In small organizations, persons with numerous responsibilities not limited to purchasing must fulfill purchasing responsibilities. All activities must be undertaken regardless of the organization's size.

Organization Size Affects Purchasing Duties

Hotels with 500 or more guest rooms will likely have a full-time purchasing director and perhaps clerical or other staff members to assist with necessary procurement

---

Key Terms

Green purchasing   The placement of purchasing priority not only on price and quality, but also on a product's effect on the environment.

Benchmarking   A search for best practices and an understanding of how they are achieved to determine how well a hospitality organization is doing and to learn ways to become even better.

Purchasing director   The top-level manager in a large hospitality organization with responsibilities for that organization's procurement function; also called purchasing manager.

Purchasing agent   A staff member in a large hospitality organization with responsibilities to purchase specific lines of products, services, supplies, or equipment; also called buyer.

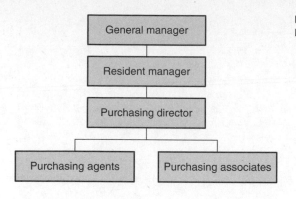

FIGURE 1.6 Organization of Purchasing
Functions in a Large Hotel

responsibilities. These, as well as smaller hotels, will have clerical and accounting staff members assigned to invoice payment activities.

As a lodging property becomes larger, one or more purchasing agents may be needed. Multi-unit hospitality organizations may employ specialized purchasing staff in district, regional, or other offices to assist with and coordinate purchasing activities of individual units. Very large restaurant operations with high volume levels may require specialized positions for procurement responsibilities, and chains frequently have purchasing specialists to assist individual units. Multi-unit foodservice organizations may use a **centralized purchasing system,** in which requests for additional products and services are routed to those with purchasing responsibilities who then assist property personnel with their purchasing needs.

A section of an **organization chart** for a large hotel showing purchasing-related positions is shown in Figure 1.6.

As noted in Figure 1.6, the hotel general managers supervise resident managers. These individuals direct the work of department heads, including the purchasing director. Purchasing agents and associates (secretarial and clerical employees) may report to the purchasing director.

Smaller, single-unit hospitality organizations typically use a **decentralized purchasing system.** With this plan, department heads become more responsible for the completion of each purchasing step, often with input and/or approval by the property's general manager, especially for high value and/or large quantity purchases.

Purchasing specialists occupy **staff positions** within a hospitality operation. They are technical "purchasing experts" who assist department heads and, perhaps others, in user departments who are in **line positions.**

Key Terms

Centralized purchasing system A purchasing system in which all (or most) purchases are made by the designated purchasing agent for the entire organization.

Organization chart A graphic showing positions and reporting relationships within a hospitality organization.

Decentralized purchasing system A purchasing system in which all (or most) purchases needed by a department are made by department heads or someone within their department who is designated to do so.

Staff positions Organizational roles (positions) occupied by technical, advisory specialists such as purchasing agents who provide advice to, but do not make decisions for, those in the chain of command.

Line positions Organizational roles (positions) occupied by decision-makers in the chain of command. Line decision-makers have authority that flows from one level of management to the next.

On-the-Job Challenges in Purchasing (1.2)

"We can never get what we want when we want it," complained Juanita to Peggy. Juanita is the director of housekeeping at the Sunrise Hotel, and she was speaking to the property's general manager.

"We have had the best experience using certain guest room cleaning supplies, but do you think we get them? The thread counts of our bed linens are down to about zero—I'm exaggerating!—but they are certainly low, and we must continually buy new linens to replace those that are worn. Sometimes it takes weeks, or longer, to get the products we need, and our housekeepers must continually go back and forth between the guest rooms and the laundry to get items that, literally, have just been washed. We don't have enough inventory."

"I've heard similar comments from other department heads," said Peggy, "What do you think we should do?"

"That's easy," replied the director of housekeeping, "I think we should decentralize our purchasing system, and then each department can assume its own purchasing responsibilities. We could eliminate the costs incurred to operate the purchasing department, everyone would get what they want when they need it, and everyone, including our guests, will be much happier."

Case Study Questions

1. Assume you are Peggy: What are your thoughts about the "pros and cons" of decentralizing the purchasing function in the property?
2. Assume that you believe the advantages of centralized purchasing outweigh its disadvantages; what would you do to improve the purchasing system at the property?
3. What would you say and do as you explain your decision to department heads, including the purchasing director, as you move forward to improve the centralized purchasing system so it will help, rather than hinder, departmental operations?

Purchasing System Affects Purchasing Duties

Figure 1.7 reviews the basics of a possible purchasing process in a large hotel. Although oversimplified, it indicates departments and personnel involved in the purchasing process. Let's review the figure, while assuming food products are being purchased. As we do so, the "who does what" of the process should become clear.

All of the furniture, fixtures, and equipment (FF&E) in this function room in a private club were purchased after consultation with an interior designer.

Lein de Leon Yong / Shutterstock

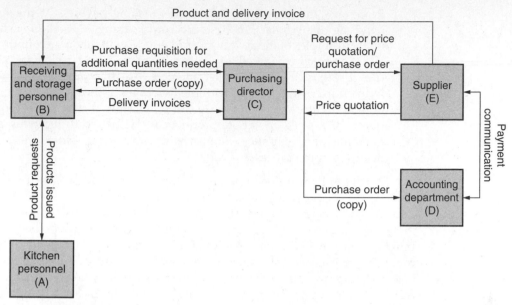

FIGURE 1.7   Basic Purchasing Process in a Large Hotel

As you review Figure 1.7, note the following:

- **(Box A) Kitchen personnel**—Kitchen personnel request (requisition) required food products from receiving and storing personnel who **issue** the products from the hotel's central storage area.
- **(Box B) Receiving and storage personnel**—These staff members have several specific procurement functions. First, they inform the purchasing director (Box C) when additional product quantities are required to maintain inventory levels. They also receive incoming product deliveries from the suppliers, and route the applicable **delivery invoices** to the purchasing director.
- **(Box C) Purchasing director**—The purchasing director performs several tasks in the basic purchasing process. When additional products must be purchased, he or she requests price quotations from suppliers, makes the supplier selection decision, and places product orders. A copy of the **purchase order** is routed to the receiving and storage personnel who use it during the receiving process, and a copy may also be sent to the accounting department.
- **(Box D) Accounting department**—The accounting function plays a significant role in the purchasing process. As noted in Figure 1.7, the purchasing director notifies the accounting department that an order has been placed. (A copy of the purchase order sent to the supplier is routed to the accounting department.) When the order is received, the delivery invoice sent by receiving and storing personnel to the purchasing director is forwarded to the accounting personnel.

Key Terms

Issue (product)   The task of transferring products from storage areas to user departments in quantities that enable user personnel to meet production needs.

Delivery invoice   A document signed by an authorized representative of the hospitality operation when products are delivered to transfer product ownership to the property. The delivery invoice is the source of supplier charges to the property.

Purchase order   A document used by the hospitality operation to solicit prices from suppliers, and to inform the appropriate supplier that a shipment should be delivered.

Processing (matching) the documents, making payment to the supplier, and handling many other purchasing, record keeping, and related tasks are additional examples of the accounting function. Details about accounting personnel and their role in the purchasing process are discussed in Chapter 12.

- *(Box E) Supplier*—The supplier interacts with all property personnel involved in the purchasing process, with the exception of those in the user department (kitchen). Information is sent to the purchasing director in response to a request for a price quotation, products are delivered to receiving and storage personnel, and suppliers interact with accounting staff as the payment and record-keeping processes evolve.

As might be imagined, there are numerous variations of the process outlined in Figure 1.7. For example, the chef may communicate directly with the purchasing director, and receiving and storing personnel may route copies of delivery invoices to the chef and/or food and beverage director for review before they are sent to the purchasing agent. Additional copies of one or more purchasing documents may be routed to an external entity such as a regional purchasing office in multi-unit organizations. Also, all, some, or none of the above steps may be accomplished electronically, with little or no face-to-face or hard-copy communication being necessary.

Purchasers affiliated with relatively small-volume units in chain organizations may route purchasing requirements to a district, regional, or other centralized source. There a purchasing director and his or her staff may combine orders from each unit, solicit price quotations, select suppliers, and arrange for delivery to the individual properties. This purchasing method works very well in chain organizations with the same ownership because it is relatively easy to agree on quality requirements (Step 2 in Figure 1.4).

Centralized purchasing by individual properties in other types of chain organizations (e.g., an organization comprised of both company-owned properties and franchised units owned by several or more owners) may involve combining purchasing needs after quality requirements are agreed upon. It is unlawful in the United States for franchisors to require franchisees to purchase specific products from, for example, the franchisor's commissaries. However, franchisors typically require that minimum quality standards be maintained in the products that are used. This requirement can reduce supplier sources for small franchisees, but not necessarily for their larger counterparts.

Close Look at Purchasing Director

What exactly does a purchasing director do? Figure 1.8 illustrates a composite list of tasks in a **job description** that helps to explain what someone in this position might do.

PURCHASING PROS NEED TO KNOW (1.2)

Purchasing pros know that purchasing systems are complex and require the successful completion of numerous activities. Each step is necessary and must be accomplished regardless of the organization's size. Persons such as a department head in a small organization may need to assume purchasing responsibilities in addition to operating duties to perform all of the steps that, in a larger property, would be the responsibility of persons in several specialized positions.

Key Term

Job description   A list of tasks performed by an employee working in a specific position.

- Identifies potential suppliers.
- Selects suppliers; negotiates prices and contracts.
- Coordinates activities involved with procuring products, services, equipment, and supplies.
- Reviews requisitions.
- Confers with suppliers to obtain product or service information such as price, availability, and delivery schedules.
- Selects products for purchase by testing, observing, and examining items.
- Estimates product prices using knowledge of current market prices.
- Determines method of procurement such as direct purchase or bid.
- Prepares purchase orders or bid requests.
- Reviews bid proposals, and negotiates contracts within budgetary limitations and scope of authority.
- Maintains manual or computerized procurement records such as items or services purchased, costs, delivery, product quality or performance, and inventories.
- Discusses defective or unacceptable goods or services with property personnel, vendors, and others to determine source of problems, and to take corrective actions as necessary.
- Approves invoices for payment.
- Expedites delivery of products to users.
- Recommends improvements in overall purchasing programs that result in more competitive bidding and product improvements.
- Researches guest counts and sales histories to determine optimal purchase quantities.
- Analyzes demand changes.
- Keeps current with suppliers and their media to forecast costs and availability of required products.
- Meets with managers to establish **bartering** (trade out) parameters and specific purchasing guidelines.
- Interacts with all members of the supply chain to determine appropriate procurement channels.
- Stays informed about new product developments of interest to the property.
- Develops and monitors purchasing department's budget.
- Reviews, develops, and revises purchasing policies and procedures, systems, best practices, and goals for the purchasing department.
- Reviews, revises, and maintains purchase specifications for all products purchased.
- Evaluates competitive bids received relative to cost, quality, service, availability, reliability, and selection variety.
- Develops standard price solicitation documents and forms to facilitate product and supply purchases.
- Ensures that all purchasing files are kept current, complete, and available for audit.
- Resolves problems with suppliers relating to defective or unacceptable products, delivery delays, invoice discrepancies, and account coding.
- Maintains supplier handbook and vendor information.
- Establishes and maintains supplier relationships to maximize pricing discounts and service.
- Interacts with property managers and suppliers to establish, improve, and maintain electronic purchasing systems.
- Assists in the training of property personnel about purchasing procedures.

FIGURE 1.8   Tasks in Job Description for Purchasing Director

EVOLUTION OF PROCUREMENT SYSTEMS

Many business organizations have reconsidered the goals of their procurement efforts to determine the best ways to use resources to gain a competitive advantage and financial success. Executives in large, multi-unit hospitality chains are also reconsidering the role of procurement and every other aspect of management and

Key Term

Bartering   A type of business transaction in which goods or services are exchanged for other goods and/or services without money changing hands; also known as "trade outs."

Internet Purchasing Assistant (1.3)

The American Purchasing Association maintains a career center that helps connect prospective employees with employers. This site posts numerous job listings that provide details about tasks that are important in the work of many purchasing directors, managers, and buyers.

To review this site, go to www.american-purchasing.com.

When you reach the site, go to "Check Out Our Career Center" and then click on "View Job Listings."

To obtain perspectives about hospitality industry purchasing positions, go to www.hcareers.com.

When you reach the site, click on "Management Positions" in the top-right search box and select "Purchasing." Also indicate your desired location in the top-left search box (e.g., All USA), and click "Search Jobs." Numerous purchasing-related positions will be displayed.

Internet Purchasing Assistant (1.4)

The hospitality industry has an association dedicated to persons interested in purchasing. The International Society of Hospitality Purchasers (ISHP) addresses a wide range of concerns to professionals in the industry.

To review its site, go to www.ishp.org.

At the site, you can review information about the society and review a statement of ethical purchasing practices and a code of professional conduct, among other information that is available.

marketing to help ensure that they can capitalize on the benefits that can arise from doing so.

Figure 1.9 reviews the evolution of procurement systems and provides an introduction to the final section of this chapter.

All of the items in this golf pro shop were purchased for retail sale to club members and guests.

Linda Whitwam © Dorling Kindersley

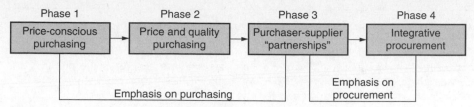

FIGURE 1.9 Evolution of Procurement Systems

Let's review the philosophies that are integral to each of the phases in the evolution of procurement systems noted in Figure 1.9.

Price-Conscious Purchasing

In this traditional approach to purchasing, an organization emphasizes tactics that can be used to purchase products at the lowest price. Although perhaps somewhat overstated, the preferred relationship with suppliers is one of "I win; you lose!" and the relationship is often much more adversarial than one of partnering. Most of the purchaser's time and efforts are spent ordering products and determining ways to reduce costs. The purchasing function is evaluated on the basis of lowest cost per unit and efficiency, and there is little recognition of the purchasing function and how it can affect nonsupply aspects of the organization. The primary purchasing goal is to "get the products here on time at the least expensive price."

Price and Quality Purchasing

Organizations with this purchasing philosophy are still concerned about product and service prices, but the quality of what is being purchased is also of concern. Purchasers are driven by value from the customer's perspective, and they recognize that the "best" product is not necessarily the "cheapest" product. Organizations in this purchasing phase also recognize the importance of information provided by their suppliers. They know that purchase prices have several important components (product, information, and service), and are willing to pay for each of them. Those with purchasing responsibilities interact with others in the organization to determine quality requirements. Also, top-level managers recognize that the procurement function can help the organization to be profitable in ways beyond reducing purchase costs to the lowest possible levels.

Purchaser–Supplier "Partnerships"

Organizations at this stage of procurement are moving away from the philosophy of "purchasing" to one of "procurement." Those within the organization recognize a broader role for purchasing, and they see how it can become a strategic advantage. Suppliers are considered a resource, and their expertise is an important consideration as supplier decisions are made. Products and suppliers are continuously monitored, and the procurement function becomes much proactive as it works within and outside of the organization to address and resolve problems.

Integrative Procurement

At this phase of procurement system evolution, purchasing is integrated into the organization's competitive strategy. Cross-functional training of purchasing professionals and other executives is available, and the performance of applicable staff is measured in terms of contributions to the organization's success.

PURCHASING PROS NEED TO KNOW (1.3)

Wise purchasers ask for, appreciate, use, and are willing to pay for the information they receive from their suppliers. They prefer suppliers who are experts in the products and services they sell, and they know the cost of supplier information is a component in the price being paid for the products and services that are purchased.

Assume that a property's wine merchant informs the buyer that the price of several wines will be increasing dramatically, and that there is an advantage to purchasing in larger-than-usual quantities now to take advantage of the current lower prices.

Purchasing pros know that **speculative purchasing** is not typically within the bounds of their responsibilities. They may not, for example, be aware of the organization's cash flow (does it have funds to pay for additional wine purchases?), or even about forthcoming menu changes which may deemphasize certain wines. They know the best tactic to use in this situation is to inform the appropriate property manager about the pending price increases. Then the manager can make a "go" or "no go" decision about purchasing in large quantities. This is in line with the role of a staff purchasing specialist who provides advice to, but does not make decisions for, line managers.

THE SUPPLIER'S SIDE (1.1)

Good suppliers work hard to gain and retain the business of hospitality organizations. They understand that it is a competitive marketplace and that purchasers have numerous supplier options. They also recognize that contemporary buyers want—and appreciate—the information and services that their favored suppliers provide.

Suppliers also recognize that a purchaser's time is important. They want to provide as much service as the purchaser desires, and some of these services can save time for the purchaser. Consider, for example, the distributor's sales representatives (DSRs) who sell foodservice equipment to independent restaurant owners and many other public and private sector organizations. Many DSRs have previous food production and/or management experience. In addition, they call on many different businesses and, as they do, they learn about creative solutions to common problems. DSRs can provide advice to their accounts about work flow, layout and design, and equipment alternatives (among other types of assistance).

This information can include drawings of equipment placement and specifications, and they can also provide access to manufacturers' catalogs. (The latter are especially helpful to give purchasers ideas about alternatives.) These resources can all be supplemented with face-to-face conversations at numerous times as projects evolve, or as specific equipment purchase decisions are being made. Furthermore, DSRs can request the assistance of manufacturers' representatives, and both of these equipment specialists can visit the property to provide specialized alternatives.

The list of ways that DSRs can help purchasers is not limited to the above examples. Suggestions about alternatives to resolve problems related to food products, paper supplies, and almost any other items being purchased can be provided. Also, this information and consulting assistance are typically provided at no cost to the purchaser. There are, then, numerous ways that professional suppliers provide value-added information and services to their accounts.

Key Term

Speculative purchasing   Making decisions about the quantities of products to purchase based on forecasted future prices. If prices are judged to be increasing, larger quantities of items may be ordered. Conversely, if prices are judged to be decreasing, smaller quantities with more frequent deliveries may be purchased.

Much planning is required at every step in the procurement process.
Photodisc/Getty Images

PURCHASING PROS NEED TO KNOW (1.4)

Should purchasing be **outsourced?** Hopefully, traditional price-conscious purchasing philosophies are giving way to a broader view of the role of purchasing in the organization. However, the clerical and repetitive activities required to perform purchasing (not procurement) tasks might be outsourced because they do not require advanced levels of decision making. However, as the purchasing function becomes fully integrated into the development and implementation of strategic plans, the importance of managing the organization's supply chain will be better recognized, and these aspects of the procurement function should not (cannot) be outsourced.

As an alternative to outsourcing, some hospitality organizations may decentralize specific purchasing tasks involved with the processing of routine orders to departmental users. This will allow purchasing specialists to devote more time and energies to the big picture "strategic concerns." Details about outsourcing are presented in Chapter 5.

Leading-edge concepts throughout the **supply chain** are used, and value addition rather than cost reduction is seen as the primary role of purchasing. Technology is used whenever possible, and there is a total focus on the customer being served.

Purchasing Resources on the Internet

In addition to the Web site references in this chapter's "Internet Purchasing Assistant" features, the following sites provide detailed information to enhance your purchasing knowledge and skills.

Key Terms

Outsourcing   The act of purchasing a product or service from an external provider that could, alternatively, be provided by the organization's own employees.

Supply chain   A coordinated system of organizations, people, activities, information, and resources used to move a product or service from the supplier to the customer. Activities in the supply chain change raw materials and components into finished products delivered to the end customer.

Purchasing Resources on the Internet

Site	Information About
	Professional Associations
www.ism.ws	The Institute for Supply Management
www.american-purchasing.com	The American Purchasing Society
www.cscmp.org	The Council of Supply Chain Management Professionals
	Professional Trade Magazines
www.purchasing.com	*Purchasing* (an online purchasing magazine)
www.sdcexec.com	*Supply and Demand Chain Executives*
www.ism.ws/pubs/ismmog	*Inside Supply Management*
www.scmr.com	*Supply Chain Management Review*
www.supplymanagement.co.uk	*U.K. Supply Management*
	Other References
www.capsresearch.org	The Center for Advanced Purchase Studies
www.greenbiz.com	Green (environmentally friendly) operations
www.nfib.com	The National Federation of Independent Businesses (Enter "purchasing" in the site's search box)
www.cio.com	e-procurement (Enter "e-procurement" in the site's search box)
www.careeroverview.com	Career information for purchasing managers (Click on "Management" and then "Purchasing Manager")
www.thepurchasinggroup.com	Group purchasing and outsourcing
www.sysco.com	Services and products provided by a full-line food-service distributor
www.mcdonalds.com/usa/good/products.html	The concept of "Responsible Purchasing" as practiced by McDonald's Corporation

Key Terms

travel and tourism industry 2	procurement 5	distribution channel 15	staff positions 17
hospitality industry 2	purchasing 5	e-commerce 15	line positions 17
independent operator 2	capital equipment 5	one-stop shopping 15	issue (product) 19
chain 2	full-service hotel 6	green purchasing 16	delivery invoice 19
franchise 4	FF&E 6	benchmarking 16	purchase order 19
franchisee 4	value 8	purchasing director 16	job description 20
franchisor 4	call brand (of liquor) 9	purchasing agent 16	bartering 21
revenue 4	quality 11	centralized purchasing system 17	speculative purchasing 24
public sector 4	make (do) or buy analysis 11	organization chart 17	outsourcing 25
private sector 4	cash flow 12	decentralized purchasing system 17	supply chain 25
consumer market 4	price quotation 12		
demographic factors 4	expedite 13		

Think It Through

1. Assume that you are the manager of a small restaurant with three departments: food production, dining room service, and lounge (beverage) operations. How might you organize the purchasing function for your restaurant? In other words, "Who would do what?" Also, assume that you are the manager of a small limited-service hotel property (one that does not offer food and

beverage services beyond a simple continental breakfast). The property is organized into three departments: front office (front desk), housekeeping, and maintenance services. How would you organize the purchasing function in this operation?

2. Assume that you are the manager of a large hotel. What would be the advantages of using a centralized purchasing system? A decentralized system? Which type of system would you use? Why?

3. What, if any, role should a property's purchasing director play in interacting with other property department heads as the organization's strategic plans are developed? As property-wide operating budgets are planned and monitored? As strategic

marketing-related decisions are made? What are examples of the types of information and assistance these professionals can bring to the decision-making process?

4. What, if any, role do you think that a hospitality organization's suppliers should play in helping the organization make procurement-related decisions? What are examples of information and assistance that suppliers can give to organizations? What kind of information and assistance should they *not* provide to hospitality organizations?

5. What are examples of some of the most important responsibilities of a purchasing director? How do these responsibilities influence the success of the organization?

Team Fun

For this exercise, assume that you are the general manager of a large and successful hotel property. It uses a "traditional" centralized purchasing model in which the major function of the purchasing department is to assist user departments in obtaining the products and services that the user departments indicate are needed. You are attending a national meeting of your brand's hotel managers (your hotel is part of a large national chain), and some of your colleagues are talking about an expanded role of purchasing, and how it could help the organization.

One of the session's internationally known speakers has had recent experience as a vice president of a large parts manufacturer that supplies the automotive industry. You have a chance to talk with him during a breakout session about how suppliers might interact with purchasers in a way that benefits both organizations, and you learned much about the future of hospitality purchasing from the speaker.

Each team is assigned one task relating to the information exchanged during this lengthy conversation:

1. The assignment of the first team is to speculate about the broad range of information and services that suppliers might provide to an "enlightened" hospitality organization.

2. The assignment of the second team is to list ideas that the speaker might have noted about how the purchasing function can save the hospitality organization money without reducing the quality of products that are purchased.

3. The assignment of the third team relates to developing suggestions that the speaker might have made about the factors that should be considered when supplier selection decisions are made.

Each team should be prepared to explain and justify their suggestions to the rest of the class.

2

Product Flow Through the Marketplace

In This Chapter

A restaurant requires new kitchen equipment to replace items that are malfunctioning, and it must also purchase lettuce (among numerous other products) for this weekend's production needs. Across the street, a hotel needs new bed linens and additional floor cleaning supplies. The restaurant buyer calls a local equipment supplier to request that a salesperson make a sales call and faxes a produce order that includes lettuce to a supplier for delivery on Friday. The hotel buyer e-mails a requisition for bed linens to a regional distributor that has negotiated a contract for all the chain properties within a fifteen-state area. His or her ordering task for cleaning supplies is even easier: The hotel's computer is interfaced to that of the approved supplier to enable electronic ordering without personal communication.

In each of the above instances, how do the required restaurant equipment and food products, and the hotel's bed linen and cleaning supplies, move from where they were manufactured (the equipment, bed linen, and cleaning supplies) or grown (the lettuce)? In this chapter, you'll learn how these and all other products move through intermediaries to reach their final destination: the hospitality operation.

Traditionally, most of a buyer's interaction with organizations within the marketplace occurred with those from whom orders were placed. This happened as they "shopped around" to determine who sold needed items, and as these products were purchased, delivered, and paid for. Purchasers still continue to interact with their traditional points of contact within the marketplace. However, they also increasingly obtain information and other value-added services from other organizations to better help them serve their customers.

There are numerous intermediaries (often called "middlemen") who add value to products as they move from the point of manufacture or where they are grown to the hospitality buyer. We will examine these, and in the process, you'll gain a better understanding about the "behind-the-scenes" activities that occur as products reach suppliers' warehouses for their final distribution to the hospitality organization.

Products do not flow through the marketplace to the purchaser until they have first been ordered. Traditionally, as suggested above, purchasers made direct contact with sellers. However, there are numerous other alternatives including several variations of group (centralized) buying, which add another intermediary to the process. These alternatives will also be examined because they are frequently used by chain organizations, which represent a significant part of the hospitality industry.

Several management and procurement concerns must be addressed as product purchase decisions are made. Many relate to cost, the needs of internal customers, transportation issues, distribution centers, and inventory management. Each will be discussed to provide further background to the core of basic purchasing knowledge that is necessary for all effective purchasers.

A final section of this chapter presents a "case study" of a fictitious restaurant chain that has some company-owned and operated units and many franchised properties. You'll learn about one possible way products move through the very complex market distribution channels and concerns that managers (of company-operated properties) and franchisees (in the remaining properties) have when some procurement decisions are made by persons outside of the immediate property.

■ ■ ■

Outline

DISTRIBUTION CHANNELS

The equipment, lettuce, bed linens, and floor cleaning supplies noted in the introduction to this chapter, along with all other equipment and products needed by the hospitality operation, move through distribution channels to end users. Distribution channels differ for many products but, along the way, there are typically several **intermediaries,** each of whom adds value before products move to the next point on their way to the hospitality property.

Overview

Distribution channels vary by types of products that move through them. For example, many parts are needed to manufacture an equipment item. Some may be produced by the manufacturer and/or its subsidiaries; others may be purchased

---

Key Term

Intermediaries (distribution channel)   All organizations and/or individuals involved in the flow of products from their source to the hospitality buyer; often called the "middleman."

from the manufacturer's suppliers. These are used to produce equipment for which equipment sellers have negotiated sales with hospitality buyers. Items may be available for immediate delivery but, often, they must be ordered from the equipment manufacturer.

Most food items flow through different types of distribution channels. For example, fresh produce may be harvested and then move without further processing through several intermediaries to produce suppliers' warehouses. Processors of items such as frozen desserts and soups purchase required ingredients, manufacture products, and ship through intermediaries to distributors' warehouses for delivery to hospitality operations when they are ordered.

A distribution channel begins with a **manufacturer, processor,** or **grower** who produces the items desired by the hospitality organization.

Basic Functions of Intermediaries

Intermediaries perform one or more of three basic functions as they move products through distribution channels:

- *Business functions.*   These activities relate to buying and selling. For example, an intermediary may purchase fresh produce from local farmers for resale to restaurants. Others serve as sales representatives as they generate orders for the companies they represent that will then produce or manufacture items for hospitality buyers.
- *Logistical functions.*   Some intermediaries add value by sorting products. For example, a supplier for airline in-flight foodservices may purchase soft drinks, water, juices, and other beverages along with snacks from various suppliers and provide these as a single-source to the airline. Other intermediaries may purchase items in large volumes and sort them into the smaller quantities desired by customers. For example, cookies may be purchased in large quantities and packaged into smaller units (e.g., one or two cookies) that are provided to hotel guests as in-room amenities. Still other logistical intermediaries are involved in the transport of products to the next point in the distribution channel and, finally, to the hospitality operations. An example is fresh seafood that may be transferred from the local airport to a restaurant in a nearby city.
- *Facilitating functions.*   Examples of these activities include financing (extending credit to an organization that purchases expensive equipment items) and leasing organizations (that purchase equipment and then make it available to users).

Types of Intermediaries

Figure 2.1 illustrates how many products flow through hospitality industry distribution channels.

Key Terms

Manufacturer   An organization that transforms raw materials into finished products. Examples include kitchen ovens and cleaning supplies.

Processor   A business that combines food items or ingredients to yield new food items. Examples include a company that bakes fresh bread from flour, shortening, yeast, water, and other ingredients.

Grower   A business that grows foods such as lettuce or raises animals such as beef cattle that will be used as food.

Many products used by hospitality operations are transported by truck.

Irene Springer/Pearson Education/PH College

Let's take a closer look at Figure 2.1. You've already learned that intermediaries separate product sources (manufacturers, processors, and growers) from product users (such as hospitality operations).

• *Agents.*   **Agents** represent product producers, but they do not purchase (take title to) the items they sell to hospitality operations. Instead, their profits are generated from the commissions or fees that producers pay them for their sales assistance.

There are two basic types of agents. A **manufacturer's representative** represents several producers and sells complimentary (not competitive) items within an exclusive territory. A representative of a food service equipment manufacturer may sell the **product lines** of several equipment manufacturers. They might, for example, represent a manufacturer of several lines of production equipment and another company that manufactures

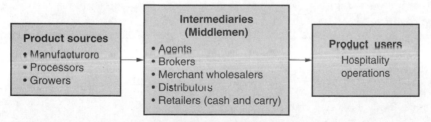

FIGURE 2.1   Flow of Products Through Hospitality Industry Distribution Channels

---

Key Terms

Agent (distribution channel intermediary)   An intermediary who does not take title to the products and makes a profit from commissions and fees paid for services provided; see manufacturer's representative and selling agent.

Manufacturer's representative (distribution channel)   An intermediary (agent) who represents several producers and carries noncompetitive (complimentary) merchandise in an exclusive territory.

Product line   A group of closely related products that satisfy similar needs, are sold to the same type of customers, and/or that fall within a specific range of prices.

dish washing equipment. A **selling agent** represents only a single manufacturer and may have more involvement in the advertising and selling plans of the producer than would a manufacturer's representative. Hospitality purchasers typically interact with manufacturer's representatives when they purchase equipment items.

- *Brokers.* **Brokers** are similar to agents in that they do not purchase (take title to) the products being sold. They receive a commission or fee from the producer for the services they provide. The primary purpose of brokers is to connect sellers and buyers by negotiating contracts between the two parties. Although most hospitality purchasers will not interact with brokers, they are used, for example, as food or vegetable crops are sold to manufacturers for processing into products that are ultimately sold to hospitality operations.

- *Merchant wholesalers.* **Merchant wholesalers** purchase products for resale and generate profits from the sale of the items.

  There are two basic types of merchant wholesalers. **Full-line** wholesalers carry a wide assortment of products but not a significant depth of variety within each specific product line. Some full-line merchant wholesalers serving the hospitality industry sell, literally, thousands of products ranging from swizzle sticks used in bar operations to dish machines (and almost everything in between!). By contrast, **limited-line** wholesalers sell a narrow range of items, but an extensive variety of products within the product line. Traditional fresh produce and seafood suppliers are examples of limited-line merchant wholesalers. Merchant wholesalers of both types represent the intermediaries with whom hospitality purchasers have most traditionally interacted when purchasing products and supplies.

- *Distributors.* **Distributors** sell specific (branded) products within a defined area. Examples include those who sell Coca-Cola or Pepsi soft drink products and specific brands of beers, spirits, and wines.

- *Retailers.* These "cash and carry" outlets are the same places of business where consumers buy their groceries and other products. Some, such as Costco and Sam's Club, charge an annual membership fee. These outlets

Key Terms

Selling agent (distribution channel) An intermediary (agent) who represents one producer and may assist with that producer's marketing and selling functions.

Broker (distribution channel) An independent organization or individual who negotiates a contract between a buyer and a seller.

Merchant wholesaler (distribution channel) An intermediary that purchases (takes title to) products handled and who generates a profit from the sale of these items; see full-line merchant wholesaler and limited-line merchant wholesaler.

Merchant wholesaler (full-line) An intermediary who carries a broad assortment of products but not much variety within each product line for resale to hospitality organizations; also called "broad-line" and "general" wholesaler.

Merchant wholesaler (limited-line) An intermediary who carries a relatively narrow range of products, but an extensive variety of products within that line for resale to hospitality organizations; also called "specialty" wholesaler.

Distributor An intermediary who sells specific (branded) products within a specifically-defined sales territory.

Retailer (cash and carry) An outlet that sells products to hospitality organizations and to individual consumers at retail prices.

PURCHASING PROS NEED TO KNOW (2.1)

Purchasing pros know that the technical definitions of supply chain intermediaries are frequently not known nor are they in common use by many in the hospitality industry. Instead, generic terms such as "supplier," "vendor," "jobber," and "dealer" are often used to represent those from whom equipment and products are purchased. These terms are well understood, if not technically accurate, and are commonly accepted as descriptions of supply sources for the industry. In keeping with the industry terminology and because the technical source of supply does vary with the situation, this text will use the term "suppliers" to represent the organizations with whom purchasers directly interact as equipment, products, and supplies are purchased for their organizations.

---

may offer products in larger **purchase unit** sizes and, because of their large volume purchases, may offer products at less-than-normal retail prices. Some grocery stores also stock popular items in larger container sizes and market them to small hospitality operators (and large families!). Many restaurants and hotels of all sizes sometimes find the need (hopefully only occasionally!) to purchase "emergency" items for which they are out of stock at a neighborhood retail store. Also, small properties may use retailers as their normal supply source for office supplies, light bulbs, maintenance items, and other low-volume purchases.

Close Look at Distribution Channels

Most hospitality purchases involve **indirect channels of distribution** because intermediaries separate hospitality buyers from the initial source of the product.

PURCHASING PROS NEED TO KNOW (2.2)

Years ago, many government-owned noncommercial facilities, such as retirement centers (nursing homes) and prisons, frequently operated farms and even raised cattle to provide some of the raw products required for their foodservices operation. These were forerunners of modern **vertical distribution systems** developed, in part, to minimize costs and to ensure a constant supply of necessary products.

Some, especially large hospitality organizations, do this today. For example, Starbucks controls some coffee bean fields, and McDonald's Corporation has interests in some cattle ranges and potato farm operations. However, because of their large-volume needs, they also purchase additional products from other sources to complement the products they produce themselves.*

*Source: Stowe Shoemaker et. al., *Marketing Leadership in Hospitality and Tourism: Strategies and Tactics for Competitive Advantage*, 4th ed. Upper Saddle River, NJ: Pearson/Prentice Hall, 2007.

Key Terms

Purchase unit   The unit weight, volume, or container size in which a product can be purchased. For example, salad oil might be purchased in pint, quart, or gallon-sized containers.

Channels of distribution (indirect)   Distribution channels involving intermediaries who perform channel functions between the producer of the item and the hospitality organization buyer.

Vertical distribution system   A distribution system in which one or more functions normally performed by an intermediary is undertaken by the hospitality organization.

These organizations and individuals provide value-added services to items before they reach the hospitality buyer. There are, however, a few **direct channels of distribution** that link hospitality organizations and producers. Examples include small organic farmers who provide locally grown items to community restaurants, and local craftsmen who provide interior decorating items for hotel public areas.

Traditionally, and still today, hospitality organizations sought out supply sources that provided products of the desired quality at a selling price judged to be reasonable (see Chapter 8 for further information about supplier sourcing decisions). They may purchase, for example, produce from a "produce supplier," guest room linens from a "linen supplier," and dining room table-top items from a "restaurant supplier." As the product user at the end of their distribution channel, hospitality buyers have not typically been concerned about from where the products originated (point of origin) nor how they moved to the property's back door (receiving dock). Significant exceptions relate to the need for buyers to know about the origin of wines, certain seafoods, and even potatoes and orange juice if there are menu descriptions of these items. Most, if not all, interaction with the distribution channel was with the end seller. Exceptions occurred, for example, when an equipment manufacturer's representative made a sales call (sometimes with the representative of a local equipment supply company), and as buyers met with agents, brokers, and others at professional trade shows.

Although contact with end-channel suppliers is likely to continue, the expectations that hospitality buyers have for those with whom they do business is likely to change. Many of these concerns will be addressed later in the text (see Chapter 8); however, some relate to distribution channel concerns, and these are discussed next.

CHANNEL FLOW BEGINS WITH THE ORDER

Products do not begin to flow through the distribution channels until they have first been ordered. A traditional method in common use throughout the hospitality industry has already been described: The purchaser contacts a designated supplier and places an order. The contact can be made by traditional alternatives

---

Key Term

Channels of distribution (direct) A distribution channel in which the producer and the hospitality organization interact directly with each other.

THE SUPPLIER'S SIDE (2.1)

Effective suppliers can help purchasers gain access to distribution channels. Examples include manufacturers' representatives who are specialists in the products produced by their companies. They can provide access to hardcopy and electronic catalogs useful for the purchaser's research purposes. Suppliers can also represent purchasers in problems with freight haulers and other middlemen who handle the products as they move through the distribution channels. The best suppliers know how to expedite products and applicable "paperwork" (perhaps not an accurate term because much of the supportive documentation is now electronic) from others in the supply chain. They will do so in efforts to provide value to the professional relationship that they have with hospitality purchasers.

Containers such as these containing nonperishable products for hospitality operations are transported by ship around the world and by trucks and trains across the country.

Mira.com

(telephone, fax, or person-to-person, or it can be electronic: Internet, **extranet,** or **electronic data interchange**).

Traditional Method

Traditionally, a purchaser interacted with each supplier who provided products to the organization. Figure 2.2 illustrates this process for a restaurant, and it is repeated on a larger scale for hotels and some other hospitality organizations where the variety of purchasing needs is larger.

Internet Purchasing Assistant (2.1)

Order placement is an important logistics function in every hospitality organization. Increasingly, it is being done electronically with transmittal over the Internet, by extranet, or electronic data interchange. Orders received by suppliers are, in turn, electronically transmitted to a centralized location where the orders are prepared. At some point, new quantities must be ordered from the suppliers' own vendors, and this is also done electronically.

After products are received, invoices can be routed through the hospitality organization electronically, and the purchaser can issue payment order or remittance advice documents and use electronic funds transfer (EFT) payments. (*Note*: Details about electronic order processing and electronic payment procedures will be discussed in, respectively, Chapters 10 and 12.)

To learn more about EFT, check out the Web site of the Financial Management Service, a bureau of the U.S. Department of the Treasury: www.fms.treas.gov/eft/

Key Terms

Extranet Private electronic network using Internet protocols and the public telecommunication system to securely exchange a hospitality organization's business information with suppliers.

Electronic data interchange (EDI) Computer-to-computer exchange of information between the hospitality organization and a supplier using a standard and machine-processable format.

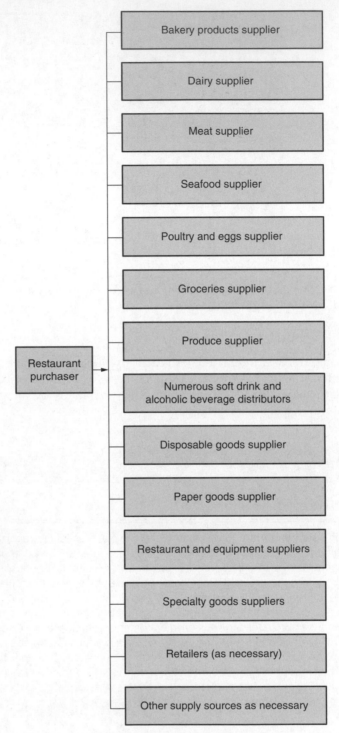

FIGURE 2.2 Traditional Restaurant Order Entry into Distribution Channels

The purchase needs of the restaurant noted in Figure 2.2 are for example only. Cleaning supplies, uniforms, and other nonfood items are also required. In addition to these routine and recurring purchases, food production and service small-wares, and major equipment items must also be purchased on an occasional basis.

As suggested earlier in this chapter, some streamlining (condensing) of the purchasing process becomes possible as full-line merchant wholesalers are used, because purchasers must interact with fewer suppliers. These supply sources become attractive when purchasers require more generally available products from

Many food items required for commercial food service operations may be purchased local markets such as this Hong Kong produce market.

Stefan Mokrzecki/Photolibrary.com

these wholesalers at lower prices than those offered by their specialty wholesaler counterparts. Also, full-line wholesalers attempt to provide an increasingly wider variety of popular products to gain market share. They can do this by purchasing large volumes of products available to purchasers from other sources, purchasing directly from manufacturers who affix the wholesaler's label to the product (this is discussed later in the chapter), and even buy companies who manufacture products that will broaden their product lines. All of these actions reduce a hospitality purchaser's dependence upon specialty wholesalers.

As orders are placed with suppliers, those suppliers use their own distribution channels to obtain products required to fill the orders. Typically, these suppliers carry an inventory and "draw down" on it as orders are fulfilled in the same way that hospitality organizations maintain storeroom inventories, and withdraw products with an issuing process until it is time to reorder from a supplier.

Figure 2.2 indicates the need for numerous soft drink and alcoholic beverage distributors. Recall that these suppliers typically have the exclusive rights to be the only source for specific products within a specified area. In other words, if a purchaser wants to use Pepsi-Cola products, only the distributor can provide it. Details about the purchase of alcoholic beverage distributors

---

PURCHASING PROS NEED TO KNOW (2.3)

Sometimes, even when the "best" suppliers are used, hospitality purchasers must expedite product purchases. In much the same manner, suppliers may need to interact with their own supply sources to obtain products required for their **accounts.** Hospitality purchasers who "do all the right things" may still not always be able to obtain the "right" products at the "right time" in the "right condition" at the "right cost." They can, however, work with suppliers who, in turn, can help to facilitate an acceptable flow of products through the distribution channels. Larger hospitality organizations (as measured by volume of purchases) are generally able to better influence organizations in their distribution channels. However, hospitality organizations of all sizes working through hospitality-related and other organizations can become spokespersons for the need to better serve hospitality customers. The role of intermediaries in the supply chain to assist with this goal can be employed by the entire industry and all the organizations that comprise it.

Key Term

Account   Hospitality and other organizations that are clients of a supplier.

HIGH-TECH PURCHASING (2.1)

The term "e-procurement" refers to an electronic system that connects hospitality organizations with their suppliers and manages all interactions between them. Its overall goal is to streamline purchasing. Buyers typically use e-procurement with their most important suppliers: those providing the highest dollar volume of purchased products. Properly implemented systems help to monitor costs, maintain an open line of communication with suppliers as business is transacted, and allow managers to confirm pricing and note variations between order periods.

Other advantages of online procurement include the ability to keep applicable information organized and updated. Because most transactions are template-driven, they are standardized and trackable so buyers can use cumulative information to obtain better pricing. E-procurement can also help to maintain inventory at optimal levels while minimizing the chance of stock outs.

Using technology to assist in the procurement process can help to lower prices without sacrificing quality. However, its net effect can also include improved productivity of purchasing personnel, faster processing, and a greater assurance that unplanned purchasing will not occur. The "best" candidates for e-procurement include items that comprise a significant part of the purchasing budget, items for which there are several (or more) competitive suppliers, and when internal procurement processes are relatively inefficient.

---

and, in some states, state-operated distribution networks, will be discussed in Chapter 16.

The purchasing tasks just described are repetitive and time-consuming and, because of the sheer number of suppliers and purchasing interactions that are required, some "communication problems" and other challenges typically arise.

On-the-Job Challenges in Purchasing (2.1)

"Why should we even consider changing our purchasing system?" asked Raul, as he spoke with Ferdinand, the general manager of Green Hills Hotel.

"Well, Raul, you're the long-time purchasing manager here at the property, and I've heard you mention numerous problems over the past year or so with the procedures we're currently using. Remember that stretch of about six months when almost every seafood delivery was accompanied with price increases? How about problems you have had with drastic inventory fluctuations and the effect they had on inventory values when food costs were calculated? And just yesterday weren't you talking about the increased time it's taking to evaluate supplier price quotations?"

"Yes," Raul replied, "I have mentioned those things, and I am aware of some other issues that I haven't bothered you about. However, many of these concerns relate to employee turnover and an inability to train new staff members to make the decisions necessary to address the purchasing problems we've encountered."

"I understand that, Raul," said Ferdinand, "However, when do you think the turnover problems will settle down? What's wrong with exploring electronic purchasing processes used by other hotels that are even smaller than ours to see how, if at all, our system can be improved? Wouldn't it be great if we could find ways to make our purchasing system more effective and, at the same time, reduce the stress that these problems create for you and your staff?"

Case Study Questions

1. What are potential reasons that Raul might be resisting Ferdinand's request to consider ways to automate the purchasing tasks at the Green Hills Hotel?
2. Assume that Raul agrees (or is required!) to evaluate (benchmark) purchasing systems used by other properties. How, if at all, might his attitude affect the process? What tactics should Raul use to complete this evaluation assignment?
3. What assistance can Raul obtain from suppliers and other distribution channel intermediaries in his efforts to assess purchasing technology alternatives?

PURCHASING PROS NEED TO KNOW (2.4)

Franchisors frequently offer franchisees the opportunity to purchase from preferred vendors who, in turn, offer products at discounted prices. The case is made that prices charged to franchisees using these services will be less than they (the franchisees) would pay on the open market. Also, franchisors note that there is better assurance that products of the required quality will be purchased.

To review the Web site that Choice Hotel International uses to inform and update franchisees about this program, go to: www.ChoiceBuys.com

Although one cannot access some parts of the site without a user name and password, it is possible to review the general types of information made available to this company's franchisees.

Alternative Methods

Independent hospitality operators, and even relatively small multi-unit organizations, may use the traditional purchasing process involving many different suppliers for all products needed. Sometimes, however, they consolidate suppliers. Also, even larger multi-unit organizations may not consolidate their purchases. Remember that hotels "flying the same flag" (those of the same brand) frequently have different ownership and/or are operated by different management companies. This makes the coordination of purchasing much more difficult and, even when there is centralization, significant **"contract leakage"** can occur. (*Note*: Very large, multi-unit hospitality organizations may require units to purchase through their centralized system [this occurs when properties are company owned], and those with franchised units frequently offer opportunities for individual units to purchase through their system or through "approved" suppliers.)

Some organizations use **group buying** procedures for some items and, as you'll learn, consolidated buying is used by many multi-unit organizations.

Key Terms

Contract leakage   A term referring to the purchase of products "out of contract" by a property whose product purchase needs can be addressed in group purchase contracts with affiliated properties.

Group buying   A purchasing system in which orders for products of a specified quality are combined for participating properties. Suppliers receiving the order deliver products to and receive payment from the participating properties; sometimes referred to as "centralized" purchasing.

Internet Purchasing Assistant (2.2)

Internet-based buying groups for small hospitality organizations exist, and they offer a variety of procurement-related services to their members.

To view the Web site of one such group, go to: www.hsgpurchasing.com

When reviewing this Web site, you'll note that a wide range of services are available for those desiring them. Detailed product purchase specifications and purchasing forms based upon the organization's inventory system can be developed. Representatives of the buying group also assist with the purchaser's ordering procedures, and the buying group maintains a computerized database of product information and prices. (*Note*: Orders are delivered and invoiced to the organization by participating suppliers.)

Internet Purchasing Assistant (2.3)

Hospitality purchasers can increasingly use the business-to-business (B2B) marketplace to "connect" with suppliers. To view a listing of online business exchanges, marketplaces, and even auctions that match buyers and sellers in the food and beverage industry, go to: www.business.com

Group buying generally arises from the realization that costs per purchase unit of a product typically decrease as the quantity (volume) of purchases increase. A buying group might, for example, agree on the purchase specifications for selected items, and then regularly pool the quantity needs of participating organizations for these products. Eligible suppliers are asked to quote a price based upon the total quantity of products to be ordered with the understanding that products will be delivered to and paid for by individual properties. Buying groups are typically used more frequently by educational and healthcare facilities, although some state professional associations offer these services to their members for selected items, and some for-profit organizations also exist.

Variations in point of entry of hospitality orders into distribution channels arise with increased frequency in multi-unit hospitality organizations.

Some hospitality purchasers use a large number of suppliers with the thought that competitive pricing alternatives will yield price reductions. Although this may be true, it also reduces the possibility of strategic alliances with supplier partners that allow in-depth supply chain management initiatives.

Many multi-unit lodging organizations have moved away from the traditional model (each property purchases for its own needs) to centralization (consolidation) alternatives. Here are two examples:

- Regional purchasing programs may be developed. Individual properties initiate orders using suppliers recommended by regional purchasing staff.
- Some organizations outsource specific purchasing functions. Outsourcing opportunities include the development of purchase specifications, bidding, and purchase cost analysis. Organizations may also outsource the purchase of furniture, fixtures, and equipment (FF&E) for the hotel's guest rooms and public areas. This may be done in companion with design services offered by the same or different supplier (partner). A typical property's FF&E project may involve the purchase of more than 250 items from more than seventy companies. The need for careful analysis to assess savings from outsourcing parts of the procurement process is obvious.

Internet Purchasing Assistant (2.4)

Large hospitality organizations can outsource major procurement functions to organizations that specialize in performing these activities. To review the Web site of one company that does this internationally, go to: www.technexxus.com

When you reach the site, click on "Solutions" then "Outsourcing" in the section's banner to review information about the services they offer.

PURCHASING PROS NEED TO KNOW (2.5)

Hospitality purchasers representing franchisees are not always confident that the purchasing services offered by their franchisors are cost-effective. They may voice concerns about higher product costs, lower product quality, and/or supplier service concerns. At the same time, franchisors have concerns about product quality and consistency when products are purchased from vendors who are not in their approved supplier base. These issues are often addressed at franchisor/franchisee national or regional meetings, in direct communications, and as alleged problems arise. These issues can affect franchisor/franchisee relationships, reduce the franchisees' perceptions of the benefits they receive, and create the need for franchisees, if they wish, to discover alternative supplier sources and develop purchasing systems that accommodate them.

Franchisors confronted with these and related problems have an ongoing challenge to manage their approved vendors and to carry on public relations efforts to "sell" their franchisees on the benefits of using approved vendors.

SUPPLY CHAIN MANAGEMENT AND HOSPITALITY PURCHASES

Before discussing how supply chain management affects hospitality purchasers, let's review the definition of the term provided in Chapter 1: A supply chain is a consolidated system of organizations, people, activities, information, and resources used to move a product from suppliers to the customers. As such, it is broader than a distribution channel, because a supply chain includes sources of the raw materials used by a manufacturer to produce products. Let's consider the example of a vineyard that produces the wine that moves through a distribution channel to finally reach a hospitality organization. The distribution channel for wine would begin with the vintner. By contrast, the supply chain for the wine used by the hotel or restaurant would begin with those who sold grapes, wine bottles, and other products to the vintner for his or her use in producing wine. A supply chain is, then, a series of suppliers and customers who are linked: Every customer is a supplier to another customer until the finished product (e.g., a meal in a restaurant) is purchased by the final consumer (a restaurant guest).

Logistics Management Practices: Acquisition Costs

Concerns about differences between distribution channels and supply chains are not as important for small hospitality organizations as they are for their larger counterparts. Consider the local restaurant planning an "All you can eat" shrimp special for next weekend. To do so may only require that the purchaser order an additional 100 pounds of shrimp that is readily available from his or her seafood suppliers. Contrast this with the planning required by a large seafood restaurant chain with hundreds of units across the country. Then negotiation for and contracts with suppliers will need to begin many months (or longer) before the time that the seafood special is to be offered in the restaurants. The task of coordinating purchases, transporting products to regional or other distribution centers, and moving them to the individual restaurant outlets represents significant **logistical** challenges related to the management of the supply chain that are beyond the purpose of this book. However, purchasers in single-unit hospitality organizations of

---

Key Term

Logistics   Activities designed to best ensure that the correct quantity of the correct products are at the correct place at the correct time, and that they were moved there at the lowest possible cost.

any size and those in small hospitality chains, who are the direct focus of this book, can still benefit from the use of some basic **logistics management** practices.

When one purchases a product, such as a food, furniture, or equipment item, the purchase cost involves three basic considerations: the cost of the item including charges to transport it to the property (and, in the case of equipment, to install and make it ready for use); services associated with the purchase; and information applicable to the product. The **total logistical costs** associated with moving the product through the distribution channel to the hospitality organization is typically borne by the property, and these costs can be significant. One might initially think that this cost only involves transporting the product from a supplier's place of business or other location to the hospitality organization. This is an obvious transportation cost. However, costs for transportation are also included in the price the supplier paid his or her own supplier, and so forth back to the original product source. Because each intermediary includes his or her costs in the charges to the next intermediary, the hospitality operator is paying for the total of all of these costs in the purchase price to the last supplier in the distribution channel.

Components of the total logistics cost affect each other. For example, transportation costs might be reduced as larger quantities of products are purchased. This, in turn, will reduce order-processing costs because fewer purchase orders and payments must be handled and increased inventory levels will reduce stock outs. However, storage costs will increase, and there is a greater chance of theft, pilferage, and quality deterioration (for perishable products).

Internal Customers and Logistics

Purchasers must consider the organization's **internal customers** when logistics decisions are made.

How much time is required when an order is placed until it is received? Timing is an important consideration in inventory management decisions, and the trade-off between higher inventory levels and stock outs in terms of logistics costs has already been mentioned. However, the possibility of production and employee schedule changes, and the inconvenience to the ultimate customers (guests), when a desired item is not available are also important considerations.

Consistency (dependability) is another logistical concern that influences users. Products are needed at specific times, and orders are placed based upon these timing concerns. Consistent lead times and delivery of complete orders in which all products meet quality requirements are important. It is the purchaser's responsibility to identify and use suppliers who are dependable.

Communication between the hospitality purchaser and the seller is important before, when, and after orders are placed. Status reports for in-process orders are helpful at all times, and they are critical if there may be anticipated "surprises." Good sellers provide this information without being requested to do so, and good buyers deal with suppliers who provide it.

Key Terms

Logistics management   The practice of planning and implementing the cost-effective flow of raw products, in-process inventory, and finished products from product source to product user while satisfying customer requirements.

Total logistics cost   All costs related to transportation, handling and warehousing, inventory, stock outs, order processing, and return of unacceptable products.

Internal customers   The organization's employees who use the products that are purchased.

Frozen foods are a popular market form for many products, but they must be carefully handled and transported to ensure that no food safety problems occur in the buyers' operations.

Mark Richards/PhotoEdit Inc.

Buyer convenience is another logistical concern that demands attention. Simply asked, is it easy to do business with the supplier? What seller requirements make the relationship difficult? What buyer requirements? Ongoing communication between both parties can help smooth out logistical concerns, and improve the relationship of and benefits to both parties.

Other Supply Management Concerns

Products purchased by hospitality operations are frequently transported by railroad, motor, or air carrier. Not surprisingly, much freight is hauled by water carrier in areas like the Caribbean, from the mainland to Hawaii, and in other parts of the world.

Transportation alternatives can be evaluated on the basis of cost, time, dependability, and frequency. Railroads are often used to transport farm products and, relative to alternatives, offer a low cost, if sometimes slow, transportation alternative. Other types of hospitality products move by motor carriers. They have extensive routes (anywhere there is a road!), and offer another service that cannot be matched by alternative modes of transportation: door-to-door service. Although rates are higher than rail rates, they typically have less loss and damage problems and can provide fast and reliable service.

Although airfreight is expensive, it is often the transportation mode of choice when the freight is relatively light weight and time sensitive.

Some large hospitality operations use **distribution centers** to store products in decentralized locations, consolidate products from different suppliers, and sort them into shipments to specific properties. What are the service and financial implications to the development and use of distribution centers by multi-unit hospitality organizations? Answers to this question move beyond the intent of this text, but they are at the heart of supply chain and logistics management decisions for large organizations. Small hospitality organizations benefit from consolidation

Key Term

Distribution centers   Locations used by multi-unit hospitality organizations to store products, consolidate products from different suppliers, and sort them into shipments to specific properties.

This property uses numerous logo items such as stationery, guest room amenities, and disposable napkins. How do they move through market channels to international locations?

Courtesy of Real Resorts

services in their distributor channels when **freight forwarders** perform some of the same services provided by distribution centers operated by larger properties.

Inventory management is also an integral part of procurement concerns, and it is a critical responsibility of purchasers (in small organizations) and supply chain managers (in larger organizations). The effective management of inventory is addressed in Chapter 11.

On-the-Job Challenges in Purchasing (2.2)

Martin's Soups and More Restaurant has just opened its fourth outlet in the suburbs of a large city. Its menus feature a variety of soups and sandwiches that are well liked by its strong customer base.

The size of the building that Martin purchased for his newest outlet is larger than those of the existing units. The twenty-year lease was really a "good deal," and the property is in an excellent location. His business plan suggests that the new unit could probably generate a larger business volume (more dining space would be needed), but he also has two other ideas. Perhaps he could design one or even two banquet rooms and develop a group business. Alternatively, he wants to seriously consider building a commissary that would supply soups, process produce, prepare sandwich fillings, and prepare or preprocess many other items sold in his various locations.

Case Study Questions

1. What are the potential advantages and disadvantages to developing a commissary to supply menu items and some ingredients to his outlets versus using his current on-site preparation process for each outlet?
2. How, if at all, could his current suppliers help him with the analysis task? What other, if any, distribution channel intermediaries might assist him with information helpful in his commissary analysis activities?
3. Assume that Martin constructs the commissary. How will inventory management and product ordering procedures likely be affected at the outlets without the commissary? How will the presence of the commissary in the new outlet affect inventory management and ordering procedures there?
4. How, if at all, will the presence of the commissary affect Martin's supplier selection decisions?

Key Term

Freight forwarders Businesses that accumulate small product shipments into larger lots, and then contract with a carrier to transport them to, for example, a local merchant wholesaler; also called freight consolidator.

COMPONENTS OF FRANCHISOR'S FOOD DISTRIBUTION SYSTEMS

Most customers ordering a sandwich or salad at the drive-through window or counter of their favorite quick-service restaurant have no idea or concern about the complex and expensive series of events that enabled the sandwich or salad ingredients to be available when their order is placed.

Introduction

Each large restaurant chain in the United States operates food distribution systems that enable their company- and/or franchisee-operated properties to procure menu items and ingredients of the correct quality at a reasonable price. Although there are variations in the "mechanics" of how these distribution systems operate, there are also some basic similarities. Figure 2.3 highlights a composite of possible entities in a distribution system that moves products into the restaurants of a chain organization. It will be used as the background to discuss the structure of a possible product distribution system and logistical and other concerns that must be addressed as products flow through it.

A review of the composite franchisor's distribution system shown in Figure 2.3 is best undertaken by discussing each of the entities that it identifies.

National Buying Group (NBG)

The basic purpose of the National Buying Group (NBG) is to purchase products on behalf of the properties in the chain. As this is done, concerns about product quality, price, and service (especially distribution including adherence to delivery schedules) are very important. In our example, separate NBGs are used to procure fresh produce, refrigerated/frozen items, and dry goods, including groceries and disposable supplies. In some organizations, one NBG may be responsible for different categories of, or perhaps all, product purchases; in others, NBGs may be responsible for regional (or other) buying needs.

Multi-unit operators have good reason to be concerned about the products used by their units. They know that their total purchase needs represent a very large (perhaps hundreds of millions of dollars) market. If the purchasing needs of individual units are combined, the resulting large product volumes can yield

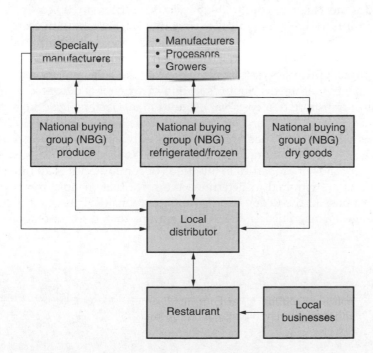

FIGURE 2.3 Possible Franchisor's Distribution System

significant price concessions by bidders. These savings benefit franchisees, and franchisors can then point to another value-driven advantage of the relationship between the two parties. Hopefully, the savings realized enable units to offer lower selling prices. This, in turn, may increase business revenue volume to the benefit of both parties. The franchisor receives, among other franchisee fees, a specified percentage of the latter's revenues. Franchisors also benefit from the purchasing programs because there is better assurance that the products used in the units will be of a quality that meets the franchisor's standards.

Personnel from each NBG interact with manufacturers, processors, and growers to:

- identify applicable products that meet the chain's quality requirements.
- negotiate reasonable prices for the products that meet these specifications.
- address myriad contractual details that favor the organization's restaurant owners (including franchisees). (*Note*: In the discussion that follows, the term "owner" is used to represent the entity owning the restaurant: the franchisor [if it is company-owned] or the franchisee [if it is operated under a franchise agreement].)

Sourcing becomes a more significant challenge as the volume of purchasing needs and the area within which restaurants are located increases. It may, for example, be possible for the NBG to procure all meat items required for a specified time for all units from one manufacturer. However, this may not be possible for fresh produce or other products where there are numerous small producers but few, if any, very large ones that can meet the needs of a large multi-unit hospitality organization. NBGs must then negotiate with regional sources for the needs of the restaurants within that region.

NBGs employ full-time purchasing specialists. They receive advice from franchisee representatives who are elected by their peers to serve as directors of the NBG. These volunteers advise NBG personnel as quality standards are established, price quotations are analyzed, and supply and distribution-related problems arise.

The movement of products through distribution channels from their source to the restaurants is very expensive, regardless of the transportation method(s) used. As products move from one point in the distribution channel to the next, value is added. For example, products are sold to the next middleman for a price that includes the: (1) price paid to the previous middleman, (2) cost of adding the value, (3) profits to the selling middleman, and (4) transportation costs to the next point in the distribution system. This process is repeated as the product moves from point to point until it reaches it final destination: the restaurant.

The product price successfully negotiated by the NBG may (or may not) be the product's final cost at the distributor's facility or when it is delivered to the restaurant. Because transportation costs vary due to many factors, including transportation, distance, those bidding on NBG products must identify and conduct their own negotiations with the intermediaries who will move products between their locations and the restaurant locations. Large franchised organizations can have hundreds and even thousands of properties in hundreds of communities in all fifty states. Significant efforts are required to determine the price that manufacturers provide to NBGs in response to the Request for Price Quotations (RFPs) issued by the NBGs. The challenge is magnified if the NBGs require that price quotations be for a

---

Key Term

Sourcing (product)   Procedures used to determine the source from which products will be purchased.

national delivered price that includes transportation costs to the distributors that service all restaurants in all states, including those outside of the contiguous United States (Alaska and Hawaii). This "group-sharing" requirement for inclusive transportation costs may apply to all, some, or none of the products being purchased.

NBGs may be physically located at the franchisor's national and/or regional headquarters, or they may operate out of other locations. They may be organized as a "purchasing division" of the franchisor or, alternatively, a separate operating entity. Costs of operating NBGs may be directly borne by restaurant owners when the costs are included in the prices owners pay for the products by way of an add-on to product costs. Alternatively, franchisees may pay their share of the NBGs' operating costs indirectly as part of their franchise fees.

Franchisors are very concerned about the products used by their franchisees. Quality is especially important because of the need for consistency in each restaurant. The sandwich and salad ordered at the beginning of this section cannot look, smell, or taste the same in every restaurant unless the same ingredients in the same quantity and of the same quality are used in their preparation. Also, franchisees cannot own profitable restaurants if they charge essentially the same basic menu selling prices, but incur widely different product costs required for production of the sandwich or salad. For these and numerous other reasons, franchisors desire, and work very hard to help ensure that, ingredients used to prepare menu items in their properties are of consistent quality and available at the same or similar price to all restaurant owners.

The duties of NBGs are much more voluminous and complex than that suggested to this point. Consider, for example, that the NBG with purchasing responsibilities for dry goods may need to make purchasing arrangements for thirty (or more) ingredients or menu items. Assume also that they negotiate with three or more manufacturers or processors who are capable of meeting their restaurants' supply needs. One can quickly see that a significant amount of effort is involved in the communication and negotiation processes necessary to award contracts for all the products for which it is responsible. Also, each of the contracts can be worth millions of dollars, and those for edible products may need to be renegotiated twice yearly or, sometimes, more frequently.

Our discussion about the role of NBGs to this point has centered on the assistance they provide to franchisees as food products are procured. However, some NBGs have expanded their services to franchisees and offer savings from aggregated purchases of:

- business insurance programs.
- capital equipment.
- cooking utensils and other smallwares.

NBGs may also negotiate with banks and other lenders for **payment card discounts.** They may also bundle preparation and/or customer service equipment packages to provide, for example, almost everything that a franchisee might require to remodel (update) the production or service side of his or her restaurant.

Key Terms

National delivered price   A product price negotiated by a National Buying Group (NBG) that reflects a common price for the products including transportation delivered to a local distributor that serves each restaurant in the chain.

Discount (payment card)   Processing fees that payment card issuers charge to merchants (restaurants) typically based upon a percentage of the transaction, and often including an additional standard fee per transaction.

PURCHASING PROS NEED TO KNOW (2.6)

Purchasing pros know that the "fewer in the middle, the better it is!" They use this expression to mean that each intermediary in the distribution channel increases the final product charge to the restaurant. The value added by each intermediary must be "worth" more than the additional cost that it charges for its services. For example, is an intermediary required to process produce as it moves through the distribution channel? Alternatively, is it more cost-effective for the lettuce to be shredded at the restaurant? The answer to this question depends upon numerous factors. However, asking and answering it should be the responsibility of NBG staff members as they interact with those in the distribution channel including restaurant owners.

Manufacturers, Processors, and Growers

Figure 2.3 indicates that NBGs interact with the manufacturers, processors, and growers who produce and supply the food and other products that will be purchased by the organization's restaurant owners. The potential need to determine the national delivered price when submitting a response to the RFP issued by the NBG request for price quotations has already been noted. Large manufacturers with the capacity to produce products meeting quality requirements in the quantities required by NBGs may, but will not necessarily have, relationships with local distributors for all areas in which the franchisor requires purchase commitments. Frequently, for example, produce growers and those with seafood-related businesses form marketing or other cooperatives whose members can collectively provide the quantity of products that a large franchisor may require. In other instances, NBGs may contract with several product sources to provide products meeting quality requirements for restaurants in specific areas of the country.

One's perception of a manufacturer may be that it is an organization that employs a marketing representative (salesperson) who makes sales calls on "accounts," takes orders, and transmits them to the "plant" where products are manufactured, and then shipped to customers. This process seldom, if ever, occurs in the large-volume product distribution system used by large franchisors.

Some nonperishable food products may be stored in several locations before reaching the buyer's location.
Vincent P. Walter/Pearson Education/PH College

Instead, manufacturers employ their own staff of marketing and sales experts who work full time to address the purchasing concerns of the company's **national accounts.**

Although a major responsibility of manufacturers is to produce and/or coordinate production and to arrange for transportation of products required under NBG contracts to local distributors, they do perform other services. Some of these are value-added amenities for franchisees. For example, manufacturers' representatives may provide in-store (restaurant or corporate dining area, for example) marketing materials or displays advertising their company's products and may provide samples of food products to individual properties. They may do this, for example, when a franchisee's agreement allows multiple soups from among an allowable variety to be available. These samples then allow franchisees to measure customers' reactions and to learn about their preferences. Representatives of manufacturers may also provide indirect assistance to franchisees as they work with local distributors to address product quality or usage concerns and distribution-related problems. They may, as well, accompany representatives of local distributors to property operations for public relations purposes and/or to assist owners with problems encountered with the manufacturer's products.

Specialty Manufacturers

You have learned about the role of NBGs as they interact with manufacturers, processors, and growers to purchase products of the proper quality at a fair price for franchisees. Most NBG interactions are with organizations that can provide several (or more) of the ingredients and/or menu items needed by restaurant owners. Menus may, however, require other items such as cheese, and promotional campaigns may require **"kids pack" toys** that are produced by **specialty manufacturers.** Contracts negotiated between the NBG and these manufacturers will be limited to only one or a very few specific items. The role of the NBG as it interacts with specialty manufacturers is basically the same as it is with other manufacturers; to: ensure quality requirements, negotiate and award contracts for orders, and solve distribution and related challenges as they occur.

More than one local distributor may be used to provide all private label and other products purchased by the NBG on behalf of the individual properties. This may be the case even when the local distributor is owned by the franchisor. If refrigerated and dry products are delivered by the same distributor, specially designed trucks that can transport both types of items at proper temperatures may be used. Alternatively, dry food products may be transported at refrigerated temperatures.

Local Distributors

As noted in Figure 2.3, local distributors order and receive products shipped from the manufacturer's (or another) location, and then store and transport them in quantities required to the owners' restaurant(s). They also bill the owners for the products that have been received and collect payments from them. The numerous interactions that an owner's employees have with a distributor's delivery and

---

PURCHASING PROS NEED TO KNOW (2.7)

Purchasing pros know that chain restaurant operators often use **private label** products. These are items that are manufactured according to the franchisor's standards, and which are then wrapped and/or packaged in materials or containers that predominately display the name. Sometimes they actually own the franchisor that manufactures the product. More often, however, the manufacturer does this as a concession to the franchisor as a result of the large quantity of products that are purchased. As this is done, additional emphasis is placed on product standardization and consistency because, as you will learn in Chapter 4, a brand (especially that of the company) is one way to express (define) quality.

Sometimes private label brands are produced according to relatively unique specifications, and they represent a product that is different from those made by the manufacturer. In many other instances, however, specifications for the private label product are identical, or at least very similar, to those used by the manufacturer to produce its own products. In these instances, the same products produced and shipped by the manufacturer may be labeled differently. Some products may carry the franchisor's brand, which is shipped through its own distribution channels to its customers. Other products carrying the manufacturer's brand are shipped to the manufacturer's own distributors. Also, if a franchisor's quality standards are relatively generic, the same product carrying the labels of other franchisors may also be produced. (*Note*: Contracts of some large-volume franchisors may prohibit the production or shipping of other franchisors' products from a common manufacturing plant.)

---

accounting record keeping personnel typically represent the most interactions that the owners have with any other entities in the distribution system. Although franchisees typically are more limited than their independent restaurant owner counterparts to select local distributors, they do have opportunities to influence the relationship that evolves, and a wide range of these alternatives are discussed in Chapter 8.

Local Businesses

Figure 2.3 indicates that local businesses may be another product source for franchisees. Items including fresh dairy products, eggs, and, sometimes, baked goods may be purchased from local sources in large part because few, if any, organizations can provide these products on a national or regional basis. Franchisors work hard to minimize the need for these purchases, and their efforts begin at the time menus are planned. If, for example, no menu items require the use of fresh eggs, these products do not need to be purchased. If a recipe requiring eggs can

---

Key Term

Private label (products)   Products that are typically manufactured or provided by one company that are made available under the brand (label) of another company.

PURCHASING PROS NEED TO KNOW (2.8)

Purchasing pros know that a franchisor's contracts with soft drink companies represent significant dollars to both soft drink bottlers (distributors) and franchise organizations. The campaigns of major soft drink manufacturers to win the business of quick service restaurant chains are well publicized in the trade literature. The stakes are made higher when one considers that the length of contracts for exclusive distribution to an organization may be 5–8 years, which is very dissimilar to normal contract lengths of 1 year or less for many commodities purchased by franchisors.

be standardized to permit the use of a frozen egg product, numerous large-volume suppliers become possible sources because of their ability to provide this alternative market form.

Fresh produce (fruits and vegetables) are among the greatest purchasing challenges for many franchisors, and some or all of the purchase needs of restaurant owners may be provided by local businesses or, at least, from sources other than those contracted by NBGs. Products that meet a specified grade (quality) level at the originating point in the distribution channel may deteriorate in quality during transportation and storage, and it can be difficult to recognize required quality standards at the owner's restaurant. Additional problems include frequent and unexpected product shortages and resulting price fluctuations. Interestingly, an inverse correlation often exists between the quality of produce and its price. For example, when a product is in short supply, what is available is typically of a relatively low quality, but it is sold at an unusually high price!

Sometimes, especially when produce may be purchased in relatively small quantities from a large number of growers, NBGs negotiate a product purchase price for restaurant owners that is exclusive of transportation or, at least, that limits the inclusion of transportation costs to only those owners operating restaurants in the contiguous United States. Additional costs to transport fresh produce to Alaska and Hawaii (the two states affected by this exclusion) are very expensive, and the perishable status of produce means that shipping delays and/or improper holding environments while under transport can cause significant quality deterioration problems for the franchisees.

Franchisees that are directly affected by produce or other problems involving NBG sources typically have only three alternatives to manage them:

- Accept higher prices, anticipate delays, and/or related quality problems. Comply with existing franchise agreements relating to the purchase of these

---

PURCHASING PROS NEED TO KNOW (2.9)

Purchasing pros know that, especially for complex distribution channels, there can be exceptions to general principles about "what's best."

Example: It might appear reasonable to suggest that a manufacturer who provides products under an NBG contract must be able to deliver products "to each state" or that it must make arrangements for a distributor "in each state." Don't modern transportation systems allow distributors to move products by rail or truck to any franchisee location within a state?

Now for an exception: There are four major islands in the state of Hawaii where most, if not all, major quick-service restaurant franchisors have locations. Cost limitations require that most products be transported from the mainland to the state's major port of entry (Honolulu on the island of Oahu). To transport these products to franchisees on the other islands (Big Island, Kauai, and Maui) requires that they be off-loaded from ocean-going freighters, reloaded onto barges that make regularly scheduled trips to these islands, and then off-loaded at the destination port. Then, as is true with Oahu-bound shipments, products must be trucked to the distributor's warehouse, and off-loaded from the truck for storage, and then later loaded onto a truck for transport to each restaurant.

The number of times that products must be handled and the distances that they must be shipped create significant cost differentials from products shipped within the contiguous United States.

Franchisees must make incremental additions to menu selling prices to compensate for the higher product costs they incur. However, nominal increases in selling prices frequently do not offset the higher product costs that include the transportation expenses that they must pay. The alternatives just noted (comply with the franchisee contract, "work around it," or work within the organization to address inequities) all become relevant alternatives in these extraordinary situations.

Air shipments are expensive but necessary to quickly move highly perishable products such as fresh seafood.

Gary Conner/Photolibrary.com

products and, hopefully, work within the franchisor's organization to discover successful solutions to these issues.

- Attempt to obtain contract exclusions that permit, for example, local, statewide, or regional franchisee associations to develop their own produce purchasing groups to procure produce that meets the franchisor's quality standards at reasonable prices.
- Ignore and/or work around contractual obligations, especially when there are no other reasonable alternatives.

Purchasing Resources on the Internet

In addition to the Web sites referenced in this chapter's "Internet Purchasing Assistant" features, the following sites provide detailed information to enhance your purchasing knowledge and skills.

Purchasing Resources on the Internet

Site	Information About
www.adacoservices.com	Purchasing and inventory management software for the hotel industry
www.restaurantsoftware.com	Restaurant software (directory) including that for purchasing and inventory management
www.hotelinteractive.com	Supplier Interactive Hospitality Network: a service that helps buyers locate suppliers for hospitality products
www.dotfoods.com	Redistribution: buying groups that assist individual food distributors
www.nathosp.com	Single-source purchasing of in-room and other amenities including retail sales
www.chrisgarrod.com	Outsourcing FF&E and operating equipment purchases
www.gfs.com	Broadline foodservice distributor
www.don.com	Broadline distributor of foodservice equipment and supplies
www.novationco.com	Largest healthcare contracting service (group purchasing organization)

Site	Information About
www.dmoz.org/business/hospitality/	Foodservice equipment manufacturers' representatives (directory)
www.hobartcorp.com	Services of broadline foodservice equipment manufacturers
www.hospitalitynet.org	Distribution strategies (Click "marketplace," then "online distribution")
www.ehotelier.com	Equipment suppliers, manufacturers, distributors, and other intermediaries in hotel distribution channels
www.hospitalityupgrade.com	Hospitality technology applications
www.foodservice.com	Foodservice distributors
www.sysco.com	The largest foodservice distributor in the United States
www.htmagazine.com	*Hospitality Technology Magazine* (Enter "supply chain management" in the site's search box)
www.business.com	Food and beverage companies (directory) (Enter "food and beverages" in the site's find it! box)
www.hotel-online.com	E-procurement (Enter "e-procurement" in the site's Search Hotel Online! box.)

Key Terms

intermediaries (distribution channel) 29
manufacturer 30
processor 30
grower 30
agent (distribution channel intermediary) 31
manufacturer's representative (distribution channel) 31
product line 31
selling agent (distribution channel) 32

broker (distribution channel) 32
merchant wholesaler (distribution channel) 32
merchant wholesaler (full-line) 32
merchant wholesaler (limited-line) 32
distributor 32
retailer (cash and carry) 32
purchase unit 33
channels of distribution (indirect) 33

vertical distribution system 33
channels of distribution (direct) 34
extranet 35
electronic data interchange (EDI) 35
account 37
contract leakage 39
group buying 39
logistics 41
logistics management 42
total logistics cost 42

internal customers 42
distribution centers 43
freight forwarders 44
sourcing (product) 46
national delivered price 47
discount (payment card) 47
national account 49
kids' pack toys 49
specialty manufacturers 49
private label (products) 50

Think It Through

1. Assume that you are the purchaser for a franchised hotel that is affiliated with a large national lodging organization and are employed by the management company that operates the hotel. What procedures would you employ to keep current on the products that are used by your hotel? What tactics would you use to learn about new products that department personnel request?

2. You've learned that transportation costs are one of the expenses "built-in" to products that are purchased. When, if at all, would you ask a supplier to provide a product price exclusive of transportation to reduce your costs? In other words, when would you consider allowing someone from your organization to pick up the products at the supplier's place of business? Defend your answer.

3. Assume that you are a restaurant manager. How, if at all, might intermediaries in a distribution channel help you directly? Help your supplier to help you?

4. What are examples of purchases that a large hotel or restaurant organization might make that would

involve transactions directly with a grower, processor, or manufacturer and, in turn, eliminate the need to deal with other distribution channel intermediaries?

5. What factors would be important to you as the general manager of a large hotel as you considered the possibility of outsourcing all or part of the purchasing function at your property?

Team Fun

This chapter has suggested that intermediaries in the distribution channels providing products to the hospitality organization may assist hospitality organizations to better serve its customers. Each team will be given one assignment as this concept is explored more in depth.

1. The assignment of the first team is to consider how a property's suppliers and other distribution channel intermediaries can assist the property with inventory management tasks.

2. The assignment of the second team is to consider how suppliers and other intermediaries in the distribution channel can assist the property with improving the property's product ordering and receiving procedures.

3. The assignment of the third team is to identify ways that suppliers and other intermediaries in the distribution channels can assist in helping the hospitality organization to best identify and address evolving customer preferences.

3

Legal and Ethical Aspects of Procurement

In This Chapter

Buyers in the United States, as well as many other developed countries, are fortunate because very specific laws and enforcement entities regulate the procurement process. In the United States, many of these laws are administered and enforced by specific federal governmental agencies. Buyers should understand the procurement-related roles of the most important of these federal agencies and their responsibilities to buyers and sellers and, in this chapter, you will learn about them.

There has also been (and continues to be) significant procurement-related legislation passed at the national level. This legislation directly affects the manner in which the buying and selling process is managed in the United States, and as a professional buyer, it is important that you recognize its influence. State and local governmental units also consider and pass legislation related to the buying process. Although it would be impossible to know every law in every state or local area, in this chapter you will examine examples of state and local legislation related to buying and learn the best way to stay current about it.

When a purchase decision is made, a buyer and a seller make an agreement. In effect, the buyer says, "*I will do this, if you will do that.*" Conceptually, such agreements seem to be quite straightforward. In reality, these buying/selling agreements (called *contracts*) can be exceptionally complex and subject to a wide range of interpretation. For that reason, professional buyers must know the basic types of buy and sell contracts, as well as the essential elements that must be present to create a legally binding contract. In this chapter you will learn about these different contract types and the elements they must contain.

Experienced hospitality buyers know that contract disputes between buyers and sellers are quite common. Unfortunately they can also be expensive, time consuming, and result in long-term bad feelings between buyer and seller. To minimize disagreements, contracts should be clearly written and well understood by both parties. In this chapter you will learn about very specific contractual terms and clauses that professional buyers should carefully review and understand before they enter into a legally binding contract.

In addition to laws that dictate their actions, experienced buyers know that there is another set of principles that directly affects all buyers' behavior. These behavioral principles are called *ethics*, and they are the set of principles that guide an individual's behavior toward others. Ethics are usually based upon an individual's moral standards and beliefs. In this chapter you will learn how to use a system for determining if a course of action is ethical.

Although you will learn about the importance of ethics, it is important to recognize that not all individuals have the same ethical standards. Therefore, some buyers and/or their hospitality companies have formalized ethical conduct for their organization. These formalized ethical standards are called *Codes of Ethics*, and this chapter presents one such code that can be used as is, or modified by those professional buyers seeking to communicate their own view of ethical buyer behavior.

■ ■ ■

Outline

LEGAL ASPECTS OF PROCUREMENT

Although professional buyers need not be lawyers to adequately perform their jobs, the legal aspects of procurement are very significant. In the United States, a large number of federal agencies control and monitor various aspects of the purchasing process. These agencies issue rules and regulations that buyers and sellers must follow. Also, Congress itself has passed a variety of bills that directly affect the purchasing process. In the next section of this chapter you will learn about some of these agencies and the most important federal laws affecting the purchasing process.

The various states (and some local area governments) have their own agencies and regulations related to purchasing, and buyers must also recognize their importance in the purchasing process. Whether federal, state, or local, the legal aspects of buyer–seller agreements (purchasing contracts) and the promises (warranties) made by sellers, should be well understood so purchasing professionals can be most effective. Let's take a look at the legal issues that are important to buyers.

Federal Agencies Affecting the Buying Process

It would be difficult to identify every federal agency that can influence a hospitality buyer. However, several federal agencies affect every buyer.

FEDERAL TRADE COMMISSION (FTC)   When the FTC was created by Congress in 1914, its purpose was to prevent unfair methods of competition in commerce. Over the years, Congress passed additional laws giving the agency greater authority to police anticompetitive practices. In 1938, Congress passed a broad prohibition against

Accuracy in menu terminology is one area in which hospitality buyers must recognize the authority of the Federal Trade Commission.

Picture Press/Corbis/Bettmann

"unfair and deceptive acts or practices." Since then, the FTC also has been directed to administer a wide variety of other consumer protection laws.

All hospitality buyers should be familiar with the agency because one of its current responsibilities is to ensure truthful advertising. If, for example, a hospitality buyer is purchasing "Colorado" trout for service at a restaurant that is advertising this item to guests, the FTC is the agency responsible for ensuring the buyer chooses, and the restaurant serves, only trout that is, in fact, from Colorado. To serve trout from a different origin would be a deceptive trade practice and illegal. Hospitality buyers must be familiar with the laws requiring truthful advertising and prohibiting unfair pricing practices. Both of these areas of federal law are administered by the FTC.

FOOD AND DRUG ADMINISTRATION (FDA)   Formed in 1906, the FDA is an agency of the U.S. Department of Health and Human Services and is responsible for regulating food, dietary supplements, drugs, blood products, radiation-emitting devices and cosmetics, as well as some other products. The FDA has the power to regulate products in a manner that ensures the safety of the American public and the effectiveness of marketed foods. Regulations can take several forms, including outright bans of some items the FDA deems as unsafe, controlled distribution of others, and controlled marketing of still others. Because it relates directly to the hospitality industry, Congress has given the FDA the authority to ensure that the foods and beverages sold in the United States are safe, wholesome, and truthfully labeled. You will learn more about this agency's specific regulatory functions in other chapters of this book.

U.S. DEPARTMENT OF AGRICULTURE (USDA)   Also called the Agriculture Department, the original purpose of the USDA was to meet the needs of American farmers and ranchers. It addressed this goal by promoting agricultural trade and production, helping to ensure food safety, and protecting natural resources. The USDA Food Safety and Inspection Service (FSIS) is responsible for ensuring that all meat, poultry, and processed egg products are safe to consume and accurately labeled. This includes any food product that contains more than 2–3 percent meat. As you will learn in future chapters, the USDA and its inspection and food grading programs play an important role in the marketing and procurement of food products used in the hospitality industry.

ENVIRONMENTAL PROTECTION AGENCY (EPA)   The EPA is charged with protecting human health and with safeguarding the environment including air, water, and land. The EPA began operation in 1970. Lesser known to hospitality buyers than some other agencies, the EPA sets a variety of standards related to food. One of the most important is enforcement of the Food Quality Protection Act (FQPA) limiting the type and amount of pesticides permitted for use in food for human consumption.

OCCUPATIONAL SAFETY AND HEALTH ADMINISTRATION (OSHA) This agency was founded in 1970 and is housed in the U.S. Department of Labor. Its mission is to prevent work-related injuries, illnesses, and deaths by issuing and enforcing rules (called standards) for workplace safety and health. As you will learn in later chapters, OSHA standards directly affect the products you should buy and the information you must supply to workers who will use them. Although sometimes criticized as overly aggressive, OSHA has had a significant influence on hospitality workplaces in a relatively short period of time. Among the changes in safety regulation brought about by OSHA are:

Guards on all moving parts: In the past, many (but not all) manufacturers produced foodservice equipment such as slicers and meat saws, with guards to prevent inadvertent contact with their blades. With OSHA, the use of guards was expanded to cover essentially all parts where contact is possible.

Personal Protective Equipment (PPE): In the hospitality industry, broader use of gloves, coveralls, and other protective equipment when handling hazardous chemicals and blood was an important OSHA initiative.

Lockout/tagout: In the 1980s, OSHA developed requirements for locking out energy sources in an "off" condition when performing repairs or maintenance.

Hazard communication: Also known as the "Right to Know" standard, this rule was issued in 1983 and requires the development and communication of information on the hazards of chemical products used in the workplace.

Blood-borne pathogens: In 1990, OSHA issued a standard designed to prevent hotel, health care, and other workers from being exposed to blood-borne pathogens such as hepatitis B and HIV (the AIDS-causing virus).

INTERNAL REVENUE SERVICE (IRS) AND BUREAU OF ALCOHOL, TOBACCO AND FIRE-ARMS (ATF) Jointly, the IRS and the ATF regulate the production and sale of alcoholic beverages in the United States. The role of the IRS is one of administrative oversight of alcohol sales. As a result, it seeks to separate alcoholic beverage sellers who are in compliance with the tax laws from those who fail to satisfy their tax obligations. To do this, the IRS focuses on identifying unreported income, monitoring product usage (costs), and unreported tip income. These activities affect procurement in a variety of ways, from developing record-keeping systems that ensure compliance with tax payments, to selecting revenue-recording systems that confirm actual sales levels.

Internet Purchasing Assistant (3.1)

The areas of responsibilities for federal agencies are quite varied and not always easily identified. It would seem, for example, that OSHA would be the logical agency for information related to all working conditions. However, the Department of Health and Human Services houses the Centers for Disease Control (CDC). The CDC publishes recommendations on a variety of topics, including how bakers, food production personnel, laundry workers, and those who buy protective gear for them can reduce threats related to working in areas with high levels of heat. To see some of their information about this issue, go to: www.cdc.gov/niosh/topics/heatstress/

At the site, click on "Working in Hot Environments."

The ATF was established in its present form and with its present name in 1972, but it traces its roots to the days of Prohibition (1920s–early 1930s). The ATF controls the production, labeling, and advertising of alcohol and the relationships between producers, wholesalers, and retailers. The agency's efforts are directed mainly at protecting consumers against products that are impure or mislabeled or otherwise potentially harmful.

Other federal agencies and departments also affect the procurement process. In fact, the buyer–seller relationship and how it is controlled is one of the most regulated and carefully controlled of all commercial activities in the United States. However, even with its considerable oversight and assistance, professional buyers must use their own good judgment and knowledge when performing their tasks. Also, they must recognize that, despite assistance from the federal government, **caveat emptor** remains an important concept for buyers to remember.

National Legislation Affecting the Buying Process

Hospitality buyers researching the effect of law on the purchasing process will find that many significant acts, orders, laws, and regulations have been enacted. In fact, legislation related to buying and selling products continues to evolve as new information and facts influence the process. Although much can be learned by a historical study of national legislation affecting the entire hospitality industry, buyers should be especially familiar with two specific areas of legislation: the **Uniform Commercial Code (UCC)** and federal legislation.

UNIFORM COMMERCIAL CODE (UCC)   The Uniform Commercial Code (UCC) is not a federal law, but rather an effort by the states to harmonize their own commercial laws across state borders. Thus, the UCC has the effect of governing interstate commerce in much the same manner as federal laws related to buying and selling. The importance of such laws is clear when, for example, a buyer in one state purchases goods grown in another state, manufactured in yet another state, from a seller located in still another state. The UCC, in its entirety, has been adopted in 49 states (Louisiana has enacted most, but not all, of the provisions of the UCC, preferring to maintain its own civil law traditions to govern the sale of goods), the District of Columbia, Puerto Rico, Guam, and the U.S. Virgin Islands.

Under the UCC, a vendor is obligated to sell only goods that are fit for their intended use and free of defects. From a practical standpoint, this means that a foodservice buyer selecting, for example, a food product to be served to guests can be assured in the usage the product is wholesome and safe to eat (fit for its intended use). In a similar manner, a piece of equipment advertised by its manufacturer as suitable for brewing coffee should do so in a manner that does not endanger its operator (the product is free from defects). The UCC covers a variety of commercial buyer–seller transactions. Figure 3.1 outlines the provisions of the UCC under its consecutively numbered Articles.

As you will learn later in this chapter as well as in others, the UCC governs many important aspects of buyer–seller relationships, including the stated and implied promises made by sellers about their products' appropriateness for intended use.

Key Terms

Caveat emptor   Latin for *"Let the Buyer Beware"*; the long-established commercial principle that the buyer is responsible for checking the quality and suitability of goods before purchasing them.

Uniform Commercial Code (UCC)   A model set of laws regulating commercial transactions, including banking and credit but especially those related to the sale of goods.

Article	Title	Subject Addressed
1	General Provisions	Definitions, rules of interpretation
2	Sales	Sale of Goods
2A	Leases	Lease of Goods
3	Banking	Banknotes
4	Bank Deposits	Banks and funds transfers
4A	Funds Transfers	Transfers of money between banks
5	Letters of Credit	Transactions involving letters of credit
6	Bulk Transfers and Bulk Sales	Auctions and asset liquidation
7	Ownership of Goods	Storage of goods
8	Investment Securities	Securities and financial assets
9	Secured Transactions	Transactions secured by assets

FIGURE 3.1 Uniform Commercial Code (UCC) Topics

THE SUPPLIER'S SIDE (3.1)

"Insider" Tips on Purchasing: From the Supplier's Perspective

Buyer's Question: Why would Louisiana be the only state not to totally accept the UCC?

Supplier's Answer: Louisiana has a different legal system than the rest of the country.

Buyer's Question: How is it different?

Supplier's Answer: Louisiana, because of its French heritage, is the only state that uses a "civil," not "common" law system. Common law and civil law are the two major systems of law in place in the Western world. Common law is the body of law that descended from Great Britain and is used in the United States and most countries influenced by the British Commonwealth. Civil law descended from the laws of the Roman Empire and is used by most Western European countries, as well as those in Latin America, Asia, and Africa. Although an oversimplification, in general, common law is guided heavily by reviewing decisions made by previous courts in cases of similar situations or facts. In civil law, decisions are based on written laws or codes. Judges in civil law are less interested in what other judges have decided before them, and more interested in the law as written. Given the historical influence on the United States of both Great Britain and France, it is no wonder that these two distinct legal systems might sometimes be at odds in methodology, if not their actual intent to promote fairness and justice.

Internet Purchasing Assistant (3.2)

Professional buyers should familiarize themselves with the major provisions of the UCC. The information it contains is practical and intended to inform both buyers and sellers about their legal rights. For example; "What are buyers legally allowed to do when a shipment of goods they purchased contains, upon delivery, some acceptable and some unacceptable products?"

To see the answer to this and other issues related to Article 2 (Sales of Goods) of the UCC, go to: http://www.law.cornell.edu/ucc/ucc.table.html

1. At the site, click on Article 2, "Sales"
2. Next, click on "Part 6 (2-601) Buyer's Rights on Improper Delivery" to learn about a buyer's options when sellers attempt to deliver defective goods.

1906   The Federal Food and Drugs Act and the Federal Meat Inspection Act authorizes the federal government to regulate the safety and quality of food. The responsibility falls to the U.S. Department of Agriculture and its Bureau of Chemistry (predecessor to the FDA).

1913   The Gould Amendment requires food packages to state the quantity of contents.

1938   The Federal Food, Drug, and Cosmetic Act replaces the 1906 Food and Drugs Act. Among other things, it requires the label of every processed, packaged food to contain the name of the food, its net weight, and the name and address of the manufacturer or distributor.

1957   The Poultry Products Inspection Act authorizes the USDA to regulate, among other things, the labeling of poultry products.

1969   The White House Conference on Food, Nutrition, and Health addresses deficiencies in the U.S. diet. It recommends that the federal government consider developing a system for identifying the nutritional qualities of food.

1973   The FDA issues regulations requiring nutrition labeling on food containing one or more added nutrients or whose label or advertising includes claims about the food's nutritional properties. (Nutrition labeling is voluntary for almost all other foods.)

1990   The FDA proposes extensive food labeling changes, which include mandatory nutrition labeling for most foods, standardized serving sizes, and uniform use of health claims.

2003   Mandatory nutritional labeling of nearly all foods in full effect.

FIGURE 3.2   Highlights in U.S. Food Labeling Law

FEDERAL LEGISLATION   The legislative branch of the federal government has long been involved in developing rules and regulations regarding the buying and selling of goods. This involvement takes many forms. Among the most important are legislation affecting free and fair trade (e.g., the Sherman Antitrust Act of 1890 and the Clayton Act of 1914), food inspection (e.g., the Food, Drug and Cosmetic Act of 1906), deceptive advertising (e.g., the establishment of the Fair Trade Commission in 1914 and the Perishable Commodities Act of 1930), and food labeling (the Hart Act of 1966 and additional ongoing legislation). Historically, food labeling (including the current interest in labeling of restaurant menu items) is of concern to federal legislators and regulators. Figure 3.2 summarizes some of the most important food labeling legislation.

Federal legislation affects hospitality buyers in areas beyond ensuring the quality of food and beverage products. For example, the Americans with Disabilities Act of 1990 (ADA) mandates the purchase of special products and building design features intended to ensure equal access to facilities (including hospitality operations) for Americans who are disabled. In another area, a variety of franchise-related laws dictate what franchisors may and may not require their franchisees to buy, and legislation related to the Robinson–Patman Act of 1936 spells out instances in which preferential (discount) pricing may be legally offered to buyers.

It is inevitable that federal legislation will continue to affect the procurement process in hospitality and other industries. For that reason, professional buyers' membership in trade associations to monitor changing requirements, and to make their own views known to federal legislators prior to the enactment of new legislation, is vitally important.

State and Local Legislation Affecting the Buying Process

The number of state and local laws, ordinances, codes, and rules related to the buying and selling of food and beverages, as well as other hospitality services, would fill many books. Also, in many cases, state and local governmental agencies often work cooperatively with federal agencies, thus creating yet another entity directly affecting the buying process. For example, the federal government is responsible for a wide variety of food safety and consumer protection programs. An important part of that responsibility is an inspection and testing program for food processing plants, food storage, and food distribution points. In most cases, businesses such as

HI-TECH PURCHASING (3.1)

What's in a (Menu) Name?

Increasingly, food service operations face the same challenges as any other food labeler when selling foods they have purchased. One of those challenges includes understanding the highly technical use of words legally allowed to be used to describe increasingly popular menu items identified with labels such as "free," "low," or "light." The FDA has very tightly defined definitions of such words when the terms are used on food service menus. These include:

Free. This term means that a product contains no amount of, or only trivial or "physiologically inconsequential" amounts of, one or more of these components: fat, saturated fat, cholesterol, sodium, sugars, and calories. For example, "calorie-free" means fewer than 5 calories per serving, and "sugar-free" and "fat-free" both mean less than 0.5 grams (g) per serving. Synonyms for "free" include "without," "no," and "zero." A synonym for fat-free milk is "skim."

Low. This term can be used on foods that can be eaten frequently without exceeding dietary guidelines for one or more of these components: fat, saturated fat, cholesterol, sodium, and calories.

Descriptors of "low" are defined as follows:

low-fat: 3 g or less per serving
low-saturated fat: 1 g or less per serving
low-sodium: 140 mg or less per serving
very low sodium: 35 mg or less per serving
low-cholesterol: 20 mg or less and 2 g or less of saturated fat per serving
low-calorie: 40 calories or less per serving

Synonyms for "low" include "little," "few," "low source of," and "contains a small amount of."

Light. This descriptor can mean two different things:

First, that a nutritionally altered product contains one-third fewer calories or half the fat of the reference food. If the food derives 50 percent or more of its calories from fat, the reduction must be 50 percent of the fat.

Second, that the sodium content of a low-calorie, low-fat food has been reduced by 50 percent. In addition, "light in sodium" may be used on food in which the sodium content has been reduced by at least 50 percent.

Note: The term "light" can still be used to describe such properties as texture and color, as long as the word explains the intent—for example, "light brown sugar" or "light and fluffy."

Professional buyers should visit the FDA's Web site regularly to monitor changes in official definitions of these terms and other modifications of food labeling requirements.

these must first be **licensed** by the state in which they operate by demonstrating compliance with that state's sanitation and related requirements.

These facilities are then inspected on a regular basis to ensure continuing compliance with established standards during all phases of food handling and storage.

A number of other consumer protection issues are typically included as part of each state inspection activity. Packaged foods are test-weighed to verify net

Key Term

License A legal document granting the authorization to operate a business or provide a service.

Ensuring the quality and wholesomeness of meats was the original goal of the Meat Inspection Act of 1907, a goal that is equally important to today's hospitality buyers and customers.
Paul Poplis/FoodPix/Jupiter Images-FoodPix-Creatas

contents labeling; ground beef is tested for fat content and extenders; labels are reviewed to preclude misrepresentation to the public; and eggs, bottled water, and other food products are inspected to ensure the purity, grade, and accuracy of informational labels. In many cases, state agencies, working under contract with the Food and Drug Administration (FDA), manage these very specific sanitation and production inspections.

In a similar manner, to provide grading services nationwide, the USDA maintains cooperative grading agreements with the various State Departments of Agriculture and other state agencies. The grading services performed under these agreements are operated jointly by the USDA's Food Safety and Quality Service and cooperating state agencies and are known as the Federal-State Grading Service. Under these federal–state agreements, federally licensed graders perform their work throughout the country at product points of origin. Often, these shipping point graders work in the fields while a crop is being harvested. In addition, a federal grading service is provided in seventy-five of the largest wholesale terminal markets in the country with assistance from cooperating state agencies.

Although much state activity is performed in conjunction with federal agencies, in some cases, states have passed legislation that mandates state-specific inspection or grading programs. For example, The Florida Department of Citrus (FDOC) is an executive agency of state government established in 1935 by an act of the Florida legislature as the result of an industry request. The act, called the Florida Citrus Code, 601 F.S., states that the FDOC's purpose is to protect and enhance the quality and reputation of Florida citrus fruit and processed citrus products in both domestic and foreign markets. As a result, this product is subject to stringent state, as well as federal, oversight.

Maintaining up-to-date information on state and local legislation affecting the buying process is an important responsibility of purchasing professionals. Because of their complexity, for most hospitality buyers a thorough understanding of the laws related to their own location is the best way to gain an appreciation for the legal influence of state and local regulations. State restaurant, lodging, or other industry segment trade associations are the best place to begin to identify these state or area-specific rules and regulations.

Contractual Issues Affecting the Buying Process

When buyers and sellers agree to do business they create a special legal relationship. The agreements made between buyers and sellers are called **contracts,** and professional buyers should know about the different types of contracts they will encounter.

It is also important to understand that not every agreement between two parties is a contract. Legally enforceable contracts have very specific, identifiable components. Also, contracts related to the purchase of hospitality goods and services work best when they are clearly understood by both contracting parties. To help minimize disagreements that could result from differences of opinion about the specifics of a contract, key contract terms should be directly and clearly addressed. Because of the vital importance of these contract issues, in the next portion of this chapter you will learn about:

- types of contracts
- elements needed in legally binding contracts
- key contract terms and clauses

TYPES OF CONTRACTS   For professional buyers, the word "contract" often has two different, but important, meanings. As a verb, it is frequently used in sentences such as:

"Let's *contract* with Miller's Gourmet Blend to provide our coffee next year."

Even when used as a verb, however, the term *contract* actually refers to a noun that describes an agreement or promise that is legally enforceable.

Contracts, and the laws surrounding them, have been established so that both parties to an agreement understand exactly what they have agreed or promised to do. Professional buyers often make a multitude of agreements on a daily basis, so they must have a through understanding of contracts and their enforcement.

Contracts may be established either in writing or verbally. In most cases, written contracts are preferred over verbal contracts because it is easier to clearly establish the responsibilities of each party when agreements are well spelled out. In addition, time can cause memories to blur or fade; seller representatives may leave their jobs and be replaced with new staff members, and honest recollections, even among the most well-intentioned of parties, can differ. All of these factors can create discrepancies in verbal contracts.

Despite the fact that written contracts have many advantages over verbal agreements, in the hospitality industry, many buyer transactions are established orally, rather than in writing. It is important to recognize that verbal (oral) contracts are enforceable by the courts. When a buyer for a nightclub calls a beverage vendor and orders, by telephone, five cases of beer, an enforceable contract is established via telephone. The buyer agrees to pay for the beer when delivered, just as the vendor agrees to deliver the product.

In a similar manner, if the manager of a restaurant is required by local law to have the operation's fire suppression system located above the deep-fat fryers inspected twice a year, the agreement to do so may not be committed to writing each time an inspection is made. In fact, if the same company has been performing the inspection for several years, it may be that, to efficiently schedule its staff, the inspection company rather than the restaurateur decides on the exact day of

---

Key Term

Contract   An agreement made between two or more parties that is enforceable in a court of law.

On-the-Job Challenges in Purchasing (3.1)

Tim Thatcher hired "Life Support," the area's most popular vocal and dance band, to play at his hotel's New Year's Eve Gala. Tickets were $300 per couple and, due in part to the featured entertainment, tickets quickly sold out.

One of the biggest reasons for the popularity of the band was the talent of Poco Miller, the band's lead singer. Tim was stunned when, on the night of the gala, Bruce, the band's manager, announced that Poco was ill and being replaced by Sara Sipes, a singer unknown in the local area.

As he feared they would, many guests expressed their disappointment at not being able to hear the singer they had "paid" to see. Tim ended up refunding a large amount of money to satisfy the significant number of guests who complained to Tim about the hotel's "false advertising."

At the end of the night, Bruce approached Tim and asked for the band's full payment.

Case Study Questions

Assume you were Tim:

1. Would you want to pay the band the full amount you had agreed to when entering into this service contract?
2. If this issue was heard by a court of law, who do you think the judge would support?
3. In the future, what could Tim do to avoid problems such as this one?

inspection. Then presence of the inspector, access to the facility, an invoice for services performed, and a written inspection report are indications that a verbal or written inspection agreement existed, even if there was no verbal or written agreement for that specific inspection.

ELEMENTS NEEDED IN LEGALLY BINDING CONTRACTS   Regardless of whether a contract is verbal or written, it must include specific elements to be **enforceable** in a court of law. If any of the components are missing, the courts will consider the contract unenforceable.

To be enforceable, a contract must be legally valid, and it must consist of an **offer, acceptance,** and **consideration.**

Not all agreements or promises made between two or more parties are legally valid. If, for example, a restaurant buyer "agrees," even in writing, to purchase an endangered species of animal for a menu item, the buyer would have no recourse if the seller did not deliver the product. The reason: Courts will not enforce a contract that requires breaking a law. Agreements to perform illegal acts are not enforceable. Thus, to be considered legally enforceable, a contract must be made by parties who are legally old enough to make the contract, and the activities specified in the contract must not be in violation of the law.

Key Terms

Enforceable (contract)   A contract recognized as valid by the courts and subject to the court's ability to compel compliance with its terms.

Offer   A proposal to perform an act, or to pay an amount that, if accepted, constitutes a legally valid contract.

Acceptance   Agreement to the exact terms and conditions of a specific offer.

Consideration   The payment to be made in exchange for the promise(s) contained in a contract.

If two parties are legally capable of entering into a contract, and the contract involves a legal activity, the initial element required in a legally enforceable contract is an offer.

An offer states, precisely as possible, exactly what the offering party is willing to do, and what he or she expects in return. The offer may include very specific instructions for how, where, when, and to whom the offer is made. The offer may include deadlines for acceptance. In addition, the offer will include the price or terms of the offer.

To illustrate, when a school foodservice director places an order for produce with a vendor, an offer is made. The foodservice director offers to buy the necessary products at a price quoted by the vendor. The reason that an offer is a required component of a contract is clear. The offer sets the term and responsibilities of both parties. The offer states, "I will promise to do this, if you will promise to do that." Despite the recognized importance of clearly defining the terms of a contract offer, a great deal of litigation today involves plaintiffs and defendants who seek the court's help to define what is "fair" in regard to a specific offer, when that offer was not clearly spelled out in a contract. It is important for buyers to recognize that the courts will enforce contracts that have clearly identifiable terms, even if those terms are heavily weighted in favor of one of the parties. Therefore, buyers must understand all of the terms of an offer before making or accepting it.

Consideration is the second essential element in an enforceable contract, and it can best be viewed as the part of the contract that identifies the value, payment, or cost. For a contract to be valid, each party to the contract must receive consideration. In the case of the foodservice director buying produce, the consideration to the buyer is the produce. The consideration to the seller is the price charged for the products purchased.

Consideration can be something other than money. If, for example, a hospitality buyer agrees to host an employee holiday party for a professional decorating company in exchange for having the company decorate its own restaurant for the holidays, the consideration paid by the restaurant would be the hosting of the employee party. The consideration paid by the decorator would be the products and time required to decorate the restaurant. **Trade-outs** such as these are common in the hospitality industry.

Courts are interested in the existence of consideration, not its size. Thus, a meat supplier may sell a steak for $1, $10, or even $100. The buyer has a right to agree or not agree to purchase the steak at the vendor's price. As a result, as long as both parties to a legitimate contract are in agreement, the amount of the consideration is not generally disputable in court. The important point for buyers to recognize is that the courts will ordinarily not declare a contract unenforceable simply because of the size of the consideration. It is the agreement to exchange value that establishes consideration, and thus the contract's enforceability. Buyers who willingly agree to "pay too much" for something will not, at a later date, find the courts sympathetic to their complaints if the seller in fact delivers the product or service the buyer had agreed to purchase.

Because it takes at least two parties to create a contract, a legal offer and its consideration made by one party must be clearly accepted by a second party before the contract comes into existence. It is important to note that the acceptance must duplicate exactly the terms of the offer in order for the acceptance to make the contract valid. If the acceptance does not mirror the offer, it is considered a

Key Term

Trade-out   An agreement between two businesses in which the contract's consideration is not in the form of cash.

PURCHASING PROS NEED TO KNOW (3.1)

Purchasing pros know legal *acceptance* of a contract may be established in a variety of ways. In the hospitality industry, these generally take the form of one of the following:

1. *Verbal or nonverbal agreement.* In its simplest form, acceptance of a contract offer can be done verbally, with a handshake or even with an affirmative nod of the head.
2. *Acceptance of full or partial payment.* Full or partial payment of the amount indicated in a contract is viewed as accepting the terms of the contract. If, for example, to replace a hot water heater in a school cafeteria a vendor requires "1/2 the price down upon acceptance," the offer of the buyer's deposit would indicate buyer acceptance of the hot water heater's price and the vendor's terms.
3. *Agreement in writing.* In most cases, the best way to indicate acceptance of an offer is by agreeing to the offer in writing. Although a large number of purchase contracts in the hospitality industry are made orally, when the sum of money involved is substantial, contracts should be confirmed in writing, if at all possible.

---

counteroffer (and a new contract) rather than an acceptance. When acceptance mirrors the offer is made, an **express contract** has been created.

An offer may be accepted orally or in writing; however, it must be clear that the terms of the offer were accepted. It would not be fair, or ethical, for example, for a contractor who offers to change the lightbulbs on an outdoor sign for a hotel to quote a price to the hotel's manager and then proceed to complete the job without a clear form of contract acceptance by the manager.

KEY CONTRACT TERMS AND CLAUSES In nearly all cases, there are essential parts of any contract in which a professional buyer agrees to purchase a product or service. The following are some of the important contractual terms and clauses that buyers should review carefully and, for each contract, ensure they understand.

1. *Payment terms* One of the most significant components of a contract for buying products and services is the payment terms. Consider the case of a nightclub owner who wants to purchase a new roof for the club. The owner gets four bids from building contractors, each of whom quotes a similar price. In one case, however, the builder wants full payment prior to beginning work. In the second case, the builder wants half the purchase price prior to beginning the job and the balance upon a "substantial completion" of the work. In the third case, payment in full is required within 30 days after completion of the job. In the final case, the builder is willing to take 12 equal monthly payments with no interest charges on the unpaid balance. Obviously, in this case, the payment terms could make a considerable difference in which contractor gets the bid.

   Required down payments, interest rates on remaining balances, payment due dates, and penalties for late payments are important terms that should be clearly specified in the contract and reviewed carefully by the buyer.

2. *Delivery (or start) dates* For some delivery dates, a range of times may be acceptable. For example, when purchasing replacement TVs for guest rooms, a hotel buyer could insert contract language, such as "within 60 days of contract signing" as an acceptable delivery date clause. Similarly, food and

---

Key Term

Express contract A contract in which the components of the agreement are clearly understood and stated, either orally or in writing.

beverage deliveries might be accepted by a kitchen manager "between the hours of 8:00 a.m. and 4:00 p.m."

In some cases, the delivery or start date may be unknown. Consider, for example, the country club with an older heating unit. Replacement parts are no longer available for the unit, so they must be custom machined when needed. In this case, a vendor/repair company may simply state that the repair will be made when the replacement part becomes available.

3. *Completion or end date* Completion dates let the contracting parties know when the contract terms end. In the case of a painter hired to paint a dining room, this date identifies when the painter's work should be finished. If the contract is written to guarantee a price for a product purchased by a restaurant, the end date is the last day that price will be honored by the vendor. Some contracts are written in such a way that the completion or end date of the contract is extended indefinitely unless specifically discontinued (in writing).

4. *Performance standards* Performance standards refer to the quality of products or services received. This can be a complex area because, especially in the case of services purchased, quality can be difficult to quantify. The thickness of asphalt paving concrete, quality of carpeting, and brand or model of a piece of equipment, for example, is easily specified. The quality of an advertising campaign, a training program, or interior design work purchased by a buyer can be more difficult to evaluate. Effective buyers, however, will quantify performance standards in contracts to the greatest degree possible. In Chapter 4, you will learn how professional hospitality buyers carefully identify the product and **market form** they wish to purchase.

In all cases, terms and clauses that specify performance standards give both buyers and sellers an added level of protection, because the extra detail helps to clearly spell out the expectations of both parties.

5. *Licenses and permits* Obtaining licenses and permits, which are normally required for contracted work, should be the specific responsibility of the product or service seller. Trade persons such as carpenters, electricians, plumbers, security guards, air conditioning specialists, and the like, who must be licensed or certified by state or local governments, should be prepared to prove they have the appropriate credentials. It is the job of the buyer, however, to require verification of these licenses or permits. Contract terms should clearly indicate how evidence of appropriate licensing and permits will be supplied.

6. *Timing of ownership transfer* In most cases, buyers assume ownership of goods when they are delivered in good condition and accepted by the buyer's representative. In some cases, however, transfer of title to goods can take place at a different time. This can be the case, for example, when international goods are purchased and must pass through many parts of the product distribution channel before they are delivered to the ultimate buyer. If buyers are to assume ownership of products prior to their actual delivery, transfer of ownership terms should be clearly spelled out in the contract and mutually agreed upon.

7. *Indemnification (if applicable)* Accidents can happen while a contract is being fulfilled. When they do, buyers should ensure, in writing, their organizations will be **indemnified** by the seller's organization.

Key Terms

Market form Alternative ways that food products can be purchased. For example, one can purchase frozen bread dough or baked sliced bread, and hamburger is available fresh either in bulk or preportioned patties, and can also be purchased frozen either in bulk or preportioned patties. Each of these alternatives represents a market form.

Indemnify To reimburse for a loss.

To illustrate the importance of this contract clause, consider the case of Ron Morris. Ron is the manager of a restaurant located near an interstate highway. Ron contracted with Twin Cities Signs Company to change the lights in a 60-foot-high road sign advertising the restaurant. While completing this work, a Twin Cities truck collided with a car parked in the restaurant's parking lot. The car owner approached Ron, demanding that the restaurant pay for the car's damages. Without an indemnification clause in the contract for services with Twin Cities, Ron would likely have to pay for the customer's car repair. Although it is a good idea to have all important contract clauses reviewed by competent legal advisors, because of the significance of indemnification, this clause in a contract should be written (or reviewed) only by a qualified attorney.

8. *Nonperformance clauses*   In many cases, it is a good idea for buyers to decide beforehand what the two contracting parties will do if the contract terms are not fulfilled. In the case of purchasing products and services, the best solution may be for the hospitality buyer to buy from a different vendor.

   If, for example, a fresh-produce vendor who has a long-term contract with a group of family-owned restaurants frequently misses delivery deadlines or has poor product quality, the nonperformance solution may simply be to terminate the contract. Language would need to be written into the contract that would address the rights of the restaurant group to terminate the agreement if the vendor consistently performed unsatisfactorily.

9. *Dispute resolution terms*   In many cases, it is a good idea for contracting entities to agree on how to settle any disputes that may arise. When a contract is between two parties that are not located in the same state, contract language such as the following could be inserted into the contract.

   This agreement shall be governed by and interpreted under the laws of the State of _____.

   This is done to ensure both contracting parties are aware of the location in which disputes are to be settled. Additional terms and clauses may address the use of agreed-upon, independent third parties to assist in problem resolutions. Court costs are another area of potential disagreement that can, and often should, be addressed before any contract problems actually arise.

Product Warranties

Those who sell products and services know that the promises and claims they make about the items they sell can help sell them. For example, if the buyer for a restaurant decides to purchase a copy machine for the restaurant's office, the promises, or **warranties,** made by the copy machine's manufacturer may play a significant role in the machine selected.

If two copy machines cost approximately the same amount, but the manufacturer of one warrants (promises) that it will provide free repairs if the machine breaks down in the first two years, whereas the other manufacturer does not, the warranty of the first manufacturer would probably be a deciding factor in the selection of the copy machine.

Key Term

Warranty   A promise about a product, made by a seller, that is a legal part of the sales contract.

Even honest disagreements regarding the terms of poorly drafted contracts can lead to expensive and time-consuming litigation, so contract terms should be spelled out, in writing, as clearly as possible.

© Royalty-Free/CORBIS

Before finalizing a purchase of goods or services, it is critical that buyers establish what warranties, if any, are included in the purchase. It is important to remember that a warranty is part of the sales contract. Therefore, it is always important to make sure that any warranties offered verbally are documented in writing.

Warranties can be considered to be either expressed or implied. An expressed warranty is created when a manufacturer makes a statement of fact about the capabilities and/or qualities of a product or service. These statements can be made either by a salesperson or in their sales literature. Examples include statements such as: "This copier will make forty-five copies per minute," or "This dishwasher uses six gallons of water for each rinse cycle," or "These sheets are made from Egyptian cotton." When the seller makes a claim about the capabilities of a product or service, that seller is required, by law, to deliver a product that meets all of the capabilities described. When professional buyers rely on factual representations to purchase a product or service, and those statements later prove to be false, then a breach of the sales contract has occurred, and the buyer may be entitled to recover damages from the seller.

Recall that, under the UCC, every product sold is required to be fit for its use and free of defects. As a result, even if a seller does not specifically claim that his or her products are free of defects, a buyer would expect that any product purchased would be fit for consumption (if a food or beverage), or in good working order (if equipment or machinery). This type of unwritten expectation is called an **implied warranty.**

Key Term

Implied warranty   An unstated promise about a product that is always a legal part of the sales contract.

Product warranties may be either expressed or implied.
David Roth/Getty Images Inc.-Stone Allstock

In most cases, the products sold in the United States must, by law, conform to two implied warranties. One implied warranty is that the item is fit to be used for a particular purpose. This is known as an implied warranty of fitness. The second implied warranty is that the item will be in good working order and adequately meet the purposes for which it was purchased. This is called an implied warranty of merchantability.

Buyers should understand that sellers have the right to disclaim, or negate, any expressed or implied warranties by inserting applicable language into their sales contract. The disclaimer must be in writing and be agreed to by both parties. As a result, it is important that professional buyers read their sales contracts carefully.

Just as price is a negotiable part of any contract, so too are warranties. Many hospitality buyers try to negotiate additional or extended warranties before making a purchase. Professional buyers should seek to negotiate the longest, strongest, most comprehensive warranty possible and insist that the warranty be in writing. Specific warranty-related questions buyers should ask sellers include:

- How long is the warranty?
- When does the warranty begin?
- Will the warranty include the charges for any parts and/or labor to make needed repairs? Are any parts of the purchase not covered by the warranty?
- Will the warranty be voided if we do not follow the manufacturer's guidelines for routine service and maintenance?
- Who is authorized to perform routine service and maintenance?
- Who pays the charges to deliver the defective product to the repair location?

ETHICAL ASPECTS OF PROCUREMENT

Some people believe that any activity that is not illegal must be legal, and therefore must be permissible. For professional buyers, that simply is not the case. For buyers, as well as many other hospitality professionals, an activity may be legal, but still be the wrong thing to do. As a professional buyer, it is important that you learn to make the distinction between legality and **ethics.**

Key Term

═══

Ethics   The proper conduct of individuals in their relationships with others which is guided by their own moral principles.

In many companies, ethical behavior on the part of managers, including buyers, is formalized by the use of a set of ethical guidelines or codes of ethics. These codes will spell out very clearly the preferred conduct of the company's buyers. In the following section, you will learn how to identify behavior that is ethical (not merely legal) and review a sample buyer's code of ethical conduct.

Ethical Behavior

Ethical behavior refers to behavior that is considered by society to be the "right thing to do." For professional buyers, choosing ethical behavior over behavior that is not ethical is an important tactic for avoiding legal difficulty. This is so because a buyer may not, in a specific situation, know exactly what the law requires. If buyers' actions are ever questioned by their supervisors, or even in a court of law, determinations will inevitably be made about whether a buyer's actions were intentionally ethical or unethical.

Although it may sometimes be difficult to determine precisely what constitutes ethical behavior, the following six guidelines can be of help when buyers evaluate a possible course of action:

Ethical Behavior Guidelines:

1. Is it legal?
2. Does it hurt someone?
3. Is it fair and honest?
4. Would I care if it happened to me?
5. Would I publicize my action?
6. What if everyone did it?

How any particular individual determines the conduct that constitutes ethical behavior may be influenced by his or her cultural background, religious views, professional training, and personal moral code. Each, however, could apply the six ethical conduct guidelines. To illustrate their use, consider the following hypothetical situation:

JeAnna Baker is the food and beverage director and the food and beverage buyer at a downtown hotel. She is planning for the property's annual New Year's Eve gala and requires a large amount of wine and champagne. She conducts a competitive bidding process with the vendors in her area and, based upon quality and price, she places a very large order (in excess of $10,000) with a single purveyor. One week later, JeAnna receives a case of very expensive champagne, delivered to her home, with a nice note from the purveyor's representative that begins "Happy Holidays," and then states how much they appreciated the order and that they are really looking forward to doing business with her in the years ahead. What should JeAnna do with the champagne?

Before JeAnna decides to keep the gift, she should ask herself the following:

1. *Is it legal?*   It is not likely an illegal act for JeAnna to accept the case of champagne. However, there could be liquor laws in her state that prohibit the vendor from making a gift of alcoholic beverage. She also must consider whether keeping the gift is allowed within the purchasing guidelines established by her hotel. Many companies have established gift acceptance policies that limit the value of the gifts that employees are eligible to accept. In this case, violation of a stated or written company policy may subject her to disciplinary action or even the termination of her employment. If so, the acceptance of the gift might be considered "illegal" from her company's perspective!

Assuming that it does not violate a law and/or hotel policy for JeAnna to accept the gift, she should go on to question 2.

2. *Does it hurt anyone?*   It probably would not hurt JeAnna to drink the champagne but, realistically, is it likely that she could be fair and objective when evaluating future vendor bids or will she be reminded, while doing so, of the free case of champagne that she received? Assuming, however, that she does not think that it is hurting anyone, (including her own ability to be impartial), she should proceed to question 3.

3. *Is it fair and honest?*   The answer to this question will cause JeAnna to consider who is affected in this particular situation. How might others in the hotel feel about the gift she received? If benefits are gained because of decisions she makes while on duty, fairness dictates that she should assess whether those benefits should accrue to the hotel or to her. Assessing the honesty of a situation gives JeAnna the opportunity to second-guess herself when answering questions 2 and 3. Does she really believe she can remain objective in the purchasing aspect of her job and continue to seek out the best quality for the best price, knowing that a purveyor rewarded her for last year's choice and may do so again?

   Assuming, however, that she has decided that it is fair and honest for her to keep the champagne, she should go to question number 4.

4. *Would I care if it happened to me?*   If JeAnna owned the hotel and she knew that one of the managers she had hired was given a gift of this magnitude from a vendor, would it be natural for her to question the objectivity of that manager? Would she like to see all of her managers receive gifts of this type, or would she likely be concerned if they did?

5. *Would I publicize my action?*   If JeAnna honestly answers *"It's O.K."* to all of the above questions, she must ask herself this question. In many cases, it will be the most important question of all. Would JeAnna choose to keep the champagne if she knew that tomorrow morning the headlines of her city newspaper would read: *"Food and Beverage Director of Local Hotel Receives Free Case of Expensive Champagne after Placing Large Order with Purveyor"*?

   The General Manager of JeAnna's hotel would see the headline, the hotel's owners would see it, her fellow employees would see it, all of the other purveyors that she is going to do business with would see it, and even her potential future employers would see it. If she knew that were going to be the case, would JeAnna care?

6. *What if everyone did it?*   If JeAnna can still justify her choice of keeping the champagne, consider: Would this process ever stop? What would happen if the executive housekeeper had a set of towels delivered to her home every time she ordered new terry products for the hotel? What would happen if every time she ordered new TVs for the guest rooms, she received a new one at home?

Most readers would likely agree that, in this case, it is unethical (even if it is legal) for JeAnna to keep the champagne. Under the circumstances, what are some of the realistic alternatives to keeping it? She could:

1. Return it to the purveyor with a professional note stating how much she appreciated it, but that company (or her own) policy will not allow her to accept it.
2. Ask her boss (the general manager) what she should do.
3. Turn the gift over to the general manager to be placed into the normal liquor inventory (assuming that local liquor laws will allow it).
4. Donate it to the hotel's own employee holiday party.

As an exercise in the ethical actions process, use the six questions listed above to assess each of these alternative courses of action. Which would you advise JeAnna to choose?

On-the-Job Challenges in Purchasing (3.2)

Wilma Gates is the vice president of operations for Pizza Pan Pizzerias. She directly supervises three regional vice presidents, each of whom is responsible for approximately 50 stores. Wilma just announced a new daily sales reporting system that requires each store to e-mail their prior day's sales revenue totals to their regional vice president. The data collected by each regional vice president will then be combined and sent to her so Wilma receives an accurate daily revenue report.

When discussing the new plan, Steven, one of the regional vice presidents, pointed out that, although all of his store managers had a personal computer, not all of them were equipped with Microsoft Office. "The cost of outfitting all of my stores with new versions of Microsoft Office will be pretty significant," he stated.

"No problem," replied Nate, another of the regional vice presidents, just buy one copy at Office Max and pass it around to each store manager. You'll saves thousands of dollars that way. And besides, Microsoft already makes a lot more money than we do!

Case Study Questions

Assume you were Wilma:

1. Would you allow the software program to be purchased and re-used on the individual unit manager's computers as Nate suggests?
2. What steps should (could) you take to ensure this was not done despite your opposition?
3. Assume, for this illustration, that the action suggested by Nate was not actually illegal, and that it could not be easily detected by Microsoft. Use the six-step questioning process introduced in this chapter. Would you, at some point in the questioning process, decide the purchasing action proposed by Nate was unethical?

Buyers' Codes of Procurement Ethics

Purchasing professionals must have a highly developed sense of professional ethics to protect their own and their operation's reputation for fair dealing. To strengthen ethical awareness, and to provide guidelines for its buyers, some organizations have developed buyers' codes of ethics. In many cases, even those buyers' whose organizations do not have formal buyer conduct codes will, voluntarily, develop and subscribe to their formalized code of ethics.

Professional buyers who have served in their jobs a long time know that the temptation for sellers to offer additional inducements to the buyer can be immense. If, however, the buyer accepts such gifts, they are effectively giving away some of the profit that could have gone into their company's operating margins. Some buyers claim that the acceptance of purchasing inducements does not actually influence their choice of supplier in the least. Although this could possibly be true for some, it is unlikely for most. In most cases:

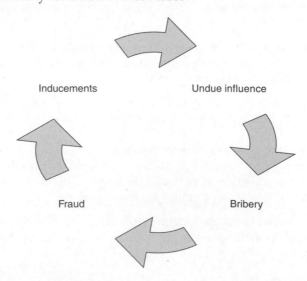

Inducements → Undue influence → Bribery → Fraud → (Inducements)

Buyer's Code of Ethics

Objective:

The objective of ____ (*insert company name*) _____ Buyer's Code of Ethics is to ensure purchasing staff will never use their authority for personal gain and shall seek to uphold, at all times, the standing and reputation of the company.

To achieve the objective, buyers will:

1. Always give first priority and consideration to the financial objectives and operating policies of the company.
2. Seek to obtain the maximum value for each dollar of expenditure.
3. Decline all personal gifts or gratuities.
4. Grant all competitive suppliers equal consideration based solely on their ability to supply our company with products and services.
5. Conduct business with potential and current suppliers in an atmosphere of good faith, devoid of intentional misrepresentation and in keeping with all applicable laws.
6. Demand honesty in sales representation whether offered through verbal statements, advertisements, or product samples.
7. Make every reasonable effort to negotiate an equitable and mutually agreeable settlement of any controversy with a supplier.
8. When conditions permit, provide a prompt and courteous reception for all sales persons who call on legitimate business missions.
9. Cooperate with trade and professional associations for the purposes of promoting and developing ethical business practices.
10. Counsel and guide those buyers within the organization in upholding this ten-point code of purchasing ethics.

Presented by: *Read and understood by:*

_____   _____

(Company official)   Buyer

_____   _____

Date   Date

FIGURE 3.3   Model Buyer's Code of Ethics

In some cases, purchasing fraud can lead to even more serious acts of deception on the part of buyers, many of which may actually be criminally illegal and subject the buyer (when caught) to imprisonment. It is to avoid just this type of temptation and potential confusion that buyers' codes of ethics are implemented and followed. Figure 3.3 is an example of such a code.

In some cases, a company president or other operating officer will relay the ethical philosophy of a company to its employees in a section of the employee handbook or, as in Figure 3.3, through a direct policy statement that may be signed and placed in the buyer's personal file. Notice that item 5 of the model code shown in Figure 3.3 makes reference to the importance of following the law. Laws do not exist, however, to cover every situation that future hospitality buyers will encounter. Also, society's view of acceptable behavior, as well as of specific laws, are constantly changing. Ethical behavior, however, is consistent and is consistently important to the long-term success of professional hospitality buyers.

Purchasing Resources on the Internet

In addition to the Web sites referenced in this chapter's "Internet Purchasing Assistant" feature, the following sites provide detailed information to enhance your purchasing knowledge and skills.

Purchasing Resources on the Internet

Site	Information About
www.ftc.gov	Federal Trade Commission
www.fda.gov	Food and Drug Administration
www.usda.gov	U.S. Department of Agriculture
www.fsis.usda.gov	Food Safety and Inspection
www.osha.gov	Occupational Safety and Health Administration
www.law.freeadvice.com	Free online advice regarding contract law
www.smallbusiness.findlaw.com	Contract-related standard business forms
www.businessnation.com/library/forms	Free contract clause language
www.answers.com/topic/implied-warranty	Implied warranties
www.hospitalitylawyer.com	Free and "For a Fee" advice regarding varied areas of hospitality law

Key Terms

caveat emptor *59*

Uniform Commercial
    Code (UCC) *59*

license *62*

contract *64*

enforceable (contract) *65*

offer *65*

acceptance *65*

consideration *65*

trade-out *66*

express contract *67*

market form *68*

indemnify *68*

warranty *69*

implied warranty *70*

ethics *71*

Think It Through

1. The UCC was established to voluntarily harmonize commercial laws across states. Do you believe that task would be better accomplished by passage of a federal law mandating such harmonization? Why or why not?

2. Describe three specific instances that you believe a buyer would find using a verbal contract superior to a written contract.

3. Describe three specific instances that you believe a buyer would find using a written contract superior to a verbal contract.

4. Explain the difference between an expressed and implied warranty.

5. Do you believe it is essential that all buyers in a large multi-buyer organization subscribe to the same ethical code of conduct? Explain your answer.

Team Fun

For this exercise, assume that each team consists of members of a hotel corporation's procurement division. The corporation has recently purchased a group of 50 hotels from a large investment company. The hotels operate in the United States, Japan, Latin America, and Australia. The hotels are all full service, offering food and beverage service as well as meeting space. The hotels average 500 rooms each, and the typical hotel has two or three individuals on property who are assigned full-time to the procurement process. The company's CEO has instructed the procurement division to address the issue of buyer codes of conduct.

1. The assignment of the first team is to write a five-point "Code of Ethics" related directly to the issue of buyers' gift acceptance from vendors. Topics addressed should include items such as when, if at all, gifts are allowed, the amount or value permitted, reporting requirements, and so on.

2. The assignment of the second team is to write a five-point "Code of Ethics" related directly to the issue of buyers' acceptance of "hospitality" from vendors. Topics addressed should include items such as when, if at all, it is permitted to attend events such as after-work cocktail parties, meals, golf outings, theater or concert events, holiday and other parties, as well as any reporting requirements related to accepting hospitality invitations.

3. The assignment of the third team is to write a three-point "Code of Ethics" related directly to the issue of a company-employed buyer's financial interest in vendor companies (i.e., permitted ownership of stock, partnerships, and reporting requirements) *and* to recommend an appropriate company action and/or response to employee violations of the proposed ethical codes.

Each team should be prepared to present and discuss their recommended ethical codes and conclusions, as well as explain their reasoning for them.

Quality and Purchase Specifications

In This Chapter

The first step in the procurement process is to identify the products and services that are needed. This statement at first appears obvious (you cannot purchase something until you know what you are going to purchase), and simple to accomplish (a hotel needs bed linens and a restaurant requires ground beef if hamburger patties are on the menu). However, it is not a simple step to attain because needs must be customer focused. That is, "What do customers want that will best address their value concerns?" Yes, it is true that bed linens will be required for guest rooms, but what quality should be purchased? The concern is even more complicated with food and beverage products: It is first necessary to determine that hamburger sandwiches are desired by the customers before the need for ground beef can be finalized. Assuming this item should be on the menu, the issue of beef quality then becomes important.

The phrase, "You get what you pay for," is useful when making purchasing decisions for hospitality organizations as well as for considering product and service alternatives in our personal lives. Although selling price is always important, it must be considered in the context of quality, and the term "value" describes the relationship between both of these factors (price and quality).

This chapter explains the importance of quality concerns as procurement decisions are made, and it will emphasize the need for a property's quality requirements to be defined and described in purchase specifications.

Purchase specifications identify and explain the hospitality organization's quality requirements. These documents are very important at the time of purchase to ensure that suppliers know the quality requirements for the products and services that best meet the organization's needs. Prices to be charged vary based upon numerous factors, and suppliers who are aware of the desired standards can quote prices appropriately.

Specifications then become important when supplier selection decisions are made. Although other issues may affect (or create) differences between quoted prices, quality variations should not be among them. Purchasers can make "apples to apples" rather than "apples to oranges" comparisons as supplier selection decisions are made.

You will also learn in this chapter that specifications are required when products are received and services are inspected to help ensure that the property "gets what it pays for": the proper quality of product or service that was ordered.

Purchase specifications should contain basic information that is important to organizations of any size as they undertake purchasing activities. Purchasing staff (or those with these responsibilities in smaller organizations), representatives of the department that will be using the products or benefiting from the services, and those who are potential suppliers can all help to ensure that necessary information is identified and addressed in the specifications that will be used.

Busy hospitality purchasers develop specifications not because "it is nice to do so," but, rather, because these tools are an integral part of the procurement process. In other words, after specifications are developed, they must be used. Initial drafts of specifications are reviewed, and revised, as necessary, and value analysis tactics can help ensure that the specifications are as good as they can be. Trial orders can then be placed to ensure that product descriptions accurately reflect those items needed by the property. After confirmation by user department personnel that the purchase "specs" are ready for use, they should be circulated to potential suppliers with the insistence that the organization requires products meeting these specifications whenever orders are placed.

The extent to which detailed product descriptions are included in purchase specifications varies depending upon the needs of the specific organization. Frequently, organizations with high-volume purchasing requirements develop more detailed and lengthy purchase specifications than do their smaller counterparts. This chapter concludes by showing specifications in different formats to illustrate the range of specifications used in the widely diverse hospitality industry.

■ ■ ■

Outline

PURCHASE DECISIONS ARE DRIVEN BY NEEDS

Figure 4.1 (originally shown as Figure 1.4) indicates that the first step in the procurement process is to identify the need for products and services to be purchased. This figure is shown again here to provide the context within which this step will now be discussed.

Some readers may think it is a waste of time to state that products not needed should not be purchased. However, one only needs to walk through many food service storerooms and notice dusty case goods to learn that food products in storage for the time it takes to accumulate dust were purchased without need for them. Likewise, consider food products in storage that must be discarded because of quality deterioration before they can be used. Then walk through storage areas in a hotel and discover excess parts in the maintenance room, items in linen storage areas, and supplies in the front office or administrative offices that were purchased but never used.

There may be a reason why "old" food products remain in the dry storeroom: They are no longer needed because of menu changes. However, couldn't creative production personnel have found a way to use them in daily specials, in

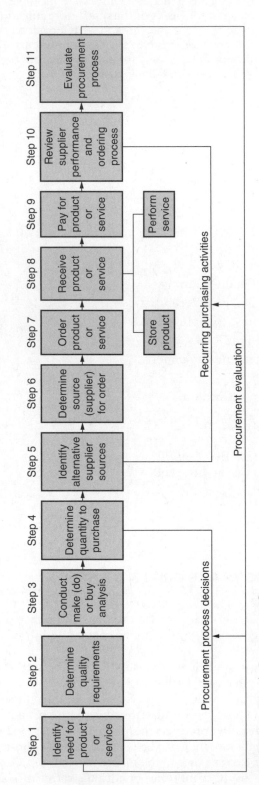

FIGURE 4.1 Steps in Procurement Process

salad bars, or for other purposes? Excess parts remaining from equipment that is no longer used, and supplies for office equipment that have been replaced with newer equipment, are more difficult to use or to receive credit for and may have to be considered a "cost of doing business." However, every purchaser must be concerned that only required products in necessary quantities are purchased. (Decisions about purchase quantities will be addressed in Chapter 6.)

You've learned that product and service purchases should reflect customers' needs, but who determines what customers want? In chain hospitality organizations, brand managers mandate many standards that have been identified by corporate-level marketing and other experts who "translate" identified needs into the products and services that the branded units will offer customers. In independently owned and operated properties, entrepreneurs use their best judgments along with experience to determine what customers want and need, and these decisions then drive the purchase of products and services. In both instances, although purchasing specialists may provide advice (input) as customer needs are determined and incorporated into purchase requirements, purchasers do not unilaterally make these decisions. Although much oversimplified, the responsibility of purchasers begins after the "big picture" determination of product needs has been made.

Purchasing staff do become involved in purchase need decisions when, for example, the quality of the needed products is determined and as decisions are made about whether products should be prepared on-site or purchased in a convenience market form (see Chapter 5). A primary role of the purchaser is, then, to help those who make product need decisions to obtain the "best" product or service available in the marketplace.

The definition of "best" refers to quality. This is the second step in the procurement process, and the topic of the remainder of this chapter.

WHAT IS QUALITY?

A review of Figure 4.1 indicates that step 2 in the procurement process is to determine quality requirements for the products and services that are needed (and which were identified in step 1).

For some hospitality buyers, the concept of "quality" is hard to define or even conceptualize. Instead, they perceive that a product or service either is—or is not—of proper quality, and they make this decision when they see the product or observe service results. Unfortunately, this subjective assessment cannot be made until a product is received (so it can be looked at) or a service is delivered (so it can be experienced). Although assessment at these points is important to ensure that quality standards *have been* met, it is also important to plan and communicate to best ensure that quality standards *will be* met.

Different purchasers have different perspectives about the proper quality of products and services needed by their organizations. This is appropriate and necessary as long as the hospitality organization has focused on what its customers want and has assigned a priority to meeting (or exceeding) their expectations.

Definition

From a purchasing perspective, the quality of a product or service relates to its intended use. In other words, the purchaser must, first, define what a product will be used for or what a service is expected to accomplish. The proper quality of product will then be that which comes closest to being suitable for its intended use. Also, the proper quality of a service will be that which best accomplishes its intended purpose.

Some examples will help explain the concept of "suitability for intended purpose" just noted. Assume a cook is going to prepare spaghetti sauce following a simple recipe that requires tomato products, vegetables including onions and green peppers, ground beef, and several seasonings. What kind of tomato products should be used for the source: fresh whole tomatoes? Tomato pieces of relatively uniform size? Tomato sauce and/or puree? Other **market forms** of tomato products provide additional alternatives for consideration.

If the cook is employed by a **high-check average** restaurant where customers believe that "fresh is best," and high-selling prices help to offset the high labor costs incurred to process fresh foods, there may be little or no canned tomato products used in the recipe. Conversely, if the cook is employed by a family-service restaurant where the use of convenience foods is well accepted by customers, there may be little or no fresh tomato products in the sauce.

Purchasers must know the intended use of the product to identify the quality of the required product. In the example above, fresh tomatoes may be used for numerous products in high-check average restaurants. They may be used only in fresh salads and/or for plate garnishes in another type of property.

Hospitality purchasers must also consider quality standards as services are purchased. Consider the "simple" decision to use an **external service provider** to maintain a hotel property's landscaping. Is the required service limited to cutting the grass? Does it also include "edging" the curbs? Sweeping and/or blowing cut grass off sidewalks and parking lots? How often are services required? Other questions can be posed and should be addressed as the purchase decision for landscaping services is made. The proper quality of needed services can be determined only after the purchaser considers the perspectives of the guests about the exterior appearance.

What is the food service buyer's definition of quality for these items?

Ricardo Arias, Latin Stock/Photo Researchers, Inc.

Key Terms

Market form   Alternative ways that food products can be purchased. For example, bread can be purchased in fresh baked and sliced, or frozen preweighed dough portions, among other alternatives.

High-check average (restaurant)   A restaurant offering relatively expensive meals to compensate for the higher cost of products, service, and other features of the dining experience that is provided.

External service provider   A person or organization that provides a service for a hospitality organization.

Quality Is a Priority

Customers of hospitality organizations of all types increasingly demand value as they purchase products and services. As noted above, their concept of value is the same as that of purchasers when they buy products and services for the organization. They consider the selling price of a product or service relative to its quality. In other words, they ask, "Is the product and/or service that I am considering to purchase worth what it costs?" In fact, customers and purchasers really want to "get more than what they are paying for."

Concerns about quality do not begin nor end with the procurement function. Top-level leaders must emphasize a quality commitment in everything that everyone in the organization does at all times. To this point, we have discussed quality in the context of a product or service. However, an organizational definition of **quality** is also important. Quality is simply the consistent delivery of a hospitality organization's products and services according to expected standards. This goal is always difficult to attain, but it is impossible to accomplish if the products and services that enable staff members to deliver quality are not available. Purchasing personnel, because of their emphasis on procuring products and services of the proper quality, "do their share" in helping the organization to meet its total quality commitments.

Although the term can have different meanings, some hospitality observers use the concept of **quality assurance** to refer to all of the activities that an organization undertakes to attain quality. In the context of purchasing, these can relate to several activities:

- Decisions about necessary products and services to determine those that provide the best value to customers.
- Determination of quality and the development of purchase specifications that incorporate quality standards.
- Assessments of suppliers to best ensure that they can consistently deliver the proper products and services (those desired by customers) at a fair price.
- An ongoing emphasis (motivation) for all purchasing staff to maintain quality concerns.
- Ongoing training to help ensure that purchasing personnel know the best way to accomplish required purchasing activities.
- Inspection of products that are received and services that are performed to ensure that quality standards are met.
- Decisions about corrective actions that address procurement-related defects.
- Feedback in an ongoing purchasing improvement process.

Another quality concept, **"total quality management,"** describes the active pursuit of organization-wide quality by all staff members. The emphasis is

---

Key Terms

Quality (organizational perspective)   The consistent delivery of a hospitality organization's products and services according to expected standards.

Quality assurance   All activities that relate to the attainment of quality by a hospitality organization.

Total quality management   An organizational-wide commitment that focuses on the encouragement and support of quality management in all activities to best meet the needs of internal customers (employees) and external customers (guests of the hospitality operation).

placed on improving **processes** and **procedures** rather than on identifying **defects** after they occur. The processes and procedures used by purchasing staff are integral to a property's total quality emphasis. Purchasers fulfill this expectation as they improve existing, and discover new, ways to better help the organization meet its quality requirements. Increasingly, quality improvements in purchasing involve assistance from suppliers. They can provide value to the organization by contributing their knowledge, expertise, and access to information to help improve the processes and procedures used to deliver quality to the organization's customers.

Economics of Quality

Careful readers might have concerns about an overriding emphasis on providing value to customers that is a priority when purchasing (and all other) decisions are made by hospitality managers. In fact, one could ask the following question: "If the priority need is to provide customer value, why not just reduce the selling price?" In fact, a guest room normally rented for $300 a night would certainly be a value to almost any guest if the rental rate were reduced to $50 nightly. Also, a dinner with a "reasonable" menu-selling price of $35 would be a great value to an increased number of customers if it were priced at $15. In these examples, customer value would be significant, but the organizations would likely be unprofitable and go out of business.

Concerns about customer value perceptions must be addressed in the context of competitive alternatives. The guest who rents a room for $300 per night must believe the room is "worth" $50 more than a room renting for $250, and "value" perception occurs when that room is perceived to be better than any other room at that rate or lower and, hopefully, at even higher rates. Guests paying $35 for a meal will think it is a value if it is "worth" more than any other meal that they can purchase at that price or lower. Hospitality operators are consistently challenged to provide better value for their customers and better value than their competitors.

Purchasing staff help external customers receive value in at least two ways. First, they ensure that the products and services purchased are integral to the customers' hospitality experience. The thread count of sheets and quality of furnishings create a certain environment in the guest room. The quality of ingredients used to prepare an entrée in the restaurant is a small, but critical, element in a guest's total experience from which a value determination is made. The managers of these organizations must determine what their guests want. Purchasers must then help to define these needs in objective quality terms and ensure that only products meeting these standards are purchased.

Purchasers also help the organization achieve quality by eliminating excessive costs from items that are purchased. This is done as higher-than-necessary quality is removed from purchases, and as unnecessary costs are reduced. This is not a suggestion to "buy cheap." Instead, it is reinforcement of the quality definition cited earlier: The proper quality of a product or service is that one which is most suitable for its intended use.

Key Terms

Process A series of actions (procedures) developed to achieve a result.

Procedure One step in a process; see process.

Defect A variation from the expected standard for a product or performance of a service.

PURCHASING PROS NEED TO KNOW (4.1)

Purchasing pros know that there are three basic types of purchasers, and, typically, one type is better than the others:

- *Price-conscious purchasers.*   They are concerned about price ("cheap is best"), and their primary purchasing goals relate to buying the least expensive products.
- *Quality-conscious purchasers.*   They are not overly concerned about costs. Instead, they want to purchase products of the highest possible quality. Perhaps these purchasers believe that "You get what you pay for," and think that higher prices represent higher quality and, therefore, less purchasing diligence is required. Perhaps, as well, they believe that higher costs associated with higher-quality products "can just be passed on to the customers."
- *Value-conscious purchasers.*   They recognize and search for the relationship between product price and quality as purchase decisions are made. These purchasers recognize that neither the lowest or highest *price* nor lowest or highest *quality* product is likely needed. Instead, the "right" product is the one that represents the greatest value based on the price of the product that is most suitable for its intended use at their properties.

Super colossal olives are very expensive and not suitable for most "help yourself" salad bars. Ground beef containing 20 percent fat is less expensive to purchase by the pound than a lower fat content product. Which type olive or ground beef item is "best"? It depends on many factors including how the ingredient will be used and what the organization's customers want, and wise purchasers know and consider each of these factors. Savings made from effective purchasing yield reduced costs that can be passed on to the customer to encourage greater value perception and/or used to help the organization remain financially viable.

Although difficult to quantify, there are four different costs of quality:

- *Prevention costs.*   Examples: costs to develop a purchase specification that describes a product that is "perfect" for its intended use, and time spent to negotiate a contract specifying desired services.
- *Appraisal costs.*   Examples: costs incurred to inspect incoming products to ensure that they meet purchase specification requirements, and to confirm that a service is completed as agreed upon.
- *Internal failure costs.*   Examples: costs of errors and rework created by use of inappropriate products, and for services performed by an organization's employees that do not meet standards.
- *External failure costs.*   Examples: costs incurred by using suppliers' products that were not recognized to be out of compliance with purchase specifications, or to accept services performed by external suppliers that do not meet quality requirements.

Unfortunately, there is typically no simple or practical way for hospitality managers or purchasers to determine (quantify) the financial effect of each of the four costs of quality just noted. What is the relationship between prevention and appraisal costs relative to internal and external failure costs? Proactive purchasers incur the former (prevention and appraisal costs). Their counterparts without effective purchasing systems incur the latter (internal and external failure) costs.

Value perceptions of customers will be increased as prevention and appraisal activities occur, and perceptions will likely decrease if internal and external quality failure results, even though these costs may not be quantifiable.

PURCHASE SPECIFICATIONS: OVERVIEW

Purchase specifications describe the quality requirements to be met by products and services purchased by a hospitality operation. They are, then, a most important communication tool that helps to ensure that user department personnel, purchasers, and suppliers mutually understand the meaning of "proper quality" in reference to a specific product or service.

Effective purchase specifications meet several requirements. They are:

- simple (short) as possible while still providing an accurate description of the product or service.
- capable of being met, whenever possible, by several suppliers to encourage **competitive bidding.**
- identifiable, when possible, with currently available products in the marketplace to minimize customization costs.
- capable of being verified to ensure that proper quality is received.
- reasonable; tolerances to yield compliance are practical. Example: a **tare allowance** is typically permitted when portion-controlled products are purchased. A 5-ounce preportioned meat item might have a tare allowance of 1/4 ounce. An item could, therefore, weigh between 4⅞ and 5⅛ ounces, and still be acceptable (meet specifications).
- as fair to suppliers as possible to encourage multiple sources of supply so that competitive bidding will result.

Purchase specifications are useful when products are purchased and received. These topics will be discussed separately.

Specifications and Quality: Purchasing

As you have learned, purchase specifications are used at the time of product purchase to inform prospective suppliers about the standards required for the products

The buyer for this hotel developed and used specifications to define the quality requirements for the bedding in this guest room.
Courtesy of Real Resorts

Key Terms

Purchase specification A tool that describes the quality requirements to be met by products and services purchased by a hospitality organization.

Competitive bidding A tactic used by purchasers who compare suppliers' prices for products and/or services of equivalent quality to determine the least expensive price; also called competitive pricing.

Tare allowance The allowable variation in the weight of a portion-controlled product purchased by weight.

or services being purchased. With knowledge of the required quality, suppliers can quote prices they will charge for the product when a specified volume and other order requirements, if any, are met. There are several ways that specifications can be described:

- *Brand or trade name.* A purchaser who specifies a specific brand of ketchup (Heinz, for example) or food mixer (Hobart) is indicating a quality preference. It is probably based upon his or her experience with the product (actual usage) and/or the product's reputation. Many of us prefer a specific brand of automobiles, hotels or restaurants, and electronic manufacturers, for example, and our preferences are based on our positive experiences with one or more brands and, perhaps, our negative experiences with others. Although we may never have purchased an auto, its positive (or negative) reputation may influence our purchase decisions. Hospitality purchasers likewise frequently equate quality to brand. (There is typically at least one advantage and one disadvantage to using a brand for a purchase specification.) The good news: The specification is quick and easy to write because it simply involves specifying the brand. The bad news: There are typically a limited number of (perhaps only one) suppliers who can provide the desired product, and the potential of competitive pricing is reduced or eliminated.

- *Blueprint.* New building construction, additions, and remodeling projects are examples of times when blueprints help to specify quality requirements and expectations. Although they do help to quantify the quality of the project, blueprints do not address the quality requirements of the construction materials used to build or remodel a hospitality building. However, in most communities, projects that require blueprints are affected by local building codes and other requirements, and responsible officials inspect the project as it evolves. (The role of building inspectors to confirm compliance with building codes is similar to that of receiving personnel who inspect incoming shipments to ensure that product quality requirements are attained.)

- *Certification with specifications commonly used by the industry.* The U.S. Department of Agriculture's Institutional Meat Purchasing Specifications (IMPS), the North American Meat Processors Association (NAMP), and its Meat Buyer's Guide (MBG) numbers are examples. When a purchaser specifies, for example, NAMP #1185, a bottom sirloin butt steak meeting specific quality standards has been specified. (Details about the use of IMPS and MBG numbers to purchase meat products are presented in Chapter 13.)

  In the United States, grading standards are also available for many fruit and vegetable products, and these serve as additional examples of widely circulated and recognized trade specifications that are used.

- *Careful description of required product.* Unfortunately, many products and almost all services cannot be quickly summarized by a brand name or trade-recognized product number. Fresh seafood, dairy products, and bakery items are among the products used by food and beverage operations for which purchase specification statements are needed. Uniforms, office supplies, and guest room linens and bedding are examples of product purchases that require written specification descriptions in lodging properties.

PURCHASING PROS NEED TO KNOW (4.2)

Grading standards used to evaluate products are applied at the locations where the applicable products are grown or processed. Considerable quality deterioration can occur if products are mishandled after quality has initially been determined, and when products are finally received by the hospitality organization. This reinforces the importance of receiving tasks, which are discussed briefly in the next section and more fully in Chapter 11.

Internet Purchasing Assistant (4.1)

The U.S. Department of Agriculture's Institutional Meat Purchasing Specifications (IMPS) are widely used as a standard for quality descriptions of products as government agencies, schools, restaurants, hotels, and other food service users specify quality requirements to suppliers. To review these specifications, go to: www.usda.gov:

When you reach the site, enter "IMPS" in the search field, and you can review general requirements and quality assurance provisions of grading systems, and then review details for beef, lamb and mutton, veal and calf, pork, and a variety of processed meat items.

• *Use of samples.* Samples of products currently used by the hospitality organization may serve as specifications in some instances. Consider, for example, a restaurant that produces specialized bakery or dessert products, and a hotel food and beverage operation that produces a variety of hors d'oeuvres for banquet events. Purchasers at these properties may investigate the possibility of buying these items ready-made for a number of reasons, and samples may be provided to prospective suppliers to identify the quality standards required for purchased products. (Information about make and/or buy analysis determinations is presented in Chapter 5.)

Purchase specifications must be carefully developed, and they must be updated when user needs change because of evolving customer preferences or new marketplace alternatives. When specifications are in use, and when competitive bidding systems are in place, all suppliers can quote prices on the same quality of product. This will help to eliminate one reason (quality differences) to be considered as supplier selection decisions are made.

Earlier in this section, you've learned that purchase specifications must be capable of being verified. This is important when products are received, and this activity will be addressed next.

Specifications and Quality: Receiving

Although it occurs all too frequently, it does little or no good for a hospitality operation to develop purchase specifications if they are not used at the time of product delivery to confirm that quality standards are met.

Experienced purchasers know that they are very likely to pay for the quality of the product or service that they order, even if they do not receive that quality of product or service. Suppliers must know about an operation's specifications, so they can base their price quotations on products and services meeting these

---

PURCHASING PROS NEED TO KNOW (4.3)

Purchasing pros know that purchase specifications may not be required for every product that is purchased. It is always best to first develop specifications for the relatively few items that represent the largest purchasing costs. For example, expensive meat and seafood items are typically of greater concern to the purchasers than inexpensive condiments and dry supply items such as baking soda and lower-cost spices, herbs, and seasoning ingredients.

Purchasers working for hospitality organizations without specifications may develop a schedule (e.g., development of one purchase specification every month) so that, over time, the organization can benefit from these important purchasing tools.

On-the-Job Challenges in Purchasing (4.1)

"Don't we have enough work to do already?" Gayle asked during a coffee break conversation with Jessie. Gayle was a cook at the Pacific Island Restaurant, and Jessie had receiving and storage responsibilities.

"I'm not aware that we've had really big problems about the quality of the food products we purchased," Gayle continued. "Sometimes products we need aren't available and then we just substitute something else. At other times we get deals on products we don't normally use and find ways to incorporate them in the menu."

"Yes, I agree," said Jessie, "And sometimes products that are delivered don't really meet our quality requirements, but we're able to negotiate lower prices for them so nobody loses, do they?"

"I think you and I and others who work in this restaurant realize some things that the owners, executive chef, and accounting department don't understand," said Gayle. "We don't need detailed purchase specifications because we've always been able to cope with every situation that ever arose, and I'm sure we will be able to continue to do so in the future." "I'm not concerned whether we have purchase specifications as long as they don't affect me. However, it is going to be frustrating if this new emphasis on specifications affects my work."

Case Study Questions

1. What are some positive ways that the use of purchase specifications can influence the work of the cooks at the Pacific Island Restaurant? In what ways, if at all, might their work tasks be negatively affected?
2. What can the manager do to address the negative feelings that these cooks have about the implementation of purchase specifications at the restaurant?
3. How will the use of purchase specifications improve the overall operations at the Pacific Island Restaurant?

standards. Hopefully, the proper quality of products and services will be delivered. However, in the case of products, if receiving staff do not have knowledge about purchase specification requirements, or do not take the time to check incoming products against these requirements, quality variations can occur. Receiving personnel have no more important task than to ensure that the products

A STORY THAT MAKES AN IMPORTANT POINT!

One of this book's authors served for several years on the food and beverage committee of the American Hotel & Lodging Association with another committee peer who represented a very large and reputable hotel linen supply company. This executive lamented about the large number of orders for bed linens that his company routinely lost because his prices were "too high." Interestingly, the winning bidder was frequently the same competitor.

After visiting a nearby property, he noticed that the products delivered by the supplier whose price quotations were often accepted were of a lower quality than that required by the specification.

He taught the author that a less-than-ethical supplier might quote a price for a product of lower quality than that specified by the purchaser with the knowledge that products were not likely to be inspected during the receiving process to ensure that quality requirements were met. If, in the unlikely event that a problem was noted, the supplier "cheerfully" exchanged the product, apologized for the "error," and delivered the correct product. The low price quoted meant that the supplier would lose money on that transaction. Over the long term, however, the supplier could be very successful quoting a slightly-lower-than-reasonable price for a higher quality product, and substituting a product of lower quality (and much lower cost) during the delivery.

The "bottom line" for buyers? Use specifications at the time of receiving to best ensure that you receive the quality of item that you purchased (and that you will pay for).

being received meet required product standards as noted in purchase specifications. As this occurs, the property will receive what it paid for: an item that represents value for the organization and, in turn, enables it to provide value for the customers.

DEVELOPMENT OF PURCHASE SPECIFICATIONS

How are purchasing specifications developed? Purchasing staff, user department personnel, and suppliers may assist in development efforts.

Role of Purchasing Staff

Purchasing staff in large organizations make a significant contribution as they facilitate the development of purchase specifications. Time-consuming efforts are often required to research, communicate about, and develop these important purchasing tools, and busy user department personnel cannot typically undertake these tasks. This relates to another observation: Large organizations (those with staff purchasing agents) typically have more detailed purchase specifications than do their smaller counterparts. Hopefully, the director of purchasing has approval of top-level property officials to commit a specified and significant amount of time, if necessary, to fulfill this responsibility.

Purchasing staff can assist in several ways as purchase specifications are developed:

- They can study the exact needs for items to be described in the specifications. Recall our earlier discussion about quality requirements being related to intended use. Purchasing staff can discover the specific answers to the question: "For what exactly will the item be used?" Effective purchasers keep current by reading industry trade publications, meeting with suppliers, and attending trade shows, among other tactics. They might, for example, be able to make suggestions as product use questions are addressed. Recall the examples of tomatoes and olives noted earlier in this chapter. A questioning process coupled with input solicited from suppliers could be very helpful in reducing product costs without compromising product quality standards.
- They can research alternative products and suppliers after intended use decisions are made. Discussions with existing suppliers, requests for referrals to other suppliers if new items are not part of existing suppliers' product lines, and discussions with purchasing peers in other hospitality organizations may yield helpful information.
- After potential suppliers are identified, purchasing staff can obtain information and product samples, if necessary, and provide these resources to user department personnel.
- They can facilitate in-house analyses of products currently used (for which specifications are being initially developed or revised), and for new products for which in-house specifications do not exist. Meetings, including taste panels, if necessary, comprised of department staff, other property officials, and even guests, if applicable, can be conducted.
- They can develop purchase specification drafts. Generic information from applicable suppliers and trade organizations, along with specific characteristics suggested by in-house personnel, can be useful as they do so.
- They can share drafts of proposed purchase specifications with suppliers to obtain feedback including additional suggestions and to ensure that the resulting specification does not limit the number of suppliers who can provide necessary products.
- They can finalize and implement the use of specifications by the organization. Implementation procedures are discussed later in this chapter.

The managers and purchasing staff in this restaurant had to consider the quality standards that these guests would likely expect when they ordered from the menu.

Real Life/Getty Images Inc.-Image Bank

Role of User Department Personnel

The hospitality employees who will use the product addressed by a specification will likely have insight about the product's intended use, and this information can be shared with purchasing staff. Additionally, they may have suggestions about "good" and "bad" features of existing products and will be able to highlight quality characteristics that are important in the products that are needed.

Staff members with extensive industry experience may be able to suggest potential supply sources and/or have a network of peers in other hospitality organizations who keep current on product alternatives. All of this information can be shared with purchasing personnel.

The role of user department employees continues as they help to evaluate alternative products, review early drafts of purchasing specifications, raise issues to be addressed with purchasing staff and/or with potential suppliers, and as they make modifications, if any, in procedures to use new items.

Role of Suppliers

We have already identified several ways that suppliers can help to develop specifications. Purchasers will benefit from technical information provided by suppliers during the development process and from the ongoing information and support they provide. Also, as suppliers observe the employee's sincere interests in using specifications, they are more likely to consistently ensure that the products they provide meet the applicable specifications.

Some might caution about significant supplier involvement in specification development. They may believe that those who provide help will believe that they will be the preferred source for product purchase. There may also be a risk that some confidential information will be "leaked." Examples include advance notice of new menu item roll-outs and/or information about an organization's expansion or downsizing. Also, other suppliers who are not involved in the specification development process may believe that the organization's relationship with other suppliers increases the likelihood that their price quotations will not be considered. As this occurs, competitive pricing benefits may be lost.

In the increasingly complex discipline of hospitality procurement, the advice and counsel of specialists can frequently be very helpful. Suppliers are experts in the products or services they provide. Also, supplier input to the specification development process provides another example of how purchasers can receive benefit from those in the marketplace distribution channels.

THE SUPPLIER'S SIDE (4.1)

A midsize food and beverage operation in a lodging property may require 800 or more food and beverage products for its à la carte, banquet, room service, and bar/lounge operations. It is not, therefore, practical to develop detailed purchase specifications for all of these items. Suppliers can, however, provide advice, information, and samples as necessary to help purchasers as they consider and develop quality standards for their organizations.

Specifications can also be developed for equipment. Consider, for example, a small multi-unit food service operation that is expanding its number of units. The organization's owners and managers can work with equipment suppliers and applicable manufacturers' representatives to develop ("spec") production or dining service equipment modules that can be replicated in new units as they are built.

Suppliers recognize that purchasers consider the information and service they receive to be a value-added benefit to the relationship between both parties. Suppliers interested in a long-term relationship encourage purchasers to request assistance, and they will provide it whenever it is possible to do so.

Internet Purchasing Assistant (4.2)

Hospitality purchasers can use the Internet to identify potential suppliers for products that are needed and can use supplier Web site information as input to the development of purchase specifications.

Assume that you are the buyer for a hotel and are interested in developing purchase specifications for mattresses for the guest rooms. Go to the Web site www.sealy-contract.com where you can learn about that manufacturer's commercial sleep systems and programs specifically designed for the hospitality, cruise, and other industries.

On-the-Job Challenges in Purchasing (4.2)

"I guess I'm from the 'old school' of buyers who think that there should be a very long arm's length between our organization and our suppliers," said Roaul as he spoke with the food services director of a school district in a large metropolitan area. Roaul was responsible for all purchasing in the school district including food and other products for the food services program.

"You're absolutely correct about our need to be transparent, and to have a very conservative fiscal management policy because we are spending the public's money. I would have many of these concerns even if we were an organization in the private sector without this element of external security," replied Nancy, the foodservices director.

"At the same time, however, we also have the obligation to use the monies in our budget as prudently as possible, and we cannot be experts in everything that is involved in providing very complex school food services to almost 20,000 students every day in 55 locations around the area," she continued. "My thought is that we are experts in certain areas such as menu planning, nutrition, governmental regulations, and food production and transportation systems. However, as experts, we should also know when we need external expertise, and I think the development of purchase specifications for new food items is an example."

"Roaul, I know you buy thousands of items to meet our district's needs including educational resources, school maintenance and repair items, furniture, safety supplies, and so many other things. Now let's add food products to the list, and you simply must be overwhelmed. Wouldn't it be good to obtain advice from food suppliers and other experts

(Continued)

who can help us make these important decisions? I'm sure that we can do so in a way that does not obligate ourselves to them. As we do so, we'll be able to make better use of the taxpayers' money to benefit our students."

"You're right, Nancy, I'm not an expert who knows everything about purchasing all the items that we need. I'll admit that, in the past, sometimes we've made purchases on a trial-and-error basis, and we probably did lose money in the process. I'm just concerned about the public's perception of involvement with suppliers, that some less-than-ethical suppliers might take advantage of us, and that the benefits of our interactions with suppliers may not be worth the time, money, and publicity costs."

Case Study Questions

1. How, if at all, do you think the role of suppliers in establishing purchasing specifications might differ for hospitality organizations operated by government agencies versus those that are owned and operated by those in the private sector?
2. Assume that Nancy can convince Roaul to receive input from suppliers as purchase specifications are developed. What are the examples of the types of assistance that might be considered "conservative" and, therefore, useful at the beginning stages of supplier involvement in the process?
3. What other types of external assistance besides that from suppliers is probably available to Roaul and Nancy as they seek information that can be helpful in the development of purchase specifications?

PURCHASE SPECIFICATION INFORMATION

What information should be included in a purchase specification? A simple, but not very helpful, answer is, "Whatever information is required to accurately describe the product and enable potential suppliers to determine the required quality."

Content of Specifications

Many hospitality organizations use a template of basic information for all (or most) of the products for which specifications are developed. Examples of this information are identified in the composite specification form illustrated in Figure 4.2.

A review of Figure 4.2 will reveal many details that a purchaser and a supplier would normally expect to see on a purchase specification. However, to emphasize two important points noted earlier in this chapter, Figure 4.2 also includes two features that are less commonly included: product use and inspection procedures.

When purchasers provide product use information (recall this chapter's definition of quality that considers a product's intended use), the supplier will better understand the context in which the product is needed. He or she may be able to provide suggestions about alternative products that were not considered, or which were not available when the purchase specification was initially developed.

Including product inspection procedures on purchase specifications provides reinforcement that the hospitality organization is very serious about ensuring that quality requirements described in purchase specifications are met. Also, because there are no "secrets," and because the specification was developed with input from suppliers, still another opportunity for supplier input is possible. A supplier might, for example, be able to suggest additional practical methods for product inspection. Why are suppliers concerned that the purchaser receives the proper quality of products from their counterparts? They recognize that some competitors may be unethical and substitute products of lower quality to enable them to quote low prices. Details about this and related theft and security issues are noted in Chapter 11.

Product Name: _____ Specification No.: _____

Menu Item Name (if applicable): _____

Product Use: _____

_____

General Product Description: _____

_____

_____

Specific Information (as applicable)

• Count/portion size: _____

• Tare allowance (if applicable): _____

• Processing requirements: _____

• Drained weight (canned items): _____

• Trade number or grade: _____

• Weight: _____

• Variety, style, type: _____

• Packaging requirements: _____

• Geographic origin: _____

• Edible yield: _____

• Other special information: _____

_____

_____

Quality Inspection Procedures: _____

_____

Other Requirements and General Information: _____

_____

Specification Implementation Date: _____

FIGURE 4.2 Format for Purchase Specification

Sample Specifications

Figures 4.3 and 4.4 show several purchasing specification formats that address some of the factors identified in Figure 4.2. They also illustrate the concerns that a hospitality organization should use systems that are "best" for their own purposes, and that there is no "one size fits all" generic specification format that should be used.

Brand names are a common way to express quality standards for draft beers, liquors, and wines.

Stephen Whitehorn © Dorling Kindersley

Menu Item	Sirloin steak on a bun
Product	Bottom sirloin butt steak; 6-ounce boneless portion
NAMP Number	1185
Grade	USDA Choice
Weight range	6-ounce with a .25 ounce tolerance
Trim level	Zero trim
Packaging	Individual vacuum packaged; 12 portions per box
Special considerations	Aged at least 10 days
State of refrigeration	Fresh product; temperature not to exceed 40°F (4°C)

FIGURE 4.3 Sample Specification Purchased by Industry Standard

Note: The "NAMP Number" refers to a reference number for the desired product that has been established (assigned) by the North American Meat Processors Association (NAMP).

Product Purchased by Quality Factors

Name: TOMATO SAUCE

Description: Tomato sauce is a lightly concentrated version of tomato juice in which other seasonings besides salt are added to the product. The additional seasonings in this product are normally sweetenings such as sugar or corn syrup, vinegar, onion, and garlic. Generally, the product is of medium texture and practically free from defects.

Quality Factors	Maximum Possible Points	Required Fancy Minimum	USDA Grade A Fancy Minimum
Color	25	23	21
Consistency	25	23	22
Defects	25	22	21
Flavor	25	23	21
Total Score	100	91	85

USDA EXPLANATION OF QUALITY FACTORS USED IN GRADING CANNED TOMATO SAUCE

COLOR	Color in tomato sauce is currently determined by the Munsell Color/Disc method. The color should be typical of tomato sauce made from well-ripened tomatoes that have been properly prepared and processed.
CONSISTENCY	Refers to the viscosity of the product and its tendency to hold its liquid portion in suspension. Consistency is determined using the Bostwick Consistometer Method. To meet U.S. Grade A, there should be no more than a slight separation of free liquid when the product is poured on a flat grading tray.

Maximum Bostwick Value

Required Fancy	11 cm
USDA Grade A	14 cm

Note: Lower value is best.

ABSENCE FROM DEFECTS	Refers to the degree of freedom from defects such as dark specks or scale-like particles, seeds, particles of seed, tomato peel, core material, or other similar substances. This factor is evaluated by observing a layer of the product on a smooth, white, flat surface.
FLAVOR	The product should possess a good, distinctive flavor characteristic of good quality ingredients. Such flavor should be free from scorching or any other objectionable flavor of any kind.

Purchase unit is case (six #10 cans; 106 ounces net weight per can).

FIGURE 4.4a Sample Purchase Specification Information

Chicken (Hogie Breaded)

Chicken (hogie breaded)
Fully cooked   Breast meat   Formed/Natural shape

Approved manufacturer: Pilgrim's Pride
Manufacturer's product number: 044707

FIGURE 4.4b   Frozen Product Purchased by Manufacturer's Product Number

Note: Product is Individually Quick Frozen (IQF); 4-ounce portions
Purchase unit = 10-lb. case (two 5-lb. packs/case)

Battered Chicken Breasts

Manufacturer:	Center Plate
Product code:	20341
Type of meat:	Chicken breast with rib meat
Total weight of portion:	3.20 ounces
Weight of temperature batter:	0.88 ounces
Weight of raw chicken breast meat:	2.32 ounces
Weight of seasoning and marinade:	0.18 ounces
Weight of meat before cooking:	2.14 ounces
Weight of meat after cooking:	2.01 ounces

FIGURE 4.4c   Specification Based on Manufacturer's Processing Information

Notes: All breast meat. No fillers or starch.
Purchase unit = case (four 5-lb. bags; net weight = 20 lbs.; gross weight = 21.5 lbs.)
One portion = 3.20 ounces (as purchased); 2.01 ounces (edible portion)

Courtesy: Division of Housing and Food Services, Michigan State University.

Internet Purchasing Assistant (4.3)

The U.S. Department of Agriculture has developed details of food purchase specifications for the products that it purchases for federal feeding programs. Although these may be too detailed for the purposes of many hospitality buyers, they do provide a benchmark of information that can be revised as necessary to fit the needs of specific food service organizations.

To review these specifications, go to: www.ams.usda.gov/cp/specindex.htm

When you reach this site, you can review specifications for meat and poultry products, dairy, eggs, fish, grains, and a variety of other commonly purchased items.

IMPLEMENTING PURCHASE SPECIFICATIONS

After initial drafts of purchase specifications have been developed, they must be revised as necessary and implemented. Specifications can be developed for products already being purchased and for which no specifications currently exist and for new products not currently being used by the organization. The steps used to develop and implement specifications described in this chapter are applicable to both situations.

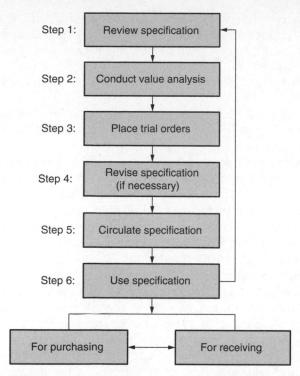

FIGURE 4.5 Implementing Purchase Specifications

Figure 4.5 provides an overview of steps that can be used to implement purchase specifications.

Let's review the steps useful in implementing purchase specifications that are noted in Figure 4.5:

- *Step 1: Review Specification.*   The purchaser should have a useful draft of the purchase specification after receiving input from user department personnel, suppliers, and his or her own research. Alternatively, the organization may have an existing specification that is being evaluated. Professional purchasers know that these early drafts can still benefit from further analysis. The result: a "better" specification (one that most effectively describes expected quality standards), or a confirmation that the existing specification accurately reflects quality requirements.
- *Step 2: Conduct Value Analysis.*   The concept of **value analysis** relates to efforts to increase the value for the money spent, and/or to increase the satisfaction that results from using the product that is purchased. Results of successful value analysis can yield reduced costs and, although less quantifiable, can also increase cooperation between departments and improve relationships with suppliers.

    To illustrate the process, a cross-functional team comprised of purchasing and user department personnel, along with others who provide diverse perspectives, can address questions such as: "What is this product?" "What is it for?" "What does it cost?" "Is there anything else that would fulfill this

Key Term

Value analysis   Techniques used to increase value for the money spent for a product, and/or to increase the satisfaction that the product provides.

product's purpose as well or better than this product and, if so, what would it cost?" The team's efforts can evolve through several phases:

- Reviewing information used to develop the present version of the purchase specification.
- Speculating about alternative products and alternative uses for the products being examined.
- Investigating ideas generated during the speculation stage.
- Recommending proposals, ideas, and suggestions to further improve the specification.

- *Step 3: Place Trial Orders.*   Ideally, the purchase specification has been developed in a way that allows several (or more) suppliers to provide products of acceptable quality. Trial orders that yield samples of products from several suppliers can help confirm that the written specification yields products meeting quality standards. (The hospitality organization may wish to address the need, if any, for a policy about payment for product samples in their Codes of Ethics [see Chapter 3]).

- *Step 4: Revise Specification (if necessary).*   At this point, significant research, analysis, and deliberation efforts have, hopefully, yielded a purchase specification that accurately reflects the organization's quality standards for the product being described. However, changes, if any, noted as a result of samples received during trial orders can be considered.

- *Step 5: Circulate Specifications.*   Suppliers who will be asked for price quotations should receive a copy of specifications for products applicable to them. These may be sent to the suppliers' headquarters electronically, hardcopies can be given to the supplier's representative who interacts with the property, and/or copies can be included in a supplier handbook that is given to all suppliers (see Chapter 8).

- *Step 6: Use the Specification.*   As noted earlier, current and accurate specifications are useful to identify quality standards required for products being purchased. They are also useful at time of product receiving to confirm that incoming products meet the property's quality requirements. Figure 4.5

PURCHASING PROS NEED TO KNOW (4.4)

Purchasing pros know that there are advantages to using one product for several purposes when it is possible to do so without sacrificing quality standards. This process is called **"menu rationalization,"** and when this is done, a fewer products must be purchased, received, stored, issued, and placed into production. Product knowledge and skills relating to handling procedures can also be lessened.

An example from a restaurant or food and beverage department in a hotel provides a good example: Is it necessary to purchase different sizes of shrimp for use in shrimp cocktail appetizers, shrimp plates, shrimp casserole dishes, and shrimp salads? If it is, different sizes should be purchased because it is important to define required quality in terms of intended use. However, if the number of required shrimp sizes can be reduced, the above-noted benefits may result.

Wise purchasing professionals consider the relationship between products, their purchase specifications, and other similar products as an integral part of the specification development process.

Key Term

Menu rationalization   Analysis of existing menu items and the ingredients used to produce them with the goal of reducing the number of different items that must be purchased.

These expensive items of serviceware are purchased by brand name to ensure that the property's quality requirements are attained.

EyeWire Collection/Getty Images-Photodisc

also reminds us that the process of implementing purchase specifications is cyclical. The availability of new products, changing customer preferences, and results from future value analysis teams may yield specifications that describe new or revised products that are judged most helpful for the organization.

HIGH-TECH PURCHASING (4.1)

Communication Is Key

The process of developing purchasing specifications is straightforward, and requires a great deal of communication, cooperation, "common sense," and dedication to the emphasis on value (cost relative to quality). This chapter has suggested that suppliers can provide input to the process. It is likely that, when possible, purchasers would request assistance from suppliers with whom they already interact, and this will typically be possible unless very specialized items available from only a relatively few suppliers are needed to meet specification standards.

Purchasers may maintain an electronic database of information about suppliers and can access electronic market information to discover and research additional suppliers. Meetings with suppliers can be arranged by e-mail and/or text messaging, and teleconferencing may be helpful when purchasers and suppliers in remote locations operated by chain organizations are involved.

Sample orders can be placed through the existing electronic purchasing networks that connect purchasers with their suppliers, and payment for these products (if policy so requires) can be made with existing electronic funds transfer (EFT) systems.

Large hospitality organizations may use customer survey methods in which input is gathered over the Internet, and data is cumulated electronically in response to questions about, for example, the desired quality characteristics of alternative food items.

Technology is of increasing use in determining quality and developing purchase specifications just as it is becoming more useful in almost all other aspects of hospitality purchasing in one way or another. Today, people communicate, control, manage, and purchase using technology to supplement the process of making quality decisions that are integral to insuring value that can be passed onto the hospitality organization's customers.

Purchasing Resources on the Internet

In addition to the Web sites referenced in this chapter's "Internet Purchasing Assistant," the following sites provide detailed information to enhance your purchasing knowledge and skills.

Purchasing Resources on the Internet

Site	Information About
www.foodqualitynews.com	Food safety and quality control
www.braywhaler.com	Services helpful in the purchase of a wide range of products for lodging properties
www.hotelinteractive.com	Suppliers offering a wide range of hotel-related items
www.foodproductdesign.com	Commonly purchased food products and overview of quality issues
www.foodproductiondaily.com	Food processing news that affects food quality
www.findarticles.com	Taste panels (Type "taste panels" in the site's search box)
www.usda.gov	Detailed food purchase specifications (Type "purchase specifications" in the site's search box)
www.sysco.com	A quality assurance program developed by one large food distributor (Click on "QA Database" on the site's home page)
www.usfoodservice.com	Procedures used by one distributor to maximize food safety before products reach the hospitality operation (Click on "Services", then click on "Food Safety & Quality Assurance" on the site's home page)
www.freshfoodgroup.com	Seasonal calendar for fresh foods noting availability, quality, and pricing concerns (Click on "Seasonal Calendar" on the site's home page)

Key Terms

market form *82*
high-check average
   (restaurant) *82*
external service
   provider *82*

quality (organizations
   perspective) *83*
quality assurance *83*
total quality
   management *83*

process *84*
procedure *84*
defect *84*
purchase
   specification *86*

competitive pricing *86*
tare allowance *86*
value analysis *97*
menu rationalization *98*

Think It Through

1. The chapter suggests that some hospitality operations develop purchasing specifications (or, alternatively, have them available from "headquarters" in the case of chain organizations) and use them only when price quotations are solicited. They do not use them to check incoming products to ensure that quality standards are met. Do you agree or disagree with this approach? Defend your response. What would you do or say to receiving personnel if you were the new general manager at a property and noticed the receiving process excluded the use of these tools?

2. Do you agree that the primary responsibility for the development of purchase specifications in large organizations should rest with purchasing rather than user department staff? Why or why not?

3. The chapter notes that some hospitality organizations have a purchasing policy requiring that samples (trial orders) be purchased rather than solicited from suppliers on a complementary basis. What is your position on this issue? Defend your answer.

4. Assume you are the new general manager of a restaurant where purchase specifications had not previously been used. The chef indicates that there are no problems with the quality of products purchased, and you are able to confirm this during your first several weeks on the job. Would you still want to implement purchase specifications at the property? Why or why not?

5. The process described in the chapter for developing purchase specifications involves input from several sources including suppliers and will require some time and effort. Is the process practical in a large organization? A small organization? What, if any, "shortcuts" can you suggest to simplify the process?

Team Fun

A regional restaurant chain is rolling out a new menu item that has never been offered previously. Market research has indicated that the organization's customer market will purchase chicken strip entrées if they are available. Plans are being made to oven-bake or deep-fry them. Also, several dipping sauces will be served with a smaller appetizer portion in a "Spice it up yourself" campaign. The analysts believe that these new menu items will appeal to existing guests, and to others who currently do not frequently visit the restaurants.

Each team is assigned one task relating to the development of a purchase specification for this new chicken strip item:

1. The assignment of the first team is to suggest how potential suppliers of this product can be identified and what, if any, role they should have in developing the purchase specification for the item.
2. The assignment of the second team is to suggest how top-level restaurant managers and their staff specialists can determine the effect of offering this new menu item on kitchen operations in specific restaurants. In other words, what can be done to best integrate the production of this new item into the existing operation while least disrupting conduction of other items?
3. The assignment of the third team is to suggest the categories of information that must be addressed in the purchase specification for the new entrée item.

Each team should be prepared to give an explanation for their suggestions to the rest of the class.

5

Make or Buy Analysis

In This Chapter

What, if any, products and services that could, respectively, be produced and performed by employees of the hospitality organization should be purchased from external suppliers? An easy, but not very helpful, response is: "Those products and services that would be less expensive if purchased." Food and beverage operations in freestanding restaurants, in hotels, and that serve healthcare, educational, and other noncommercial organizations can prepare required menu items by purchasing the individual ingredients that are needed or, alternatively, they can purchase the items partially prepared or ready-to-serve. Which of these market forms is best? Also, hospitality organizations of all types have needs for custodial, pest control, landscaping, window washing, and numerous other services that could be done by the organization's employees or by external service providers. What is best?

Like most other procurement concerns, there is no easy answer to these questions other than, "It all depends." The numerous factors that influence these decisions and the process of making the "right" decisions are the topics of this chapter.

We begin our study by considering the responsibilities for make or buy decisions. Numerous factors influencing the analysis process can be identified and should be carefully considered as product or service production or purchase alternatives are evaluated. These will be explored in depth, and they will be described in the context of the sequential steps helpful in an objective decision-making process.

Next we'll recognize the importance of the old saying, "A picture is worth a thousand words," by illustrating two practical examples of make or buy analysis. They will reinforce the need for specific procedures that yield the most appropriate decisions about the potential purchase of products and services.

Finally, the decisions that are made must be implemented. Although this seems obvious, the way in which this occurs is likely to significantly affect how the decision will be judged. To this end, short- and longer-term evaluation procedures are needed to evaluate the initial decision. As a result, the decision might be considered effective or, alternatively, problems discovered may suggest that the decision-making process should be repeated to update the considerations of ever-changing customer needs, supplier availability, and changing marketplace alternatives.

■■■

Outline

Key Terms
Think It Through
Team Fun

BACKGROUND

Assume you are the manager or purchasing director for a large restaurant that currently offers a menu with 35 entrée selections and an extensive variety of "homemade" desserts. Several hundred individual ingredients must be purchased to prepare these items. Should any of these entrées and/or desserts be purchased in a ready-made market form to reduce purchasing requirements and to meet other objectives? What about the numerous bookkeeping, window washing, pest control, custodial, and/or other services that are required to keep the restaurant in operation? Should these services be performed by restaurant employees or should these services be outsourced?

Hotel general managers and their staff in the same community have similar purchase considerations as their restaurant counterparts but, in addition, they even have the option of contracting with a separate company to operate the foodservices or to provide housekeeping (and other) functions.

The foodservices director or business manager of the large hospital in the community has the same decision-making concerns in addition to another dimension: Should food services be provided by the facility or by a **contract management company?** If the latter, should nonmanagement personnel be employees of the management company or the facility? These and related issues are important, and they are addressed in this chapter.

As noted in Figure 5.1 (originally shown as Figure 1.4), the subject of this chapter, make (do) or buy analysis, is the third step in the procurement process.

Is this hotel restaurant managed and staffed by the property's employees or by a contract management company?

Ian Aitken © Rough Guides

Key Term

Contract management company   A for-profit business that contracts with an organization to provide foodservices as specified; the management company may be a chain with many contracts or an independent management company with only one or a few contracts.

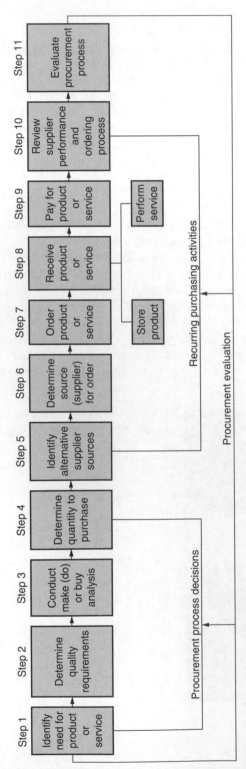

FIGURE 5.1 Steps in Procurement Process

It occurs after the first two steps (Identify Need for Product or Service and Determine Quality Requirements) have been completed.

You've learned (in Chapter 1) that "make or buy analysis" decisions relate to deciding whether selected food products should be produced by hospitality employees or, alternatively, whether they should be purchased with some or all of the labor "built in" that otherwise would need to be provided on site. "Do or buy analysis" relates to the same type of decisions except that they relate to services that could be performed by the organization's staff members or by external service providers. These decisions are very important because they have significant marketing, financial, human resources, and other implications.

Note: Throughout this chapter, we will use the term, "make or buy analysis" when referring to decisions about product or service alternatives and the terms "make or buy" and "do or buy" when referring to, respectively, product and service purchase decisions.

RESPONSIBILITIES FOR MAKE OR BUY DECISIONS

In large hospitality organizations with staff purchasing departments, make or buy analysis activities are typically the responsibility of purchasing personnel. Concerns that prompt make or buy analysis can originate with user department personnel who are confronted with a challenge and wish to consider resolution alternatives. A make or buy analysis can also be prompted by proactive purchasing personnel desiring to provide assistance (potential solutions to resolve operating concerns with which they are familiar). In smaller properties without this specialized assistance, these decisions must be made by managers, supervisors, or line operating personnel.

Figure 5.2 provides the basis for discussing the responsibilities for make or buy analysis in large organizations.

As noted in Figure 5.2, the responsibilities for make or buy analysis in large organizations is typically shared between the purchasing director, department heads, and/or top-level managers. Any of these staff members can initiate and suggest that make or buy analysis is needed. Typically, the actual process is facilitated by the purchasing director and his or her staff with significant input from the requesting department head or manager and his or her staff. Note also that input from line operating personnel should follow the **"chain of command."** The department head should consider whether a make or buy analysis would be useful and, if so, make a request to the purchasing director.

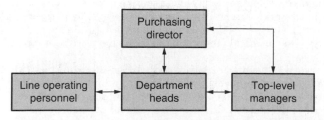

FIGURE 5.2   Responsibilities for Make or Buy Analysis: Large Organizations

Key Term

Chain of command   The path by which authority (power) flows from one management level to the next within the organization.

For example, the executive chef may believe that costs can be reduced without sacrificing quality if preportioned beef patties were purchased instead of (current practice) purchasing bulk ground beef that is portioned on-site by food preparation personnel. After discussion with the department head (food and beverage director), the purchasing director and his or her staff might be asked to conduct a make or buy analysis of the alternatives.

As a second example, the executive chef or food and beverage director in a hotel may believe that money could be saved by purchasing and installing a dishwasher in the banquet service area to reduce the time required to transport dishes back to the dishwashing unit in the central kitchen. Significant costs would be required to implement this alternative. Therefore, discussion with the top-level managers including the property's general manager might be required before the purchasing director is contacted to request that an analysis be undertaken.

As a third example, a hotel's top-level managers, probably after extensive consultation with department heads, regional managers (if a multi-unit organization), and owners may wish to objectively evaluate the outsourcing of employee foodservices or housekeeping services. In each of these examples, managers at higher levels of the organization become more involved as the influence of the make or buy decision becomes more significant.

FACTORS INFLUENCING MAKE OR BUY ANALYSIS

The saying, "There's always a better way," clashes with the philosophy that "If it isn't broken, don't fix it." Managers in contemporary hospitality organizations frequently are confronted by problems that demand resolution, others that would be "nice" to address, and still others that are causing challenges of which they are unaware. An overriding concern for all of these is the desire to increase value for the customer while reducing costs. These concerns could never be addressed if they are relegated to the status of "We'll consider alternatives when we get around to it."

Numerous factors should be considered as make or buy decisions are made. Figure 5.3 identifies some concerns that might be relevant when products are currently being produced or services are currently being provided by the organization's employees.

Now let's consider the opposite of the above discussion: Assume that the hospitality organization is purchasing a product or service from an external

---

- Are changes in necessary production volumes causing difficulties for our staff?
- Are there significant price increases in the products or ingredients needed to produce the item?
- Is there an interest in increasing the variety of menu items without increasing labor costs?
- Is new (expensive) equipment necessary to continue on-site production?
- Is there management interest in allowing staff to focus on their core competencies?
- Are we experiencing difficulty in obtaining a consistent source of supplies?
- Are we experiencing difficulty with the limited number of suppliers that are available?
- Are alternative products and/or services available in the marketplace?
- Does purchase from an external supplier impact other items? For example, a menu item might require a sauce as an ingredient that is also used for other menu items.
- Is equipment and/or space available to store products purchased in other market forms?
- Are there special concerns about decision reversal (returning to on-site production if there are unforeseen problems with outsourcing)?
- Will required purchase quantities be of interest to external suppliers?
- Will future costs of on-site production of products or services change? If so, why, and how much?

FIGURE 5.3 Make or Buy Decision Factors: Products and/or Services Provided by On-site Staff

- Have product or service quality requirements changed?
- Have volume requirements changed?
- Are there problems with the consistency of the product or service quality that is purchased?
- Are costs higher than anticipated?
- Has our need for the product or service changed?
- Are there supplier relationship difficulties?
- Are there special concerns about decision reversal (returning to product or service purchase) if there are unforeseen problems with on-site production?

FIGURE 5.4   Make or Buy Decision Factors: Products and/or Services Purchased from External Suppliers

supplier. Should it continue to do so? Factors to be addressed as this decision is made are listed in Figure 5.4.

The lists of factors in Figures 5.3 and 5.4 that are useful in answering questions about on-site production or product or service purchases are not inclusive. Numerous other special concerns are applicable to make or buy decisions about specific products and services. However, two very important concerns are integral to every make or buy decision:

- Which alternative consistently yields the product or service of appropriate quality (customers' perspective)?
- Assuming equivalent (acceptable) quality, which product or service alternative is the least expensive?

The only general response that can be given to both of the above critical questions is, "It all depends!" Most of the factors identified in Figures 5.3 and 5.4 address components of the quality and price issues. The make or buy analysis process itself that is detailed in the following section, "Close Look at Make or Buy Analysis Process," also focuses in large measure on answers to various dimensions of these two questions. Some hospitality managers subjectively consider quality and cost concerns in a fast and less-than-deliberate manner. However, experienced purchasing professionals know that thoughtful study is required, and the more the decision affects customer value and costs, the more carefully decisions must be made.

Internet Purchasing Assistant (5.1)

Wise hospitality purchasers must be alert to possible ways to reduce costs without sacrificing product quality or services. To do so, they can conduct do or buy analyses relating to a wide range of services that might be provided by in-house personnel or external service providers.

Some services, however, are probably best left to professionals. Specialized knowledge, skills, equipment, and sometimes even licenses issued by state or other regulatory agencies are required to provide some services. To view examples of these services, and to learn why specialists are required, view the following:

- *Pest control services www.orkincommercial.com.*   When you reach this site, review the general information, and then click on "Industry Solutions" to review specific information about hospitality and food services.
- *Ventilation duct cleaning www.nadca.com.*   This site provides certification information for members of the National Air Duct Cleaners Association. Few, if any, food service operators clean kitchen ventilation systems because of the ongoing concerns about safety. Information at this source will help to justify the need for professionals to provide this service.

Most restaurants purchase bread because they do not have the equipment, space, or trained personnel (bakers) to bake it on-site.

Getty Images-Stockbyte, Royalty Free

PURCHASING PROS NEED TO KNOW (5.1)

Which professional sport is "better": baseball or football? The most avid fans of both sports will, from their perspectives, adequately defend their position and be able to cite numerous anecdotes and statistics to defend their position. It is unlikely that anything can be said or done to change their opinion.

Which is better: beef stew **"made from scratch"** or a frozen market form of the product? The most common response is likely to be one or the other, depending, in part, upon the experience that one has had with one or both alternatives. However, a better response to the question is, "It is not possible to generalize." Numerous factors must be addressed to best answer this question for the specific hospitality operation. It is also necessary to objectively consider the alternatives. The purpose of make or buy analysis is not to "confirm" what those conducting the analysis already think or know. Instead, it is to determine the most appropriate alternative for the specific organization by considering those factors judged most important in their own decision-making process.

CLOSE LOOK AT MAKE OR BUY ANALYSIS PROCESS

Earlier sections of this chapter have emphasized the need for careful analysis in make or buy decisions. In fact, several steps are involved, and they are outlined in Figure 5.5.

Before discussing the steps in the make or buy process, note that Figure 5.5 identifies a very significant point: The quality of alternative products or services must be assessed before their costs are determined. As seen in Figure 5.5, the first six steps relate to quality aspects of the decision. Only two steps (Steps 7 and 8) relate to costs of the decision. A point emphasized earlier must be reinforced: Make or buy analysis is not a decision about costs. It is, instead, a decision about quality and costs. Quality must be considered from the perspective of customers (which alternative provides them with greater value?). It does little good to determine the

---

Key Term

Scratch (made from) The use of individual ingredients to make items available for sale; for example, a stew may be made on-site with vegetables, meat, and other ingredients, and a Bloody Mary mix can be made on-site with tomato juice and seasonings.

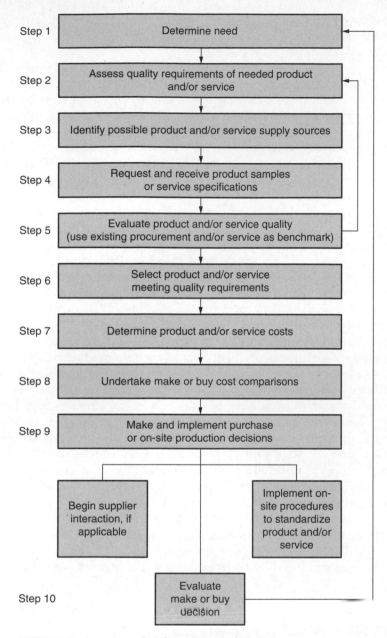

FIGURE 5.5 Overview of Make or Buy Analysis Process

costs of product or service alternatives (Steps 7 and 8) if the product or service cannot be purchased because of unacceptable quality. The purpose of make or buy analysis, then, is to assess cost differences between products or services of equal (or, at least, acceptable) quality.

Having emphasized the need for quality, let's begin a review of Figure 5.5:

- *Step 1: Determine Need.*   In the context of purchasing, need relates to intended use. If a product or service is not needed, it should obviously not be purchased. Although this statement is obvious, it happens all the time! Many hospitality organizations, for example, must discard food products that have deteriorated because of extensive storage time (some products that were purchased were not needed or, at least, were not used!). A second example is bookkeeping services. If purchased, they should be used to help establish an effective record-keeping system, and to then collect data applicable to it. An all-too-common tactic is purchasing bookkeeping services to develop an accounting system rather than use, at least as a basis, the uniform system of accounts recommended by the applicable trade association.[*] The result is a purchased service is that is not needed.

- *Step 2: Assess Quality Requirements of Needed Product and/or Service.* How is the quality of the existing product produced by the organization's employees described? What type, quality, and amount of ingredients are used in the item? What is the portion size? What are the most important factors suggesting a make or buy analysis for it?

  If the analysis concerns a service, how are questions about the "who, what, when, why, and where" of the service answered? What factors are prompting the analysis, and what would be the most distinguishing characteristics of a "better" service?

  This step in the make or buy analysis process is critical because the result should be a definition or description of an exemplary product or service that provides a benchmark (standard) against which to evaluate alternative products or services. A dilemma may arise at this step in analysis: If an acceptable product or service cannot be produced, it will either have to be purchased, or it cannot be offered. If the desired quality cannot be described, it cannot be measured, and it will be difficult (impossible) to evaluate as alternative products or services are evaluated (see Step 5 below).

- *Step 3: Identify Possible Product and/or Service Supply Sources.* Employees in the user department considering an alternative product or service may be aware of external suppliers used by their previous employers. (This is one of the few advantages of employee turnover!) Purchasing staff may have collected information about alternative supply sources as part of the research function of their job responsibilities. Department managers and others with knowledge about a "problem" product or service may also learn about potential suppliers as they visit trade shows, review trade magazines, and discuss challenges with current suppliers of similar products and services. The numerous electronic buying guides are another easy way to identify potential sources of supply.

- *Step 4: Request and Receive Product Samples or Service Specifications.* Potential suppliers of the products or services being considered for outsourcing should be contacted by purchasing personnel. They can be informed that the organization is considering the purchase of products or services currently being produced by its employees. When detailed information about

Internet Purchasing Assistant (5.2)

Assume that you are considering the purchase of a convenience product such as frozen beef stew or canned spaghetti sauce. Where might you go to find alternative manufacturers or suppliers of these products? In addition to contacting the distributors with whom you are currently doing business, you can check out the Internet.

For example, Business.com provides a wide variety of services for hospitality purchasers including a marketplace search for food products and supplies of all kinds. To view this site, go to: www.business.com

When you reach the site, enter the menu entrée or dessert item in the site's search box (e.g., canned spaghetti sauce, frozen beef stew, or cheesecake).

---

[*]See, for example: *Uniform System of Accounts for Restaurants*, 7th ed. Washington, DC: Natinal Restaurant Association. 1996; and *Uniform System of Accounts for the Lodging Industry*, 9th ed. Lansing, MI: Educational Institute of the American Hotel & Lodging Association, 1996.

Suppliers are great sources of information required for make or buy analysis.

Photolibrary.com

the desired products or services is provided (see Steps 1 and 2), it is easier for potential suppliers to assess whether they might be of assistance to the organization.

Hospitality buyers should be knowledgeable about their organization's policies relative to product samples. Some organizations, for example, have policies requiring that samples be purchased (no complementary products are accepted) in efforts to eliminate any concerns about supplier favoritism. This is sometimes of special concern when samples for new products are requested from suppliers of existing products and when organizations or employees request larger-than-necessary quantities for company or personal benefit.

If a product sample is desired, the request is fairly straightforward. However, the process depends upon whether the product will replace one currently being produced (the applicable purchase specification should be provided), or whether the item would be new to the menu. In that case, the purchaser must request a sample of alternative products that meets general quality requirements described by the purchaser. By contrast, if a service is being evaluated, responses to specific questions in addition to the direct descriptions of service requirements may be necessary. (Specifics of outsourcing hospitality services will be examined in more detail in Chapter 19.)

If a do or buy analysis applicable to the potential purchase of a service is being conducted, the purchaser should develop a **Request for Proposal (RFP)** that provides details about the desired service. The RFP should emphasize exactly what is desired (what and how frequently) and, if possible, suggest the quality standards to be attained and the procedures to evaluate the adequacy of the service. Prospective suppliers can also be asked to provide service references.

Key Term

Request for proposal (RFP)   A request made by a purchaser to prospective suppliers to learn the selling price of a product or service that meets identified quality requirements and other purchase concerns including quantity and timing of product delivery or service provision.

Internet Purchasing Assistant (5.3)

Hospitality buyers considering a do or buy analysis for a service should require information from potential external suppliers who provide the desired service. Requests for proposals are useful tools in obtaining information about potentially eligible suppliers and their services. Also, the financial information including alternative prices provided can help determine whether the do or buy analysis is potentially worthwhile.

To read information about procedures helpful in developing an RFP, go to: www.interne-training.com/6art2.htm

- *Step 5: Evaluate Product and/or Service Quality.* Product samples that are received should be evaluated using the product currently produced on-site as a benchmark. Historically, evaluation of alternative product samples has been called **"can-cutting."** This is in reference to cans of food products that are "cut open" to enable contents such as corn or string beans from alternative suppliers to be compared relative to factors such as consistency of size, proper color and shape, and **drained weight** (amount of content that is food product versus canning **liquor**). This term is still used in some organizations to describe the comparison of any food products, even if they are not canned goods.

  Who participates in these product evaluations? A cross-functional team of food production staff, purchasing personnel, food and beverage managers, service staff, and individuals from other departments (if in a hotel) might participate in taste comparisons. In some organizations, guests may be given samples and asked about their opinions. Formal **taste panels** may be used within a controlled environment in large organizations considering large volume purchases.

  When alternative products are being evaluated, **"blind testing"** is necessary to ensure the anonymity of the brand and/or supplier to help ensure that there is no bias or favoritism.

  As noted in Figure 5.5, if the product being considered will replace an existing product, it (the existing product) should be used as an evaluation benchmark.

  If service alternatives are being considered, evaluators should consider proposal responses received from the Request for Proposals issued in Step

---

Key Terms

Can-cutting   A term used to describe the comparison of alternative food products relative to each other and against desirable purchase characteristics.

Drained weight   The amount of a food product in a container after the liquid in which it is packed is removed; also called servable weight.

Liquor (canning)   The liquid in which canned vegetables are packed.

Taste panel   A formal process used to sample food or beverage products being considered for volume purchase. Evaluation factors include taste, color, and smell.

Blind testing   The process of evaluating alternative product samples without knowledge about the brand or of the supplier from whom the product was received.

4. This process will be easier if the RFPs specify details about the services to be provided, and if references provided by prospective service providers are queried about the service qualities of the alternative suppliers.

- *Step 6: Select Product and/or Service Meeting Quality Requirements.* As a result of the focused evaluation of product and/or service alternatives (Step 5), those that meet the property's quality requirements (Step 2) will be identified. It then becomes necessary to assess the costs of products and/or services meeting quality requirements and to compare the costs associated with their counterparts provided by the organization's employees.

- *Step 7: Determine Product and/or Service Costs.* All significant costs associated with producing the product or service should be identified. The definition of "significant" must be addressed by the organization and its planning team. For example, the utility costs incurred as an oven is used to bake loaves of bread may be easy or difficult to determine and may or may not be considered "significant" when cost comparisons are developed. Conversely, the replacement costs for several mop heads may (or may not) be considered worthwhile to include in a cost comparison of custodial services when an outsourcing decision is made. A good "rule-of-thumb" is to determine the estimated cost for all expenses that are incurred to produce a product or service if it is considered practical (cost-effective and reasonable) to do so. (*Note*: Examples of cost comparisons for a product and a service being considered for outsourcing are included in the next section.)

- *Step 8: Undertake Make or Buy Cost Comparisons.* As a result of determining the product or service costs associated with in-house production and external supplier sourcing, the cost for both alternatives will be known and should be compared. If the process described in Figure 5.5 has been followed, it should be an "apples-to-apples" comparison (one based on products or services of equal quality) rather than an "apples-to-oranges" comparison in which products of different quality and, therefore, different production costs, are being compared.

- *Step 9: Make and Implement Purchase or On-Site Production Decisions.* At this point, the planning team is aware of quality and cost factors relative to the products or services being evaluated in the make or buy analysis process. Although these are important factors, others, including those noted in an earlier section of this chapter, must also be considered. For example, it is unwise to select a product of acceptable quality and at a very favorable price from an undependable supplier (hopefully, these suppliers were eliminated in Step 3). However, service factors are among those that should be part of the "big picture" evaluation that is part of the final make or buy decision.

  After the decision is made, further interaction with the applicable supplier will be necessary if a "buy" decision has been made. Alternatively, if the make or buy analysis indicates that external supply sources will not be used, procedures must be implemented to ensure that products purchased for on-site production are standardized (consistent). If the decision relates to the use of the organization's employees to provide a service, then ongoing training, coaching, use of error-prevention controls, and defect analysis may be needed.

- *Step 10: Evaluate Make or Buy Decision.* Was the decision to produce or buy the product or service a good one? The phrase, "Only time will tell," is relevant to answering this question. Situations do change that can affect the validity of the decision. As suggested in Figure 5.5, the make or buy process is cyclical. At a future point and time, further analysis, beginning with the need for the product or service, may be necessary or, at least, helpful.

On-the-Job Challenges in Purchasing (5.1)

"What are the folks in food and beverage and maintenance thinking about?" Greg asked himself as he waited for an elevator that would take him to a meeting with the hotel's general manager. "I really like our management team, but there has to be some coordination because this is getting out of hand!"

Greg was the hotel's director of purchasing, and his concerns centered on the recent request for make or buy analysis assistance he had received from the food and beverage department and three additional requests during the same time period from the maintenance department.

"Why is this happening all at once?" was the next concern in Greg's thoughts. "Right now I'm working on some new menu items, and I'm evaluating new equipment alternatives for floor and wall cleaning for maintenance staff. The need for new guest-room bedding and other linen is also high on my "to-do" list. I wish everyone could remember that my staff members have to place and receive numerous orders for our ongoing product needs every day, and there's only so much we can do."

During Greg's meeting with Adele, the hotel's general manager, he related the above issues as, first, a concern (not a complaint), and then asked a question to introduce his proposal for addressing the situation.

"What about the possibility of us discussing this situation at the next meeting of the **executive committee** when all department heads will be present?" asked Greg, "I think we should develop a system in which nonemergency purchasing assistance that is requested can be coordinated, prioritized, and planned. If I'm correct, Adele, you'll need to be involved because you have the best understanding of how our purchasing department can best help this hotel."

Case Study Questions

1. What do you think are the problem(s) causing Greg's stress and concerns?
2. What would you now say to Greg if you were Adele?
3. What are examples of short- and longer-term solutions to address the problems that are now confronting Greg?
4. What is likely to happen if these problems are not satisfactorily addressed?

An off-site payroll service prepared this employee's check, and a do or buy analysis determined this tactic to be the most cost-effective.

Michael Newman/PhotoEdit Inc.

Key Term

Executive committee   Members of a hotel's top management team (generally department heads) responsible for departmental leadership and overall property administration.

Internet Purchasing Assistant (5.4)

Some specialty restaurants and other food service operations offering menu items with hard-to-find ingredients may discover that difficulty in locating specialty food items limits their options for make or buy alternatives.

Check out the following Internet site, and note the extremely wide range of specialty food items that are available: www.foodservicedirect.com

This site has more than 50 categories of specialty food items and, within each category, numerous ingredients and other items available for purchase.

EXAMPLES OF MAKE OR BUY COST COMPARISONS

The previous section presented a ten-step process that can be used by purchasers as they consider make or buy decisions. In Chapter 4 you learned details about quality, how to describe it, and how best to ensure that quality standards are adequately addressed as products are purchased. Most, if not all, of these principles apply to quality aspects of the make or buy decision-making process discussed in this chapter. However, there is more to be said about costing concerns in make or buy analysis, and these will be discussed now. We'll do so by considering the potential purchase of a restaurant food product and a hotel service.

Make or Buy Analysis: Convenience Food Products

The Mountain-View Restaurant does a great luncheon and dinner business during the six days it is open for business each week. It offers a luncheon buffet with a modest variety of items during the week along with its standard variety of salads, soups, sandwiches, and some "luncheon specials" during the midday meal. During the evenings, a salad bar is offered as a "no additional cost" complement to the entrées on the dinner menu. Each Sunday a fairly expansive buffet line featuring a wide variety of items including several fresh salads is offered.

A tossed salad is available for **à la carte** purchase or as a meal accompaniment with each meal period during the week, and it is very popular. Because salads are selected by the guests as they pass down the buffet/salad bar, they can help themselves to the amount and type of salad ingredients they desire. The serving line offers a large and frequently replenished bowl of fresh chopped lettuce and numerous accompaniments including shredded carrots, sliced radishes and cucumbers, spinach leaves, and numerous other ingredients, toppings, and dressings.

For the past twenty years (probably longer), the food production personnel have been purchasing iceberg lettuce several times weekly to best assure a fresh product. The outside leaves and core are removed, and the product is carefully washed, quartered, and chopped. The amount of lettuce judged sufficient based upon the specific meal forecast (number of guests) is prepared in advance, placed into plastic transport tubs covered with damp (and clean) foodservice towels, and placed in the walk-in refrigerator. Tubs of chopped lettuce are then transported to the serving line as needed. Lettuce remaining at the end of the meal period is

Key Term

à la carte   Individually priced; not included in the price of a meal.

placed back in plastic tubs, covered with a damp cloth, and held in refrigerated storage until the next meal period.

Over the years, the restaurant manager has worked with the cooks to reduce costs without sacrificing quality. However, rising produce costs, increased labor rates, and the difficulty in finding qualified production personnel to compensate for turnover is taking its toll.

The restaurant's produce supplier, in efforts to provide value-added information and service, has made a suggestion to the restaurant manager: "Perhaps you should purchase fresh chopped lettuce in a plastic bag that is ready for service without any required preparation."

Intrigued by the suggestion, the manager received product samples and, after consultation with the production staff, confirmed that the quality of the two alternatives (on-site processed and preprocessed chopped lettuce) were acceptable (of appropriate quality).

Because there were no quality differences between the two products, the manager decided to undertake a make or buy analysis of the two alternatives (continue to purchase and prepare head lettuce, or purchase chopped lettuce as a **convenience food.** Figure 5.6 reviews the estimated costs associated with the on-site processing of the lettuce and are based on several assumptions.

To calculate food cost for one portion (2 ounces):

STEP A.   DETERMINE NUMBER OF EDIBLE PORTIONS (EP) OF ONE HEAD OF LETTUCE

   1 head = 1.08 pounds (AP): 26 pounds per case ÷ 24 heads (count per case)

   1 head = 12 oz. (EP): 1.08 pounds (AP weight per head) × 70% (yield)* = .75 pounds or 12 ounces (16 ounces per pound × .75 pounds)

   Number of 2-oz. servings per head of lettuce = 6 (12 ounces per head ÷ 2 oz. per serving)

STEP B.   DETERMINE FOOD COST PER PORTION

   1 head of lettuce = $1.37 ($32.96 ÷ 24 heads)

   1 portion of lettuce = $ .228 ($1.37 ÷ 6 portions)

STEP C.   DETERMINE LABOR COST PER PORTION

   Labor cost (one case) = $7.47 $9.75 (hourly rate) + $1.46 (fringe benefits; 9.75 × 15%) × ⅔ hour (40 minutes = ⅔ of 60 minutes [one hour])

   Labor cost (one head) = $.311 $7.47 (labor cost per case) ÷ 24 (number heads in case)

   Labor cost per portion = $.052 $.311 (labor cost per head) ÷ 6 (number servings per head)

STEP D.   DETERMINE TOTAL FOOD AND LABOR COST PER PORTION OF LETTUCE

   Food cost $.228
   Labor cost   .052
                   ‾‾‾‾‾
                   $.280
                   ‾‾‾‾‾

FIGURE 5.6   Alternative 1: Chop Lettuce On-Site

*If there is 70% yield, then there is 30% waste (100% − 70% = 30%). Waste represents lettuce not used (outer leaves and core).

Key Term

Convenience food   A food product that has been totally or partially processed to reduce the amount of on-site labor required for its preparation.

Assumptions: On-site Processing:

- 70% **yield**
- Purchase unit = case (24 heads)
- Case weight (**as purchased** weight) = 26 pounds
- Case cost = $32.96
- Portion size = 1 cup (2 ounces **edible portion**)
- Cook's hourly rate = $9.75
- Cook's benefits = 15% of hourly rate
- Preparation time = 40 minutes per case (24 heads)

Note: Cost estimates are used for illustrative purposes only and are not meant to suggest that the least expensive alternative is the best alternative. Ounces per cup (head lettuce) is from: Lynch, F. *Table of Food Yields & Equivalents: A Food-Costing Aid for Chefs.* Chef Desk (www.chefdesk.com). 1997.

When reviewing the information in Figure 5.6, note that the first calculations determined the number of edible portions (EP) of one head of lettuce and the food cost for one portion of lettuce (see, respectively, Steps A and B). The labor cost per portion was then calculated (in Step C), and a total food and labor cost per portion ($.280) of on-site processed lettuce was then calculated (in Step D). Now let's learn about the costs of a two-ounce portion of preprocessed chopped lettuce. Several assumptions are made, and the results of the analysis are shown in Figure 5.7.

Assumptions: Preprocessed (chopped) Lettuce:

- 100% yield
- Purchase unit = 5-lb. bag
- Cost per purchase unit = $18.47
- Portion size = 1 cup (2 ounces edible portion)

To calculate food cost for one portion (2 ounces):

STEP A.   DETERMINE NUMBER OF EDIBLE PORTIONS (EP) OF ONE BAG OF PROCESSED LETTUCE

　　　　　　1 bag = 80 oz. (5 lbs. × 16 ounces per pound)

STEP B.   DETERMINE NUMBER OF PORTIONS PER BAG

　　　　　　1 bag = 40 portions (80 ounces ÷ 2 oz. [portion size)])

STEP C.   DETERMINE FOOD COST (ONE PORTION)

　　　　　　One portion = .462 ($18.47 (cost for one bag) ÷ 40 [number of portions per bag])

FIGURE 5.7   Alternative 2: Purchase Processed Chopped Lettuce

---

Key Terms

Yield (%)   The amount (%) of the as-purchased weight of a food item that is edible after it is processed; see "as-purchased (weight)."

As purchased (weight)   The weight of a product before it is processed, prepared, or cooked; also called AP weight.

Edible portion (weight)   The weight of a product after it is processed, prepared, or cooked; in other words, the amount that is available for service to guests; also called EP weight.

FIGURE 5.8 Per Portion
Cost Comparison of
Chopped Lettuce
Alternatives

Bagged lettuce	$.462
(On-site processed; includes labor)	.280
Cost differential	.182

Weekly Cost Difference

Assume: 100 guests/day (lunch)	×	5 = 500
125 guests/day (dinner)	×	6 = 750
200 guests (Sunday brunch)		200
		1,450 guests/week

Weekly cost savings (on-site preparation) $263.90 (1,450 guests × $.182)

Note that it was much easier to calculate the per-portion cost of bag (processed) chopped lettuce, and that the cost per portion was $.462. Figure 5.8 reviews the cost comparison of the two alternatives (process chopped lettuce on-site or purchase processed chopped lettuce).

Figure 5.8 indicates an estimated savings of $.182 per portion and $263.90 per week if the manager continues to purchase lettuce for on-site processing.

THE SUPPLIER'S SIDE (5.1)

"Insider" Tips on Purchasing: From the Supplier's Perspective

Question: How can suppliers help purchasers as make or buy decisions are made?

Answer: Suppliers can provide extensive assistance as purchasers perform make or buy analysis. Ideas about convenience food alternatives and equipment to reduce tasks now being performed manually might remain unknown to some purchasers if they were not suggested by their suppliers. The provision of product samples, access to small equipment items for a "trial" period, and locating and providing a wide range of information from their "contacts" in the distribution channels are additional examples of supplier assistance as make or buy analysis activities evolve.

Question: Wouldn't most suppliers automatically suggest an operation "buy" (from them!) rather than "make"? How can suppliers help purchasers as make or buy decisions are made?

Answer: The best suppliers know their customer's best interests are truly the same as their own; if they are not, consider a new supplier!

PURCHASING PROS NEED TO KNOW (5.2)

Purchasing pros know that you "can't bank a paper savings!" In the example illustrated in Figure 5.8, the purchasing team identified a savings of approximately $.182 cents per portion when head lettuce was purchased and processed by the restaurant's employees. However, notice the assumptions made in the calculations, including the:

- As-purchased cost per case of head lettuce.
- Yield (servable portion of the head lettuce).
- Purchase cost of bagged lettuce.
- Portion size of salad.
- Labor costs including fringe benefits for the processing employee(s).
- Length of time required to process a case of lettuce.

If any of the above assumptions are wrong or change, the "numbers" leading to the "make" decision will change as well. Costs do change, processing tactics may yield more or less edible portion sizes, and the time required for an efficient or less-than-efficient staff member to process head lettuce will differ.

Careful study is required as make or buy cost comparisons are planned and undertaken, and ongoing study of changing conditions that affect the study's results is also required.

Internet Purchasing Assistant (5.5)

Most broad line food distributors offer several (or more) market forms of popular menu items and the ingredients needed to prepare them. Prepared and precooked convenience food items are often among the alternatives.

To review information about convenience food items offered by one supplier, go to: www.sysco.com

When you reach the site, click on "Products," then click on "Food and Beverage," and then click on the items you wish to review, such as appetizers, desserts, and main dishes.

Do or Buy Analysis: Landscaping Service

The basic process described above to determine the estimated costs for making or buying a convenience food product also applies to analyzing costs associated with "doing" or "buying" a service. For example, assume that the Elmwood Place Hotel meets all of its community's building code requirements for parking spaces and access roads, but still has a significant amount of "green space" planted in grasses, trees, bushes, and flowers. The property is located in a North/South "border state" where the growing season is basically all year around. As a result, grass must be cut about every ten days, and shrubs and other ground cover landscaping and driveway and sidewalk edging must be attended to approximately once every three weeks.

Although the existing service provider does an excellent job, his proposal response for a renewed contract indicates a significantly increased price. Personnel from the property's maintenance department could be used to perform those tasks that do not involve pesticide control, fertilizing, tree trimming, or other activities that involve specialized skills or out-of-the-ordinary equipment. (These are excluded from the service provider's price quote and are included in a separate contact.) However, there are some difficult-to-define costs associated with the "do" alternative that will need to be considered in addition to the "numbers." For example, space must be found to store the required grounds equipment (lawn mower, weed trimmer, and other items), and a possible danger is associated with the storage of flammable gasoline and oil required to operate the equipment. Also, even though new equipment would be purchased, some "number of dollars" must be included for equipment maintenance and repair.

Figure 5.9 reviews the cost if landscaping maintenance is done by the hotel's maintenance staff.

As you review Figure 5.9, note that the cost of outsourcing landscaping maintenance appears to be about $190 more per year than the cost of using maintenance department personnel to perform the landscaping services. Is this differential enough to continue the relationship with the external service provider? Recall that some difficult-to-quantify costs including equipment fuel and repair parts are not addressed in the calculations. Consider also the interest the hotel could earn on the $1,750 investment required for equipment purchase. More importantly, are there existing part-time maintenance staff who would work additional hours to complete landscaping tasks or, alternatively, would the additional labor hours be provided by a new staff member? If the productivity of maintenance personnel is such that these additional labor hours cannot be "found," many hoteliers would be pleased that the do or buy analysis was undertaken, but would opt to continue the contract with the external supplier at the increased cost. Alternatively, if quality and service standards could be maintained with another landscaping service, RFPs could be sent to other service providers.

Alternative 1: Perform Services with Hotel Maintenance Employees

Assumptions:
- Total grass cutting time = 1.25 hours
- Total time for other landscaping services = 2.5 hours
- Hourly rate = $15.25
- Benefits = 17% of hourly rate
- Landscaping equipment purchases = $1,750.00
- Equipment/maintenance/repair = 18 hours annually
- Grass mowing = 1 time each 1.5 weeks
- Landscaping = 1 time each 3 weeks

STEP A.   DETERMINE REQUIRED ANNUAL LABOR HOURS

Frequency of grass mowing = 35 times   (52 weeks in year ÷ 1.5 weekly mowing cycle)
  Labor hours (mowing) <u>43.75</u>   (35 times per year @ 1.25 hours cutting time)

Frequency of ground cover service = 17 times   (52 weeks in year = 3 week cycle)
  Labor hours   = <u>42.50</u>   (17 times per year @ 2.5 hours cycle)

Total Annual Labor Hours
Mowing	43.75
Ground cover	42.50
Maintenance/repair	<u>18.00</u>
Total hours	<u>104.25</u>

STEP B.   DETERMINE HOURLY RATE INCLUDING BENEFITS

$17.84 = $15.25 (hourly rate) + $2.59 ($15.25 [hourly rate] × .17 [tax and benefits rate])

STEP C.   DETERMINE ANNUAL LABOR COSTS

$1,859.82 = $17.84 (hourly rate with benefits) × 104.25 (total annual labor hours)

STEP D.   DETERMINE REQUIRED ANNUAL EQUIPMENT COSTS

$350.00 = $1,750.00 (equipment purchases) ÷ 5 (number years of useful life)

STEP E.   DETERMINE TOTAL ANNUAL COSTS

Labor costs (Step C above)	$1,859.82
Equipment costs (Step D above)	<u>350.00</u>
Total annual costs	<u>$2,209.82</u>

Note: Excludes costs of gas and/or oil and repair parts, if any, extended under warrantee.

Alternative 2: Contract with External Landscaping Supplier

The price quotation from the landscaping service was $200/month ($2,400 annually). Annual cost comparison of landscaping maintenance alternatives:

External supplier services	$2,400.00
Use of hotel's employees	$2,209.82
Annual cost differential	<u>$ 190.18</u>

FIGURE 5.9   Do or Buy Analysis: Hotel Landscaping Services

IMPLEMENTING RESULTS OF MAKE OR BUY ANALYSIS

Undertaking a make or buy analysis is, by far, the easiest part of the process by which the hospitality organization improves. As noted above, "paper savings" do not contribute to cost minimization. Instead, affected managers must "work their assumptions," and implement the tactics assumed by those who developed the make or buy analysis. Although this is obvious, there is frequently a significant difference between what the make or buy analysis assumes and the actual practices that occur after decisions are implemented.

PURCHASING PROS NEED TO KNOW (5.3)

Purchasing pros certainly know about the importance of procurement. However, does this mean that all activities relating to purchasing should be performed by the organization's employees or, alternatively, can some purchasing activities be outsourced? This is a fair question to ask because, if a hospitality organization is to focus its resources on its **core competencies,** the tasks of procuring required products and services might be less important than delivering them to the customers.

 The evolution of procurement from simple and repetitive clerical order processing to an integral part of the organization's strategic function is changing the role of purchasing personnel as they interact with distribution channels and manage the supply chain to best achieve organizational goals. As this evolution occurs, it may be possible for routine aspects of purchasing to be outsourced with external suppliers or, at least, to be resourced to user departments. Examples include determining purchase quantities (increasingly this is done electronically), monitoring incoming products versus purchase specifications, issuing requests for proposals and analyzing proposal responses, and monitoring incoming products (delivery invoices) versus purchase orders. Additional routine activities may include the conduct of make or buy analysis, specialized accounting tasks relating to storage (inventory management), and supplier payment processing.

 As the role of purchasing changes within the organization, some responsibilities will be considered more important than others. Those that don't "make the cut" need to be done by someone, and the use of an external service provider is an increasing possibility.

Consider, for example, an analysis that determines the labor costs that will be saved if preportioned hamburger patties are purchased, and it is no longer necessary to spend on-site labor hours for this task. Preportioned hamburger patties of the same quality as their bulk-purchased counterparts will likely be more expensive. Will labor hours be reduced to compensate for the higher per-unit cost? If so, the savings suggested by the make or buy analysis may be realized, and costs will initially be reduced. Conversely, if the preparation schedule is not actually revised to reduce labor hours, food costs will be higher (because a more expensive market form of ground beef will be purchased), and labor costs will remain the same. The result: higher operating costs.

As a second and related example, assume that specialized patty-forming equipment is purchased as a result of a make or buy decision to reduce labor hours required to preportion hamburger that is purchased in bulk. Because equipment costs will increase, this cost must be more than offset by the reduced labor cost if the decision is to be a "good" one. Instead, if labor hours are not reduced, equipment costs will be higher, labor costs will remain the same, and the financial effect of the make or buy analysis will be harmful rather than beneficial.

Hopefully, all details that are practical to consider are addressed as a make or buy study evolves. If so, there is a lessened chance that "surprises" will arise as the decision is implemented. Changes in "how we have done things in the past" and the need to defend the "status quo" represent aspects of make or buy decisions that cannot be quantified during the analysis. However, they can cause a

---

Key Term

Core competencies The sum of employee knowledge and skill sets required to attain the hospitality organization's mission. These concerns relate to answering the question, "What business are we in, and what business do we want to be in?"

Was this hamburger patty manually portioned and shaped on-site, purchased already portioned and shaped, or purchased in bulk, portioned, and then shaped with equipment on-site?

Getty Images, Inc.-PhotoDisc

significant concern as decisions are implemented. The best approach is to solicit input from affected personnel including those who will be working with revised products and/or work methods. First, their input to the analysis can be helpful and, second, their "buy-in" will quickly help to lessen the resistance that is otherwise possible.

HIGH-TECH PURCHASING (5.1)

In the not-too-distant past, hospitality purchasers undertaking a make or buy analysis were confronted with two time-consuming tasks; they had to (1) determine alternative supply sources, and (2) assess other information required for quality and cost comparisons.

Contemporary hospitality purchasers can use technology to ensure that the very best information is available as make or buy decisions are made. For example, the Internet can be used to obtain information about alternative suppliers carrying a wide range of potentially useful products from frozen desserts to very unique and hard-to-find ingredients for regional specialty dishes. Buyers wanting to view and/or revise recipes as part of their make or buy analysis efforts have access to numerous electronic recipe sources.

What volume of products are sold? The answer to this question is important to learn about the quantity of items that will need to be purchased. In-house purchasing and point-of-sale software answers this question for any desired period of time for many foodservice operators.

What are possible sources of supply for services? What are components of an exemplary request for price quotations for specific services, and what types of value-added services might be available? Careful review of suppliers' Web sites provides background information helpful to lay a foundation for face-to-face meetings with potentially eligible suppliers.

After make or buy analysis decisions are made, product inventory assessments, ordering, receiving management, invoice processing, and related tasks can be managed electronically for the items that are purchased. Procedures to purchase products and services used by many hospitality organizations are increasingly automated. This provides purchasers with more time for creative decision-making because less time is needed for repetitive and clerical routines.

PURCHASING PROS NEED TO KNOW (5.4)

Purchasing pros are aware of the **"Hawthorne effect,"** which relates to the tendency of persons being observed to act differently than they might act if they were not observed.

For example, a cook being timed as the lettuce was chopped might be more productive (work more quickly or efficiently) than he or she would normally. If this occurs, the production time noted for the make or buy study might be shorter than required, and the time spent on the task after the study might be longer than the "actual" time the task should take.

EVALUATING MAKE OR BUY DECISIONS

As noted in Step 10 in Figure 5.5, make or buy decisions require evaluation. This task can be done much more objectively if the data used for the analysis, such as the affected number of labor hours or dollars of anticipated costs, can serve as a benchmark against which to prepare actual "numbers."

Unfortunately, systems to track make or buy analysis data are frequently not in place. For example, a restaurant would not typically track the number of hours of preparation labor required to process a case of lettuce (recall Figure 5.6) nor would the managers identify the number of hours required to portion bulk ground beef into patties (recall our example above). Instead, the times required for both of these tasks would probably have been tracked several (or fewer!) times for the primary purpose of generating information for the make or buy study.

It becomes difficult to monitor (evaluate) the effectiveness of make or buy decisions when special procedures are required to do so. For example, should a cook be asked to "keep track" of his or her time as lettuce is chopped for the analysis? Should the purchasing agent be responsible for this task if he or she collects information and develops the make or buy analysis, or should another busy person such as the chef assume this responsibility?

Managers and others addressing make or buy results are less likely to give a priority to evaluating the effect of a study that has already been implemented. This is especially true if changes implemented from the study were originally suggested or agreed to by those who are now responsible for its evaluation.

It is especially necessary to evaluate the results of the analysis when cost changes occur. For example, wage rates increase, and/or costs of convenience food items fluctuate. New labor-saving equipment, revised work processes, and different market forms of required food products are all examples of factors that can make "yesterday's" make or buy analysis out-of-date.

Busy hospitality managers are likely to, at least subjectively, evaluate changes stemming from a make or buy analysis immediately and for a short time after changes are made. After a relatively short time, however, the "new" product or process will replace its earlier alternative and become the accepted product or process. However, wise hospitality professionals recognize that the journey toward optimal customer value never ends. They recognize the need to use make or buy analysis as one tool in their efforts to ensure that what they are currently doing represents the best alternative in their efforts to please the guests and minimize costs as they do so.

Key Term

Hawthorne effect The tendency of people to act differently when they are observed than when they are not observed.

On-the-Job Challenges in Purchasing (5.2)

"Whose idea was it to start baking bread?" asked Beverly. She was talking about the meeting of the food services employees at the North Chester Hospital that was held earlier in the day. "We've been buying our bakery products forever—if not longer—and no one has ever complained. Teresa is a great foodservice manager, and I know she means well when she says that the baking program can be done by employees in the early evening when the kitchen and equipment is not in use. However, I wonder how long that will last, and I'm also concerned about the spin-off effects of additional work that will be required from all of us who work so hard on the day shift."

Beverly was talking to Warren, another cook who had also attended the meeting. "Well," he said, "Teresa did do a good job of defending how an on-site baking program would upgrade our operation. I also agree with her ideas that it might be less expensive to do so, and that we can generate some additional revenues from an employee take-home program because people like to sit down with their family for a quick meal at the end of a work day with a freshly made dessert. I agree, however, that there is likely to be an awkward transitional period where our jobs might change. I am also worried about what will happen if the program is 'kind of' successful, but also becomes more difficult to justify if several people make just a few bakery products every night."

"You know Warren, you are mentioning some of the same concerns that I have. Why did Teresa spring this on us? Why weren't we told earlier? What are we supposed to do now?"

Case Study Questions

1. What, if any, role should Beverly, Warren, and their peers have played in the make or buy analysis leading to Teresa's decision to implement a baking program at the hospital?
2. What can (should) Teresa do now to help reduce the type of problems you have just read about?
3. How, if at all, is the make or buy analysis different when an analysis is primarily concerned with the more traditional approach of minimizing costs without reducing quality, and when a study such as Teresa's addresses this concern as well as revenue-generation tactics?

Purchasing Resources on the Internet

In addition to the Web sites referenced in this chapter's "Internet Purchasing Assistant," the following sites provide detailed information to enhance your purchasing knowledge and skills.

Purchasing Resources on the Internet

Site	Information About
www.outsourcing.com	Outsourcing (use of external suppliers) (Click on "Buyers" when you reach the site)
www.strategicpurchasingservices.com	Professional supply decision consulting for the hospitality industry
www.icgcommerce.com	Procurement outsourcing
www.procurementoutsourcing.net	Procurement outsourcing
www.threecore.com	Procurement outsourcing
www.outsourcing-center.com	Outsourcing as a business solution
www.connellpurchasing.com	Purchasing assistance to hospitality organizations
www.hotel-online.com	Numerous articles about hotel outsourcing practices (Enter "outsourcing" in the site's search box)
www.rimag.com	Numerous articles about outsourcing in food service operations (Enter "outsourcing" in the site's search box)

Site	Information About
www.saraleefoodservice.com	Convenience products (bakery and meats) for volume purchasers
www.affi.com	History of frozen foods
www.findarticles.com	Processed produce in restaurants (Enter "processed produce in restaurants" in the site's search box)
www.soupbase.com	Prepared soup bases sold through distributors
www.windsorfoods.com	Web site of frozen food manufacturers
www.tyson.com	Information about convenience food products manufactured by the world's largest poultry company
www.chefdesk.com	Purchasing ideas for chefs (supply sources, food links, and information about Book of Yields)
www.preparedfoods.com	Prepared foods (Enter the item of interest, for example, "frozen desserts" or beef stew," in the site's search box)
www.chow.com	Sous vide (a cooking method that expands alternatives in make or buy analysis for foods) (Enter "sous vide" in the site's search box)
www.hollymatic.com	On-site food processing equipment
www.careamerica.com	Outsourcing of custodial services

Key Terms

contract management company   *103*

chain of command   *105*

scratch (made from)   *108*

Request for Proposal (RFP)   *111*

can-cutting   *112*

drained weight   *112*

liquor (canning)   *112*

taste panels   *112*

blind testing   *112*

executive committee   *114*

à la carte   *115*

convenience food   *116*

yield (%)   *117*

as purchased (weight)   *117*

edible portion (weight)   *117*

core competencies   *121*

Hawthorne effect   *123*

Think It Through

1. Who should be responsible for make or buy analyses relating to food alternatives in a small restaurant? Beverage alternatives? Labor (savings) alternatives? Defend your answers.

2. Assume that a make or buy analysis indicated that a desired product of the proper quality could be procured from several suppliers at approximately the same cost. How should the supplier selection decision then be made?

3. Assume that a new food outlet is opening in the student union of the college or university where you are in charge of the purchasing department. You are working with the campus foodservice director as purchasing decisions are made. What factors would prompt you to consider purchasing a dish machine and using washable items (plates, bowls, flatware, and related items) versus disposable products in the food outlet?

4. You are the general manager of a small lodging property close to an airport, and you "try" to offer shuttle service to and from the terminals for your guests. Despite your best efforts, you sometimes need to pay the taxi fare for guests arriving and departing when the bell person who drives your shuttle van is busy with other activities. You know that the general manager of another small property directly across the street from your own is having exactly the same difficulties. What factors are important in the decision that considers two properties combining (sharing) shuttle services?

5. You are the food and beverage director of a mid-size hotel that has a very "temperamental" chef. His personal decisions represent the only way that something can be done relative to food production. You want to begin serving appetizers in the lounge during the late afternoon and early evening to build that business. The chef has absolutely no interest in considering convenience food alternatives because he "knows" these products are of inferior quality and will hurt the reputation of his food production efforts. What, if anything, should you do?

Team Fun

For this exercise, assume that each team is responsible for advising a limited-service hotel property about a special concern. The general manager wants to begin offering cookies to guests as they check in, and she would like to have them along with coffee and milk available in the lobby throughout the evening. The property has a small oven that is used to heat pastries as part of its complimentary continental breakfast program. The manager is trying to determine whether cookie dough should be purchased and then portioned and baked on-site or, alternatively, if prebaked cookies should be made available. Each team will be given one task that will help the manager make this decision.

1. The assignment of the first team is to identify the biggest challenges to the "make" decision.
2. The assignment of the second team is to identify the most significant challenges related to the "buy" decision.
3. The assignment of the third team is to make suggestions about how the new program (whichever alternative is used) should be "rolled out" (introduced) to hotel employees and the guests.

6

Determining Purchase Quantities

In This Chapter

Among a purchaser's many responsibilities is the need to ensure that employees who require products and services will have them available when they are needed. This concern, by itself, does not seem difficult. However, taken in the context of quality assessment, pricing concerns, and supplier selection, the task becomes more formidable.

Many food and beverage products are perishable and prone to quality deterioration if held in storage for excessive periods. Storage space is itself an expensive asset (excess and unused storage areas are expensive and undesirable), and some products are theft-prone. It is clear, then, that purchasing in larger-than-necessary quantities is not appropriate. Inventory depletion due to insufficient purchase volumes is equally unacceptable. As a result, purchasers must be concerned about the balance of "too much" and "too little" as they make purchase quantity decisions. Numerous factors affect the quantity of products to be ordered. Production volumes, quantity discounts, and available storage space are just a few special concerns to be considered.

Hospitality purchasers have traditionally used two basic approaches to purchasing based upon their interests in receiving items for immediate use or for storage in inventory (longer-term availability). Both of these methods will be discussed, and the pros and cons of both alternatives will be presented. Product yields can affect purchase quantities when on-site processing occurs, and these important considerations are addressed in this chapter. Also, both purchasing systems require forecasting of production requirements, so the relationships between forecasting, production schedules, and purchasing needs will be discussed. Not surprisingly, technology can help purchasers forecast needs so product quantity requirements will be better known. These systems are typically an integral part of a more complete procurement system, but we will focus on forecasting modules in this chapter. As we do, you'll learn that basic procedures for manual forecasting are incorporated into contemporary (electronic) production and purchase quantity decisions.

Strategies useful as hospitality purchasers interact with suppliers and others in distribution channels have been emphasized (see Chapter 2) and will continue to be considered in this chapter. For example, two nontraditional purchasing systems help to remove purchase quantity decisions from inventory-related decisions. Just-in-time purchasing and supplier-managed purchasing systems allow purchasers to make long-term purchase commitments without assuming responsibility for on-site storage of the products that are purchased. Are these useful systems? Will they be in the future? You'll be better able to answer these questions by the conclusion of the chapter.

■ ■ ■

Outline

Correct Purchase Quantities Are Important
    Purchase Needs Can Be Forecasted
    Improper Product Quantities Create Problems
        Excessive Quantities
        Inadequate Quantities

CORRECT PURCHASE QUANTITIES ARE IMPORTANT

Up to this point in our discussion of the procurement process, we have explained the importance of identifying needs for products and services. As you have learned, purchasing staff typically provide only nominal, if any, assistance in the marketing (customer)-related responsibility (Step 1), determining quality requirements (Step 2), and conducting make and/or buy analysis (Step 3). As a result of this last step, buyers will know the proper market form of the product to be purchased.

Figure 6.1 (originally shown as Figure 1.4) indicates that we have now reached Step 4 in the process: Determine quantity to purchase (e.g., individual ingredients needed to prepare a known quantity of beef stew or an equal amount of frozen beef stew convenience product).

Purchase Needs Can Be Forecasted

Many hospitality operations have recurring purchase needs. Examples include most restaurant and hotel food and beverage operations with preplanned menus, noncommercial foodservice operations that use **cyclical menus,** and lodging operations that routinely order specific bed linens, guest room amenities, cleaning supplies, and other items. One possible exception may be a catering business whose only revenue source is special catered events. However, even these operations typically offer preplanned menu suggestions to event sponsors that feature entrées, salads, desserts, and other items that have been served in the past.

Key Term

Cyclical menus   A menu that is repeated on a recurring basis (e.g., every 21 days); cyclical menus are most frequently used in noncommercial foodservice operations. Also known as a "cycle" menu.

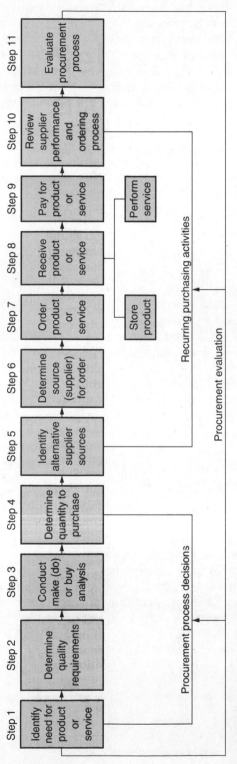

FIGURE 6.1 Steps in Procurement Process

These examples make the point that typically there is a relationship between forecasted customer volumes, production requirements and inventory levels, and the quantities of items to be purchased. Therefore, it is possible to develop policies and procedures relating to the quantities of products to purchase that consider the relationship between these functions. Purchasers typically use different procedures to determine necessary quantities for different products. Highly perishable items such as dairy products and fresh produce, for example, cannot typically be purchased in quantities greater than those that will be used over a several-day period. Frozen and canned foods can, if one desires, be purchased for several months (or longer) usage, and other products such as cleaning supplies and paper goods could be purchased in quantities sufficient for many years (if any purchaser wanted to do so!).

Improper Product Quantities Create Problems

Problems can occur when products are purchased in quantities that are greater than necessary and less than necessary.

EXCESSIVE QUANTITIES   Numerous problems can arise when excessive quantities are purchased, including:

- It ties up **capital** that otherwise could be used for another purpose.
- It affects cash flow. Products that are purchased and placed in inventory for excessive times must be paid for before they are used. The money used for these payments would otherwise be available for other purposes.
- It can affect flexibility. For example, purchasers may be less interested in taking advantage of special buys at significant discounts when excessive quantities are already on hand. Also, the adoption of new products may be slowed.
- More space must be available to store products.
- There is an increased risk of **theft** and **pilferage.**
- Quality deterioration may occur with perishable products.
- There is an increased risk of product damage or destruction because of fire or other natural disasters.
- Handling costs increase (e.g., additional time is required to conduct inventories and to perform cleaning duties.)

Are excessive inventory quantities ever acceptable? Ideally, the answer is "no." However, excessive products may be purchased to compensate for poor or inadequate forecasting ("We need to have some products available in case our customer counts are wrong") and to allow for inconsistent supplier performance. This occurs, when, for example, deliveries are frequently late and/or are frequently under count. In these instances, respectively, more effective management planning and supplier selection decisions can reduce the need for excessive **safety levels** and, in the process, reduce the quantities that must be purchased to maintain them.

Key Terms

Capital   The amount invested in a hospitality operation by its owners (stockholders), and the amount, if any, of income retained by the organization that is invested in it.

Theft   The act of unlawfully taking another's property.

Pilferage   The act of stealing small quantities over a relatively long time period.

Safety level   The minimum quantity of a specific product that must always be available in inventory.

INADEQUATE QUANTITIES Inadequate purchase quantities create their own difficulties. When inventory levels become lower than desired, stock outs and the problems that they can create then arise. These include the:

- Inability to meet production requirements.
- Need to revise production plans to compensate for **stock outs.**
- Possibility of disappointed customers who, for example, visit a specific property for a preferred menu item that is not available because of the stock out.
- (Probably) unknown effect on consumer choices that affect sales data used for future purchase forecasts. For example, customers who would have ordered the stock-out item now must select other menu items; this, in turn, overstates the "popularity" of that item and understates the popularity of the stock-out item.

As you've seen, problems arise when there is an excessive or inadequate supply of products on hand. Although these challenges can be due to numerous factors, they typically relate to the quantity of products that are ordered.

Basic Inventory Concerns

Products that are purchased and received are either moved into storage areas or, alternatively, enter production immediately. Examples of the latter occur when, for example, special steaks required for a catered event are received today for production this evening, and when a specific liquor has been out of stock at the bar, or on **back-order** from the supplier, and is now delivered. Numerous inventory control procedures become important when products enter storage areas and are discussed in Chapter 11.

For reasons including convenience, cost, and practicality, most hospitality buyers do not purchase individual products when the quantities on hand reach an ideal order point for each item. Instead, items are typically divided into several categories, and all or most products within that type are ordered at the same time. For example, all fresh produce, fresh meats, and dairy products may be grouped into their specific categories. Then orders are placed for all items within these categories at the same time (and, typically, from the same supplier for that order).

This system means, in effect, that the quantity of each product ordered may be different (more or less) than would be purchased if the order were being placed for a specific product. Common purchasing practices also require that forecasted business volumes and planned inventory levels minimize, when possible, the potential problems that occur when excessive or inadequate quantities of products are available in inventory. The "bundling" of product purchases increases the challenges that the "right" quantity of every product always be available.

FACTORS AFFECTING PURCHASE QUANTITIES

Traditionally, the primary factors related to purchase quantity decisions involved the estimated sales forecast (production needs); consideration of possible volume purchase discounts, available storage space; and cash flow. These are important considerations today as well; however, nontraditional purchasing systems that involve more significant buyer–supplier "partnerships" can revise decisions about the quantity of products to be delivered to the property at a single time.

Key Terms

Stock out   The condition that arises when a product is no longer available in inventory.

Back-order   The situation in which a product normally available in a supplier's inventory is out of stock and has been ordered from the supplier's own product source.

PURCHASING PROS NEED TO KNOW (6.1)

The quantities of products ordered must consider safety levels: the amount of stock to be available in on-site inventory at all times. Maintaining a safety level is important to:

- Ensure that products are available if supplier delivery schedules are not maintained.
- Hedge against production forecasting errors (production volumes are greater than anticipated).
- Compensate for planning errors.
- Replace products that, for any reason, are found to be unusable.
- Consider miscounts in the quantities of products that are actually available.
- Compensate for product theft or pilferage.

These concerns are important and should be considered. However, it is not appropriate to have safety levels that are excessively conservative (too large) because of cost, space needs, and quality deterioration (of perishable products), among other reasons.

All purchasers should have the goal of determining the "right" amount of inventory of each product to be available. The balance between "too little" and "too much" is a necessary challenge that this effort must address. Wise purchasers look to nontraditional ways to do so, and several of these alternatives are discussed in this chapter.

For example, purchase commitments made by buyers typically address the quantity of items to be delivered as the result of a specific purchase order. Newer alternatives consider the total quantity of products for which the purchaser is committing to buy over longer time periods. Products may be delivered over many months (or longer) or can even be delivered very frequently (even daily) in efforts to minimize storage space and other problems related to inventory management. These newer systems require purchasers to think about purchase quantities in a new way: The amount of product for which a commitment will be made and delivery frequency become separate negotiation concerns. Purchase quantities, then, do not necessarily refer to the amount of product to be delivered at one time for (relatively) immediate use.

These new purchasing alternatives also change another factor in the procurement process: The quantity of products ordered (committed) may not be the quantity needed to replenish inventory levels for a specific order period. Again, the purchase decision is separated into factors (quantity, number of deliveries, and on-site inventory levels) that used to be an integral part of one purchase decision.

The possibility of delivery delays needs to be considered when products are ordered.

John W. Warden/Stock Connection

On-the-Job Challenges in Purchasing (6.1)

I know they're expensive, but we're careful, aren't we?" questioned Katie as she talked to Natava. "And besides, we can always use them, so they'll never go to waste." Katie was the second in charge in the kitchen of the Sandy Waters Inn & Spa, and she was talking with the executive chef. Natava had just met with the property's purchasing director and food and beverage director about several concerns prompted by unplanned rising food costs.

"I share your concern about our problems, and what we might do about them, Katie" said Natava. "It does make sense to pay particular attention to our 'A' items, and the beef tenderloins we purchase are certainly in that category. As you know, they are a regular on our menu, and I wonder if they should be because of price fluctuations. In the past, it was always my plan to have more than we needed on hand so we wouldn't run out. I wasn't really concerned about having too much because I knew we could always process some additional loins into more tenderloin tip casseroles that we could sell for daily specials."

"Well, Natava, those sound like great ideas to me, and they've worked well for a long time, so what's the problem now?" asked Katie.

"Well, the problem is that 'now' is different than before," replied Natava, "The property manager has asked the food and beverage director to identify ways to reduce costs without reducing quality. He, in turn, has asked the buyer and me for ideas. The purchasing guy—he has less to do than me—has reviewed past purchase orders, and he is suggesting that there isn't always a direct correlation between what we need, what we get, and what we sell, and he used the beef tenderloin item as an example."

"Well," said Katie, "What's next? What are you going to do now?"

"Well, Katie, I guess I don't know. The cost of the product is high, and I guess I need to accept some responsibility for that. I don't know what I'm going to do, but I've got to do something, and I need to show some results on next month's food and beverage departmental income statement."

Case Study Questions

1. What, if any, problems do you see that can arise with chef Natava's current tactics for using beef tenderloin? What are specific examples of how his use of this item could excessively increase food costs?
2. Assume you are the food and beverage director: What types of specific assignments to analyze food costs would you give to the purchaser? To chef Natava?
3. What problems might arise at this property if tenderloins were purchased in excessive quantities? In inadequate quantities?

In addition to these factors, several other concerns may be important when purchase quantities are determined:

- *Minimum orders.* Many suppliers specify that a minimum dollar value of products be delivered to help compensate for delivery costs that will be incurred.
- Anticipated increases or decreases in market prices for products. For example, in times when product prices are increasing, purchasers may receive permission to buy in larger-than-normal quantities. Conversely, when market prices are decreasing, buyers may purchase in smaller quantities than normal to increase the turnover of these items and to take advantage of lower prices when additional purchases are made.
- Larger quantities may be purchased when, for example, suppliers offer **"close-outs."** This occurs as manufacturers or others in the supply chain

Key Term

Close-out Tactic used by suppliers or manufacturers to quickly move (sell) unwanted inventory by reducing selling prices.

THE SUPPLIER'S SIDE (6.1)

"Insider" Tips on Purchasing: From the Supplier's Perspective

There are numerous ways that suppliers can offer service and information that can influence purchasers' decisions about the quantity of products to be ordered. Each of these suggests opportunities for purchasers to gain value in their interactions with applicable suppliers.

Question: How can suppliers help purchasers reduce purchasing costs when quantities of items to be purchased are being considered?

Answer: Suppliers desiring a favored relationship with purchasers must try to assist them in meeting purchasing needs in efforts to deliver value in the ongoing relationship. There are numerous examples depending upon the purchaser's needs. Purchasers will not know about close-out specials unless they are informed about them. They cannot take advantage of trial orders, or obtain samples, unless the suppliers are willing to consent to these concessions that typically are costly to the suppliers. Rigid definitions of minimum orders for delivery may be "bent" in some instances. Advanced information about increases or decreases in future market prices may be known by purchasers who keep up with changing market conditions. However, suppliers may have more current and insightful perspectives about marketplace changes that can be shared.

One suggestion: Purchasers should ask suppliers for suggestions about how they (purchasers) can save purchase dollars without reducing quality. The answers they receive may be surprising and very useful.

---

offer short-term promotional discounts to introduce new products and/or to quickly sell products with outdated packaging.

- Trial orders, samples, or other unusually small quantities of products may be ordered at times when new menu items are being considered. A proposed item might, for example, be offered as a "daily special" on several occasions to test for customers' interests. Purchasers may also buy small quantities of products for personnel in other departments to allow for usage comparisons in make–buy analyses relating to cost-effectiveness.
- Machine parts and supplies for equipment being discontinued by the manufacturer may be purchased in a large quantity to expand the property's useful life of the equipment, and/or to gain cost savings because these items will, in the future, need to be purchased from other sources if they will be available at all.

TRADITIONAL PURCHASING METHODS

Traditional hospitality purchasing methods are designed to purchase necessary items for immediate use or, alternatively, longer-term requirements. We'll look at both of these systems in this section.

Quantities for Immediate Use

Perishable food products such as fresh produce, bakery, and dairy items must be purchased in a quantity that enables their consumption within a short time period. Less perishable items such as frozen foods and grocery items, along with materials and supplies used by personnel in other departments of the hospitality organization, can be purchased for immediate use or, alternatively, to store for use over a longer time period.

The quantities of perishable products to be purchased require knowledge about the quantity of products still available and an estimate of the quantity of products needed for the order period.

For example, assume that the purchaser determines that 8 cases of lettuce will be needed during the three days for which an order is being placed:

8.00 cases	(−)	1.50 cases	(=)	6.50 cases
Quantity Needed	(−)	Quantity Currently	(=)	Quantity to
for Order Period		Available		Purchase
(3 days)				

Number of cases to order = 7.0

In this example, the purchaser, working in cooperation with the chef or other representative of the food and beverage department, determines that 8 cases of lettuce (24 heads per case) will be required for the next order period (3 days). However, he or she also notes that 1.50 cases (approximately 36 heads) are currently available for use. This means, then, that 6.50 cases are required (8.00 cases − 1.50 case = 6.50 cases). The purchaser knows that there is a significant increase in product cost when less than a total purchase unit (case) is purchased. It is an easy decision, then, to "round up" and order 7 full cases to meet the property's needs for 6.50 cases. Some suppliers who sell exclusively to large wholesale accounts will not even ship **"split cases."** Higher charges for broken case quantities are one reason that many small-volume hospitality organizations buy from retail outlets such as buyer "clubs." These businesses routinely sell commercial-size containers (e.g., one #10 can containing approximately 12 cups) at a price lower than a wholesale supplier who would prefer to sell by case lot (six #10 cans per case) only.

The process used above to determine the quantity of lettuce to be purchased would also be used to determine the quantities of other perishable items to be purchased for the upcoming order period. After the purchaser knows the items and quantities of each item needed for the order period, he or she can request price quotations from eligible suppliers using a price quotation system (detailed in Chapter 10).

The above-described system works well when purchasers can accurately estimate the quantity of items needed for the order period. Typically, the general usage rates of these products are known. For example, assume that a foodservice operation's

Some cities limit times when trucks can make deliveries to properties in downtown areas. Buyers must consider non-traditional delivery schedules if these restrictions apply.

Peter Byron/PhotoEdit Inc.

Key Term

Split cases A case of less-than-full purchase unit size sold by a supplier. For example, a supplier sells five #10 cans of peaches rather than a full case containing six #10 cans. Also called a broken case.

business is relatively slow during the first several days of the week (Monday–Thursday) and much busier for the weekend (Friday–Sunday). Purchasers may know the normal usage rates for perishable products during the slower first part of the week and use the process just described to determine purchase quantities for orders to be placed on Friday or Saturday for Monday delivery. Because the quantity of each product that will be available at the end of the weekend will not be known when the order for the first part of the week is placed, a conservative estimate [perhaps no inventory] will be factored into the quantity-to-purchase decision.

Continuing with our example, the purchaser will then also place an order for perishable goods on Thursday for delivery on Friday. The estimate of higher weekend usage will be known, and the quantity of product currently available when the order is placed can be accurately determined. It is, then, factored into the decision about purchase quantities for the (relatively) busier weekend.

The quantities of products routinely needed must be adjusted as business volume fluctuates. For example, additional quantities will be needed when business volume is expected to increase because of celebrations, holidays, community events, and other activities that will likely increase business volumes during the period covered by the perishable product order. Conversely, business volume estimates will be reduced at other times because of, for example, periods of poor weather and when business has been reduced for explainable or unexplainable reasons. Forecasting business volumes and production schedules is discussed later in this chapter.

Professional purchasers are always alert to the need to revise the "normal" quantities of products ordered. Consider situations such as excessive spoilage or waste (that suggest quantities of purchased items should be reduced), and when stock outs and "emergency" orders consistently occur (which suggest that purchase quantities should be increased).

Generally, purchasers with experience in a specific hospitality organization can establish a foundation of normal ("routine") purchase quantities for perishable products and adjust these to compensate for changes in estimated business volumes.

Quantities for Long-Term Use

Hospitality organizations of all types require numerous products that are not limited to the time spent in inventory because of perishability concerns. For these items, purchasers can, and typically do, purchase in quantities that will last more than just several days. However, the factors affecting purchase quantities noted earlier in the chapter apply to these items as well, and purchasers have several purchasing and inventory options for each product to be purchased. When nonperishable products are received, they are typically physically placed into storage areas and, depending upon the item, information about the purchase may be entered into the property's perpetual inventory system. Receiving and inventory procedures are discussed in-depth in Chapter 11.

Several systems can be used to determine purchase quantities for nonperishable items when the products are to be delivered to the property at the same time. Procedures used to determine purchase quantities can differ for different products. As expected, more attention is paid to managing the consequences of the relatively few **"A" items** that represent the most significant financial commitments for the organization.

Key Term

"A" items   The relatively few products that represent the largest percentage of purchasing dollars to buy. As a rule of thumb, 20 percent of all products purchased cost a hospitality operation 80 percent of its purchase dollars.

MINIMUM–MAXIMUM PURCHASE SYSTEM   The **minimum–maximum inventory system** requires the purchaser to determine, for each product for which the system will be used, the minimum and maximum quantities of allowable inventory.

Minimum–maximum inventory system procedures involve determining the quantity of each product that should be ordered to bring the existing inventory level back to the maximum point allowable when the order is received.

The minimum–maximum inventory system is best used when:

- There are standard quality specifications for the products being purchased, and quality requirements do not change between orders.
- Product prices are relatively constant.
- Products are used in relatively consistent quantities.
- Products are expensive (and, therefore, require more extensive purchasing and inventory control).
- Products will continue to be used in the future.
- Products are not perishable. In the hospitality industry, few products, if any, are purchased with the intention that they will remain in inventory for extensive time periods. Exceptions may include some wines, noncapital equipment such as kitchen utensils, and supplies used by maintenance personnel.
- Reasonable maximum quantities do not present storage space problems.
- Inventory and storage procedures are in place to ensure that stock is rotated and that theft and/or pilferage is minimized.

This list supports the point made earlier that the minimum–maximum system is best used to control the relatively few and most expensive "A" items. The system is not typically applicable to inexpensive, low-volume, and nonperishable products without a long storage life. Instead, the par inventory system discussed in the following section is often most useful for these items.

Several concepts (terms) must be understood as the minimum–maximum inventory system is discussed:

- *Purchase unit.*   The standard size of the package or container in which the product is typically purchased. For example, many canned fruit and vegetable products are typically purchased by the case (six #10 cans per case), and frozen shrimp may be purchased by the case (ten 5-lb. boxes or bags per case).
- *Product usage rate.*   The number of purchase units (see above) that is used during a typical order period.
- *Order period.*   The time (number of days or weeks) for which an order is normally placed. For example, canned goods may be purchased once monthly, and frozen shrimp may be purchased biweekly.

Key Terms

Minimum–maximum (inventory system)   A system to calculate product purchase quantities that considers the minimum quantity below which inventory levels should not fall, and the maximum quantity above which inventory levels should not rise.

Purchase unit (minimum–maximum system)   The standard size of the package or container in which the product is typically purchased.

Usage rate (minimum–maximum system)   The number of purchase units used during a typical order period.

Order period (minimum–maximum system)   The time (number of days or weeks) for which an order is normally placed.

- *Lead time.* The number of purchase units typically used during the time between placement and delivery. For example, if three cases (50-lbs. each) of frozen shrimp are normally used during the several days separating product order and receipt, the lead time for this product is three cases.
- *Safety level.* The minimum number of purchase units that must always remain in inventory to compensate for late deliveries and unexpected increases in product usage rates.
- *Order point.* The number of purchase units that should be available in inventory when an order is placed.

Let's assume that a seafood restaurant uses a large quantity of frozen shrimp, which is an expensive "A" item included in the property's minimum–maximum inventory system, and let's further assume the following:

- Purchase unit (frozen shrimp): Case—10 boxes (5-lbs. each; 50-lbs. total)
- Product usage rate—42 cases per order period
- Order period—2 weeks (14 days)
- Daily usage rate—3 cases (42 cases per order period ÷ 14 days)
- Product lead time—4 days
- Number of cases used during lead time—12 cases (3 cases/day × 4 days)
- Product safety level—12 cases

The purchaser can now address several questions about the purchase quantities for frozen shrimp.

Question #1: What is the maximum number of cases of shrimp that should ever be available in inventory?

42 cases	(+)	12 cases	(=)	54
Usage rate cases	(+)	Safety level	(=)	Maximum cases

Question #2: What is the order point for the shrimp?

12 cases	(+)	12 cases	=	24 cases
Lead time	(+)	Safety level	=	Cases at order point

The order point (24 cases) can be verified:

Number of cases available when shrimp is ordered	24 cases
Number of cases used until shrimp is delivered (product lead time)	(12 cases)
Number of cases available when shrimp is delivered (safety level)	12 cases

Question #3: How many cases of shrimp should be ordered at the order point (when there are 12 cases in storage)?

42 cases	(+)	24 cases	(=)	66 cases
Usage rate	(+)	Order point	(=)	Cases to order

The number of cases to order at the order point can be verified:

Cases available	=	66 (24 cases [order point] (+) 42 cases [usage rate])
Less lead time cases	=	−(12)
		54 cases (maximum inventory level)

Key Terms

Lead time (minimum–maximum system) The number of purchase units typically used during the time between order placement and delivery.

Order point (minimum–maximum system) The number of purchase units that should be available in inventory when an order is placed.

Question #4:   How many cases of shrimp should be ordered if an order is placed when there are 30 cases in inventory (the order point for shrimp has not been reached)? This could occur, for example, when an order must be placed for other frozen seafood products, and all products to be purchased from a specific supplier are to be placed at the same time.

Step A: Calculate the number of cases of shrimp that exceed the order point:

30 cases	(−)	24 cases	=	6
Cases in storage	(−)	Order point	=	Excess cases

Step B: Calculate the number of cases to order:

42 cases	(−)	6	=	36 cases
Order point	(−)	Excess cases	=	Cases to order

The number of cases of shrimp to order when there are 6 cases in excess of the order point can be verified:

36	(+)	30	=	66
Cases ordered	(+)	Cases in inventory	=	Total cases available when order is placed

66 cases	(−)	12 cases	=	54 cases
Cases available	(−)	Lead time cases	=	Maximum number of cases

When reviewing the purchaser's questions above, note that data for the product being controlled with the minimum–maximum inventory system relating to product usage rate, order period, lead time, and safety level can be used to determine the:

- Minimum number of cases that should be available in inventory.
- Maximum number of cases allowable in inventory.
- Order point (number of cases).
- Number of cases that should be purchased if an order is to be placed before that product's order point is reached.

The safety level for the product represents the minimum number of purchased units below which product quantities cannot decrease. Factors to consider when establishing the safety level include:

- *The lead time required for reorders.*   For example, as the frequency of deliveries decreases, the number of lead-time units should increase. When delivery timing and schedules are not predictable, minimum inventory levels must be increased to compensate for this uncertainty and to reduce the possibility of stock outs.
- *The product's usage rate.*   As the volume of product usage increases, safety levels may need to be increased accordingly. It is more likely to expect greater volumes of unexpected purchases for high-sales volume items than from lower-sales volume items. Likewise, more customers are likely to be dissatisfied with stock outs of higher popularity items. The real goal is to reduce and/or eliminate stock outs so no customer or user department employee will be, respectively, dissatisfied or frustrated.

An ideal safety level will minimize the possibility of stock outs without the need to maintain excessive quantities of products in inventory.

Several factors also influence the decision about the lead times established for products controlled by the system. They can be established by considering the amount of time generally required for an order of a specific type (e.g., fresh dairy products or grocery items). If usage and safety levels incorporate a margin ("cushion") to compensate for unanticipated problems, a small variance in the length of lead time is not critical. However, as these usage and safety level quantities are minimized, greater concerns about lead-time problems are warranted, and it is more likely that time-consuming expediting will be required to obtain needed items.

Conditions that affect the length of product delivery lead times include:

- When suppliers are not dependable (and this should be an important factor in deciding whether to continue to do business with them).
- When the hospitality operation is in a remote location and, therefore, long delays are more likely.
- When market situations, including distribution channels, cause unpredictable conditions that affect the availability of products and potential need for back orders of some products.

These instances suggest times when the purchasers normally increase allowable lead times for product delivery.

Several advantages and disadvantages to the minimum–maximum inventory system can be cited. Potential advantages include:

- Excessive stock build-up is less likely if a reasonable maximum inventory level has been established.
- The minimum level provides a cushion against stock outs.
- The system is easy to understand, explain, and use; in other words, it is practical.
- Actual performance can be monitored versus expected performance. Reasons for inventory levels that exceed and are less than those established for the system can be investigated, and corrective actions can be taken, as necessary.
- Analysis of inventory levels may yield changes in product order quantities that might not otherwise have been perceived.

Potential disadvantages include:

- It may not be the optimal way to calculate required quantities. There are, for example, computer-assisted systems that provide more detailed and accurate forecasts of quantity purchase needs and the timing for purchases. These systems are increasingly used by larger and even relatively small hospitality organizations. This topic is discussed later in this chapter.
- The assumptions used to establish the system's safety and lead-time calculations may decrease its accuracy, which can result in excessive inventory or stock outs.
- Quantity discounts may not be possible when maximum inventory quantities cannot be exceeded, and when these levels are below supplier-specified quantities for which discounts are applied.
- Some time is required to initially consider and calculate safety and lead-time estimates.

PURCHASING PROS NEED TO KNOW (6.2)

Purchasing pros know that special attention is always necessary to control "A" items: those relatively few products for which the majority of purchasing dollars are spent. They know that every product purchased is important. However, items that are expensive, theft prone, and used frequently require special attention.

This special emphasis begins when product needs are established and continues as quality requirements and purchase quantities (the topic of this chapter) are determined. They continue as purchase costs, supplier selection, and negotiation strategies are planned and are emphasized through the final steps in the procurement process: ordering, receiving and storing, and accounting.

In the fast-paced hospitality industry, where purchasers seldom, if ever, have the time to do everything they would like to do, priorities must be established. A special management and control emphasis must be placed on "A" items at every step in the procurement process.

PAR INVENTORY SYSTEM   A **par inventory system** is similar to the minimum–maximum inventory system because buyers must determine the quantity of products needed to bring inventory levels to an allowable maximum (par). The system is commonly used for alcoholic beverages (beer, wines, and spirits), dishwashing and other chemicals, and linen supplies and other nonperishable products.

The quantity of product to be used as the par is determined on the basis of experience, "trial and error," and many of the other factors discussed above—safety stock levels and usage rates established for the minimum–maximum system. The same concerns about quantity normally used and an additional amount (safety stock) that may be necessary in "just in case" situations are integral to the system.

HERE'S AN EXAMPLE OF HOW THE PAR SYSTEM WORKS   The manager (and also the purchaser) of the Desert Oasis Bar and Grill has established a par level of 10 cases of Desert Waters beer (a popular product produced by a local brewery). She orders the item once per week (on Tuesday for delivery on Thursday) to maintain this par level. Before ordering, the manager counts the number of cases available and "rounds down" to the nearest full case. For example, this week she notes that there are 4 full cases and an opened case with 7 bottles in a 24-bottle case. Because she includes only full cases in her par calculations, there are 4 cases in inventory.

The manager also knows that she normally uses "about one case" each on Tuesdays and Wednesdays (lead time: the two intervening days between order and delivery), and also recalls the 7 bottles in the open case. Therefore, she believes her estimate of a 2-case usage for Tuesday and Wednesday will not yield a stock out.

Next, she determines the need to order 8 cases from the local supplier:

(10 cases)	(−)	4	(−)	(2)	(=)	8
Par level	(−)	Number of cases available	(−)	Number of cases used before delivery	(=)	Number of cases to order

If her usage estimate is correct, the par inventory level will be maintained when the delivery arrives:

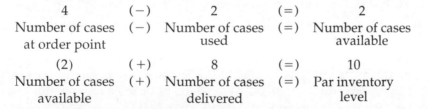

4	(−)	2	(=)	2
Number of cases at order point	(−)	Number of cases used	(=)	Number of cases available
(2)	(+)	8	(=)	10
Number of cases available	(+)	Number of cases delivered	(=)	Par inventory level

You'll notice that the owner of the Desert Oasis Bar & Grill was able to make an easy and fast determination about the number of cases of Desert Waters beer to order by considering:

- The established par level.
- The number of cases of product currently available.
- The number of cases that were likely to be used during the time lapsed between product order and delivery.

Key Term

Par inventory system   A system in which purchase quantities are calculated on the basis of the number of purchase units required to return inventory quantities to a predetermined level.

The quantities of a specific product ordered can affect the price per purchase unit, and this may be a negotiating point.

Photolibrary.com

The par inventory system has advantages (fast and simple) that must be countered with the potential disadvantages of stock outs. These can occur, for example, if the par level is low, the usage rate is higher than expected, and/or the owner is unable to expedite another delivery if unforeseen problems occur (e.g., higher-than-expected usage during the 2-day interval or a special event that was not anticipated when the order was placed).

Par system inventories do not typically create problems with excessive quantities on hand because wise buyers decrease the par level if they notice that quantities on hand are increasing because of decreased usage rates. Conversely, decreased quantities available immediately before deliveries are made will likely be noticed, and anticipated usage rates are considered so par levels can be adjusted. This process is the "trial and error" method noted earlier, and over time, it works well in many hospitality operations.

OTHER SYSTEMS TO DETERMINE PURCHASE QUANTITIES   The widely diverse situations within which purchasers must work sometimes require that additional methods be used to determine quantity needs. These include:

- *Exact requirements system.*   This method involves the purchase of specific products in the exact quantity needed for a specific function. For example, a special banquet function may be planned with an entrée item not generally used for other purposes in the food and beverage operation. The exact quantity required for that special event would be ordered on a one-time basis, and no inventory of that product would be desired.
- *Cyclical ordering system.*   This method involves a periodic assessment of quantities of products available in inventory with a decision made at that time about the need, if any, for additional quantities of products to be purchased. This might be done, for example, at the time physical inventory counts are

Key Terms

Exact requirements system   A purchasing system in which specific products in specific quantities are purchased for a specific function or for a nonrecurring purpose in a hospitality organization.

Cyclical ordering system   An ordering method that involves a periodic assessment of quantities of products available in inventory with a decision made at that time whether additional quantities should be purchased.

taken (see Chapter 11). Consider, for example, unopened cases of light bulbs used by the maintenance department. Assume that a large quantity was purchased and that, over time, the inventory level has decreased. At some (probably subjectively determined) point, a decision would be made to purchase additional quantities of light bulbs.

This process is, perhaps, the most popular method to determine the quantity of many items purchased by hospitality operations. It would not be a useful method for expensive and frequently used "A" items, but it is a useful method for other items, especially when there are suppliers available who can provide short delivery lead times.

- *Cooperative (pool) buying system.*   This method involves several organizations that combine orders for a similar quality of products and then submit one rather than separate orders to a supplier. Although this method does not, in itself, directly affect the quantity of products to be purchased by a specific organization, participants in the buying pool may be required to purchase a minimum quantity of products to place an order for a specific item, and/or to remain members of the cooperative buying system.

- *Economic order quantity (EOQ) method.*   This method involves the use of mathematical calculations and is typically computerized. It allows purchasers to analyze the costs involved related to numerous variables including product price, usage rates, and internal (handling) costs to indicate an order quantity that yields the lowest total of variable costs. When used properly, the EOQ formula can yield lower stock levels and fewer orders with no reduction in service (chance of stock outs).

- *Definite quantity contract.*   Large quantity buyers may enter into an agreement with a supplier to provide a definite quantity of products over a specified number of deliveries. To use this plan, purchasers estimate the total quantity of product that will be required for the contract period. This amount is a function of product needs driven by production anticipated by business volumes during the period. Delivery charges, if any, imposed by the supplier and available storage space are also considerations when delivery frequency is determined.

This method may have merits when quantity discounts are involved (a likely incentive for the purchaser to make a long-term commitment), a supply source is ensured, potential inventory excesses can be used, and purchasers desire to minimize the time and effort required to select suppliers for more frequent orders.

- *Requirement contracts.*   This method is similar to the definite quantity contract just discussed, except that the quantity to be purchased over the

Key Terms

Cooperative (pool) buying system   An ordering method that involves several organizations that combine orders for a similar quality of products and then submit one rather than separate orders to a supplier.

Economic order quantity (EOQ)   This involves the use of mathematical calculations that allow purchasers to determine product order quantities that yield the lowest total of variable costs.

Definite quantity contract   A commitment made by a purchaser to a supplier that a specified (definite) quantity of products will be purchased and delivered to the organization in a specified number of deliveries.

Requirement contracts   Commitments made by a purchaser to a supplier to purchase a minimum quantity of a specified product during a specific time period.

Internet Purchasing Assistant (6.1)

The process of detailed information about economic order quantity (EOQ) purchasing systems is beyond the intent of this text. However, to read articles detailing the process, go to: www.inventoryops.com

At the site's home page, type "economic order quantity," into the site's search box. You may also wish to use the search feature to discover information about numerous other topics applicable to inventory management, including quantity purchase decisions.

extended time period is not fixed. For example, a purchaser may have an agreement with a dairy to deliver varying quantities of milk based on sales volume needs at the same per-gallon price for a specific time period. There may, however, be an agreed-upon minimum quantity. The advantages to this system are similar to those discussed for a definite quantity contract. One further advantage to the purchaser (with, possibly, a higher per-unit cost attached) is that the purchaser can be more flexible; only a range of quantity needs, rather than a fixed quantity, must be estimated and negotiated.

- *Open market purchasing.* For products purchased in small quantities and at minimum value, the calculation or even estimation of exact quantity needs is less important. A workable procedure may be that items such as office supplies in a small organization will be purchased in a quantity roughly equal to consumption with a petty cash system at a local retail business. Petty cash systems are discussed in Chapter 12.

Product Yields Affect Purchase Quantities

The purchasing task would be very easy if all products purchased had a 100 percent yield, and some products do. For example, frozen preportioned 8-ounce hamburger patties have an approximate 8-ounce (100 percent) yield. The menu should indicate that the patty has a **portion size** weight of 8 ounces as purchased [AP], because there will be some cooking loss resulting in an edible portion [EP] weight of slightly less than 8 ounces.

The quantity to purchase is relatively easy to determine when there is a 100 percent yield. Consider the 8-ounce frozen portions of hamburger noted above:

$$
\begin{array}{ccccc}
\text{Estimated} & & \text{Number of} & & \text{Quantity of} \\
\text{portions} & & \text{portions} & & \text{8-ounce} \\
\text{required for} & (-) & \text{in} & (=) & \text{portions} \\
\text{order period} & & \text{inventory} & & \text{required}
\end{array}
$$

Purchasers typically buy preportioned meat products by the pound (1 pound = 16 oz.), and there are two 8-oz. portions per pound (16 oz. ÷ 8 oz. = 2 portions). Standard packaging containers may be 10-lb. boxes or bags (10 pounds × two 8-oz.

Key Terms

Open market purchasing A purchasing method involving the use of petty cash systems to purchase small quantities of items.

Portion size The quantity (weight, count, or volume) of a menu item to be served to a guest.

portions per pound = twenty 8-oz. portions per container) or 25-pound purchasing units (25 pounds × two 8-oz. portions per pound = fifty 8-oz. portions per container).

Many products, however, do not have a 100 percent yield, and then it is more difficult to determine the quantity of these items to purchase even when the number of portions required is known.

Assume that a manager for an upscale restaurant is planning a banquet for 100 guests, and the host has requested that 6-oz. tenderloin filets be served. The restaurant purchases whole tenderloins weighing about 10 pounds that have an AP cost of $14.75 per pound. This entrée is a popular choice, and the restaurant's buyer, working with the chef, has performed **yield tests** that reveal there is an approximate 60 percent yield for the desired product.

The buyer can use yield test information for numerous purposes. For example, he or she can calculate:

- *Production loss.* The amount (weight and/or percent) of a product's AP weight that is not servable because of, for example, trim loss from fat and bones and from cooking (roasting) shrinkage.

    In our whole tenderloin example, a 10-pound (AP) loin will have a 40 percent production loss:

    $$100\% \quad (-) \quad 60\% \quad (=) \quad 40\%$$
    $$\text{AP weight} \quad (-) \quad \text{yield} \quad (=) \quad \text{production loss}$$

- *Weight after processing and cooking.* The loin will weigh only 6 pounds after on-site trimming and roasting:

$$10 \text{ lbs.} \quad (\times) \quad [100\% - 40\%] \quad (=) \quad 6 \text{ lbs.}$$
$$\text{AP weight} \quad (\times) \quad [\text{AP yield} - \text{production loss}] \quad (=) \quad \text{weight after processing}$$

- *Amount of product to purchase (no inventory).* The purchaser knows that only 60 percent of the quantity of whole tenderloins purchased will be servable for the banquet. The amount needed for the event, assuming no product is currently available on-site, can be easily calculated:

$$\frac{100 \text{ portions needed } \times 6 \text{ oz. per portion}}{60\% \text{ yield}} = \frac{600 \text{ oz.}}{.60} = 1{,}000 \text{ oz.}$$

$$\frac{1{,}000 \text{ oz.}}{16 \text{ oz.}} = 62.5 \text{ pounds}$$

    Because each tenderloin weighs approximately 10 pounds, the purchaser will need to buy seven loins (62.5 pounds ÷ 10-pound loin = 6.25 rounded to 7 pieces).

- *Amount of product to purchase if some product is available in inventory.* Assume the purchaser has three whole 10-pound loins in storage that are not needed for another purpose. He or she must then purchase 4 additional loins to meet banquet production requirements:

    7 loins needed (−) 3 loins available = 4 loins to purchase

Key Terms

Yield test A carefully controlled process to determine the amount (weight and/or percent) of the as-purchased quantity of a product remaining after production loss has occurred.

Production loss The amount (weight and/or percent) of a product's as-purchased weight that is not servable.

- *Cost per servable pound.* The cost per servable pound is the cost of one pound of product that can be readily served to guests. In our example, the whole tenderloin costs $14.75 (AP) per pound and has a 60 percent yield. The cost per servable pound is $24.58:

$$\text{Cost per servable pound } = \frac{\text{AP price/lb.}}{\text{yield}\%} = \frac{\$14.75}{.60} = \$24.58$$

- *Food cost for one portion.* The restaurant manager will likely establish the selling price for the banquet based, at least in part, on the food cost that is incurred. Food costs for all items to be served must be determined and, for the tenderloin, it is:

$$\frac{\text{Food cost}}{\text{(one portion)}} = \frac{\$24.58 \text{ (cost per servable lb.)}}{16 \text{ oz.}} = \$1.54 \text{ (cost per ounce)}$$

$$\$1.54 \text{ (cost per ounce)} \times 6 \text{ oz. (portion size)} = \$9.24 \text{ (portion cost)}$$

The tenderloin cost would increase if, for example, it were served bacon-wrapped and/or with a sauce.

- *Selling price information.* Some of the most popular menu pricing methods use mark-ups based on food cost. We know only the entrée cost in this example ($9.24). Assume that the salad **accompaniment costs** (the cost of all other food items served on the entrée plate), bread and butter, and dessert are $6.75 when prepared according to applicable standard recipes that have been **precosted** with current market costs. The manager can use this information to calculate the banquet's **base selling price** (assume the meal should be priced at a 35 percent food cost) based upon its total **plate cost:**

Step 1: Determine Total Plate Cost

$15.99	(=)	$9.24	(+)	$6.75
Total food cost	(=)	Entrée cost	(+)	Accompaniment cost

Step 2: Calculate the Base Selling Price

$45.69		$15.99		.35
Base selling price	(=)	Total food cost	(÷)	Desired food cost percent

---

Key Terms

Cost per servable pound   The cost of one pound of a product in a form that can be served to guests.

Food cost (portion)   The cost of one portion of a food item when it is prepared and portioned according to its standard recipe.

Accompaniment costs   Items such as salads, potatoes, and/or other choices that are offered with, and included within, the price charged for an entrée.

Precost (recipe)   The process of establishing the cost to produce all (or one) serving of a recipe by considering the recipe's ingredients, current ingredient costs, and the number of portions that the recipe yields.

Base selling price   The benchmark selling price of a menu item calculated by the use of a mark-up or other objective pricing method. After its calculation, managers may determine the actual selling price based upon marketing issues, competitive pricing structures, and the "psychology" of menu pricing.

Plate cost   The sum of all product costs included in a single meal (or "plate").

PURCHASING PROS NEED TO KNOW (6.3)

You've learned that buyers must know about product yields and production losses as they determine purchase quantities. What can they do to help ensure that the yield of an item is the same (or, at least, very similar) each time it is purchased so production quantities, costs, and selling price calculations can be reasonably accurate?

The following operating tactics are helpful. Each involves a management (not purchaser) responsibility, but each becomes especially important as the buyer's input about "real" product costs is shared with production managers:

- *Conduct yield tests.* Yield depends upon a product's grade, AP weight, preparation and preparation methods, and cooking times and temperatures. Purchasers working with managers and food production personnel can obtain product samples, conduct yield tests, and make decisions about products that should be purchased.
- Incorporate yield test results into purchase specifications, share them with potential suppliers, and require that price quotations be based upon the quality described in the purchase specification.
- Assume that all operating controls are consistently used. For example, when incoming products are received, they must be checked against applicable purchase specifications (see Chapter 2), ovens must be **calibrated** to ensure that desired temperatures are maintained, and cooking times and temperatures must be closely monitored.
- Consider use of industry standards such as the U.S. Department of Agriculture's Meat Purchasing Specifications (IMPS) and standards developed by the North American Meat Producers Association (NAMPS). See Chapter 7.

In this example, the manager may price the banquet meal at $45.50, $45.75, or another amount, which includes the base selling price as a pricing factor.*

FORECASTING AND PRODUCTION SCHEDULES

Most, if not all, methods to determine the quantity of products to be purchased relate to production needs for the items. As more products are used, inventory levels are depleted, and additional quantities must be purchased. The purchasing methods described in this chapter have, directly or indirectly, been driven by estimates (forecasts) of business volumes that drive purchasing needs.

There are exceptions to this relationship. Consider, for example, a routine practice of lodging properties to stock bed linens and guest room amenities on the basis of the number of rooms available at the property (not on the number of guests who will occupy the rooms during a specific time period). Managers and their purchasing staff know that (hopefully) all of the rooms will be occupied sometimes (the more frequently, the better!) and products and supplies required to serve the highest occupancy needs must be available even though (unfortunately) fewer items will actually be needed for lower occupancy periods.

---

*For details about menu pricing, see: J. Ninemeier and D. Hayes, *Restaurant Operations Management: Principles and Practices*. Upper Saddle River, New Jersey: Pearson–Prentice Hall. 2006. (See Chapter 6.)

Key Term

Calibrate (oven)   To verify, check, or adjust the heating control of an oven versus the actual internal temperature of the equipment.

For example, custodian supplies needed to clean the public spaces of a hotel are required in large amounts because these areas must be cleaned daily (or on another scheduled basis) without regard to the number of hotel guests. Exterior window cleaning, swimming pool, and sidewalk and parking lot maintenance supplies are additional examples of purchases that depend upon variables other than guest counts.

Wise purchasers understand that the types of products being discussed are costly and should not be purchased without consideration of reasonable inventory levels. They also know, however, that these products are not perishable, and judgment errors will not lead to the waste that occurs when their perishable product counterparts must be discarded.

Most perishable products in hospitality operations are purchased for use in food and beverage operations, and it is here where careful attention to production needs based upon forecasted sales volumes is absolutely critical.

The method to make a production forecast is relatively straightforward. Food and beverage managers track historic sales, make adjustments for anticipated events, and use this information to establish customer counts for future periods. This data, in turn, drives the quantities of products required for the planning period.

Manual Systems

Traditionally, and even in many food and beverage operations today, these calculations are done manually. Managers might, for example, record the number of total guests served for each meal period and can use this data to develop future sales estimates. The average total number of customers served on Friday evening for the past 5 weeks (or another time period) might be averaged for use as a base for estimating consumer counts for next Friday. This process can then be repeated to generate customer count estimates for all meal periods for the planning period. These manual systems can also be more specific. For example, managers might consider the percentage of customers likely to order specific menu items, and this detailed information is even more helpful to determine purchase quantities.

Consider, for example, the following example:

- The anticipated total customers to be served during the evening meal periods next week based upon forecasts made from customer counts for evening meal periods for the last 5 weeks = 670
- The percentage of customers who ordered the steak entrée based upon actual sales records for the last 5 weeks = 9%
- The estimated number of steak entrées to be purchased by customers next week = 60 (670 estimated customers × .09 steak purchase percentage = 60 steaks estimated to be sold).

In this example, note that the estimate of customers being served next week (the order period for frozen steaks) is 670, based upon the average served during the evening meal period for the past 5 weeks. Because no out-of-the-ordinary events are anticipated that will affect customer counts, this base (670 customers) is used.

Historical records also note that approximately 9 percent of evening meal customers order this entrée. Therefore, the estimated number of steak entrée portions (60) can be easily determined. This process would be repeated to calculate the number of other entrée portions to be ordered, and managers can use spreadsheet programs such as Microsoft's Excel to quickly make such calculations.

With estimates of production needs for menu items known, food and beverage managers can provide this information to purchasing personnel who can, then, consider existing inventory levels and other information as purchase quantity decisions for the coming week are made.

The proper quantity of products must be ordered to ensure that production personnel have the ingredients necessary to prevent stock outs and customer disappointment.

Mira.com

Ingredients required for other items, including entrée accompaniments, salads, desserts, and beverages, might be ordered on the basis of one or more of the inventory management systems discussed earlier in this chapter.

Manual systems are made easier with the use of **point-of-sale (POS) systems** that automatically generate customer count, menu item sales, and (seemingly) innumerable other information as a result of tallying transaction information.

Many POS systems routinely generate this predictive information that can help to forecast the quantities of numerous items that should be purchased.

Because these calculations are made electronically, they are probably not considered manual systems. However, as we've discussed, a significant amount of manual effort is still required to determine quantity needs for all non-entrée products required for the order period.

Computerized systems that provide more detailed quantity-to-purchase information are also available and are discussed next.

Computerized Systems

The system to forecast the quantity of products needed discussed thus far can make use of information from basic computerized POS systems if they are used at the property. However, systems that assist purchasers with more electronically generated information helpful in purchasing tasks are also available.

For example, advanced POS systems can track the sale of every menu item to determine the quantity of ingredients that should have been used to produce them. This information can be used for food cost control purposes to answer the following question: To what extent does actual product usage match theoretical usage based upon actual sales? The data can also be used to assist in determining product purchase quantities for subsequent order periods.

In an oversimplified example, assume that **standard recipes** have been interfaced with the POS system. The number of customers ordering each menu item is

Key Terms

Point-of-sale (POS) system   A computerized device that records sales information, among numerous other functions; typically abbreviated "POS."

Standard recipes   Instructions to produce a food or beverage item that, if followed, will help ensure that quality and quantity standards are attained.

Internet Purchasing Assistant (6.2)

Many useful point-of-sale systems are available to help food service managers and purchasers determine purchase quantities (among numerous other planning, control, and evaluation tasks).

To learn about one of these systems, go to: www.pcamerica.com

This site allows you to download several demos to gain a fuller understanding of how the system can assist managers and purchasers.

easily determined, and this information is used to determine the quantities of ingredients that should have been used.

Assume, for example, that 2 ounces of tomato sauce are used in each chili portion, and 1 ounce of tomato sauce is used in each meat loaf portion at the Home Town Restaurant. Assume also that tomato sauce is not an ingredient in any other product served at the property in the evening. Because the number of persons ordering chili and meat loaf are known, the quantity of tomato sauce used as an ingredient in these items can also be calculated. The total quantity of tomato sauce used to serve customers during the evening meal period can be combined with the total amount of this product used to produce menu items for other meal periods (e.g., tomato sauce is used in the sauce for breakfast omelets and for casserole dishes used at lunch. The total quantity of tomato sauce used can be "converted" into purchase units (e.g., the number of cases of #10 cans).

Because the quantity of tomato sauce is known for the number of customers served during previous order periods, this information can help in making decisions about purchase quantities for future periods. For example, the fractional amount of each product required for each customer can be multiplied by the estimated number of customers to be served to determine the quantity of product needed. For example, if approximately 1/8 cup of tomato sauce is, on average, used for each customer, this estimate (1/8 cup) can be multiplied by the estimated number of customers to be served to determine the quantity of tomato sauce likely needed.

Although computerized systems do not replace the need for food and beverage managers and purchasing staff to use judgment as purchase quantity decisions are made, these calculations do provide a benchmark of information that can be helpful in determining the actual quantity of product that should be purchased.

HIGH-TECH PURCHASING (6.1)

This and the previous section have previewed the role that technology increasingly plays in helping purchasers to determine the quantity of products that are needed. Basic information provided by most point-of-sale (POS) systems can be used to estimate the quantity of each menu item that has been sold. Because many of these are "A" items, these electronic systems help purchasers to control their most expensive items.

In this section, you learned that POS systems can also use information from standard recipes to provide usage information about their ingredients that can provide assistance in determining product quantities needed for future purchases.

Both of these technology advancements can be compared to traditional methods of tallying manual guest checks and making manual arithmetic calculations to determine sales forecasts. Modern systems are more accurate and, as importantly, help managers and purchasers to use their time to make creative decisions based upon information generated rather than spend significant time generating necessary information.

On-the-Job Challenges in Purchasing (6.2)

"There is never a good time to run out of a product, but today is absolutely the worst time," shouted Harry as he grabbed the telephone.

Flora, a cook at the Calvin Avenue Retirement Center, had seldom seen Harry, the head cook, so angry.

"Well, I guess I fixed the problem this time, but I'm sure going to lose some bargaining power the next time this happens with this supplier," said Harry as he put down the phone. "The salesperson is going to drop off the two cases we need this afternoon, and that will be plenty of time for us to do the preprep necessary later this afternoon."

"All of this started when our facility administrator decided to centralize purchasing and to coordinate our purchase needs with the other three retirement centers that our company operates locally. I certainly see the advantage—volume discounts—but I don't know why we don't receive the quantity of product that we order. Before this change, I could determine the number of cases needed, contact the supplier mandated by the company, and simply place an order. What could be easier?"

"Well, I'm glad you noticed that we didn't have what we needed to prepare our special holiday dinner for the residents tomorrow," said Flora, "It's great that we have good suppliers, but it's a shame they don't deliver the quantity of items that we need."

"There's got to be something wrong with our purchasing system," replied Harry, "and I hope they fix it soon!"

Case Study Questions

1. What procedures should chef Harry be using to determine the quantities of products he is requesting the company's purchasing agent to obtain for him?
2. Assuming that Harry is specifying the appropriate quantity of items, what problems could create the present situation in which the desired product quantities are not being delivered?
3. What, if any, concerns would you have about a centralized purchasing system that allows an individual in a specific unit (the retirement center) to contact suppliers directly? Is this a good idea or a bad idea? Defend your response.

NONTRADITIONAL PURCHASING SYSTEMS

This chapter concludes with a discussion of two nontraditional purchasing systems used by some manufacturing and other organizations and that, with modifications as necessary, may have application to the hospitality industry. Both of these systems incorporate a "partnership" relationship between buyer and seller, and they provide examples of how the value added by a supplier can be more cost-effective than traditional methods that emphasize only lowest cost.

JUST-IN-TIME (JIT) PURCHASING   Most purchasing methods discussed to this point in the chapter have involved ordering a specified quantity of product for an order period of some duration with one delivery for all products in the order. Two systems (definite quantity contracts and requirements contracts) did incorporate the concept of deliveries being negotiated separately. **Just-in-time purchasing** might be considered a variation of these two methods.)

The goal of a JIT system is to have the necessary quantity of required products arrive when they are needed for production. For example, a food service operation

Key Term

Just-in-time (JIT) purchasing   A purchasing system in which a long-term commitment is made with a supplier to make frequent product deliveries that enable the hospitality organization to minimize on-site product storage.

may have products required for the next day's production delivered during the previous afternoon. Some additional storage space would also likely be available to store very small quantities of products for use on an "emergency" basis.

Potential advantages to JIT systems include:

- Reduced need for on-site storage space.
- An improved "partnership" relationship with suppliers.
- Longer-term relationships with suppliers that minimize time and problems caused as interactions with numerous suppliers occur.
- Reduced waste from spoilage.
- Fewer opportunities for theft and pilferage.
- Reduced amount of monies tied up in inventory.

Purchasers using a JIT system must "qualify" a supplier to help ensure that a long-term relationship would be beneficial, and that concerns about **single sourcing** could be overcome. These typically relate to concerns about being dependent on one supply source: "What do we do if we can't get necessary supplies from our single supplier?"

It is also necessary to select a supplier that is in a relatively close location to the hospitality operation to reduce the potential for transportation-related problems that can slow JIT deliveries.

Potential concerns about JIT include the obvious:

- Production concerns if products are not delivered.
- Apprehension about making significant changes in existing purchasing systems.
- The need for significant analysis planning to: (1) ensure that a system is cost-effective and (2) develop procedures for its implementation and operation.

Figure 6.2 reviews some of the major differences between traditional and JIT purchasing systems.

Traditional Purchasing	JIT Purchasing
• Purchase in relatively small quantities.	• Purchase commitment for greater quantities of products.
• Fewer deliveries of greater quantities.	• Frequent deliveries of smaller quantities.
• Products rejected at time of delivery are reordered.	• Items rejected are redelivered without an additional order.
• Lowest price is the primary purchasing objective.	• Total acquisition cost is the primary objective.
• Supplier determines delivery schedule.	• Purchaser determines delivery schedule.
• Formal communication (e.g., purchase orders).	• Less formal communication.
• Innovations are discouraged.	• Innovations are encouraged (required).
• Significant time spent on purchasing functions.	• Less time spent on direct purchasing activities.
• Purchaser–supplier "partnership" is not a consideration.	• Purchaser–supplier "partnership" is critical.

FIGURE 6.2 Traditional and JIT Purchasing Systems

Key Term

Single sourcing The concept of relying on only a single supplier as the source of one or more specific products.

How might a JIT system actually work in a hospitality organization? Let's consider the food and beverage operation in a very large hotel in a relatively large metropolitan area with a strong base of tourist business yielding a consistently high occupancy rate (e.g., a branded hotel in Waikiki [Honolulu, Hawaii]). It has used a traditional purchasing method with several produce suppliers and several dry good suppliers for many years. The property has had an excellent long-term relationship and experience with each supplier who is requested to submit a price quotation. Top-level hotel managers and their purchasing specialists meet with suppliers to explain their potential interest in a JIT system with a long-term (one year) commitment to a single supplier who can provide specific products needed by the property. The hotel will require daily deliveries (six days weekly), and the supplier must provide an agreed-upon normal quantity of on-site "back-up" products. Numerous other details must also be considered and agreed upon.

Suppliers are asked to quote a product **mark-up price** based upon an agreed-upon standard such as the published market price available from several available sources. The supplier chosen is the one submitting the lowest mark-up price above the current market price for each delivery.

Two basic types of quantity purchases are involved in this system. Some produce items (e.g., lettuce and spinach) and grocery good items (e.g., canned tomato paste and paper goods) are used on a fairly consistent basis, and a **standing order** is established for these items. Unless adjustments are made, the same quantity of these products will be delivered daily.

Other products, including produce required in significantly larger quantities than the standing order because of very large banquet and specialty items required for catered events, are electronically ordered on a daily basis.

Products required for the next day's production are delivered in the afternoon of the previous day. Receiving personnel perform normal receiving tasks (see Chapter 11), and they move items into applicable storage areas. Products remain on the transport dollies used to move them from the loading dock or receiving area to the storeroom. The next morning, products are transported to the applicable production areas, and carts are returned to the receiving area for that afternoon's delivery.

Internet Purchasing Assistant (6.3)

"Just in time" purchasing has another name in other industries: "Lean Manufacturing." To review a history of Lean Manufacturing and learn about some of its present-day applications, go to: www.strategosinc.com

When you reach the site, click on "Search Site" and then type "just in time" in the search box.

Key Terms

Mark-up price   The amount (price) for a product that a supplier would charge above a base price agreed upon by the buyer if the product were purchased by the buyer.

Standing order   An agreement made between a purchaser and a supplier that the same quantity of a specified product is required each time a delivery is made.

Although this composite case study is oversimplified, it includes aspects of a JIT system that might be useful in some situations (e.g., large hospitality organizations located in metropolitan or suburban areas). It also illustrates the commitment that both the purchaser and supplier must make to the other party and suggests the types of value-added services that are integral to a successful partnership.

Supplier-Managed Inventory

With traditional purchasing systems, products are ordered and received, and the hospitality organization takes ownership of, and responsibility for, products when the receiving task is completed. Is it possible to use another approach in which the supplier maintains an inventory at the hospitality organization, and ownership (cost) is transferred to the organization when products are issued?

A variation of this approach occurs in many food and beverage operations when representatives of suppliers providing dishwashing chemicals maintain a property's consumption (usage) rates, existing inventory levels, and suggest purchase quantities based upon historic usage patterns. In a similar manner, a chemical supply company may monitor a hotel's laundry facility and provide their products as needed. In these examples, decisions about purchase quantities are reversed from traditional methods; the supplier rather than the purchaser has significant input to the quantity purchase decision.

A supplier-managed inventory has potential advantages for the hospitality organization and the supplier. The former incurs no financial responsibility for care or carrying costs applicable to product inventory until the time of issue. The latter will likely generate a larger dollar value of product sales to the hospitality organization as the single-source supplier than he or she might otherwise. Benefits to the hospitality organization should also include higher levels of service and improved cash flow, and suppliers should receive significant **customer loyalty** from the hospitality organization.

Produce must be purchased in the correct quantity to help reduce spoilage that can occur if these items remain in storage for an excessive amount of time.

Vincent P. Walter/Pearson Education/PH College

Key Term

Customer loyalty   The concept of purchasers giving priority to a specific supplier because of past positive experiences they've had with the supplier.

Internet Purchasing Assistant (6.4)

The concept of supplier-managed inventory traditionally relates to the roles and responsibilities of manufacturers and their distributors. Manufacturers receive electronic information about the distributor's sales and stock levels; this information then helps manufacturers create and manage the distributor's inventory plan.

The discussion about supplier-managed inventory in this chapter is a derivation of that concept. To learn more about vendor-managed inventory, go to: www.vendormanagedinventory.com

Both the supplier-managed inventory system and the JIT system have several characteristics in common:

- They encourage or require collaboration between the purchaser and the seller. Hopefully, this encourages the trust and "transparency" that is a prerequisite to a partnership relationship.
- The emphasis moves away from minimizing cost (perhaps at the expense of the other party) to minimal costs for both companies. In effect, then, the emphasis changes to "cost removal" rather than cost transference.
- A foundation or framework for an ongoing agreement means that both the purchaser and seller will understand their responsibilities and have a shared goal: to assist each other.
- There is an emphasis on continuous improvement. Both the purchaser and the supplier make mutual efforts to ensure quality and to reduce waste.

Purchasing Resources on the Internet

In addition to the Web sites referenced in this chapter's "Internet Purchasing Assistant," the following sites provide detailed information to enhance your purchasing knowledge and skills.

Purchasing Resources on the Internet

Site	Information About
www.purchasing.com	Obtaining value from distributors (Enter "distributor value" in the site's search box)
www.scmr.com	*Supply Chain Management Review*—inventory management (Enter "inventory management" in the site's search box)
www.microsoft.com	Supply chain management and interactions with suppliers (distributors) (Enter "supply chain management" in the site's search box)
www.adacoservices.com	Food and beverage product control including inventory quantities.
www.culinarysoftware.com	Food and beverage product control including inventory quantities
www.foodtrak.com	Food and beverage product control including inventory quantities
www.menulink.com	Food and beverage product control including inventory quantities

Key Terms

Think It Through

1. The text stated that hospitality purchasers do not typically purchase products for inventory. What do you think this statement means? Do you agree or disagree? Defend your response.
2. What are examples of ways in which purchasers should closely interact with user department personnel to determine the quantities of products to be purchased?
3. What, if any, special purchasing-related concerns are important when determining the quantity of "A" items that should be purchased that may not be applicable to the purchase of "B" and "C" products?
4. What are the pros and cons of just-in-time purchasing? Of supplier-managed inventory systems?
5. What are practical ways that small hospitality operations might use technology to help determine quantities of products that are needed?

Team Fun

You and your team have been asked to provide consultative assistance to a new restaurant that will soon be opening. The owner is concerned about product purchasing and cash flow, and wants to minimize the quantity of products in inventory while minimizing the occurrence of stock outs.

1. The assignment of the first team is to determine general "rules of thumb" about how to classify items into two categories: perishable products and nonperishable products. After this determination is made, the team should suggest general policies applicable to determining purchasing quantities for both categories of items.
2. The assignment of the second team is to make suggestions about how to determine purchase quantities when the property initially opens and has no "track record" of previous sales information that would normally influence purchase quantity decisions. This team should also develop suggested procedures for using historic sales information that can be useful after the property has been opened for several months.
3. The assignment of the third team is to suggest an extensive list of specific ways that suppliers to this new restaurant can provide value-added services of benefit to the managers when the restaurant is in its final stages of planning and then later in its initial stages of operation.

7

Managing the Purchase Price

In This Chapter

Knowledge about price is an important element in every buyer's understanding of the procurement process. It is critical, however, that buyers move beyond an oversimplified notion of price (i.e., "cheapest means best") to a full appreciation of the role price plays in effective purchasing. You will begin your study of price by examining core concepts sellers consider when determining their prices, as well as key points buyers must remember about these price determination concepts.

Nearly all buyers perceive price in their own way. As a result, what is seen as a fair price to one buyer may not be perceived as fair by other buyers. Therefore, buyers should understand their own perceptions of price and how they influence their purchase decisions.

Although buyers and sellers are generally seen as the most important factors in price determination, there are other important factors. Among these are governmental entities, contract terms, and the actual amount purchased. Buyers must understand the importance of these factors, and how they and other factors directly affecting pricing will be examined.

Not surprisingly, discounts are as popular with hospitality buyers as they are with any other types of shoppers! Recognizing this, sellers offer a variety of discounts to buyers, and in this chapter you will learn about the most common types of discounts offered, why they are offered, and how, when appropriate, buyers can take advantage of them.

Any person who has shopped in a grocery store knows it can be difficult to compare prices when the containers in which foods and beverages are sold vary in package size. Also, comparisons between fresh and minimally or fully processed foods increase the complexity of price comparison. Professional hospitality buyers also face these challenges. In this chapter you will learn how buyers make the calculations necessary to knowledgeably and accurately compare vendor prices.

Although many hospitality buyers devote a great deal of their time to the purchase of food and beverage products, most also purchase a variety of services. Buying services is challenging. Comparing alternative suppliers' prices for services can be especially challenging. In this chapter you will learn some of the techniques buyers use to make good price-related decisions when they evaluate alternative service providers and their prices.

■ ■ ■

Outline

DETERMINANTS OF SELLERS' PRICES

In Chapter 1 you learned that the primary objectives of effective procurement are to obtain the *right* product or service at the *right* **price** from the *right* source in the *right* quantity at the *right* time.

Figure 7.1 (originally presented as Figure 1.3) illustrates the central importance of price in the overall procurement process.

Certainly, price can be thought of as the amount of money needed to purchase an item, but a careful review of Figure 7.1 will reveal that obtaining the "lowest" price is *not* an objective of effective procurement. It is the "right" price, not the "lowest" price that is best. This should come as no surprise to professionals in the hospitality industry. Few restaurateurs would maintain the best meals are the cheapest meals, nor would most hoteliers argue that the best hotels are always those that charge the least per night for their rooms. In fact, a focus on lowest price alone usually indicates, on the part of the buyer, a misunderstanding of the economic determinants of pricing.

A review of pricing-related literature intended for buyers reveals that, too often, important information about securing the "right" price is presented to buyers only from their own perspective. Although a buyer's viewpoint is important (and much of this chapter will focus on buyer-related activities), to truly appreciate

---

Key Term

Price   The amount (usually of money) that is required to purchase a product or service.

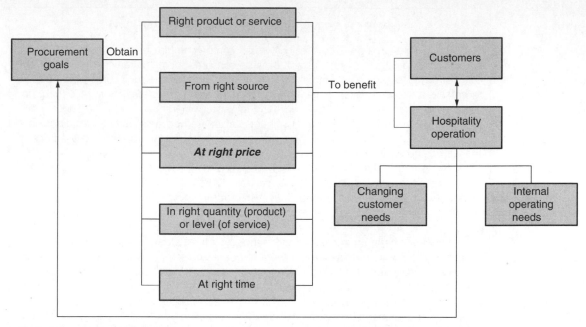

FIGURE 7.1 Procurement Objectives

the rationale for pricing, and to fully understand its complete role in the procurement process, professional buyers must know how sellers establish their prices.

Four primary considerations influence prices charged to customers. Each of these is worthy of examination, and the key point professional buyers should remember from each is noted.

1. ***Prices reflect product costs:*** Few people are in business just for the "fun" of it. Assume you were the seller of a product for which you paid $10. If you are to recover your costs, make a profit, and maintain your business, you will be able to do so only if, on average, you sell your product for more than $10. Assuming the $10 you paid for the item was fair and reasonable, if your own customers do not value your product enough to pay you more than $10 for it, your own business will eventually cease to exist.

   Key Point: Professional hospitality buyers understand that their own suppliers who do not make a profit on their sales will, eventually, go out of business. When they do, it reduces the number of potential suppliers available, diminishes competition, and as a result can place the buyer's organization at risk of paying even higher prices in the future. This book has emphasized the "partnership" between buyer and seller, and a fair (reasonable) profit is given by the buyer in return for the products, services, and information that the seller provides in return.

2. ***Prices reflect consumer demand:*** In many cases, prices are influenced by consumer **demand.** When products are scarce and highly desired, the prices for those products will generally be high. In some cases (e.g., rare wines of limited quantity) the price will reflect the limited supply. In some other cases (e.g., expensive bottled waters) it is not scarcity, but rather simply consumers' willingness to pay, that most influences price.

Key Term

Demand   The total amount of a good or service buyers want to purchase at a specific price.

> ### PURCHASING PROS NEED TO KNOW (7.1)
>
> Understanding what a product is really "worth" can be complex because demand for food and beverage products is not constant. Because consumer demand can change rapidly, the value of products can change rapidly as well. Bottled water is one such current example. As recently as a decade ago, significant sales of bottled water in restaurants were virtually unheard of. Few people would "pay" anything for water when dining out. The 2000s, however, saw an explosion in the sale of still and carbonated bottled waters, including those served in food service operations. Menu prices were high relative to the purchase price of the water, and profits were good.
>
> Beginning in the latter 2000s, however, concern for the environment caused many consumers, including buyers in the food service industry, to question the wisdom of their purchases. As one operator of an upscale restaurant in California stated: "*The whole goal of sustainability and conservation means using as little energy as we have to. Shipping bottles of water from Europe doesn't make environmental sense to me.*"
>
> When increasing numbers of food service customers started asking: "*Does it come in plastic or glass? How much energy is spent to bottle and ship it? Is the plastic bottle safe? Is the water really superior to filtered water from our local water supply?*", it was clear that the consumer's view of value (and thus the price they were willing to pay) was changing. In most cases, the move away from bottled water reflects concerns not about high price, but about the environmental costs of bottling and transporting water, the energy spent recycling the plastic or glass containers, and keeping plastic out of landfills. It will be interesting to see if the trend continues, but it should be clear to professional buyers that the value of products (what they can be sold for) can readily change in the mind of consumers, and these changes should be carefully monitored.

Key Point: As is true for all consumers, the purchase price professional buyers pay for goods and services will be affected by the supply of and demand for them. Buyers should understand when they are paying for scarcity and when they are merely paying a premium price for a consumer fad. This is important because consumer willingness to pay for fads can vary widely (or stop) based upon factors completely beyond the control of the buyer.

3. *Prices reflect service features and enhancements:* This factor can be easily understood by considering two food service buyers. One pays $100 for a case of fresh turkey breasts, but must pick it up at the vendor's location several miles away. The other pays $101 for the case, but the product is delivered to the buyer's restaurant. It is easy to see in this case that the second buyer got the "best" price. Despite the fact that the price was one dollar more, the second buyer received a service enhancement (delivery) that easily justified the increase in price.

Key Point: Food service operators know that when they supply a meal to a guest, the guest receives a product (the food and beverage items consumed), but the guest also benefits from the location, furnishings, ambiance, and service levels provided. In a similar manner, hospitality buyers purchase products and in doing so they will experience the enhancements (or lack of enhancements) offered by the seller. The importance of these added features cannot be overlooked. Timely delivery, condition of facilities, quality of vendor personnel, accurate invoicing, payment processing, and ease of order placement are examples of service enhancements that will be directly reflected in a vendor's pricing structure.

4. *Prices reflect supplier quality:* Much as food service operators with a reputation for quality food and outstanding service can charge more for their products, vendors who have established reputations for consistently providing excellent products and services can reap the benefits of their efforts via increased prices. If buyers truly place a high value on the seller's quality reputation, the additional prices paid for products and services will be paid willingly.

Key Point: If buyers focus only on a product's per pound or per unit purchase price without considering the reputation of the vendors with whom they are doing business, they will frequently fall prey to vendors who provide neither quality nor value. Those suppliers who do not operate ethically and who do not stand behind their products and services often end up costing buyers more (sometimes much more!) than the prices originally quoted to them.

A buyer's recognition of the above factors is important because it reveals the complexity of vendor pricing and illustrates the importance of considering all aspects of price (not merely per unit price) when buying hospitality goods and services.

BUYERS' PERCEPTIONS OF PRICE

Now that you understand the major factors vendors consider when developing their prices, it is important to examine your own view of pricing. Understanding your own perceptions will be helpful when you are considering alternative prices.

Although much has been written about the psychology of pricing and buyers' reactions to price, one fairly straightforward way for hospitality buyers to examine their own pricing perceptions is to consider them as being either traditional or nontraditional. Knowledge about these two basic types of perceptions enables buyers to understand their own responses to price and areas to be carefully examined as price-related assumptions are made.

Traditional Views of Pricing

A traditional consumer's view of pricing assumes that vendors have carefully evaluated their own cost structures and arrived at a price that is low enough to attract customers and high enough to cover the seller's costs and allow for a reasonable profit. Under this view of pricing, buyers routinely make one or more of the following three price-related assumptions:

Increased Price = Increased Quality   This is often an attractive and reasonable assumption, and one that can help hospitality buyers make informed decisions. For example, guest room furniture made from solid wood is of higher quality than similar products made from pressed board, and the quality of the "better" furniture will most certainly be reflected in its price. In a similar manner, a twenty-year-old Scotch whisky will likely taste better, and cost more, than a five-year-old Scotch produced by the same distillery. To avoid purchasing errors, however, buyers who embrace this assumption must ensure they are comparing similar products. Pressed board furniture prices should not be compared directly to those of solid wood furniture. Nor should twenty-year-old Scotch prices be compared to those of five-year-old products. The assumption that increased quality = increased price should be considered true only when it is used to compare products and services that are truly identical in nature (e.g., two brands of solid wood furniture, or two brands of equally popular twenty-year-old Scotch).

Increased Price = Scarcity and Value   Purchasers subscribing to this assumption believe that "rarity" justifies higher pricing. Buyers purchasing imported Russian caviar, steaks of the very highest quality, or rare French wines readily understand the importance, and often the truth, of this assumption. Recall that "demand" was previously defined as "the total amount of a good or service buyers want to purchase at a *specific price*." In many cases, when demand for a product is significantly strong, it will be reflected in the price. A danger in this assumption, however, is the mistaken belief that scarcity alone is a reason for increased value that justifies an increased price. If that were always true, the drawings you undoubtedly made in first and second grade, although unique, and certainly one-of-a-kind (and no doubt highly valued as refrigerator-worthy by your own family!) would be worth a large sum as "rare art." Unfortunately, in fact, scarcity of a product frequently reflects widespread lack of consumer interest and often justifies a lower (not higher) price.

Increased Price = Increased Image   Buyers in the hospitality industry are subject to the same levels of peer pressure and self-image confirmation issues as are any other consumer. Thus the temptation, for example, to buy a Lexus to transport very important hotel guests to the airport (instead of a Chrysler minivan, which would take guests to the airport in the same amount of time) is real. In a less dramatic but similar situation, guests dining at a food service operation that places ketchup bottles on the table will likely perceive the restaurant more favorably if a well-known "Heinz" or "Hunts" product is displayed, rather than an unknown, generic bottled product.

In both of these examples, hospitality buyers make purchase decisions, in part, based upon the image the product portrays. Buyers should understand, however, that paying for image makes sense only when the image paid for is truly appreciated, or demanded, by guests. If it is not, the price paid for "image" is simply wasted. To further illustrate, consider your own buying behavior. Would you pay $100 for a pair of popular, name brand jeans? Would you pay $500 for jeans manufactured by a famous and very exclusive manufacturer? Finally, would you pay $5,000 for a pair of jeans designed specifically for you by the world's top jeans designer? Obviously, there are no "right" answers to the previous questions. They do illustrate clearly, however, the importance of unmistakably recognizing when you are purchasing image (as well as the product) and clearly identifying the incremental price you are willing to pay for it.

Less-Traditional Views of Pricing

Traditional perceptions of price most often relate the selling price of an item to the costs incurred by the item's seller. This is also a typical way of viewing price in the hospitality industry. For example, it is common for a food service operator to establish a product cost and then multiply it by a constant number to achieve a desired product cost percentage. For example, an operator computing a menu item cost of $2 might multiply that cost by "4" to arrive at an $8 selling price with a 25% product cost ($2 product cost/$8 selling price = 25% product cost). There are, however, less-traditional views of pricing that, at first, might appear radical. However, upon further examination they reveal important aspects of pricing. Three of the most useful, but less-traditional, perceptions about pricing will be discussed.

PRICE AND COST ARE UNRELATED   This less-than-traditional view of pricing recognizes that a seller's cost and selling price may be unrelated. This situation is the case more often than some buyers suspect, and when it is true, significant buyer savings can result. Readers accustomed to relating product prices directly to vendor costs may not readily recognize the potential savings. To illustrate, assume that a ban on smoking tobacco was enacted. Because it could not be used any longer, the price of tobacco would likely fall significantly and immediately. This would be true despite the fact that the cost of producing tobacco (planting, fertilizing, harvesting, and manufacturing) would not have changed at all. What would have changed significantly is the inclination of consumers to buy tobacco. It is not the cost of producing tobacco that justifies its (or any other product's) price, but rather price is justified by consumer demand for the product.

Hospitality buyers who encounter situations in which sellers must, for any of a variety of reasons, sell below their true costs can significantly offset one of the basic premises of seller pricing (*prices reflect seller costs*) presented earlier in this chapter. These circumstances do arise, and buyers should be alert to take advantage of them. This first nontraditional understanding of pricing leads directly to the next.

COST PLUS VALUE = PRICE   An examination of most cost accounting textbooks would reveal a common and very traditional view of the manner in which businesses should establish their prices. This approach to selling price determination can be summarized by the following formula:

$$\text{Cost} + \text{Desired profit} = \text{Selling price}$$

A less-traditional, and less commonly taught, view restates the formula as follows:

$$\text{Cost} + \text{Value to Buyer} = \text{Selling price}$$

This less-traditional view demonstrates that it is the buyer, not the seller, that ultimately determines price. Value to buyer, as presented in this equation, represents the notion that the value of goods arises from their relationship to consumer needs and is not inherent in the product itself. In this view, value, like beauty, is in the eye of the beholder. To illustrate, in the long run it is true that only hospitality buyers, not growers, product manufacturers, distributors, or brokers, determine prices that will be paid.

It is also important to note that, in this equation, cost is not weighted more heavily than value to buyer. This is so because, in reality, buyers are inevitably uninterested in a seller's cost. The fallacy inherent in the concept, "cost plus desired profits equals price," can be easily observed by the large number of restaurant operations that go out of business. If business simply involved computing costs and adding desired profits to arrive at a fair selling price, even the least skilled persons could remain in business. In fact, however, when a sufficient number of customers do not visit a restaurant (and thus ultimately contribute to its closing), they do not care about the restaurant's operating costs nor the owner's desired profits. They care only about whether the restaurant provides value to them. If it does, they will gladly pay the restaurant's posted prices. If they do not perceive value they will not pay the price, regardless of how accurately the owner of the business computed costs and desired profits.

The important point for hospitality buyers to recognize from this pricing perception relates to the value they place on an item or service to be purchased. The "value" they should place on a less-than-essential item should be low, and thus its price, if purchased, should also be low *regardless* of the seller's proposed price (or costs). Alternatively, the value placed on some services (e.g., the hourly rate for a plumber to unstop a restaurant's guest toilets on a busy Saturday night) will be high, and excessive time and other resources should never be wasted negotiating relatively small differences in vendor prices!

DIFFERENTIAL PRICING IS NORMAL   Is it "fair" to price virtually identical products differently for different customers? The concept of **differential pricing** states that it is not only fair, it is often essential for ensuring the long-term profitability of a business.

If you are initially uncomfortable with the potential ethical conflicts inherent in differential pricing, you are not alone. Certainly, no legitimate business should charge higher or lower prices based upon a buyer's race or ethnic background. Recognize, however, that most hospitality organizations have historically practiced (aggressively) differential pricing based upon sex, age, and a variety of other factors. "Ladies" nights at night clubs, "Senior Citizen" meal discounts, and reduced

---

Key Term

Differential pricing   The process of charging different consumers different prices for the same product.

Offering "senior citizen" dining discounts is a common example of differential pricing as practiced in the hospitality industry.

Bob Thomas/Getty Images Inc.-Stone Allstock

prices for children at amusement parks, theaters, and fairs are all examples of differential pricing based upon a seller's view that different customers should be charged different prices. Savvy hospitality buyers understand that differential pricing decisions are quite frequently made independent of the seller's actual cost of providing the product or service (e.g., does it really cost an airline less to fly a child in an airplane than it does an adult?)

Hospitality buyers who find themselves in a position of receiving "preferred" prices because of differential pricing methods practiced by their vendors will pay lower prices, and they should do so. Those buyers who do not find their operations in such a situation should actively engage their vendors in discussions to discover the requirements necessary to receive favorable prices. The number of reasons for inclusion in a preferentially priced group can be many (and often can be quite surprising) and are worth investigation.

THE SUPPLIER'S SIDE (7.1)

"Insider" Tips on Purchasing: From the Supplier's Perspective

Buyer's Question: My friend also owns a restaurant in this town and he and I were comparing prices we pay for products. We buy the same items from you, but I pay a lot more for them. And I found out we buy exactly the same amount of product from you each month, so it isn't that he buys in greater quantity than I do. I thought you told me you were already giving me your best price!

Supplier's Answer: It's true, you are paying more, and it's also true I am giving you my best price.

Buyer's Question: Then why do I pay more?

Supplier's Answer: Several reasons. First, he takes delivery once per week. We deliver to you three times weekly. It costs us more to sell to you.

Buyer's Question: O.K., that makes sense, but what else affects my price?

Supplier's Answer: Well, he pays his invoice within 7 days. You pay every 30 days. That costs our company more as well.

Buyer's Question: Anything else?

Supplier's Answer: Yes, you have a higher volume restaurant. Your friend buys over 80 percent of all his products from us, and my company offers a discount to buyers who place the great majority of their orders with us. You buy the same amount of products as he does, but that represents less than 50 percent of all you buy. So now you simply don't qualify for our preferred customer discount. But you could!

SPECIFIC FACTORS AFFECTING HOSPITALITY PRICING

Professional buyers will encounter a number of industry-specific factors that directly affect the prices they pay for goods and services. Although their effect varies based upon the particular industry segment, the following are noteworthy for nearly all buyers and will be examined more closely:

>   Governmental Controls
>   Contract Terms
>   Number of Vendors
>   Payment History

Governmental Controls

Thus far our discussion of prices has included only the viewpoints of a willing seller and a willing buyer. Sometimes, however, local, state, or the federal government play a role in price determination. For example, in Chapter 19, you will learn that the prices charged for utilities (e.g., electricity, gas, water, and sewage) are, to some degree, governmentally controlled and/or regulated and not subject to normal price negotiation. Alcoholic beverage prices are another area in which some level of governmental price controls is common.

When authorized to do so, governmental entities directly affect the prices paid for products and services. To illustrate, consider what businesses pay for water. Water is generally owned by the community from which it comes and is sold to commercial accounts in 100- or 1,000-gallon increments. Water prices vary nationally based upon the scarcity of water in an area, seasonality, and the total quantity of water purchased per month by the business. In some communities, larger volume users are given a discount for quantity purchases, but in other communities, volume users are penalized with increases in per gallon prices as their water usage increases. In all cases, the price of this product will be directly influenced by the attitude and actions of the governmental entity as it fulfills its role as custodian of the community's water resources.

Contract Terms

In a **free market,** the price you pay for goods and services you choose will be determined only by the seller and yourself. As you learned in Chapter 3, however, if you voluntarily enter into a purchase contract, the terms of the contract will dictate the prices you will pay.

Contract pricing is very common in the hospitality industry. This is the case for many products but especially so for services such as exhaust hood cleaning and degreasing, window cleaning, carpet and upholstery cleaning, lawn care, and snow removal. A contract price is agreed upon for a specific period of time and is not generally subject to negotiation until that contract period expires.

Number of Vendors

Many buyers are faced with the decision of whether to buy from one seller (vendor) or a number of vendors. In most cases, buyers understand that the more potential vendors there are, the more time must generally be spent in ordering, receiving, and paying invoices. Many buyers, however, fear that if given all

---

Key Term

Free market   An economic system in which businesses operate without government control in matters such as pricing and wage levels.

(or nearly all) their business, a single-source supplier will increase prices because of a lack of competition. Therefore, on principle, buyers routinely split their business among several vendors.

In reality, the likelihood of a single-source supplier increasing, rather than reducing, the prices paid by their higher-volume customers is small. Consider that hoteliers and savvy foodservice operators are unlikely to take advantage of their best guests (and, in fact, would likely offer additional service enhancements not available to the occasional guest). Similarly, vendors tend to offer pricing in a manner that is preferential to buyers who do most of their buying from them. It is easy to see that doing so makes good business sense for the vendor, and it is in his or her best interests to give a better price to a high-volume customer to retain that buyer's business. The effect upon price of a buyer's decision to use single, versus multiple, vendors can be complex, however, and as a result is worth additional consideration.

SINGLE SUPPLIER Professional buyers understand that, in most cases, the cost to a vendor of delivering a $1,000 order is not that much different from the cost of delivering a $100 order. Each delivery will require one truck and one driver. When the vendor's cost of service enhancement (delivery) must be spread across fewer items, the inevitable result is an increase in per unit price paid by the buyer.

Those buyers who concentrate their business with one (or the fewest possible) vendors will, as a general rule, pay lower per-unit prices for the products (and services) they buy. This is why buyers employed by restaurants operating nationwide are so effective at negotiating attractive product and service pricing for their operations. For a vendor, the prospect of securing an extremely large piece of business permits significantly reduced pricing because the cost of service enhancements can be spread across many more individual sales.

MULTIPLE SUPPLIERS Using only one or two vendors tends to increase average delivery size and should result in lower per item prices. Alternatively, giving one vendor all of an operation's business can be dangerous and costly if the items to be purchased vary widely in quality and price, or if they often prove difficult to obtain. Therefore, many hospitality buyers split their orders for items such as meats, produce, and some bakery products among several vendors, most often with a primary and a secondary vendor chosen in each critical category.

For many professional buyers this logic of using multiple vendors appears fundamentally sound. Often it is, but sometimes it is not. Buyers who continually compare prices among competing vendors and choose, when quality is equivalent, to buy from the vendor offering the lowest price appear to be maximizing their own efforts and minimizing the costs to their own organizations. Buyers using such price minimization tactics, however, must also recognize that **cherry pickers** will be serviced last.

Cherry pickers is the term commonly used by vendors to describe the buyer who solicits bids from multiple vendors, then buys only those items each vendor has "on sale" or for the lowest price. If a buyer purchases only a vendor's low-priced items, that vendor will usually respond by providing limited service. It is a natural reaction to the buyer's failure to consider varying service levels, long-term relationships, dependability, or any other vendor characteristic other than lowest price. To illustrate this concept at the consumer level, assume that the town in which you live has five different pizza restaurants. As a careful shopper, you watch the newspaper for coupons and buy your pizza only from the restaurant

Key Term

Cherry picker   A buyer who purchases only a seller's lowest-priced goods.

Prompt payment of invoices is one of the best ways buyers can help ensure their organizations receive favorable pricing terms.

© Dorling Kindersley

offering the lowest priced pizza that week. Now assume that all five restaurants were well aware of your pizza purchasing strategy. Do you believe that a single restaurant, when preparing the order you placed this week, would give you the very best product and service they could possibly deliver? They might. Perhaps, however, they might not simply because they know that, regardless of their best efforts, your business will be lost to them next week if a lower-priced pizza is available. The result: You may well have minimized your per-unit price, but you likely have minimized quality and service levels as well.

Payment History

Those buyers whose organizations do not pay their bills in a timely manner would be surprised to know what their competitors are paying for similar products. In most cases, operators who are slow to pay will find that the vendor has determined it is simply good business for them to add the extra cost of carrying slow-pay accounts to the price those buyers pay for their products. They do so because, in effect, slow pay buyers are purchasing goods and services with the seller's money, not their own. Because money has real value to those who possess it (see "Time Value of Money" in Chapter 20), payment history directly affects the prices that will be paid by hospitality buyers.

PRICE DISCOUNTS

Thus far we have examined many of the factors upon which sellers (vendors) base their normal prices. After their normal prices have been established, however, many vendors will offer potential buyer **discounts.**

Buyers should understand the difference between a lowered price and a discount. To qualify as a true discount, the price reduction must be offered only to select buyers based upon some definable characteristic or action of those customers. If the reduction is offered to all potential buyers, it is not a discount at all, but rather a simple price reduction. The technique of discounting should be very familiar to those in hospitality. To clarify the difference between a discount and a reduced price even further, consider the hotelier who offers guests a "Weekend Getaway." In this promotion, guest rooms are sold for $199 per night. If guests

Key Term

Discount   A deduction from the normal price paid for something.

elect to stay a second night, however, the room rate charged for the second night is $99, a discount of $100 from the normal rate. Note that, in this example, to qualify for the discount the required characteristic of the guest (buyer) is the willingness to stay in the hotel for two nights.

Sellers are creative, and there are any number of reasons for which imaginative sellers will devise discounts. As a result, professional hospitality buyers should ask about all the discounts offered by those from with whom they do business. Doing so allows the buyer the potential of paying the very lowest possible **net price.**

Although an exhaustive compiling of all possible discount types would be impossible, buyers should routinely inquire about discounts in the following broad categories, each of which will be examined further.

> Prompt Payment
> Quantity
> Customer Status
> Special and Promotional

Prompt Payment

You have already learned that a buyer's payment history is a factor in establishing the price sellers charge them. Discounts for prompt payment are closely related to this common practice. This discount is granted because sellers frequently want to reward those customers who do not keep them waiting for their money. Buyers typically qualify for discounts of this type either because they pay the entire amount they owe within a predetermined number of days, or they pay **cash on delivery (COD)** for the entire cost of their merchandise at the time it is delivered to them.

Although sometimes difficult to qualify for, typical vendor discounts related to prompt payment can range from 1–5 percent of the normal price charged and thus, for professional buyers, are very much worth pursuing.

Quantity

Many vendors use these discounts as incentives to encourage customers to buy more of their products. This type of discount is popular with both sellers and buyers. Buyers like them because they yield lower net prices. Sellers benefit from them because, often, the cost of producing or delivering additional products is marginal after the **fixed costs** associated with producing the initial number of items sold has been recovered.

In some cases, quantity discounts are offered for the total amount purchased (order amount) rather than the increased purchase of a single item. In other cases, total order amounts and increased quantities may be added together over a given time period to lead to a cumulative discount.

Key Terms

Net price   The total or per unit amount paid for something after all discounts have been applied to the purchase price.

Cash on Delivery (COD)   The decision or requirement that a buyer pay the full amount owed (in cash or other acceptable payment form) at the time it is delivered for merchandise they have purchased.

Fixed cost   A business expense that does not vary based upon the revenues achieved by the business. Examples include rent, insurance, and lease payments.

Although quantity discounts can be significant, buyers must be cautious about them. Purchasing more product than needed can be risky and result in product waste. This is especially true with products whose quality deteriorates rapidly when they are held in storage. In addition, there may, in the short run, be significant additional costs incurred in the financing and storage of excess product purchased only for the purpose of qualifying for the quantity discount.

Customer Status

Preferred customer status is another reason for vendors to offer discounts to select buyers. Unlike restaurants, which typically maintain prices between menu reprints and generally charge the same (nondiscounted) price to all customers, vendors can offer a variety of customer status-based discounts depending upon the vendor's business objectives.

Entitlement to discounts of this type may result from such factors as reciprocal business relationships; length of standing as a customer; annual purchase volume; membership in a specific company, brand, or chain; or a desire on the part of the vendor to expand sales in a new segment of the hospitality industry. Some vendors even offer discounts based upon an operator's nonprofit business status.

Special and Promotional

Special discounts comprise a variety of vendor offerings. Many times they are associated with holidays, seasons, or exclusive events. A desire to increase brand or product awareness is often the motivation behind such discounts.

In some cases, significant discounts may be offered when a seller is interested in clearing inventories of older or discontinued merchandise. As a result, savvy buyers should inquire fully about the reasoning behind any special discount offered. If the seller's reasoning is sound, the discount may be of real value to the buyer. Buyers should never, however, accept defective or poor-quality goods simply because they are heavily discounted.

Rebates are similar to discounts, and they too are often promotional in nature. As you have learned, discounts are deductions from the normal selling price. Rebates are a discount offered only *after* a purchase has been made at the normal selling price.

Manufacturers selling goods (via brokers or others in the distribution chain) to buyers in the hospitality industry often use these special rebate offers to introduce new products or to enhance awareness and sales volume of existing products.

You have learned that a variety of factors affect the normal prices sellers charge for their goods and services. Figure 7.2 illustrates the effect of discounts and rebates on the net price of one case of sliced peaches, purchased in cases containing six cans.

If six cans are purchased for $41.96, the cost of each can is $ 6.99 ($41.96 per case/6 cans = $ 6.99 per can). This "per can" price can be compared among different vendors when a buyer evaluates the cost of canned peaches. As you're learning throughout this text, wise buyers always ensure that the quality of alternative products meets the organization's purchase specifications.

Key Term

Rebate An after-purchase discount offered by the maker (or seller) of a product. Sometimes referred to as a "cash back" offer.

	Case Price	(6/ #10)
Normal Price		$ 41.96
Less Seller's "2% Prompt Payment" Discount	$ 0.84	
Less Manufacturer's Rebate	$ 3.00	
Less Total Discounts and Rebates	$ 3.84	$ 3.84
	Net Price	$ 38.12

FIGURE 7.2 Net Price Computation

On-the-Job Challenges in Purchasing (7.1)

Did you say, "*Two Fer*?" asked Ava, the food and beverage manager and buyer for the Golden Fox Country Club.

"No," replied Jason, her sales rep from the Ready Boy Produce company. "I said '*Two Per*'; it's a special discount program we are running all summer. Two deliveries per week. So it's a called a *Two Per*!"

"Explain it again," said Ava.

"Well," replied Jason, "with all the fresh, local produce available in the months of June, July, and August, our produce company is extra busy processing it; but we can't really add more regular staff because, after summer, things return to normal. So we designed a program that helps both of us. Instead of delivering produce to you three times a week like normal, if you choose to go on a two deliveries per week schedule, just for the three summer months, we can offer you a 10 percent discount on all of your produce purchases. In an operation your size, that can mean a lot of money. You really should think about it, Ava."

Case Study Questions

Assume you were Ava:

1. Identify at least three changes that would immediately occur in your operation if you chose to reduce the number of weekly produce deliveries from three per week to two per week.
2. What additional real costs might your Country Club incur if you elect to participate in the special summer discount program offered by Ready Boy Produce?
3. Do you believe Ava should participate in this discount program? Why or why not?

HI-TECH PURCHASING (7.1)

Go Figure!

Manual calculations of the loss percentage, yield percentage, and their resulting effect on prices and thus vendor price comparisons have, in the past, been cumbersome and often time consuming. Today, quality vendors can be an excellent source of information related to loss percentage and yield percentage for standard products they sell.

Some computer software programs on the market today also have components that will conduct yield calculations and compute EP price for a variety of items. Today, a variety of printed material and computer programs exist to assist buyers in rapidly and accurately making these computations. To identify the most current of these, access your favorite search engine and simply enter "Food Yields".

It is important to understand, however, that these resources will be accurate only to the same degree that the EP weights achieved in your operation are consistent with those achieved by the resource's authors. Original AP product variety, quality, available processing equipment, and even employee skill levels will all affect the ultimate product yields achieved in any food or beverage operation.

Produce is just one of many products in which the loss percentage and yield percentage directly affect the EP price.

Richard Embery/Pearson Education/ PH College

SERVICES PRICING

A service is simply an act performed by one person or group for a hospitality business. The number of services purchased by hospitality buyers varies by industry segment but is large and quite diverse. Figure 7.3 lists some of the services hospitality buyers typically purchase.

From a pricing perspective, services buying is complex because purchase specifications for services are harder to develop and confirm (e.g., it is more complex to define "quality" in respect to legal or tax preparation services than in respect to eggs or milk). Further complications include the fact that services are either consumed when delivered (e.g., when windows are washed) or ongoing (e.g., health insurance coverage for employees or credit card processing services). Services cannot be stored, inspected prior to use, and returned if defective. In fact, in some cases, it may even be difficult to objectively quantify the quality of service after it is provided (e.g., legal services).

FIGURE 7.3 Typical Services Purchased by Hospitality Buyers

Advertising design and placement
Banking
Carpet cleaning
Computer repair/maintenance
Entertainment
Exhaust hood cleaning
Insurance
Interior design
Landscaping
Laundry/dry cleaning
Legal
Menu design
Parking lot maintenance
Payment (credit/debit) card processing
Payroll/tax preparation
Pest control
Plant care
Snow removal
Vending machine operations
Waste removal
Web design/maintenance
Window cleaning

Despite the price comparison challenges, however, buyers must purchase services, and they must do it effectively. To simplify the price comparison process, it is helpful for buyers to consider alternative service providers as performing their tasks in one of three levels of service quality variation:

- Identical quality services
- Services with objective quality variation
- Services with subjective quality variation

Buyers must understand which category they are evaluating when comparing price, or those comparisons will likely be inappropriate.

Identical Quality Services

In some cases, two vendors offer virtually identical services. This is the case, for example, when, in a hotel, two vendors bid to install carpet in guest rooms or provide overnight laundry and dry cleaning services for guests' clothes. In a food service, identical services offered by vendors include those such as cleaning exhaust hoods or draft beer lines, repairing cooking equipment, or cleaning exterior windows. When services are virtually identical, the prices for the services can be directly compared much in the same manner a buyer will compare the pricing of two tangible products, both of which meet the buyer's purchase specification.

Earlier in this chapter, you learned that vendors develop their pricing structures based upon costs, consumer demand, service features and enhancements, and quality of reputation. In cases where identical quality is offered by two vendors, service features and enhancements (e.g., the timing of the service delivery) and the vendor's reputation for quality and integrity are key factors in price comparison.

Services with Objective Quality Variation

Unlike services in which quality is identical and price is easily comparable among vendors, in some cases, the quality of a service to be provided by a single vendor will vary from those offered by alternative vendors. In these situations, quality or some other important aspect of the service may vary markedly, making direct price comparison more difficult.

To illustrate, consider the case of the buyer seeking to buy employee health insurance. Two insurers submit very similar proposals. Insurer "A" has supplied a bid that calls for employees themselves to pay $25 each time they visit a doctor (a $25 employee copay) and the insurance coverage will provide payment for the doctor's remaining charges. Insurer "B" offers, at a lower per-employee cost to the buyer, a plan that requires a $50 copay per doctor's visit. In this case, the buyer cannot compare identical services because they simply are not offered. It would be a mistake, however, for the buyer in this example to automatically assume that the "lowest" price is the right price, or best price to pay. Because the difference in costs can be quantified (the average number of doctor's visits per employee can be computed or estimated), and the variation in insurer bids can be calculated, these activities must be undertaken before a legitimate price comparison can be made.

Service vendors are frequently fond of stating that the services they provide are "specialized," "unique," or even "one-of-a kind." Although this may be the case, it can complicate a buyer's price comparison tasks. If vendor prices for services do vary, it is often the result of measurable variations in the quantity or quality of service provided. When that is true, buyers must objectively quantify the quality differences in vendor service offerings before they can make a valid price comparison.

Services with Subjective Quality Variation

This is the most difficult situation in which to compare vendor prices. To fully understand the complexity involved, recall that, when buyers purchase a service, they generally do not become the owner of a tangible good. Rather, they gain an experience or, in many cases, benefit from an effort expended on their behalf. As you have learned, when the experience or effort is identical, buyers examine price and the quality of the vendor prior to making a purchase decision. When the experience or effort varies in an objectively measured way, buyers can calculate the effect of these differences. In some cases, however, it may be difficult or even impossible to objectively quantify the difference in service provided. In such cases, the buyer must make a **subjective evaluation** of quality.

To illustrate, consider the buyer who must select musical entertainment for a resort hotel's grand opening. The decision has been made that the entertainment provided will consist of light, swing-jazz music, performed on the resort's outdoor stage. The audience will consist of 2,000 local dignitaries, political notables, and the press. The buyer can choose from three groups recommended by its selected talent agency. Each of the groups offers to play for 4 hours, with one 15-minute break per hour.

The first group is a newly formed jazz ensemble and not well known. They are, however, supposed to be very good (a real "up and coming group" according to the talent agent). Their fee is $1,000 for the night's performance. The second group is very well known in the area and in fact is widely considered to be one of the state's top jazz ensembles. Their fee is $3,000 for the night.

The talent agent also has recommended a nationally known jazz trio. The trumpet player for this group is an internationally renowned musician who has appeared frequently on television. The fee for this group is $15,000 for the evening. In the purchase of a service such as this, objective price comparisons are meaningless. The decision of which group to select will be the result of a subjective evaluation based, in part, upon the values, beliefs, and opinion of the buyer. Of course, if a budget has been established, it may be that budget constraints determine the decision. Professional buyers recognize, however, that in many cases subjective evaluations will, in fact, be employed when evaluating competitive prices of service providers.

The employment of advertising specialists, interior designers, consultants, the hiring of specialized training companies, and retaining legal service are all examples of areas in which buyers must make fairly subjective decisions about the

---

PURCHASING PROS NEED TO KNOW (7.2)

Choosing important service providers on the basis of price alone is a dangerous practice. Consider your own health in the hypothetical case of a life-threatening situation that was the result of a serious heart attack. Although a specific heart transplant surgeon might be the low bidder among ten alternative doctors, would that really be the most important factor in your selection of a heart transplant specialist? Probably not! In fact, some buyers would avoid such a service provider simply because the price proposed is perceived to be "too low" relative to other providers.

Just as hoteliers can rightfully justify the price of their rooms, and food service operators can justify the price of their products based upon the quality and service they provide, so too can quality service providers who excel in their own businesses. Purchasing pros know that, in many cases, the axiom "you get what you pay for" holds as much truth for services as many other products. Experienced buyers know this and are glad to pay the right price for outstanding service quality.

Key Term

Subjective evaluation   An assessment based upon personal opinions, feelings, or beliefs rather than facts or evidence.

The cost of health care insurance for employees varies greatly based upon the specific health care services offered in the employer's chosen plan.

Patrick Watson/Pearson Education/PH College

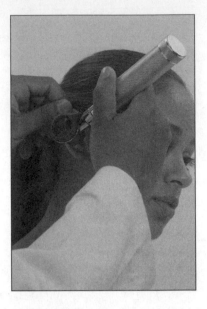

INTERNET PURCHASING ASSISTANT (7.1)

Booking musical and other entertainment is one of the most complex tasks faced by hospitality buyers. Understanding contract terms when purchasing such services is critically important. Music Contracts.com, developed by a well-known entertainment lawyer, provides a wide variety of standard music business contracts for your use. You can view the site at: www.musiccontracts.com

At the home page, click on your own area of interest to review summaries of the wide range of entertainment-related contracts they make available for purchase.

---

quality of service to be purchased and the appropriateness of the price to be paid for that service. When they do, these buyers must be especially aware of the influence of their own values on the price comparison process and carefully consider their effect on the price evaluations they undertake.

Purchasing Resources on the Internet

In addition to the Web sites referenced in this chapter's "Internet Purchasing Assistant" feature, the following sites provide detailed information to enhance your purchasing knowledge and skills.

Purchasing Resources on the Internet

Site	Information About
www.ishp.org	Hospitality Purchasing Association
www.purchasingsolutions.co.uk	International Purchasing Association
www.bn.com	Resources related to hospitality purchasing
www.amazon.com	Resources related to hospitality purchasing
www.borders.com	Resources related to hospitality purchasing

Key Terms

price 158	free market 165	net price 168	fixed cost 168
demand 159	cherry picker 166	cash on delivery	rebate 169
differential pricing 163	discount 167	(COD) 168	subjective evaluation 173

Think It Through

1. This chapter established the concept that a seller's integrity is an important factor in evaluating the prices charged by that seller. Identify five specific actions buyers can undertake to determine a seller's reputation for providing quality products and services.

2. From flavored energy drink products to entire franchises, hospitality buyers are often faced with new purchase options, many of which do not ultimately gain popularity. Consider hospitality products that did not prove to be well accepted (consult back issues of your favorite trade magazines to discover them). Which specific buyer perceptions presented in this chapter did sellers seek to use to sell these products? How could potential purchasers have identified them as ones that would not be worth the prices charged for them? How can you do the same thing with today's "new" products?

3. You have learned that some sellers value prompt payment so much that they give significant discounts for those buyers who pay COD. In other cases, a buyer's payment history can be so poor that vendors will sell to him or her only on a COD basis. In cases such as these, discounts are not offered, and in fact, the prices paid by such buyers will likely be high relative to buyers with better payment records. What do you think would be some disadvantages associated with COD-only deliveries? What can buyers do personally to minimize these disadvantages if they find themselves operating in a COD situation?

4. Bacon is one example of an item that is not typically portioned by weight, but by "slices." What are some other items that are not portioned by weight? How could an unscrupulous vendor demonstrate very low EP prices when selling such items? What can wary buyers do to guard against such actions?

5. Tax preparation service is one example of a service in which there should be identical quality between competing service providers (i.e., taxes should be filed promptly and accurately). In many cases, however, even services that should be identical will vary in quality. List three factors you could use (excluding price alone) to make a knowledgeable decision when comparing price quotes from alternative tax preparation specialists as well as why you identified those factors.

Team Fun

Richard Basso is a highly successful dentist who has always wanted to be in the restaurant business. He finally decided to do it. For three million dollars, he purchased *Giardino's*, an upscale Italian restaurant that was open in his hometown but recently closed due to low sales volume.

The restaurant is in good physical condition, and Richard is excited about his new venture, which he plans to visit each evening after his dentist practice closes, as well as all day on Saturdays and Sundays. Richard recognizes his inexperience and has assembled a team of qualified hospitality professionals to plan and implement the restaurant's new reopening.

For this exercise, assume that each team consists of members of the food and beverage buying team Richard has assembled.

1. The assignment of the first team is to draft a memo to the restaurant's owner making a clear case for using a single source supplier for all meat and seafood purchases required by the restaurant as a means of minimizing per-unit costs.

2. The assignment of the second team is to draft a memo to the restaurant's owner making a clear case for using three different vendors, in roughly equal proportion, for all meat and seafood purchases required by the restaurant as a means of minimizing per-unit costs.

3. The assignment of the third team is to prepare, for the owner, a memo summarizing the activities that he must undertake to ensure the restaurant will always receive the lowest possible per unit prices from the vendor(s) ultimately selected by the food buying team.

Each team should be prepared to present and discuss their guidance and the rationale for it.

8

Supplier Sourcing and Relations

In This Chapter

This section of the book presents basic information about the general management of the purchasing process. It began by examining how specifications detailing quality requirements for needed products and services are developed and continued with an explanation of the make–buy analysis. Quantity requirements were also considered, and numerous pricing considerations were discussed. It now becomes appropriate to consider the topic of this chapter: how product suppliers and service providers are selected, and how to manage and evaluate the ongoing professional relationship required to maintain a solid purchaser–supplier "partnership."

How are suppliers selected? Hopefully, you now know that determining who offers the least expensive products or provides the lowest-priced services is not a reasonable approach. Instead, the time, effort, and creativity allocated to selecting potential suppliers should reflect its importance. The "best" suppliers are those who can assist the hospitality organization in attaining its other purchasing goals: to purchase the "right" products and services at the "right" time in the "right" quantities and at the "right" price. The organization cannot attain its customer-driven goals (it cannot be financially successful) unless all of these objectives are met, and each is affected by the suppliers chosen to interact with the organization.

What are the traits of the most desirable suppliers? This is the next question addressed in this chapter. Not surprisingly, effective purchasing "partners" (suppliers) should have a wide range of characteristics to maintain the desired relationship with the hospitality organization. You'll learn about each of them.

With these important characteristics in mind, those few suppliers among the sometimes many who sell products required by the property must be selected. Numerous sources of information are available to help purchasers make this decision, and a formalized preselection assessment process can be used. Both of these topics will be discussed to help you understand how preferred suppliers are identified.

Hospitality buyers have two basic ways to order products from their supplier base: They can select one with whom they will make relatively long purchase commitments (e.g., three or more months), or they can make supplier selection decisions each time specific quantities of products are needed (sometimes two or more times weekly). In this chapter, you'll learn about factors to consider as both of these alternatives are considered, as well as specific procedures useful for both processes.

Several other important supplier sourcing issues are discussed in this chapter's comprehensive treatment of this topic. How are suppliers chosen for multi-unit organizations? Should broad line suppliers carrying many different products be used or, alternatively, are their counterparts with very narrow product lines the best sources? What about supplier tiering (use of priority and secondary suppliers)? Finally, how are some hospitality organizations "partnering" with suppliers as nontraditional purchasing systems are used? All of these issues will be considered.

You have learned about the benefits of long-term relationships with selected suppliers in which both parties (the hospitality organization and the suppliers) receive mutual benefits. This exemplary "partnership" is best ensured when there are policies in place that define, from the purchaser's perspectives, the most important "dos and don'ts" of the relationship. These policies can be included in a supplier handbook that can address a wide range of concerns, and both of these topics are discussed in depth.

Finally, the chapter concludes with a discussion about supplier evaluation. Did the purchaser make "good" decisions when primary suppliers were selected? Should the organization continue its relationship with them? If "yes," what, if anything, should be addressed in efforts to maximize the benefits that the supplier and organization bring to their interactions?

Supplier sourcing and relations are important considerations in the success of an organization's procurement program. This chapter details many of the most important policies and procedures that wise purchasers must know and be able to do to best benefit their organizations.

■ ■ ■

Outline

IMPORTANCE OF SUPPLIER SOURCING DECISIONS

Figure 8.1 (originally shown as Figure 1.4) shows the context of this chapter's topic, which addresses Step 5 (Identify Alternative Supplier Sources).

Top-level hospitality leaders recognize that their organizations benefit from carefully chosen suppliers who provide much more than products or services for the purchasing dollars that are spent. You've learned that the information and services provided by the best suppliers are well worth the (typically) incremental costs that are incurred as the organization enters into contractual relationships with them.

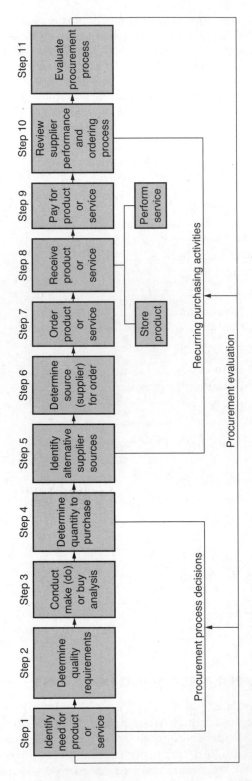

FIGURE 8.1 Steps in Procurement Process

What is a **supplier?** In this chapter, we'll use the term to mean any business (large or small located within or away from the community) that sells products or services to the hospitality organization. It includes merchant wholesalers and any other entities in the distribution channels that were discussed in Chapter 2, but it also includes many other supply sources (hence the name, "supplier").

Many hospitality observers would not use the term "partnership" to describe an exemplary relationship between the hospitality organization and its suppliers. The term can imply persons who share in the financial rewards of the business, and this benefit should be reserved for the organization's owners and employees. However, it can also mean those with joint interests who are on the "same side" because they maximize efforts to benefit from their interactions. When this latter definition (perhaps more of a philosophy!) is used, then the term "partnership" is very relevant to the hospitality organization–supplier relationship. In this context, then, the importance of selecting suppliers who will become "partners" with the organization is very useful.

Supplier sourcing decisions affect the organization's ability to attain its objectives, and much more attention is required than the concerns expressed all-too-often such as "Let's purchase from our usual suppliers," or "Let's buy at the best price we can get." Both of these approaches do have some relevance in the broad supplier sourcing decision. However, they are far from the only—or even most important—concerns.

Customers cannot be satisfied unless the organization has the appropriate resources, including products and services, required to meet (or exceed) their expectations. Many products (e.g., food and beverages and bed linens) must be available when needed. Services such as window cleaning can have a direct effect upon the customer (they will enjoy the clean, or, at least, not be distracted by the dirty, windows). Other services are indirect; eliminating fire danger when kitchen ventilation systems are cleaned is an example. Effective suppliers enable hospitality organizations to best serve their customers, and this makes it easy to defend the importance of the selection decision.

Large organizations with centralized purchasing systems derive another benefit from making the "right" supplier sourcing decisions: There is a lessened chance that "supply" problems will result that would hinder the team relationship between purchasing staff and their peers throughout the organization.

Supplier sourcing involves the initial decision about which suppliers will be asked to submit prices for products and services that are needed. However, it can also involve the development of relationships with other potential supply sources that, in the future, may be used. These supplier alternatives may become important as the organization's products and service needs change and/or if the best efforts of purchasers and their staff do not yield the desired "partnership" with a current supplier.

CHARACTERISTICS OF DESIRABLE SUPPLIERS

Many of the most desirable characteristics of suppliers are really "common sense," and others relate to the needs of the specific hospitality organization. However, most buyers of hospitality-related products and services tend to be

---

Key Terms

Supplier   Any business (large or small located within or away from the community) that sells products or services to the hospitality organization.

Sourcing (supplier)   Activities undertaken to determine which, often from among many, suppliers will be requested to quote prices for the products and services to be purchased by the hospitality organization.

Supplier selection decisions can be influenced by the actions of delivery persons who represent their employer.

Michael Newman/PhotoEdit Inc.

interested in many of the following concerns as they purchase for their employer (and also in their personal lives!). A "good" supplier is one who:

- Consistently provides the quality of products and/or service specified by the buyer.
- Offers products or services at a reasonable price.
- Meets product or service delivery schedules.
- Provides proper supportive services.
- Volunteers information useful to the purchaser.
- Takes ownership of applicable problems and is responsive to the organization's needs.
- Informs the buyer about order or delivery problems.
- Enjoys a stable financial position (which is necessary for the supplier to remain in business).
- Is mutually interested in providing value to customers and does so, in part, by suggesting how costs can be reduced without sacrificing required quality.
- Has similar values about ethical business relationships.
- Is oriented to a quality emphasis.
- Enjoys a workforce with high morale levels (to minimize problems from high employee turnover rates and/or union-related work stoppages).
- Has a genuine interest in helping the hospitality organization.
- Is accessible; communication between purchaser and supplier is "easy."

Most, if not all, of the above characteristics can be summarized as "a desire to work cooperatively together so that both parties can maximize the benefits from their relationship."

Purchasers in some hospitality organizations may need to be "salespersons" to advocate for this type of relationship with suppliers to maximize its benefits to the organization. It is often necessary to direct management peers away from the posture that suppliers provide only products or services. Because purchasers can do this, the characteristics of a "good" supplier become similar to those of a "good" employee, manager, or even hospitality organization.

SUPPLIER SOURCING DECISIONS

A large full-service hotel may do business on a regular basis with 150 or more suppliers as it purchases a thousand or more different products. Food service organizations, likewise, need numerous vendors to provide the products and services needed to help them serve their customers. How should supplier sourcing decisions

---

PURCHASING PROS NEED KNOW (8.1)

Purchasing pros know that "good" suppliers provide information and are ethical. It is obvious, problems can arise despite the best intentions of knowledgeable and honorable suppliers.

A "case study" from Florida shows how concerned suppliers can help hospitality organizations. Fresh Florida grouper caught in the Gulf of Mexico wholesales for $10 a pound (or more). Frozen grouper from Asia and South America sells for less than $5 per pound. A similar product (ponga) sells for less than $3 a pound.

Some seafood wholesalers were receiving bulk shipping containers with contents labeled "grouper," which really contained lower quality and lesser-priced products. Restaurant owners who thought they were buying fresh grouper (and paying the higher price for it) were misled, and in the process, their customers were as well: Menu item descriptions were incorrect and, therefore, illegal. Most restaurant owners and customers couldn't tell the difference, and some seafood suppliers were also unable to note the product discrepancy.

What could be done? At least one supplier now requires its seafood providers to provide DNA certificates with fish to identify their species. This enables them to confirm the authenticity of products and to pass this assurance on to their hospitality customers. Excerpted from www.sptimes.com/2007/01/29/news on January 30, 2007.

---

be made? The answer begins by learning as much as is reasonably possible about potential suppliers and by using the information gained to assess which are most likely to meet the needs of the hospitality organization.

Supplier sourcing decisions may not be as commonplace as are other responsibilities of the purchaser. However, they will be necessary if challenges arise with existing suppliers, as new suppliers enter and other suppliers leave the marketplace, and as new suppliers must be identified to provide products and/or services that will best help the organization to address the changing wants and needs of its customers.

Sources of Information

Purchasers must make selection decisions about two basic types of suppliers: those who provide the products and services that are routinely purchased by the organization, and those that can supply products and services needed on a one-time or less frequent basis. Purchasers are typically more likely to have experience with and "keep up with" supplier alternatives for frequently used items. Conversely, they often do not have time that can be devoted to identifying the suppliers of other products, services, and equipment items. Ironically, then, purchasers must typically spend more time and effort selecting suppliers for relatively infrequent purchases than they do for commonly used items that represent larger financial and volume commitments.

There are numerous sources of information about potential suppliers, and the organization's previous experience with them is likely to be among the most useful. In fact, some purchasers consider this to be the most important factor and, after identifying a "good" supply source, they continue to use it (the supplier) unless (until) problems arise. In fact, many of us use this approach as we make our own personal buying decisions: We are loyal to specific merchants to the exclusion of others.

The concept of identifying and entering into long-term mutually beneficial relationships with suppliers has been noted throughout this book. However, periodic identification of potential suppliers and analysis of how, if at all, they can assist their organizations can help the purchasers to:

- Confirm that the suppliers currently being used are the most beneficial.
- Determine whether any changes in purchasing procedures or relationships can be helpful.
- Provide an opportunity for the suppliers to address concerns that will improve the relationship from their (the suppliers') perspectives.

Procedures for supplier sourcing range from using detailed tactics to learn about or screen suppliers about whom the purchaser is unfamiliar to a reaffirmation that an existing supplier should continue to be the primary source of a product or a provider of a service.

Note: Some purchasers use one or more suppliers for each required product or service as their primary source(s) for a specified time period (e.g., six months), and then the supplier sourcing (reaffirmation) process is repeated.

There are numerous other sources of information about potential suppliers. Hopefully, the identification of possible supply sources is an ongoing research and information responsibility of purchasers, and this activity is not undertaken just when there is an immediate and specific need for a supply source. Supplier information sources include:

- *Reputation of supplier.*   The purchaser's knowledge of the marketplace in general and those providing products and services to the local area more specifically will provide reputational input to the supplier sourcing decision.
- *Trade publications.*   Effective purchasers keep up with "industry-related" information. For example, they keep current with electronic and print magazines and newsletters and bulletins to learn about manufacturers, suppliers, and others in distribution channels that may be supply sources.
- *Electronic marketing information.*   Numerous "buyers' guides" are made available by industry publications, trade associations, Chambers of Commerce, and other sources that allow purchasers to search on the basis of, for example, a needed product, to identify numerous possible sources.
- *Supplier representatives.*   The emphasis about "good" suppliers providing information to their accounts has been consistently stated throughout this book. Purchasers asking their suppliers about others who sell noncompetitive products and services might identify other useful supply sources.
- *Trade shows and other professional meetings.*   Many **trade shows** offer extensive opportunities for **qualified buyers** to learn about suppliers and their products or services. These professional meetings typically include time for attendees to visit exhibits and to meet with and sample, if applicable, the exhibitor's (supplier's) products.
- *Other employees of the organization.*   Staff members working at the purchaser's property and purchasing peers in other properties (especially if the property is affiliated with a multi-unit organization) may have knowledge

HIGH-TECH PURCHASING (8.1)

The computer makes it very easy to identify potential supply sources for products and services required by the hospitality operation. Assume your restaurant wants to purchase new dinnerware. One tactic is to contact a local restaurant supply company, perhaps the one with whom you normally do business, to obtain information.

However, another useful technique is to use the services of an electronic buying guide. This can help you obtain a significant amount of information about the product that can influence your purchasing needs, identify one or more specific manufacturers, and locate a local supply source for the product.

To learn how this process works, use the buying source for *Restaurants and Institutions Magazine* (www.foodservice411.com)

When you reach the site, click on the "Restaurants and Institutions" magazine cover. Next, click on "Products," then click on "Supplier Search." You can then browse industry supplier sectors or search for specific product information. For example, if you enter "china" in the search window, you can follow the links to information about china suppliers. Clicking on the links will take you directly to the china supplier's website, where you can learn about available products and related information.

Trade show attendees can learn much about suppliers and their products, and some suppliers even offer product demonstrations.

David Young-Wolff/PhotoEdit Inc.

about potential products, suppliers, and service providers. Cooks, for example, who have worked in other food service operations, may be asked about supply sources with which they are familiar.

- *Other sources of information.* Supplier catalogs, the "yellow pages" of the local telephone directory, and brochures and other information that have been collected and cataloged are examples of additional supplier information sources that can be helpful.

Supplier Preselection Assessment

The same basic factors used to evaluate the performance of existing suppliers (this topic is discussed at the end of the chapter) are important when evaluating all potential suppliers to determine those who will be asked to submit price quotations. As noted earlier, a purchaser's experience with existing suppliers will likely determine whether that relationship should continue. Unfortunately, supply sources with whom the purchaser has no experience can be evaluated only by means of a subjective assessment of capabilities and the desired relationship that might evolve.

The time and effort spent on assessing potential suppliers relates, at least in part, to the financial importance of the potential relationship. Purchasers should be aware of the **Pareto principle,** the concept that the majority of an organization's purchase dollars are spent with relatively few suppliers and relatively few of the products and services purchased require the largest percentage of dollars spent for all product purchases. Not surprisingly, then, a priority effort to identify these suppliers for repetitive purchases is required. Also, as noted above, purchases of products or services for which the buyer has relatively little experience will also require more extensive supplier sourcing assessment.

Key Terms

Trade show An industry-specific event that allows suppliers to an industry to interact with, educate, and sell to individuals and businesses that are part of the industry; also called exhibition.

Buyers (qualified) Persons with the authority to make purchase decisions for an organization.

Pareto principle The "rule" that the majority of results is due to a minority of contributors; also commonly called the "80–20" rule, or the "law of the vital few."

Efforts to consider the quality of service likely to be provided by potential suppliers are very important. Unfortunately, it is not possible to evaluate service until after it is delivered. This is a reason why reputation is so important: It is probably reasonable to assume that a supplier who, in the past, has provided exemplary service, will continue to do so. This occurs as the supplier provides timely and accurate price quotations, meets delivery schedules, makes it easy for purchasers to contact the **distributor sales representative,** and is willing to assist in problem solving. These are examples of desired and expected services that are integral to the preferred purchaser–supplier relationship.

You've learned that the quality of information provided is another special concern of purchasers as they interact with suppliers. This factor is, therefore, very important when supplier sourcing decisions are made. Will high-quality technical advice be provided, and to what extent will a potential supplier be interested in providing information to help the hospitality organization address its challenges? Answers to these questions should help purchasers in their decision-making process, especially when a supplier enjoys that reputation with a large number of purchasers.

The financial stability of the hospitality organization is of obvious importance to suppliers who want assurance that they will be paid for the products and services they provide. However, the reverse is also true: Purchasers should be concerned that suppliers pay their own bills on a timely basis to help ensure that they (the suppliers) can continue to help the organization meet its customer service needs. Purchasers want to develop a business relationship with suppliers who will, first, remain in business, and whose financial stability results from the same practices used by the hospitality organization: The best suppliers are concerned about improving work methods, reducing costs, and providing better products and services with fewer defects to their customers.

Some purchasers conduct on-site inspections of a potential supplier's facilities to observe factors such as work methods, cleanliness, and the general organization of the facilities. The condition of transport equipment is also important when, for example, fresh produce, meats and seafood, and dairy products must be delivered during warm summer seasons. Increasingly, the potential supplier's e-commerce capabilities must be evaluated. Electronic communication including requests for price quotations (RFPs), the resulting supplier-provided price quotations, and payment statements are examples of business-to-business capabilities of potential suppliers that are important to many hospitality purchasers.

Determining Preferred Suppliers

Communication with potential suppliers and with others who can comment on the suppliers' capabilities, the purchaser's own research, visits to the supplier facilities, and consideration of each supplier's reputation will, taken together, assist in the supplier sourcing decision. Figure 8.2 shows a sample Supplier Preselection Assessment Form that can be used by a purchaser to subjectively assess the worth of using a specific supplier to provide products or services. It presents a composite of the information useful to make this important decision. This form is not the same as the form used to evaluate suppliers already providing products

---

Key Term

Distributor sales representative   The person who is the purchaser's most immediate contact with the supplier; often abbreviated "DSR"; commonly called "salesperson" or "account executive."

Supplier Name: _____

_____

Products/Services Provided:_____

Contact Information:

_____

Representative:_____
Telephone: _____
E-mail: _____
Address: _____
_____
_____

Sources of Information about Supplier (check all that apply):

☐ Interviews with supplier references
☐ Interviews with supplier representative
☐ Distributor's sales representative
☐ Sales manager
☐ Other interviews: _____
    _____

☐ On-site visit
☐ Trade publications
☐ Electronic marketing information
☐ Other: _____
    _____

Assessment

Assessment Factors	Unacceptable 1	Acceptable 2	Comments
Quality (Adherence to Standards)	☐	☐	_____
Service Procedures	☐	☐	_____
Service Philosophy	☐	☐	_____
Management Systems	☐	☐	_____
Facilities/Delivery Equipment	☐	☐	_____
E-Commerce Applications	☐	☐	_____
Financial Stability	☐	☐	_____
Reputation	☐	☐	_____
Information (Technical Support)	☐	☐	_____
Input from Others	☐	☐	_____
Sanitation/Food Safety (if applicable)	☐	☐	_____
Current Customer Recommendations	☐	☐	_____
Experience (years in business: _____)	☐	☐	_____
Total Points	_____	_____	

Other Information:_____
_____
_____

Supplier Sourcing Decision:_____
_____
_____

Purchasing Director: _____   Date: _____

FIGURE 8.2 Preselection Supplier Assessment Form

and services to the hospitality organization. The supplier evaluation process, including this form, will be discussed later in this chapter.

Approved suppliers offering products commonly used by the organization may initially be used as a secondary supply source if a tiering system (discussed later in this chapter) is used. Small orders placed over time will provide purchasers with additional insights about the worth of maintaining an ongoing relationship with the supplier. Unfortunately, supplier sourcing decisions for one-time and/or infrequent purchases such as a new dishwashing machine do not provide opportunities for "trial and error" selection. As will be seen in Chapter 20, these decisions are typically made on the basis of buyer experience with equipment manufacturers and the local distributors who sell and service the equipment, along with their reputation.

Suppliers and Ordering Methods

As you learned in Chapter 6, buyers must consider numerous factors when purchase quantities are determined, including expected usage rates; perishability issues, if any; and volume purchase discounts. These and other factors were very important when buyers traditionally determined the short times within which purchased products would be used. For example, a restaurant buyer using fresh ground beef typically received products several times weekly. If a frozen ground beef product was used, suppliers could deliver products on the same basis (small quantities several times weekly) or larger quantities for use over much longer time periods.

However, today's purchasers have other options. A perishable product can be purchased frequently or infrequently (if, for example, a long-term purchase commitment for the perishable product is made). If this purchasing option is desired, the supplier sourcing decision must consider suppliers who are willing to enter into longer-term contracts.

Assume that the purchaser believes that purchase discounts are possible if a commitment is made to a supplier for several months' usage of a perishable item. The purchaser must then identify those suppliers who meet all other requirements of the organization and, in addition, will make selling commitments under this arrangement. Other purchasers may be interested in just-in-time (JIT) purchasing and inventory systems. A supplier's willingness to provide products under a JIT plan would then be a requirement for the supplier sourcing decision.

As you've seen, then, purchasers can determine the quantity of products needed for a short or longer time period. This is not, however, an "all or nothing" decision. Buyers may determine that some products may be purchased frequently, or they may need to use this traditional ordering method if no suppliers will sell under another arrangement. Also, the purchasing arrangements made by a purchaser with a supplier may be different for different products provided by the supplier. For example, purchasers may consider the prices quoted by a one-stop shopping distributor along with those quoted by other suppliers for twice-weekly produce orders and may use the same supplier to provide canned goods delivery twice monthly.

Like other aspects of the procurement process being discussed in this book, supplier sourcing can be complex and will be affected by policies and procedures applicable to the specific organization, supplier, and situation. New supplier sourcing decisions may need to be made almost never (in the case of a small hos-

Buyers can learn much about suppliers by visiting their Web sites and can typically use the site to order products from them electronically.

Andreas Pollok/Getty Images, Inc.-Taxi

pitality operator who is content with his long-standing relationship with existing suppliers) or more frequently when a purchaser makes periodic decisions about suppliers for specific products.

OTHER SUPPLIER SOURCING ISSUES

Hospitality purchasers may have special concerns about several additional supplier sourcing issues, including those used for multi-unit organizations, broad line suppliers, use of supplier tiering, and selecting suppliers when nontraditional purchasing systems are desired.

Suppliers for Multi-Unit Organizations

As you learned in Chapter 2, multi-unit hospitality organizations can be comprised of company and/or franchisee-operated units. Perhaps the only generalization that applies to purchasers in these organizations is that they may have less discretion in selecting suppliers than their counterparts in independently operated single-unit properties.

Purchasers in chain organizations may be required to use specific suppliers, including subsidiaries owned and/or operated by the company. Also, purchasers in franchised operations frequently use franchisor-approved suppliers or, at least, must use suppliers whose products meet franchisor-mandated quality standards. Within these broad parameters, purchasers in some organizations do (or do not) use local supply sources, do (or do not) use the chain organization's "approved" vendors, and do (or do not) participate in buying cooperatives operated at national, regional, or state levels. It is difficult to generalize further about supply sources for multi-unit organizations. However, within this context, one can note that, whatever the process used to select suppliers, product consistency between properties is typically necessary, and this occurs by using purchase specifications developed for organization-wide use.

Use of Broad Line Suppliers

You have learned that broad line suppliers are those providing a wide (broad) range of products, in contrast to specialty-line suppliers that provide a narrow (focused) product line. Broad line suppliers tend to offer a wide variety of items with few choices of each item in contrast to specialty-line suppliers, who offer few items but a deep selection within their available product lines. One might, for example, purchase frozen bread dough from a full broad line supplier who has just a few variations of this product, but who also offers hundreds or even thousands of additional products. The frozen bread varieties offered are those that would be acceptable to the majority of product users. By contrast, specialty frozen food suppliers may offer buyers the choice of many additional varieties of frozen bread

Internet Purchasing Assistant (8.1)

Avendra is the largest procurement services company serving the hospitality industry, and it offers a wide range of purchasing programs for hotels, restaurants, private clubs, spas, and other organizations. Also, it helps suppliers reach their own hospitality industry customers.

To review detailed information about the company and its services, go to: www.avendra. com

Internet Purchasing Assistant (8.2)

Gordon Food Services (GFS) is a large, family-owned regional foodservice distributor offering over 1,500 private labels and nationally branded, specialty, and exclusive products. It serves more than 45,000 customers in 15 states within the United States and throughout Canada.

In addition to deliveries made to the buyers' properties, GFS also operates marketplace stores that are open to the public and do not require a membership fee. These stores offer commercial savings programs to businesses desiring restaurant-quality and quantity foodservice and related products.

To learn more about GFS, it marketplace stores, and its commercial savings program, go to: www.gfs.com

When you reach the home page, click on "Marketplace Stores."

dough and, if purchase quantities warranted it, could even produce special products to meet a hospitality organization's exact requirements. This frozen food supplier would, however, likely offer few, if any, items outside of its specialty lines.

Advantages of one-stop shopping suppliers are those related to reducing the number of suppliers with whom purchasers must interact:

- Increased purchase volumes typically yield reduced per-unit costs.
- Decreased costs associated with the purchasing and accounting aspects of order placement.
- Less purchasing time required for purchasing (not procurement) tasks.
- Less time required for product receiving activities.

There are potential disadvantages to reliance on one-stop shopping suppliers, including the lack of detailed product knowledge and information that can be provided by the supplier's representatives and a lack of variety if very specialized products are required. One-stop shopping sources include very large wholesale distributors and, increasingly, wholesale buying clubs in which hospitality purchasers buy products at the supplier's location.

Many hospitality purchasers use broad line suppliers, and these organizations are becoming more prevalent as distribution channels evolve. Some of these companies are also becoming still larger as they merge purchasing with other distributors, including those with specialty lines. As this occurs, "the large get larger" in much the same way that hotel and restaurant chains purchase other hotel and restaurant chains as a growth strategy.

Supplier Tiering

Most hospitality organizations limit the number of suppliers of a specific product or service with whom they will interact (solicit price quotations and place orders) during a specific time period. We have used the term "primary suppliers" to refer to this select group from among the larger category of all potential suppliers who might sell to the organization.

As noted earlier, suppliers with whom the organization does not have previous experience might initially be given occasional and/or small-volume (trial) orders to help confirm the tentative decision to use that supplier.

The concept of primary ("first tier") suppliers relates to a purchaser's interest in doing business with suppliers who, themselves, are interested in moving toward a more exemplary relationship in which both parties benefit as much as possible from their mutual relationship.

PURCHASING PROS NEED TO KNOW (8.2)

Purchasing pros know that many hospitality organizations, including those in the non-commercial segment, want to invest in their communities. One way to do so is to "buy locally" and thus minimize the time from "farm to fork"! Food and beverage operations may have few, if any, nonlocal sources for fresh products such as breads, pastries, and dairy products, and the purchase of many services typically involves the consideration of local service providers. For many other products, however, most hospitality buyers do have choices. Purchasers should realize that they should not make local purchases if quality standards will be compromised or if significant financial disadvantages result. However, with these restraints in mind, many organizations buy from local sources when equal or better products can be purchased at the same or lower prices than elsewhere.

Some hospitality purchasers are also concerned that, for whatever reason, a primary supplier could become less dependable or even go out of business. To this end, additional suppliers may be used to provide some products as back-up to their primary supplier counterparts. These purchasers reason that, in doing so, they are better guaranteed a continuing source of supply. Also, they are managing for the future and preparing for contingencies that they hope will never happen but for which they will be better prepared.

Supplier Partners: Nontraditional Purchasing Systems

The number and types of suppliers who are willing to participate with hospitality organizations in nontraditional purchasing systems (e.g., long-term order quantities and JIT systems) are typically fewer than the total number of suppliers who can provide necessary products to the organization. This is important because of the correlation between the use of these systems and purchaser–supplier "partnerships." Increasingly, purchasers are looking beyond the ability of a supplier to "sell," and toward suppliers who are able to provide products, services, and information that helps the hospitality organization to best serve its customers. As they do so, they increasingly consider the use of a single supply source for a period of time before the supplier sourcing decision is reconsidered.

PURCHASING PROS NEED TO KNOW (8.3)

Purchasing pros know that there are several potential advantages to a single supply source:

- Reduced purchase unit costs are applicable to larger volume purchases.
- Incentives for the supplier to maximize the provision of supportive services and information.
- Better assurance that the purchaser will receive products if there are shortages (because the purchaser's organization will likely be favored because it is a larger volume buyer).

At the same time, there are at least two potential concerns to a single supply source: (1) unplanned supplier interruptions caused by, for example, a serious weather problem (e.g., hurricane) or labor dispute; and (2) a concern about the supplier becoming dependent on the hospitality organization. Many very large volume purchasers may also want to limit the amount of a supplier's business that they (the purchasers) represent so the supplier does not become dependent upon the purchaser. Severe problems for a supplier "partner" can occur, if, for example, the hospitality organization changes purchasing requirements and no longer needs the products that represent a substantial segment of a supplier's business.

How should buyers determine possible suppliers for new ingredients required for new menu items?

Tomas del Amo/PacificStock.com

On-the-Job Challenges in Purchasing (8.1)

"I just don't like it, and they are doing it just to save a couple of pennies," said James as he spoke about the decision to formalize the supplier sourcing process at the Good Eats Café. James was the head cook, and he was talking to Sandra, the head bartender.

"I think you're right, James," said Sandra, "We've been successful using our present system, where you buy the food products, and I purchase for the bar. I know it's harder for you because you have more supplier choices and I have only a limited number of distributors for beers, wines, and liquors. However, I do think both of us have helped the owner because our excellent relationships with our suppliers have brought benefits to us. Remember just a week or so ago when you had a product problem, and a salesperson delivered a couple of extra cases on a Saturday afternoon. I also remember the time that we received some decorator mirrors for our bar area from one my beer distributors."

"Well, that's all changing now, isn't it?" replied James, "Our restaurant has been successful, and the boss is building another property across town. I understand we're supposed to determine what we need and send the information to her in her office at the new place. She's going to combine the orders from our restaurant and the new operation, send them out to bid, and accept the order from the least expensive supplier. What do you think?"

"Well," said Sandra, "I don't think it will work as well as she wants it to. First of all, we're in the hospitality business, and we ought to be hospitable to our suppliers as well as to the customers. Basing every purchase decision on 'who's the cheapest,' doesn't seem to fit that philosophy. Second of all, I'm not even sure that the customers will be the same or that the products that will be required are going to be the same for both properties. How is she going to get around those problems?"

"I certainly don't know, Sandra," said James, "But I do know about one thing: The first time that I don't have a product that I need, I'm going to complain. The second time it happens, I'm out of here!"

Case Study Questions

Assume that you are the owner of these two restaurants:

1. What must you do to best ensure that this new centralized purchasing system will accomplish your goals?
2. What, if anything, should you say to James and Sandra to address the concerns that they are now having and the morale problems that are likely to occur when the new purchasing system is implemented?
3. How should the suppliers for the centralized purchasing system be selected? What, if any, priorities should be given to the existing suppliers, and how will they "fit into" the supplier sourcing process that you have planned?

SUPPLIER RELATIONS

The concept of **supplier relations** relates to the way that purchasers interact with their suppliers. An appropriate professional relationship is important, and purchasing policies expressed in, if applicable, purchasing handbooks are helpful in enhancing and maintaining this relationship. These are the topics of this section.

Purchaser–Supplier Relationships

What is the appropriate relationship between the purchaser and his or her suppliers? Figure 8.3 shows the continuum of purchaser–supplier relationship possibilities.

As you review Figure 8.3, note that the traditional (I win; you lose) philosophy anchors one side of the continuum and, at the other extreme, is the "partnership" relationship (we win together). A middle point along the range is labeled "contemporary" (I win; you win).

Purchasers and their hospitality organizations typically have differing relationships with each of their many suppliers that may include each of the points along the continuum noted in Figure 8.3. These supplier-specific relationships are based upon numerous factors, including many described earlier in the chapter. This is to be expected, and it is appropriate that purchasers do not attempt to develop a "one size fits all" relationship with each supplier. In addition, several general factors often influence the relationship:

- *Relative size (business volume) of both organizations.* A very large hospitality organization is not likely to prioritize the development of a "partnership" with a supplier providing a tiny fraction of the purchaser's needs for a product or service, and the reverse is also true: A very large supplier is not likely to devote significant time and effort to develop an extensive relationship with a small, independent restaurant or hotel. This why multi-unit organizations develop centralized and coordinated procurement systems that warrant the attention of supply chain entities.
- *Reliance on a supplier.* This can occur when, for example, one supplier is the only source of a very unique specialty item, and when a supplier has exclusive distribution rights to specific products sold in the purchaser's location.
- *Compatibility.* This is the extent to which the purchaser and supplier share cultural, moral, and ethical (among other) beliefs that help shape their respective businesses. If there is not a good fit, one or both parties may wish to limit the purchaser–supplier relationship to a position on the more "traditional" end of the continuum noted in Figure 8.3.
- *Extent of asset commitment.* Manufacturers who commit research and development efforts to extend product lines for, and/or increase production capacities to better serve, large-volume hospitality organizations desire a long-term relationship (commitment) from the purchaser.

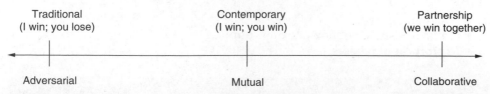

Traditional (I win; you lose)	Contemporary (I win; you win)	Partnership (we win together)
Adversarial	Mutual	Collaborative

FIGURE 8.3 The Purchaser–Supplier Relationship Continuum

Key Term

Supplier relations The ways that purchasers interact with their suppliers.

Importance of Professional Relationships

Purchasers want their suppliers to treat them fairly and, hopefully, recognize that there is reciprocity: Suppliers are likely to treat purchasers in a manner similar to how they are treated. Long-term relationships allow for collaborative efforts that emphasize trust, flexibility, and innovation as total acquisition costs relative to quality concerns are addressed. Both parties benefit from the improved communication and increased levels of trust that result.

The "best" supplier relations occur as a result of supplier qualifications made on the basis of effective selection assessments (recall this chapter's earlier discussion of this topic) and the sound business decisions that result.

What factors are typically among those that affect the relationship between the purchaser and supplier from the former's perspective? Hopefully, these are the same concerns that were considered as the decision to select the supplier was made. The purchaser's experience with suppliers will be based on factors including:

- Consistency of product quality.
- Adherence to delivery schedules.
- Effectiveness of communication.
- Value pricing.
- Interest in addressing the purchaser's concerns.
- Level of service provided.
- Quality of information supplied.
- Process of payment processing concerns.

The extent to which the above and related factors are satisfactorily addressed by the supplier directly affects the purchaser's perception of the relationship with the supplier. Also, the relationship is likely to become stronger when few, if any, problems related to these concerns arise over time. As this occurs, purchasers have a greater incentive to continue and expand upon their business relationships with these suppliers.

Supplier-Related Policies

Purchasers working with top-level managers typically develop numerous policies that help guide them as they make decisions about, and take actions relating to, important purchasing issues. These policies are used, then, to provide guidance about appropriate actions to be taken when buyers are confronted with a specific situation. Purchasing policies help to provide consistency because issues will always be addressed the same way, and problems will be resolved appropriately according to the applicable policy.

Hospitality organizations typically require policies that address a wide range of concerns. Some that affect the relationship between purchasers and suppliers relate to topics such as:

- Accepting gifts.
- No favoritism to be shown to any supplier.
- **Reciprocal purchases.**

Key Term

Reciprocal purchases   A transaction in which a supplier agrees to purchase something from the purchaser if the purchaser agrees to purchase something from the supplier. For example, the purchaser makes an advertising commitment with a local newspaper and, in return, newspaper managers agree to spend a specified amount of money on food and beverage purchases at the property; also called counter purchasing.

- Use of local suppliers.
- **Conflicts of interest.**
- The need to obtain competitive bids.
- **Back door selling** (which occurs when a supplier attempts to contact and/or influence user department personnel without approval of the purchasing department).
- Trial orders.
- Samples.
- Free meals and/or entertainment.
- Use of **sharp practices.**
- Taking advantage of suppliers such as, for example, when one supplier's price is provided to a second supplier with the hope that the latter will reduce his or her selling price.

For a review of ethical concerns relating to purchasing policies, including those relating to relationships between purchasers and suppliers, review the information in Chapter 3.

Purchasing Handbooks

Many, especially large, hospitality purchasers develop a **purchasing handbook.** These become excellent communication tools to inform new, and to remind longer-term, suppliers about the organization's purchasing policies and procedures.

The topics that can be addressed in a purchasing handbook are broad and include:

- General information about the hospitality organization, including a brief statement of its history, an organizational chart showing key positions, customer market descriptions, and mission statement.
- Basic procedures required for purchasing, with an emphasis on contacts and communication between the organization and its suppliers. This may include statements about the need for competitive bidding, alternate supply sources, and procedures used to select suppliers.
- Procedures for product receipt, including inspection.
- Payment policies and procedures.
- Purchasing policies.
- Details about electronic purchasing procedures.
- Copies of (or references to) purchasing forms.

Key Terms

Conflict of interests (purchasing policy)   A business situation in which an employee has an interest in another organization that could (or does) compromise his or her loyalty to the employer.

Back door selling (purchasing policy)   The act of a supplier attempting to contact or influence a user department employee without approval of the purchasing department.

Sharp practice (purchasing policy)   Bargaining between the purchaser and potential seller in such a way that the purchaser unethically takes advantage of the seller.

Purchasing handbook   A document developed by the hospitality organization to inform suppliers about the organization's purchasing policies and procedures that must be followed at all times.

Internet Purchasing Assistant (8.3)

Some hospitality organizations are increasingly interested in "green" (environmental) purchasing, and their concern about this contemporary issue applies to their suppliers.

To learn significant information about the evaluation and certification of suppliers providing products to organizations concerned about environmental improvement, go to: www.pprc.org

When you reach the site, type "supplier" in the search box.

- Information about preferences for "green" (environmentally preferable) products.
- General information about the procurement of services, construction and remodeling, equipment, and supplies.

Once developed, the organization's purchasing handbook should be provided to all suppliers with whom the organization does business. Hard or e-copies should be provided to representatives of suppliers who make unannounced visits ("cold calls") and purchasing staff, and they should be provided with RFPs sent to respective suppliers of one-time purchases.

As with all other materials developed by the organization, purchasing handbooks must be maintained (kept current) and, most importantly, used as a foundation for how the purchasing department operates.

SUPPLIER EVALUATION PROCEDURES

The quality of each supplier's products and/or services and information must be evaluated to ensure that the hospitality organization is receiving the anticipated value in its relationships with its suppliers. Some evaluation is ongoing and occurs as the routine day-to-day interactions with the supplier occur. Although it is not reasonable that the supplier must be "only as good as its last interaction" with the purchaser's organization, it is also true that these routine interactions affect longer-term relationships.

You've learned that selected factors are important when initially determining the suppliers to be used and that these same factors affect the relationship between the two parties. (Examples of these factors were noted in Figure 8.2). However, in addition to these informal and ongoing evaluations, it is also appropriate to conduct a more formal assessment. This is especially important for suppliers of high-cost and/or high-volume products, new suppliers, and those in which an expanded ("partnership") relationship is desired.

In large organizations, the process can begin as purchasing staff meet with user department personnel to discuss supplier performance, and the rating form used to select the suppliers can be helpful as a benchmark for this assessment. Information from other persons in the organization, including the accounting and purchasing staff themselves, is also useful, as are discussions with supplier representatives, including sales managers. In smaller organizations, the manager may perform all of these assessment tasks.

The timing of formal supplier evaluation activities is important. Assessment should, at least, be done as decisions about primary suppliers for future procurement cycles are made. If, for example, the purchaser wants to award a contract for disposable paper supplies for a six-month period, an assessment of performance

THE SUPPLIER'S SIDE (8.1)

Hospitality purchasers who want to improve their relationship with suppliers should undertake an evaluation process similar to that described in this chapter. However, they should also recognize that suppliers may have suggestions about how, from their own perspective, the relationship can be improved. The supplier evaluation discussions just suggested in this chapter can be useful tactics to discover this information.

If they thought about it objectively, many purchasers create awkward situations for their suppliers that are no fault of the suppliers in much the same way that customers of the hospitality organization create problems for it. For example, every hotel and restaurant manager has customers who try (sometimes successfully) to take advantage of them. Examples range from restaurant guests who do not "enjoy" their meal and request a refund after the meal is almost completely consumed, and hotel guests wanting a free room because of an alleged problem that, even if true, was relatively minor (e.g., discovering a clean but water-spotted decanter in the complimentary in-room coffee maker provided in their guest room).

Suppliers are also placed in positions where purchaser-induced challenges create concerns. Consider, for example, the common (and reasonable!) supplier policy that incoming deliveries should be carefully checked to verify accuracy, and that the responsibility for and ownership of products transfers to the purchaser when delivery invoices are signed. Every supplier has anecdotes about minor requests for "policy exceptions" when after-delivery quality concerns are noted for products of relatively low value. Most suppliers will allow a purchase credit for these items so as to not jeopardize their relationship with the purchaser. However, most suppliers also have experience with purchasers who later allege that many cases of products "signed for" at time of delivery were never received, or that large equipment was later found to be damaged in a location that would have been easily noticed at time of delivery.

What is the proper response to these credit requests? Although the "answer" probably relates to the volume of business provided by the purchaser, purchasers should be alert to the need to improve their receiving practices, and their supplier "partners" should urge that this be done. (Some suppliers add a slight up-charge in product prices for some organizations in which these problems routinely occur to compensate for the "give backs" that will likely be necessary.)

---

of existing suppliers is important when determining to whom RFPs for this purchase should be sent.

Supplier evaluation is a critical component of the evaluation of the entire procurement process (see Chapter 23), and Figure 8.4 shows a Sample Supplier Rating Form.

The owners of this family-owned restaurant can get help to resolve equipment operation problems from their equipment suppliers.

Michael Newman/PhotoEdit Inc.

Part 1: About Supplier

Supplier Name: _____

Contact Information: _____

Representative: _____

Telephone: _____

E-mail: _____

Part 2: General Assessment Factors

	Assessment			
	Unacceptable	Acceptable	Excellent	No Opinion
Assessment Factors	0　　　1	2	3	
Consistent Quality (Adherence to Standards)	☐　　☐	☐	☐	☐
Service Procedures	☐　　☐	☐	☐	☐
Service Philosophy (Cooperation)	☐　　☐	☐	☐	☐
Management Systems	☐　　☐	☐	☐	☐
Facilities/Delivery Equipment	☐　　☐	☐	☐	☐
E-commerce Applications	☐　　☐	☐	☐	☐
Financial Stability	☐　　☐	☐	☐	☐
Reputation	☐　　☐	☐	☐	☐
Information (Technical Support)	☐　　☐	☐	☐	☐
Input from Others	☐　　☐	☐	☐	☐
Sanitation/Food Safety (if applicable)	☐　　☐	☐	☐	☐
Current Customer Recommendations	☐　　☐	☐	☐	☐
Experience (years in business: _____)	☐　　☐	☐	☐	☐
Total Points	____　____	____	____	____

Part 3: Specific Information

Accurate Orders	☐　　☐	☐	☐	☐
On-time Deliveries	☐　　☐	☐	☐	☐
Emergency Requests	☐　　☐	☐	☐	☐
Purchase Costs	☐　　☐	☐	☐	☐
Total Acquisition Costs	☐　　☐	☐	☐	☐
Payment Policies/Procedures	☐　　☐	☐	☐	☐
Discounts	☐　　☐	☐	☐	☐
Total Points	____　____	____	____	____

Part 4: Other Information

_____

_____

_____

Part 5: General Recommendations

☐ Continue Use of Supplier　　　　　☐ Discontinue Use of Supplier

Comments: _____

_____

Director of Purchasing: _____　　Date: _____

FIGURE 8.4 Sample Supplier Rating Form

On-the-Job Challenges in Purchasing (8.2)

"I have been saying for a long time that I've got to do something about it, and now it's time," said Laura as she began her conversation with Thomas. "I'm the purchasing manager here, I think I know what I'm doing, and this just can't happen any longer. Thomas, you're doing an excellent job as a receiving and store room clerk, and I really appreciate it."

"Thanks for your compliment, Laura, I appreciate it. I just thought you would want to know that it happened once again."

"Yes," replied Laura, "I'm glad you did tell me. Abbott Provisions is an excellent company; they provide high-quality products (you know that because you receive them!), they give us good prices and value, and the service and information we receive from the sales staff are great. However, your stories about delivery personnel are unbelievable. Either they are always in a hurry to make the next delivery, and try to rush you through the receiving process, or they've got lots of time, and want to have a cup of coffee and talk to our production staff who just don't have the time for these unnecessary and unproductive visits. Traveling through nonpublic areas, making deliveries at inappropriate times, and being foulmouthed are among the actions you've told me about in the last few months."

"I've talked to the sales representative and have also called the sales manager. Now you've brought it to my attention again, and the third time is the final time."

"I know you will be able to resolve this, Laura," said Thomas, "I just don't know how you will do it without changing suppliers."

Case Study Questions

Assume that you are Laura:

1. What are the actual and potential problems created by Abbott Provision's delivery personnel?
2. What action(s) should you take right now?
3. Assume you were going to develop a new section in your organization's purchasing handbook that relates to expectations of delivery personnel while they are on-site. Make a list of the points you would include in that section.

Purchasing Resources on the Internet

In addition to the Web site references in this chapter's "Internet Purchasing Assistant," the following sites provide detailed information to enhance your purchasing knowledge and skills.

Purchasing Resources on the Internet

Site	Information About
www.businesslink.gov.uk	Supplier sourcing factors and concerns for small businesses (Type "supplier sourcing" in the site's search box)
www.homewoodfranchise.com	Information of interest to suppliers for this Hilton lodging brand (Click on "Suppliers' Corner)
http://www.marriott.com/corporateinfo	Marriott's program to work with suppliers in local communities (Click on "Diversity" under "Corporate Information," and then "Suppliers")
www.mcdonalds.com	Corporate responsibility concerns applicable to many issues including those that are supplier-related (Click on "Corporate Responsibility")
www.4hoteliers.com/4hots_news.php	Selection of suppliers for hospitality technology
www.cvmsolutions.com	Supplier diversity programs (Click on "Supplier Diversity" on the site's home page)

(continued)

Site	Information About
www.rimag.com	Supplier sourcing and relations in the foodservice industry (Enter "supplier sourcing" in the site's search box)
www.ism.ws	Supplier evaluation (Enter "supplier evaluation" in the site's search box)
www.purchasing.com	Supplier sourcing procedures (Enter "supplier sourcing" in the site's search box)

Key Terms

supplier *179*
sourcing (supplier) *179*
trade show *183*
buyers (qualified) *183*
Pareto principle *183*

distributor sales
   representative *184*
supplier relations *191*
reciprocal
   purchases *192*

conflicts of interest
   (purchasing policy) *193*
back door selling
   (purchasing
   policy) *193*

sharp practices
   (purchasing
   policy) *193*
purchasing
   handbook *193*

Think It Through

1. What specific characteristics of a "good" supplier would become the foundation upon which you would evaluate the performance of your existing suppliers?
2. Assume that you were the director of purchasing for a large hotel that required major quantities of cleaning and other chemicals for your on-site laundry. How many suppliers of these chemicals would you prefer to have? How would you select them? Defend your answers.
3. The chapter suggested that hospitality buyers may not want to purchase more than a specified percentage of a supplier's total business volume out of concern that changes in the hospitality organization and/or its purchasing system may negatively affect the supplier. What are your thoughts about this issue?
4. How would you, as the director of purchasing for a large hotel with a significant banquet operation, decide whether to maximize the use of broad line suppliers who can provide, in effect, a "one-stop shopping" service versus the use of numerous specialty suppliers with a large variety of fewer categories of items?
5. What would be the pros and cons of developing and using a purchasing handbook if you were a director of purchasing for a large foodservice organization. Would you develop and use one? Why or why not?

Team Fun

You are the director of purchasing for a large healthcare facility. The director of foodservices working with the facility's dietitian has decided to begin using a line of food products especially formulated for diabetic patients. You have determined that products meeting required specifications may be available through several local suppliers. These specialty products are more expensive than their counterparts without special formulation and, although the foodservice department's budget is "tight," they are judged to provide value for their purpose. Each team will be given one assignment to help the director of purchasing make a supplier sourcing decision.

1. The assignment of the first team is to suggest how the director of purchasing should identify potential suppliers of this specialty food item.
2. The assignment of the second team is to explain how the director of purchasing should determine how frequently prices should be negotiated: each time orders are placed or for longer time periods. How does this decision, then, affect the supplier sourcing decision?
3. The assignment of the third team is to consider the advantages and disadvantages of using a broad line supplier for these products (assume one is available) or, alternatively, whether a supplier specializing in food products for persons with special nutritional needs should be used.

9

Procurement Negotiations

In This Chapter

Which procurement task must be completed first: Negotiate with several suppliers and select one from whom orders will be placed, or select a supplier and then negotiate important concerns with him or her? At first, it might appear that this question has an obvious answer: Negotiate with several suppliers, and then select the one that best meets the organization's needs. However, as is true with numerous other procurement issues, the correct answer is: "It all depends."

Many hospitality purchasers use both approaches to negotiate—but at different times. First, as you learned in the previous chapter, they make supplier-sourcing decisions to identify those who can potentially meet their organization's needs for products, information, and service. They may do this through a "give and take" (negotiation) process to determine which suppliers can best and most consistently meet the organization's procurement objectives (to receive the right products in the right quantities, at the right time, and at a fair price). Those that are acceptable after this "first-round" negotiation process become primary ("first choice") suppliers who will then be asked to quote (submit) prices for products as decisions about specific orders are made. The supplier selection and ordering process for specific orders is discussed in Chapter 10, and you will learn then that further and more specific negotiations about prices, delivery schedules, length of contract period, and other factors may be necessary. In this chapter, you will learn about the basics of negotiation that assist with both supplier sourcing and more specific ordering tactics.

The chapter begins by defining negotiation. It suggests that, at least for a long-term relationship, both parties must "win" at the negotiation table. This observation is consistent with the emphasis throughout the text that a "partnership" (not a "winner take all") relationship is preferred between the purchaser and his or her suppliers. Negotiation topics are often much broader than "What will you sell it for?" and "How much will you pay?" Value (the relationship between price and quality) must be held consistent so the purchaser is ensured that price differences quoted by suppliers are not related to quality variations between alternative products or services.

To help provide the context for a discussion that follows, we'll review some situations where negotiation can be helpful and, perhaps, even necessary. This will further justify the need for purchasers to have effective negotiation skills.

What types of skills and characteristics are useful as one assumes negotiation responsibilities? There is a wide range of knowledge and abilities that are useful to successful negotiators, and these will be reviewed in this chapter.

Our next concern will focus on necessary steps in negotiation: preparation, participation, and "follow-up," and this discussion will help explain why effective negotiation skills are important.

Significant time and effort is needed to prepare for a negotiation session, especially as the significance of the outcome increases. It begins with careful attention to the question, "What exactly are the objectives?" With these identified, facts can be assembled, and the negotiator can consider those benefits that are most critical (and which are necessary for successful negotiation) and other benefits that are less important (and can be conceded to the other party).

The actual negotiation session has three parts. The introduction can help to set the proper environment for the session. Discussion (the actual negotiation process) then follows, and the conclusion allows both parties to review and summarize their perspectives of the negotiation outcomes.

Negotiation agreements must be implemented, and the several follow-up activities required to ensure this occurs are also detailed in the chapter.

■ ■ ■

Outline

What Is Negotiation?
   Definition
   "Win–Win" Negotiation Is Important
   Negotiation and Emphasis on Value
   Negotiation Situations
      Identify Alternative Supplier Sources
      Determine Source (Supplier) for Order
      Other Negotiation Situations
Successful Negotiation Traits
Steps in Negotiation Process
   Preparation
   Participation (Negotiation)
      Meeting Introduction
      Meeting Discussion
      Meeting Conclusion
   Follow-Up
Purchasing Resources on the Internet
Key Terms
Think It Through
Team Fun

WHAT IS NEGOTIATION?

Purchasers must be effective negotiators as they procure the products and services required by their organizations. Sometimes negotiation involves only one issue such as price. Frequently, however, several (or more) concerns such as price, service, timing, payment terms, and other issues are important as the purchaser attempts to receive value as supplier agreements are made. Negotiation sessions can involve only a single representative of the hospitality organization (the purchaser) and the supplier or, alternatively, they can involve numerous representatives of both organizations. Negotiations can be face-to-face and/or undertaken electronically. Time required for negotiation can be a few minutes or several months or even longer. This chapter focuses on negotiation between the hospitality organization and external entities. However, purchasing staff must also negotiate with their peers when, for example, departmental operating budgets are developed, as roles and responsibilities of purchasing and user department staff are determined, and while procedures for specific procurement activities are planned and implemented.

Definition

Negotiation is a process in which parties with mutual interests reach agreement about disputes, determine courses of action, and bargain as necessary for their individual and mutual advantage. Compromise and agreement between parties who have an incentive to overcome each other's concerns are an integral part of most successful negotiation efforts.

There are three possible outcomes from any negotiation process:

- The parties can reach a mutually acceptable agreement (compromise).
- The parties can fail to compromise; they can, in effect, "agree to disagree."
- The negotiation can be unsuccessful with an understanding that the parties will renegotiate in the future.

"Win–Win" Negotiation Is Important

The perception of hospitality purchasers with a traditional view of negotiation is that one party must "win" and the other party must "lose" when the process is effectively undertaken. This can occur when the parties are negotiating about the cost of a product for a single order, an equipment purchase on a "one-time-only" basis, or a nonrecurring service such as a construction project. For example, a caterer requires a wild game entrée from a specialty supplier, a restaurant owner purchases a piece of equipment from an exhibitor at a trade show, and a hotel wants to construct a storage shed in a back area of a parking lot. If both parties believe that it is unlikely that there will be a future business relationship (and these scenarios may suggest that), the issue of price is likely to be very important. As the purchase price is negotiated in the examples just cited, the seller "wins" as the price goes up, and the purchaser "wins" as the price goes down.

However, there are even instances in these examples where issues other than cost can be negotiated. Perhaps, for example, the caterer needing the wild game entrée can travel to the distributor's location to reduce incurred transportation costs. Perhaps the restaurant owner purchasing the trade show equipment will transport it to his or her property at the completion of the show. Also, the cost of the hotel's shed construction project may be influenced by payment terms.

More commonly, successful negotiation allows both parties to the process to "win," and this is the desired outcome when a long-term relationship is preferred. For example, a supplier granting a price concession might be interested in the possibility of a long-term relationship with the purchaser and/or to "grow" his or her business in another way. In the above situations, the specialty game supplier may carry other products of potential interest to the purchaser, and the equipment distributor may be interested in selling a newly introduced item because its presence in the community makes it convenient for other restaurant operators to see the equipment, and to learn the new owner's experience with it. The contractor who builds the hotel's storage shed may be looking for a hospitality industry-specific reference for a marketplace "niche" to expand his or her business.

The concern that suppliers should provide value to the hospitality organization has been emphasized throughout this book, and it is now addressed in our

Key Term

Negotiation A process in which parties with mutual interests reach agreement about disputes, determine courses of action, and bargain as necessary for their individual and mutual advantage.

PURCHASING PROS NEED TO KNOW (9.1)

Purchasing pros know that their relationships with suppliers must be "win–win." They understand, for example, that a hotel or restaurant manager has no long-term interest in renting a guestroom or selling a meal at a loss. Instead, hospitality organizations must realize a fair profit from their efforts. Their best customers (those who are frequent guests) recognize that the value they receive for the money they spend is not sustainable unless the property remains in business—and a reasonable profit is required for them to do so.

Would a supplier want to continue to do business with a hospitality organization if a fair profit did not result? Just as we saw above, the answer is "no." Hospitality purchasers look for value as purchase decisions are made, and they recognize that long-term success requires that their suppliers can achieve a reasonable profit. The price of items purchased from a supplier does include a mark-up for profit. However, because it is part of the cost, the supplier's profit is factored into the purchaser's value decision.

---

discussion of "win–win" negotiating. In fact, the term **mutual gains bargaining** is often used to describe negotiating with the purpose of attaining "win–win" results.

Negotiation and Emphasis on Value

The cost (price) of a product or service is important, but value (the relationship between price and quality) is more important. Good suppliers provide more than just products to hospitality organizations. The service and information they provide is part of a product's cost, and they are components of the "deliverable" provided by the supplier. Hospitality purchasers should remember that price is a concern and may, in fact, be a most significant issue that is frequently addressed as the negotiation process evolves. However, wise purchasers realize that the supplier's information and service is bundled with the purchase price and, like the price, can be negotiated.

How much is it "worth" to a hospitality organization to consistently receive the correct quality of products in the right quantities at the agreed-upon price? Alternatively, how much does it cost from financial, operational, and marketing perspectives, if these purchasing goals are not consistently attained? How important is the supplier's information about products and the possibility of price changes, and specialized expertise to help address product-related problems, that the organization is encountering? Do purchasers prefer to see their suppliers' representatives only when orders are placed, or is it helpful for a salesperson to hand carry products to the property on the very occasional times that this may be necessary? The answers to these questions are obvious. However, they provide examples of value components of purchase decisions. To negotiate on price to the exclusion of the above and related services is typically shortsighted. Unfortunately, many purchasers learn this principle when they pay a low price for a product they do not receive (or do not receive by the time they require it). These and service-related difficulties might have been avoided if a nominal increase in price was agreed to when another supplier's price quotation was accepted.

We have been examining reasons why purchasers might consider paying more for one supplier's product than for the quality-equivalent product from another supplier. It is also possible to consider price negotiation tactics from the

---

Key Term

Mutual gains bargaining   Negotiation with the objective that both parties attain a lasting (ongoing) benefit from the negotiation process.

PURCHASING PROS NEED TO KNOW (9.2)

Purchasing pros know that negotiation is only one way for nonagreeing parties to reach an agreement. Other approaches involve:

- *Conceding*—One party totally accepts the other party's offer. This may, for example, be the only alternative when there are limited suppliers and/or limited product availability. Conceding to a supplier's price for rare vintage wines or to an art gallery for rare artworks for display in the hotel lobby are examples of the "take it or leave it" conditions of some sellers. Conversely, very large hospitality organizations that purchase in very significant volumes may, within reason, be able to "dictate" prices they're willing to pay, and their suppliers can accept the offered price or risk loss of the business to a competitor. However, conceding to the other party's demands is not representative of the "win–win" negotiating posture that is desired when long-term, value-added relationships are important.
- *Solving the problem*—Consider the hospitality purchaser who is experiencing difficulty obtaining a necessary food ingredient for a specialty menu item. A menu change may eliminate the need for the specialty item and the ingredient. The results of a make–buy analysis (see Chapter 5) may yield a decision to purchase equipment to undertake lawn care and eliminate the need for purchase of the service. Problems with existing sources of supply are frequently the reason that a make–buy analysis is undertaken.
- *Persuading*—Frequent and reasonable defense of one's position, information sharing, and explaining the circumstances surrounding a purchase need are examples of tactics that may encourage a supplier to accept the position of the hospitality purchaser without negotiation.

---

supplier's perspective. Would a supplier want to do business with a purchaser who paid a very high product price when the chances for payment are risky, at best, and **accounts receivable** payments will likely be slow? Do suppliers seek to do business with hospitality organizations that consistently allege product defects that probably don't exist, or who have all-too-frequent stock outs with the need for expedited supplier deliveries? What about purchasers who have excessive product quality deterioration because of improper storage conditions and, as a result, place distributors in jeopardy of "**deep pocket**" lawsuits related to food safety concerns?

Although overstated, hospitality organizations want to purchase from "good" suppliers, and suppliers want to do business with "good" hospitality organizations. Tactics used during, and the results of, the negotiation process may be affected by the relationship between these two parties. The better that relationship, the greater will be the benefits to both parties. Also, the greater is the likelihood that subsequent negotiations will help move both parties further along on their journeys toward increased mutual benefits.

Negotiation Situations

The introduction to this chapter indicated that there are typically several times during the procurement process when negotiation is necessary or, at least, helpful.

Key Terms

Accounts receivable   Money that is owed to, but has not been received by, an organization.

Deep pocket   A slang term referring to a large company with greater financial ability to compensate a victim than another company who is also party to a lawsuit.

Buyers for chain operations can often negotiate price discounts because of their large volume purchases.
Jeff Greenberg/PhotoEdit Inc.

Figure 9.1 (presented originally as Figure 1.4) provides an overview of steps in the procurement process, and it provides the context for our present discussion about negotiation.

The most common times when negotiation will occur are as part of Step 5 (Identify Alternative Supplier Sources) and Step 6 (Determine Source [Supplier] for Order) in Figure 9.1. Let's look at these steps more carefully.

IDENTIFY ALTERNATIVE SUPPLIER SOURCES Hospitality purchasers in most locations within the United States typically have numerous alternative sources for the products and services they require. This is advantageous because an increased competitive base makes it easier for purchasers to obtain the value that they desire. Also, this increases the likelihood that there may be suppliers who can provide products that are relatively unique and specific. Assume that a hospitality operator is located in an area where there are numerous produce suppliers. It is probably impractical for him or her to routinely consider all of them when several-times-weekly produce purchasers are made. It would be an effort to distribute purchase specifications outlining the operator's quality requirements (Step 2 in Figure 9.1), and it would not be cost-effective for the purchaser to solicit price quotations (part of Step 6 in Figure 9.1) from numerous suppliers. Also, consider the difficult-to-quantify but still very significant accounting costs incurred when invoices must be processed for, and payments must be made to, numerous suppliers. Even if this could be done, it may not be in the purchaser's best interests to interact with numerous produce suppliers. Over time, some will want to do business with the purchaser (they have received orders) and other suppliers (those who have not been granted orders) will not want to do so. Small-volume purchasers with few supplier options are likely to incur cost challenges that are likely to occur as potentially interested suppliers lose interest in the operation's business.

How might a purchaser decide which of the numerous suppliers should receive purchase specifications and be asked for price quotations? Details about supplier sourcing were presented in the previous chapter. Although general information about product price will be of concern at this time, the primary objective when selecting potential supply sources is to determine from whom products might be purchased. Topics of potential concern during these negotiation sessions might include

- Minimum order quantities
- Contract prices for extended order periods

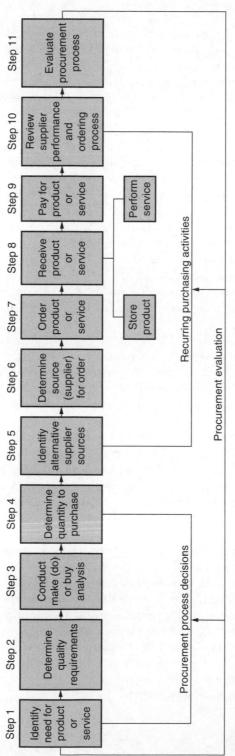

FIGURE 9.1 Steps in Procurement Process

- Delivery times
- Payment processing alternatives
- Procedures for placing and receiving orders
- Policies for return of defective products
- Alternatives for provision of services

Note that each of these topics relates to general concerns applicable to all product orders or service needs. They do not relate to orders for specific products in specific quantities for specific deliveries.

As a result of exploratory and negotiating sessions with selected suppliers serving the organization's location, relatively few (perhaps three or four) produce suppliers will be identified. These would be the ones to be contacted when specific orders are placed (Step 6 in Figure 9.1).

DETERMINE SOURCE (SUPPLIER) FOR ORDER   As indicated in Figure 9.1 and discussed above, orders for specific product or service needs will be placed with a relatively few primary suppliers. A routine system of issuing Requests For Price Quotations (RFPs), and the analysis of quotations received from these suppliers, typically eliminates the need for extensive negotiation as specific orders are placed. Procedures for placing orders are detailed in Chapter 10. However, during times of price escalations and product scarcity (the latter can create the former), negotiation becomes important. Also, when order periods are for long time intervals (e.g., several months or more), or when significant product volumes or purchase dollars are at stake, purchase terms become much less "routine," and much more negotiable.

OTHER NEGOTIATION SITUATIONS   Our discussion to this point about alternative negotiation situations has focused on recurring product purchases and necessary services. However, hospitality buyers must also negotiate when specialized services and capital equipment items, among other needs, are purchased.

Equipment items such as food mixers or lobby furniture are not frequently purchased. However, these and related items are typically available from suppliers who carry a variety of related products, so interactions with equipment suppliers may be relatively frequent as other necessary products and supplies are purchased. Some hospitality organizations use the same tactics to select suppliers for these items as they do for products noted above. They determine primary suppliers, and then request price quotations for specific items from these suppliers. When an occasional equipment item must be purchased, negotiation sessions with these primary suppliers occur.

The purchase of pest control, landscaping, window cleaning, and a wide variety of other services might also involve the consideration of several (or more) service providers. However, unlike products and supplies, contracts for services may be for extended periods of time up to, and beyond, one year. Sometimes a pricing clause is tied to a **cost of living** or other index that may extend throughout the contract period. However, contracts will need to be reconsidered at some point, and this is when negotiation is important as new service providers, schedules, responsibilities, and costs are considered.

Key Term

Cost of living (index)   A measure of the difference in the price of goods and services over time; a related term, cost of living adjustment ("COLA") refers to price changes for goods and services based upon index changes.

> ### PURCHASING PROS NEED TO KNOW (9.3)
>
> When the purchasing process for recurring products and supplies is properly planned and well organized, there are relatively few times when significant negotiation efforts between purchasers and their suppliers will be necessary. Purchasing pros know, however, that the importance of negotiation is not related to the frequency with which this activity is undertaken. If, for example, the negotiation process yields several primary suppliers who can meet the organization's product and service requirements, little or no further negotiation with them may be necessary for many months, or longer. Although price quotations will likely be solicited, extensive negotiations will not be needed. All primary suppliers (those to whom RFPs are sent) are known to provide proper quality and to meet other concerns of the purchaser. Therefore, analysis of price quotations can help to select the supplier for specific orders without the need for negotiation.
>
> By contrast, "big ticket" capital equipment purchases, and the need to select special service providers such as designers and contractors for building remodeling and vendors for technology upgrades, will likely require significant negotiations for these "one time" purchases.
>
> Fortunately, necessary skills are similar regardless of the purpose of the negotiation, and successful negotiators are those who use these principles most effectively.

HIGH-TECH PURCHASING (9.1)

Reverse Auctions

The traditional model of negotiation is one in which the seller attempts to obtain the highest price for the products being sold. A new approach using technology, however, is one in which potential suppliers compete against each other to sell their product at the *lowest* price. As this is done, the need for more traditional negotiation is minimized.

To prepare for a **reverse auction,** the buyer contracts with an intermediary who identifies and alerts potential suppliers, informs those who have not participated in a reverse auction about the process, organizes and manages the event, and provides information to buyers helpful in decision making.

The buyer issues an RFP to purchase one or more items. Then, at the designated time, interested suppliers input quotes into an Internet auction site over a relatively short time period. Quotes indicate the price for which suppliers are willing to sell the product meeting the requirements in the RFP. Buyers typically reserve the right to purchase from the supplier submitting the lowest price, the supplier with a higher price, or from a supplier that has not participated in the auction.

If you want to learn more about reverse auctions, type the term into your favorite search engine, and select one or more of the numerous information sources that will appear.

SUCCESSFUL NEGOTIATION TRAITS

As the negotiation process evolves, two types of concerns must be successfully addressed: corporate concerns relating to the interests of the hospitality organization, and human concerns relating to those involved in the negotiation session. These concerns are interrelated, and the eventual success (or failure) of negotiation is affected by:

- The personality and skill levels of the negotiators
- The extent to which the personalities of negotiators are compatible

Key Term

Reverse auction A business-to-business procurement tactic in which suppliers bid against each other to provide a purchaser's desired products at the lowest price.

- Each negotiator's expectations about the other party's strengths and weaknesses, intentions and goals, and commitments to positions
- The ability of each negotiator to use persuasion and other tactics to modify the other party's bargaining position, and to move both sides toward a mutual outcome

Many skills used by effective negotiators are the same as those necessary for success in any management or business position. For example, effective negotiators are excellent communicators. They possess and use general communication skills including those for speaking, listening, and organizing thoughts before expressing them. They can also use facts to defend their decision in efforts to persuade the other party. They can build rapport and recognize the importance of using cross-cultural communication skills. The negotiation process in many cultures involves tradition, special considerations about positions of negotiators in their organizations, and even the time required for negotiation. Those negotiating in global situations must be very aware of and use proper negotiation protocols.

All good negotiators are effective communicators. Some persons believe that communication is an art; one is either a "good" communicator, or he or she is not. Persons who are creative thinkers, and who are dedicated to their organization and empathetic about the interests of the other party will likely be more effective negotiators than their counterparts without these traits. Each of these characteristics can be learned or, at least, improved upon. The old saying, "Experience is the best teacher," is often true, and it applies to becoming a better negotiator.

Successful negotiators know that the process involves more than just making mutual compromises. People skills, especially listening ability, is critical.

Hospitality purchasers who negotiate must have a command of problem solving, decision making, and critical thinking tactics. Their ability to spot shortcomings in the logic used by the other party, and the potential need to determine when the other party is being deceptive, are important. For example, a negotiator may make a questionable statement (fallacy) that, when observed, can weaken his or her argument (position). An equipment supplier might, for example, say that his or her equipment is widely used and is, therefore, the "best." You have learned that the definition of "best" refers to that which is most suitable for the intended use of one's own organization. This will create a need for the supplier to discuss the equipment's features relative to the buyer's specific organization rather than to the entire hospitality industry more generally.

Deceptive information is an intentional effort to mislead and, in the process, to gain an advantage. A negotiator might, for example, indicate the utility consumption

Internet Purchasing Assistant (9.1)

One's cultural background can significantly affect the negotiation process and negotiation styles that are used. For these reasons, persons planning and participating in negotiation sessions within the global marketplace must be very knowledgeable about the "dos and don'ts" of business negotiation when interacting with those from diverse backgrounds.

To view basic information about culture-based negotiation, go to: www.beyondintractability.org

At the site's home page, type "culture and negotiation," in the search box.

Internet Purchasing Assistant (9.2)

The Negotiation Center of Excellence (NCE) of the United States Air University offers a very comprehensive and all-inclusive primer on negotiation. The skills, competencies, and tactics that it discusses are useful in any business including hospitality organizations, just as much as they are in the military. To view this site, go to: http://negotiation.au.af.mil/

When you reach the site, browse any of the listed negotiation areas to learn more about the negotiation process.

rate for a specific equipment item. That rate might be correct for one, but not all phases of equipment operation, and actual consumption might be significantly greater than what was suggested.

How can one identify fallacies and outright deception? It is not easy, but skilled negotiators are able to consider statements, analyze them objectively, and quickly discover what questions should be asked and what statements should be questioned.

Although the term "professional" refers to all of the successful negotiation traits discussed in this section, the need for the purchaser to be polite and courteous, be respectful, show concern, and recognize the other party as a person (not just an "adversary") in a negotiation situation should be obvious.

On-the-Job Challenges in Purchasing (9.1)

"We all keep up with news about the markets," said Herman, general manager of the Merigold Seafood Restaurant. He was speaking to Betty, the executive chef, as he continued. "The price of seafood is going up with every order. I know it is partially a seasonal thing—and we're coming into the wrong season! But I also think that we're paying our seafood suppliers more than we need to. Fortunately, because we're right on the ocean and close to several large cities, we've got some supplier choices. I'm thinking about calling some other possible seafood sources. What do you think?"

"I like the suppliers we use now because they bring us pretty good products, and they give us pretty good service," replied Betty. "They were all helpful when we made our recent menu changes, because their suggestions and product samples allowed us to make some good decisions. You're the boss, so I think we should do what you think is best. However, my suggestion is that maybe I can mention our concern about prices to our current supplier's sales reps when they stop by for our orders, and then we can perhaps wait and see what happens to the prices after we tell them about our concerns."

"Okay, Betty, let's give your approach a try," said Herman, "However, if prices continue to increase and, especially if they do so dramatically, I'm going to do more than tell the suppliers to be careful with their price increases. Instead, I'm going to shop around for some new ones."

Case Study Questions

Assume you were Herman:

1. Would a planned and formal negotiation activity be of benefit now? Why or why not?
2. What, if any, concessions could you make to suppliers in efforts to reduce seafood costs without sacrificing quality?
3. What would you think about Betty's suggestions to speak with the salespersons as a tactic to reduce cost?

This purchaser knows that the most effective negotiations occur between the buyer and the supplier's representative who is authorized to make price concessions. It is important to identify this person before negotiation begins.

Stockbyte/Jupiter Images Picturequest-Royalty Free

STEPS IN NEGOTIATION PROCESS

Figure 9.2 provides an overview of the steps in the negotiation process. As seen above, the negotiation process can be divided into three steps: preparation, participation, and follow up. Let's review these steps in detail.

Preparation

Preparation (prenegotiation) is sometimes de-emphasized with negative consequences. There is no "rule-of-thumb" about the amount of time or effort required for negotiation preparation. It is obvious, however, that the complexity of the negotiation and its importance to the hospitality organization will likely correlate with the amount of preparation that will be needed. In the context of the preferred value-driven relationship with suppliers emphasized throughout this book, the negotiation process is, in effect, continual.

The purchaser assumes the ongoing responsibility to research the marketplace, address challenges experienced by user department personnel, and consider ways that purchase value can be enhanced. In the fast-paced world of change in which hospitality organizations operate, it is likely that the marketplace will have changed, perhaps significantly, since the time of previous negotiations. Also, the organization's requirements may differ because they are driven by the wants and needs of the customers whose preferences change or, at least, evolve over time. Purchasers preparing for negotiations must carefully analyze the situation at the time of the earlier negotiation, consider what has occurred since then,

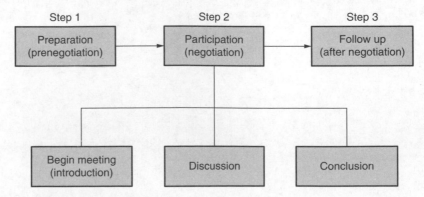

FIGURE 9.2 Steps in Negotiation Process

and, to the extent possible, forecast the future and its implications on purchasing current decisions.

Purchasers preparing for negotiation have several primary concerns. First, they must know exactly what they want. Often, the answer(s) to the following question can assist in this consideration: "If the negotiation process is ideally effective, what will happen?" Related questions include (in an ideal situation): "How will we know?" "What benefits will accrue to our organization?" "What will be our relationship with this supplier?" "How will our customers benefit?"

Some objectives of a forthcoming negotiation activity may be relatively easy to quantify. Examples include a lower price, a larger discount, and faster or different delivery times. By contrast, other objectives may be more difficult to quantify. Desired product or service quality changes (especially if quality is difficult to assess) and ways to improve value in the products, services, and information provided by the supplier are examples. Wise negotiators establish **"going in"** positions that prioritize desired outcomes from the negotiation. For example, desired quality changes may be very important, and different delivery times might be less of a concern. An analogy between an auction and a negotiation activity may be helpful: one knows when to start bidding (when bids are initially solicited for the desired item) and the level of the highest bid one is willing to make. The purchaser must also know his or her **fallback** position when negotiation on a specific point must be concluded. For example, a purchaser desires twice-a-week delivery of a specific product instead of the current once-weekly delivery, and that is his or her going in position. However, the purchaser knows that delivery on another day will minimize the time in inventory for the majority of products required for the week and, perhaps, a once-weekly delivery is acceptable if it is on a specific day. This, then, becomes the purchaser's fallback position.

Careful preparation can yield going in and fallback positions for a negotiator's most important concerns. However, this is where our analogy with an auction ends. If the bidding continues beyond the highest price the auction bidder will pay, the bidder will stop bidding and lose the item. However, a party in the negotiation process may change his or her fallback position if the other party makes a concession on a different issue that is sufficient to encourage a revised fallback position.

In the example above, the supplier is concerned about delivery cost and will likely be disinterested in providing twice-weekly delivery unless compensated for it. The supplier also recognizes the hospitality purchaser's perspective: two deliveries each week reduces inventory quantities, and fewer quality, theft, and "cramped" storage space concerns are likely. The delivery schedule can be revised to bring products in on Friday (most of the organization's business is on the weekends). There will be little or no additional cost for the supplier to do so, the hospitality organization will benefit, and in the process, the purchaser will realize greater value for purchasing dollars spent. Also, the supplier who has made this negotiation concession has likely gained an "edge" when the next negotiation point is discussed. As this process evolves, the relationship between the two parties will be improved or, at least, will not deteriorate. Hopefully, the purchaser will consider these alternatives (compromises) when planning as the negotiation evolves.

Key Terms

Going in (negotiation position)   The initial offer made on a negotiating point by one party in the negotiation process.

Fallback (negotiation position)   The point beyond which a negotiator will not compromise on a specific issue.

Internet Purchasing Assistant (9.3)

You've learned that proper planning is important for successful negotiation. To view a worksheet that identifies special concerns important when preparing for a negotiation session, go to: www.mindtools.com

At the site's home page, type "negotiation worksheet" in the search box.

Figure 9.3 reviews the specifics of two situations that can occur during the negotiation process, and it suggests how the purchaser should anticipate and prepare for them.

Figure 9.3 reviews the going in and fallback positions of the purchaser and supplier for the cost per purchase unit (such as pound) for a product of agreed-upon quality. Let's look at Possibility A first. The purchaser desires to pay $2.00 per purchase unit for the product, but is willing to pay up to $2.25 per purchase unit for it. The supplier would like to charge $2.50 per purchase unit, but is willing to accept $2.30 per purchase unit. Possibility A clearly indicates that there is a gap of five cents per purchase unit ($2.30 supplier's lowest price [−] $2.25 purchaser's highest cost). Possibility A (the inability to reach an agreement about cost) should be considered by both parties as they prepare for the negotiation. For example, the purchaser might anticipate this gap and consider concessions to attain a lower selling price. Possible tactics might include a willingness to buy the product in larger

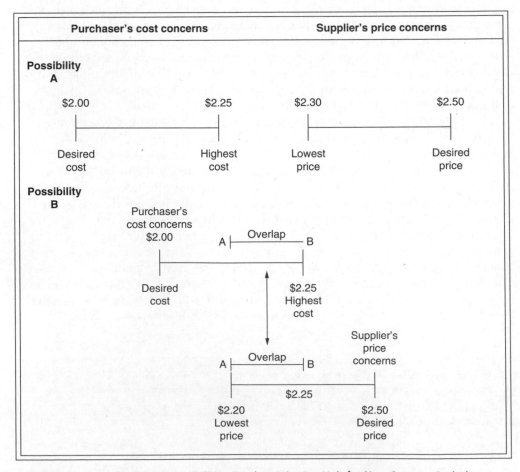

FIGURE 9.3 Two Negotiation Possibilities: Product Price Per Unit for New Contract Period

volumes, purchase in larger unit sizes, and/or purchase other products at agreed-upon prices. These concessions would probably be favorable to the supplier and might create an inducement for him or her to lower the product's selling price.

The supplier should also prepare for the negotiation and recognize that his or her lowest price may be higher than that which the purchaser will pay. He or she can be prepared to counter a lower offering price by suggesting one or more of the alternatives just noted. Effective negotiators consider the range of alternatives that might be possible if and when a negotiation gap occurs, and they know what they will do (and will not do) in efforts to reach agreement.

Note that the list of alternatives that might be offered to address the price gap did not include anger, threats, the raising of voices, or other emotional outbursts that probably do more to firm up one's irrevocable position than it does to make one's position more flexible. Successful negotiators must undertake effective planning (the topic of this section). They must also be able to think creatively about alternatives that will benefit their organization while making concessions of benefit to the other party.

Now let's look at Possibility B in Figure 9.3. In this situation, the purchaser desires to buy the product for $2.00 per purchase unit, but is willing to pay up to $2.25 per purchase unit. The supplier desires to receive $2.50 per purchase unit but, depending upon certain variables, will drop the price to $2.20 per purchase unit. In this situation, there is an overlap of five cents between what the purchaser is willing to pay, and what the supplier is willing to accept ($2.25–$2.20). This five-cent overlap represents the range within which negotiation leading to an acceptable price agreement is possible. Although five cents per purchase unit does not seem significant, it probably is for both the purchaser and the seller, especially as the volume of purchase units affected by the negotiation increases. Also, five cents represents a potentially very large range of final agreed-upon prices because negotiation can yield a final cost per purchase unit of several decimal places. Both parties may agree, for example, to a final price of $2.217 per purchase unit or any other amount within the range of $2.20–$2.25.

This discussion of Possibility B in Figure 9.3 suggests, to this point, that the negotiation process represents an "I win," and "you lose" emphasis because the example focuses on the product's selling price: The lower the purchaser's cost, the less benefit there is for the supplier. The reverse is also true; the greater the cost to the purchaser, the greater the profit for the supplier.

Let's examine Figure 9.4, which expands on this concept.

First, let's review Figure 9.4a and assume that the single negotiation concern relates to product cost. If this is the only factor being considered, there is a point

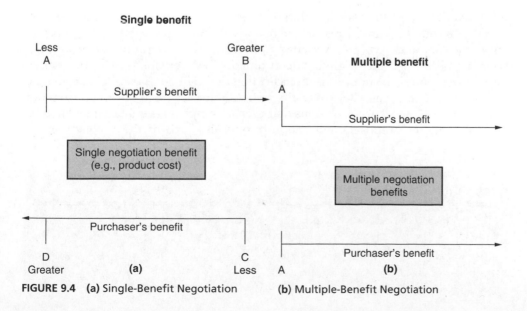

FIGURE 9.4   **(a)** Single-Benefit Negotiation   **(b)** Multiple-Benefit Negotiation

(A) that represents the supplier's lowest selling cost. (It provides the least benefit to him or her.) There is also a point (B) representing the highest price the purchaser will pay, and it is a greater benefit to the supplier. Beyond this point, the supplier cannot benefit because the negotiation process will unsuccessfully end. From the purchaser's perspective, there is a point (C) beyond which he or she will not pay (there is little or no benefit to the purchaser), and another point (D) that greatly benefits the purchaser, but it may be beyond the lowest point that the supplier will sell the product.

In this example, negotiation can occur only between points A and B for the supplier and points C and D for the purchaser. However, as negotiation moves from point A to B, the supplier benefits more, and the purchaser benefits less. Conversely, if the negotiation process moves along the purchaser's position from points C to D, the purchaser benefits to the detriment of the supplier. In this situation, unless the price–cost position can be offset by a mitigating factor (e.g., the selling price is lower but fewer deliveries are needed, or the purchaser's price is higher but more deliveries will be provided), this type of negotiation represents a **zero-sum** situation.

Figure 9.4b allows us to consider another type of negotiation situation. Perhaps, as noted above, the supplier's cost considerations can be offset by the purchaser's price concession(s). Perhaps additionally (or alternatively), additional nonprice issues such as quality and additional product purchase concerns must be negotiated. In this situation, both the supplier and purchaser can begin at the mutual point "A" and obtain benefits from negotiation in such a way that both parties benefit from the process. This "win–win" result is referred to as **positive sum** negotiation.

In the business world, including the hospitality industry, purchasers and suppliers can mutually benefit from their relationship and, in the context of the above discussion, positive sum rather than zero sum negotiation is best for a long-term positive relationship. Unfortunately, the actual negotiation process will likely be much more complicated than that suggested by the simplified examples just presented, and both parties must prepare for all reasonable contingencies. Remember also that the existing relationship of the two parties will influence their interests in moving away from their desired positions. For example, wouldn't you rather pay $2.21 per purchase unit if you were very confident that you will receive the right amount and quality of a product rather than pay $2.19 per purchase unit to another supplier if his or her quality control and reputation in the industry suggest the probability of inconsistent quality? What about paying a lower price to a supplier whose fleet of delivery vehicles does not suggest that delivery schedules will be reliable? (You know this because you observed the trucks and also the sanitation conditions of the supplier's warehouse when you initially viewed his or her operation.) You know that these types of suppliers should have been eliminated from further consideration when supplier sourcing decisions were originally determined. However, one's favorable experience with a potential supplier is an indication of the likely (positive) future relationship. This, then, may help to justify a slightly higher price. As noted from our discussion of Figure 9.3, it is obvious that even a "simple" negotiation may involve a wide range of proposals and counterproposals. Each of these will be more

Key Terms

Zero-sum (negotiation)   A situation that exists when only one benefit is negotiated, and only one party "wins" as the second party "loses."

Positive sum (negotiation)   The negotiation process in which both parties create value for the other as a result of the negotiation.

Almost anything about the purchase of these products can be negotiated by willing buyers and sellers.

David Parker/Photo Researchers, Inc.

clearly focused if it has been considered as an integral part of the preparation step in the negotiation process.

Purchasers planning for negotiation sessions should also consider "common ground" agreements and use them as a foundation upon which the subsequent negotiation can be built. For example, both parties may be (and hopefully are) in agreement about the need for quality and appreciate the lengthy and mutual rewarding relationship that their organizations have enjoyed. They both also likely share an interest in better serving customers to enable their business relationship to continue and grow.

The purchaser will require significant information and input from user department personnel during the negotiation planning stage. What are the best estimates of business volumes? (These will drive quantity needs.) How, if at all, will changing customer preferences affect what is purchased (such as ingredients for menu items) during the length of time covered by the upcoming negotiations? Are competitors doing anything now that may influence what we do—and what we will need to purchase—in the near or long-term future? Our list of possible questions can continue, but the point relates to the importance of obtaining the most current and accurate estimates of future needs. The ability of a negotiator to distinguish between facts (e.g., a specified number of conventions are coming to town that will have a specified number of attendees) is much better than assumptions (e.g., the business climate of our community is getting "better," and we should get more business as a result of it).

Figure 9.5 reviews examples of factors that may affect the negotiating abilities of purchasers and suppliers.

As you review Figure 9.5, think about how these factors would affect your interest in negotiating with the other party. Chances are, you will agree that these

---

PURCHASING PROS NEED TO KNOW (9.4)

Purchasing pros know that suppliers want to do business with them, or they would not be willing to negotiate. A successful negotiator is proud of his or her organization and what it is trying to accomplish. He or she perceives that suppliers will want to be a part of these accomplishments. Although effective negotiators know their own strengths (and will favor them in the negotiation process), they are also aware of their weaknesses (and will work hard to overcome them during negotiation sessions).

Purchasers Have a Better Negotiating Position When:	Suppliers Have a Better Negotiating Position When:
• They pay their bills on time.	• The quality of their delivered products consistently meets the purchaser's standards.
• Large quantities are purchased.	• The purchaser's service expectations are met.
• Their quality standards are reasonable.	• There are few errors in product delivery.
• They have a long-term relationship with the supplier.	• Payment processing problems are minimal.
• Commonly used (not specialty) products are purchased.	• Company representatives are professionals.
• They practice ethical purchasing procedures.	• They provide important information to the purchaser.
• They provide value in the supplier–purchaser relationship.	• They help the purchaser to solve problems.
• Their organization has a reputation of being a good "community citizen."	• They provide value in the purchaser–supplier relationship.
• They desire a "win–win" relationship with the supplier.	• They have a long-term relationship with the purchaser.
	• They desire a "win–win" relationship with the purchaser.

FIGURE 9.5 Factors Impacting Negotiation Abilities of Purchasers and Suppliers

factors affect one's ability to negotiate. A wise negotiator will consider these factors as they apply to the other party and, especially if they are favorable, address them as the meeting begins. (See below.)

As already noted, much information must be collected, analyzed, addressed, and considered for its use, if any, during the negotiation session. Figure 9.6 provides

Negotiation Preparation Questions	
Purchasing Agreement Issues	**Quality Specification Issues**
• When will the current contract end?	• Has the supplier attempted to improve product quality?
• Are current product costs reasonable?	
• What is the organization's experience with the supplier?	• What specific quality problems have been observed?
• To what extent have product quality requirements been met?	• Are changes needed in how quality is measured?
• Has there been a need to resolve any serious problems during the contract term? If so, what are the problems?	• Is it possible to replace the product with another item for which quality problems are less likely?
• When must a supplier decision be made?	
Delivery Issues	**Financial Issues**
• What is the desired frequency of deliveries?	• What credit terms, if any, are appropriate?
• What are the desired quantities of products to be purchased?	• What, if any, changes in payment policies are desired?
• What is the supplier's preferred delivery time? Can it be altered?	• What, if any, changes in procedures for payment is desired?
• What have been specific delivery problems, if any, and how have they been resolved?	
• What are the supplier's suggestions about resolution of delivery problems?	

FIGURE 9.6 Important Negotiation Planning Considerations

examples of considerations that might be of importance if the negotiation session will involve an existing supplier.

Purchasers can also do the following as they prepare for an effective negotiation meeting:

- They can establish objectives for the negotiation meeting. They should write down what should ideally be accomplished and carefully consider what concessions they will and will not make to attain these objectives. Unfortunately, it is not possible to predict with certainty what will occur during the negotiation session. Therefore, ideal and unacceptable limits to each objective should be defined with a goal to negotiate toward the end of the preferred range.
- They can develop strategies and tactics designed to achieve these objectives. These probably involve "going in" and "fallback" positions that may require applicable information to support their position.
- If persons besides the purchaser will be involved in the negotiation, it is important to consider the basic responsibilities of each party and, to the extent possible, determine "who will say what and when" during the session.
- Arrange for the meeting. Numerous details about location, time, and other concerns are important and should be confirmed.

Participation (Negotiation)

The preparation stage of negotiation is followed by the participation (negotiation) step. This is where all of the purchaser's preplanning activities should benefit the organization. Figure 9.2 indicated that there are three dimensions to the actual participation (negotiation) activity: begin the meeting, undertake discussion, and reach a conclusion. We'll discuss each of these in this section.

On-the-Job Challenges in Purchasing (9.2)

"It's really a shame because their produce is so good, and their prices are so competitive," said Jojender in a frustrated tone of voice as he spoke to Melissa. Jojender was the receiving and storeroom manager for the 600-room Cambridge Hotel, and Melissa was the purchasing director.

"You are confirming what I already know," said Melissa in response. "The chef makes the same point. Her obvious concern is that a good product at a good price isn't really very good if it's not available when she needs it. Late deliveries, no deliveries, and short deliveries just don't work, and we've got to do something about it."

"Well," said Jojender, "Good luck finding a new and better produce company!"

Left to her thoughts, Melissa considered the upcoming round of negotiations that would yield a decision about the primary fresh produce suppliers with whom the hotel would request price quotations during the next six months. There were a couple of good reasons (product price and quality) why Melissa wanted to continue to do business with the current company. There was, unfortunately, one important concern; service, and especially timely delivery, that worked against the ongoing relationship.

Case Study Questions

Assume that you are Melissa, and participating in a negotiation meeting with your current produce company's representative:

1. What would be your negotiation style, position, and attitude as you began the negotiation process?
2. What, if any, type of agreements would you make with the produce representative about remedial actions you could take if products were not delivered on time?
3. What, if any, concessions might you make to help the supplier meet his service (delivery) commitments?

Buyers from reputable hospitality operations negotiate only with representatives of reputable supply sources.

Gunnar Kullenberg/Stock Connection

MEETING INTRODUCTION Being on time and ready for the negotiation session is an obvious first tactic as the meeting begins. Hopefully, the purchaser can help to establish an environment that is professional, positive, and conducive to successful negotiation. Emphasizing the benefits of the historical relationship, if applicable; indicating an interest in reaching mutually successful negotiation conclusions; and suggesting the foundation upon which both parties will agree are among useful introductory actions.

The beginning of the meeting is an appropriate time for the purchaser to remember the need for a positive emphasis, to recall the importance of making considered (not necessarily quick) decisions, and to make a personal promise to use the three most important skills of negotiation: questioning, listening, and observing.

MEETING DISCUSSION The situation and negotiation process will dictate helpful procedures during the actual negotiation process. As it evolves, several tactics might be of benefit:

- Remember that arguments are never helpful. When problems are noted, the proposal of a helpful solution is better than pointing blame or becoming offensive.
- Providing summaries of important points as they are agreed upon can help to minimize later "communication problems."
- Be aware that **body language** can help knowledgeable persons to understand what the other party thinks.

Successful negotiators use the following concepts when appropriate:

- They remember that, in one way or another, everything is negotiable. They don't necessarily accept the other party's going in position. They recognize that a supplier typically has "fallback" positions just as they do.
- They quickly ensure that they are negotiating with the person or persons with the authority to make a decision. For example, although the purchaser

Key Term

Body language Nonverbal actions such as gestures, poses, movements, and expressions that a person uses to communicate.

Internet Purchasing Assistant (9.4)

People "speak" (and many times they "say" very much) about their thoughts and feelings even when they do not use words. Nonverbal communication can be a helpful tool as the negotiator interacts with another party during the negotiation process.

To learn more about nonverbal communication issues, go to: www.coping.org

When you reach the site, click on "Tools for Communication," and then on "Nonverbal Communication Issues."

might most frequently be in contact with a distributor's sales representative (account executive), it is likely to be that individual's supervisor (the sales manager), or someone at even a higher organizational level who has the final authority to make negotiating concessions.

- They know the advantages of listening, "of reading between the lines," and of listening much more than they speak. They ask open-ended questions that can't be answered with a "yes" or "no."
- They are patient, desire a deliberated discussion, and do not appear to be in a hurry.
- They don't accept the first offer.
- They don't make one-sided concessions; for example, if a purchaser receives something (e.g., frequent deliveries), he or she gives up something (e.g., less frequent payments).

PURCHASING PROS NEED TO KNOW (9.5)

Purchasing pros know that body language can be a significant assistance to, or determent in, the negotiation process. Here are some examples:

Body Language	What Action "Says"
• Tapping fingers, drifting eye contact, and moving one's body away from the other person	• Being untruthful
• Hands and arms open, good eye contact, and sitting on the edge of one's seat	• Ready to take action
• Expansive gestures, chin raised, leaning forward in chair	• Dominance
• Arms close to body; head down	• Submissiveness
• Rubbing back of neck, increased eye blinking, legs crossed	• Nervousness
• Tapping fingers or pencil on table, yawning, body angled away from speaker	• Information overload
• Arms crossed over chest, frown or superficial smile, positioning one's body toward the exit	• Closed mind or disagreement
• Avoiding eye contact	• Not telling the truth
• Looking away or at one's watch	• Wants to avoid further discussion or leave the negotiation session.
• Good eye contact	• Interested in conversation

It is sometimes difficult to interpret body language, and it is also possible to "receive" the wrong message. However, purchasers who must negotiate frequently become skilled at using every one of their abilities, including the interpretation of body language, to best represent their organizations during the process.

- They wait to learn the supplier's position before stating their own.
- They know it is not possible to negotiate without options, and one option should always be the ability to "walk away" from the negotiation.
- They don't pretend to know everything about the supplier's situation. Instead, they ask inquisitive questions, make simple points, and don't get involved with technical details, unless it is necessary to do so.
- They take the time to consider their response to a question or situation before they react to it.
- They know the limits of their authority.
- They have applicable data, information, and notes available. However (and hopefully), they will refer to them only minimally because of their planning and preparation that preceded the negotiation session.
- They think in "real money" terms. For example, assume a supplier indicates that an additional (but unnecessary) processing step in a convenience food will cost only an additional fraction of a cent per serving. However, if this is not what the organization really needs, the "fraction of a cent" can represent tens of thousands of dollars (or more) during the life of the contract.
- They remain focused on the issues. Although the purchaser may (or may not) have control over the sequence with which concerns are discussed, he or she does, however, understand their importance and, therefore, knows their priority.
- They end the meeting by congratulating the other party. Hopefully, the negotiation session yields a "win–win" outcome. (Imagine the effect that a negotiation session would have on their long-term relationship if, after the negotiation session is concluded, the purchaser informs the supplier about numerous critical concessions that the supplier made).

THE SUPPLIER'S SIDE (9.1)

Suppliers negotiate with purchasers as an integral part of their job. Not surprisingly, "good" suppliers are effective negotiators. They know and practice the same basic negotiation principles used by effective purchasers. (There are no negotiation "secrets.")

What advice do suppliers give that, from their perspectives, can help maintain a long-term mutually beneficial relationship between purchasers and suppliers? Here are some examples:

- Allow ample time to plan for the negotiation. Not surprisingly, suppliers also require some time to communicate with their sources, to consider how they can best offer value to the purchaser, and to plan for their own negotiation needs.
- Consider whether it is necessary to identify all recipients in the memo sent to suppliers to solicit price quotations. (Many suppliers do not like this, nor do they see any advantage to a purchaser who informs all suppliers about whom price quotes are being solicited.)
- Inform suppliers who do not submit a successful price quotation that they did not receive the order.
- Don't "use one supplier's price quote against another supplier." This occurs, for example, when a purchaser tells a supplier the price quoted by a competitor in the hopes that the second supplier will sell the product at a lower price. Ethical suppliers appreciate a "best price first" policy that encourages all suppliers to submit and be evaluated upon their first (and only) price provided in response to an RFP.
- Be sure that the quality of desired product has been identified, and that all suppliers submitting price quotations are aware of quality requirements. Also, be sure to confirm that the desired product quality is received. If it is not, purchasers should realize that other suppliers might also have been able to quote a lower price if the purchaser desired a lower quality product or service.

Win–Win Philosophy	Win–Lose Philosophy
• Participants solve problems.	• Negotiators are adversaries.
• Goal is win-win.	• The goal is to win.
• Disconnect people from the problem.	• Focus on the problem and the people.
• Both parties trust each other.	• Don't trust the other party.
• Focus on and explore common interests.	• Don't compromise your position.
• Do not have a "bottom line."	• Focus on the bottom line.
• Develop options that allow both parties to win.	• Search for one-sided gains.
• Develop multiple options; make decisions later.	• Insist that your position is correct.
• Use objective factors to evaluate compromises.	• Win a "contest of will."
• Yield to principle rather than to pressure.	• Apply pressure.

FIGURE 9.7 Factors of Concern in Negotiating Philosophies

Purchasers will not, unfortunately, always be negotiating with suppliers with whom they have had, or with whom they desire, a long-term "win–win" relationship. They are, therefore, likely to be confronted with negotiation tactics that are designed to gain an unfair advantage over them. These **ploys** can be countered when recognized and, as they are, they hinder the development of a long-term relationship.

Examples of common ploys include

- *Easy negotiator/difficult negotiator.*   When two or more persons represent one party, one person can be aggressive while the other is conciliatory. The hope is that the other party will make concessions to the "easy negotiator."
- *Add-ons.*   This tactic involves negotiating a price for a basic purchase with other "add-ons" being optional and provided only at extra cost.
- *Two poor choices.*   This tactic involves offering two choices, neither of which is good and to have the other party accept the "best" of the two poor options.
- *"No more to offer."*   This tactic involves convincing the other party that there is no more that can be compromised; the offer that has been made is the best possible offer.
- *"I must ask my boss."*   This tactic is implemented when one party indicates that agreements beyond certain limits can be made only with the approval of someone not present at the negotiation. The goal is to encourage the other party to agree to details that do not require additional approval.
- *Deadlines.*   This tactic occurs when one party indicates that agreement must be reached by a certain time.

Purchasers representing their organization in negotiations may also be confronted with negotiation philosophies that differ from their own, and more professional and principled negotiating postures. Examples of these are noted in Figure 9.7.

Key Term

Ploy (negotiation)   A tactic designed to manipulate the other party during a negotiation session.

If this negotiation session ends properly, it should signal the beginning of a successful "partnership."
Michael Newman/PhotoEdit Inc.

MEETING CONCLUSION   The final part of the negotiation session should include a review of the major points and an agreement about what both parties expect to occur as a result of the negotiation. Details should be recorded (the purchaser could have agreed to do so at the start of the meeting), and these "minutes" can be session summary points that are circulated to confirm approval of the negotiation results.

Follow-Up

The negotiation agreements made during the discussion must be implemented. As a result of the meeting, both parties should, hopefully, "know who will do what and when." What occurs immediately after the negotiation will affect the future of the relationship under the agreement. This is important in all purchaser–supplier relationships. However, consider the case of a broad line supplier who might conduct several negotiation sessions with the purchaser over a relatively short period of time. If the purchaser is beginning a relationship with a new supplier, he or she is likely to be evaluated on the basis of adherence to recently negotiated agreements. By contrast, as you learned, if negotiation involves a long-time supplier, purchasers are likely to consider their experience with the supplier and believe it to be a relatively accurate forecast of what to expect relative to compliance with future negotiated agreements.

Clarifications made by both parties about the summary of the negotiation results can best help to ensure communication, consistency of opinion, and the mutual understanding that is necessary to implement the agreement.

Final steps in negotiation follow-up include

- Ensuring that persons in the purchaser's organization will act in accordance with the negotiated agreement; a negotiation is not successful until this occurs.
- Persons responsible for doing so should prepare the (written) contracts, if any, that incorporate the agreement provisions.
- Evaluating the negotiation process beginning with prenegotiation activities, continuing through negotiation discussions and follow-up. Also, the extent to which the agreement is implemented is a special evaluation concern (see Chapter 23).

Purchasing Resources on the Internet

In addition to the Web sites referenced in this chapter's "Internet Purchasing Assistant," the following sites provide detailed information to enhance your purchasing knowledge and skills.

Purchasing Resources on the Internet	
Site	**Information About**
www.negotiatormagazine.com	General negotiation topics
www.changingminds.org	A wide variety of negotiation topics (Click on "Negotiation Tactics")
www.ezinearticles.com	General negotiation topics (Type "negotiation" in the site's search box)
www.findarticles.com	General negotiation topics (Enter "negotiation" in the site's search box)
www.karrass.com	Negotiation training
www.smithfam.com	Successful negotiating tips and strategies (Enter "negotiation" in the site's search box)
www.negotiationresources.com	Negotiation procedures (Click on "Articles/Research" on the home page)
www.freeworldacademy.com	Practical business negotiation advice (Click on "negotiation")
www.negotiationskills.com	Negotiation questions and answers (Click on "Click Anywhere to Continue, then "Advice," and then "Interest-Based Negotiation")

Key Terms

negotiation *201*

mutual gains bargaining *202*

accounts receivable *203*

deep pocket *203*

cost of living (index) *206*

reverse auction *207*

going in (negotiation position) *211*

fallback (negotiation position) *211*

zero-sum (negotiation) *214*

positive sum (negotiation) *214*

body language *218*

ploy (negotiation) *221*

Think It Through

1. Figure 9.5 lists some factors that affect the negotiation abilities of purchasers and suppliers. What are examples of problems created for purchasers when suppliers do not have these attributes? To suppliers when purchasers do not have these attributes?

2. What are examples of comments that purchasers can make during the introductory part of the negotiation meeting to enforce the "win–win" and long-term relationship that is desired with the supplier?

3. Assume that you are a buyer conducting a negotiation session with a long-time supplier with whom you have had an excellent working relationship. How, if at all, would this past experience affect the style and tactics you would use in the current negotiation? How does your response change if you are negotiating with a supplier with whom you have had only a marginally positive relationship?

4. Assume that the purposes of your negotiation session with a supplier are to obtain a reasonable

price for a product that you buy in large quantities, resolve current delivery problems, and obtain a purchase price for a new product that will be used in relatively small quantities. Ideally (although you may not be able to control the actual sequence), what order would you like to discuss these issues? Defend your response.

5. You are negotiating with a supplier who has consistently provided excellent products and service for several years. You are meeting with her in efforts to establish pricing for several products that you purchase in high volumes. During the meeting you learn that the supplier's delivery schedule for your area will be changing and, beginning in three months, the supplier will be coming to your relatively remote location only one day per week—and it is the day your restaurant is closed. Prepare a list of the alternatives you have and the concessions, if any, you can make in response to this situation. Recall that this is a desirable supplier.

Team Fun

You are the purchasing director for a multistory hotel in Florida. The humidity level in the area creates an ongoing mildew problem that requires exterior high-pressure cleaning three times yearly to maintain your building in the sparkling clean condition that is important for it to achieve high average daily rates (ADRs). Your business is not the only one that experiences mildew-related problems, and a number of commercial businesses in the area provide this service.

Your property has just completed a fairly large building addition that adds another forty guest units to the room inventory. Because the annual contract for exterior building cleaning must be renegotiated, this new building addition must obviously be addressed. Each team will be given one assignment to provide advice to the hotel's purchaser about negotiating with potential service providers. The goal is to determine the service provider that will "best" meet your exterior building cleaning needs.

1. The assignment of the first team is to suggest how potential suppliers should be identified and screened to determine those with whom a negotiating session should be scheduled.
2. The assignment of the second team is to identify two important concerns that should be addressed in the agreement covering these services and to identify basic concerns that would be important in the negotiating process for these priorities.
3. The assignment of the third team is to identify how, if at all, the negotiation process will need to differ for the current service provider.

10

Selecting Suppliers and Placing Orders

In This Chapter

Throughout this book, you're learning that procurement is a very important function and is more complex than it first appears to be. This is the case once again as we focus on selecting suppliers for specific orders and then placing orders with them. We'll study details about both of these processes in this chapter, and you'll discover the task involves much more than just "calling in an order to the cheapest supplier" or inputting information at the supplier's Web site.

The ordering process is most effective when procurement-planning procedures, including those discussed in earlier chapters, have been followed. Then buyers will be assured that they will receive the correct quantity and quality of, and price for, the product or service being purchased. Much internal and external communication must precede the ordering process as the supplier for a specific order is chosen from among those selected during the supplier sourcing decision (see Chapter 8).

Although the specific requirements for ordering are the same regardless of the type or size of hospitality operation, procedures tend to become more formalized as the volume of business increases. An early part of this chapter will review ordering procedures in small, decentralized operations and in their larger, centralized counterparts.

When should orders be placed? In this chapter, we'll answer this question, and you'll learn that factors such as anticipated production volumes and available storage space may (or may not!) be a factor in ordering decisions.

Buyers for large-volume hospitality organizations frequently use a purchase order system to place orders. Although buyers for smaller operations may not use a formalized purchase order method, they still want to do whatever is reasonably possible to ensure there are no "surprises" as orders are received and payment obligations are incurred. To this end, we'll review some basic terms and conditions that should be addressed as the foundation for agreement between buyers and sellers is established.

Unfortunately, even when the best planned ordering and other procurement procedures are implemented, there will still likely be times when the "right" products in the "right" quantity at the "right" time are not delivered. What can buyers do then? We'll address possible answers to this question as we consider the task of expediting, an activity that can be a stressful but very integral aspect of a purchaser's professional responsibilities. Throughout earlier chapters, we have reviewed the increasing role that technology plays in the procurement process. We will take a close look at how buyers can use technology to help them place orders. You'll learn that even relatively small hotels, restaurants, and other hospitality organizations can use technology in a way that yields practical and cost-effective advantages to the activity that is the focus of this chapter: ordering products and services from suppliers.

■■■

Outline

OVERVIEW OF ORDERING PROCESS

Let's begin our discussion of the **ordering** process by defining the term: The ordering process occurs when a buyer makes specific commitments to a seller or service provider relating to a specific purchase. As you'll learn in this chapter, the commitment, either formally or informally, involves much more than just an agreement to purchase a specified quantity of products or services meeting predetermined quality requirements at agreed-upon prices. These factors are of obvious importance and must be addressed in the ordering process. However, numerous other considerations are also integral to the agreement.

Importance of Effective Ordering Procedures

Figure 10.1 (originally shown as Figure 1.4) reviews steps in the procurement process as they are being discussed in this book.

Key Term

Order (product or service) The process by which a buyer makes specific commitments to a seller or service provider relating to a specific purchase.

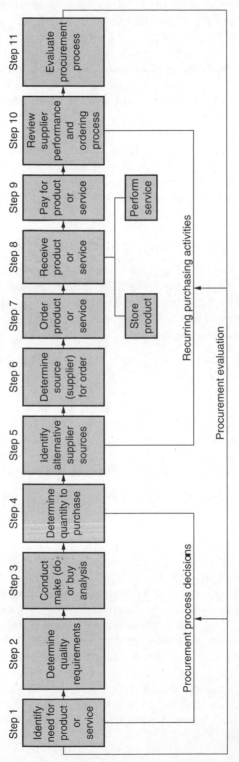

FIGURE 10.1 Steps in Procurement Process

In this chapter, you will learn about Steps 6 and 7 in Figure 10.1. You'll discover that ordering a product or service involves a sequence of activities that enables the buyer to learn all the necessary information about a potential purchase commitment with the supplier. In fact, the creative effort and energies expanded in the earlier procurement steps are wasted if thoughtful follow-through does not occur when the supplier for a specific order is determined and that order is placed. The results of these decisions represent significant legal and financial commitments that will help or hinder the hospitality organization's user department personnel as they provide products and services for their customers.

Because no single step in the procurement process is more important than any other, the task of selecting suppliers and ordering products and services must receive equal attention to the other activities. Unfortunately, some hospitality managers and buyers believe that procurement ends when the order is ready to be placed. However, you're learning that the procurement process never ends! In fact, the last step in procurement (Step 11 in Figure 10.1) is evaluation, which can yield never-ending improvements to better help the hospitality organization meet its customers' needs.

Internal Communication Precedes Ordering Process

Managers in small-volume hospitality organizations may undertake purchasing activities as one among many responsibilities. Large-volume organizations typically employ one or more staff members with full-time purchasing responsibilities. However, regardless of the organizational structure, a significant amount of internal communication is required to:

- Determine exactly what products and services must be purchased.
- Assess proper quality requirements for the products and services to be purchased.
- Determine which products should be produced and which services should be provided by the organization's employees and conversely, which should be purchased from external suppliers and service providers.
- Identify the quantity of products needed and length of time for which products and services should be purchased or purchase commitments should be made.

Managers in small operations may make these decisions by themselves or do so in cooperation with their staff members. Affected managers in larger operations may use the services of purchasing personnel to facilitate decision making relating to these issues. In both instances, those who purchase must have the information necessary to determine alternative supply sources and, from among them, to determine those with whom specific orders should be placed.

Each of the above activities may involve no more than oral communication in small properties, whereas extensive written communication may be necessary in larger organizations. Examples include purchase specifications (discussed in Chapter 4) and purchase requisitions and purchase orders (which are discussed in this chapter). One major theme of this book has been that the basic principles required for effective purchasing are the same regardless of an operation's size. It is always the buyer's responsibility to know and to tell suppliers and service providers exactly what is required. This cannot be done unless the buyer is the user or has interacted with others within the organization to determine the exact product and service needs.

External Communication Precedes Ordering Process

Another central theme of this book has been the emphasis on a "partnership" relationship between the buyer and seller in the hopes that value-added services provided by the latter benefit the buyer and encourage a continued relationship between both parties. Although the ordering process involves specific communication between both parties, other interactions are ongoing in a preferred relationship. Examples include the provision of information when purchase specifications are developed (see Chapter 4), when make–buy analysis is undertaken (discussed in Chapter 5), and as supplier sourcing and negotiation activities occur (see, respectively, Chapters 8 and 9). The ordering process is important, then, because it helps ensure that the operation's purchase requirements are met as an integral aspect of the ongoing relationship.

Unfortunately, "communication" or other problems can occur when orders are placed. If this happens infrequently, the buyer and the seller will likely cooperate to resolve the problem. As they do, their relationship improves, and the satisfaction that results encourages a continuing "partnership." However, if there are frequent problems that, from the buyer' perspective, are caused by the supplier, this works against the purchaser's ongoing interest in continuing to place orders. Conversely, suppliers are less likely to provide value-added services for their "problem" accounts.

Common Ordering Challenges

There is an old saying that, "You can't solve a problem unless, first, you are aware of it." Unfortunately, receiving and user personnel may be aware of problems with incoming products that are not shared with purchasing personnel. As this occurs, buyers cannot address these concerns when orders are placed. Examples include

- *Quality problems.*   Purchasers who are unaware of inconsistent product quality cannot reemphasize the need for specified quality when orders are placed. Also, conversations with the supplier's representative and/or sales manager can be undertaken only if purchasers know about quality issues.
- *Frequent back orders.*   If, for example, a supplier is experiencing difficulty obtaining one or more items for resale, purchasers will need to obtain these items from another source.
- *Problems with quantities or purchase unit sizes.*   Some suppliers freely substitute different packaging sizes for those that are ordered. Consider, for example, an order for one 50-lb. bag of all-purpose flour, which is met with five 10-lb. bags of this product. The price per pound of flour is likely to be less when ordered in a 50-lb. bag than in a smaller unit. Even if the supplier makes a price adjustment (and he or she should because the problem should be noticed by the observant receiving clerk), the operations production staff

---

PURCHASING PROS NEED TO KNOW (10.1)

Purchasing pros know that there are times when market-related problems affect the supply sources of all vendors normally carrying an item. A recurring example is fresh produce. Adverse weather conditions can destroy or damage crops for an entire growing season. The resulting disruption in availability then creates significant shortages and unanticipated high prices. Large-scale outbreaks of food-borne illness traced to products such as tomatoes and spinach are other examples of problems that create availability issues. They, in turn, create a paradox: Purchasers must pay more for products that are typically of lower quality during these times. Wise buyers consider how, if at all, they can substitute other products, or discontinue the offering of some items until the market recovers.

must still spend excessive time opening and dispensing numerous bags of flour as they fill flour bins.

- *Problems with on-site shortages.*   Purchasers must always be careful when determining the quantities of product to order. Numerous examples of potential problems were noted in Chapter 6. However, product theft, pilferage, and spoilage, among other factors, can create unexplained ("surprise") decreases in inventories, which create the need for ordering before purchasers may normally expect to do so.

- *On-site storage capacities.*   Storage equipment and space is always expensive, and kitchen designers work hard to plan ideal storage requirements. Unfortunately, the "ideal" capacities for an operation being planned may be significantly over- or understated for food service operations, which may follow in the future. Purchasers for high-volume operations with inadequate storage space have ongoing ordering challenges, which often involve more frequent and expensive deliveries. They may also need to create additional storage space when, most often, there is none available without converting ("repurposing") other space.

- *Coordination between receiving and user personnel and purchasers.*   Purchasers should "manage by walking around" and be physically present on random occasions when products are received. They can observe products in storage and production areas and participate in conversations and meetings to receive input from receiving and production personnel about the products being ordered.

Our list of examples could continue. However, this discussion emphasizes the need for close cooperation and communication between receiving and both user personnel and purchasers.

CLOSE LOOK AT ORDERING PROCESS

In this section, we'll discuss basic ordering procedures in small hospitality organizations with decentralized purchasing and in larger operations using more centralized purchasing procedures.

Ordering Procedures in Decentralized Operations

You've learned that small hotels, restaurants, and other hospitality organizations do not employ full-time purchasing staff. Instead, a decentralized purchasing process that incorporates some or all of the following steps is often used:

- Persons responsible for purchasing are identified. For example, in a very small operation, the owner/manager may assume responsibility for the purchase of all required products and services. In operations of sufficient size to have designated department heads, they may be responsible for purchasing products and services required by their department. In a hotel, for example, the housekeeping, maintenance, and foodservice managers may assume this task for their departmental needs. In a small restaurant, the chef, beverage manager, and dining room manager may be responsible for the purchase of, respectively, food, beverage, and dining service-related products and supplies.

- Department heads are given purchasing authority to spend up to a pre-established limit (e.g., $1,000), after which approval of the owner or unit manager is required.

- Departmental buyers make basic purchasing decisions such as the quantities of products to order (typically to bring product inventory levels to a predetermined par level) and quality requirements. They may also make

Orders can be placed by telephone.
Pearson Education/PH College

supplier selection decisions which frequently involve little more than purchasing products and services from those from whom products and services have satisfactorily been purchased in the past. Many franchised operations are small and, therefore, use a decentralized procurement system. In many respects, the purchasing task is easier because franchise buyers are required to buy logo and other items meeting franchisor-mandated minimum specifications.

• Departmental purchasers are required to complete purchase documentation as determined by property policy. In some organizations, they retain this until orders are delivered. They, or a department representative, sign delivery invoices for incoming orders, and the original documentation and delivery order are then provided to the person with accounting responsibilities. In other properties, purchase documentation is routed immediately to the accounting employee, who then holds it until the signed delivery invoice is received by the accounting staff member.

The basic procedures just described suggest one practical way that the ordering process might be undertaken in a small organization. However, the method used must share at least one characteristic with the ordering process in larger organizations: Approved documentation must authorize the purchase. Details about the payment process will be discussed in Chapter 12.

Internet Purchasing Assistant (10.1)

The general manager or accountant for a small hospitality operation using a decentralized purchasing system may wish to create a standardized purchase order format to be used by all departmental purchasers. Numerous alternatives to do so are available using inexpensive windows-based software. For example, go to: www.formdocs.com

When you reach the site, review the information for "Small Business Owners," including the sample purchase order form and suggestions for its use.

Departmental purchasers using a form approved for property-wide use are more likely to have the proper documentation available to assist with the accountant's payment procedures. Increasingly, suppliers use electronic ordering systems that generate appropriate documentation, and details about these are discussed later in this chapter.

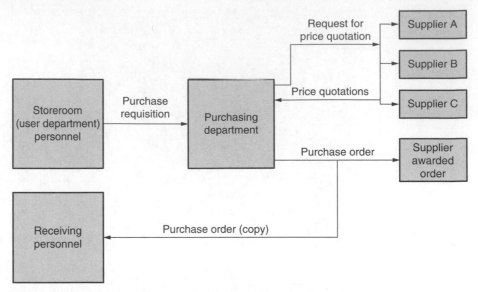

FIGURE 10.2 Ordering Process in Large Hospitality Organization

Ordering Procedures in Centralized Operations

You've learned that the procurement process becomes more formalized in a large hospitality organization. Figure 10.2 reviews the basic steps that might be required. All of the steps identified in Figure 10.2 can be automated, and details of an automated system will be discussed later in this chapter.

Let's review the ordering procedures noted in Figure 10.2:

• How do purchasing personnel know when additional quantities of products must be ordered? Traditionally, orders have been placed when current inventory levels relative to forecasted production requirements indicate that stock outs are likely unless additional quantities are purchased. Details about the quantity of items to be purchased are explored in Chapter 6, as are more contemporary systems in which purchase agreements are made for longer time periods with a minimum quantity to be shipped in intervals during that period. Food and beverage products are held in storerooms with inventories controlled by designated storeroom personnel (see Chapter 11). These staff members are responsible for informing purchasing staff when additional product quantities are needed. Housekeeping, maintenance, and other departments in a hotel also have dedicated storage areas, but they are not typically staffed with full-time storeroom personnel. A **purchase requisition** can be used by food and beverage storeroom and user personnel in other departments to indicate when additional quantities must be purchased.

Figure 10.3 shows an example of a purchase requisition.

Key Terms

Purchase requisition   A document used by food and beverage storeroom and user personnel in other departments to inform purchasing employees when additional quantities of products are required to build inventory levels to pre-established par levels.

Request for price quotation (RFP)   A document used by a purchaser to inform eligible suppliers that specified additional quantities of products meeting quality specifications are required by a specified time and asking the suppliers to indicate their current price for the product.

Requesting Department: _____		Requisition Number: _____	
Date Needed: _____			
Item	**Purchase Unit**	**Number of Units Needed**	**Specification Number**
Authorized by:_____		Current Date: _____	

FIGURE 10.3   Purchase Requisition

- Upon receiving the purchase requisition, the purchasing department issues a **request for price quotation (RFP)** to the suppliers with whom the organization normally purchases the items.
- Suppliers interested in selling the product and/or services to the buyer's organization return a price quotation to indicate their current selling price.
- After analyzing the price quotations submitted, purchasing department personnel issue a purchase order to the supplier selected to provide the order. A copy is also routed to receiving personnel so they will know the details about incoming deliveries. (Details about receiving tasks are discussed in Chapter 11). When manual procurement systems are used, the RFP and purchase order are frequently the same document. Prices are requested, the RFP is returned, and a copy is then used (returned to the supplier) as a purchase order to confirm the buyer's acceptance of the seller's prices.

Depending upon the system used, purchasing personnel may also route a copy of the purchase order to the accounting department. There, it will be held until the applicable delivery invoice and copy of the purchase order sent earlier to receiving personnel are returned to the accounting department.

PURCHASING PROS NEED TO KNOW (10.2)

Many symbols and abbreviations are commonly used in request for price quotations, purchase orders, delivery invoices, and other purchasing documents. Hospitality purchasers must know what they mean, and they must use and interpret them correctly. Some examples include:

Symbol/Abbreviation	What it Means
# or lb	pound (# can also mean "number")
oz	ounce
ea	each
bu	bushel or bunch
pu	purchase unit
tsp or t	teaspoon
Tbsp, T, or Tbs	tablespoon
Pt	pint
Qt	quart
gal	gallon
doz	dozen
c	cup
%	percent
AP	as purchased
°F	Fahrenheit (degrees)
°C	centigrade (degrees)

MORE ABOUT THE ORDERING PROCESS

Like many other aspects of procurement, the physical task of ordering has undergone significant change. In the past, salespersons visited their buyers on a regularly scheduled basis. They explained current specials; worked with buyers to resolve problems, if any; and wrote down the order on a hard copy document typically preprinted with the supplier's most popular items. A copy of this document was provided to the purchaser for use as an in-house record of the purchase agreement.

Other ordering variations existed as when, for example, buyers used the telephone or a facsimile machine to place orders and, more recently, as e-mailed orders became commonplace. Today, even relatively small suppliers may prefer (or require) that orders be placed over the Internet on the company's Web site. Details about these procedures will be addressed in an in-depth discussion about ordering using technology later in this chapter.

Increasingly, purchasers order products electronically from their suppliers.

Ken Chernus/Getty Images, Inc.-Taxi

Internet Purchasing Assistant (10.2)

Automated solutions are available to help purchasers automatically fax, e-mail, and Web-deliver purchase orders, change orders, and RFPs. To learn about one system, and to view screen images of the activities it automates, go to:www.merkur.com

On-the-Job Challenges in Purchasing (10.1)

Flora and Harry had been friends since high school, and they kept up with each other during college. Now Flora was the purchasing director for Championship Golf Club, the largest and most prominent club in the state. Harry had also done well professionally; he was the sales manager for one of the largest broad line distributors in the region that included Flora's location.

Their professional relationship was mutually beneficial; Harry was able to receive occasional complimentary golfing, and Flora frequently received helpful information about purchasing challenges as they were encountered.

One day, Harry called Flora with some good news. "Flora, our company is changing some supply sources, and we want to move some products in our inventory very quickly. I have a list of these items and would be happy to e-mail it to you so you can have a first choice of anything you want."

"Thanks so much, Harry," replied Flora, "We are always on the lookout for ways to reduce our purchasing costs, and I hope there's some special deals that we can take advantage of."

"Sure thing, Flora," said Harry, "I always think of you first. You are one of our best accounts, and I think giving you a 'heads-up' about this is certainly the right thing to do."

"Okay, Harry," said Flora, "I'll let you know what we want as soon as I see the list."

Case Study Questions

1. Assume there are products on Harry's list that the Championship Golf Club uses. Assume, however, that these products are of a different quality level, and/or are available in purchase unit sizes not used by the club. Should Flora purchase the items if there are significant savings? Defend your response.
2. Assume there are some products on Harry's list that Flora currently purchases; in other words, they are exactly what her organization can use. How should Flora determine the quantity of these special-priced items that she should purchase?
3. Assume the club's general manager is aware of Flora's long-term personal and professional relationship with Harry. What, if any, types of special procurement-related procedures are in order to best ensure that the club's interests are being safeguarded?

What About Competitive Bids?

Many hospitality organizations, especially services affiliated with governmental agencies, require the use of **competitive bids,** even if it is not necessary to

Key Term

Bid (competitive)   The act of sending requests for price quotations to more than one supplier with the goal of receiving a lower price from one supplier for a product or service of agreed-upon quality.

PURCHASING PROS NEED TO KNOW (10.3)

The process of requesting price quotations from alternate suppliers is designed to help the buyer to receive the "best" price for products of comparable quality from suppliers whose services are acceptable to the buyer. Does this protocol always yield accurate information about price differences and an assurance that the "best" price is known?

Purchasing pros would answer this question with a resounding "no!" They know, for example, that representatives of competitive supplier organizations know and interact with each other in much the same way that hospitality managers from hospitality organizations have professional relationships with their peers. Information about organizations who are "slow payers," whose ethics are questionable, and who are otherwise "hard to get along with" are likely known by the circle of suppliers with whom the buyer interacts. Suppliers are not, then, likely to "sharpen their pencils" to provide the lowest possible price for business that is less-than-optimally desired. Although several price quotations may be received, each is likely to be higher than if the supplier were dealing with a more "preferable" buyer.

A second example occurs when one supplier is commonly asked to submit a price quotation but seldom, if ever, receives a purchase order. He or she knows that the buyer may be obligated by an organizational policy to solicit competitive bids even if the lowest price does not have to be accepted. In this instance, the supplier may submit a high price with the knowledge that an order is not likely to be forthcoming and, if it is, a financial return for his or her "wasted time" in the past is justification for a higher-than-necessary mark-up.

Purchasing pros know that their previous experience with suppliers is a significant factor that will affect prices to be quoted for the products and services they need. They consistently interact with all suppliers from whom prices are quoted in efforts to ensure that prices received are the "best" prices rather than just the "lowest price of all the high prices" that are submitted.

---

award the purchase to the entity submitting the lowest bid. An applicable policy might, for example, require the purchaser to send RFPs to at least three suppliers who carry the product or offer the desired service. The purpose of this tactic is to determine the supplier with the lowest price, and to ensure that the price offered by the supplier awarded the order is, in fact, reasonable (similar to that posed by other competitive suppliers).

A supplier offering a much lower price might be offering a great deal to the buyer. Perhaps, for example, he or she desires to break into the market by initially offering low prices. However, in today's competitive marketplace, it may also mean that supplier is offering a product of a different quality or excluding some services that may have been overlooked in the RFP, and which are included in the price quotations of competitive suppliers.

Some may question whether a requirement for competitive bids with its emphasis on lowest cost is contrary to a point emphasized throughout this text: Purchasers should be value conscious, and value (the relationship between product or service price and the quality) is a more important factor than price alone. Buyers requiring competitive bids will be emphasizing not only the lowest cost when they have completed other activities described in previous chapters, including

- Determining quality requirements for desired products and services, expressing these in purchase specifications, and distributing these to the suppliers from whom prices will be solicited.

Key Term

Award (to supplier)   The act of selecting and notifying the supplier that his or her response to a request to a proposal was accepted, and that the product and/or service will be purchased from that supplier.

- Considering the quantity of products or the length of services to be purchased, and clearly communicating this information to prospective suppliers. This activity is necessary because many suppliers reduce the price per purchase unit for products and lower service costs for extended time periods when the purchaser's quantity commitment increases.
- Making supplier sourcing decisions by considering the purchaser's experience and objective factors to assess the supplier's commitment to quality, value-added service, and the provision of information. These "eligible" suppliers will, then, have the capacity to contribute to the professional "partnership" that enables both the buyer and seller to be successful.
- Undertaking negotiations, if necessary, with prospective suppliers to best ensure that details about the products and services being ordered are known. As you've learned, negotiation does not need to precede each order. Instead, it is most useful for unique (one-of-a-kind) orders, for very expensive orders, and when beginning a relationship with new suppliers.

When the above and related activities have been undertaken, buyers can be reasonably ensured that the prices being quoted by all suppliers are for the same quality and quantity of product or service, and that the services provided by each supplier submitting a proposal response will be equal or, at least, acceptable, to the purchaser. With these assurances, the only difference in the price of the product or service being proposed will relate to the supplier's interest in doing business with the purchaser: the extent to which the supplier will accept a lower product or service mark-up to do business with the hospitality organization.

Wise buyers know that suppliers operate their businesses in much the same way as hospitality organizations: They work hard to reduce costs without sacrificing the quality of their products or services. They innovate, use technology when applicable, and work to ensure that their labor force is fairly treated and productive. The use of these and other tactics enable suppliers (and hospitality organizations!) to operate more efficiently. They can then pass savings on to the customers while still generating a fair financial return for their efforts.

Analysis of Proposal Responses

What concerns do buyers have as they review proposal responses from suppliers who have received RFPs? A first review should ensure that the supplier is submitting a **bid** for the same products and/or services in the same quantity/length of time that was specified in the RFP. If there are no variations, the buyer's next concern relates to each supplier's proposed cost. If there is a variation (e.g., the supplier does not submit a price for one or more specific items listed on the RFP), the buyer may exclude that supplier's proposal response from further consideration. Whether this is done depends upon how the buyer intends to select the supplier:

- The buyer may select the supplier quoting the lowest total price for all items noted on the proposal responses. (In this case, a supplier quoting a price for only some products would be excluded from further consideration.) An advantage to this method is the ability to purchase all items from one supplier and to avoid the need to issue purchase orders, accept incoming deliveries from, process "paperwork" for, and make payments to more than one

Key Term

Bid   Another term for price quotation, as in "The supplier bid (submitted a price quotation of) $17.12 for a specific product."

Analysis of RFP No. 5736512

Product	Purchase unit	Supplier A	Supplier B	Supplier C
Ground beef	lb.	3.29	3.24	3.31
Tenderloin steak	lb.	9.87	9.59	10.03
Chicken	2½-lb. bird	5.29	5.47	5.54

FIGURE 10.4   Sample Supplier Competitive Bid Analysis

supplier. Although costs associated with issuing purchase orders and completing follow-up documentation processing is difficult to quantify, some observers believe it is much in excess of $10 per purchase order. These costs must be considered when suppliers are selected on a by-item rather than by-product basis. A likely disadvantage to this supplier selection method is the concern that the buyer may be paying a higher price for some of the products in the order.

• The buyer may select the supplier based upon the prices quoted for each product in the proposal response. For example, supplier A may have submitted the lowest price for several products, and she will receive a purchase order for these products. Supplier B may, in turn, have submitted the lowest prices for other products, and they will be purchased from him. An advantage to this method is that the lowest price will be paid for every item. A disadvantage (noted above) is the time and expense required to interact with more than one supplier as the orders for all products are placed.

Figure 10.4 illustrates a sample supplier competitive bid analysis for three items. Supplier A submitted the lowest price for chicken, and Supplier B will be awarded the ground beef and tenderloin steak purchase. Buyers reserving the right to accept only specific products on an RFP should indicate this. Furthermore, many organizations also specify that they reserve the right to not award a bid to any supplier submitting a price quotation in response to a specific RFP.

PURCHASING PROS NEED TO KNOW (10.4)

Suppliers know that some organizations may purchase only some products based on their (the supplier's) price quotations. They may, then, increase their prices for specific items out of concern that they will be awarded only a relatively small portion of the forthcoming purchase order. Experienced buyers realize this, and they may request that suppliers indicate the percentage discount, if any, that they will offer on the total order if the buyer purchases all products on the RFP from the supplier.

Some purchasers request that suppliers provide their price quotations two ways: one price including delivery to buyer's location, and a second price for buyer pick-up at the supplier's location. The latter alternative might be useful in certain situations. Examples include for food specialty products purchased in small quantities and for purchases of a single or few products in larger quantities when the supplier's location is close to that of the buyer.

Knowledge of delivery costs can help purchasers make a decision based upon cost that must, in the case of pick-up at the supplier's dock, also consider the buyer's labor-related and transportation costs that will be incurred.

Purchase order

From/ship to:		Purchase from:		PO No.	34X135
Townville Hotel 1717 W. 17th Ave. Townville, NV, 00000 Telephone: 000-000-0000		Acme Grocers 2451 Elm Rd. Center Place, NV, 00000		PO Date:	7/16/xx
				Delivery Date:	7/20/xx
				Contact:	John Davis
				Terms:	Net 30

Item	Quantity	Purchase	Purchase unit price	Total price	RFP #
Green beans	4	Unit case (#10)	34.50	138.00	1715700
Flour, all purpose	3	Bag (50-lb.)	22.17	66.51	1715700
			Total	**204.51**	

Terms and conditions:	Buyer:	John Davis	Date:	7/16/xx
This purchase order expressly limits acceptance to the terms and conditions stated above and included on the following page. Any additional terms and conditions are rejected.				

Page_____ of_____ pages

FIGURE 10.5 Sample Purchase Order

THE PURCHASE ORDER

As you've learned, purchase orders are used by buyers to authorize (approve) the purchase of products or services of a required quality in a specified quantity at an agreed-upon price. Figure 10.5 illustrates a sample purchase order that might be in a hardcopy or electronic form.

When reviewing Figure 10.5, we'll assume that the Townville Hotel sent RFPs for products needed to several suppliers, including Acme Grocers, and the Townville Hotel buyer selected Acme Grocers to provide the order. Specifications have previously been sent to and are on file at Acme Grocers, and both the buyer and seller are aware that RFP prices supplied by Acme and the purchase order prices agreed to by Townville Hotel are based on products meeting these quality requirements.

Note that (in the upper-right-hand corner) the purchase order (PO) number and date are included as is the preferred delivery date and the name of the property contact if the supplier has questions. The purchase order also indicates that the "terms" are "Net 30." This means that the buyer will pay the total amount of the invoice ($204.51) within 30 days of the delivery date. Sometimes buyers negotiate

---

PURCHASING PROS NEED TO KNOW (10.5)

Some hospitality organizations have a policy indicating that discount offers should routinely be accepted. These policies, then, guide buyer decisions. In the absence of a policy, buyers should discuss taking significant discounts with accounting personnel before accepting them. The reason: There may be ongoing or temporary cash flow problems that make the discount offer less attractive. If there is, accounting staff, perhaps working with top-level managers, may wish to consider the advantages, if any, of short-term borrowing to pay invoices before they are due. The analysis can, then, focus on the discounted savings compared to the costs of the short-term loan that must be taken to do so.

---

a discounted price for faster payment. For example, payment terms might be: "2/10; net 30." In this instance, the buyer will receive a 2 percent discount if the total invoice is paid within 10 days; otherwise the total amount of the invoice is due within 30 days of the invoice date.

Procedures for Using Purchase Orders

Procedures for using purchase orders are straightforward. A copy is sent to the supplier and the operation's receiving personnel. Depending upon the hospitality operation's procedures, additional copies will be retained by the purchasing department and may be forwarded to accounting personnel. In large properties, all orders, except small purchases for which a petty cash fund will be used, should be authorized with a formal purchase order. In small organizations with a decentralized system, those authorized to purchase may use a standardized purchasing format (preferred) or another form approved by the person(s) with accounting responsibilities.

Unfortunately, there may be times when the purchaser's needs change after a purchase order has been issued. An example occurs when unforeseen problems arise during a construction or remodeling project for which a purchase order has been issued. Perhaps design changes are required, or structural challenges arise during remodeling. In these instances, the buyer may desire (or a building code may require) changes that involve activities and costs not addressed earlier. Hopefully, these are minimized because a purchase order typically represents a binding contract (see Chapter 3), and because there are likely to be additional costs, which have budget implications. However, when changes in a purchase order are required, a **change order** becomes necessary.

Terms and Conditions

Suppliers and purchasers typically have **terms and conditions** that apply to all, respectively, selling and purchasing transactions that the other party agrees to as a condition of the transaction. For example, suppliers typically mandate minimum purchase values that must be met before deliveries are made, and they may deliver only on specified days when their delivery vehicles are near the purchaser's location.

Key Terms

Change order   A revision to a purchase order that has been issued by a buyer to a supplier or service provider.

Terms and conditions   General provisions that apply to a supplier's price quotations and a buyer's purchase orders that apply regardless of the specific products or services addressed in the price quotation or purchase order.

Purchasers may have numerous general concerns when orders are placed that must be addressed in their agreements with suppliers. Often these are included in **"boilerplate" language** that is part of or affixed to purchase orders.

There are numerous boilerplate clauses for purchase orders that can address special concerns of purchasers that apply unless separate written agreements are negotiated. Examples include

- *Purchase order to be exclusive agreement.*   The purchaser order represents all of the responsibilities of the buyer and seller.
- *Services and deliverables.*   Seller agrees to perform the services or to provide the products described in the purchase order including compliance with all terms and conditions.
- *Delivery schedules.*   Deliveries are to be made within a reasonable time to the location specified by the buyer.
- *Risk of loss.*   Unless otherwise specified, the seller assumes the risk of loss until received (e.g., the delivery invoice is signed) by the buyer.
- *Packaging and crating charges.*   All packaging and crating charges are included in the product price or stated clearly as a separate charge on the RFP carried forward in the purchase order.
- *Payment of invoices.*   Buyer will pay the seller the amount agreed upon in the purchase order.
- *Guarantees and warranties.*   Service providers warrant that services will be completed according to currently sound professional procedures. Sellers of products warrant that products will be free from defects and conform to workable specifications (see Chapter 3).
- *Sellers are independent contractors.*   They do not have any authority to bind the buyer to pay under another contract.
- *Sellers are responsible.*   Sellers must pay taxes and maintain records required by governmental authorities relating to the products or services sold to the buyer.
- *Insurance.*   Sellers must maintain those types of insurance that are required by law.
- *Indemnification.*   Seller will hold the buyer and his or her organization harmless from claims, liabilities, damages, and other costs related to the goods or services purchased with the purchase order.
- *Disposition of rejected products.*   Seller will pick up any items that are refused at the time of delivery.
- *Confidentiality.*   Information related to the sale of any product or service to the hospitality organization will not be shared with anyone.
- *Noninterference with business.*   The seller will not solicit or encourage any employee or independent contractor to terminate or change a relationship with the hospitality operation.
- *Termination.*   The buyer can terminate the purchase order or agreement if the seller fails to perform in accordance with it. Also, the seller can terminate the agreement if the buyer does not pay the seller for products delivered, or services received, within a specified time period.
- *Legal remedies.*   The buyer specifies how it will recover damages incurred if the seller fails to perform.

Key Term

Boilerplate (language)   Clauses (portions) of a contract that do not change through repeated uses in different applications; in other words, general language that is applicable for different applications with different entities.

PURCHASING PROS NEED TO KNOW (10.6)

Some less-than-reputable suppliers may submit their bid for one product listed on an RFP at a very low price or for a product that it does not currently have in stock, and that it does not intend to carry in the future. The low price quoted for this product may, in turn, allow the supplier to receive the order if the buyer places it based on the total price for all products addressed in the supplier's proposal response. When delivery is made, the price that is **"low-balled"** will not be delivered (perhaps with a "back order" notation).

Wise hospitality buyers recognize the potential for this unethical tactic and address it with a boilerplate remedy: "The buyer reserves the right to purchase, at current market prices, any missing products in the quantity specified in the purchase order with that amount deducted from the amount due to the supplier."

- *Failure to perform.* Neither the buyer nor the seller will be penalized for failing to perform for reasons beyond his or her control (e.g., fire, flood, acts of war, or labor difficulties).
- *Limitations on subcontracting.* Sellers, including service providers, must indicate the extent, if any, to which part of the services covered by the purchase order will be subcontracted.

The quantity of products on hand is frequently an important factor that determines when orders are placed.

Vincent P. Walter/Pearson Education/PH College

Key Terms

Low-ball (selling price)   A selling price that is significantly below current market price that a supplier might quote for a product that he or she does not intend to sell.

Subcontract   A contract that is part of another contract; a person may enter into a contract with someone else who, in turn, contracts with a third party to perform part of the original contract's obligation.

Internet Purchasing Assistant (10.3)

There are, seemingly, innumerable topics that organizations may consider important terms and conditions to be addressed in boilerplate clauses for purchase orders.

To view examples of topics and the specific language used to address them, type "sample purchase order terms and conditions" into your favorite search engine. You will find the actual provisions used by many private industry and government organizations.

- *Invoice information.* Invoices should be sent to a specified location on or after the date of shipment (or delivery). Separate invoices are required for each specific purchase order, and invoices should indicate applicable purchase number orders.
- *Quantities.* Shipments must be in the quantities ordered.
- *Provisions for packaging.* Requirements relating to the construction of shipping containers, packing materials, marking information, and bar coding can be specified.
- *Work on-site.* Service providers agree that those furnishing services under a purchase are employees or agents of the seller who is, then, liable for all clauses and regulations applicable to his or her employees or agents. Sellers must hold the buyer harmless for claims and liabilities caused by or related to employees and agents, and they must carry insurance coverage in specific amounts for applicable service providers.

Governmental buyers, such as noncommercial foodservice operations, may include terms and conditions applicable to nondiscrimination in employment relative to persons employed by the supplier.

Special Concerns: Equipment Purchases

Purchases of expensive equipment require attention to details such as those already discussed in this section, and as well, several additional issues become important. Purchasers must ensure that the RFP soliciting prices and the purchase order confirming product orders identify exactly what the buyer desires to purchase. For example, it may be obvious that a purchaser desires to buy a specific brand and model number of a dishwashing machine. However, does the buyer expect the equipment to be delivered only to the property's back door? Should it be uncrated with crating materials removed from the buyer's location? Should the machine be set in place (if so, must the existing machine be removed)? Should the new machine be installed? Is training of dish machine operators expected? What about warranties and guarantees? These are among the factors that suppliers must know about so they can include costs in their proposal response for the exact products and services desired by the buyer.

"Good" equipment distributor representatives ask these questions to learn exactly what the buyer wants. "Good" buyers know about these variables, and they concisely indicate their expectations on RFPs and follow-up purchase orders. Both buyers and sellers must work closely together to ensure that there are no "surprises" or "communication problems" that can cause difficulties when equipment is purchased.

THE SUPPLIER'S SIDE (10.1)

"Insider" Tips on Purchasing: From the Supplier's Perspective

Question: How do distributor sales representatives determine the price that a manufacturer charges for a product?

Answer: As background, consider the number of linear feet of bookshelf space a restaurant supplier would require to hold catalogs from the, perhaps, 100 or more manufacturers of products that he or she sells. Consider, as well, the frequency with which catalogs must be updated to reflect ongoing equipment and product changes. Most equipment manufacturers use electronic catalogs, but consider the time required for a sales representative to develop a price quotation for all of the major equipment, tools, and supplies that would be required for production, service, storage, and other areas of a new restaurant or food and beverage outlet in a hotel.

Today, many suppliers have access to a computerized system ("auto quote") that makes it fast and simple for them to provide price quotations to purchasers. The system can be used when a buyer has requested prices for a routine order, and when the supplier is asked to quote prices for numerous items of equipment from several manufacturers.

The "auto quote" system allows sales representatives to quickly consult on-line catalogs and to complete a price quotation or develop a price list for a purchaser. The supplier's representative must enter only the name of the desired manufacturer and product. Product numbers, list prices, photos, specification information (if available), and other relevant information can then be reviewed. The sales representative can add items to an electronic quotation sheet being compiled and can also view dealer discount and other distributor-related information.

The price quotation listing all purchase information desired by the purchaser can be e-mailed or printed and sent to the purchaser. Also, the document can be electronically filed for future reference by both parties.

If you want to learn more about this system, go to: www.aqnet.com

Question: How do supplier representatives determine freight charges for heavy equipment that has been purchased?

Answer: The easiest way is to quote a price for the equipment cost and to then alert the purchaser that transportation costs will be billed by the freight company directly to the purchaser. However, even if the purchaser agrees, he or she will likely desire an estimate of these costs, and the supplier will want to provide it as value-added service to maintain a favored relationship with the buyer.

There is no "secret" formula that suppliers use to determine freight and related costs. First, they base their costs on exactly what the buyer specified in the RFP. If, for example, the buyer has not specified anything to the contrary, a seller typically assumes that the buyer will be responsible for uncrating and moving the equipment after it reaches the buyer's back door. Professional sales representatives make this known to perspective buyers. They indicate the options and suggest that buyers specify exactly what services should be provided so that they can be cited, along with the respective charges, on the supplier's price quotation. If equipment is to be shipped from the manufacturer to the buyer's location, applicable (estimated) freight charges can be determined by the supplier when he or she contacts freight companies. Rates for the supplier's own personnel to perform on-site uncrating, within facility relocation, and other tasks can be estimated if he or she is aware that the buyer desires these services. The same basic process is used to estimate these costs regardless of whether the supplier includes them in the equipment cost (the price paid is for the equipment delivered to the buyer), or whether negotiated costs are identified as separate "line items" on the proposal response.

An interesting anecdote: Equipment sellers to hospitality operations in island locations such as Hawaii have unique challenges. They may, for example, submit a price for equipment based upon shipment to the property's dock side location and a specific site within the property. Each of these alternatives requires suppliers to identify costs associated with each alternative, and each detail can significantly influence costs. As an example, suppliers must determine the type of palleting and crating that will be used because these

(continued)

factors affect the weight and cubic footage upon which costs for sea transport will be based. Also, several freight transport companies will be involved (from the site of manufacture to the seaside dock, across the ocean, and from the dock to the buyer's location). Numerous other details relating to insurance and responsibility for damage represent additional factors of which suppliers must be aware and that many buyers are not frequently concerned about unless boilerplate language in freight hauler contracts identifies the party responsible for these costs.

TIMING CONCERNS

You've learned that, when traditional purchasing systems are used, orders are placed when inventory levels must be increased to accommodate future production or service requirements. Details about alternative systems to determine purchase quantities were presented in Chapter 6. That chapter also discusses other types of purchasing systems such as just-in-time and supplier managed systems, which are less dependent upon the need to build inventories to meet short-term needs.

In addition to the need to purchase products for use at a specific time in the future, the timing of order placement typically includes consideration of factors such as:

- Delivery schedules of preferred suppliers. Deliveries may be possible several times weekly in major metropolitan areas but much less frequently in rural locations.
- Safety levels and order lead times for inventory management.
- Budgets and fiscal periods. Funds for major equipment purchases may be available only after a specific period (e.g., the next budget year). Also, unspent funds remaining in specific accounts near the end of the budget year may be released for applicable purchases.
- Out of stock, "emergency," and other unexpected purchases may need to be made with little or no lead time. Use of effective purchasing practices should minimize these "last minute" purchase requirements but, unfortunately, they are likely to occur on, at least, an occasional basis.

Many, especially smaller, hospitality purchasers are increasing their use of "club" outlets such as Sam's Club (Wal-Mart) and Costco. They, along with numerous grocery, outlet, and other stores, provide an alternative source of supply for hospitality operations of any size for occasional or more frequent purchases. When these alternatives are used, the timing for order placement becomes, basically, whenever an employee of the hospitality organization is asked to make a purchase during the store's operating hours. Many of these warehouse outlets offer account-charging opportunities to businesses just as their competitive suppliers do, and their prices can be very competitive. Deliveries to the buyer's location may also be arranged. Buyers must consider employee labor and/or benefits and transportation expenses involved when comparing prices to those offered by suppliers who make deliveries. As importantly, buyers must ensure that quality standards of alternative products are equally acceptable. Buyer's clubs often sell popular name brands and, as you learned in Chapter 4, brand names are commonly used as quality specifications.

Standing orders are another example of an ordering method, which involves minimal, if any, ordering time. For example, a restaurant may have an agreement with a coffee company, soft drink vending company, or dishwashing chemical supplier to provide, respectively, coffee packets, soft drinks, and dishwashing chemicals. A route person may visit the property on a predetermined basis (e.g., every Tuesday morning) and replenish applicable products to a predetermined par level. A delivery invoice is signed by and left with an authorized person at the property and is used as the basis for payment.

Many owners of small-volume restaurants purchase products at local grocery stores. Even managers of large properties may purchase from this source when there are stock outs.

Vincent P. Walter/Pearson Education/PH College

AN INTERESTING OBSERVATION!

The term "menu" is French and it means "detailed list." Perhaps surprisingly, the first menus were used by the chefs who prepared the meals rather than the guests who consumed them. In effect, the earliest menus were "shopping lists" used by chefs to help recall items that had to be purchased for use as meals were prepared.

Today, as hospitality managers, including chefs, take their shopping lists to retail businesses, they are repeating the visits made by chefs hundreds of years ago to the public marketplaces. There, they could purchase products that met the needs of their employers or the guests of the local taverns and lodging places that employed them just as contemporary buyers visit these "retail warehouse" outlets for the same purpose.

EXPEDITING PROCEDURES

Purchasers will, at some time, need to expedite deliveries.

Suppliers and service providers doing business with a hospitality organization will have been preselected based upon the purchaser's experience and/or the suppliers' reputations. The delivery of agreed-upon items according to a predetermined delivery schedule will have been a significant factor influencing the supplier selection decision. Likewise, the purchaser will be using internal procedures designed to best ensure that desired product quality and quantity concerns are addressed when orders are placed. Also, the timing of RFPs, analysis of incoming price quotations, and issuing of purchase orders should be planned to minimize the need for special tactics to expedite deliveries.

In spite of the best planning, however, internal problems can occur that affect orders. For example, the needs of user departments can be misunderstood, purchase requisition problems can arise, unexpected variations in business volume affecting lead times can occur, and inventory management issues may misstate quantities available on site. Also, weather conditions, strikes, equipment breakdowns, and problems creating errors as delivery vehicles are loaded provide

Problem	Possible Expediting Tactic
1. Inadequate quantity at time of delivery.	1. Purchase product from another supply source.*
2. Improper product quality.	2. Purchase the product in the public marketplace.
3. Purchaser error; product needed quickly.	3. Pick up product at supplier's location; buy product in public marketplace.
4. Product shortage (multi-unit property).	4. "Borrow" product (complete proper inter property transfer form).
5. Product on back order (but available at the supplier's location before time of need).	5. Request that supplier make special delivery, or request that the product be delivered by a sales representative.

*Recall a possible purchase order clause (terms and conditions) relating to the buyer's option of purchasing the missing product in the marketplace with a credit to the amount owed to the supplier.

FIGURE 10.6 Examples of Expediting Tactics

examples of supplier-related reasons for product shortages. In all of these and numerous other instances, expediting may become necessary.

A passive reaction ("we'll just have to wait until the product is delivered") should be among the last approaches to problem resolution. Useful tactics vary according to the situation, but several alternatives are noted in Figure 10.6.

Purchasers should consider the need to expedite as an opportunity to consider alternatives to minimize problems associated with the need to do so. They should also work with suppliers to anticipate and resolve supplier-related causes of product shortages and quality issues. More than very infrequent problems caused by the purchaser's organization must be corrected, and those caused by the supplier may create the need for an examination of a continued relationship with him or her.

TECHNOLOGY AND THE ORDERING PROCESS

As you've learned throughout this book, purchasers can use technology in numerous ways at every step in the procurement process to replace manual processes with their computerized counterparts. In this section, we'll explore how technology enables earlier steps to provide information required at the time of ordering. Also, we'll review automated ordering alternatives.[1]

Production personnel depend upon purchasers to order products required to meet production needs so guests will not be disappointed.

Tony Souter © Dorling Kindersley

On-the-Job Challenges in Purchasing (10.2)

"We better see that truck first thing tomorrow morning, or this problem will be officially out of hand!" said Flicia to herself as she slammed down the telephone.

Flicia, the kitchen manager at the Pine Hill Retirement Center, had ordered some boneless turkey rolls as a special entrée for the holiday luncheon to be served to her senior citizen residents and their families. She had ordered the frozen products about five days ago, and they should have been delivered two days ago. Her salesperson had called her to advise that they were on back order from his supplier, and they were due to be special-delivered to the retirement center today. Deliveries were normally in the afternoon, so she didn't start to worry until late in the afternoon. She had just completed her third unsuccessful attempt to reach the supplier's office phone and her sales representative's cell phone. Although she didn't expect an answer at the former number (it was after 7:00 p.m.), she did think her sales rep would respond to the two earlier messages she had left him.

Flicia arrived at her office about 7:00 a.m. the next morning and had two messages. One was from the supplier's office that explained the delivery truck had broken down and, coincidentally, there was a telephone service interruption because a new internal-office system was being installed. The second call was from her salesperson who indicated that an (unexplained) personal emergency kept him away from the telephone throughout the evening and much of the night.

"Well," thought Flicia, "Maybe the supplier and my account rep have reasonably good excuses for not delivering the product, and for not contacting me yesterday. However, what should I do now that I've spent several hundred dollars at the local buyer's club to purchase the product that I knew required thawing and preparation today?"

Case Study Questions

1. If you were Flicia in this situation, would you have purchased the turkey rolls even though you had an outstanding purchase order for the product with this supplier? Explain your response.
2. If you were the supplier, what, if anything, would you have done to reach Flicia? (Assume that there were about 25 customers affected by the truck breakdown.)
3. What should Flicia do now?
4. Assume you are Flicia's account representative and that you did have a personal situation that kept you out of telephone contact. What, if anything, would you do right now? After you learn at some point that Flicia has purchased the product from another source?
5. What, if anything, can Flicia learn from this experience? What can her account representative learn?

Many software developers have rolled out systems that integrate most of the procurement functions that can, for example, determine menu item sales and resulting decreases in product inventory based on the sales, calculate remaining product inventory levels based upon theoretical usage required to generate the sales, and alert purchasers and others when product order points are reached. These subsystems, taken together, allow technology and its numerous advantages to assist managers and purchasers with control information required to make the most effective procurement and other decisions. Details about the use of technology for the management of hospitality operations are beyond the scope of this book.[2] However, in this section, we'll review two aspects of the ordering process that are increasingly automated: determining inventory levels and communicating with suppliers.

Determining Inventory Levels

As you've learned, traditional ordering systems consider existing levels of inventory and are implemented when order points were reached. Alternatively, orders can be placed on a regularly scheduled basis (e.g., orders on Tuesday for delivery on

Thursday). Then existing inventory levels are considered, and orders are placed to return storage quantities to a pre-established par level. Both tactics require knowledge about the quantity of products in inventory as a prerequisite to ordering.

As you'll learn in the next chapter, automated systems are available to maintain an ongoing count of products in inventory. Systems can track the quantity of products entering inventory (which increase inventory balances) and record the quantities of products leaving inventory (which reduce inventory levels). This data can be accessed at any time by authorized personnel, and it provides an instant answer to the question, "How much product should we order?"

As suggested in our introduction to this section, systems can use much more sophisticated methodology than simple tracking of products into and out of storage areas. Point-of-sale (POS) systems are increasingly used to track customer counts, revenues, and other information that allows restaurant managers to tally the number of each menu item sold. If standard recipes are used, it is possible to track the quantity of ingredients used to produce each menu item, and to then adjust remaining inventory balances accordingly. For example, assume that POS data indicate that 325 hamburger steaks were sold during a specified time period. If the standard recipe for this menu item requires 5 ounces (as purchase weight) of ground beef for each entrée, approximately 101.6 pounds of ground beef should have been used for this purpose: 325 hamburger patties $\times$ 5 oz. (ap) = 1,625 oz. $\div$ 16 (number of oz. in pound) = 101.6 pounds.

Similar tallies can be made for the number of pounds of ground beef (let's assume that only one ground beef product is used) to determine the total quantity of this ingredient that should have been used. If inventory management software is interfaced with POS software or if software containing both sales and inventory applications are used, it is possible to calculate the approximate quantity of ground beef that should remain in inventory: Beginning quantity of ground beef + incoming shipments of ground beef − amount of ground beef used = amount now available.

As seen above, technology provides at least two methods to determine the quantities of products on hand to help purchasers with ordering decisions: track product movements in and out of storage areas, and track quantities of specific ingredients based on sales.

In practice, some hospitality operations use both methods: After verifying theoretical quantities with physical count information provided by accounting personnel, purchasers have inventory quantity information necessary for ordering. At the same time, their food and beverage management peers can consider reasons, if any, for differences between theoretical counts from inventory movement and ingredient usage and the actual physical count of product on hand. Although some variation may be expected for reasons including over-portioning and leftovers, significant variation requires the application of food and beverage cost control practices.

Communicating with Suppliers

There are numerous times during the routine ordering process that require communication between buyers and sellers. These were mentioned earlier in this chapter, and automated examples were briefly noted. Examples include when the:

- Purchaser requests prices for specific products with a request for price quotation (RFP)
- Supplier provides a price quotation (bid) in response to the RFP
- Purchaser awards an order to the supplier with a formal purchase order

Each of these steps can be, and increasingly is, automated. You've even learned that many organizations provide terms and conditions related to their purchase orders on the Internet. The use of technology streamlines the ordering process, reduces time-consuming "paperwork," and allows for a much less cumbersome information tracking and storing process.

Many suppliers allow (encourage) purchasers to place their orders online rather than rely on salespersons taking orders physically (in person) or by telephone, facsimile or, even, with e-mail messages.

A commonly used online ordering system uses several steps. For example, purchasers:

- Enter the supplier's Web site and use a protected identification code to reach their accounts.
- Enter products desired into an order template on the screen. They can review previous orders and note current prices for desired and/or alternative products as ordering information is entered.
- Provides other information and completes the ordering process.

Although purchasing technology applications such as those just discussed apply to the ordering process, they are useful for numerous other procurement-related responsibilities as well. Many of these are discussed in applicable chapters throughout the text.

Purchasing Resources on the Internet

In addition to the Web sites referenced in this chapter's "Internet Purchasing Assistant," the following sites provide detailed information to enhance your purchasing knowledge and skills.

Purchasing Resources on the Internet

Site	Information About
www.samsclub.com	Buyer's club (warehouse retail chain) (Click on "Restaurant & Foodservice")
www.costco.com	Buyer's club (warehouse retail chain) (Enter a zip code into the "Shop for Business Products" tool bar, then click on "Shop by Business," and then "Catering & Restaurant" and/or "Hospitality & Hotel")
www.bellwethercorp.com	Purchase order software (Click on "Purchasing")
www.sysco.com	Large foodservice distributor (Click on "Order Entry")
www.adacoservices.com	Automated procurement management system
www.costguard.com	Automated procurement management system
www.htmagazine.com	Automated procurement system (Enter "automated procurement" in the site's search box)
www.crunchtime.com	Automated procurement system (Click on "Products")
www.hotel-online.com	E-procurement (Type "e-procurement" in the site's search box)
www.hospitalitynet.org	Requests for proposals (Type "request for proposals" in the site's search box)

Key Terms

order (product or
   service)   226
purchase requisition   232
request for price
   quotation (RFP)   232

bid (competitive)   235
award (to supplier)   236
bid   237
change order   240

terms and
   conditions   240
boilerplate
   (language)   241

low-ball (selling
   price)   242
subcontract   242

Think It Through

1. How would you determine the types of "terms and conditions" that you as a buyer for a hospitality organization would use for purchase orders? What, if any, assistance would you request from your organization's attorney?
2. How would you determine the need, if any, for the additional automation of the ordering process for your organization?
3. How would you determine the role, if any, that a local buying club might play in your hospitality organization's purchasing program?
4. Assume that you were the owner or chief operating officer (COO) for a multi-unit hotel operation that uses a centralized purchasing system, and your lodging properties are located over a several state region in the Southwestern United States. How would you determine the products, if any, that purchasers in specific properties could order themselves from their own (approved) supply sources? In your response, provide examples of food/beverage and non-foodservice items that properties could order locally. Also, provide examples of categories of products that you would require to be ordered from the centralized procurement department.
5. Assume that you were a restaurant manager and your organization has typically used a coffee distributor to replenish inventories of coffee packets used for the brewing of this beverage. Your operation has three separate dining rooms and a large banquet facility in an adjoining building at the same site. Explain the basic procedures that you would use to:
   • Select the "best" coffee distributor.
   • Ensure that the number of coffee packet cases delivered (and billed for) are correct.
   • Develop procedures (what would they be?) to ensure that cases of coffee packets are properly rotated so the oldest products were used first.

Team Fun

You and your team are serving as consultants to the manager of a 100-room limited-service hotel. The property is not franchised, so it does not have access to policies and standard operating procedures that franchisors make available to their franchisees.

Your project involves developing policies and procedures related to the roles and responsibilities of department heads for purchasing in the decentralized system that is used. There are three department heads (for front desk operations, housekeeping, and maintenance), and each reports to the manager.

1. The assignment of the first team is to determine the factors that should be used to determine whether the department heads require approval from the manager before purchase.
2. The assignment of the second team is to specify the need for documents and their flow through the organization as a prerequisite for approval of, and payment by, the part-time accountant (who is supervised by the manager).
3. The assignment of the third team is to indicate the process that the manager should use if he or she wished to consider replacing the existing decentralized purchasing system with a part-time purchaser.

Each team should be prepared to present and discuss their findings and conclusions.

Endnotes

1. Note: Other chapters in this book contain an element, "High-Tech Purchasing." This topic is reviewed at length in this section and replaces a briefer discussion of computerized aspects of purchasing in the other chapters.
2. Interested readers are referred to: Michael Kasavana and John Calhill. *Managing Technology in the Hospitality Industry*, 5th ed. East Lansing, MI: Educational Institute of the American Hotel & Motel Association, 2007.

11

Product Receiving and Storing: Principles and Procedures

In This Chapter

How can an entire chapter be written on the (seemingly) "mundane" activities of receiving and storing? Doesn't the task of receiving merely involve "signing some paperwork" and moving products to storage areas? Isn't storing just the simple process of holding products until they are needed? Unfortunately, these descriptions represent how receiving and storing responsibilities are undertaken in some hospitality organizations. However, these two activities are critical steps in ensuring that the organization's concerns about quality and the management of costs are addressed as an integral part of the procurement process.

Purchasers must receive the quantity of products that were ordered, and the tasks required to do so are integral to effective receiving practices. Other concerns relating to financial management and record keeping also point to the importance of using effective receiving procedures.

Properly trained staff members are required to recognize quality characteristics of incoming products. Physical concerns (facility, tools, and equipment) also affect how well receiving activities can be implemented. Policies and related procedures that guide how receiving should be done must be implemented and consistently used to best ensure that purchasing expectations are met. Two additional concerns, use of technology and security precautions, are also important and will round out our discussion of product receiving.

Trained personnel, appropriate storage spaces, and tools and equipment are important product storage concerns. These, along with the policies and procedures necessary to ensure that quality, cost, and record-keeping concerns are addressed, must be in place to avoid quality deterioration and excessive costs during storage that work against the goal of providing customer value. Also, many hospitality operations have inventories containing tens of thousands of dollars or more of products and supplies. Some fine-dining restaurants boast wine inventories valued at hundreds of thousands of dollars! These products must be protected from theft and pilferage while in storage.

Not surprisingly, technology is increasingly available to help in the generation and analysis of storage-related information and with security and accessibility concerns, and these issues will be discussed in detail. The ultimate goal of purchasing is to make the "right" products available to those in user departments. This chapter is important because it addresses the two steps (receiving and storing) that must occur from the time products reach the hospitality organization until they are issued to those who will use them to produce the products and services required by the organization's customers.

■ ■ ■

Outline

RECEIVING AND STORING: INTEGRAL TO PROCUREMENT

Figure 11.1 (shown earlier as Figure 1.4) reviews the steps in the procurement process discussed in this book. It sets the context for our receiving and storing discussion by identifying where these activities fit into the process. The location in the sequence (Step 8) indicates that they are among the concluding tasks in a wide range of activities designed to attain procurement goals. It is important to ensure that the products ordered (Step 7) and that will be paid for (in Step 9) were, in fact, received. After receipt, products must be stored before they can be issued for production and service.

Overview

Let's begin our study of **receiving** and **storing** with some definitions.

> **Key Terms**
>
> **Receiving** The transfer of ownership from a supplier to a hospitality operation that occurs when products are delivered.
>
> **Storing** The process of holding products under optimal storage conditions until they are needed for production or use.

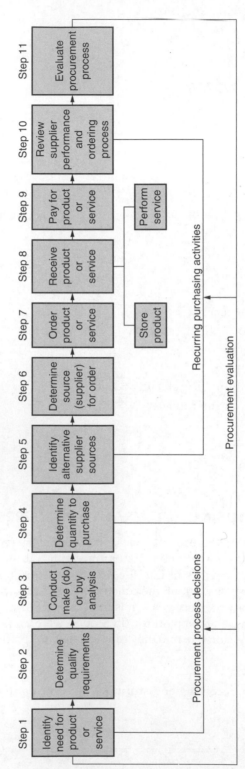

FIGURE 11.1 Steps in Procurement Process

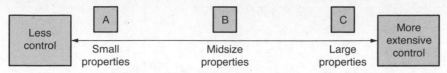

FIGURE 11.2 Range in Control of Receiving and Storing Practices

Who is responsible for the receiving and storing tasks? The answer to this question depends upon several factors, of which organizational size is among the most important. Responsibilities for, and the procedures used to receive and store, products typically become more defined as property size increases. Figure 11.2 illustrates the concept that control procedures for receiving and storing tend to increase with property size. Generalizations and stereotypes are sometimes incorrect: Some small properties have excellent receiving and storing systems, and some very large properties use less-than-desirable procedures.

Consider the range of control emphasized in Figure 11.2. In a very small operation (point "A"), the manager or person responsible for food production or beverage service may receive incoming products and move them to appropriate storage areas. In these operations, "everyone" may be responsible for storing (meaning, in fact, that sometimes "no one" is responsible for storing!). Products are simply placed in designated storage areas, and they are removed by applicable personnel as needed for production or other use. In many small properties, beverage storage areas, unlike those for food products, may be locked to limit unauthorized access.

Midsize properties are noted at point "B" in the range of control for receiving and storing. These include many franchised multi-unit hotel and restaurant units. Operating procedures such as those for product receiving and storing are among the foundation of assistance that franchisers provide to franchisees in return for the several types of fees paid by the latter to the former.

Properties with intermediate levels of receiving and storing controls (point "B") tend to have designated people who, although often not occupying full-time applicable positions, have received specific training for their receiving and storing duties. Procedures designed to better ensure that quantity, quality, security, and record-keeping concerns are addressed during receiving and storing tasks are likely to be used in these operations.

Large properties (point "C" in Figure 11.2) employ purchasing persons with full-time purchasing responsibilities. They also typically employ staff members whose primary responsibility is receiving and storing. In the largest properties, these duties are split, and different people have specialized receiving and storing obligations.

Importance of Receiving and Storing

You've learned about the importance of each of the procurement activities discussed in earlier chapters. However, without effective receiving and storing, all of the time, efforts, concerns, and creativity expended to best ensure that proper products and services are available to the hospitality organization will be wasted. Some (but fortunately few!) suppliers and/or their employees who handle products at a supplier's facility and deliver them to the hospitality organization are dishonest. Given an opportunity, they will take advantage of weakness in the organization's control system, if possible. All suppliers and their employees (and all staff members of hospitality organizations!) can make mistakes that have a negative effect on the organization. The goal of every property should be to reduce the incidence of these problems by the consistent use of effective receiving practices.

The potential for quality and cost problems do not end when products are properly received and "safely" moved into their designated storage areas. Environmental problems can seriously affect the quality of products in storage. In fact, with few exceptions, the quality of food and beverage products available for use by production staff will never be better than when they are

Procedures for receiving and storing fresh fruits and vegetables must help ensure that the products available for production and service are just as fresh as when they are harvested.

Veiga, Luis/Getty Images Inc.-Image Bank

received. Unfortunately, quality can deteriorate quickly unless procedures are in place to prevent this from happening.

Security is another concern at time of product storage and must be addressed by appropriate control measures. In their absence, pilferage and/or theft can occur when, for example, products are consumed or unlawfully removed from the property by dishonest employees.

An easy justification of the importance of effective storing is possible even if the only advantages are those related to an increased assurance of quality and minimized security concerns. However, there is another reason why attention must be paid to products while they are in storage: record keeping. This concern relates to the need to know about the quantity and cost of products in storage. You learned in Chapter 6 that the amount of products on hand, available in storage, influences the quantity of products that must be purchased when a traditional purchasing system is used. You can note this relationship again by reviewing Figure 11.1: Step 4 (determining the quantity to purchase) precedes product ordering (Step 7), which results in its receipt and storage—the topics of this chapter.

The amount of product in storage affects the cost of products in storage, and storage (inventory) costs are of concern for several reasons, including

- They are used to calculate the product cost **(cost of goods sold).** This is a critical element in the **income statement** of a restaurant as well as the food and beverage department's income statement in a lodging, healthcare, private club, educational, or other organization that offers food services.
- The cost of inventory is also reflected on an organization's **balance sheet** as a **current asset.**

Key Terms

Cost of goods sold The cost of the food or beverage incurred during a specific period to generate food or beverage revenue during that same period; simplified to "food cost" or "beverage cost"; sometimes referred to as COGS.

Income statement A summary of a business's profitability that details the revenues generated, expenses incurred, and profits or losses realized during a specific accounting period (such as a month); also known as the Statement of Income and Expense, Profit and Loss, or P&L Statement.

Balance sheet A summary of a business's assets, liabilities, and owner's equity at a specific point in time (typically the last day of the month); also called Statement of Financial Position.

Asset (current) An item of value owned by an organization, such as cash or other items, that can be converted into cash within one year.

On-the-Job Challenges in Purchasing (11.1)

"I've been working here almost five years, and now I guess I can't be trusted!" exclaimed Douglas as he sat across the table from Zachary. Both were seated at a dining room table in the Cider River Restaurant when the property was closed. They had just attended a mandatory meeting called by the property's new owner. The session had been lengthy, and the new owner had used most of the time to tell the employees about his plans.

"I've been here longer than you have, Doug," replied Zachary, "And I feel the same way. I know that this new guy has invested a lot of money in this place. He really does have some good ideas, and I know he wants this to work out. However, his concerns about how to manage costs are pretty radical. The present owner had this place for many years, and it was always successful. What's wrong with just continuing to do what we've been doing? Does the new guy really think he will make more money by weighing every single item that comes in here, by locking the storeroom doors when we are here, and by challenging us to find a way to steal food and beverage products?"

"I get what you mean, Zach," said Douglas, "I don't want to steal anything, and I wish him the best of luck because our futures are tied to his success. I just wish he would recognize that we're honest, treat us like we are, and keep things the way they've been . . . at least until he has a reason to change!"

Case Study Questions

Assume you are the new owner of the Cider River Restaurant:

1. Should you anticipate that there will be resistance to change when you implement new procedures? Why or why not? If so, what are some tactics that you can use to address them?
2. What are your thoughts about the general strategy of learning how existing systems work before making any (or, at least, significant) changes?
3. What are the potential advantages and disadvantages to implementing tight receiving and storing control procedures in a relatively small restaurant operation when you have no knowledge about problems, if any, that create a definite need for them?

As you can see, the receiving and storing functions are critical aspects of the procurement process that cannot be overlooked. Instead, significant attention to each step in these activities is important. Examples of receiving and storing concerns, and appropriate ways to address them, are the topics of the remainder of this chapter.

RECEIVING ESSENTIALS

A "recipe" for effective receiving includes attention to personnel, the receiving area, and tools and equipment. These ingredients for success will now be examined.

Receiving Personnel

In Chapter 1, you learned that much of the revenue generated by restaurants and food and beverage operations in hotels are required to purchase the food and beverage products needed to generate the revenues. This justifies the use of trained and qualified personnel as product ownership and responsibility transfer from the supplier to the hospitality operation. The (unfortunately all-too-common) practice that "whoever is closest to the back door when the delivery person arrives should sign the invoice and put the items in storage" has always been an indefensible procedure with no place in today's professionally managed operation.

As you'll learn, many of the procedures necessary for effective receiving are clerical or physical; however, the most important tasks, including the ability to recognize the quality of incoming items and to confirm that they meet the property's standards, require training and experience. This is especially important when products such as fresh produce, meats, and seafood are received. These products are not typically purchased by brand (name), and product observation in comparison to the standards identified in purchase specifications is necessary. In the best operations, those in receiving positions work shoulder-to-shoulder with experienced food production personnel to learn about and observe firsthand all of the features found in proper quality products.

Among the other attributes of successful receivers are the ability to:

- *Maintain sanitation standards.* Food safety and/or sanitation concerns are incorporated into the property's purchase specifications, and these are integral aspects of quality. However, sanitation concerns also apply to the receiving area, the tools and equipment used, and the procedures implemented to handle products while being received.
- *Know about appropriate technology.* There are numerous technological advances that expedite the receiving and storing process while, at the same time, provide more accurate information and more appropriate reports.
- *Lift and carry products, if applicable.* Some cases of products can weigh 30 pounds or more. Flour and sugar are routinely packaged in 50-pound or even 100-pound bags, and packages of these sizes are often purchased because of lower purchase unit prices. The Americans with Disability Act [ADA] prohibits discrimination against persons with disabilities who seek employment. The ability to lift heavy packages and containers may, or may not, be a **Bona Fide Occupational Qualification (BFOQ).** Hospitality managers must be aware of these potential legal issues, and may need to consider ways to modify the work of receiving employees to accommodate persons who would otherwise be qualified.
- *Resolve problems.* What should be done if some or all incoming products do not meet the property's quality requirements? If incorrect quantities are delivered? If delivery personnel attempt to rush the receiving clerk to "catch up on the delivery schedules"? These and other challenges can arise and help make the receiving clerk's job responsibilities anything but routine.
- *Maintain an attitude of concern.* Although this is likely to be a function of hospitality managers and how they do (or don't) respect receiving clerks and their efforts, exemplary staff members want to assist the organization and the department within which they work. Concerned receiving personnel are committed to helping the hospitality organization attain its goals. They recognize, because they are told about it, their important role in helping the property to better serve customers and are contributing members of the hospitality team.

Receiving Area

Hopefully, the importance of the receiving area was recognized when product flow concerns were initially planned. Typically, receiving areas are close to a back door in a small operation but, in large organizations such as hotels, they are often part of or adjacent to the loading dock. In small properties, they may be little more than relatively large spaces around or close to a back door where no other equipment is located. Adequate space to assemble all incoming products is necessary for counting and/or weighing tasks, as is space to accommodate a receiving scale.

Key Term

Bona Fide Occupational Qualification (BFOQ) Job qualifications legally judged to be reasonably necessary to safely or adequately perform the job.

Space for transport equipment is likely required, and this can be significant if **pallet** loads of incoming products are received.

There may also be some space for a desk, file cabinet, or other equipment and, increasingly, access to a computer is required because of the increasing use of technology for product receiving.

Receiving Tools and Equipment

Tools frequently used by receiving personnel include plastic tote boxes or other containers to transport ice for products such as fresh poultry or seafood that require it, and cleaning tools and equipment used to keep the area in clean and proper condition. Increasingly, personal digital assistants (PDAs), notebook or laptop computers, and/or other wireless devices are also required to access purchasing and inventory records required at time of receiving.

Receiving scales should be of two types: those accurate to the fraction of a pound (for large items) and those accurate to the fraction of an ounce (for smaller items and preportioned meats). Scales should be calibrated regularly to ensure accuracy. Wheeled equipment, such as hand trucks, carts, and/or dollies, should be available to move incoming products quickly and efficiently to their proper storage areas. Box cutters must be properly maintained and safely used as receiving personnel remove excess packaging to verify the quality of delivered products.

Thermometers are used to ensure that foods are delivered at their proper storage temperatures. For many operators, these temperatures are

Item	Acceptable Temperature Range	
	°F	°C
Frozen foods	10°F or less	−12°C or less
Refrigerated foods	30°F–45°F	1°C–7°C

A calculator or adding machine may be needed to check suppliers' calculations on delivery invoices, especially if they have been prepared manually. This task may be done by receiving staff in some operations and by accounting personnel in others. A printing calculator is best and will be used if the original delivery invoice is changed because of incorrect vendor pricing or items listed on the invoice were not delivered. In addition, invoice totals will change when all or a portion of a delivery is rejected because items were of substandard quality.

The receiving area should include a desk, telephone, computer/fax, copy machine, file cabinet, and ample office supplies such as pens, pencils, and a stapler. Although larger operations are more likely to have such an area, small-volume operations still have a need for basic equipment. In all cases, the records area should include copies of all purchase specifications to avoid confusion about whether a delivered food or supply item meets quality requirements.

BASIC RECEIVING PROCEDURES

Several important procedures should be used when receiving incoming products and supplies. They apply to all types of hospitality operations regardless of size in all industry segments and can be used when receiving almost any type of product or supply for any department within a hospitality operation. They

Key Term

Pallet A portable platform (rack) typically made of wooden slats used to store and/or move case goods of products that are stacked upon it.

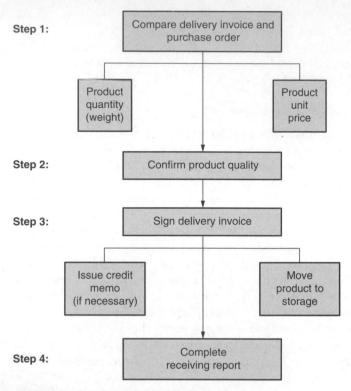

FIGURE 11.3   Steps in Effective Receiving Process

address the three basic receiving concerns already identified: quality, record keeping, and security.

Figure 11.3 reviews the steps required for effective receiving.[1]

As you review Figure 11.3, note that several steps are involved in the receiving process. First, the supplier's delivery invoice that accompanies the incoming product order should be compared to the copy of the purchase order that specifies what is being purchased from the supplier. This will help ensure that the quantity and price of products agreed upon at time of purchasing are correct when they are delivered and summarized on the delivery invoice. Some items such as cases of canned goods can be counted because a specified number of cases were ordered. Other items such as fresh meats ordered by the pound must be weighed to confirm that the required amount (weight) was received.

Figure 11.4 shows a sample (composite) delivery invoice.

When reviewing the sample delivery invoice in Figure 11.4, note that it summarizes a delivery made by Kornell Provisions to Oakville Family Diner on 7/16/xx. The invoice number and date, along with other information (the Oakville Family Diner's account number and purchase order number) and Kornell Provision's delivery number and purchase terms, are also noted.

The delivery invoice lists each item that was ordered and delivered. Note the provision for a signature by the receiving clerk ("received by") and, as well, the detachable slip that is to be sent along with payment for the delivery. There are typically several copies of the delivery invoice, and both Oakville Family Diner and Kornell Provisions will retain at least one complete copy.

Figure 11.3 indicates that the second step in the receiving process involves confirming that the product quality meets the property's purchase specification. This step is very important and probably the most challenging. Standards incorporated into purchase specifications must be easily observable. Then incoming products can be compared with the written specifications. If there are concerns

Delivery Invoice	Invoice No. 100001	Invoice Date: 7/15/xx

Sold by: Kornell Provisions 236 Spruce Street Campusville, NY 00000 Telephone: 111-111-1111 Fax: 111-111-1112	Sold to: Oakville Family Diner 132 N. 10th Street Anyville, NJ 00001 Account No. 7891011	Ship to: Oakville Family Diner 132 N. 10th Street Anyville, NJ 00001

Buyer's Purchase Order No. 6800105	Delivery No. X314YZ	Delivery Date: 7/16/xx

Item	Product No.	Quantity	Purchase Unit	Price/Unit	Total Price
Ground beef	170	4	10-lb. poly bag	34.70	138.80
Pork links	321	2	Case (20-lb.)	49.80	99.60

Terms: Net due in 14 days	Total Amount Due	$238.40

Received by: _____   Date: _____

Distribution: Retain original copy; second copy to buyer.

FIGURE 11.4   Sample Delivery Invoice

about quality, the restaurant manager and/or chef should be asked to decide whether the purchase specification requirements are met.

If no problems are observed, the delivery invoice can be signed. However, if there are product shortages or other problems, a **credit memo** should be cosigned by the receiving employee and the supplier's delivery person to confirm that adjustments to the delivery invoice will be necessary. These will require special handling as payment processing tasks are undertaken. (See Chapter 12.)

After the delivery invoice has been signed, receiving personnel must quickly move products to their appropriate storage areas to:

- Help prevent the quality deterioration of those products that should be stored at refrigerated or frozen temperatures.
- Reduce the possibility of product theft by employees.

Key Term

Credit memo   An accounting document used to adjust information about product quantities and/or costs as initially recorded on a delivery invoice.

"Where Do These Eighty Televisions Go?"

One of this book's authors is aware of a hotel that purchased approximately eighty television sets because of its franchisor's requirement that existing sets in guest rooms be upgraded. Managers had planned for maintenance personnel to cart the incoming sets a few at a time from the hotel's receiving area to the affected guest rooms. There sets would be unboxed, and the old units would be returned to the receiving area. The used televisions had been sold ($25 each) to a hotel furniture reseller.

Shortly after the exchange process began, it became clear that the number of old sets being returned to the receiving area was less than the number of new units being transported to guest rooms. Some were, apparently, being stolen by hotel staff.

They quickly implemented a solution: Boxes containing new sets were marked with the designated guest room and name of the employee responsible for transporting the unit to the room. The old set was placed in the empty box that originally contained the new television, and the same employee returned the old set to the receiving area. This tactic eliminated the problem because it attached responsibility for the new and old televisions to an identified staff member.

One other tactic was used in response to the problem: The reseller was contacted, and subsequently picked up the used sets on that day to eliminate the possibility of additional theft of sets from the receiving/storage area.

Figure 11.3 suggests a final step in product receiving: complete a **receiving report.** This document is used in food service operations that calculate food costs on a daily basis because it helps separate information on delivery invoices into the components required for daily food costing (see endnote 1).

Figure 11.5 shows a sample receiving report.

When reviewing the receiving report, note that supplier A delivered two cases of eggs (among other items not shown in this sample report) and that the cost of this product is considered to be a **"direct"** charge against daily food costs. By contrast, supplier B delivered sirloin steaks (among other products) and, be-

Date: _____

Supplier	Invoice	Product	Purchase Unit	No. of Units	Unit Price	Cost	Directs (Food)	Stores (Food)	Beverages
A	10735	Eggs	Case[a]	2	$34.50	$69.00	$69.00		
B	221	Sirloin Steaks	Pound	55	$14.70	$808.50		$808.50	

[a]*Note:* There are 30 dozen eggs in a commercial–packed case of eggs.

FIGURE 11.5 Daily Receiving Report

Key Terms

Receiving report   A document that separates incoming food costs into components required for daily food cost calculations.

Direct (food cost)   A food product that is charged to daily food costs on the day it is received.

PURCHASING PROS NEED TO KNOW (11.1)

In some, especially small owner-operated, restaurants the owner/manager is likely to be responsible for receiving on an occasional (if not more frequent) basis. In larger operations, the restaurant manager may delegate this task to the chef or kitchen manager. In a still larger property, a specific person (receiving or storeroom clerk) may have this responsibility. Regardless of the organizational structure, however, the manager has some responsibilities for receiving that cannot be delegated. These include the need to:

- Develop and implement a policy requiring the use of effective receiving techniques every time every product is received.
- Ensure that persons responsible for receiving are properly trained. They must know and use the proper procedures and be able to identify the quality standards that have been incorporated into the property's purchase specifications.
- Provide the proper receiving equipment and ensure that it "works." For example, a receiving scale must be available in the receiving area, and it must be routinely calibrated to ensure accuracy.
- Inform suppliers about the need for delivery personnel to spend the time necessary for the receiving process to be implemented. (Alternatively, some managers arrange with suppliers for the receiving steps to be undertaken after delivery personnel leave, with the understanding that delivery invoices will be adjusted retroactively if product problems are noted.)

---

cause of their much higher cost, the charge for this item is considered a **"stores"** expense. Some properties using manual control systems calculate a daily food cost by summing "directs" delivered that day and "stores" that are issued from storage areas.

SPECIAL RECEIVING CONCERNS

Procedures for receiving are influenced by numerous concerns.

Ensuring Quality

You have learned that it does little good to develop purchase specifications describing product quality requirements unless these specifications are then used during the receiving process to confirm that incoming products meet those quality requirements. Experienced purchasing professionals recognize that the property will pay for the quality of products identified in the purchase specification even if this quality is not received. It is, then, very important that receiving personnel be able to recognize the desired and actual quality of all products coming into the operation with a priority established for the "A" items (those relatively few products that involve the property's largest financial commitment).

An exhaustive list of ways to confirm quality would be difficult to develop because it would depend upon those items being received by a specific property. For example, Chapters 13 and 14 relating to, respectively, entrées (meat, poultry, game, and seafood) and produce, dairy, and egg products, note special quality requirements for these items that would be important *if* your operation is using one or more of them. These chapters also list numerous Web site sources for additional information that can be useful in developing a property's specifications.

Recall that a property's purchase specifications (see Chapter 4) may include a description of procedures to be used during receiving to help confirm that quality requirements are addressed.

Key Term

Stores (food cost)   A food product that is charged to daily food costs on the day it is issued from a storage area.

THE SUPPLIER'S SIDE (11.1)

"Insider" Tips on Purchasing: From the Supplier's Perspective

Question: Everyone says that it is very important for receiving personnel to check incoming products before the delivery invoice is signed. Although this is correct, shouldn't suppliers wanting to improve or maintain the relationship with purchasers make concessions if problems are noted after the delivery invoice has been signed? Can't suppliers just absorb the cost and/or pass them on back to their own sources in the distribution channel?

Answer: Most suppliers recognize that there are likely to be occasional instances where human error can yield oversights about products that should have been refused by receiving personnel but, instead, are accepted. Reputable suppliers are not likely to create difficulties about the "letter of the law" that typically applies when ownership is assumed by the buyer.

These types of problems can become much more extensive and expensive when, for example, capital equipment items are received. Here's an example: An item of food production equipment is valued at several thousand dollars and is delivered to a hotel by a freight company that transported it directly from the manufacturer. An employee signs for the equipment without knowing what to check for, how to properly receive the item, or realizing the need to alert someone with receiving knowledge about the delivery. Two days later, the equipment supplier is notified that the equipment is damaged, and a replacement request is made. The supplier does not know whether the equipment was shipped in damaged condition, the problem occurred during cross-country transport, and/or after it arrived at the hotel. Neither the manufacturer nor the freight company will assume responsibility (for the delivery invoice), and the supplier would not be "reimbursed" by anyone for a several thousand dollar "refund" or "repurchase." What would a reasonable business person, including the hospitality purchaser, expect the supplier to do?

Question: What is your advice from the supplier's perspective about how the receiving practices of a typical hospitality operation can be improved?

Answer: First, develop, implement, and supervise to ensure that effective receiving practices are consistently used. Second, recognize the value-added services that reputable suppliers can provide. For example, simply ask suppliers about: (1) general receiving practices that should be used, and (2) specific factors to look for as specific products are being received. Reputable suppliers want to provide products meeting a property's specification at a reasonable price. It is to their (the suppliers') benefit to educate hospitality buyers about how less-reputable suppliers can offer lower prices, provide still-lower quality products, and benefit themselves while doing a disservice to other suppliers and the hospitality buyer.

Effective receiving personnel are able to determine whether incoming products meet quality requirements. Sometimes this involves determining that a **"slack out seafood"** item is being represented as a fresh product. At other times, they can determine that the lengthy and sometimes confusing names of imported wines do not match those on the property's purchase order. They also know to check the expiration dates on containers of applicable items and understand that produce in the center of a shipping container may not be of the same quality as those on top levels (which are more visible). As noted earlier, purposeful fraud and inadvertent error have the same effect on the operation: products will be paid for that cannot be used and will not, therefore, generate revenues.

Key Term

Slack out seafood   Seafood that has been frozen and is then thawed and represented to be fresh so that it can be sold at a higher price than if it were in a frozen market form.

Technology and Receiving

This chapter, especially Figure 11.3 and its discussion about receiving procedures, has identified basic procedures that should be incorporated into any receiving process regardless of whether it is a manual system or has been computerized to the greatest extent possible with current technology. As you'll learn throughout this book, many procedures at every step in the procurement process can be, and increasingly are, computerized. The purpose is to provide more accurate data and reports useful for decision making and to free managers' time that would otherwise be needed for mundane record-keeping tasks.

How has technology affected receiving tasks? First of all, "paperwork," can be eliminated and the resulting "communication problems" that often occur reduced. For example, traditional hardcopies of purchase orders that identify a property's purchase commitments to suppliers can be electronically routed to receiving personnel for subsequent use when products are received (Step 1 in Figure 11.3). Wireless technology allows receiving personnel to check incoming products without the need to print a copy of the purchase order for on-site use. Those who purchase in very large volumes can specify **bar code** labels to be used on the containers of incoming products to enable quantity and cost information to be scanned by receiving personnel and "automatically" entered into the property's inventory management system. Almost all case products are now shipped with bar codes. Properties of any size with bar code readers and accompanying software programs can use bar code technology to assist with purchasing and inventory management.

Radio frequency identification (RFID) technology uses wireless transponders affixed to the products in inventory. These systems "expand" applications beyond noting product inventory information applicable to specific locations (where bar codes are read). They also enable wireless tracking of inventory in real time throughout the specific property.

Bar code scanning technology is available to help hospitality managers count quantities and assess values of products in inventory.

Spike Mafford/Getty Images, Inc.-Photodisc.

Key Terms

Bar code   Numerous machine-readable rectangular bars and spaces arranged in a specific way to represent the letters, numbers, and other symbols used to identify a product.

Radio frequency identification (RFID)   An electronic wireless tracking system that uses a transmitter to provide noncontact and automatic location of stock throughout the hospitality operation.

Internet Purchasing Assistant (11.1)

Bar code and radio frequency identification (RFID) technology enables managers to obtain and track desired information for product inventories at a much faster and more accurate pace than is possible using manual paper systems.

To learn more about bar coding and RFID systems for the hospitality industry, review the following Web sites:

Barcoding, Inc.—www.barcoding.com
IntelliTrack—www.intellitrack.com
ASAP Systems—www.asapsystems.com (Click on "Solutions")
eBarcode—www.ebarcode.com (Catalog of bar coding hardware)

A review of these sources will provide an overview of available technology and suggest numerous applications for inventory management beginning at the point of receiving.

Technology enables electronic versions of purchase specifications, schedules of suppliers expected to make deliveries on specified dates, and communication between user department, purchasing, accounting, and receiving personnel to be more conveniently transmitted. Also, information from daily invoices can be electronically summarized on daily receiving reports (see Figure 11.5) that generate information needed for daily food costing or other purposes.

Security Concerns

Security concerns at times of receiving relate to any reason why the property does not receive the products it has ordered and agreed to pay for. Effective receiving personnel guard against problems such as:

- *Short weights.* A carton containing, for example, 45 pounds of fresh steaks should be weighed. Ideally, steaks will be removed from the shipping carton to determine their exact weight. The problem of container weight (which the property does not want to pay for!) becomes more significant when fresh seafood or fresh poultry is packed in heavy, waxed cardboard containers encasing the product in shaved ice. Then the weight of the container and its packing can be quite heavy, and product removal for weighing is very necessary.
- *Assorted contents.* A carton containing 30 pounds of ground beef and 20 pounds of preportioned steaks will weigh the same (50 pounds) as a carton containing 20 pounds of ground beef and 30 pounds of fresh-cut steaks, even though the value of the former container is much less than that of the latter container. Different items must be weighed separately because of their different costs.
- *Missing items.* The use of proper receiving procedures will identify these type of problems. However, a suggestion from the delivery person to "Just sign the delivery invoice; I'll deliver additional products without putting it on the invoice next time," cannot be heeded. First of all, the same receiving person may not be on duty or may forget when the next delivery is made. Also, a delivery person is unlikely to have the authority to request that products not listed on delivery invoices be placed on the delivery truck.

On-the-Job Challenges in Purchasing (11.2)

"I'm really in a hurry, Scottie, because my truck broke down this morning and I've got lots of people on my route waiting for their deliveries. Just like you guys, they're prepping for the big football weekend, and every minute counts." Freddy was a delivery person for Swanson Produce and was talking to the storeroom manager for the Big Time Restaurant. Scottie's duties included product receiving, and he was now involved in this task.

"You know, Scottie," Freddy continued, "You folks pay more attention to the products you receive than just about anybody else on my route. I guess I see the importance of what you're doing, but you hardly ever find any problems, and you know that we always take care of everything when you do. I think just this once you should sign the delivery invoice, and let me go on my way. Everyone will be happy including me; I want to see my son's ball game, it's an early one: 5:30 tonight."

"Thanks for the compliment about our receiving procedures, and I share your concern that everyone else on your route must have," said Scottie. "I really do know because our cooks have been waiting during your two-hour delivery delay, and I know what they were thinking and what they said!"

"I don't know what to do, Freddy, because everything you say makes sense. However, we've got procedures to follow here, and I'm supposed to use them without exception."

"Well, I think you should make everybody happy, and sign the ticket. I just know there isn't any problem," replied Fred, who was starting to sound increasingly frustrated and anxious.

Case Study Questions

1. What would you do at this moment if you were Scottie? Defend your response.
2. Is this problem (a late delivery) a situation that should normally be anticipated, and for which a policy and procedure should be developed? Why or why not?
3. Assume you were the property's general manager, and you walked into the receiving area while this situation was evolving. What would you say and/or do? What, if any, alternatives are available to resolve this situation?

PURCHASING PROS NEED TO KNOW (11.2)

The receiving procedures described above may be modified for multi-unit organizations. For example, recall that product orders for individual units in a chain may be forwarded to, and cumulated by, purchasing staff in a centralized location. Orders are sent out for bid and awarded to a specific supplier with knowledge of the organization's standard purchase specifications, and deliveries are made to individual properties.

Incoming products may be accompanied by a delivery invoice. Receiving procedures similar to those just discussed may be used. There are, however, two other alternatives:

- A copy of the delivery invoice may be routed to the centralized purchasing office, where it is later "matched" with the delivery invoice that accompanied the order and which was routed through the property to the centralized purchasing office.
- A **blind receiving** method might be used when a purchase order indicating the products, but not the quantities, is sent to the receiving personnel in each property, who can then note the incoming quantities of each product by count or weight. This information is routed to the central purchasing office, where it is matched with the applicable delivery invoice indicating the quantities delivered, and then sent to the central purchasing office.

Key Term

Blind receiving A receiving method in which receiving personnel are aware of the products, but not quantities, delivered. Receiving personnel forward the information about product count and/or weight to the central office, where information is matched with a delivery invoice sent by the supplier.

A potentially much more significant security-related problem at the time of receiving occurs when delivery personnel gain access to nonpublic areas of the hospitality operation. Consider, for example, the possibility of theft when they are in storage areas (especially where liquor is stored) or, even worse, if they gain access to back-of-house corridors and employee-only elevators in hotels. Then access to other storage areas and even guest rooms may be possible, and employees or guests could be harmed by people who should not be **trespassing** in these areas.

Multi-unit and very large hospitality operations may use an automated invoice review system, which highlights the products for which prices have increased beyond a specified amount between orders or over a specified range of dates. Products with accelerated price increases can then be evaluated in efforts to control them: Are the prices correct? Are specifications still appropriate? Should a new source of supply be investigated? (Invoice price analysis is sometimes outsourced to a service provider that performs just this or other purchasing services for the organization.)

STORING ESSENTIALS

We'll begin our study of product storage concerns by discussing the personnel, areas, and storage tools and equipment involved in the activity.

Storeroom Personnel

In small properties, storeroom personnel are likely to be the same people who receive products. By contrast, very large hospitality organizations may have people with specialized storeroom management responsibilities. Storeroom employees must have the same basic qualities as those who receive the products, including the knowledge required to maintain sanitation standards and to use appropriate technology. They must be able to perform required physical tasks (recall our earlier discussion about the Americans with Disabilities Act) and to resolve the numerous storage-related challenges that can occur. Their interest in performing as a committed member of the operation's team is also a prerequisite for successful performance.

Storeroom personnel may be involved in the inventory procedures discussed later in this chapter, and they will likely be responsible for product **issuing** to user personnel in the food production and beverage operations departments.

Storage Area

The location of storage areas is of concern. The ideal location of storage space is close to the receiving area and between the receiving and food/beverage production areas. However, the ideal arrangement from a work-flow perspective has at least one potential disadvantage in free-standing properties: It may be easier for employees to steal items from unlocked storage areas when they leave the property through its back door. Also, storage areas are frequently affected by restaurant

---

Key Terms

Trespass   Unlawful (without permission) entry of a person onto the property of another person.

Issuing   The process of moving products from storage areas to the point of use (place of production).

Special controls are necessary to prevent theft of alcoholic beverages while they are being stored.
Getty Images-Stockbyte

remodeling, which can occur several times (or more) during the life of a building. Sometimes, for example, frozen storage space is relocated to outside the building to convert interior space for other uses. Sometimes, as well, storage space is moved to very inaccessible spaces, including on different levels of the building than that used for food preparation and/or service. Hopefully, managers recognize that storage space should be an integral part of the work flow patterns, and it should not be relegated to "leftover" space.

Small foodservice operations may have one dry storage area ranging in size from a few shelves to a small room and a small (several-door) refrigerator and freezer. In contrast, large-volume operations may have separate dry storage areas for foods and alcoholic beverages and multiple walk-in freezers and refrigerators. Large hotels may have several dry, refrigerated, and frozen storage areas in different locations throughout the property. The need for storage space in any property relates to production requirements and the frequency of product deliveries.

Storage Tools and Equipment

Shelving units are a major item of storage equipment. These are typically removable and adjustable in small refrigerators and freezers, but are frequently mobile units when used in walk-ins and dry storage areas. Metal shelving is easy to clean and contributes to proper air circulation. Frequently, local sanitation codes require that shelving units keep stored food or beverage products at least six inches off the floor and six inches away from the walls to allow for air circulation and to reduce the possibility of rodent infestation.

Pallet storage is often used in large operations to allow products to be stored in the same containers in which they were shipped. This practice avoids the "double-handling" that would otherwise occur if products were removed from their cases, placed on shelving units, and then later placed on mobile transport carts when issued. Transport equipment including, perhaps, carts, dollies, and rolling bins (for flour and sugar in properties with large on-site baking operations) may also be needed. Also, computer hardware, even in a wireless environment, is increasingly available in storage areas.

Internet Purchasing Assistant (11.2)

Shelving units are an important concern in foodservice operations to maximize storage capacity while making it easy to retrieve necessary items. To review the Web site of one of the largest manufacturers of commercial shelving, go to: www.metro.com

At the home page, click on "Storage." You'll note a wide range of information about, and pictures of, numerous storage systems.

BASIC STORING PROCEDURES

There are three basic types of storage in foodservice operations (see endnote 1):

- *Dry storage (50°F–70°F; 10°C–21.1°C).* This is for grocery items such as canned goods, cereal products such as flour, and alcoholic beverage products such as liquor.
- *Refrigerated storage (less than 41°F; 5°C).* This is for items such as fresh meat, produce, and dairy products.
- *Frozen storage (less than 0°F; –17.8°C).* This is for items such as frozen meats, seafood, french fries, and other vegetables purchased in this market form.

Figure 11.6 reviews the storage guidelines for some commonly used food products.

Product	Storage Period	
	In Refrigerator 40°F (4°C)	In Freezer 0°F (−18°C)
Fresh meats:		
Beef: Ground	1–2 days	3–4 months
Steaks and roasts	3–5 days	6–12 months
Pork: Chops	3–5 days	4–6 months
Ground	1–2 days	3–4 months
Roasts	3–5 days	4–6 months
Cured meats:		
Lunch meat	3–5 days	1–2 months
Sausage	1–2 days	1–2 months
Gravy	1–2 days	2–3 months
Fish:		
Lean (such as cod, flounder, haddock)	1–2 days	up to 6 months
Fatty (such as blue, perch, salmon)	1–2 days	2–3 months
Chicken: Whole	1–2 days	12 months
Parts	1–2 days	9 months
Giblets	1–2 days	3–4 months
Dairy Products:		
Swiss, brick, processed cheese	3–4 weeks	*
Milk	5 days	1 month
Ice cream, ice milk	–	2–4 months
Eggs: fresh in shell	3 weeks	–
hard-boiled	1 week	–

*Cheese can be frozen, but freezing will affect the texture and taste.

FIGURE 11.6 How Long Will It Keep?

(Sources: Food Marketing Institute for fish and dairy products; USDA for all other foods.)

Some foodservice operations use additional storage areas, including **broken case** storage rooms, and sometimes provide for relatively extensive storage in workstations, including food preparation and serving areas.

Product **marking** is often an early step in the storage process. This involves marking information, including the date of receipt and invoice cost, on the actual product containers in storage. This helps managers to check stock rotation (products in storage the longest should be used first) and to assess product cost information for **issue requisitions** that can be used to calculate daily food and beverage costs and to assign values when inventory costs are determined.

Quality Concerns

Products can deteriorate in quality even under the best environmental conditions when, for example, appropriate storage times are exceeded.

Product quality is also affected when the environment is not properly maintained. Proper storage temperatures should be maintained and monitored with appropriate and accurate thermometers. Raw food products should be stored beneath cooked/ready-to-eat foods. Items should not be stored under water or sewer lines located overhead because they can be a source of contamination. Foods should never be stored near sanitizing, cleaning, or other chemicals. If practical, chemicals should be stored in a different room to reduce misidentification and related problems.

Managers and their purchasing staff who emphasize a clean storage environment, minimize the time that products are in storage, and regularly monitor storage areas are taking important steps to manage product quality during times of storage.

Record-Keeping Concerns

Several record-keeping concerns should be addressed as storeroom-related procedures are developed. First, inventory cost calculations must be addressed because costs must be assessed for several control-related reasons and to develop income and balance sheet statements.

Many food service operations make these calculations manually using forms similar to that illustrated in Figure 11.7 as they conduct a **physical inventory.**

Key Terms

Broken case (storage)   Some large operations issue products such as canned goods in full purchase units even if only partial units are needed. If four cans of vegetables are removed from a case containing six cans, the two remaining cans are kept in small storage areas for quick access as needed.

Marking (product storage)   The act of recording information about the date of product receipt and product cost information on the containers of products in inventory.

Issue requisition   A document used to identify the products, and their quantities, removed from storage areas when formal inventory control procedures are used.

Inventory (physical)   A procedure used to determine the quantity and cost of inventory on hand at a specific point in time (typically end-of-month). Information is used to develop income and balance sheet statements and for product control purposes.

Item	Purchase Unit	No. of Units[1]	Purchase Price	Total Price
Green beans	Case	3	$26.50	$79.50

[1]If local health codes permit, items should be stored in the same containers in which they were purchased. This can reduce double handling and provide a convenient way to mark information about the date of receipt and product costs. It is also, for example, easier to count one case of six #10 cans of fruits or vegetables than it is to count six individual cans of the product.

FIGURE 11.7 Physical Inventory Form

When reviewing Figure 11.7, note that there are three cases of green beans in the storage area with a purchase price of $26.50, and a total price (inventory cost) of $79.50 (3 cases [×] $26.50 = $79.50). Ideally, the count of this item, along with that related to all other items in storage, is undertaken by two people. One might be a manager, and the second should be someone not involved with ongoing storage responsibilities. One person can count inventory units, and the second can complete the form.

When the inventory valuation process is completed at the end of the month, the restaurant manager will have the information required to calculate the actual food costs for that month, and as well, he or she will know the beginning inventory value needed to calculate food costs for the subsequent month.

Inventory counts are also important to determine actual beverage costs. However, the cost of this inventory is typically "defined" as the total cost of beverages in both central storage and behind-bar areas, so a more extensive inventory assessment process is necessary.

Internet Purchasing Assistant (11.3)

Handheld wireless technology is available for hospitality managers to quickly and efficiently enter physical inventory counts and upload this information into the property's inventory management system. To review details of one company's system, go to www.culinarysoftware.com/ This site also has information about optical scanning with bar codes, and you will learn about other ways that modern technology can assist with inventory control.

Internet Purchasing Assistant (11.4)

Technology is available to assist restaurant and bar managers with the task of calculating the cost of beverage inventories in behind-bar areas. For an example of one system, go to www.accubar.com.

As you review this information, think about its speed and accuracy (advantages) as well as other concerns, including cost and acceptance by beverage managers who favor more traditional methods.

Item: <u>Sirloin Steaks (6-oz.)</u>

Date	No. of Purchase Units		Balance
	In	Out	
Start			37
9/7/xx	–	25	12
9/8/xx	35	20	27

FIGURE 11.8   Perpetual Inventory Form

A second record-keeping issue relates to the need to maintain **perpetual inventory** information for selected products so managers and purchasing staff can know, at any point in time, the quantity of products available in inventory.

Although it may not be practical or even useful for many food and beverage operations to maintain all products under a perpetual inventory system, this will likely be a useful tactic for the relatively few and expensive "A" items. Because alcoholic beverages are expensive and theft-prone, they are prime candidates for control using a perpetual inventory storage system.

A perpetual inventory system works just like someone uses a personal checkbook: As money (food and beverage products) is deposited in the bank (brought into the storeroom), the balance in the checking account (food and/or beverage products in the storeroom) is increased; conversely, as money is withdrawn from the bank (food and/or beverage products are issued to production areas), the balance of money (food and beverage products) in the bank (storeroom) decreases. Therefore, at any point in time, the restaurant manager is aware of the quantity of products available in inventory.

Figure 11.8 shows the format for a perpetual inventory form.

Managers must first identify those "A" value and other items appropriate for monitoring via the use of perpetual inventory system. When reviewing Figure 11.8, note that there were 37 individual (6-ounce) portions of this item on-hand when the new form was begun. On the first date (9/7), 25 steaks were issued, leaving a balance of only 12 steaks in inventory. On the next date (9/8), 35 steaks were purchased, and 20 steaks were issued. This left a net balance of 15 steaks, which increased the inventory balance to 27 portions: The calculation:

For 9/8:

12 steaks (beginning balance) + 35 (in) − 20 (out) = 27 steaks (ending balance)

On an occasional basis, the general manager, chef, and/or purchasing agent should physically spot-check (count) the number of sirloin steaks to ensure that the number of portions actually available in inventory is equal to the balance noted on the perpetual inventory form.

Key Term

Perpetual inventory   A system that tracks all products entering and being issued from storage areas so managers know, on an ongoing basis, the amount of product that should be available in storage areas.

PURCHASING PROS NEED TO KNOW (11.3)

Must all foodservice operations use both a physical and perpetual inventory system? The technically correct answer is "no," but all commercial operations must report income (profit and/or loss) information to regulatory authorities for tax purposes. Food cost is an expense that reduces the organization's profitability and, therefore, must be reported. However, some properties using a cash accounting system assume their food costs to be the value of the checks written to pay for food purchases during the accounting period. By contrast, properties using an accrual accounting system make a cost of goods sold calculation (Beginning Inventory [+] Purchases [–] Ending Inventory) as part of the process to calculate food costs. These operations must, then, use a physical inventory system.

What about perpetual inventory management? No food and/or beverage operation is required by taxing authorities to maintain perpetual inventory balances. However, most would benefit from their use for, at least, the "A" items in efforts to manage and control these expensive products more closely.

Typically, as operations grow larger, they use accrual accounting systems (physical inventories become necessary) and, as well, they take advantage of the benefits derived from the use of perpetual inventory methods.

Another record-keeping concern applicable to storage involves the calculation of **inventory turnover rates** that measure the frequency with which food and beverage products are ordered and sold. It answers the question, "How many times per accounting period must the quantity of food and beverages on hand be purchased to generate the food and beverage revenues for the accounting period?"

The basic formula for the inventory turnover rate is:

Inventory Turnover Rate = Cost of Goods (Food or Beverage) Sold ÷ Average Inventory ($ value)

(The same calculation is used for food [Cost of Food Sold] and beverages [Cost of Beverages Sold]). Some managers calculate a separate inventory turnover rate for beer, wine, and spirits. Others combine all alcoholic beverages into a single turnover calculation. Inventory turnover rates in the hospitality industry are typically computed monthly, but other periods (e.g., every two weeks) may also be useful for a specific property as long as the amount of time covered by the analysis is consistent.

Let's examine how the turnover rate for food is established. Assume the manager takes a physical inventory of all food products in inventory and finds the following:

- food inventory (beginning of accounting period)   = $129,500
- food purchases (during accounting period)   = $276,000
- food inventory (end of accounting period)   = ($127,500)
- cost of goods sold: food (used during accounting period) = $278,000

Key Term

Inventory turnover   A mathematic calculation that measures the frequency with which food and beverage products are purchased and sold:

$$\text{Inventory turnover rate} = \frac{\text{Cost of Goods (Food or Beverage)}}{\text{Average Inventory}}$$

The food inventory turnover rate equals:

$$\frac{\text{Cost of Goods Sold : Food}}{[\text{Beginning Food Inventory} + \text{Ending Food Inventory}] \div 2}$$

$$\frac{\$278,000}{\$129,500 + \$127,500 \div 2}$$

$$\frac{\$278,000}{\$128,500}$$

2.16 turns

The above result indicates that the dollar value of its food inventory for this operation turns over approximately 2.16 times per month. In other words, on average, the food products in inventory will last about 14 days (30 days in month ÷ 2.16 turns). This rate, by itself, may not be especially helpful to the manager or purchaser. Some managers believe that a turnover rate below 1.00 each month indicates excessive inventory levels, and turnover rates above 3.00 times may indicate that too few products are kept on hand (which could result in unnecessary product stock-outs). The ideal turnover rate for any operation, however, must be evaluated in view of: (1) its goals, and (2) the combined value of inventory that managers and purchasers determine should always be available.

Regardless of the target established for the operation, when the rate is calculated each fiscal period, it becomes possible to note any changes between fiscal periods. Why is the rate increasing (or decreasing)? What are the implications of this change? What is the desired trend that the turnover rate should take? The answers to these and related questions can help to better control the inventory and the costs associated with it.

Security Concerns

Food and beverage products available in inventory have been purchased with the intent that they will be used to generate revenues. If, instead, they are stolen, money will have been spent, thus expenses will have been increased, but there will be no resulting revenue and, therefore, costs will be greater than necessary, and profitability will be lower than expected.

Storage areas should be considered bank vaults, and procedures used for storage should address the question, "How should money be managed in a bank vault?" Simple procedures such as keeping products in lockable areas with walls

Security concerns are important for the storage of alcoholic beverage products in behind-bar areas.

Joe Cornish © Dorling Kindersley

extending to the ceiling, and limiting access to storage areas to authorized persons, can help reduce the incidence of employee theft. Differences between perpetual inventory quantities of "A" items and the quantities actually available in storage should be investigated. Some properties use employee package inspection programs to reduce the possibility of unauthorized "carry outs."

When it is not practical to have full-time storeroom clerks, there are some reasonable alternatives. Consider, for example, keeping storage areas locked with scheduled issues at which time the manager, chef, and/or beverage manager issue items from storage. Alternatively, consider keeping "A" items locked and under perpetual inventory, and allow more general access to the storage areas used for other, less expensive and less theft-prone items.

SPECIAL STORING CONCERNS

This final section of the chapter addresses two special storing concerns: technology applications and storing requirements in nontraditional purchasing systems.

Technology and Storing

Computerized applications that have modified the traditional product ordering system (see Chapter 10) and that influence product receiving systems (discussed above) also have changed the way many hospitality operations manage inventory. The use of bar coding and RFID inventory systems has reduced much of the manual work required to maintain inventories. For example, when items enter inventory through the receiving process, quantity and cost balances automatically increase. Conversely, when products are issued, inventory quantities and costs are automatically decreased. The usage rates that are derived are very useful in controlling food and beverage costs and planning purchase quantities, and they can be generated with relatively little manual input. Outputs of these computerized processes also allow perpetual inventory balances to be maintained with minimal effort.

Physical inventories undertaken to verify the accuracy of perpetual inventory balances can be automated with optical scanning. Manual counts can be taken with entries into a personal digital assistant (PDA) that is connected wirelessly to the computer system or, alternatively, data can be electronically transferred after the unit is connected to the computer. It is no longer necessary to print out or carry issue requisitions to enable storeroom clerks to retrieve products to be issued to a user department. Instead, they can use wireless hardware to determine the items and quantities to be retrieved from the storeroom for issue. In large storerooms or storehouses, these electronic systems can even indicate the shortest travel routes to collect items.

Records of items nearing expiration dates, information about items that have been discarded because of spoilage, and listings of items that have reached order points are additional examples of technology applications affected by storeroom management.

Technology affects storeroom management in at least one other way: Computerized locking systems, similar to those used for hotel guest room doors, are in increasingly common use. They indicate who entered the storage area (the person to whom the key was issued), and the date, time of entry, and length of time in the storage area. This information is of significant assistance to managers desiring to control and monitor storage area access.

Surveillance equipment is now relatively inexpensive and is increasingly used to record who has entered storage areas.

Storing in Nontraditional Purchasing Systems

Traditional procurement systems have been focused on purchasing, receiving, and storing the quantity of items needed for a relatively short period of time. The gen-

HIGH-TECH PURCHASING (11.1)

This chapter has reviewed some exciting ways that technology can assist purchasers and user department personnel as they manage product receiving and storing tasks. The chapter presented two separate discussions in two different sections of the chapter. In practice, however, a property typically uses a single software package for both applications, which are integral components of most automated purchasing systems.

Chapter 10 listed some organizations offering procurement and inventory management software for the hospitality industry. The following are some additional businesses providing these products. A review of the Web sites listed in this and the previous chapter will provide a fairly comprehensive overview of the advantages and applications of technology for a property's procurement activities.

- Cost Guard—www.costguard.com
- Eatec Corporation—www.eatec.com
- Food Software—www.FoodSoftware.com
- EGS Enggist & Grandjean Software SA—www.calcmenu.com
- IntelliTrack—www.intellitrack.net

eral rule-of-thumb was that, the larger the quantity of products purchased, the greater would be the space (cubic footage) requirements of applicable storage areas.

Modern purchasing systems that emphasize a more fully integrated network with suppliers are drastically altering this traditional model. In fact, there can almost be an inverse relationship between the quantity of product for which purchase commitments are made and the storage capacities that are required. Consider, for example, just-in-time and supplier-managed systems in which purchasers make commitments for large product quantities over an extended time period with deliveries made to the property on a very frequent basis. Although some storage space will likely always be necessary, these systems reduce on-space requirements significantly. In new operations, space savings result in capital savings or, at least, allow capital expenditures to be diverted to other areas of the organization. In existing operations, new systems that reduce storage capabilities may be used for other creative purposes. Can an existing office space be relocated for a small banquet area in a restaurant or for a retail shop in a hotel? Can an employee dining room be relocated to the now unused storage space with additional purposeful use found for the space currently used for employee dining?

Only large hotel, restaurant, and other hospitality operations have dedicated loading docks and receiving equipment necessary to handle large-volume deliveries.

Mark Richards/PhotoEdit Inc.

Purchasing Resources on the Internet

In addition to the Web sites referenced in this chapter's "Internet Purchasing Assistant," the following sites provide detailed information to enhance your purchasing knowledge and skills.

Purchasing Resources on the Internet

Site	Information About
www.traulsen.com	Commercial refrigeration equipment
www.ballyrefboxes.com	Commercial refrigeration equipment
www.food-management.com/article/12418	Prevention of storeroom theft
www.orkincommercial.com	Pest control in commercial foodservice operations including storage areas (Click on "Industry Solutions" and then "Foodservice"; Also, click on "Services" and then "Pest Management")
www.restaurantreport.com	Receiving practices for independent restaurants. (Enter "receiving" in the site's search box)
www.barvision.com	Beverage inventory management system
www.hiendsecurity.com	Numerous types of security concerns.
www.mt.com	Storeroom receiving scales (Enter "receiving scales" in the site's search box)

Key Terms

receiving 253
storing 253
cost of goods sold 256
income statement 256
balance sheet 256
asset (current) 256
Bona Fide Occupational
   Qualification
   (BFOQ) 258

pallet 259
credit memo 261
receiving report 262
direct (food cost) 262
stores (food cost) 263
slack out seafood 264
bar code 265
radio frequency identifi-
   cation (RFID) 265

blind receiving 267
trespass 268
issuing 268
broken case
   (storage) 271
marking (product
   storage) 271
issue requisition 271
inventory (physical) 271

perpetual inventory 273
inventory turnover
   rates 274

Think It Through

1. The chapter makes the point that the property will pay for the quality of products identified in the purchase specification even if this quality is not received. What does this statement mean? Do you agree or disagree? Why?

2. The need for recognizing and accepting only products meeting the property's quality requirements has been emphasized throughout this chapter. Assume the following situation: A special order product (of which none is available in inventory) has just been delivered for a large banquet this evening. The receiving clerk has noticed that it is of a slightly lower quality than that which has been ordered. The chef is notified, and she agrees with the receiving clerk's quality analysis. What should be done? Defend your response. What would you do in the future to reduce the potential for reoccurrence of this type of problem?

3. You are the food and beverage controller in the accounting department of a very large hotel that typically has a receiving clerk and a storeroom clerk on duty during the weekdays. A recent physical inventory count shows a one-case (12-bottle)

difference in the inventory balance of a specific alcoholic beverage. The receiving clerk said the case was brought to the storeroom. However, the storeroom clerk said he did not receive it so he did not enter it into inventory records. What is the problem? How can it be resolved? What are exemplary procedures to separate the duties of these two people? How, if at all, can technology help to reduce this problem in the future?

4. This chapter notes several ways that technology can be used to assist in the product receiving and storing functions. Who should be involved in planning for the increased use of technology, if any, in a hospitality operation? What factors should be considered as decisions about replac-

ing manual with computerized systems are made?

5. You are the director of purchasing for a small (15-unit) pizza organization that uses a centralized procurement system. Product orders from each unit are routed to your office, and your staff combines orders, selects suppliers, and arranges for products to be delivered to each individual unit. Your accounting office pays suppliers for all products delivered to all of the units. What procedures would you want in place to ensure that each property received the products that were ordered on their behalf? How would you confirm the payment amount that is due to each supplier for products received by each unit?

Team Fun

Your team has been requested to advise the food and beverage controller of a large hotel about improvements in record-keeping systems for the property's centralized alcoholic beverage (beer, wine, and spirits) storage procedures. The advice is to be given by submitting a standard operating procedure (SOP) manual describing the procedures that should always be in use for handling these products to maximize quality and to minimize the possibility of theft or pilferage. Each team will be given one assignment to help in the development of this SOP manual.

1. The assignment of the first team is to develop a detailed list of procedures that should be fol-

lowed when these products are received in the receiving area by a designated receiving clerk.

2. The assignment of the second team is to develop a detailed list of cleaning and sanitation tasks applicable to the beverage storage area.

3. The assignment of the third team is to develop a policy and procedure that should be used during off-hours (no storeroom or receiving clerk is on duty) to retrieve the necessary supplies for the bar operations in the event that additional products are needed.

Endnotes

1. This section is adapted from: Ninemeier, J. and Hayes, D. *Restaurant Operations Management: Principles and Practices.* Upper Saddle River, NJ: Pearson Prentice-Hall. 2006. (See Chapter 10.)

12

Procurement Accounting and Follow-Up

In This Chapter

In this chapter, you'll learn that paying suppliers for their products and services involves significantly more than just "writing a check." A great deal of communication is required between accounting, purchasing, and receiving personnel in preparation for vendor payment. For example, documentation, including copies of purchase orders and the suppliers' delivery invoices, must be routed from receiving to accounting personnel. Then document verification is required to confirm that product purchase agreements were complied with, and to ensure that arithmetic extensions are correct. Verified bills may be paid on a by-invoice and/or by-statement basis, and specific procedures for both of these payment methods are necessary and must be consistently followed.

Communication is also required between accounting and supplier personnel as needed credit memos are processed and as payments are made. Accounting staff should inform their purchasing peers about their relationships with suppliers because this is important input to supplier selection decisions made by purchasing staff.

A number of important payment policies and procedures will be reviewed in this chapter. However, perhaps none is more important than a trail of responsibility to confirm that all purchases have been approved by authorized management personnel. Payment approval procedures for single-unit properties and multi-unit organizations are addressed. Although electronic funds transfer (EFT) payment systems are evolving, most hospitality organizations still pay for purchases with traditional checks. Security concerns important in reducing opportunities for theft at the time of payment disbursements are detailed. Also, because some relatively minor low-value purchases may be made by cash, details about petty cash systems are also explained.

It is absolutely critical that accounting and purchasing personnel work closely and cooperatively as they perform their important functions. A final section of this chapter emphasizes the importance of this relationship.

■■■

Outline

Purchasing and the Accounting Process
Accounting Requires Documentation
    Documentation Is Critical
    Internal Documentation Flow
    Communication between Accounting and Suppliers
Payment Policies and Procedures
Special Accounting Concerns
    Payment Approval Procedures: Single-Unit Properties
    Payment Approval Procedures: Multi-Unit Organizations
    Petty Cash Systems

PURCHASING AND THE ACCOUNTING PROCESS

The role of the accounting department requires special attention in our discussion about procurement because all products and services ordered by the purchasing department must be paid for. Accounting activities are, therefore, an integral part of the procurement function.

In small hospitality organizations, the owner may be the property manager, purchaser, and bill payer. As organizations become larger, procurement and accounting tasks may be split into two support departments: purchasing and accounting. At this point, responsibilities for receiving and storage may be assumed by operations personnel or by purchasing staff. As the organization grows still larger, receiving and storage duties may be assumed by the accounting department to separate tasks as a security safeguard. Note that this **separation of duties** helps to reduce the possibilities of theft and/or fraud, which become more probable when one manager or department is responsible for combined functions. Procedures for effective receiving and storage are the same regardless of which department is responsible for the tasks.

Figure 12.1 (originally shown as Figure 1.4) identifies the steps in the procurement process as we have been discussing them. You'll note that this chapter on **accounting** relates to Step 9 in the figure. This step is vitally important because hospitality managers must ensure that they pay only for those products and services that they have ordered and which have been received.

The responsibilities of accountants in hospitality organizations extend far beyond their role in procurement.[1] However, because a large percentage of all revenues generated by a hotel, restaurant, or noncommercial foodservices operation is used to purchase required products and services, accounting personnel must give this aspect of their responsibility a very high priority.

When **accrual accounting systems** are used (as they are in all but the very smallest of **"Mom and Pop"** hospitality operations), the largest effect of purchasing-related transactions is on the balance sheet.

Figure 12.2 reviews how the balance sheet is affected when food products, supplies, and equipment are purchased for cash or on account.

Key Terms

Duties, separation of   The management control principle that ensures that no single person controls all steps in a process.

Accounting   The process of summarizing and reporting financial information related to the hospitality organization.

Accrual (accounting system)   An accounting system that matches the expenses incurred with revenues generated during the same accounting period (such as a month). This is done with the use of accounts receivables, accounts payables, and other accounts.

"Mom and Pop" (hospitality operation)   Industry jargon referring to a small and independently owned single-unit hotel or restaurant.

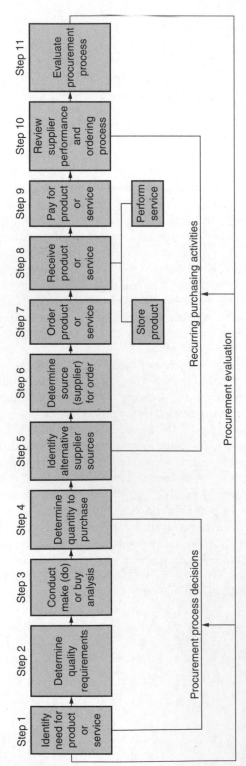

FIGURE 12.1 Steps in Procurement Process

Purchasing Activity	Effects
• Purchase food products or supplies (for cash)	Decrease cash (current asset) Increase inventory (current asset)
• Purchase food products or supplies (on account)	Increase **accounts payable (current liability)** Increase inventory (current asset)
• Purchase equipment (for cash)	Decrease cash (current asset) Increase **equipment (fixed asset)**
• Purchase equipment (on account)	Increase **notes payable** (current liability; for amount to be repaid within one year) Increase **long-term debt** (noncurrent part of equipment cost) Increase equipment (fixed asset)

FIGURE 12.2 Purchasing: Effect on Property's Balance Sheet

Figure 12.2 suggests that a hospitality operation has two basic ways to pay for its purchases: cash or on account. When cash is paid, the available cash on-hand that could otherwise be used for another purchase or other use is reduced. When a purchase is made on account, the amount owed to the supplier (accounts payable) is increased. Regardless of the method of payment for products and supplies, purchases increase the inventory (amount of product available).

When equipment is purchased for cash, the amount of available cash is reduced, and the applicable equipment account (a fixed asset) is increased. When equipment is purchased on account, part of the liability (that which must be paid within one year) is current and the remaining liability is long term. As with one's personal purchases, part of the payment for equipment may be for cash with the remainder paid for with short-term (current) or longer-term debt.

To this point, we have been discussing how accounting for purchasing activities affects the organization's balance sheet. However, the income statement is also directly affected by purchasing activities because the purchasing department, like all others, will incur expenses for direct labor (e.g., the director of purchasing and his or her staff) and all other **allocated** expenses. These costs increase a property's operating expenses and decrease its **operating income.**

Key Terms

Accounts payable   Money owed by the hospitality operation for products or services it has purchased but not yet paid for.

Current liability   An obligation that must be satisfied (paid) within one year of the balance sheet date.

Equipment   A fixed asset; also called capital equipment (see fixed asset).

Fixed asset   Resources of the hospitality operation that are tangible, material in amount, used in operations to generate revenue, and that will benefit the organization for more than one year into the future.

Notes payable   A current liability representing the amount of a long-term debt that must be repaid within one year of the balance sheet date.

Long-term debit   Debt that will not be paid within one year of the balance sheet date; also called noncurrent liability.

Allocate   The process of distributing expenses as applicable among departments within the hospitality organization.

Operating income   Income (profit) before interest and income taxes.

PURCHASING PROS NEED TO KNOW (12.1)

A restaurant owner who purchases food products valued at $1,000 does not incur an immediate $1,000 increase in food costs when an accrual accounting system is used. Instead, the cost of products or goods reported on the property's income statement are calculated on the basis of changes in inventory using the following calculation:

Value of beginning inventory (+) Purchases (−) Value of ending inventory = Product cost

Although there are numerous adjustments that can affect this "cost of goods sold" calculation, the activity of purchasing most immediately affects the value of inventory on the balance sheet rather than the product cost on the income statement.

Similarly, furniture, fixtures, and equipment, when purchased, affect a fixed asset account on the balance sheet that is expensed by a **depreciation** process to determine the amount applicable to an income statement for a specific period.

For details about the cost of goods-sold calculations, see: J. Ninemeier and D. Hayes, *Restaurant Operations Management: Principles and Practices.* Upper Saddle River, NJ: Pearson Prentice-Hall. 2006 (see Chapter 16).

ACCOUNTING REQUIRES DOCUMENTATION

The task of "paying the bills" incurred by purchasing obligations involves much more than assembling some paperwork and writing checks. You've learned that a significant amount of the revenue that accrues to a hospitality operation is spent as products and services required to generate that revenue are purchased. The saying, "Every penny counts!" has never been truer than it is today. Businesses must reduce costs without sacrificing quality, and wise hospitality managers look at the purchasing function as a prime way to do so. It is absolutely critical that all suppliers be paid what they are owed. However, it is equally important to ensure that they are not paid more than they are owed. The responsibility for ensuring that correct payments are made begins when initial product purchase decisions are made, continues as they are received and, as importantly, concludes when payments are made.

Documentation Is Critical

Figure 12.3, originally shown as Figure 1.7 and slightly modified to identify applicable **source documents,** illustrates the flow of documentation for the purchase of food and beverage products throughout a large hospitality organization and between it and its suppliers.

You have learned (in Chapter 10) about the interactions between the receiving and storage personnel and purchasing staff as additional quantities of products are required. Production staff inform storeroom personnel about their needs with an issue requisition. When inventory levels require additional quantities of product, storeroom personnel use a purchase requisition to inform purchasing staff members, who then use a request for price quotation to obtain prices from approved suppliers (see Chapter 8). A purchase order signifies order acceptance for a specific supplier, and a copy is provided to receiving and storeroom staff. When

---

Key Terms

Depreciation   The process used to determine the value of a fixed asset during a specific accounting period that is assumed to have been "used up" during that period to generate revenue applicable to the period.

Source document   The source of initial entry of financial information into an organization's accounting system.

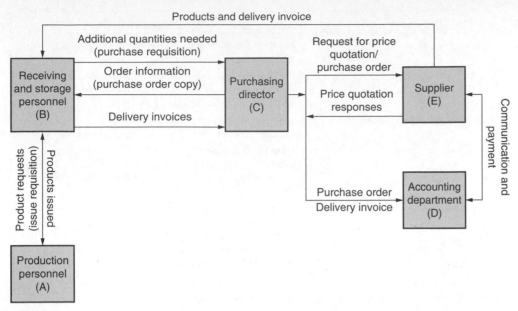

FIGURE 12.3   Basic Food and Beverage Purchasing Process in Large Hospitality Organizations

products are delivered, receiving personnel must match the applicable purchase order and delivery invoice with the incoming products, and these documents are then routed to the purchasing department. In this section, details about interactions between purchasing and accounting department staff and between accounting staff and suppliers at time of payment are addressed.

Internal Documentation Flow

Accounting personnel must prepare bills for payment, and the task requires communication, information (source documents), and coordination between purchasing, receiving, and accounting personnel. The process is basically the same regardless of whether a manual or electronic system that eliminates some hard copy "paperwork" is used. However, as noted earlier, a small organization has fewer specialized positions, and one or a very few persons must perform all purchasing- and accounting-related tasks.

Technology available for procurement begins to track information at the point of sale.

David Young-Wolff/PhotoEdit Inc.

Document	Purpose
Issue requisition	Used by production staff to request the withdrawal of products from storage areas.
Purchase requisition	Used by storeroom personnel to alert purchasing employees that additional quantities of products are required to replenish inventory levels.
Request for price quotation	Used by purchasing personnel to solicit prices from eligible suppliers for products of specified quality.
Purchase order	Used by purchasing personnel to formally order products from suppliers. Requests for price quotations and purchase orders may be combined into one document in some organizations.
Delivery invoice	Used by suppliers to indicate products (including quantities and prices) that are delivered to the hospitality operation. Purchasers must pay the amount specified by the delivery invoice after it is signed by a representative of the hospitality operation.

FIGURE 12.4 Review of Basic Purchasing-Related Documentation

Figure 12.4 reviews the basic types of documentation reviewed above. Each becomes increasingly important as the size of the hospitality operation increases, and as more specialized positions become involved in the procurement and accounting processes.

Let's consider what and how documentation is forwarded to accounting personnel in preparation for payment in varying sizes of hospitality operations:

- *Small hotel or restaurant; owner/manager present.* Products are ordered by the manager and may be received by him or her. A copy of the purchase order (or, in some cases a copy of the supplier's order form) and applicable delivery invoice is used by the owner/manager for payment purposes. The owner may pay the bill himself or herself or transfer documentation to a bookkeeper for payment.
- *Small hotel or restaurant; absentee owner.* In this situation, the manager of the property is employed by the owner. Procedures for purchasing and receiving may be undertaken by the manager and his or her staff with documentation routed to the bookkeeper for payment. However, the supplier may be requested to send a separate copy of each delivery invoice directly to the absentee owner or bookkeeper to enable reconciliation of delivered items by comparing both copies of the delivery invoice. This additional step recognizes the separation-of-duties principle discussed earlier in this chapter.
- *Large hospitality operation with separate purchasing and accounting departments.* As noted above, document flow becomes more formalized as the size of the operation increases, and Figure 12.3 reviews document flow in a large operation. A copy of the purchase order is sent from purchasing to receiving and storage personnel. Incoming orders are checked against the purchase order (which indicates the property's purchase commitments). The purchase order and signed delivery invoice are then routed to the purchasing department for reconciliation before being forwarded to the accounting department as authorization for payment. In some hospitality organizations, purchase orders and applicable delivery invoices are routed from receiving personnel to the chef, food service director, or hotel department manager who, in turn, forwards them to purchasing personnel. These staff members have significant knowledge about the needs of the organization, and they can review this documentation: "Do we normally purchase all of these items and in these quantities?" "Do prices seem reasonable and

Technology makes it easy for hospitality operations to pay invoices for products purchased by the property.
Terry Vine/Getty Images Inc.-Stone Allstock

in line with other recent purchases?" "Is the delivery invoice from one of our regular suppliers?"

Once documentation from purchasing personnel is received, accounting personnel have several responsibilities that are less likely to vary by size of the operation. However, when more people have been involved in processing documents as they move forward, the likelihood of "communication problems" that must be addressed as bills are prepared for payment increases.

Careful "auditing" of purchase and delivery documents will often identify and resolve most potential problems and enable bills to be paid when due. Concerns that are identified can then be corrected as accounting department personnel interact with the purchasing and/or receiving staff about the products ordered and received.

PURCHASING PROS NEED TO KNOW (12.2)

Purchasing pros know that the same basic procedures described for purchasing food and beverage products also applies for the purchase of furniture, fixtures, and equipment and other items. However, as the value of the purchases increases, additional steps may be required. For example, in some organizations, "large dollar" purchase orders are sent to the accounting department before orders are placed with suppliers. Accounting personnel can then confirm that these purchases have been budgeted for and approved. Also, required funds are then **encumbered** to help ensure that the purchases will not cause an "overbudget" situation.

Another example is when purchases exceeding a specified dollar value may require additional authorization from higher management levels, and checks written in excess of a designated amount may require the second authorization signature of a management executive.

Key Term

Encumbrance (accounting)   The act of setting aside (identifying) funds to be spent from a specific account to help ensure that any future purchases chargeable to that account will not bring it over budget.

Communication between Accounting and Suppliers

Accounting personnel will have reduced need to interact with suppliers about pricing and related concerns if proper documentation has been received from within-property sources. However, one potential problem that arises as bills are prepared for payment relates to credit memos that are issued when products are received.

Well-trained and observant receiving personnel may identify problems during delivery that must be corrected with a credit memo. Examples include:

- *Incorrect price charged.*   For example, the purchase order price is $3.17 per pound; the delivery invoice is $3.27 per pound.
- *Back order.*   For example, the product is not available and cannot be delivered, but included on the delivery invoice.
- *Short weight or count.*   For example, 30 cases per purchase order were ordered; 25 cases were received.
- *Items rejected because of unaccepted quality.*   For example, the items do not meet the purchase specification requirements and are rejected upon attempted delivery.

Depending on the property's policy, receiving staff may be empowered to sign credit memos relating to the first three problems noted above, but they may need to receive a "second opinion" from a chef or manager about perceived variances between the quality of products ordered (per purchase specifications) and what is delivered.

As you learned in Chapter 11, hospitality operations typically become responsible for products and obligated to pay for them when they take delivery. Unless there is contractual language to the contrary, this is normally assumed to occur when delivery invoices are signed. Several exceptions to this practice are explained in Chapter 3. Therefore, it is critical that any product delivery problems be noted. A credit memo can then be issued to adjust the delivery invoice that represents the amount the hospitality operation owes the supplier for the order.

Figure 12.5 shows a sample credit memo.

When you review the sample credit memo, notice that it is issued to the organization purchasing the product(s) by the supplier's representative (typically the route delivery person), and that it is applicable to a specific invoice. Items to be excluded from the amount owed to the supplier (total invoice amount) are listed along with the reason that credit is being granted. The signature of the supplier's representative confirms that the products noted in the credit memo were not received or accepted and that their value should be deducted from the amount owed to the supplier.

Multiple (at least duplicate) copies of credit memos are required to provide one copy for the supplier, and one copy for the hospitality organization. Some suppliers and/or purchasers may require more than one copy for their use.

Credit memos are typically issued by the supplier at the time of delivery. However, wise purchasers have copies (even if they are generic) available in case the delivery person does not have one available.

Credit memos should be treated like cash because they represent a credit (reduction) of the amount otherwise owed to the supplier based on the delivery invoice. They must be routed to the accounting department in a way that best ensures they will not be lost, discarded, or ignored. Most frequently, they are attached to the applicable delivery invoice for routing to purchasing and then on to accounting personnel for their use in adjusting (reducing) invoice amounts and subsequent payments.

Special procedures sometimes used when processing credit memos include

- Accounting personnel may contact the supplier from whom a credit memo has been issued to confirm that it was received, that no processing problems

Date: _____   Credit Memo No.: _____

Supplier: _____

_____

_____

_____

_____

Issued to: _____

_____

_____

Account No. _____

For Invoice No.: _____

Item	Purchase Unit	Number Purchase Units	Price/Purchase Unit	Total Price
			Total	**$**

Reason for Credit (Check):		
☐ Back order	☐ Incorrect quality	☐ Incorrect item
☐ Short start count/weight	☐ Incorrect price	☐ Not ordered
☐ Other: _____		

Authorized Signatures:	
Supplier's Representative	Purchaser's Representative

FIGURE 12.5 Sample Credit Memo

exist, and that credit will be reflected on the next statement to the hospitality organization.

* When the applicable purchase order and delivery invoice are received in the accounting department and filed for payment, the credit memo is included with that documentation along with a notation about the applicable credit memo for the delivery invoice.

Adequate documentation is required to ensure that a property has received all of the products that are being paid for by this check.

Getty Images-Stockbyte, Royalty Free

PURCHASING PROS NEED TO KNOW (12.3)

Purchasing pros know that their organization's relationship with suppliers is based upon the interactions of all personnel, including accounting staff. The need for more-than-occasional credit memos issued by a specific supplier typically suggests that the continued relationship between the hospitality operation and supplier should be evaluated. Problems relating to the need for frequent credit requests leading to the issuing of credit memos are also of concern. Differences between agreed-upon and delivery prices, and quality and quantity concerns, for example, should be investigated. If problems are found to be caused by employees of the hospitality organization, reasons for their occurrence should be investigated and procedures revised to minimize future occurrence. If problems are caused by suppliers, they should be directed to take corrective action.

Purchasers, not accounting personnel, typically make supplier selection decisions. As they do so, input from all affected personnel within the organization, including accounting staff, should be considered and used as an integral part of supplier evaluation and selection decisions. Excessive credit memos increase: (1) the likelihood that the operation will not have products required when needed, (2) the amount of effort required to process bills for payment, and (3) the likelihood that suppliers may be paid for products that were never delivered.

Internet Purchasing Assistant (12.1)

Procedures for developing, issuing, and using credit memos, like numerous other aspects of the procurement process, are increasingly computerized. To view a demo about the automated development of credit memos and their use for numerous purposes, go to: http://www.ezysoft-dev.com

While you are at the site, review several of the numerous credit memo formats that are shown.

An internal record-keeping system is also necessary to ensure that the hospitality operation does not pay bills until they have been adjusted by any applicable credit memos.

PAYMENT POLICIES AND PROCEDURES

We have reviewed the preliminary procedures required to prepare bills for payment by emphasizing the need to collect and carefully review supportive documentation that justifies (confirms) the hospitality organization's obligation for payment. Now let's examine the procedures for bill payment.

Because delivery invoices indicate the products and quantities of items for which suppliers make a payment request, they must be carefully studied for accuracy. Details include the need to:

- Ensure that there are no quantity or price differences between the items ordered (listed in the purchase order) and the items received.
- Ensure that all arithmetic **extensions** on the delivery invoice are correct.

Key Term

Extensions Arithmetic calculations made on delivery invoices. For example, item quantity ($\times$) unit price for each item must be multiplied to determine the total cost for the item. This total cost must be summed for all items to confirm that the total amount of the invoice is correct.

On-the-Job Challenges in Purchasing (12.1)

"I'm sure glad the Spartan's won this week's game," said Ned to Mannie, as all of the "paperwork" was signed.

Ned was the long-time receiving clerk for the Golf Pro Country Club, and Mannie was the delivery person for the Green Course Produce Company.

Over the years, Ned and Mannie had become pretty good friends because they saw each other several times weekly as Mannie made his product deliveries. Also, over time, Ned had begun to make "short cuts" in the receiving procedures he had been taught while training for the position. He knew these procedures were important, at least when checking deliveries of new suppliers and for suppliers and delivery persons whom he didn't "trust." However, it was a different situation with Mannie. Both men followed the same sports teams, had a similar sense of humor, and even had some mutual friends.

For these reasons, there was typically more personal conversation than professional procedure compliance as Ned checked in Mannie's produce deliveries.

"Okay, Mannie," said Ned, "It looks like this order is okay, except I think there must still be two cases of apples on the truck; I don't see them here."

"No, Ned, they aren't here and I was going to mention that to you," replied Mannie, "I guess they never made it on the truck this morning, and I don't know what happened. However, I'll be back here in two days for the next delivery. Why don't you just go ahead and sign the delivery invoice now, and I'll bring the two cases along next time and not charge you for them. Then we'll be even, and neither your office people nor mine will have to mess with extra paperwork."

Case Study Questions

1. What is the proper procedure that Ned should use in this instance? Why is it important to do so?
2. What potential problem(s) can arise if Ned accepts Mannie's suggestion and signs the delivery invoice without a notation about the two-case shortage of apples?
3. What tactics might you, as Ned's supervisor, do to help ensure that all required receiving procedures are consistently followed?

- File the invoice with the applicable purchase documentation for future payment.
- Pay the invoice at the appropriate time (payment procedures are discussed later in this section).

Two basic methods can be used to pay suppliers for purchased products and services:

- *By invoice.* After review of supportive documentation, delivery invoices and other information are filed (manually or electronically) for payment by a specific due date, and these bills are paid when due. For example, if an approved invoice must be paid by July 16, it may be "pulled" on July 10 for final review, signature, and mailing on July 11 to allow time for mail delivery. A copy of a delivery invoice was shown in Figure 11.4 in the previous chapter.
- *By statement.* Process documentation is filed by name of supplier while the accounting personnel await receipt of a statement of account. For example,

Key Terms

Invoice (payment method) A method of paying supplier bills on a by-delivery basis; the amount specified by the delivery invoice is paid at or before the time specified in the invoice.

Statement (payment method) A method of paying supplier bills for a specific time period; payment is based upon the sum of delivery invoices indicating the amount due for each delivery during the period.

PURCHASING PROS NEED TO KNOW (12.4)

Purchasing pros know that the need to confirm arithmetic extensions applies to machine-processed delivery invoices just as it does to manual tallies. Some purchasers, however, believe that "machines don't make mistakes," and verification of the accuracy of machine-generated data is overlooked. However, errors can occur because people must input the data, so it is important to review all delivery documentation as one step in payment processing.

Two special concerns can be addressed as electronic-generated financial information is reviewed. First, careful study is important to confirm that there are no "hidden" charges such as order processing fees, delivery charges, or other costs that were not agreed to at the time of the order. Also, "rounding" calculations can be programmed that increase charges from, for example, $189.95 to be printed as $189.99 (or another number). Over time, these excessive charges can become significant. Purchasing pros know, then, that (at least) random, if not routine, verification of machine-processed financial information is an important control tactic.

---

a produce supplier who delivers daily may request payment every two weeks, and does so by submitting a statement listing delivery invoices applicable to the two-week period for which deliveries were made and payment is requested. When the supplier's statement is received, applicable invoices are retrieved. Then all invoices covered by the statement, less adjustments (if any, required by credit memos), are paid at the same time.

Figure 12.6 shows a sample supplier's statement.

When invoices are to be paid, either singularly or as part of several covered by a statement, a check in the correct amount of the supplier's bill should be prepared for signing. If a manual system is used, each invoice that is paid should be

---

Statement 107643

Hilotown Produce
117 Bay Street N.W.
Hilotown, Any State, 00000
Telephone: xxx-xxx-xxxx
Fax: 111-111-1111

Account No.: ___ 1735210 _____
Delivered to: Hilotown Eatery
              300 Ocean View Lane
              Hilotown, Any State 00000
              Attention: Jack David, Director of Purchasing
              Telephone: 222-222-2222

Invoice No.	Delivery Date	Amount Due	Adjustment	Net Amount Due
10711	2/10/xx	$173.59		$173.59
10928	2/13/xx	$310.80	($21.55)	$289.25
12541	2/18/xx	$190.51	Credit memo	$190.51
13401	2/23/xx	$290.18	#2138	$290.18

Payment due upon receipt. Please send payment to the above address.

Duplicate: Please return top copy with payment, and retain second copy for your records.

Thank you.

FIGURE 12.6   Sample Supplier's Statement

Internet Purchasing Assistant (12.2)

Increasingly, hospitality purchasers and their suppliers are using e-business protocols, including electronic funds transfer (EFT), to simplify the payment process and to reduce associated payment costs. For example, purchasers can authorize that automatic payments be charged to a business credit card or be withdrawn from a business checking or savings account with the funds collected being directly deposited into the supplier's business account. Vendors can communicate with purchasers about the amount of the direct deposit being made via e-mail.

One advantage to suppliers offering EFT options is the faster receipt of payments that are due to them. The loss of this several-day "float" (the time required for checks to reach suppliers and clear the hospitality operation's account) is a disadvantage to the purchaser. However, this may be offset by the often significantly reduced costs to the purchaser for check processing. For example, the U.S. government estimates that it cost .89 cents to manually process a check and, by contrast, .09 cents to process an EFT payment. (Source: http://www.fms.treas.gov/eft)

A relatively new term, **"electronic invoice presentment and payment (EIPP),"** is used to identify the process by which bills are created, delivered, and paid over the Internet, and this provides one additional alternative to suppliers as they bill their customers and to buyers as they consider the best way to pay supplier bills.

To review information about EIPP, go to: http://www.ebilling.org. At the home page, click on "EIPP."

marked to indicate the date and amount of payment, and check number. Marking and processing should be done in a way that is possible to verify that payment has been made and to minimize the possibility that an invoice would be paid twice.

SPECIAL ACCOUNTING CONCERNS

In this section, we will discuss payment approval procedures for single- and multi-unit organizations and petty cash systems.

Payment Approval Procedures: Single-Unit Properties

As you learned in Chapter 3, those with purchasing and accounting responsibilities serve as agents (representatives) of the organization's top-level managers and/or owners as they make decisions about those matters for which they have delegated authority. This is both convenient and necessary to eliminate the need for purchasers and accounting personnel to, respectively, obtain permission for the order of every product and the payment of every bill. In effect, then, the general authorization for product purchasing and bill payment is inherent in the position, and the approval is implied in the appropriate documentation that moves forward in the process. To illustrate these points, let's review Figure 12.7.

Key Term

Electronic invoice presentment and payment (EIPP) The process by which companies present invoices through, and use the Internet, to make payments to one another for goods and services received.

FIGURE 12.7   Payment
Approval Process (Single-
Unit Properties)

12.7 (A) : For routine purchases (small hospitality operations)

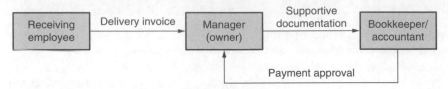

12.7 (B) : For routine purchases (large hospitality operations)

Notes:

(1) Delivery invoice and/or other documentation may be routed through the applicable department head in some organizations.

(2) Accounting personnel in some large hospitality organizations that are part of chains may be located in area or regional locations away from their individual property to further reduce opportunities for collusion between on-site managers and accounting department directors.

12.7 (C) : For nonroutine purchases (large hospitality operations)

Special Approval Needed:

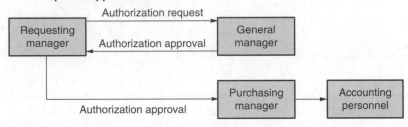

Note: The general manager's preorder approval becomes part of the support documentation sent from the purchasing manager to accounting personnel (12.7B).

Note that Figure 12.7 reviews the payment approval process for three situations:

- *12.7(A): Payment approval process for routine purchases (small hospitality operation).*   In this situation, the employee signing the delivery invoice confirms the type and quantity of products received. The delivery invoice moves forward to the manager or owner, who confirms compliance with the original purchase agreement (e.g., purchase order). He or she then routes all documentation with payment approval to the bookkeeper/accountant who: (1) verifies agreement between purchase and delivery documents and, at the appropriate time, (2) prepares the check for payment. The final payment approval occurs as the manager (owner) signs the check before mailing.

- *12.7(B): Payment approval process for routine purchases (large hospitality organization).*   In this example, the signed delivery invoice is routed to the purchasing manager, who compares the information with the applicable purchase documents and forwards this information to the accounting personnel. Within specified limits, the director of accounting is authorized to process payment after the documentation has been approved and verified.

- *12.7(C): Payment approval process for nonroutine purchases (large hospitality operation).*   Recall from our discussion above that purchasing and accounting personnel are, in their role as agents of their employers, authorized to perform their duties within defined parameters; in other words, to make and pay for "routine" purchases. Beyond limits established by the specific organization, special authorization (approval) is typically required. In these instances, the requesting manager (e.g., the director of housekeeping who needs new laundry equipment and the maintenance engineer desiring to repave a service driveway) will likely require permission to make these purchases. Approval is obtained when each department head's capital budget is approved, and when final authorization to proceed with the project is granted by the property's owner or general manager. This official, if managing a property in a multi-unit chain, may also need approval from a management official at a still-higher organizational level for **capital purchases.** The documentation providing formal approval for these nonroutine purchases are provided by the requesting manager to the purchasing manager as part of the purchasing process. After the product is delivered or the service is provided, and after all the suppliers'/service providers' contractual obligations are met, this approval documentation is forwarded to the accounting personnel by the purchasing manager.

Each of the above examples of payment approval incorporates, to the extent practical, the principle of separation of duties noted at the beginning of this chapter. Concerns relate to both position specialization (a "good" purchaser may not have significant knowledge about accounting and vice versa) and to resource control. Those designing purchasing and accounting systems should implement safeguards that include reducing the opportunity for one person working alone to fraudulently obtain products or funds. Security concerns applicable to procurement accounting are detailed in the next section.

Payment Approval Procedures: Multi-Unit Organizations

Figure 12.8 provides one model of payment approval for purchasing obligations in multi-unit (chain) organizations.

PURCHASING PROS NEED TO KNOW (12.5)

Before paying for services it is necessary to ensure that they were performed (i.e., the work was done). Although this seems obvious, it is difficult to observe and confirm the completion of many routine services such as:

- Lubricating air handlers on the top of the hotel's seven-story roof.
- Cleaning drains in all guest room showers with a "snake" (drain router) per the plumber's quarterly invoice.
- Cleaning the lines in the beer dispensing system last Thursday night after the bar closed per the vendor's invoice.
- Spreading the autumn weed treatment on the grassy areas of the restaurant's property last week.
- Cleaning the exterior second-story windows on Sunday when it is hard to confirm this because it rained Sunday night.

In these and numerous other cases, a responsible person such as the buyer or person in the affected department must be involved. He or she should have sufficient knowledge about the service to know whether it was actually performed. This staff member can then sign off that the work was done, and that the quality of the work met the agreed-upon quality level. Perhaps, for example, the invoice from the service supplier should be routed to the department for which the service was performed for a confirming signature. In other cases, the vendor may be required to sign in and out, and leave verification with someone on the property at the time the work is completed.

Key Term

Capital purchase   Any purchase made by the hospitality operation that is expected to benefit it for more than one year; also called a capital expenditure.

THE SUPPLIER'S SIDE (12.1)

"Insider" Tips on Purchasing: From the Supplier's Perspective

Question: Is the "paperwork" that accompanies the delivery of equipment or other capital items the same as that which accompanies routine product and supplier deliveries?

Answer: The best response to this question is, "It depends!" If, for example, an equipment supplier sells an item that is available in his or her (the supplier's) inventory, it will likely be transported to the hospitality organization's loading dock accompanied by a routine delivery invoice.

Assume, however, that the equipment supplier sells a **special order** equipment item that must be ordered from the manufacturer. In this instance, it may be easier for the freight company that transports the equipment item from the manufacturer's location to deliver it directly to the **end user.** When this is done, the distributor sends a **delivery note** along with the order to inform the manufacturer that the delivery location is that of the purchaser rather than the distributor. A **shipping confirmation** is sent by the manufacturer to the distributor regarding the specifics of transportation and delivery when the item leaves the manufacturer's plant. Then, when it is delivered to the hospitality operation, a delivery note or other **proof of delivery (POD)** document is signed by a property representative to confirm that the equipment item has been received and is in good condition.

Documentation for this purchase transaction includes two purchase orders: one from the buyer to the distributor, and one from the distributor to the manufacturer. Other documentation includes a copy of the delivery note or other proof of delivery and a specific invoice (bill) sent to the purchaser by the distributor.

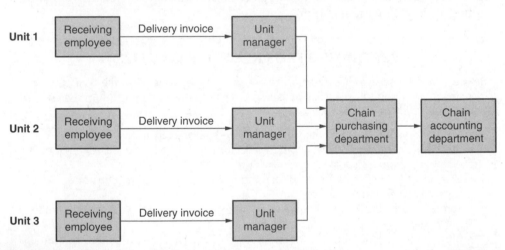

FIGURE 12.8   Payment Approval Process (Multi-Unit Organizations)

Key Terms

Special order   An order taken by a distributor for an item that is not available in the distributor's inventory and which must be ordered from the manufacturer.

End user   The hospitality organization; the buyer of the product.

Delivery note   A request made by a distributor to a manufacturer that a specific equipment item should be delivered to a hospitality operation rather than to the distributor.

Shipping confirmation   Document sent by an equipment manufacturer to a distributor indicating that an equipment item has been shipped or is due to be shipped to the end user or the distributor's warehouse.

Proof of delivery (POD)   A signed document such as a delivery invoice, delivery note, or packing slip verifying that the purchaser has received the goods and they are acceptable.

Chain purchasing or accounting personnel may receive copies of the supplier's invoices that accompany deliveries to each unit. These are matched with those signed by the receiving employee in each unit as part of the invoice processing procedures. The chain purchasing department will have copies of the purchase orders because it placed the orders for delivery to each unit with the suppliers.

Figure 12.8 shows the approval process for a three-unit chain. Receiving employees in each unit certify (by signature) the receipt of specific items and/or quantities on the delivery invoices that are routed to the unit managers. Unit managers review this documentation and forward it to the chain's purchasing department (perhaps located in one of the three units). The purchaser, who originally accumulated the product needs from the three units and ordered the products, compares the invoices with the purchase information and routes this documentation to the chain's accounting department (which also may be located in the same or a different unit in the chain). Purchasing or accounting personnel may receive copies of the supplier's invoices applicable to the deliveries to each unit. If so, these are included with the documentation and used to further support the purchase and delivery of the products to the units. As we discussed with single-unit purchase approval, the movement of source documents from the point of receiving to payment incorporates the payment approval by those who have "signed off" on the documentation.

On-the-Job Challenges in Purchasing (12.2)

Koji and Andrea had worked together at the Mountain Town Hotel for several years. In addition to their professional relationship, they also had a mutual interest (bowling), and they worked together to form a company bowling team that played in one of their community's bowling leagues.

Andrea was the purchasing manager for the hotel, and Koji was in charge of the accounting department. The Mountain Town Hotel was managed by a large regional hotel management company, and as did others in the chain, standard operating procedures for purchasing and accounting had been implemented. Among these were control safeguards designed to ensure that management approval for payment preceded each step in the bill payment process.

Andrea was intrigued by a current scandal occurring in her community: The business manager of the local public school has recently been indicted for theft of public funds that occurred as he submitted fictitious invoices for services rendered into the school district's purchasing system. After his approval, the invoice was routed to another department in the business office for payment.

In addition to her membership on the hotel's bowling team, Andrea had another interest: She really enjoyed gambling and, unfortunately, had incurred significant credit card debt to support her losses.

"The school district's business manager was caught by the district's accountant and he should have known better because of the effective way the school district separated the duties of the people responsible for managing expenses and for paying them," thought Andrea. "However, Koji and I are good friends. He's always telling me about the new car he'd like to have, and the vacations he'd like to take. I know he needs more money to do these things. We're a good team at the hotel and in our bowling league. I wonder if we could also be teammates in a venture that would help both of us?"

Case Study Questions

1. What are exemplary procedures that should be implemented to separate the duties between the purchaser and the accounting manager in this (and all other) hotels to reduce opportunities for collusion?

2. What, if any, tactics can the general manager and other officials use to routinely determine whether collusion between a buyer and accounting personnel may be occurring?

3. Assume that the general manager determines that collusion between Andrea and Koji may be occurring. What should he or she do?

Policies and procedures guiding the actions of purchasing and accounting personnel are needed to ensure that the communication between both departments is effective.

PhotoDisc/Getty Images

Petty Cash Systems

Normally, hospitality organizations should minimize the use of cash payments to satisfy their purchase obligations. Checks allow for better control of expenses and are easier to classify for accounting purposes because **audit trails** can be developed and more easily traced. There are, however, typically numerous minor expenses that are best paid in cash because it is more practical and less expensive

HIGH-TECH PURCHASING (12.1)

The accounting function, including that applicable to procurement, was one of the first areas within hospitality operations to become automated. Today, even the smallest of operations or the accounting/bookkeeping services that they hire use "off-the-shelf" or other software to develop the organization's financial statements. As you learned in Chapter 10, almost every step required to manage products in inventory, determine when additional products should be ordered, and interact with suppliers can be and, increasingly is, automated. "Paperless" purchasing can continue as purchasers communicate with accounting personnel to electronically route delivery and purchase information necessary to substantiate supplier payment and claims. Electronic rather than manual filing systems are increasingly used to separate purchasing data on a by-supplier basis and to record and track supplier payments with further input to systems used to determine financial statement data. Electronic funds transfer by several means is available to automate this step in the purchasing process. The end result: Perhaps, with the exception of the front office department in a hotel, no other area within a hospitality organization is more automated than its accounting department.

Key Term

Audit trail   A chronological (step-by-step) record that allows financial data to be traced to its source. An example for a food purchase is a purchase order—delivery invoice—check number used for payment of the delivery invoice.

to do so. Examples of minor expenses include miscellaneous hardware and some office supplies, and even "emergency" purchases from grocery stores. These and related expenses are often paid for with monies from a **petty cash fund.** These cash banks can, however, be misused, and security procedures governing their use for purchasing should be established and consistently used.

Petty cash funds must be housed in secure locations and administered by responsible management personnel. For example, a petty cash bank in a restaurant might be housed in the property manager's office. A large hotel may have a petty cash fund at the front desk administered by the front office manager, another in the chef's office for use by the food and beverage personnel, and, perhaps, one or more other cash banks for use by other departments such as maintenance or housekeeping. Policies and procedures governing the use of petty cash banks, and the frequency with which their current balances are verified, should be developed and consistently used for all cash purchases throughout the property. Petty cash funds should be established on an **imprest** (cash advance) system:

- The amount of money in the petty cash fund should be based upon the normal value of petty cash purchases for a specific time period (e.g., two or four weeks).
- A check charged to "petty cash" is written, and its proceeds are used to establish the petty cash fund.
- As cash purchases are made, cash is removed from the petty cash bank as needed for the specific purchase. The change from the purchase transaction along with the receipt for the purchase is returned and, after verification that the amount (change [+] receipt) equals the amount removed, both the change and receipt are placed in the petty cash bank. In many organizations, the original petty cash voucher is attached to the receipt.
- When the petty cash fund must be replenished, a check is again written to "petty cash," and this time it is for the value of paid receipts in the fund. This check, converted to cash, will replenish the fund to its original value.
- At any point in time, the actual value of the petty cash fund should equal the original amount of money allocated to petty cash: cash in the bank (+) paid receipts for all purchases.

Figure 12.9 shows a sample petty cash voucher that is deposited in the cash bank when cash is withdrawn for a small item purchase. This voucher, along with the purchase receipt and cash change, should be deposited in the cash bank at the completion of the transaction.

The responsibility for keeping the petty cash funds secure and authorizing its use should be vested in one individual. Policies should be established relating to items that can be purchased, frequency of purchases, and the dollar value of cash purchases that can be made with petty cash.

Numerous other procedures typically apply to the management of a petty cash fund, including:

- All items to be purchased must be approved by the appropriate management official (the person who is the fund custodian). This occurs as the petty cash voucher (see Figure 12.9) is completed.

Key Terms

Petty cash fund   A small amount of cash on hand used to make relatively low-cost purchases.

Imprest (petty cash system)   A petty cash fund in which payments to the fund are always in the amount required to bring its balance to the original amount. The petty cash balance is always maintained by cash and the receipts for cash payments.

```
┌─────────────────────────────────────────────────────────────────┐
│                      Pleasant Town Club                           │
│                      Petty Cash Voucher                           │
│   Date: _____          Voucher No.: _____      │
│                                                                   │
│   Description of purchase: _____  │
│   _____  │
│                                                                   │
│   Amount of cash issued: _____                 │
│                                                                   │
│   Signatures:                                                     │
│                                                                   │
│   _____            _____            │
│     Funds Issued by                 Funds Received by             │
│                                                                   │
│   Instructions:                                                   │
│   Institutions: This petty cash voucher, along with the purchase  │
│   receipt and change equal to the voucher amount, must be         │
│   returned to the cash bank custodian.                            │
└─────────────────────────────────────────────────────────────────┘
```

FIGURE 12.9   Petty Cash Voucher

- All purchases must be supported with receipts, and if necessary, a notation should be written on the receipt to identify the item that has been purchased.
- The petty cash fund must be kept secure at all times; money should not remain in unlocked and easily accessible areas.
- Petty cash funds should not be commingled (mixed together with) cash register or other cash bank funds.
- Unless the employee responsible for the petty cash fund is the property's owner/manager, the fund custodian should not be empowered to write a check to replenish the fund. Also, the check should be made out to "petty cash," rather than to "cash" or the staff member responsible for fund management.
- Funds used to replenish the petty cash fund should be charged to a "petty cash" expense account.
- There should be no unauthorized "borrowing" of money from the petty cash fund; cash advances or payments, if any, for employees should not originate from this fund.
- When the petty cash fund is reimbursed to its approved level, all receipts should be examined for compliance with fund usage policies and guidelines.
- Petty cash funds should be spot-checked on a routine but random basis to ensure that they remain intact; the amount available in the fund (cash and paid receipts) should equal the authorized amount of the fund.

SECURITY CONCERNS AND PROCUREMENT ACCOUNTING

Hospitality managers must ensure that basic security controls are in place in the accounting department to minimize opportunities for dishonest staff members to commit **embezzlement.** Reasonable accounting procedures in common use in any business can be very helpful for this purpose. Few, if any, hospitality-specific fund

---

Key Term

Embezzlement   The act of stealing financial assets, including cash, from a hospitality operation.

control procedures are typically used. It is also important to note that the objective of a security system is not to "catch crooks," but, instead, to "keep honest people honest." In other words, sound security systems reduce opportunities for theft.

Details about security procedures to control the organization's funds as purchase payments are made are beyond the intent of this section.[2] However, security control at the time of disbursement begins with the development of effective policies and procedures that are consistently used. Employees who handle the organization's assets can be **bonded** and, when possible, specific employees should be responsible for specific activities. The need for the separation of duties has already been discussed, and systems must be in place that require managers to authorize each business transaction. Adequate records providing audit trails and the use of auditors to verify financial statements, to assess existing control systems, and to make recommendations for improved controls can all be helpful.

The previous section discussed the importance of minimizing cash payments for purchases and provided detailed control procedures helpful when cash purchases are made. An extensive list of procedures for control of noncash (check) payments for purchases can also be developed, and these include the following:

- Check protectors that mechanically imprint the amount of checks should be used.
- The person who signs the checks should mail them; they should not be returned for mailing to the individual processing invoices for check writing.
- More than one signature by a management or accounting official might be required on checks in excess of a specified amount.
- Invoices and vouchers are clearly identified as being "paid" when checks are written.
- Invoices are filed, along with the purchase order or other authorizing documents, by supplier name for future reference.
- Blank checks for "emergency" or other use are never signed. Checks should be signed only after they are prepared.
- A system to control spoiled, voided, or other unused checks is used. There should be no way that such checks can be fraudulently converted by dishonest employees. Any checks that are not used should be mutilated to avoid reuse.
- All checks should be imprinted with the name of the property or business identity and should be marked, "Void after 60 days."
- All checks should be prenumbered by the printer.
- Supplies of blank checks should be kept under lock. When check-signing machines are used, signature plates must be securely controlled when not in use. Also, the counting device on the machine, which shows the number of checks processed, should agree with the number of checks actually used.
- Banks are notified of personnel authorized to write checks; copies of their signatures are on file at the bank, and all authorized documents have been completed.
- All checks written are made payable to a person or company; no checks should be made payable to "cash" or "to bearer." Managers should routinely examine the check registry (list of processed checks) to learn and inquire about new suppliers and one-time transactions.
- Unless checks are signed by the owner/manager, other signatories should not have access to petty cash funds and should not be authorized to approve cash disbursements and record cash receipts.

Key Term

Bond (insurance agreement)   A contract in which, for a fee, an insurer guarantees payment to a hospitality organization for a financial loss caused by the action(s) of a specific covered employee.

The price paid for the furnishings in this guest room will only be that which was agreed upon if accounting personnel do their job correctly.

Courtesy of Real Resorts

- A system is in place that makes it impossible for an invoice to be submitted two or more times for payment.
- Outstanding checks that are not returned or cashed promptly are followed up on and controlled.
- Bank records should be carefully examined to confirm that all checks issued have been processed. No checks should be missing. Checks should be used in number sequence without skipping (jumping ahead).
- The name of the payee must be the same on the check, check record, and invoice.

Some hospitality properties use an accounts payable check voucher system to manage the flow of information with accompanying checks through the accounting department. This system is useful regardless of the extent to which the purchasing and accounting procedures are automated, and it is an element in the computerized accounting systems of many hospitality operations. Figure 12.10 shows a sample accounts payable check voucher system.

							Charge to Account			
Date	Invoice No.	Purchase of	Amount	Less Discount	Net Due		No.	No.	Check No.	Date Paid

Voucher No. _____   Payable to: _____

Note: The above voucher enables accounting personnel to provide details about twelve sequential invoices for the supplier when a payment check is written.

FIGURE 12.10 Sample Accounts Payable Check Voucher

Internet Purchasing Assistant (12.3)

Modern technology can be used to automate the check-signing process. For example, in one system, a computerized check signer is interfaced (electronically connected) with the computer and printer. Before checks are printed, the equipment is activated with a special security system. Checks are then printed and signed. Systems allow for signatures to be required for checks beyond a predetermined dollar amount to ensure that no check is signed above that amount without required authorization. Valid checks can be printed and signed only when a check is requested from accounting software and the check signer is activated to provide an additional level of security.

Some automated check-signing equipment embosses checks to eliminate forgery. Other machines require that two persons complete security measures to enable check writing (dual lock controls).

Machines can use programmable passwords to limit machine, resetable batch counters to determine the number of checks written at a single time, and nonresettable display counters to determine the total number of checks written.

For more information about computer interfaced check signers, go to: http://www. pbsoffice.com

Use of a voucher system helps to control (track) vendor invoices and to match the property's check number and date with each specific invoice.

RELATIONSHIP BETWEEN ACCOUNTING AND PURCHASING STAFF

Purchasing and accounting personnel must closely and cooperatively interact with each other and with suppliers, service providers, and others external to the hospitality organization. It is critical that they work closely together in ways that maximize benefits to their employer. Some interaction will be assisted by formal meetings as document flow, report development, and other processes are finalized and implemented. However, it is just as important to ensure that all daily and informal contacts (and there are likely to be many!) between personnel in the two departments are cordial and cooperative. This is best done by involving representatives from both departments in the (hopefully) cross-functional teams that are assigned to policy and procedure development tasks.

Purchasing Resources on the Internet

In addition to the Web sites referenced in this chapter's "Internet Purchasing Assistant," the following sites provide detailed information to enhance your purchasing knowledge and skills.

Purchasing Resources on the Internet

Site	Information About
www.findarticles.com	Embezzlement information (Enter "embezzlement" in the site's search box)
www.insurehedge.com	Employee bonding (fidelity) insurance (At the home page, click on "Coverages" and then "Fidelity Liability")
www.ganson.com	Check-writing software (At the home page, click on "Check Software")
www.medlin.com	Payroll software

(continued)

Site	Information About
www.suretyone.org	Insurance against embezzlement
www.irislink.com	Scanning, archiving, and encoding supplier invoices for processing and payment (At the home page, click "Products" and then "Invoice Reading")
www.PayPal.com	Electronic Funds Transfer—many people associate this company with eBay; however, it has applications for other merchants as well (At the home page, click on "Merchant Services")
www.microsoft.com	Accounts payable processing procedures for small businesses (At the home page, type "accounts payable" in the site's search box)
www.checkfree.com	Electronic payment processing products
www.lason.com	Accounts payable outsourcing.

Key Terms

duties, separation of *281*
accounting *281*
accrual (accounting system) *281*
"Mom and Pop" (hospitality operation) *281*
accounts payable *283*
current liability *283*
equipment *283*
fixed asset *283*

notes payable *283*
long-term debit *283*
allocate *283*
operating income *283*
depreciation *284*
source document *284*
encumbrance (accounting) *287*
extensions *290*
invoice (payment method) *291*

statement (payment method) *291*
electronic invoice presentment and payment (EIPP) *293*
capital purchase *295*
special order *296*
end user *296*
delivery note *296*
shipping confirmation *296*

proof of delivery (POD) *296*
audit trail *298*
petty cash fund *299*
imprest (petty cash system) *299*
embezzlement *300*
bond (insurance agreement) *301*

Think It Through

1. Assume you are the controller (director of accounting) for a large hospitality organization. List the factors that would be most important to you as you evaluate the effectiveness of the purchasing department. Then list the factors important in evaluating the suppliers with whom your organization procures products. In other words, from the perspective of an accounting employee, what is the definition of a "good" and "bad" purchasing department and suppliers?

2. What are some ways that purchasing and accounting managers can collude to defraud a hospitality organization? What are basic controls that top-level property managers can implement to help identify and address these theft methods?

3. Some multi-unit hotel organizations do not have accounting departments located within the individual properties. One reason is to eliminate the possibility for the property manager and accounting head to collude in efforts to defraud the or-

ganization. What, if any, are other advantages to locating the accounting function at an area or regional level of the organization? What, if any, are potential disadvantages?

4. Some hospitality organizations are able to negotiate with suppliers to obtain a discount for prompt payment. Perhaps, for example, a 1 percent or 2 percent discount might be allowed if payment is received within 10 days of product delivery. What role should accounting personnel play in these negotiations? How would they be affected by them?

5. The chapter notes the potential use of bonding (fidelity insurance) for accounting personnel and others who have the most significant opportunity to defraud the hospitality organization. Comment on the following observation about properties that bond employees: "It is important to bond accounting personnel because they may be dishonest, and bonding is an easy way to protect the organization against this risk."

Team Fun

Your team has been asked by the general manager of a 200-room limited-service hotel in your community to provide some assistance in the design (improvement) of the property's system used to pay suppliers for products and services that have been received. Currently, products are ordered by the three department heads (front desk, housekeeping, and maintenance) after approval by the manager. Products are delivered to, and delivery invoices are signed by, the manager who orders the products. Delivery invoices are to be checked for accuracy and submitted to the manager once weekly. After her review, all invoices are hand-carried to the area headquarters of the lodging management company that are located in the same suburban area as the property.

1. The assignment of team one is to consider the pros and cons of this decentralized system in which each property selects its own suppliers and orders its own products versus the use of a centralized system in which product and service sourcing is done at the company's area office.

2. The assignment of the second team is to assume that the existing decentralized system should be continued. Team members are to consider how, if at all, the purchasing system can be improved. For example, should the general manager or his or her department heads do any other, or discontinue doing some, activities related to the audit trail of source documents being generated?

3. The assignment of team three is to suggest how, if at all, the property's general manager should confirm that accounting-related details generated by the area office accurately reflect the financial condition of the property. Is it important for her to confirm that only invoices for the property are allocated to the property? If so, how should she do this? What basic understanding should the general manager have with the area accounting personnel about processing and paying supplier bills applicable to his or her property?

Endnotes

1. For an overview of accounting in lodging operations, see: D. Hayes and J. Ninemeier, *Hotel Operations Management: Second Edition*. Upper Saddle River, NJ: Pearson Education, Inc. 2007 (see Chapter 5); for an overview of accounting in restaurant operations, see: J. Ninemeier and D. Hayes, *Restaurant Operations Management: Principles and Practices*. Upper Saddle River, NJ: Pearson Education, Inc. 2006.

2. Readers desiring more information are referred to: R. Schmidgall, et. al., *Restaurant Financial Basics*. Hoboken, NJ: John Wiley & Sons, Inc. 2002. (See Chapter 13.)

13

Meat, Poultry, Game, and Seafood

In This Chapter

Meat and seafood are generally the most expensive menu items and are typically the most highly prized by guests. Paradoxically, meat is also one of the most avoided major foods due, in part, to concerns about the methods used to raise some animals, to religious restrictions, and, in the case of some red meats, because of health concerns. Despite those reservations, however, meat and seafood are a significant part of the diet in most cultures, including that of people in the United States.

The word "meat" generally refers to beef, veal, pork, and lamb products consumed for food. Poultry products are also sometimes called meat. In the United States, the most popular poultry products are chicken, turkey (a bird native to North America), and duck. Other animals eaten for meat include game animals of various types.

Like poultry, seafood is also sometimes referred to as meat. Although there are a variety of ways to classify the many animals taken from the ocean, lakes, and rivers for food, in this chapter, these seafoods will be categorized as either fish or shellfish.

Regardless of the type, the carcasses of all animals eaten for food consist primarily of muscle tissue, fat, connective tissue, and bones. In the past few decades, in response to increased concerns about health, the composition of the animals eaten for food has changed dramatically. Today's meats are younger, leaner, and therefore more prone to be dry and less flavorful if not properly cooked. As a result, today's meat buyer must understand meat products even better than did meat buyers in the past.

Just as the composition of meat has changed, so too have the various forms in which buyers may purchase meat. Had this book been written 30 years ago, it would have been filled with pictures of large cuts of meat and fish, with copious details about how butchers could fabricate those large pieces into smaller, more usable products. Today, it is estimated that less than 1 percent of commercial foodservice operations do any fabrication on any of the meat and seafood items they sell. Today's meat and seafood buyers choose from meats and seafood sold in a variety of "ready-to-use" cuts and market forms. In some ways, this makes the job of determining required product quality and standards easier, but it also means buyers' knowledge of available market forms must be expanded. This is so because the average foodservice buyer selecting meat items can choose from literally hundreds of popular meat items including those produced locally and those imported from around the world. In this chapter, you will learn about the meat, poultry, game, and seafood products most often purchased by foodservice buyers, as well as the market forms in which these items are most often sold.

■■■

Outline

Meat, Poultry, Game, and Seafood
  Meat
    Beef
      Cuts
      Purchasing Standards
    Veal
      Cuts
      Purchasing Standards
    Pork
      Cuts
      Purchasing Standards
    Lamb
      Cuts
      Purchasing Standards
    Charcuterie
  Poultry
    Chicken
      Market Forms
      Purchasing Standards
    Turkey
      Market Forms
      Purchasing Standards
    Duck
      Market Forms
      Purchasing Standards
  Game
    Furred Game
    Winged Game
  Seafood
    Fish
      Round Fish
      Flat Fish
    Shellfish
      Mollusks
      Crustaceans
Product Receiving and Storage
  Receiving
  Storage
Purchasing Resources on the Internet
Key Terms
Think It Through
Team Fun

MEAT, POULTRY, GAME, AND SEAFOOD

Meat

Meat is the term most often used to describe the muscled flesh of animals eaten for food. Typically, a distinction is made between muscle meats and organ meats (livers, hearts, kidneys, and the like). In the United States, the term meat is used even more specifically to describe the flesh of livestock animals (commonly beef, veal, pork, and lamb).

Meat is important because it typically serves as the **center of the plate** item for most foodservice operations.

Meat can be a very complex item to buy because each animal raised for food varies somewhat from other animals, and even from other animals in the same species. In addition, meat muscle can be cut in hundreds of ways and processed and sold in even hundreds more. The result is that meat sellers now offer virtually thousands of fresh and processed products to foodservice buyers.

Although it can be complex, buyers can better understand the meat-buying process by remembering a few key principles. The first of these is that all meat sold in the United States must be federally inspected for wholesomeness (see Chapter 3). When inspected, each animal is stamped with a round purple vegetable dye mark, "U.S. INSP'D & P'S'D," as shown in Figure 13.1

The mark is put on animal carcasses and large meat cuts, so it might not appear on smaller cuts such as roasts and steaks. However, meat that is packaged in an inspected facility will always have an inspection legend, which identifies the plant on the label.

Although voluntary in many cases, the U.S. government also assigns **quality grades** to meats (and other foods) and, in the case of some animals, **yield grades,** so that buyers may know more about the various quality and yield levels they are purchasing.

Grades are important to meat buyers because, for example, the beef to be purchased may have been graded for quality, or yield, or both. Because meat grading is voluntary, many meat processors use their own labeling systems to provide quality assurance. These private systems do not necessarily use the USDA's criteria for meat evaluation. Buyers of these products must inquire carefully about the quality level of these privately labeled items.

The second major principle for meat buyers to know is that there are highly established standards for meat products. When these standards are known,

FIGURE 13.1 U.S. Meat Inspection Stamp

Key Terms

Meat   The body tissues of animals eaten for food.

Center of the plate   The main course (entrée) in a multi-item meal most often placed in the "center" of the plate when served.

Quality grade   Designation of an item's quality rank relative to established standards of excellence. For example, Grade A, Grade B, and so on.

Yield grade   An evaluation of usable meat on an animal's carcass.

buyers can more easily develop detailed specifications for the meat items they wish to buy. To eliminate the confusing names given to meat cuts in different regions and by different product sellers, a uniform system of designating cuts has been developed. Each beef, pork, and lamb cut is identifiable by a number assigned by the IMPS/NAMP numbering system.

IMPS refers to the USDA-approved Institutional Meat Purchase Specifications (IMPS) for fresh beef, veal, pork, and lamb. Under IMPS, meats are indexed by a numerical system (e.g., specific beef cuts are numbered in the 100 series, lamb in the 200 series, veal in the 300 series, and pork in the 400 series). NAMP refers to the North American Meat Processors Association. Foodservice meat buyers, however, best know NAMP for *The Meat Buyer's Guide*, a publication that even more fully explains the IMPS-numbered items.

The Meat Buyer's Guide is intended for meat cutters and commercial meat purchasers and is the recognized reference for meat cuts. It is published annually to enable NAMP to maintain and illustrate the standard numbering system for NAMP-recognized cuts of meat. NAMP has issued its meat buyer's guide since 1963 and now also issues a *Poultry Buyer's Guide*.

A third important principle to know regarding meat buying relates to the age of meat. When an animal is slaughtered, its muscle composition will continue to change as time passes. Some meats (such as beef, veal, and lamb) improve in flavor as they continue to age for longer periods, whereas others (such as pork, as well as poultry and most seafood) do not. Those meats that are aged may be either **wet aged** or **dry aged.**

Wet aging in vacuum-sealed plastic bags allows natural enzymes and microorganisms time to break down connective tissue in meat, which tenderizes and flavors it. As this chemical process occurs, the meat will develop an unpleasant odor that is released when the package is opened. This odor will dissipate in minutes, however, and has no long-term negative effect on the wet-aged item.

Internet Purchasing Assistant (13.1)

The North American Meat Processors offers its meat buyer's guide for sale in hard copy form. The USDA-approved Institutional Meat Purchase Specifications (IMPS) for fresh beef, veal, pork, and lamb, however, is free and may be downloaded at: www.ams.usda.gov. At the site's home page, enter "IMPS" in the search box.

Large-volume purchasers such as government agencies, schools, restaurants, hotels, and other foodservice users reference the IMPS when buying meat products. The IMPS describes in great detail each cut of meat, with illustrations and photographs.

When you have downloaded the information:

1. Click on "Fresh Beef (series 100)" to see the type of detail provided by these published standards.
2. Also click on one of the processed meat PDF files (e.g., Series 500 or 600) to review the specification details provided for these types of processed meat products.

Key Terms

Wet aged (meat) The process of storing vacuum-packed meats under refrigeration for up to six weeks.
Dry aged (meat) The storing of fresh meats in an environment of controlled temperature, humidity, and air flow for up to six weeks.

Dry aging also allows enzymes and microorganisms to break down connective tissue. Dry-aged meats, however, also lose 5–20 percent of their total weight during the aging process. They can also develop external molds, which add flavor, but which must be removed before the meat is consumed. Dry-aged meats are usually of very high quality, costly, and obtained only through specialty distributors and butchers.

An understanding of quality, yield, standards, and aging principles will equip meat buyers with much of the information they need to effectively procure fresh meat products. It is important to understand, however, that increasingly, meat buyers can purchase meat products in a variety of processed forms. These include those packaged as "ready-to-eat," those sold in single-serve microwaveable containers, and "boil-in-bag" cooking systems, as well as in more traditional canned, refrigerated, and frozen forms.

BEEF   Beef is the meat of domesticated cattle and is also one of the principal meats used in European and American cuisines. It is popular in Asian cultures as well. Meat buyers should know that beef is taboo to Hindus, and its consumption is discouraged among some Buddhists.

Most of the beef eaten in the United States comes from steers, the castrated male cattle specifically raised for beef. Beef is easily the most popular meat in the United States and is increasingly sold to foodservice operators in processed forms and cuts designed to reduce labor costs and increase product quality and consistency.

Cuts   When cattle are slaughtered, carcasses are initially cut into four pieces (called quarters). This results in two front quarters and two rear (hind) quarters. Each quarter is then separated ("broken" is the word used in the industry) into **primal cuts** and, in many cases, subprimal (smaller) cuts. These primal parts are also known as wholesale cuts, and they are customarily distributed to retailers and some foodservice operators who then produce **fabricated cuts.**

Because meat preferences vary, primal cuts in Canada, Mexico, and the United States are not identical. For U.S. buyers, however, primal cuts are carefully defined by the IMPS/NAMP numbering system. Although those in the meat industry use virtually every part of each animal they process, Figure 13.2 shows the common names of the cattle parts and primal cuts important to most foodservice buyers.

It is good to have a basic understanding about the major foodservice parts taken from beef cattle. These include those from:

Chuck: Chuck meat is basically muscle, and the chuck is a heavily used muscle area. This area contains a great deal of connective tissue, including collagen. Collagen breaks down during slow cooking, making meat dishes made from chuck intensely flavorful. Cuts from this area benefit from wet cooking methods like stewing, braising, or pot-roasting. Counted from front to back, it includes the first five ribs of the animal.

Rib: This tender and flavorful part of the animal can be cooked any number of ways. It includes ribs six to twelve. Most recipes call for ribs to be roasted, sautéed, pan-fried, broiled, or grilled. Major cuts from this part

---

Key Terms

Primal cuts   The large meat cuts taken from front and rear beef quarters. Primal cuts are typically sold to retail and wholesale outlets. Subprimal cuts are products resulting from further breaking down of primal cuts.

Fabricated cuts   The individual portions cut from subprimal cuts.

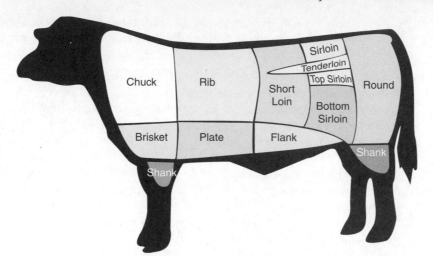

FIGURE 13.2 Beef Cattle Parts

include "rib roast," also known as a "standing rib roast (bone left in)," or as "prime rib." This section also produces the "ribeye" steak.

Short Loin: The short loin includes one rib (number 13). Fabricated cuts from this portion include Porterhouse steaks (which include a sizable portion of the tenderloin), T-bone steaks (which include smaller portions of tenderloin), and club steaks (which contain no tenderloin). When the backbone is removed, this primal cut also produces the New York strip steak. The tenderloin taken from the short loin area is often sold separately. It is boneless and produces the popular filet mignon steaks. Cuts from the short loin may be sautéed, pan fried, broiled, pan broiled, or grilled.

Sirloin: This cut produces the sirloin steak, as well as sirloin tip roasts and other flavorful fabricated cuts.

Flank: The meat from this portion of cattle is lean, muscular, and very flavorful. Flank is used primarily to produce flank steaks. Flank steaks have great flavor but must, when served, be carefully sliced thin and against the grain. It is used to make the classic dish London broil.

Short Plate: This section is most often used for stew meat, where its rich, beefy flavor can be appreciated. It also produces the skirt steak (used in classic fajitas), as well as short ribs.

Round: The round consists of lean meat well suited to long, moist cooking methods. Steamship rounds are very large roasts from this cut. Round may also be used as pot roast or cut into thick steaks for braising in dishes such as Swiss steak.

Shank/Brisket: Traditionally used for **corned beef,** or Bar-B-Q, brisket is best prepared with moist heat or very low dry heat. Suitable preparation methods for shank/brisket include stewing, braising, and pot-roasting.

With all the possible products made from the primal beef cuts, there are virtually hundreds of beef forms. When selling to foodservice operators, most packers and distributors sell **box beef.**

Key Terms

Corned beef   The process of preserving meat with salt. Corned beef (preserving beef with "corns" or large grains of salt) is an ancient form of meat preservation.

Box beef   The industry term for primal and subprimal cuts of beef that are vacuum-sealed and shipped to the buyer in cardboard boxes.

Fresh beef sold in the United States may take many forms; however, overwhelmingly, the majority of beef selected for use in foodservice is purchased as either ground beef or steaks.

Ground Beef: The incredibly popular "ground" beef is sold in a variety of forms and sizes and under a variety of names. This is so because, year after year, "hamburgers" are the single most popular menu item in America. Buyers should know, however, that in the United States "ground beef" is not the same as "hamburger." Beef fat may be added to "hamburger," but not "ground beef," if the meat is ground and packaged at a USDA-inspected plant. However, a maximum of 30 percent fat by weight is allowed in either hamburger or ground beef. Both hamburger and ground beef must be labeled in accordance with federal law and marked with a USDA-inspected label, but these products are not typically graded. When it comes to buying "ground" beef, buyers should carefully do their research and understand exactly what they are buying.

Generally, all ground beef products are made from the less tender and less popular cuts of beef. Trimmings from more tender cuts may also be used. Fat contents range from 5 to 30 percent. Although grinding tenderizes the beef and the fat reduces its dryness and improves its flavor, the process also creates problems. It is dangerous to eat raw or undercooked ground beef because it may contain harmful bacteria introduced during the grinding process. The USDA currently recommends that people not eat raw or undercooked ground beef. To be sure all bacteria are destroyed in meatloaf, meatballs, casseroles, and hamburgers, they recommend ground beef should be cooked to a minimum internal temperature of 160°F to ensure that it is safe to eat.

Steaks: As you learned, steaks come from selected primal and subprimal beef cuts. Steaks served as individual portions vary in quality and will vary even further based upon how they are handled prior to cooking, the cooking time and temperatures applied, and the internal temperatures at which they are served. Because of their importance to diners, meat buyers should particularly understand the cooked-steak terms culinarians use when preparing beef steaks and ground products. These are listed in Figure 13.3.

Steaks served in foodservice operations may be fabricated on site (from boxed beef) or purchased fresh or in the desired **IQF** size.

On-the-Job Challenges in Purchasing (13.1)

"We should grind our own beef," said Hendric, the executive chef at the Gaslight Steakhouse. "They quality would be much better, and I could use up the scraps left over from when the sous chef cuts our steaks. We would save a lot of money."

"We could I suppose," replied Sandy, the restaurant's manager. "Do you really think it would be a good idea?"

"Absolutely," replied Hendric.

Case Study Questions

Assume you were Sandy and were considering Hendric's request:

1. What product quality concerns might you have?
2. What cost concerns might you have?
3. What safety-related concerns might you have?

Key Term

IQF   Short for "Individually Quick Frozen."

Ordered/ Cooked	Traditional Temperature (United States)	Description
Blue	115°F–125°F	Blood-red meat, soft, very juicy
Rare	125°F–130°F	Red center, gray surface, soft, juicy
Medium rare	130°F–140°F	Pink center, gray-brown surface
Medium	140°F–150°F	Slightly pink center, becomes gray-brown toward surface
Medium well	150°F–160°F	Mostly gray center, firm texture
Well done	160+ °F	Gray-brown throughout

FIGURE 13.3   Steak Internal Temperatures

Increasingly, foodservice operators buy beef in a multitude of partially or fully precooked forms. Also, beef is a key ingredient in many canned or frozen convenience foods such as chili, stews, soups, and casserole dishes.

Purchasing Standards   As you have learned, beef processors may elect to have their beef graded. Although there are actually eight designated beef grades, commercial foodservice operators typically use only those three detailed in Figure 13.4.

Beef carcasses (as well as lamb) are also graded, on a scale of 1 to 5, for yield. Yield grade 1 represents the greatest yield (most usable meat), and number 5 the least.

VEAL   Veal is the meat of young, usually male, beef calves. Veal is actually a by-product of the dairy industry. Dairy cows must calve before they begin to give milk. Thus, calves not used in the dairy herds were traditionally killed for food at an early age. Although veal can come from any animal under the age of 9 months, most are slaughtered at 8 to 16 weeks old. Veal is lighter in color than beef, is lower in fat, and has a milder flavor. It is used in a variety of dishes and cuisines.

Product	USDA Seal	
		FIGURE 13.4 Top Three USDA Beef Quality Grades
USDA Prime: Prime grade beef is the ultimate in tenderness, juiciness, and flavor. It is highly marbled, with large flecks of fat within the lean, which enhances both flavor and juiciness.	USDA PRIME	
USDA Choice: Choice grade beef has less marbling than prime, but is of very high quality. Choice roasts and steaks from the loin and rib are very tender, juicy, and flavorful.	USDA CHOICE	
USDA Select: Select grade beef is very uniform in quality and somewhat leaner than the higher grades. It is fairly tender but, because it has less marbling, it lacks some of the juiciness and flavor of the higher grades.	USDA SELECT	

PURCHASING PROS NEED TO KNOW (13.1)

Food buyers need not be expert chefs; however, when it comes to meat, and especially beef, professional buyers need to fully understand the intended use for a meat item before they can effectively create a purchase specification for it. A basic understanding of the two most common meat-cooking procedures is helpful to doing so. This is so because a quality piece of meat, when cooked improperly, will be of poor quality. It is best to match the cut of meat purchased with the cooking method that will be used to prepare it.

Dry Heat Cooking Methods: Tender cuts of beef from the loin and rib are best cooked with dry cooking methods, such as grilling, broiling, roasting, and sautéing. Grilling is characterized by cooking the beef over a high heat source, generally in excess of 650 °F. This leads to searing of the surface of the beef, which, due to the Maillard effect, creates a flavorful crust. Broiling is similar to grilling, except that grilling is usually performed with the heat source *under* the beef, and broiling is usually performed with the heat source *above* the beef. Roasting is a method of cooking that uses hot air to cook the meat all the way around the product at the same time. Pan frying and deep frying are also considered dry heat cooking methods.

Moist Heat Cooking Methods: Tougher cuts of beef from the round, brisket, flank, plate, shank, and chuck are generally best cooked by a moist heat cooking method such as simmering, or a combination of dry and moist cooking such as braising, pot-roasting, and stewing. Stewing involves immersing the entire cut of meat in a liquid. Braising involves cooking meats, covered, with small amounts of liquids (usually seasoned or flavored).

Cuts   Veal carcasses are cut into a foresaddle (front portion), and a hindsaddle (rear portion). A veal carcass yields five primal cuts: three from the foresaddle (shoulder, foreshank and breast, and rib), and two from the hindsaddle (loin and leg). These cuts may be cooked whole or further fabricated.

Purchasing Standards   There are five USDA grades for veal and meat of calves: prime, choice, good, standard, and utility. Prime is the most juicy and flavorful. Choice cuts are somewhat less juicy and flavorful than prime cuts. Dry heat may be used to cook the most tender veal cuts such as loin roasts, rib roasts, rump roasts, loin chops, rib chops, cutlets, and ground veal. Moist cooking methods should be used for cuts such as shank cross-cuts, shoulder roasts, breasts, and round steaks.

PORK   Pork is the edible meat from pigs (hogs), or domestic swine. The domestication of pigs for food dates back to about 7000 B.C. in the Middle East. However, evidence shows that Stone Age man ate wild boar, the hog's ancestor, and the earliest surviving written pork recipe is from China and is estimated to be at least 2,000 years old.

Internet Purchasing Assistant (13.2)

Buyers responsible for quantity beef purchases should understand fully the USDA quality and yield grade programs. To learn more about these, go to: www.ams.usda.gov/lsg/mgc/beefrole.htm

At the home page:

1. Type "purpose of federal grading" in the site's search box.

   Also

2. Type "history of federal grading" in the site's search box.

Hogs were introduced to Florida by Hernando de Soto in 1525 and soon were raised in all parts of the United States. Today, with the exception of beef, Americans consume more pork than any other meat. The United States is one of the world's leading pork-producing countries. In fact, the United States is the third largest exporter, trailing only long-time world leader Denmark and Canada. U.S. production accounts for about 10 percent of total world supply. Interestingly, during the war of 1812, the U.S. government shipped pork to American soldiers packed in barrels stamped with the letters "US" and the name of the meat packer, Sam Wilson. The soldiers referred to the meat as "Uncle Sam's," thus giving rise to the government's still popular nickname of "Uncle Sam."

Despite its extensive popularity, pork is also the meat most often avoided by large numbers of people. Throughout the Islamic world, many countries severely restrict the importation and/or consumption of pork products. This is so because Muslims are forbidden from consuming pork or any of its derivatives. Pork is also one of the best known of a category of foods forbidden under traditional Jewish dietary law. Historically, pigs have been considered animals that, if eaten, could cause disease. Today, however, the pork sold in the United States is as safe and disease-free a product as is either beef or chicken.

Because of its high **myoglobin** content, fresh pork is pink or red before cooking, and then becomes lighter as it is cooked.

According to the USDA, pork is considered a red meat because it contains more myoglobin than white meat such as chicken or fish. Despite this traditional definition of pork as a red meat, in 1987 the National Pork Board in the United States began an advertising campaign to position pork as "the other white meat" due to a public perception of chicken and turkey (white meats) as more healthy than red meat. The campaign was highly successful and resulted in 87 percent of consumers identifying pork with the slogan and as a "healthy" meat item. As of the time of this book's development, the slogan is still used in the marketing of pork.

Cuts   Pork is generally produced from young animals (6 to 7 months old) that weigh from 175 to 240 pounds. Much of a slaughtered hog is cured and made into ham, bacon, and sausage. The uncured meat is called "fresh pork" and comes from one of the animal's primal or subprimal cuts.

Although the terminology used to describe fresh pork products varies somewhat by region of the United States and by country, foodservice buyers should understand the eight basic parts of a pig. Starting at the animal's head and moving clockwise (Figure 13.5), the major pork cuts and foodservice products they produce are

Pork Cuts	Foodservice Use and Cuts
Head	Processed meats products (souse, pâtés, terrines)
Blade shoulder	This section includes the "Boston Butt," a square cut located just above the shoulder. The Boston Butt is very lean and when smoked is called a cottage ham. Roasts and steaks cut from this section may be called blade roasts, boneless blade roasts, and blade steaks (pork steaks).
Loin	This section of the animal produces the chops: pork tenderloin and pork back ribs that are so popular in foodservice operations. Boneless loin is used to make Canadian bacon. Other common cuts used in foodservice include rib roasts, sirloin chops, crown roasts, butterfly chops, and boneless center-cut loin roasts.

Key Term

Myoglobin   The oxygen-transporting protein found in animal muscle.

FIGURE 13.5 Eight Pork Cuts

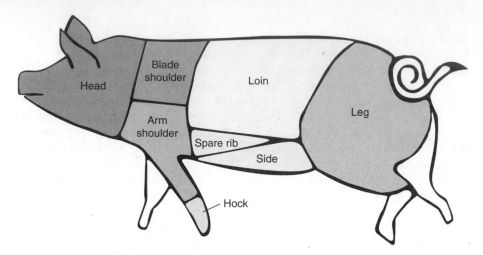

Leg	The leg of a pig includes the leg muscle and shank of the animal. The most popular use of this cut is the production of hams. These include boneless, bone-in, shank-in, and shankless varieties. This portion also includes the rear hock, used primarily in seasoning a variety of stocks, soups, and foods.
Side	Noted mainly for bacon production, this cut has a very high fat content. It is nearly always separated from the spare ribs prior to processing.
Spare Rib	Spare ribs are removed from the side of the animal for processing. They can be purchased smoked but are most often sold to foodservice operators in their fresh or frozen state. Increasingly, spare ribs are seasoned, brined, marinated or cooked prior to their sale to foodservice operators.
Hock	Used in the same manner as the hock from the rear leg, this product is most often stewed or braised.
Arm Shoulder	The arm shoulder is also known as the "picnic" or "picnic ham" portion. Picnics may be smoked but are also sold as fresh products for roasting.

Pork is a unique form of livestock because the ribs and loin are not separated into two different primal cuts, as are the ribs and loin of beef, veal, and lamb. As with all meats, it is important to know the location of bones when cutting or working with pork. This makes meat fabrication and carving easier and aids in identifying cuts for purchase.

Purchasing Standards   USDA grades for pork reflect only two levels of quality: acceptable and unacceptable. Acceptable quality pork is also graded for yield, that is, the yield ratio of lean to waste. Unacceptable quality pork, which includes meat that is soft and watery, is graded "U.S. Utility" and is not generally available for foodservice usage.

Pork, on a per pound basis, can be both very expensive and economical. This is so because the difference in cost between its various cuts is large. To better understand why, consider that a 250-pound live hog yields approximately a 180-pound carcass. Of that, approximately 145 pounds of saleable retail pork cuts will result, with fat, bone, and skin accounting for the other 35 pounds.

Demand for the various highly desired products (ribs and chops) dictates the prices charged for these cuts. It is also true that, when pork is highly processed (as for bacon and hams), its cost per pound also increases significantly.

Hospitality buyers should understand that pork can be labeled as "natural" if it complies with the USDA standards for natural processing. The standards stipulate that the product cannot contain artificial ingredients, artificial coloring, or chemical preservatives and can have only minimal meat processing done. It can be processed using traditional methods to preserve it and to make it edible and safe to consume. Methods such as freezing, smoking, roasting, drying, and fermenting can be used. Physical processes, such as cutting into component retail cuts, are allowed, but processes such as grinding, which alter the raw product, are not allowed. When producing "natural" pork, the pork producers must follow the production guidelines set up by the FDA for all federally inspected pork.

For many foodservice operators, a large amount of pork purchasing will involve processed products. Figure 13.6 is the inspection mark used on processed pork (as well as other meat) products. This mark should be on all processed pork items purchased.

Among the most popular of the processed pork items used in foodservice are smoked ham and bacon. Ham and bacon are made from fresh pork cuts by curing these with salt and/or smoking them. Shoulders and rear legs (or "hams") are most often cured in this manner. In addition to ham and bacon, pork is particularly common as an ingredient in sausage, which is popular in many foodservice operations and is most often purchased in bulk, links, or patties.

FIGURE 13.6   Inspection Mark Used on Processed (and Fresh) Meat Products

THE SUPPLIER'S SIDE (13.1)

"Insider" Tips on Purchasing: From the Supplier's Perspective

Buyer's Question: Why isn't pork graded?

Supplier's Answer: Because of the consistency of today's pork products, the USDA does not really see a need for grading.

Buyer's Question: So, are there quality differences in fresh pork products?

Supplier's Answer: Absolutely. The marbling in pork (as in beef) is an indicator of quality. The more streaks of fat you see, the more tender and flavorful the pork will be. Pork that comes from certain breeds, such as certified Berkshire pork (known in Japan as Kurobuta or "Black Hog") has dark red meat and heavy marbling and is among the best pork you can buy.

Buyer's Question: What should I know about buying fresh and processed pork products that most foodservice operators do not know?

Supplier's Answer: Because the wholesale price of pork can fluctuate widely during short periods of time, a strong relationship with your vendor is critical. This is so because, if your supplier knows you are a loyal customer, they can help cushion you against short-term, but very wide, product price variations. They will not likely do that if your continued business is unsure.

Internet Purchasing Assistant (13.3)

Hormel Foods Corporation was established in 1891 as Geo. A. Hormel & Company in Austin, Minnesota, by George A. Hormel. The company specialized in fresh pork products. A true product innovator, Hormel developed the world's first canned ham in 1926. The company's expansion into international markets received special emphasis in the late 1990s, beginning with a joint venture with Grupo Herdez, S.A. de C.V., in Mexico City to market Hormel Foods products in Mexico. Today, Hormel produces, and distributes worldwide, a tremendous variety of meat (and other) products for the foodservice industry. To view this innovative company's Web site, go to: www.hormelfoodservice.com

At the home page, click on "Recipes" to see how their products are used in a foodservice setting.

LAMB A lamb is a young sheep. Sheep were among the first animals domesticated. An archeological site in Iran produced a statuette of a wool-bearing sheep, which suggests that the selection of sheep for clothing and food had begun over 6,000 years ago.

Interestingly, the terms "lamb" and "mutton" are used to describe the meat of domesticated sheep. Both terms refer to products generally known as sheep meat. Although not extremely common on many American-style restaurant menus, sheep meats are featured prominently in the cuisines of the Mediterranean, North Africa, Middle East, and certain parts of China. In some countries, including India, the term "mutton" more frequently refers to goat (not sheep) meat, although in most Indian restaurants in the United States, sheep meat is generally served.

Cuts Technically, lamb is any sheep less than 1 year old. They are known for their tender meat. Baby lamb is customarily slaughtered at between 6 and 8 weeks old. Spring lamb is usually 3 to 5 months old and has not been fed on grass or grains. Regular lamb is slaughtered under a year of age. Lamb between 12 and 24 months is called a yearling and when it is over 2 years old it is referred to as mutton and has a much stronger flavor and less tender flesh.

Lamb carcasses generally are cut into four main parts: shoulder, rack (source of lamb rib chops), loin (source of lamb loin chops), and leg. Lamb, served in the form of rib or loin chops, which are cooked plain or after **frenching,** are among the most popular of lamb cuts. Lamb leg served as roast is also popular.

Additional foodservice cuts of lamb that are commonly available include the neck, fore shank, breast (also called the brisket), and flank.

Purchasing Standards Approximately 50 percent of the lamb sold in the United States is imported from New Zealand or Australia. U.S. lamb, because it is

The rib chop is one of the most tender (and tastiest) parts of a lamb.

David Murray and Jules Selmes
© Dorling Kindersley

Key Term

Frenching (chops) A method of trimming individual or connected chops of meat (especially lamb), in which the excess fat is cut away from the bone, leaving the eye muscle intact.

Grade	Characteristics
Prime	Has abundant marbling and is generally very juicy and tender.
Choice	Has less marbling than prime grades, but is still high quality.
Good, utility, and cull	These cuts are seldom sold to foodservice buyers.

FIGURE 13.7 USDA Lamb Quality Grades

fed on grain (not grass), tends to be smaller-boned and milder in flavor than imported lamb. As shown in Figure 13.7, there are five USDA grades for lamb based on proportion of fat to lean. Beginning with the best, they are prime, choice, good, utility, and cull. When purchasing lamb, in general, the darker the color, the older the animal. Baby lamb will be pale pink, whereas regular lamb is pinkish-red. Lamb can be purchased ground and in steaks, chops, and roasts in either fresh or frozen forms. Lamb variety meats can also be purchased.

Because the quality of lamb varies according to the age of the animal, it is advisable to buy lamb that has been USDA graded only prime or choice.

CHARCUTERIE Historically, **charcuterie** referred to sausages, ham, pâtés, and other cooked or processed pork products. Today, the art and science of the charcutier includes the use of conventional pork products as well as **forcemeat** mixtures made from all types of meat, poultry, fish, and vegetables.

In the days before refrigeration, charcuterie began as a necessary process to preserve meats before they would spoil. In many cases, the products created proved equally as popular as the fresh meats from which they were made. Today, the desirability (and purchase price) of foie gras (a pâté made from goose liver that can easily cost over $100 per pound), other specialty pâtés, terrines, and galantines is heavily influenced by the quality of the original products used to make them, as well the item's primary ingredients. The main ingredients will include the dominant meat or seafood from which the item is made and the fat that is added, for flavor, to the item. In addition, binders of starch or egg may be added, as well as seasonings that give the item its characteristic flavor and texture (e.g., chicken liver pâté). In some items, garnishes of meats, fats, vegetables, or other foods are added in limited quantities to provide contrasting flavors and textures. Common garnishes include pistachio nuts, fatback, truffles, and diced ham or sausages.

Poultry

Poultry is the collective term used to describe domesticated birds bred for eating. The USDA recognizes six categories of poultry: chicken, turkey, duck, goose, guinea, and pigeon. Each poultry type is divided into classes based upon the bird's age, tenderness, and in some cases, sex. Chickens and turkey make up the overwhelming majority of poultry sold in the United States.

The low cost and mild flavor of poultry products means they will make up a significant portion of many operations' overall entrée items. In addition, because

Key Terms

Charcuterie The processing of meat, poultry, fish, shellfish, or vegetables prepared by salt curing, brining, and cold or hot smoking.

Forcemeat A preparation made from uncooked ground meats, poultry, fish, or shellfish that is seasoned and emulsified with fat.

Internet Purchasing Assistant (13.4)

Charcuterie (from the French *cuiseur de chair*, cooker of meat) is the branch of cooking origi-nally devoted to prepared pork products. The practice is an ancient one and involves the chem-ical preservation of meats. It was initially practiced as a way to use up various meat scraps and to preserve larger cuts such as hams and bacon.

Despite its French name, the Italians are masters at charcuterie as well. To view a U.S. im-porter of classic Italian charcuterie products, go to: www.dibruno.com

When you arrive:

1. Click on "Charcuterie.
2. Next, click on "Prosciutto."
3. Next, read the information about this famous processed pork product.

of the many processed forms of poultry available to foodservice operators, poul-try consumption continues to rise. In fact, whereas red meat still comes out ahead of poultry in terms of per-capita consumption, the gap has been narrowing and will continue to shrink over the next decade, according to projections from the USDA. Based upon its data, in 2003, consumption of red meat, including beef, veal, pork, lamb, and mutton, was 118.5 pounds per person. Consumption of these items is projected to fall to just over 112 pounds in 2013. Meanwhile, poultry con-sumption, according to their projections, will rise from 100.2 pounds per person in 2003 to 108.9 pounds per person by 2013.

All poultry must be officially inspected to ensure that it is wholesome, prop-erly labeled, and not adulterated. Every poultry processing plant's premises, facil-ities, equipment, and procedures must be inspected. When sold, an inspection stamp must appear on the label. This mandatory inspection is done by the USDA's Food Safety and Inspection Service. It must be done before poultry can be graded for quality. The USDA's Agricultural Marketing Service provides grading services, on a voluntary basis, to poultry processors and others who request it and pay a fee for it. Most poultry sold to foodservice industry buyers is U.S. Grade A, the high-est quality grade.

Figure 13.8 illustrates the most common market forms of poultry sold to foodservice operators.

The USDA grade shield should be on the following ready-to-cook poultry products, whether purchased chilled or frozen:

- Whole poultry carcasses
- Poultry parts (with or without the skin, bone-in or boneless)
- Poultry roasts
- Poultry tenderloins

There are no grade standards for poultry necks, wing tips, tails, **giblets,** or poultry meat that is diced, shredded, or ground.

Although poultry grades are important, increasingly, poultry is sold and purchased in a wide variety of preprocessed forms. Today, foodservice buyers

Key Term

Giblets The edible internal organs of poultry, including heart, liver, gizzard, and kidneys.

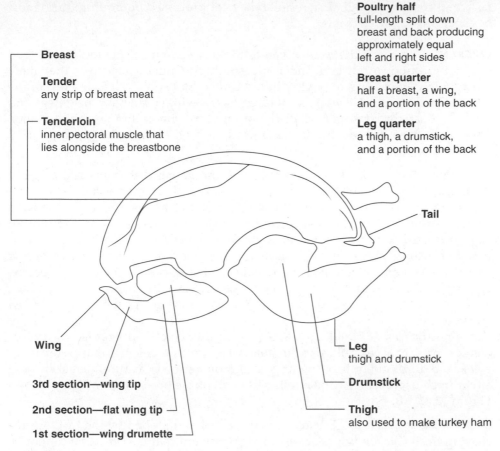

Poultry half
full-length split down
breast and back producing
approximately equal
left and right sides

Breast quarter
half a breast, a wing,
and a portion of the back

Leg quarter
a thigh, a drumstick,
and a portion of the back

Breast

Tender
any strip of breast meat

Tenderloin
inner pectoral muscle that
lies alongside the breastbone

Tail

Wing

3rd section—wing tip

2nd section—flat wing tip

1st section—wing drumette

Leg
thigh and drumstick

Drumstick

Thigh
also used to make turkey ham

FIGURE 13.8   Basic Poultry Market Forms
Source: USDA

selecting poultry products choose from processed alternatives that range from items such as poultry-based "hot dogs," "hams," and "bacon" to breaded, battered, and preseasoned poultry parts and shaped meats. Adding to the complexity of buying poultry, many poultry products of all forms may be injected with seasoning solutions that significantly increase product weight and thus affect the

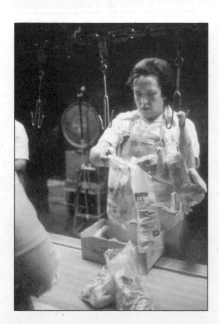

Most poultry products undergo a grading process before shipping to consumers.
Ron Sherman/Creative Eye/MIRA.com

taste and cost per pound. As a result, buyers of processed poultry products must be especially knowledgeable.

CHICKEN   Chicken is the name given to the descendents of the red jungle fowl originally found in northern India and southern China. Chicken is the single most widely eaten form of poultry in the United States, as well as the rest of the world. Chickens contain white meat (breasts and wings) and dark meat (legs and thighs). Most chickens have a relatively low fat content and are quite tender. They are served roasted, fried, and stewed, as well as, increasingly, in myriad processed forms.

Market Forms   Chickens have very specific names, based upon the age of the animal. A young chicken is called a chick. A male chicken is a cock or cockerel. Similarly, a female chicken is called a pullet or a hen. The age at which a pullet becomes a hen and a cockerel becomes a cock depends on the type of chicken raised. Typically, however, a chicken is a cockerel or pullet if it is less than one year of age. After one year of age, the chicken is referred to as a hen or cock. In the commercial industry, a female chicken is called a hen after it begins egg production (around five months of age). A sexually mature male chicken, also around five months old, is referred to as a rooster. A capon is a castrated male chicken.

Specific classes based upon age also identify chickens. A broiler or fryer is a chicken eight weeks old or younger. A roaster is a chicken that is up to 16 weeks old. Birds older than 6 months are simply termed "mature." Chicken, sold either fresh or frozen, may be purchased in all of the product forms identified in Figure 13.8.

Purchasing Standards   Because it is inspected and graded by the USDA, purchasing fresh chicken is a relatively straightforward matter. The same cannot be said about processed chicken parts and products. Chicken meat is increasingly purchased by foodservice buyers in easier-to-cook, or precooked and pre-processed forms. Those who buy processed chicken products must consider three major issues: the method for removing chicken meat from the bone, internal product modifications, and external product treatments.

Meat Removal: Not all boneless poultry meat is removed from the bone by knives. "Mechanically separated poultry" is a paste-like and batter-like poultry product produced by forcing bones with attached meat tissue through a sieve or similar device under high pressure to separate bone from the edible tissue. Mechanically separated poultry has been used in poultry products since 1969. The resulting meat has as different texture than regular poultry meat, and buyers should know whether the processed chicken they are buying has been produced using mechanically separated poultry.

Internal Product Modifications: Food additives are not generally allowed on fresh-sold poultry. However, if chickens are processed (injected with a basting solution, ground, canned, cured, smoked, dried, or made into luncheon meats), additives such as Monosodium Glutamate (MSG), salt, or sodium erythorbate may be added. When they are, these ingredients must be listed on the label in descending order from largest to smallest amount of ingredient. If injected with liquids, stocks, broths, and so on, the products should be so labeled, and buyers must be able to determine the amount of solution (by weight) that has been added to the product.

External Product Modifications: Many processed poultry products are battered (e.g., with wet batters) or breaded (e.g., with cracker meal, bread-crumbs, or cornmeal) for frying. The meat may be either cooked or raw prior

On-the-Job Challenges in Purchasing (13.2)

"You're sure it's the same item?" asked Sofie to Lars, the sales representative from Braddock foods.

"Look," said Lars, "you said you wanted a precooked, 6-ounce, breaded chicken breast for your popular Fried Chicken Sandwich right?" asked Lars. "And at a good price!"

"Yes," replied Sofie, "but you say your item costs 40 percent less than the item I'm currently buying. That seems like a big difference if your product is really the same."

"We buy in volume," said Lars, "so I can pass the savings on to you."

Case Study Questions

Assume you were Sofie:

1. What questions about meat removal would you ask Lars?
2. What questions about internal product modification are appropriate?
3. What questions about external product modification are appropriate?

to its coating. For battered and breaded poultry, the pieces are passed through a flour-based batter containing leavening and then through the breading ingredients. Nuggets, fingers, strips, fritters, and patties are all examples of recognized forms of externally modified chicken products. The USDA requires that combined batter and breading for chicken nuggets, fingers, strips, and patties do not exceed 30 percent by weight. Chicken fritters may contain up to 65 percent batter and breading and must contain at least 35 percent meat. Because manufacturers can produce any chicken products they desire within these broad parameters, it is easy to see why processed chicken product buyers must be very careful when comparing alternative products across vendors.

TURKEY Turkeys are members of the pheasant family and native to North America. Turkey is the second most popular poultry meat sold in the United States, where it is served roasted whole and in an ever-increasing variety of processed products. A longtime food favorite in the southern United States, even deep-fried turkey (despite the dangers associated with cooking it), has also quickly grown in popularity, due in large part to its promotion by food celebrities such as Martha Stewart and Emeril Lagasse.

Market Forms When purchased whole, or in parts, turkeys are classified as either a fryer/roaster (under 16 weeks old), young (8 months old or less), yearling (15 months old or less), or mature (15 months old and older). Like chicken, turkey contains both white (breast and wings) and dark meats (legs and thighs). In most areas of the country, all of these parts may be purchased fresh or frozen.

Because of its low cost and mild flavor, virtually hundreds of processed turkey products are available. Turkey ham, a meat product made from the thigh meat of turkeys, is cured and smoked like pork. The size and shape of the "ham" depends on how the meat is processed, and it is generally available in whole or half portions. Turkey ham is approximately 95 percent fat-free and is a low-fat alternative to ham made from pork. Turkey bacon is a meat product produced from smoked turkey that has a similar appearance and flavor to pork bacon. It is used just like bacon, however, because it contains less fat than bacon made from pork, and turkey bacon shrinks less when cooked (and produces a higher E.P. yield). Turkey pastrami is an increasingly popular turkey product made from skinless thigh and drumstick meat that has been ground and seasoned. Like other types of pastrami, turkey pastrami is flavored with peppercorns and other seasonings, then cured, and smoked.

Purchasing Standards   In most cases, the same purchase standards that apply to chicken and other processed meats apply to turkeys. A unique purchasing term associated with bone-in turkey products, however, is **self-basted.**

When bone-in products are sold as self-basted, the label must include a statement identifying the total quantity and common or usual name of all ingredients in the solution; for example, *"Injected with approximately 3% of a solution of* _____ (list of ingredients). Basted and self-basted solutions in poultry products are limited to 8 percent of the raw poultry weight before processing.

DUCK   The duck ("canard" in French) used most often in commercial foodservice is a roaster duckling. The USDA establishes different classes for ducks. Broiler ducklings or fryer ducklings are young ducks (usually under 8 weeks of age) of either sex. Roaster ducklings are young ducks under 16 weeks of age. Mature ducks are usually over 6 months of age. Government duck grades are USDA A, B, and C; however, most buyers will not have options beyond Grade A.

Ducks contain only dark meat and have an extremely high fat content. Duck also has a high bone and fat-to-meat ratio. As a result, buyers of this item must recognize that the edible portion yields of duck are approximately half that of commercial chickens. Thus, for example, whereas a four-pound roasting chicken could serve four people, an equivalent sized duck would serve only two people.

Market Forms   Ducks are most often sold whole or halved. Duck breasts, which may be labeled as "magrets," are also a common market form. Duck sausages and pâtés are also popular. Ducks and duck parts may be purchased fresh or frozen.

Purchasing Standards   The quality of duck meat relates most to its age and feed. There are two groups of duck typically bred for meat: the Muscovy and the Pekin. The Muscovy duck is the largest of the common duck breeds. The White Pekin duck, native to China, grows rapidly and is also a popular animal among breeders. Buyers can choose either breed, but only those that have been properly inspected.

Game

Game refers to animals that, traditionally, have been hunted either for food or sport.

Today, the increased popularity of many game animals has increased these items' presence on foodservice menus, especially in the fine dining restaurant segment. It is important to understand that, in nearly all cases, the buying and selling of wild game (animals or birds) is strictly prohibited. Farm-raised game, however, may be sold. Before they may be sold, some game animals are inspected by the USDA and others by the FDA. Game is typically divided into two basic categories: furred game and winged game.

FURRED GAME   Furred game animals can be large or small. Large, furred game animals commonly sold on restaurant menus include antelope, buffalo, beefalo (a cross between bison and beef cattle), caribou, deer, and wild boar. Small game animals sold include alligator and rabbit, although squirrel, beaver, muskrat, opossum, raccoon, armadillo, porcupine, and other species infrequently appear.

Key Terms

Self-basted   A legally recognized food term referring to the fact that the product described has been injected or marinated with a solution containing butter or other edible fat, broth, stock or water plus spices, flavor enhancers, and other approved substances.

Game   Animals hunted for food or sport.

The meat on game animals is typically dark and may have a strong flavor, but in the hands of talented culinarians can be extremely tasty. Because of potential health and safety issues, buyers of these products must be extremely careful to ensure the supplier of furred game operates legally and supplies only government-inspected products.

WINGED GAME Like furred game, the sale of wild winged game birds in the United States is illegal. Winged game birds are, however, very popular menu items. As a result, the game bird industry in the United States annually raises millions of birds for sale to commercial foodservice operators and direct to consumers. The most popular of these are pheasant, partridge, and quail, but also include grouse, guinea fowl, squab (young pigeon), and ostrich. Winged game is available whole or precut and can be purchased fresh or frozen.

Seafood

The term "seafood," unfortunately for buyers, can mean many different things to different foodservice suppliers. For some, it refers only to specific species of fish with shells (shellfish) or other small marine creatures. For other sellers, seafood refers to virtually all types of freshwater and saltwater fish, and to shellfish. This wider definition will be used in this text, although, for ease of study, seafood will be categorized as either fish or shellfish.

Today more seafood of outstanding quality is available, and more widely, than ever before. Foodservice buyers may also choose seafoods that come from all over the world, thus allowing the opportunity to offer new ingredients and creative menu items. At the same time, the variety and variability of seafood make it challenging to purchase because these items are more fragile and less predictable than other available meats.

Both fish and shellfish have become increasingly popular on foodservice menus in recent years. This is so, in part, because of the reputation of seafoods as good sources of protein, B vitamins, various minerals, and in the case of cold-water ocean fish, high levels of desirable omega-3 fatty acids. These nutrients cannot be made very efficiently by the human body and are essential to the development and function of the brain (thus fish are sometimes referred to as "brain food") and to the health of the body's central nervous system. Other documented benefits of omega-3 fatty acids include lowering the incident of heart disease, strokes, and the artery-damaging form of blood cholesterol.

In addition to consumer perceptions of health benefits, fish are increasingly available on foodservice menus because of the ways they are packaged and stored. Fish are more perishable than other meats, and in the past that limited their use on commercial foodservice menus. Today, however, improved packaging and processing techniques have resulted in ample availability of most high-quality seafood (both fish and shellfish) at all times of the year.

FISH Fish include those species of animals found living in both fresh and salt water. Fish, by definition, have fins and an internal skeleton of bones and cartilage. The number of different kinds of fish in the world is stunning. Of all the animals with backbones, fish account for over half, or about 29,000 different species. Not all of those species are eaten regularly, nor (fortunately) are they all available for purchase. Of those that are commonly eaten, fish can readily be divided into two groups, based primarily upon their shape and skeletal structure.

"Round" fish swim in a vertical position and have eyes on both sides of their head (see, for example, Black Sea Bass; Figure 13.9). These are purchased either as filets (horizontal cuts) or as steaks (vertical cuts).

Unlike round fish, "flat fish" have asymmetrical compressed bodies, swim in a horizontal position, and have both eyes on the top of their heads. (See, for

FIGURE 13.9 Black Sea Bass (a type of round fish)
© Culinary Institute of America

example, a Dover Sole; Figure 13.10). Flatfish tend to live on the bottom of ocean waters around the world. Typically, the skin on the top of their bodies is dark (to hide them from predators). Because of their body shape, these species are not generally available in steak form and are sold either whole or, more commonly, as filets.

Even when segmented into round and flat fish, identifying fish by sight and name can be hard because of the vast number of fish that look similar but are a separate species within a fish family. In addition, confusion can easily result when various names are given to fish based upon the locality in which the fish is either caught or eaten.

Generally, in comparison with most food products, seafood has been poorly labeled. In the case of meats, for example, buyers know about the animal species (i.e., turkey, cow, chicken) and cut of the meat. In addition, in most cases, it is common to get information about where the meat was produced or how it was grown (e.g., organic, free-range, grain feed). In contrast, buyers often do not even know which species of seafood they purchase (e.g., more than 100 fish species are currently and legally marketed as "Snapper," and over 20 can be legally marketed as "Red Snapper").

In most cases, neither a fish product's specific origin nor how it was harvested is included on the label. Add to these facts the reality that, in most cases, fish purchased today will not be delivered in its fresh, whole, and somewhat easily identifiable state, but rather in refrigerated or frozen prefabricated steak or filet forms, and it is easy to see why buying fish can be so challenging. The FDA does publish a list of approved market names for fish in the *Seafood List: FDA Guide to*

FIGURE 13.10 Dover Sole (a type of flat fish)
David Murray and Jules Selmes © Dorling Kindersley

Atlantic cod	Herring	Sardines
Atlantic salmon	John Dory	Scrod
Bass	Mackerel	Shark
Black sea bass	Mahi-mahi	Silver salmon (Coho)
Catfish	Monkfish	Swordfish
Chinook (King salmon)	Orange roughy	Tilapia
Cod	Pacific cod	Trout
Eels	Pollock	Tuna
Grouper	Red snapper	Wahoo
Haddock	Rockfish	Whitefish

FIGURE 13.11 Popular Round Fish

Acceptable Market Names for Food Fish Sold in Interstate Commerce (2002). The list is updated regularly. Supplier deviations from these approved names are discouraged, but historically have been difficult to enforce.

Despite the challenges and complexity of knowing what, exactly, has been selected, fish buyers can learn to better understand how to purchase round and flat fish.

Round Fish A detailed description of the types and market forms of round fish readily available to foodservice operators would fill its own book, and serious seafood buyers are encouraged to seek out the fish species-specific information they need to effectively purchase these items. Figure 13.11 lists thirty of the varieties of round fish commonly used in foodservice operations.

Flat Fish Although fewer in number, flat fish are extremely popular on many foodservice menus. Buyers of flat fish also know that they are among the most complex to buy. It is easy to realize why when you understand that, for example, the FDA permits use of the term "Sole" (a popular flat fish) to be applied to over fifteen different varieties of fish. These include English sole, Rock sole, Sand sole, and Petrale sole as well as Yellowtail flounder, Starry flounder, and Fluke. In addition to flounder and sole (often one and the same, but named differently on the menu), other popular flatfish commonly sold in the foodservice industry include halibut and turbot.

SHELLFISH Like fish, shellfish can be more easily studied if they are first divided into two major classifications: **mollusks** and **crustaceans.**

Mollusks To best understand them, mollusks can be further divided into those that are univalve, bivalve, or **cephalopods.**

Univalve mollusks include Abalone, the brownish-gray shelled species harvested off the coast of California (California law does not permit it to be canned or

---

Key Terms

Mollusk Shellfish with soft, unsegmented bodies, and no internal skeleton. Examples include conch, clams, and oysters.

Crustacean Shellfish with hard outer skeletons or shells and joints that separate the "head" from the "tail" (as in shrimp and lobster), or "leg" from the "body" (as with crabs).

Cephalopods Marine mollusks with distinct heads and well-developed eyes. They lack an outer shell of any type. Examples include squid and octopus.

Internet Purchasing Assistant (13.5)

Catfish production is the leading aquaculture (fish farming) industry in the United States. Commercial catfish production generates over 46 percent of the value of all aquaculture production in the country. The catfish market has evolved over the past several years from being an "oddity" regional item, consumed primarily in the southern United States, to a large, commercial industry that serves all major U.S. markets.

Catfish harvests are seasonal, following the growing cycle of the fish. Catfish farmers harvest their ponds at the end of the summer, after the period in which the fish experience their maximum weight gain and before the fish enter a period of slower growth during the winter. This leads to a seasonal abundance of fish between late summer and early winter, the time of year when catfish prices are usually at their lowest. Catfish is simply one example of how aquaculture techniques can influence what foodservice operators serve on their menus. To learn more about this increasingly popular fish item, go to: www.catfishwholesale.com

On the home page:

Click on "Catfish" to review the various product forms available to commercial buyers.

shipped out of state), and Conch (found off the waters of the Florida Keys and the Caribbean). Snails, too (although these are actually univalve land animals), are often considered univalve mollusks.

Bivalve mollusks are characterized by two bilateral shells attached by a central hinge. Widely served in a variety of market forms, they are often sold while still alive. Figure 13.12 lists fifteen of the most popular of these.

Cephalopods include octopus and squid (calamari is their Italian name), and they may be purchased fresh or frozen in blocks. Tender fleshed, these mollusks, like all others, must be wisely handled and carefully cooked if they are to be served safely and at the peak of their quality.

Crustaceans   Crustaceans are found in both fresh and salt water. They have a hard outer shell and jointed appendages and breathe through gills. They are among the most popular and expensive of all the seafoods. Some species (e.g.,

---

PURCHASING PROS NEED TO KNOW (13.2)

The quality of fish and shellfish vary much more than does the quality of other meats and poultry. As a result, the eating characteristics of many fish and shellfish change significantly from one season to the next. This is so because these animals live out two life cycles. During the first phase, they grow and mature, storing up energy reserves and reaching the peak of their flavor and quality. At this time, their taste will be at its absolute best.

A subsequent life phase, however, finds them expending their stored energy to migrate and create masses of eggs or sperm to ensure future generations. It is important to understand that most fish do not store energy reserves in layers of fat like land animals. Instead, the proteins stored in their meat muscles provide their energy reserves. When migrating and spawning, they accumulate protein-digesting enzymes in their muscles and thus retrieve their stored energy. Then and immediately afterward, their flesh will be soft and spongy.

Because different fish species will have different life cycles and, even within the same species, will have life cycle variations based upon where on the globe they are harvested, it is often very difficult for buyers to know whether a given fish variety will, in fact, be at its peak. In such cases, and when it is not possible for the buyer to personally inspect each fish product before it is purchased, the quality and reputation of an operation's fresh fish supplier is the key to ensuring product quality.

Atlantic oysters (Bluepoints)	European oysters	Pacific oysters
Blue mussels	Greenshell mussels	Quahogs (Atlantic clams)
Cherrystone clams	Littleneck clams	Scallops
Chowders	Manila clams	Soft-shell clams
Cockles	Olympias	Surf clams

FIGURE 13.12   Popular Bivalve Mollusks

One of the most tender and sweetest clams is also the smallest, called littleneck clams, which are harvested along the ocean's coastal line.

Sian Irvine © Dorling Kindersley

lobster) are purchased alive. Also, they are sold in a variety of market forms and in various sizes or **counts.**

When buying shrimp (one of the most popular crustaceans), counts can range from 200–400 shrimp per pound (titi) to 8 per pound (extra-colossal). Figure 13.13 lists some of the most popular crustaceans normally available to foodservice buyers.

It is important for foodservice buyers to understand that, unlike meats, fish and shellfish inspections are voluntary. The National Oceanic and Atmospheric Administration (NOAA) conducts the voluntary seafood inspection program on a fee-for-service basis. The program provides vessel and plant sanitation, product inspection, grading, certification, label review, laboratory analysis, training, and consultative and information services. Participants may use official marks on complying products, which indicate that they have been federally inspected,

Blue crab	Maine lobster	Spiny (rock) lobsters
Crayfish (crawfish)	Prawns	Stone crab
Dungess crab	Shrimp	Tiger shrimp
King crab	Slipper lobster	
Langoustines	Snow (spider) crab	

FIGURE 13.13   Popular Crustaceans

Key Term

Count (crustaceans)   When used to label crustaceans, this term refers to "the number in a pound." For example, 40–50 "count" shrimp means that, on average, 40–50 individual shrimp of that size will weigh 16 ounces.

Internet Purchasing Assistant (13.6)

Today, most foodservice operators buy their fish products in a fabricated or processed form. That can make the difficult seafood buying situation even more complex and truly serves to illustrate the "*caveat emptor*" (let the buyer beware) concept.

To better understand why, consider the humble "fish stick." Widely served (and either loved or hated), the possible variation among different fish stick-like products available to buyers is nothing short of stunning. To better understand why, review the 11-page "fish stick products" buying specifications issued by the USDA at: www.ams.usda.gov/fqa/aa20325.pdf

Clearly, those responsible for buying processed seafoods must purchase only from reputable suppliers of impeccable integrity if they are, consistently, to "get what they pay for."

Internet Purchasing Assistant (13.7)

"Surimi" is the term used to describe a food product typically made from white-fleshed fish (such as pollock or hake) that has been pulverized to a paste and attains a rubbery texture when cooked. Surimi is a much-enjoyed food product in many Asian cultures and is available in many shapes, forms, and textures. The most common surimi product in the Western market is "imitation" (artificial) crabmeat and legs. The "imitation" label applied to surimi products is mandated by the FDA.

To learn more about how this versatile and increasingly popular foodservice product is made and used on foodservice menus, go to: www.pacseafood.com

At the home page:

1. Click on "Products," then
2. Click on "Surimi."

although few choose to do so. It is also important to understand that well over half of the fish consumed in the United States comes from other countries, will likely be fabricated within hours of being caught, and would then be ice packed or frozen right on the fishing vessel. It is easy to understand why thorough and consistent inspection and grading of products caught in the remote waters of far-flung fishing beds would be very difficult to achieve.

PRODUCT RECEIVING AND STORAGE

Because of their high levels of fat and protein, the products examined in this chapter are exceedingly perishable. Great care must be taken when receiving these products (to ensure that they are at their peak of quality at the time of arrival), as well as when storing them (to ensure they maintain the highest possible quality levels).

Receiving

In their fresh forms, meat, poultry, game, and seafood should be delivered to a foodservice operation at an acceptable temperature and in appropriate packaging. For most fresh items, a delivery temperature between 30°F and 34°F (−1°C to 1°C) is appropriate. Frozen foods should arrive at temperatures at or below 0° F. The use of thermometers to check the arriving temperatures of these foods is essential.

HI-TECH PURCHASING (13.1)

I Need It by Tomorrow!

In the past, finding outstanding seafood could be more difficult than the actual cooking of the items purchased. Even if a source of good seafood was identified, transportation and shipping restrictions could easily result in poor product quality when it actually arrived at the operation's receiving area.

Just as the Internet has changed the way foodservice operations communicate with their customers, it has changed the ways buyers can communicate with their fresh fish and shellfish suppliers. Of course, knowing where to buy quality products is not the same as having them delivered fresh to your door.

Luckily, advances in modern shipping and online shopping result in the ability to buy fresh fish and shellfish products and, in many cases, "absolutely positively" have them the next day.

To better understand how such a purchasing effort can be undertaken, go online, and enter: www.fishermansfleet.com

At the home page, click on "Wholesale" to review this company's foodservice supply efforts. One word of caution with buying seafood online, however, is to check shipping costs. Overnight shipping can be very expensive, especially when half of your package may be ice!

When products like meats and poultry are delivered in vacuum-packed plastic, check the temperature by placing a thermometer between the two packages (bags) making contact with the product inside. The thermometer should read 32°F (plus or minus one degree). Fresh poultry and seafood that are delivered "on ice" should be received in clean, solid (not wet-soaked) containers. These products should be encased in crushed ice that shows no evidence of significant melting.

Fresh seafood products create special concerns for those receiving them. The FDA requires shellfish harvesters and processors of oysters, clams, and mussels to put a tag on sacks or containers of live shellfish (in the shell) and a label on containers or packages of shucked shellfish. These tags and labels contain specific information about the product, including a certification number for the processor, which means that the shellfish were harvested and processed in accordance with national shellfish safety controls. When receiving items of this type, foodservice operators should ensure that employees:

- Discard cracked/broken shellfish: Throw away clams, oysters, and mussels if their shells are cracked or broken.
- Do a **tap test:** Live clams, oysters, and mussels will close up when the shell is tapped. If they do not close when tapped, they are dead and should not be accepted.
- Check for leg movement: Live crabs and lobsters should show some leg movement. These spoil rapidly after death, so only live crabs and lobsters should be accepted.

Delivery temperatures are especially important when buying seafood because, in some species, if the catch has been left out in the sun for too long, or if the

Key Term

Tap test A procedure used to check the delivery status of certain shellfish. When lightly "tapped" by hand or kitchen tool, live shellfish shells should close. If they do not, the animal inside is likely dead and should not be served.

Product	Freezer (0°F)	Refrigerator (40°F)
Beef, roasts, and steaks	6–12 months	3–5 days
Lamb, roasts, and chops	6–9 months	3–5 days
Pork, roasts, and chops	4–6 months	3–5 days
Beef and lamb, ground	3–4 months	1–2 days
Pork, ground	1–2 months	1–2 days

FIGURE 13.14 Suggested Storage Times for Fresh Meats
Source: USDA

fish have not been transported under proper refrigeration, toxins known as scombrotoxins can develop. Serving fish with high levels of this toxin can result in food-borne illness in those who consume the items.

Storage

When possible, the storage area for items examined in this chapter should be in close proximity to the area in which the product will be used. This reduces unnecessary time lost in traveling to remote storage areas to store or secure needed products. When a storage area is well located, properly labeled, kept clean, and monitored regularly, product quality can more easily be maintained.

Meat, poultry, game, and seafood received should be immediately placed in proper storage areas. For meats, poultry, and game, refrigerator temperatures between 30°F and 35°F are best, as are freezer temperatures of 0°F or lower. Refrigerated and frozen seafood products may be held at these same refrigerator and freezer temperatures or, in the case of some crustaceans, in a regularly cleaned saltwater tank.

Properly wrapped meat cuts, frozen at 0°F, or lower, will maintain their quality for several months. This varies, however, with the kind of meat. Figure 13.14 shows a range within which you can store meat with reasonable expectation that it will maintain its quality. Meats can be kept safely frozen for longer periods than indicated, but they will suffer quality decline.

Raw poultry may safely be kept in a refrigerator (40°F) for 1 to 2 days. Frozen poultry held in a freezer (0°F) can be thawed then cooked promptly after thawing. Thaw frozen poultry or parts in the refrigerator, or in cold water, changing the water every 30 minutes. Cooked poultry may be kept in the refrigerator, but should be used within 2–3 days or discarded.

Seafood products that have been received on ice (or refrigerated) can be safely stored using the following guidelines:

- If the seafood will be used within one to two days after purchase, store it in the refrigerator.
- If the seafood will not be used within two days after purchase, wrap it tightly in moisture-proof freezer paper or foil to protect it from air and store it in the freezer.
- Always thaw fish and seafood in the refrigerator. Thawing at temperatures higher than 40 degrees causes excessive drip loss and adversely affects taste, texture, aroma, and appearance.

Purchasing Resources on the Internet

In addition to the Web sites referenced in this chapter's "Internet Purchasing Assistant" feature, the following sites provide detailed information to enhance your purchasing knowledge and skills.

Purchasing Resources on the Internet

Site	Information About
www.cryovac.com	Wet aged and other meat packaging systems
www.americangrassfedbeef.com	Dry-aged-beef advantages
www.certifiedangusbeef.com	Black Angus Beef (At the home page, click on "Beef Cuts")
www.boarshead.com	Ready-to-eat meat and poultry items
www.davidmosner.com	Natural veal and lamb products
www.siouxpremepork.com	Premium pork products
www.theotherwhitemeat.com	Pork products, facts, and recipes
www.catellibrothers.com	Lamb and veal products
www.dartagnan.com	Charcuterie products and foie gras
www.tyson.com	Fresh and processed poultry products
www.perdue.com	Poultry products (presented in Spanish)
www.jennieo.com	Turkey products
www.quakerfarm.com	Free-range geese and duck products
www.shafferfarms.com	Venison (deer) products
www.honolulufish.com	Overnight delivery of sashimi-grade fish
www.aboutseafood.com	National Fisheries Institute and Seafoods
www.freshseafood.com	Overnight delivery of high-quality shellfish
www.shellfish.org	Commercial shellfish management
www.prenhall.com	Books about the commercial purchase and cooking of meats and seafoods

Key Terms

meat *308*
center of the plate *308*
quality grade *308*
yield grade *308*
wet aged
  (meat) *309*

dry aged (meat) *309*
primal cuts *310*
fabricated cuts *310*
corned beef *311*
box beef *311*
IQF *312*

myoglobin *315*
frenching (chops) *318*
charcuterie *319*
forcemeat *319*
giblets *320*
self-basted *324*

game *324*
mollusk *327*
crustacean *327*
cephalopods *327*
count (crustaceans) *329*
tap test *331*

Think It Through

1. Private-labeled meats that use their own (rather than USDA-developed) quality standards are increasingly available from foodservice distributors. What are the advantages to a foodservice buyer of selecting such products? What are potential disadvantages?

2. For many foodservice operators, ground beef is one of the principal forms in which they will buy meat. It can also be a potential source of foodborne illness. Assume your operation uses ground beef. Draft a step-by-step "ground beef" handling statement (to be followed by all employees) that details the procedures that will be followed to handle this product from its delivery to its final service. Include your position on serving guests, upon request, "rare" hamburgers.

3. Assume you have been asked to prepare a specification for sliced bacon to be used as a garnish/topping for your 500-restaurant chain's new "Double Bacon Cheeseburger." List and explain five things you must know about the specific intended use of this item before you can "spec" it properly.

4. A supplier approaches your operation with an offer to sell you "fryer-ready" chicken consisting of first- and second-wing sections for use in your popular "Buffalo Wings" menu item. Assume you currently purchase 400 pounds of fresh, three-section chicken wings each week to meet the customer demand for this item. Explain the procedure you would use to do a cost comparison on these two alternative product market forms.

What noncost issues would you also consider? Explain your answer.

5. Many varieties of fish and shellfish have been overfished to the point that they are in real danger of being completely exhausted for commercial use (see, for example, the list found at: www. fishonline.org/advice/avoid/). Assume consumer demand for such products remains strong and that they are available for purchase from your distributor. What specific responsibility, if any, do you believe you and other buyers in foodservice have toward such overfished species? Be prepared to defend your answer.

Team Fun

For this exercise, assume that each team consists of those individuals who are partners in *Captain Jack's*, a proposed new seafood restaurant located in a large college town. The target market for customers are city residents who like fresh seafood, as well as college students seeking a casual dining experience. Based upon the available kitchen equipment and layout, the restaurant's partners believe the kitchen can support the offering of 20 different entrée items. Each team will be given one task in helping to plan the restaurant.

1. The assignment of the first team is to identify 10 seafood items that will be on the menu, as well as the exact specifications required to properly buy those items.

2. The assignment of the second team is to identify 10 nonseafood (meat) items that will be on the menu, as well as the exact specifications required to properly buy those items.

3. The assignment of the third team is to address the specific market forms best suited for each of the twenty items (i.e., should the items be purchased fresh, frozen, canned, preportioned, IQF, etc.).

Each team should be prepared to justify their suggestions to the rest of the class.

14

Produce, Dairy, and Egg Products

In This Chapter

For food buyers, produce, dairy, and egg products are second in importance only to meat and seafood for only one reason: meats and seafoods are usually more expensive. The variety of produce, dairy, and egg products, and the skill required to properly select them, however, often makes their purchase even more challenging than center of the plate items.

Adding to the importance of these foods is the growing number of vegetarians who eat no meat or seafood of any kind. Currently there are approximately seven million vegetarians in the United States (and many times that number worldwide). Even more people, for religious, ethical, sociocultural, or other reasons reduce or eliminate animal products in their diets. In fact, for many, increased consumption of fruits and vegetables simply reflects how tasty they are! As a result, fruits and vegetables, in their vast number of colors, flavors, textures, nutritional contents, and market forms, comprise the majority of healthy protein and caloric intake for many individuals.

An increasing number of people with a wide variety of eating preferences enjoy properly prepared fruits and vegetables. As a result, knowledgeable and health-conscious consumers expect food service operations to take advantage of the increased accessibility of quality fruits and vegetables and make them available on the menu. This includes many items that, until recently, were not always available but, because of advancements in growing, processing, and shipping, can now be purchased and served year-round.

Because of their popularity and nutrient density, most food service buyers will, in addition to produce, purchase significant amounts of milk and those products made from milk. These include a variety of items such as butter, yogurt, sour cream, and ice cream, each of which may, based depending upon the menu they support, be absolutely indispensable to the operation of the business.

Dairy products are versatile, and they are eaten in a wide variety of ways. Unlike some other foods, dairy products have been consumed for centuries. As a result, one of the most ancient and highly refined methods of processing and consuming dairy products involves the production of cheese. Cheeses are produced in every culture where dairy products are plentiful. Regardless of the shape, aging methods used, or resulting flavors, quality cheeses are highly prized when served alone or as a key ingredient in countless dishes. Cheeses must be carefully chosen for their best quality and intended use.

In addition to produce and dairy products, food buyers will, invariably, purchase large quantities of fresh or processed eggs. Eggs are popular when served by themselves, but they are also a key ingredient in most baked items, as well as numerous other prepared dishes.

Buying the items examined in this chapter can be complex, but when you complete it, you will have learned much about produce, dairy, and eggs, including proper techniques for receiving and storing these items.

■■■

Outline

Produce

    Fruits

        Fresh Fruits

        Processed Fruits

    Vegetables

        Fresh Vegetables

        Processed Vegetables

Dairy Products

    Milks and Creams

    Cheeses

        Fresh or Unripened

        Soft

        Semisoft

        Firm

        Hard

    Other Milk-Based Foods

        Butter

        Yogurt

        Buttermilk and Sour Cream

        Ice Cream

Egg Products

    Fresh Eggs

    Processed Eggs

    Egg Substitutes

Product Receiving and Storage

    Receiving

    Storage

Purchasing Resources on the Internet

Key Terms

Think It Through

Team Fun

PRODUCE

Produce is the broad term generally used to describe fruits and vegetables. Although most often reserved for foods that are fresh (not processed), as used in this text, the term refers to fruits and vegetables in all of their many market forms. Tasty and nutritious when fresh, but of very poor quality and nutritive value when past their prime, the purchasing of produce items can be a real challenge for foodservice buyers.

Key Term

Produce   Agricultural products, especially fresh fruits and vegetables, grown for the market.

Produce items constitute a large percentage of all the food purchased by hospitality buyers.

Nigel Hicks © Dorling Kindersley

Biologists use the term **fruit** to identify produce that develops from the ovary of a flowering plant, and, therefore, contains one or more seeds. Botanically, tomatoes, beans, eggplant, and some other items are classified as fruits, but in the foodservice industry these products are more commonly considered vegetables. In fact, regardless of their true botanical nature, in the hospitality industry, those produce items that taste "sweet" are generally referred to as fruits, whereas those that are less sweet are typically referred to as vegetables.

The term **vegetable** refers to any herbaceous (nonwoody) plant that is commonly consumed for food.

In general, vegetables contain less sugar and more starch than fruits. Like fruits, however, some vegetables are eaten raw, whereas others must be carefully cooked to be served at their peak of quality.

Fruits

Purchasing fruits is challenging because fruits may have different names in different regions of the world or country. Also, purveyors may "create" names for fruits that they feel best describe the specific item they are selling. In fact, purveyors face their own challenges when selling fruits because no other food group offers a greater variety of colors, flavors, and texture than fruit.

FRESH FRUITS   The quality of fresh fruit is judged by its outside appearance, and the USDA has established grade standards for most fresh fruits. Fruit grades are used as a basis for trading among growers, shippers, wholesalers, and retailers; however, they are used to only a limited extent in sales between wholesalers and restaurateurs because the use of USDA grade standards is generally voluntary. If a container of fruit is marked with a grade, the packer must make the contents conform to official grade requirements. Grade designations are most often seen on

---

Key Terms

Fruit   The reproductive organ of a flowering plant. All species of flowering plants produce seeds (fruits) for reproduction.

Vegetable   Any herbaceous plant that can be wholly or partially eaten, including the leaves, stems, roots, tubers, seeds, or flowers.

FIGURE 14.1 USDA Fruit Grades
Source: U.S. Department of Agriculture

> **U.S. Fancy:** Premium quality. Only the very best (a small percentage) of fruits achieve this grade.
>
> **U.S. No. 1:** Good quality. The most commonly used grade for most fruits.
>
> **U.S. No. 2 and U.S. No. 3:** U.S. No. 2 is noticeably superior to U.S. No. 3, which is the lowest grade practical to pack under normal commercial conditions.

containers of pears and apples, but some other fruits occasionally carry grade designations. Figure 14.1 details the basic fruit grades used by the USDA (grades for some specific fruits may vary slightly).

Fresh fruits have not been subjected to any processing such as canning, freezing, or drying. In many cases, they can be purchased ripe or unripened. Specific fresh fruits and their characteristics can be examined in a variety of ways. One way is to divide them into the following broad subcategories:

Berries: Berries must be purchased fully ripened because they will not ripen further after picking. Common varieties include blackberries, blueberries, cranberries, currants, raspberries, and strawberries.

Citrus: Citrus fruits are characterized by their thick rind coverings. Citrus fruits are acidic, and their flavors range from bitter to tart to sweet. Popular varieties include grapefruits, kumquats, lemons, limes, oranges, and tangerines.

Exotics: Exotic fruits come from a variety of locales. Many are available year-round and include gooseberries, guava, lychees, persimmons, pomegranates, prickly pears, rhubarb, and star fruits.

Grapes: Grapes are the single largest crop in the world, due in great part to their popularity in wine making. Table grapes (those grown for eating) include Red Flame, Thompson seedless, and Concord.

Melons: Melons are members of the gourd family. Most are eaten without cooking. Popular types include cantaloupes, Casaba, Crenshaw, honeydew, and watermelons.

Pomes: Pomes are tree fruits with thin skins and firm flesh. Within this family of fruits are apples of all types, pears, and quince.

Pit fruits: These fruits are characterized by thin skins, soft flesh, and a woody pit, or stone, in the center of the fruit. Apricots, cherries, peaches, nectarines, and plums are popular varieties.

Tropicals: Tropical fruits are native to the world's hot tropical and subtropical regions. All can be eaten fresh, without cooking. Popular tropicals, most of which are now available year-round, include bananas, dates, kiwis, mangoes, papayas, passion fruits, and pineapples.

PROCESSED FRUITS Suppliers process fruits for a variety of reasons, including reduced shipping costs, increased shelf life, improved utility, and product enhancement. Fresh fruits may be processed in a variety of ways. In some cases, the fruits are simply cleaned, trimmed, and packaged in bags, jars, or other containers. In other cases, the foods are highly processed to enhance their form or useful life.

The most popular means of preserving fruits include

Irradiation: Some fruits (as well as many vegetables and meats) can be subject to ionizing radiation to destroy parasites, insects, and bacteria. This treatment is classified as **irradiation** and is considered by the FDA as a food

Key Term

Irradiation The use of x-rays for the purpose of preserving foods.

Many tropical fruits are now imported and enjoyed all year-round.
© Dorling Kindersley

additive. Similar in many aspects to cooking foods with a microwave, irradiation also slows the ripening of the fruits treated.

Irradiated fruits are generally purchased, stored, and used like any other fresh fruit.

Canning: Many fruits are canned. Pineapple and peaches are among the most popular. In **solid pack** canning, little or no water is added to the fruits before they are sealed in the cans and heated. **Water pack** canning is accomplished by first adding water or fruit juice to the products. **Syrup packing** involves the addition of various amounts of sugar and water to the foods prior to packing. In most cases, the highest graded fruits are packed in higher sugar density syrups (higher **Brix** level) syrups.

Freezing: Freezing is a highly effective method for preserving fruit, even though the process negatively affects the texture of many fruits because freezing often damages the product's cell walls. The process does not, however, have a negative effect on the nutritive value of fruits. Many fruits are sold individually quick frozen (IQF), whereas others are sold as purees.

Drying: Drying is one of the oldest known methods of preserving fruit. As fruits lose their moisture content, their flavor intensifies, there is a concentration of sugar content, and their shelf life is extended. Unlike products such as dried beans and legumes, dried fruits are processed in a manner that results in products with 16 to 26 percent moisture. The result is fruits that are moist and soft. Raisins, prunes, apricots, and figs are among the most popular of the dried fruits.

Vegetables

The term "vegetable," as commonly used, can be considered almost any non-woody plant with edible parts used for food. A definition this encompassing,

---

Key Terms

Solid pack (canning) Canning foods with little or no water added.

Water pack (canning) Canning foods after the addition of water or juice.

Syrup pack (canning) Canning foods to which light, medium, or heavy sugar syrups have been added.

Brix A measurement of the ratio of dissolved sugar to water in a liquid. A 30 Brix (°Bx) solution contains 30 grams of sugar per 100 grams of solution. Put another way, there are 30 grams of sugar and 70 grams of water in the 100 grams of solution.

THE SUPPLIER'S SIDE (14.1)

"Insider" Tips on Purchasing: From the Supplier's Perspective

Buyer's Question: Why is food irradiated?

Supplier's Answer: Food is irradiated to provide the same benefits as when it is processed by heat, refrigeration, freezing, or treated with chemicals to destroy insects, fungi, or bacteria that cause food to spoil and to make it possible to keep food longer and in better condition in warehouses. Because irradiation destroys disease-causing bacteria and reduces the incidence of food-borne illness, hospitals sometimes use irradiation to sterilize food for immuno-compromised patients. Also, irradiation is currently the only known method to eliminate the deadly *E. coli* O157:H7 bacteria.

Buyer's Question: Are irradiated foods still nutritious?

Supplier's Answer: Yes. Irradiated foods are absolutely wholesome and nutritious. Nutrient loss with irradiation is less than or about the same as with cooking and freezing.

Buyer's Question: Does irradiation cause chemical changes in food?

Supplier's Answer: Yes, irradiation does produce chemical changes in foods. These substances, called "radio-lytic products," may sound mysterious, but they are not. They have been carefully studied by food scientists in making safety assessments of irradiated foods. Many things cause chemical changes in food. For instance, heat applied in cooking produces chemical change. Scientists have found the changes in food created by irradiation minor to those created by cooking. The products created by cooking are so significant that consumers easily can smell and taste them, whereas only a chemist with extremely sensitive lab equipment would be able to detect changes caused by irradiation.

Buyer's Question: How can irradiated foods be identified in the market?

Supplier's Answer: Irradiated food cannot be recognized by sight, smell, taste, or feel. Irradiated foods will be labeled with a logo, along with the words "Treated with Radiation," or more commonly, "Treated by Irradiation."

---

however, also includes fruits, nuts, and cereals; products that are not usually considered vegetables by foodservice buyers or by those guests for whom they buy.

A vegetable, as a generic foodservice term, has come to mean those plants and plant parts eaten raw or cooked and served with a main meal. Using this definition, rice and sweet corn are examples of cereals that, although they are not vegetables in a botanical sense, are considered vegetables by many consumers. Originating from almost any part of a plant, a vegetable can be a leaf (cabbage, lettuce, spinach), a seed (beans, lentils, peas), a root (beet, carrot, potato), a bulb (garlic, leek, onion), a flower (cauliflower, broccoli, artichoke), a fruit (cucumber, pepper, squash), or a stem (asparagus, celery, kohlrabi).

Vegetables are an important component of most menus. They add color, texture, flavor, and variety to appetizers, salads, and entrées and are often used as side dishes to accompany main courses.

The USDA has established grade standards for most fresh vegetables. Use of the grading standards is generally voluntary; however, some state laws and federal marketing programs require official grading of certain vegetables. If a package of vegetables does list a grade, the packer is legally obligated to ensure that the contents meet the grade standards. Grade designations are most often seen on packages of potatoes and onions, but other vegetables occasionally carry the grade name. Figure 14.2 lists the USDA grades that have been established for fresh vegetables.

> **U.S. Fancy:** Of more uniform shape and with fewer defects than U.S. No. 1.
>
> **U.S. No. 1:** Should be tender and fresh appearing, have good color, and be relatively free from bruises and decay.
>
> **U.S. No. 2 and No. 3:** Although these grades have lower quality requirements than Fancy or No. 1, all grades are nutritious. The differences are mainly in appearance, amount of waste, and buyer preference.

FIGURE 14.2 USDA Fresh Vegetable Grades
Source: U.S. Department of Agriculture

FRESH VEGETABLES There are few hard and fast rules for selecting vegetables because each type has its own quality characteristics. The following are broad guidelines for some of the more popular vegetables.

Artichokes: The globe artichoke is the large, unopened flower of a plant belonging to the thistle family. The leaf-like parts that make up the bud are actually the flower's petals. Size is not important with respect to quality. Poor quality artichokes have large areas of brown on the petals and/or spreading petals (a sign of age that indicates drying and toughening of the edible portions).

Asparagus: Asparagus is a member of the lily family, which also includes onions, leeks, and garlic. The edible portion of this plant is called a spear. Buy round spears with closed, compact tips and a fresh appearance. A rich, green color should cover most of the spear. Reject spears with tips that are open and spread out, moldy, or decayed.

Beans: The word "bean," like the word "vegetable," has an imprecise meaning. It is used to refer to the seeds of many different kinds of plants. Beans are widely used in quantity foodservice operations in one or more of their many forms. These include French beans, snap beans (string, stringless, and wax), bush beans, pole beans, and kidney beans, to name just a few. Beans can be purchased in their fresh state or, in some cases, dried. Common dry types include pinto, black, navy, Great Northern, red kidney, and pink beans.

When buying fresh beans, look for a fresh, bright appearance with good color for the variety of bean being selected. Reject wilted or flabby bean pods, and those with serious blemishes or decay.

Beets: Fresh beets are available year-round. Their color and flavor are unique, and they are popular in salads, as a base for soups, and as a side vegetable. Buy beets that are firm, round, have a deep red color, and are smooth over most of the surface.

Broccoli: Broccoli is a popular member of the cabbage family and a close relative of cauliflower. Buy broccoli that is firm with a compact cluster of small flower buds (none of which should be opened or showing a yellow color, which indicates excessive age). Also, reject broccoli with soft, slippery, and water-soaked spots on the bud cluster.

Cabbage: Cabbage is one of the most popular vegetables in the world. Essentially, there are three types: smooth-leaved green cabbage, crinkly-leaved green (Savoy) cabbage, and red cabbage. All types are suitable for any use, although the Savoy and red varieties are more in demand for use in slaw and salads. Buy cabbage with firm, hard heads that are heavy for their size. Avoid cabbage with badly discolored, dried, or decayed outer leaves.

Carrots: Carrots are grown throughout the world in a variety of colors and in a wide variety of sizes. The type of carrot most often purchased in the United States is the Mediterranean carrot. Freshly harvested carrots are available year-round. Buy fresh carrots that are well formed, smooth, and firm. If the tops are attached, they should be fresh and of a good green color. Reject carrots with large green "sunburned" areas at the top (which must be trimmed) and roots that are flabby from wilting.

Cauliflower: A popular member of the cabbage family, cauliflower is believed to have originated in the Mediterranean regions. In addition to white cauliflower, green and purple types are also available. The white edible portion is called "the curd," and the heavy outer leaf covering is called "the jacket leaves." Buy cauliflower with a creamy-white color and compact, solid, and clean curds. Reject cauliflower that has a spreading curd or that has dark spots on the curd because these indicate excessive age.

Celery: Celery is popular for a variety of uses and is available throughout the year. Most celery is of the "Pascal" type, which includes thick-branched, green varieties. Fresh celery should have a solid, rigid feel, and the leaf tips (if any) should be fresh or only slightly wilted. Reject wilted celery and that with flabby upper branches or leaf stems.

Chicory, endive, escarole (and other greens): These vegetables, used mainly in salads, are available practically all year-round. The shape, texture, color, and flavor of each make them interesting for mixing with more traditional lettuce in salads. Actually, a large number of widely differing species of plants are grown for use as "greens." The better-known kinds are spinach, kale, collard, turnip, beet, chard, mustard, broccoli leaves, chicory, endive, escarole, dandelion, cress, and sorrel. Buy fresh greens that are crisp, tender, and have a good green color. Reject wilted and yellowing plants or those with insect injury.

Corn: Worldwide, only wheat and rice are cultivated in greater quantities than corn. Much is used for cattle feed, but "sweet" corn is grown for human consumption. Fresh sweet corn is available in frozen form every month of the year, but in the United States, fresh sweet corn is most plentiful from early May until mid-September.

Cucumbers: Cucumbers can be purchased with or without seeds. Buy those with good green color that are firm over their entire length but not too large in diameter. Reject overgrown cucumbers that are too large in diameter, are flabby, and/or have evidence of spotty soft parts.

Lettuce: Lettuce owes its prominence to the popularity of salads. Four types of lettuce are generally available year-round: iceberg (the most common), butter-head, romaine and leaf.

Iceberg lettuce is 90 percent water and has very little flavor. Therefore, the best tasting salads are made with a combination of iceberg and other lettuce types and/or a mixture of one or more greens. Butter-head lettuce, including the Big Boston and Bibb varieties, has a smaller head than iceberg. This type will have soft, light-green leaves in a rosette pattern in the center. Romaine lettuce plants are tall and cylindrical with crisp, dark-green leaves. It is used to make the classic Caesar salad. Leaf lettuce includes many varieties—none with a compact head.

When buying fresh lettuce, look for good, bright color (in most varieties, this means a medium-to-light green). Some varieties have red leaves. Slight discoloration of the outer or wrapper leaves will usually not hurt the quality of the lettuce, but serious discoloration or decay should be avoided because of their negative affect on the yield of consumer-acceptable, visually appealing salad products.

Mushrooms: Mushrooms are naturally fat free and are popular by themselves and when prepared in a variety of ways. There are over 40,000 known varieties. In the United States, the most common is the moonlight (button mushroom). Other popular mushrooms include portabella, porcini and shitake.

Onions (dry):   The many varieties of onions grown commercially fall into three general classes distinguished by color: yellow, white, and red. Yellow onions make up 88 percent of those grown; 5 percent are white and 7 percent are red. Onions range in size from less than 1 inch in diameter (creamers/boilers) to more than 4.5 inches in diameter (super colossal). The most common sizes of onions sold in the United States are the medium (2 to 3¼ inches in diameter) and the jumbo (3 to 3 ¾ inches in diameter). Onions should be hard, dry, and have small necks. Reject those that are wet, soft, or affected by decay.

Onions (green), shallots, and leeks: Green onions, shallots, and leaks are similar in appearance but are somewhat different in size and flavor. Scallions are a type of onion, and the term is often used when referring to green onions or shallots. Shallots are an onion-like plant that produces small bulbs and edible shoots. Leeks are larger than green onions but share the characteristic of large, green, edible shoots. Green onions are simply ordinary onions harvested very young. They have very little or no bulb formation and their tops are tubular.

Peppers (green):   Most of the green peppers used in the foodservice industry are considered "sweet" or "bell" peppers. Although the taste of these vegetables is not actually sweet, the term is used to distinguish them from "hot" peppers. The best green peppers (as well as those with other colors) have a deep, characteristic color; glossy sheen; relatively heavy weight; and firm walls or sides.

Potatoes: Inca Indians in Peru were the first to cultivate potatoes more than 2,000 years ago. For practical purposes, most potatoes are of three types: russet, round white, and round red. Russets (sometimes called "bakers" or "Idaho potatoes") are the most popular type in the United States. Round white potatoes are used most often in the Eastern United States. Round red (redskin) potatoes are sometimes called "new" potatoes; however, technically, "new" refers to any variety of potatoes that is harvested before reaching maturity.

Squash: The squash varieties most used in restaurants are generally either a "summer" or a "winter" variety. The varieties of summer squash available include crookneck, straightneck, and zucchini. Winter squash includes the small-sized acorn (available year-round) and the butternut, buttercup, and Hubbard varieties. Reject squash with cuts, punctures, sunken spots, or moldy spots on the rind.

Sweet potatoes: The sweet potato is not actually a potato (tuber) at all; it is a root, which is a member of the morning glory family. They are a Native American plant. Sweet potatoes are often confused with yams. However, yams are large, starchy roots grown primarily in Africa and Asia. Yams are rarely available in the United States; however, the term "yam" is commonly used to describe sweet potatoes. Two types of sweet potatoes are available in varying amounts year-round. Moist sweet potatoes are the most common. They have orange-colored flesh and are very sweet. Dry sweet potatoes have pale-colored flesh and are low in moisture.

Tomatoes: Tomatoes, although technically a fruit, are one of the most popular and heavily used of all vegetables. The flavor of tomatoes varies greatly, and most buyers would agree that the best flavor usually comes from locally grown tomatoes. This type of tomato is allowed to ripen completely on its vine before being picked. Buy tomatoes that are smooth, well-ripened, and reasonably free from blemishes. Reject too soft, overripe, or bruised tomatoes and those with severe growth cracks (deep brown cracks around the stem) that can reduce yield.

PROCESSED VEGETABLES   Few, if any, menu ingredients have undergone more change in the past decade than have processed vegetables (and to a large but lesser degree, fruits). Today, an increased number of vegetables, processed in an ever-growing number of market forms, are readily available.

Three major factors have converged to make this so. First, labor has eclipsed food as the largest cost in many foodservice operations and has significantly increased demand for foods with "built-in" labor. In many cases, vegetables purchased raw must be cleaned, trimmed, chopped, diced, or otherwise handled. A supplier's central processing facility (or that operated by a multi-unit foodservice organization) can process food products much more cost effectively than can individual foodservice units. In addition, centralized processing can result in the increased consistency of sizes, shapes, mixtures, and assortments of such products.

A second major factor in the increased sale of processed vegetable items relates to consumers themselves. In the days when simply having adequate food stocks was an accomplishment, canned, dried and, in many cases, poor quality frozen products may have been tolerated because these methods, at least, provided a constant supply of products. Today, however, consumers demand fresher ingredients, of an increased variety, and of higher quality. The result is that food growers and suppliers are constantly challenged to manage their products in ways that result in fresher, better, faster-to-market produce. Central vegetable processing units, often located adjacent to the fields in which fresh produce is grown, helps them do just that.

Finally, and perhaps most significantly, the explosion in vegetable processing has been aided by recent, and major, advancements in packaging technology. The drying of vegetables entails methods that have existed for thousands of years. The canning process was invented in France in 1795 by Nicholas Appert, a chef who was determined to win a cash prize offered by Napoleon for a way to prevent military food supplies from spoiling. In 1923, Clarence Birdseye, an American, invented and later perfected a system of packing fresh food in waxed cardboard boxes and then flash freezing them under high pressure. As a result, the first quick-frozen vegetables, fruits, seafoods, and meat were sold to the public beginning in 1930 in Springfield, Massachusetts, under the trade name Birds Eye Frosted Foods®.

In each of the above food preservation methods, processors sought to protect food from damaging contact with oxygen to prolong its life. Today, food processors do the same thing using **modified atmosphere packaging (MAP)** technology.

Essentially, MAP lowers oxygen in a package from 20 percent to near 0 percent, to slow the growth of microorganisms and the effects of **oxidation,** both of which damage fresh produce.

In the 1970s, MAP reached the public when bacon and fish were sold in retail packs in the U.K. Since then, the interest in MAP has grown due to heightened consumer demand, and this has led to significant advances in the design and manufacturing of food packaging materials.

It has been estimated that 25 to 40 percent of all fresh produce harvested will not reach the market due to spoilage and mishandling that occurs during distribution. Yet, most consumers want fresh vegetables and fruits without the use of preservatives. As a result, the MAP technique is today's most commonly used packaging technology for fresh-cut produce. Today foodservice buyers selecting processed products can choose from a wider array of products than ever before.

Key Terms

Modified atmosphere packaging (MAP)   The practice of altering the internal oxygen ratios in a food package to improve the shelf life of the food.

Oxidation   The chemical reaction (and deterioration) that occurs when a substance is exposed to oxygen. Burning is an example of rapid oxidation; rusting is an example of slow oxidation.

Internet Purchasing Assistant (14.1)

For most produce buyers, the first step in becoming knowledgeable about produce standards and quality is obtaining the *Fresh Produce Manual* published by the Produce Marketing Association (PMA). Founded in 1949, PMA is a not-for-profit global trade association serving more than 2,100 members who market fresh fruits, vegetables, and related products worldwide. Its members are involved in the production, distribution, retail, and foodservice sectors of the industry. PMA offers its members a wide variety of services. To learn about PMA and what it does for members, go to: www.pma.com

On-the-Job Challenges in Purchasing (14.1)

"This looks awful," said chef Tony as he carefully examined a head of iceberg lettuce taken from the 24-head case that was about to be delivered by Brothers Produce Company.

"It's pretty much all like that," said Ted, the produce company's delivery truck driver.

Later, when chef Tony called Linda, his sales representative from Brothers Produce, he found out why.

"I know it looks "rusty" and the trim loss rate will be a lot higher," said Linda, referring to the patches of rust-colored lettuce interspersed with the bright green normally associated with iceberg. "Actually, Tony, it's called "Downy Mildew," and it happens when there is too much rain to harvest the heads at the right time. Our supplier tells us it won't improve for several more days. I can't change that, but we do have other unaffected greens in stock. Right now, I can send you butterhead, Bibb, looseleaf, romaine, watercress, arugula, oak leaf, escarole, or radicchio. Would you like to place a reorder?"

Case Study Questions

Assume you were chef Tony.

1. What are the advantages and disadvantages associated with keeping the iceberg lettuce and simply absorbing the higher trim loss?
2. What factors would affect your decision to switch to another green(s)?
3. Where, before you place a reorder, could you rapidly find up-to-date product information about the alternative greens available to you?

Internet Purchasing Assistant (14.2)

The standards of identity and quality developed for all of the many fruits and vegetables sold worldwide would fill many very long books. For most buyers, in-depth product knowledge is really needed only for those products they buy frequently or in large quantity.

The U.S. Department of Agriculture makes the quality standards it has developed for fruits and vegetables available to all buyers at no charge. These standards are an excellent resource. To see them, go to: www.ams.usda.gov/standards/stanfrfv.htm

At the home page:

1. Read the complete standards information provided about your favorite fresh vegetable.
2. Next, read the complete standards information provided about your favorite fresh fruit.
3. Next, read the related information about the processed forms of either your favorite fresh fruit or vegetable.

HI-TECH PURCHASING (14.1)

How Organic is It?

Things move quickly in the world of procurement. One case in point is that of "organic foods." At the time of this book's writing (2009), the author team could find no purchasing *text* that accurately defined "organic" foods. That's because buyer needs change, and it was not until October 21, 2002, that the USDA's National Organic Program (NOP) standards for food labeled "organic" went into effect. This standard applies to food grown in the United States or imported from other countries.

The National Organic Standards provide a national definition for the term *"organic,"* providing clear and consistent labeling requirements for use of the word. Before a product can be labeled organic, a USDA-approved certifier inspects the farm where the food is grown to make sure the farmer is following all the rules necessary to meet USDA organic standards.

For single-ingredient foods, such as produce, a small sticker with the USDA Organic seal identifies foods that are 100 percent organic. For foods with more than one ingredient, there are four labeling categories:

100% Organic. Must be just that—100 percent organic ingredients.

Organic. With the USDA seal, it must contain 95 percent organic ingredients by weight.

Made with Organic Ingredients. Must contain 70 percent organic ingredients by weight.

Products with less than 70 percent organic ingredients may not make any organic claims on the front of the package but may do so on the side of the package.

It is important to note that the term "natural" does not mean "organic." Neither do other truthful claims such as "free-range," and "hormone-free." Only food that has been certified as meeting USDA organic standards may carry the USDA's "organic" label (below).

How would professional buyers know about these new definitions, and stay up-to-date with the latest information? It's easy. Visit the USDA Web page regularly. You can access it at: www.usda.gov

DAIRY PRODUCTS

The term "dairy" generally refers to cow's milk and the basic foods that are produced from it. These include cheeses, butter, yogurt, cultured dairy products, and ice cream. In some cases, foodservice buyers purchase dairy products produced by mammals other than cows (goat cheeses, for example, are increasingly popular). Dairy products are consumed alone, as is the case with beverage milks, and are used as ingredients in appetizers, baked goods, entrées, side dishes, and desserts. For some buyers, the amount of money spent on dairy products exceeds the amount spent on meats or produce.

Milks and Creams

In addition to its widespread consumption as a beverage, milk contributes texture, flavor, and nutritive value to a wide variety of other foods. Although its protein, vitamin, and mineral (especially calcium) contents are significant, from a buyer's perspective, it is the milk's fat content that most influences what is purchased. In

A vast array of dairy products are on the market, all of which are derived from mammal's milk.

© Dorling Kindersley

fact, the milk fat content of beverage milk actually defines the products purchased and how they will be marketed and used in the kitchen.

In its natural form, cow's milk contains approximately 88 percent water, 3.5 percent fat (milk fat), and 8.5 percent other solids that include proteins, milk sugar **(lactose),** and minerals.

Unprocessed, or "raw," milk is not generally available in the United States. As a result, buyers choose from various forms of **pasteurized** and **homogenized** milks.

Foodservice buyers selecting beverage milks can generally select from the following widely available forms:

Whole milk: Whole milk is usually homogenized and fortified with vitamin D. For shipment in interstate commerce, it must contain a minimum of 3.25 percent milk fat and 8.25 percent milk solids (not fat).

Low-fat milk: Low-fat milk has between 0.5 and 2 percent milk fat and is fortified with vitamin A. The addition of vitamin D is optional.

Skim milk: Also called nonfat milk, this product must have less than 0.5 percent milk fat, and be fortified with vitamin A. The addition of vitamin D is optional.

Flavored milks: Flavored milks are made by adding fruit, fruit juice, or other natural or artificial food flavorings such as strawberry, chocolate syrup, or cocoa to pasteurized milk.

Dry whole milk: Dry whole milk is pasteurized whole milk with the water removed. Dry milks with reduced fat levels or no fat are also readily available. "Instant" nonfat dry milk is made of larger milk particles that dissolve easily in water. The best instant nonfat dry milk will have a sweet, pleasing flavor and a natural color. It must also dissolve immediately when mixed

Key Terms

Lactose A sugar comprising one glucose molecule linked to a galactose molecule. Lactose occurs only in milk. Natural cow's milk contains approximately 4.5 to 5.0 percent lactose.

Pasteurized To expose a food, such as milk, cheese, yogurt, beer, or wine, to an elevated temperature for a period of time sufficient to destroy certain microorganisms that cause spoilage or undesirable fermentation.

Homogenized To reduce fat particles to a uniform and smaller size and to distribute these evenly in a liquid (such as milk) to enhance its flavor and texture.

with water. Dry milk products are used mainly in baking and other recipes in foodservice operations.

Evaporated milk: Evaporated milk is prepared by heating homogenized whole milk under a vacuum to remove half its water and then sealing it in cans. Evaporated skim milk is also readily available.

Condensed milk: This concentrated canned milk is prepared by removing about half the water from whole milk and then adding sugar. Sweetened condensed milk must have at least 40 percent sugar by weight and is used primarily in baking.

The U.S. Food and Drug Administration sets the standards for milk products as well as for cream, a milk form that must, by definition, contain at least 18 percent milk fat.

Foodservice buyers selecting creams can generally choose from the following widely available forms:

Half-and-Half: Half-and-half is made by homogenizing a mixture of milk and cream. It must contain at least 10.5 percent, but not more than 18 percent, milk fat.

Light cream: Also known as coffee cream or table cream, light cream must have at least 18 percent, but less than 30 percent, milk fat.

Light whipping cream: Also known simply as whipping cream, it must have at least 30 percent, but less than 36 percent, milk fat.

Heavy cream: Heavy cream must contain at least 36 percent milk fat.

Despite being pasteurized, all milk and cream products are highly perishable, and must be carefully stored at or below 41°F (5°C) to maintain their best quality.

Cheeses

You have learned that milk and milk products are highly popular but also highly perishable. Because that is so, it is not surprising that "cheese" is one of the oldest and most widely produced foods known to man. Cheese production was originally

---

PURCHASING PROS NEED TO KNOW (14.1)

Buyers of dairy products can be challenged by the wide variety of products available. Specialized product knowledge is important. However, all buyers of beverage milk need to be aware of basic dairy product facts, including the following:

Milk available in stores today is usually pasteurized and homogenized. Very little raw milk is sold today.

In pasteurizing, milk is heated briefly to kill pathogens and harmful bacteria, after which it is rapidly chilled.

Homogenized milk has been processed to reduce the size of the milk fat globules so the milk fat does not separate, and the product stays uniform throughout.

Depending on its milk fat content, fluid milk is labeled milk, low-fat milk, or skim milk (nonfat milk). Vitamin D may be added to any of these milks, and the milk is then so labeled. If added, the vitamin D content must be increased to at least 400 International Units (I.U.) per quart.

Low-fat and skim (nonfat) milk are fortified with vitamin A (at least 2,000 I.U. per quart), usually providing more vitamin A than whole milk. The protein and other vitamin and mineral content of milks with reduced milk fat are equivalent to that of whole milk.

Source: U.S. Department of Agriculture

Some blue cheeses are injected with spores before the curds form, whereas others have spores mixed in with the curds after they form.

Clive Streeter © Dorling Kindersley

undertaken to prolong the life of dairy products. Today, foodservice buyers can select from virtually hundreds of cheeses made in a variety of styles and packaging forms to use in literally thousands of recipes, or to serve alone.

Cheeses may be broadly classified as either natural or processed. Natural cheeses have been produced in the same manner for centuries. Essentially, all natural cheeses begin with mammal's milk (cows, goats, or sheep are the most popular). To make cheese, the protein found in milk (casein) is coagulated by adding an enzyme (usually **rennet**), which is a natural ingredient found in the stomachs of cattle, sheep, and goats.

As the milk coagulates, it naturally separates into curds, which are solid, and whey, which is the remaining liquid. The whey is removed, and the solids are then either consumed immediately or treated in a variety of ways including cutting, kneading, seasoning, or cooking. The resulting product, known as "green" cheese, is then packed into molds to age (ripen). The outside (rind) of the cheese may, depending upon how the cheese is made, range from very thin to very thick.

Many factors affect the quality of natural cheeses, including the type of milk used, the skill of the cheese maker, how long the cheese is aged, and even the atmosphere in the part of the world in which the cheese is produced. The moisture level and fat contents of cheeses are good indictors of the product's texture and shelf life. The higher the moisture content of a natural cheese, the softer and more perishable it will be.

Pasteurized processed cheeses are made by combining aged and green cheeses and mixing them with emulsifiers and flavorings. The resulting mixture is then pasteurized and poured into molds. In most cases, processed cheeses are less expensive than natural cheeses. Processed "cheese food" is a variation of processed cheese. This product must contain at least 51 percent cheese, but also includes vegetable oils or milk solids designed to produce a cheese that spreads easily. These are often flavored with pimentos, fruits, vegetables, or meats.

Key Term

Rennet   An enzyme that causes the coagulation of milk. It is found in the gastric juice of the fourth stomach of certain animals such as cattle, sheep, and goats.

For most foodservice buyers, the majority of cheeses purchased are natural cheeses. There are thousands of natural cheese makers worldwide, and the number of distinct products they produce is vast. Natural cheeses can be classified based upon where they are made, the ripening method used, or their fat content. For the typical buyer, however, a convenient way to classify cheeses is by their texture. As a result, cheeses can be categorized as one of the following:

Fresh (or unripened)

Soft

Semisoft

Firm

Hard

FRESH OR UNRIPENED   Fresh, or unripened, cheeses are not cooked and have moisture contents between 40 and 80 percent. They are highly perishable and extremely popular. Among the most commonly purchased fresh cheeses are

Cottage cheese: Cottage cheese is a cheese curd product with a mild flavor. It is drained, but not pressed, so some whey remains. It is not aged or colored. Different styles of cottage cheese are made from milks with different fat levels and in small or large curd forms. Cottage cheese is a soft, tasty, and easily produced cheese. It must have a milk fat content of at least 4 percent. Low-fat cottage cheese must have a milk fat content between 0.5 percent and 2 percent, and nonfat cottage cheese must contain less than 0.5 percent total fat.

Cream cheese: Cream cheese is an unripened cheese containing at least 35 percent fat. Cream cheese originated in the United States in 1872 when a dairyman in Chester, New York, developed a "richer cheese than ever before," made from cream as well as whole milk.

Feta: Feta is a Greek or Italian product made from sheep or goat's milk. Feta is a white, flaky cheese with a distinct flavor.

Mozzarella: Mozzarella is an Italian cheese that contains 40 to 50 percent milk fat. It becomes elastic and stretches when melted, and is sometimes wrongly referred to as "pizza" cheese. Fresh mozzarella is a very mild cheese that many believe is best eaten within hours of its production.

Moscarpone: Moscarpone is also an Italian cheese and is best known for its use in sweet and savory sauces and desserts.

Queso oaxaca: This fresh Mexican cheese is kneaded, soaked in brine, and shaped into a ball. It melts easily and is used in a variety of Mexican dishes, including quesadillas and dips.

Ricotta: Ricotta is an Italian cheese similar to cottage cheese. Ricotta has a milk fat content between 4 and 10 percent. It is used in a variety of Italian-style dishes, including pastas and desserts.

SOFT   Soft cheeses are best known for their thin skins and creamy middles. The moisture content of these cheeses range from 50 to 75 percent. Among the most commonly purchased soft cheeses are

Brie: Containing approximately 60 percent fat, Brie is a French cheese made from cow's milk. Its soft, pliable rind may be eaten but is often cut away. Brie is often served as a dessert cheese and is commonly used as an ingredient in soups, sauces, or hors d'oeuvres.

Boursin: A French cheese with a high fat content (75 percent), Boursin is usually flavored with pepper, herbs, or garlic. It is delicious and rindless with a smooth, creamy texture that makes it popular as a sauce ingredient or when eaten alone.

Camembert: Camembert is a French cheese with a fat content of approximately 45 percent. Similar to Brie, this popular cheese is often served with fruit.

SEMISOFT Semisoft cheeses are smooth and sliceable. The moisture content of semisoft cheeses range from 40 to 50 percent. These cheeses include what is commonly known as the "blue" varieties, which refer to cheese types containing blue-colored molds that produce varieties with a distinctive look and taste. The most commonly purchased of the semisoft cheeses include

Gouda: Gouda is a Dutch cheese containing approximately 48 percent fat. Gouda is sold in various-size wheels covered with red or yellow wax. The cheese itself is yellow with a mild buttery flavor.

Havarti: Havarti, also known as Danish Tilsit, is a cow's milk cheese produced in Denmark. It has a mild and creamy texture and is often flavored with dill, caraway seeds, or peppers.

Fontina: This Italian cheese is from the Piedmont region, but imitation products are produced in Denmark, France, and the United States. Fontina is a popular after-dinner cheese.

Roquefort: Roquefort is a blue-veined sheep's milk cheese from France containing approximately 45 percent fat. It is intensely flavorful with a rich, salty taste and strong aroma. True Roquefort is smooth and spreadable.

Stilton: Stilton is a blue-veined cow's milk cheese produced in Great Britain. Produced in a manner similar to Roquefort, it has a pale yellow or white color and evenly spaced mold veins.

Gorgonzola: Gorgonzola is a blue-veined cow's milk cheese from Italy containing 48 percent fat. It is creamier than other blue-veined cheeses such as Roquefort or Stilton.

FIRM Firm cheeses are not hard or brittle. Some are solid and flaky like cheddar, whereas others are full of holes like Emmenthaler (better known in the United States as "Swiss"). Most firm cheeses have moisture content in the range of 30 to 40 percent and are made in a manner similar to either cheddar or Emmenthaler. Among the most commonly purchased firm cheeses are

Cheddar: Cheddar cheeses are made from cow's milk and are extremely popular. Variations of the classic cheddar cheeses originally produced in Great Britain include American Style, Colby, and Longhorn. Cheddar cheeses are made in colors that range from white to very dark orange. Flavors used in foodservice operations range from very mild to very sharp. The milk fat content of Cheddar cheeses ranges from 45 to 50 percent.

Emmenthaler: This Swiss-made cow's milk cheese is mellow and rich with a nutty flavor. It is ripened in three stages, and its characteristic "holes" are the result of gases that expand inside the cheese during the fermentation of bacteria added to the milk during production. Gruyere, made in Fribourg, Switzerland, is a firm cheese with a flavor and appearance similar to that of Emmenthaler, but with smaller holes.

Jarlsberg: Jarlsberg is a Swiss-type cow's milk cheese made in Norway.

Monterey Jack: Monterey Jack or "Jack" is a very mild, cheddar-like cow's milk cheese originally produced in California. Its color ranges from pale ivory to white, and it is often flavored with peppers or herbs.

Provolone: This cow's milk cheese was originally produced in Southern Italy and contains approximately 45 percent fat. Smoked provolone is perhaps the most popular of all the smoked cheeses.

HARD   Hard cheeses are those carefully aged for extended periods of time and dried to the point that their moisture contents are approximately 30 percent. Hard cheeses are best when grated for use as needed, and the most famous originated in Italy. Among the most commonly purchased hard cheeses are

Asiago: This sharp-flavored cow's milk cheese, when aged for one year, has a texture similar to cheddar. When aged for longer periods, it becomes brittle, hard, and suitable for grating. Asiago melts easily and is used in a variety of recipes.

Parmigiano–Reggiano: Commonly, but most often improperly known simply as Parmesan, this cheese was originally produced near Parma in Italy. It is now one of the most widely copied cheeses in the world. The name is trademarked in Europe, but not in the United States, so buyers of "Parmesan" cheese in the United States may be purchasing a very good or a very poor imitation.

Romano: Romano is a sheep's milk cheese made in Italy. It contains approximately 35 percent fat. Romano is sharper and more brittle than other grated cheeses, and is also lighter in color.

Other Milk-Based Foods

In addition to its use as a beverage and in cheese production, milk is used to make a variety of important foods. Among the most popular of these are butter, yogurt, sour cream, and ice cream. For buyers, these can be among the most complex

Internet Purchasing Assistant (14.3)

The American Cheese Society (ACS) was founded in 1982. The Society's membership includes cheese makers, academicians, marketing and distribution specialists, food writers, and specialty foods retailers from the United States, Canada, and Europe. Their Web site includes a wealth of information about the many forms of this extremely popular food. To see the site, go to: www.cheesesociety.org

At the home page, click on "Education," then click on "Tips for Cheese Consumers."

On-the-Job Challenges in Purchasing (14.2)

"Well, what do we have in the box?" asked Mellisa, the general manager at Maggiories Italian Bistro.

"I have an American Blue that I use for making dressing," replied Gene, the restaurant's kitchen manager.

"But we don't have any Gorgonzola at all for the Tuscan Gorgonzola Steak?" replied Mellisa.

"None, " said Gene, "the distributor shorted us on the last delivery."

Case Study Questions

Assume Mellisa has listed, on her menu, "Melted Gorgonzola" as the topping for her popular "Tuscan Gorgonzola Steak."

1. Would you use the American Blue cheese as a substitute?
2. What are the ethical issues associated with your decision?
3. What are the legal issues associated with your decision?

items to purchase because of their high level of perishability and the wide array of quality levels generally available.

BUTTER Butter is one of man's oldest processed dairy products. In fact, the first documented mention of butter-making occurred over 3,500 years ago. The term "butter" is used in the names of a variety of products including those made from puréed nuts (such as peanut butter), fruits (apple butter), and fats that are solid at room temperature (cocoa butter).

In general purchasing usage, however, the term "butter," unqualified, almost always refers to the dairy product. Butter is the natural substance that results when milk is churned to shake up whole milk or cream to separate the fat. Various models of butter churns have been developed by different cultures. In Europe, from the Renaissance until the Industrial Revolution, the preferred churn was simply a barrel mounted on rockers.

In the United States, the type of butter most commonly known to culinary professionals and foodservice consumers must, by law, contain at least 80 percent milk fat, not more than 16 percent water, and 2 to 4 percent milk solids. Its texture and sweet flavor make it a favorite of cooks and bakers.

In general, butter buyers select from one of three USDA-approved grades:

U.S. Grade AA: butter has a smooth, creamy texture and is easy to spread. It contains a light, fresh flavor and may contain a small amount of salt. Grade AA butter is made from sweet cream and is available from most distributors.

U.S. Grade A: butter is made from fresh cream, has a slightly stronger flavor, and possesses a fairly smooth texture. Grade A butter is also widely available.

U.S. Grade B: butter is less commonly available to foodservice operators. It is usually made from sour cream and its texture is coarser than that of regular butter. Its major application is in food manufacturing and processing.

The packages in which butter is sold display a shield surrounding their USDA-assigned letter grade (and occasionally the numerical score equivalent), indicating the quality of the contents. Grade scores are 93 or higher (for AA), 92 (for A), and 90 (for B). The highest attainable grade is AA, and the highest attainable **score** for butter is 100.

Butter may be artificially colored, and it may be sold salted or unsalted. Unsalted butter is usually labeled as such and contains absolutely no salt. It is sometimes erroneously referred to as "sweet" butter, which is inaccurate because any butter made with "sweet" cream (instead of sour cream) is sweet butter. Therefore, buyers can expect packages labeled "sweet cream butter" to contain salted butter. Unsalted butter is preferred for many cooking and baking purposes. Because it contains no salt (which acts as a preservative), however, it is more perishable than salted butter and, therefore, is often purchased and stored in a frozen state.

Butter may be purchased in a variety of packaging types. These include blocks of varying weights, ¼-pound sticks, individually wrapped patties of various sizes, and preformed shapes (such as roses, balls, and chips).

Butter may be purchased in a variety of forms. Whipped butter is made by incorporating nitrogen gas (not air, because that would encourage oxidation and rancidity) into the butter. This process is typically done to increase the spreadability

---

Key Term

Score (butter) A numerical equivalent of a quality grade. For example, grade AA butter may also be assigned a "score" of 93 or higher.

of the product. When purchased by weight, the whipping process does not affect the buyer's cost per ounce. When whipped butter is purchased by volume, however, the price is, of course, significantly affected.

Clarified butter is also called drawn butter. Clarified butter is unsalted butter that has the milk solids and water removed so that all that remains is pure liquid butterfat.

The advantages of this type of butter is its long-keeping quality (several months refrigerated) and its high **smoke point,** which allows it to be used in frying without burning as readily as nonclarified butter.

YOGURT   Yogurt is a thick, tart, custard-consistency dairy product. There is evidence of yogurt-like products being produced as food for at least 4,500 years. Yogurt was known primarily in Asia and Eastern and Central Europe until the 1900s, when its health benefits were widely publicized. In 1919, Isaac Carasso, a Spanish entrepreneur in Barcelona, developed an efficient method for mass-producing yogurt. He named the business "Danone" after his son. In the United States, Carasso's company is better known to foodservice buyers as "Dannon."

Commercially sold yogurt can be made from whole, low-fat or nonfat milk, as well as soymilk. Therefore, yogurt contains the same amount of milk fat as the product from which it is made. Yogurt is produced by bacterial fermentation of milk sugar (lactose), which produces lactic acid. The resulting effect on the milk's proteins give yogurt its characteristic consistency and tart, tangy flavor. In the United States, yogurt may be purchased plain or with a variety of fruit or spice flavorings.

The USDA recognizes three yogurt forms commonly available for foodservice buyers:

Yogurt: Not less than 3.25 percent fat, and not less than 8.25 percent milk solids (not fat).

Low-fat yogurt: Not less than 0.5 percent, nor more than 2.0 percent fat, and not less than 8.25 percent milk solids (not fat).

Non-fat yogurt: Not more than 0.5 percent fat, and not less than 8.25 percent milk solids (not fat).

The caloric content of yogurt will vary based upon its milk fat content and flavoring ingredients. Although used infrequently for cooking in the United States, it is an extremely popular ingredient in many Middle Eastern cuisines. Also, yogurt has gained tremendous popularity as a breakfast and snack food. Typically, it may be purchased in bulk containers of one to five pounds, as well as in single-service size containers of plus or minus 6 ounces (170 grams).

BUTTERMILK AND SOUR CREAM   "Buttermilk" was the term originally used to describe the liquid that was left over after producing butter from milk. Today, the buttermilk available to most foodservice buyers is actually **cultured** buttermilk; that is, milk to which lactic acid-producing bacteria has been added.

Sour cream (like yogurt) is also a cultured dairy product. Both buttermilk and sour cream are produced by adding a specific bacterial culture (*Streptococcus lactis*)

Key Terms

Clarified (butter)   Unsalted butter from which the water and milk solids have been removed. Also known as "drawn" butter.

Smoke point   The temperature at which a fat begins to break down and emit smoke.

Cultured (dairy product)   The processed food created when specific bacteria are added to liquid dairy products.

Internet Purchasing Assistant (14.4)

The National Yogurt Association is the nonprofit trade organization representing the manufacturers and marketers of live- and active-culture yogurt products, as well as suppliers to the industry. Its purpose is to sponsor health and medical research for yogurt with live and active cultures and to serve as an information source to the trade and general public. Its Web site is an excellent source of up-to-date product information. To view it, go to: www.aboutyogurt.com

At the home page, click on and read about "Live & Active Culture Yogurt."

to milk. The bacteria convert the milk sugar (lactose) to lactic acid. The acidity of buttermilk and sour cream explain their relatively long refrigerator shelf life because acid is a natural preservative that inhibits the growth of pathogenic bacteria.

Buttermilk is produced when the bacterial culture is added to fresh, pasteurized skim, or low-fat milk to yield a thick product with a tart flavor. Sour cream is made by combining the same bacterial culture to dairy cream, and cream with a higher fat content produces a thicker sour cream. The USDA has well-defined fat content minimums for regular sour cream (18 percent) and minimum established standards for reduced-fat sour cream, light sour cream, low-fat sour cream, and nonfat sour cream.

Buttermilk is most commonly used in foodservices as an ingredient in baked products and quick breads (e.g., pancakes and biscuits) because the acid in buttermilk reacts with baking soda in most quick bread recipes to form large quantities of gas bubbles that efficiently and quickly leaven these items. Sour cream is a very commonly purchased foodservice item because it is used as an ingredient in many recipes. These include dips, salad dressings, soups and baked goods, and toppings for baked potatoes and many popular Mexican-style foods such as enchiladas, nachos, and quesadillas.

ICE CREAM Ice cream (or iced cream) is a challenging product to purchase. In its basic form, ice cream is a frozen mixture of milk, sugar or other sweetener, cream, and flavorings such as fruits, nuts, or vanilla. The last, and perhaps most essential, ingredient in ice cream is air, without which ice cream would not have the texture that makes it such a popular dish worldwide.

Ice cream, which comes in many flavors, is a favorite dessert around the world.

Paul Harris and Anne Heslope © Dorling Kindersley

In the United States, ice cream is a frozen dairy product that must contain at least 10 percent milk fat and, at most, 50 percent air, and it must weigh at least 4.5 pounds per gallon. Ice creams termed "premium" and "super premium" have higher fat content (13 to 17 percent) and lower air content (called **overrun** in the ice cream trade).

Despite the fact that the USDA has established rigid standards for various ice cream quality levels, in common terminology, frozen custards, yogurts, and sherbets may also be referred to as "ice cream." The USDA, as well as the governments of other countries, also closely regulates these product standards for these items. The following is a partial list of some of the most popular ice cream-like desserts, as well as their identifying characteristics:

Low-fat ice cream (ice milk):   This product contains less than 10 percent milk fat and lower sweetening content. It is made from milk, stabilizers, sweeteners, and flavorings and contains not more than 3 grams of fat per 4-ounce serving. Ice creams advertised as "reduced fat" or "light" must have a lower fat content than "regular" ice cream, but may not meet the standard for "low fat."

Frozen custard: Also known as French Ice Cream or New York Ice Cream. This product has must contain at least 1.4 percent egg yolks.

Frozen yogurt: A low-fat or fat-free ice cream alternative made with yogurt

Gelato: The Italian word for "ice cream," Gelato is an Italian-style frozen dessert that must have a 4 to 9 percent milk fat content.

Sherbet: This product is made from milk, fruit or fruit juice, stabilizers, and has a level of sweetening much higher than ice cream. It must contain 1 to 2 percent milk fat.

Sorbet: Technically, sorbet is not a dairy product at all because it is made with fruit purée and contains no milk products.

Ice cream products are highly perishable and must be stored carefully and used fairly quickly to maintain high quality. Increasingly, consumer demand in the hospitality industry is for higher quality, more expensive ice cream products than for lower quality products.

PURCHASING PROS NEED TO KNOW (14.2)

Although the fat content of ice cream is often cited as its most important indicator of quality, purchasing pros know that overrun is equally, or more, important to a guest's perception of ice cream quality.

The percentage of overrun in ice cream products can range from 0 (no air) to 200, a theoretical figure that would indicate all air. The legal overrun limit for ice cream is 100 percent, or 50 percent air. Ice cream must have air in it or it would be hard as a rock. However, ice cream with a 100 percent overrun would feel mushy in the mouth and melt extremely quickly.

The most desirable overrun proportion is between 20 and 50 (10 to 25 percent air), which creates a product that is denser, creamier, and more satisfying. Because the overrun is not listed on the package, the only way to be absolutely sure about it is to weigh the product. Ice cream with a 50 percent overrun (25 percent air) will weigh about 18 ounces per pint (subtract about 1 1/2 ounces for the weight of the container). The net weight of other ice creams tested will be proportionally higher (or lower) with differing percentages of overrun.

Key Term

Overrun   The term used to indicate the amount of air in a frozen dairy product.

Internet Purchasing Assistant (14.5)

The International Dairy Foods Association (IDFA) is located in Washington, DC. It represents the nation's dairy manufacturing and marketing industries and their suppliers. IDFA is composed of three constituent organizations: the Milk Industry Foundation (MIF), the National Cheese Institute (NCI), and the International Ice Cream Association.

IDFA's 220 dairy processing members operate more than 600 plants, and together they represent more than 85 percent of the milk, cultured products, cheese, and frozen desserts produced and marketed in the United States. To view their Web site, go to: www.idfa.org

At the home page, click on "Industry Facts."

1. Next, click on and read about "Milk."
2. Next, read the material on "Ice Cream."
3. Next, read the information in "Cultured Products."

EGG PRODUCTS

Many animals and fish reproduce by laying eggs. Bird eggs are laid by the female of the species, and when fertilized, a single young hatches from each egg. Foodservice operators generally buy unfertilized eggs laid by chickens, although duck and quail eggs, among others, are also widely available. In commercial foodservice operations, the chicken egg product alternatives available for purchase consist of fresh eggs, processed egg products of various forms, and egg substitutes, which are egg-alternative products that can be made in whole, or in part, from regular eggs.

Fresh Eggs

The three primary parts of a fresh egg are the shell, yolk, and white **(albumen).**

The shell, which is made of calcium carbonate, prevents microbes from entering the egg, keeps the egg from drying out by retaining its moisture, and protects the egg during handling. The breed of chicken dictates the shell's color,

Chicken eggs are used in many dishes and are an excellent source of protein as well as other essential vitamins and minerals.

Dave King © Dorling Kindersley

Key Term

Albumen   Another term for the "white" of a fresh egg.

which can range from white to brown. As a buyer, it is important for you to know that the shell's color has no effect on the egg's quality, flavor, or nutritive content, despite the fact that some food distributors consistently charge a premium for brown-colored shell eggs.

The yolk of an egg contains approximately 75 percent of the egg's calories, most of the minerals, and all of the fat. The yolk also contains **lecithin,** the compound responsible for emulsification in mayonnaise and hollandaise sauce. In one large-sized egg, the yolk contains five grams total fat, two grams saturated fatty acids, 213 milligrams cholesterol, and 60 calories.

The feed eaten by chickens directly affect the color of egg yolks. As is true with shell color, however, the color of an egg's yolk is not an indicator of egg quality.

Eggs are sold by the dozen in various carton sizes. Egg cartons from USDA-inspected plants must display a **Julian date** (the date the eggs were packed).

Fresh shell eggs can be stored in their cartons in the refrigerator for four to five weeks beyond this date with insignificant quality loss. Although not required, they may also carry an expiration date beyond which the eggs should not be sold.

There are three consumer grades for eggs: U.S. Grade AA, A, and B. The grade is determined by the interior quality of the egg and the appearance and condition of the egg shell. Eggs of any quality grade may differ in weight (size).

U.S. GRADE AA eggs have whites that are thick and firm; yolks that are high, round, and practically free from defects; and clean, unbroken shells.

U.S. GRADE A eggs have whites that are reasonably firm; yolks that are high, round, and practically free from defects; and clean, unbroken shells. This is the quality most often sold in stores.

U.S. GRADE B eggs have whites that may be thinner and yolks that may be wider and flatter than eggs of the higher grades; the shells must be unbroken, but may show slight stains.

PURCHASING PROS NEED TO KNOW (14.3)

Shell eggs are sized by their minimum weight per dozen. As a result, buyers may compare prices based upon the net cost per ounce or gram.

Egg Size	Minimum Weight Per Dozen	
	Ounces	Grams
Jumbo	30	850.5
Extra Large	27	765.5
Large	24	680.4
Medium	21	595.3
Small	18	510.3
Peewee	15	425.2

Source: U.S. Department of Agriculture (ounce weights only)

Key Terms

Lecithin   A fatlike substance also called a phospholipid. A healthy human's liver produces this compound daily if that person's diet is adequate.

Julian date   A dating system that starts with January 1 as number 1 and ends with December 31 as 365. These numbers represent the consecutive days of the year. Thus, for example, February 1st would be represented by the Julian date "32."

U.S. Grade AA and A eggs are good for all purposes, but especially for poaching and frying where appearance is important. U.S. Grade B eggs, if available, are suitable for general cooking and baking.

Processed Eggs

Most distributors sell a variety of processed egg products. These include whole eggs that have been shelled and whites-only or yolks-only products. Processed egg products are sold fresh (refrigerated), frozen, or dried. Processed eggs are shell eggs broken by special machines at the grading station, and then pasteurized before being further processed and packaged. Processed egg products may contain preservatives and flavor or color additives. Because of their built-in labor savings, these products generally cost more per ounce than shell eggs.

Another special and popular form of egg processing exists when processors remove yolks from eggs, and then further process the whites only. ConAgra Foods "Egg Beaters" is such a product. "Egg Beaters," according to the nutrition information posted on their Web site (www.eggbeaters.com), contain 99 percent egg whites. The other one percent comprises coloring, salt, and other ingredients. In addition, nutrients are added to make up for those lost from the yolk, so egg products of this type will usually contain varying amounts of iron; zinc; foliate; thiamin; riboflavin; vitamins A, E, B^6, and B^{12}; and have an equivalent amount of protein as whole eggs, but with fewer total calories. Like shell eggs, it is important that proper storage and handling procedures are followed when using any processed egg product.

Egg Substitutes

Eggs contain **cholesterol,** and because significant numbers of people are allergic to eggs, the popularity of total egg substitutes has increased greatly in recent years.

Egg substitutes are generally of two types, and professional buyers must understand the difference between the two. The first type is a complete substitution made from soy or milk proteins. These may not typically be used for baking or other uses where the egg is intended to provide thickening or leavening in the item to be produced.

The second type contains real albumen, but the yolk is removed and replaced with dairy or vegetable products. Although these products taste different than whole eggs, the whites they contain do make them suitable for many cooking purposes.

Internet Purchasing Assistant (14.6)

Eggs of all types are eaten around the world, but chicken eggs are especially popular. In fact, in the United States, an "egg" typically refers to the eggs of chicken. These are high in protein, low in cost, and readily available at all times of the year. To study eggs in greater detail, and to learn more about how to best buy them, log on to the Web site of the American Egg Board, at: www.aeb.org

At the home page, click on "foodservice professionals," then click on "egg products" to learn more about eggs."

Key Term

Cholesterol   A white crystalline substance found in animal tissues and various foods. Its level in the bloodstream can influence certain conditions such as the development of atherosclerotic plaque and coronary artery disease.

Verifying product quality and quantity upon delivery is an important key to controlling cost and usage accuracy.

Vincent P. Walter/Pearson Education/PH College

PRODUCT RECEIVING AND STORAGE

Like other fresh foods, produce, dairy products, and eggs should be carefully inspected upon delivery. As is true with other categories of fresh foods, there are also some special aspects regarding the receiving and storage of these items.

Receiving

When receiving fresh produce, buyers and receivers must understand the common container sizes used to pack and ship these items. Although many produce items are sold by the pound, many are also sold in container sizes and shapes that are not readily known by all buyers. Figure 14.3 lists some of the most frequently used of these, as well as the approximate net weight of products these containers will hold.

Storage

Proper storage of produce and dairy products is essential if they are to be served at their peak quality levels. It is important to remember that produce, dairy, and egg purchases will arrive at the operation in their best condition. From the time most of these items are delivered to the time they are served, quality levels will decline. This is so because fruits and vegetables lose moisture and continue to **respire** after they are harvested, which causes them to decline in quality as they age.

The ability of an operation to produce high-quality fresh foods that maximize yield and flavor depends upon the condition of the items upon delivery and the ability to store, produce, and hold them, if necessary, before service. Vegetables with an especially high water content such as lettuce and celery quickly lose flavor and texture as they dehydrate. Therefore, water retention or replacement is important in maintaining quality vegetables. To best preserve most vegetables,

Key Term

Respire To take up oxygen and produce carbon dioxide through oxidation. Respiration rates can be controlled (slowed) when storing produce by reducing temperatures or reducing the available oxygen levels.

Items Purchased	Container	Approximate Net Weight in Pounds
Apples	Cartons, tray pack	40–45
Asparagus	Pyramid crates, loose pack	32
Beets, bunched	½ crates, 2 dozen bunches	36–40
Cabbage, green	Flat crates (1 3/4 bushel)	50–60
Cantaloupe	½-wire-bound crates	38–41
Corn, sweet	Cartons, packed with 5 dozen ears	50
Cucumbers, field grown	Bushel cartons	47–55
Grapefruit, Florida	4/5-bushel cartons and wire-bound crates	42 1/2
Grapes, table	Lugs and cartons, plain pack	23–24
Lettuce, loose leaf	4/5-bushel crates	810
Limes	10-lb. cartons	10
Onions, green	4/5-bushel crates (36 green bunches)	11
Oranges, Florida	4/5-bushel cartons	45
Parsley	Cartons, wax treated, 5 dozen bunches	21
Peaches	2-layer cartons and lugs, tray pack	22
Shallots	Bags	5
Squash	1-layer flats, place pack	16
Strawberries, California	12 one-pint trays	11–14
Tangerines	4/5-bushel cartons	47 1/2
Tomatoes, pink and ripe	3-layer lugs and cartons, 20-lb. place pack	24–33

FIGURE 14.3 Selected Produce Container Net Weights

store them in their original or airtight containers at normal refrigeration temperatures and buy only enough to last for a few days.

Some vegetables, such as tomatoes, do best if held at room temperature until fully ripe before being placed in the refrigerator. Others, such as sweet potatoes, should not be refrigerated at all. Avocados and bananas should not be refrigerated until they are completely ripe. Melons can also be held at room temperature until fully ripe before refrigerating them. Most fruits should be stored in their original containers, unwashed, until ready to use and can be held at standard refrigerator temperatures. When in doubt, discuss specific vegetable and fruit storage requirements with your produce vendor.

Fluid milks, butter, cream, yogurt, and most cheeses should be stored under refrigeration at 41°F (5°C). Dairy products easily absorb off-odors and should, therefore, be stored in airtight containers. Butter should be stored in its original container to avoid absorbing flavors from other foods. To enhance their quality, keep frozen desserts in tightly closed cartons. Frozen desserts stored at temperatures below 0°F (−18°C) will keep for about a month but have best quality when stored for shorter periods of time.

Canned milk, **aseptically** packaged milks, and dry milk powders do not need to be refrigerated.

After the can or box containing these items is opened, or after the dry milk product has been reconstituted, however, these become potentially hazardous foods that must be cared for just as if they were fresh milk products.

Key Term

Aseptic (packaging) A system of packaging, in airtight containers, products that are free from organisms that cause disease, fermentation, or putrefaction.

The quality of eggs upon delivery is most often unknown. The age of eggs (how recently an egg was laid) is only one of many factors affecting its quality. For example, the National Egg Board states that a one-week-old egg, held under ideal conditions, can be fresher than a one-day-old egg left at room temperature for 24 hours.

The ideal conditions for eggs are temperatures that do not go above 40°F (4.5°C) and a relative humidity of 70–80 percent. The quality level of fresh eggs is very important. As eggs age, the white becomes thinner, and the yolk becomes flatter. Although these changes do not affect on egg's nutritional quality, the fresher the egg is when poached or fried, the more it will hold its shape rather than spread out in the pan, which can affect the guest's perception of product quality.

Purchasing Resources on the Internet

In addition to the Web sites referenced in this chapter's "Internet Purchasing Assistant" feature, the following sites provide detailed information to enhance your purchasing knowledge and skills.

Purchasing Resources on the Internet

Site	Information About
www.dole.com	Fresh fruits and vegetables
www.unitedfresh.org	Fresh fruits and vegetables
www.freshdelmonte.com	Fresh fruits and vegetables
www.localharvest.org	Organic fruits and vegetables sources
www.organicexpress.com	Organic fruits and vegetables
www.fpfc.org	Fresh fruits and vegetables
www.freshfrommexico.com	Imported fruits and vegetables
www.landolakes.com	Butter, cheese, and dairy products
www.wisconsincheese.com	Domestic (Wisconsin) cheeses
www.realcaliforniacheese.com	Domestic (California) cheeses
www.idealcheese.com	Imported cheeses
www.ballardcheese.com	Cheese making
www.challengedairy.com	Butter products
www.horizonorganic.com	Organic dairy products
www.haagen-dazs.com	Premium ice cream
www.bluebell.com	Premium ice cream
www.icecreamusa.com	Ice cream and frozen novelty items
www.eggbeaters.com	Egg substitutes
www.nestfresh.com	Organic eggs
www.ams.usda.gov/howtobuy/eggs.htm	Buying eggs

Key Terms

produce 336
fruit 337
vegetable 337
irradiation 338
solid pack
   (canning) 339
water pack
   (canning) 339

syrup pack
   (canning) 339
Brix 339
modified atmosphere
   packaging
   (MAP) 344
oxidation 344
lactose 347

pasteurized 347
homogenized 347
rennet 349
score (butter) 353
clarified (butter) 354
smoke point 354
cultured (dairy
   product) 354

overrun 356
albumen 357
lecithin 358
Julian date 358
cholesterol 359
respire 360
aseptic
   (packaging) 361

Think It Through

1. Traditionally, restaurants and other food service operations have offered their vegetarian clientele few creative menu options. What role can purchasing agents play in collaborating with food production professionals when planning menu items that appeal to vegetarian customers?

2. "Fresh," when discussing fruits and vegetables, can mean anything from "never frozen" to "never processed." Choose one fruit and one vegetable, and write a complete menu definition of "fresh" for that item. Do you think everyone would agree with your definition? Why or why not?

3. Assume you are the buyer for a college foodservice program. What different milk fat content milks would you propose offering your residence hall students? How would you decide? What fac-tors must buyers consider as they balance their guests' desires for variety with an operation's logistical limitations?

4. The world of food, and its market forms in the foodservice industry, changes rapidly. What are three specific actions procurement professionals can take to keep their knowledge of purchasing alternatives up-to-date?

5. Like many other food products, some fruits, vegetables, and dairy products are packaged under nationally labeled brands, (e.g., Dole brand pineapples, Green Giant brand vegetables, and Ben and Jerry's brand ice cream). How important do you feel branded products in these categories are to consumers? How important do you think they are to buyers? Explain your answers.

Team Fun

For this exercise, assume that each team consists of those individuals who make up the corporate procurement team at "Salads and More," a nationwide chain of 150 restaurants featuring fresh salads and grilled sandwiches.

Each team will be given a crisis investigation task.

This is necessary because, unfortunately, the company has just been notified that an outbreak of *E.coli* O157:H7 appears to have been traced to one of your restaurants. In the past three days, 75 people reported having gotten ill after eating at the same company-operated store. The local health department states it has traced the source of the illness to fresh spinach, a key ingredient in one of your most popular salads. Its investigation is ongoing.

As the buying agents for your corporation, the company's CEO has asked that you and your team members question appropriate individuals about the issue and report back. Form your class members into three teams:

1. The assignment of the first team is to devise a series of fact-finding questions to be asked of those actually managing the operation in which the outbreak is suspected to have occurred. The intent of the questions should be to assess compliance with industry procurement standards.

2. The assignment of the second team is to devise a series of questions to be asked of the managers of the distributor from whom "Salads and More" buys its produce. The intent of the questions should be to assess compliance with industry procurement standards.

3. The assignment of the third team is to devise a series of questions to be asked of the packer/wholesaler from which the produce distributor purchased the spinach. The intent of the questions should be to assess compliance with industry procurement standards.

Each team should also consider and note the specific potential impediments (and their causes) that could affect their crisis investigation efforts.

15

Complementary Food Products

In This Chapter

A dictionary definition of "complementary" is "completing, or making whole." The foods discussed in this chapter do not fully complete the products presented in the two previous chapters or represent all items purchased by professional foodservice buyers. However, they are among the most important and will conclude our examination of food products most often used in foodservice operations. Meat, seafood, produce, dairy, and egg-based products typically constitute the highest cost of all items purchased for foodservice use, but knowledge of the foods examined in this chapter is also essential to foodservice buyers.

Bread is among the most important complements to a meal, and to understand its many forms, one must understand the cereal grains from which it is made. This chapter examines wheat, corn, rice, and other cereals used to make breads and other starchy dishes. Pastas are also an important starch. Despite its close association with Italian foods, pastas and noodles are a mainstay of many cuisines, and buyers should know how they are made and used in the foodservice industry.

Among the most important of food flavorings are fats and oils. These are used in all forms of cooking and baking, and a basic understanding of their sources and uses helps buyers make good decisions when selecting these products. Additional flavorings common to all foodservice operations are sweeteners, spices, and in many cases, nutmeats.

Natural and artificial sweeteners are important as food flavorings as well as for their role in baked products. Experienced cooks also know the importance of spices to enhance flavor and preserve foods. Thus, a basic understanding of these critical recipe ingredients is fundamental to purchasing them. Although sometimes neglected, in many dishes (e.g., pecans in pralines, walnuts or pistachios in baklava, and pine nuts in pesto), the meats from nuts (nutmeats) are an essential ingredient, as well as an indispensable flavoring that professional buyers should know about.

Increasingly, foodservice professionals purchase a variety of foods that have labor built into them. These "convenience" foods affect many areas of today's foodservice menus, and knowledge of how they are made, packaged, and labeled is essential to good buying. Entrées, baked goods, soups, dressings, and condiments are good examples of foods that are often considered (and purchased as) convenience foods.

Some food products are not a specific type, but rather are selected foods that are produced and handled in very special ways. Chief among these are Kosher products (those permitted by Jewish dietary law) and Halal foods (those permitted by Muslim dietary law). Buyer knowledge of these food types is increasingly important in a world where the diversity of foodservice customers is rapidly growing.

■■■

Outline

Starches
  Cereal Grains
    Wheat
    Corn

STARCHES

Grains (wheat, corn, rice, and others) and **pastas** are collectively known as starches. The starch category also includes potatoes, the vegetable examined in Chapter 14. Some starches are vegetables whereas others are grasses.

Starches are the staple foods in nearly all cuisines. In general, they are high in carbohydrates, low in fat, and relatively inexpensive. As a result, they are typically an integral part of a well-balanced meal, as well as a balanced diet.

Key Term

Pasta Unleavened dough, usually made of wheat flour, water, and sometimes eggs, which is molded into any of a variety of shapes and then boiled or simmered.

Cereal Grains

Of the approximately 8,000 species in the grass family, only a few are considered food. Aside from bamboo and sugar cane, **cereals** are the only grasses regularly eaten by humans. Cereal plants produce edible grains. The grain may be either a seed (e.g., rice) or a kernel (e.g., wheat).

Most grain kernels are protected by a hull or husk, which is removed prior to eating the kernel. Understanding the three main parts of the edible kernel is essential when making informed cereal grain buying decisions. These parts are

Bran: The tough outer layer covering the endosperm.

Endosperm: The largest part of the kernel, and the source of the grain's protein and starch content. This portion of the grain is used to produce **flour.**

Germ: The smallest part of the kernel. It is the source of any fat found in the grain.

Whole grain flours (and foods) are those in which all three parts of the grain—bran, endosperm, and germ—are used in the product.

The flours made by grinding grains are produced using steel rollers or are stone ground. In both cases, the miller (grinder) will expose the grain to one or more grinding processes.

- *Cracking.* The miller breaks open the grains.
- *Hulling.* The hull is separated from the grain.
- *Grinding.* The grains are reduced to powders of various sizes.
- *Pearling.* All or part of the hull, bran, and germ are removed from the grain.

Because stone grinding produces a product superior to that made with steel rollers, stone ground products are always labeled as such and will generally be sold at a higher price.

Although any grain can be used to produce flour, foodservice buyers are typically most concerned with the information needed to purchase wheat, rice, and corn and, to a lesser degree, other types of ground grains.

WHEAT Wheat is the most widely cultivated food in the world. Its grain is highly prized for a variety of reasons, chief of which is bread making. Wheat germ and wheat bran are also popular because of their nutritional value, and these may be served alone, but are most often added to other foods. Although some popular dishes use milled or processed wheat grains (e.g., tabouli and couscous), wheat is most often purchased in its flour form. In fact, in the U.S. foodservice industry, the word "flour" is most often synonymous with "wheat flour."

The character of wheat determines the character of the flour it produces. Soft wheat varieties yield flours with low protein contents, whereas hard wheat varieties yield high protein content flours. Flours with higher protein contents produce

---

Key Terms

Cereal Any plant of the grass family that yields an edible grain. Examples include wheat, rye, oats, rice, and corn.

Flour The finely crushed meal (powder) that results when an edible grain has been ground, called "farina" in Spanish.

Whole grain Foods that contain all three of the essential parts (bran, endosperm, and germ) and naturally occurring nutrients of the entire grain seed. If the grain has been processed (i.e., cracked, crushed, rolled, ground, etc.), the resulting food product should deliver approximately the same balance of nutrients as that found in the original grain seed.

Type	Protein Content	Used for
Cake	7%–9.5%	Cakes
Pastry	7.5%–12%	Pie crusts, biscuits
All-purpose	10%–13%	General baked products, cookies
Bread	12%–15%	Yeast breads
Whole-wheat	13%–14%	Breads
High-gluten	14%–15%	Bagels

FIGURE 15.1 Protein Content of Flours

more gluten: the tough, rubbery substance that is produced when wheat flour is mixed with water. Flours with lower gluten-producing characteristics make tender baked goods such as cakes and pie crusts, whereas flours with higher protein contents produce heartier products such as yeast breads and bagels.

Figure 15.1 lists the various types of flours and their protein contents typically available to foodservice buyers.

Flour develops better baking qualities if it is allowed to age for a few weeks after it is milled. Chlorine dioxide speeds this aging, but also bleaches the flour. Bleaching destroys some of wheat flour's naturally occurring vitamin E, so some bakers (and foodservice consumers) prefer unbleached flours. Professional buyers should also be aware that wheat flour is often sold as **self-rising,** but its use in foodservice is limited because, in many quantity food recipes, there are variations in the ratio of salt and leavening to flour.

CORN   Corn (in Spanish: maize) is the only grain that is eaten fresh like a vegetable (sweet corn). It is native to South America and was originally grown for its use as a ground product (flour). Foodservice buyers will typically encounter three variations of ground corn flour:

Cornmeal: This product is made by grinding a special type of corn known as field corn, or "dent." Ground field corn (cornmeal) may be yellow, white, or blue. It is used as a coating for fried foods or can be cooked and made into a variety of products.

Hominy: This product is made from dried corn that has been soaked in hydrated lime or lye. Doing so removes the germ and the hard outer hull from the kernels, making the kernels more palatable, easier to digest, and easier to process. When first cooked with an alkaline substance and then very finely ground, this version of hominy is known as **masa harina** and is used in a variety of Central and South American dishes.

In most of the United States, hominy refers to whole corn kernels, which are hulled but not ground. In most of the Southern United States, however, hominy is the coarsely ground kernels used to make the dish known as "hominy grits" or more simply "grits."

Grits: Grits are dried hominy that has been finely to coarsely ground. Grits are most often served as a breakfast cereal and are usually topped with butter or cheese. Quick-cooking and instant grits are also available to foodservice buyers.

Key Terms

Self-rising (flour)   All-purpose flour to which salt and a chemical leavening (usually baking powder) has been added.

Masa harina   Literally corn "dough flour." It may be reconstituted with water or other liquids and used to make tortillas, tamales, and other corn-based dishes.

RICE   Rice is the starchy seed of a semiaquatic grass. Rice is a staple dish in most East and Southeast Asian cuisines. It is a key ingredient, however, in many cuisines including French and Spanish. Rice is the world's third largest grain crop, behind only wheat and corn. Rice is divided into three main types based upon its seed size: long-grain, medium-grain, and short-grain. Long-grain is the most popular worldwide. Its grains remain firm, fluffy, and separate after cooking. Short-grain rices contain more starch, thus they tend to get sticky after cooking. Japanese sushi and Spanish paella are both made using short-grain rice.

"Wild" rice is a special variation of rice cultivated in the United States. The most highly prized variety is "Northern" wild rice, an annual plant native to the Great Lakes regions. Wild rice is generally available in three grades: Giant (long grain and the highest grade), Fancy (medium grain), and Select (short grain).

It is important for buyers to know that all rice is originally brown. "Brown" rice is simply rice in which the bran has been left intact. "Converted rice" has been parboiled to remove the rice's surface starch. "Instant" or quick-cooking (Minute) rice is created by fully cooking and then flash freezing or drying the cooked product.

OTHER CEREALS   Although wheat, corn, and rice are the most popular grains, others are also widely consumed and thus often purchased for use in foodservice. These include

Oats: 95 percent of the oat crop grown in the world is used as animal food. The remaining 5 percent, however, constitute important parts of American and European cuisine. Oats are consumed primarily as a breakfast cereal (oatmeal). **Rolled oats** are a popular oat form, as are **quick-cooking oats** and **instant oats.** Henry Crowell, the founder of "Quaker Oats," who turned the commodity into a breakfast cereal by packaging it with cooking instructions and labeling it "natural," refined each of these forms. Today, oats are also a very popular ingredient in breads, muffins, and cookies.

Barley: Fast growing, hardy, and nutritious, in the Middle Ages, barley (as well as rye), was the mainstay grain of peasant diets, whereas wheat flour was reserved for the wealthy. Today, barley is used in Western cuisines primarily as an ingredient in soups. It is, however, an essential ingredient in Japanese miso (fermented soy paste). In Moroccan cuisine, as well as other countries of North Africa and western Asia, it is a popular ingredient for bread making.

Buckwheat: Although not actually a grain (it is the fruit of a plant most closely related to rhubarb), buckwheat nonetheless is often treated as a grain. It can be used to make noodles and bread; however, in the United States it is most often encountered as an ingredient in pancakes, where it contributes tenderness and a nutty flavor.

Rye: Popular for its use in bread making, rye flours are readily available to foodservice buyers. Interestingly, rye flour can absorb eight times its weight in liquid (in comparison, wheat flour can absorb only two times its weight). As a result, breads made with rye flour tend to be heavier than those of the

---

Key Terms

Rolled oats   Whole grain oats that are steamed, rolled in flat flakes, and then dried.

Quick-cooking oats   Rolled oats cut into small pieces to reduce cooking time.

Instant oats   Oats that are fully cooked before drying and must be reconstituted only with hot liquid prior to consumption.

same size that are made from wheat flour. Rye flour may be purchased in four colors, or grades: white, medium, dark, and rye meal. Medium and dark ryes have the most intense flavor, and breads containing them will typically be labeled as such. Rye meal is simply whole rye grain that is ground in various coarseness levels. Some millers and food manufacturers refer to rye meal as pumpernickel. Others, however, use pumpernickel as a generic term to describe any dark rye flour.

Ready-to-eat cereals: Although not a separate type of grain, ready-to-eat cereals deserve the special attention of foodservice buyers. Despite their currently poor reputation for containing too much highly refined sugar and contributing only "empty calories," ready-to-eat cereals began as a healthy alternative to the heavy American breakfasts of the mid-nineteenth century.

Dr. John Harvey Kellogg and his brother, Will Keith Kellogg; Charles William Post; and others were actually part of the first health movement in America. They warned about the dangers of fatty, protein-rich foods. Instead, they advocated a diet based primarily on vegetables, grains, and fiber. This group of innovators created the ready-to-eat cereal industry and invented such still-popular cereal variations as shredded wheat, puffed rice, wheat and corn flakes, Grape Nuts (invented by Post), **muesli,** and **granola.** Ready-to-eat cereals may be purchased in bulk or in single-service containers.

Pasta

Pasta is primarily associated with Italian cooking; however, pastas are an important part of many cuisines. Originally made from only wheat flour, today's pasta is made from various flour, water, and egg mixtures and is produced in a wide variety of shapes and forms. Pastas are usually cooked and served with a sauce or are stuffed, and then sauced.

They are made chiefly from **semolina,** the endosperm of durum, a wheat variety highly prized for its high protein content, rich cream color, and smooth, durable dough.

Couscous, a very unique form of pasta associated with Moroccan cuisine but indigenous to Tunisia and Algeria as well, is also made from semolina. Asian pastas, commonly called "noodles," can be made from wheat, but may also be produced from rice, bean, or buckwheat flours.

Pasta is an ingredient in many common foodservice dishes and thus will be included in products purchased canned or frozen. For most foodservice buyers, individual pasta products may be purchased dried or fresh.

DRIED   Dried pasta is available in a variety of flavors and shapes. In addition to white (traditional), green (spinach-flavored), and red (tomato-flavored) pastas, foodservice buyers can choose from whole-wheat products and other flavor combinations. Although pastas can be made into literally hundreds of shapes, these can be considered more easily when divided into the three main groups of ribbons, tubes, and shapes, as shown in Figure 15.2.

Key Terms

Muesli   A mixture of thinly rolled grains, sugar, fruits, and nuts.

Granola   Rolled oats flavored with sweeteners (usually honey) and spices, enriched with vegetable oil, toasted, and then mixed with nuts and/or dried fruits. The term was originally coined by the Kellogg brothers.

Semolina   The flour preferred for pasta making.

Foodservice buyers can choose from a variety of dried and fresh pasta products.

Dave King © Dorling Kindersley

Pasta Group	Common Products
Ribbons	Lasagna Fettuccine Linguine Spaghetti Vermicelli (thin spaghetti) Capellini (Angel hair)
Tubes	Manicotti Ziti Rigatoni Penne Spira Elbows
Shapes	Conchiglie (shells) Fusilli (spirals) Farfalle (bows) Rotello (wheels) Orzo (rice grains)

FIGURE 15.2 Common Pasta Groups and Products

Internet Purchasing Assistant (15.1)

Large buyers of dry pasta products may prefer to purchase unique varieties and shapes. Several custom pasta makers can accommodate the large institutional users and chains that wish to do so. To see one such company, and to review its pasta product customization ability, go to: www.zerega.com

At the home page:

1. Review the material in "Who We Are."
2. Review the material in "What We Do."

Basil	Jalapeno	Sage
Beet	Lemon	Scallion
Black pepper	Lemon-pepper	Spinach
Buckwheat	Mushroom	Sundried tomato
Cayenne	Onion	Tarragon
Chive	Oregano	Tomato
Dill	Red (bell) pepper	Tomato-basil
Egg	Red (chili) pepper	Tricolor
Garlic	Rosemary	Thyme
Green (bell) pepper	Saffron	Whole wheat

FIGURE 15.3 Fresh and Precooked-Flavored Pastas

FRESH In addition to the dried pasta forms most commonly purchased, many operations choose to use fresh (not dry) and/or precooked pasta. Like their dried counterparts, these pastas are made from semolina. Fresh pasta cooks faster than dried pasta, and many kitchen managers believe its taste is superior. For operations serving stuffed pastas (e.g., manicotti, cannelloni, and tortellini), prefilled fresh pastas can save labor and help ensure product consistency.

For generations, culinarians have been instructed that pastas taste best when served **al dente.**

Today, foodservice buyers can purchase expertly precooked pastas guaranteed to be prepared al dente. The results: product consistency and rapid preparation times. Precooked pastas need be heated only by plunging in boiling water, or steaming (but not cooking), prior to their service. Many operators selecting precooked pastas also report reduced levels of product waste.

Packaged in a variety of forms, these precooked products, as well as fresh pastas, are increasing in quality, variety, and availability. Figure 15.3 lists some flavors of fresh or precooked pastas.

FATS AND OILS

One way for professional food buyers to understand **fats** is to recognize that they are not water. In fact, they are so unlike water that the two cannot be mixed. Culinarians use this fact to their advantage when they fry foods to brown them, when they create **emulsions,** and when they thicken sauces with microscopic but intact fat droplets.

Fat is the term most often used to identify those "lipids" (the Greek term for "fat") that are solid at room temperature. Oil is the term used to identify those that are liquid at room temperature. Both fats and oils are members of the triglyceride family of chemical compounds; therefore, oils can quite correctly be considered simply liquid fats.

Despite the fact that most fats do not actually have sharply defined melting points (they soften gradually over a broad temperature range), many foodservice buyers use these traditional "solid" and "liquid" categories when learning about them.

Because of their importance in the human diet, and their proven relationship to obesity, heart disease, and cholesterol, as well as other health-related issues, it is

Key Terms

Al dente Pasta that has been cooked just long enough to be firm to the tooth (not soft).

Fat Any of various lipid compounds of carbon, hydrogen, and oxygen that are obtained from plants and animals. They are a major class of energy-rich food and are not soluble in water.

Emulsion The dispersion of small droplets of one liquid into a second liquid with which the droplets cannot be readily mixed. For example, oil and vinegar.

more important than ever that professional foodservice buyers understand fats and oils.

Solid fats contain more saturated fats and/or trans fats than oils. Trans fats occur naturally, in small quantities, in meat and dairy products. Most trans fats consumed by foodservice customers, however, are industrially created as a side effect of partial hydrogenation of plant oils.

Hydrogenation is a process of changing the chemical properties of liquid oils to make them solids. The technique was perfected in Germany in the early 1900s and was first commercialized in the United States, in 1911, as the product "Crisco." Partial hydrogenation changes a fat's molecular structure, raising its melting point, and reducing its rancidity. Unfortunately, this same process also results in a proportion of the changed fat becoming trans fat.

Unlike other fats, trans fats are not beneficial for health. While their use is declining, trans fats can still be found in many commercial cakes, cookies, crackers, icings, margarines, and microwave popcorns. Eating trans fats has been found, among other things, to increase the risk of coronary heart disease and as a result, health authorities worldwide recommend that consumption of trans fat be eliminated or severely restricted.

In December 2006, the New York City Board of Health voted to make New York the nation's first city to ban artificial trans fats in foods served at restaurants. The board, which passed the ban unanimously, bars restaurants from using most frying oils containing artificial trans fats by mid-2007 and mandated the elimination of artificial trans fats from all of foods served by July 2008.

Solids

Solid fats are fats that are firm at room temperature and include butter and shortening. Solid fats come from many animal foods and, as previously noted, can be made from vegetable oils through hydrogenation. In commercial foodservice, the most commonly used solid fats include

- butter
- beef fat (tallow, suet)
- chicken fat
- pork fat (lard)
- margarines

In most cases, solid, nonhydrogenized fats have low smoke points (see Chapter 14). As a result, these fats are purchased primarily for the characteristic flavors they give soups (chicken fat), sauces, and baking (butter), and for flavoring other foods (beef and pork fats).

Margarine has a long and interesting history. In 1869, Napoleon offered a prize to anyone who could make a butter substitute suitable for the armed forces of France, as well as for the country's poor. A French chemist invented a substance extracted from beef fat and flavored that was called "oleomargarine" and was, over time, shortened to "margarine." The term "margarine" now refers generically to any of a range of broadly similar fats and oils made into solids (although liquid margarines are also available). Some people commonly shorten the name oleomargarine to "oleo."

Modern margarine can be made from any of a wide variety of animal or vegetable fats and is often mixed with skimmed milk, salt, and emulsifiers. Margarine made from vegetable oils is especially important in today's foodservice industry because it provides a substitute for butter, which is appreciated by vegetarians as well as those individuals who must avoid dairy-based products.

Although the USDA has not developed grades for margarines, it has established specifications to ensure quality. You can view these at: http://www.ams.usda.gov/dairy/vegoil.pdf

The three main categories of margarine most purchased by foodservice buyers are

- Solid, uncolored, or colored margarine used for cooking or baking. This product is also known as shortening, a term that refers to a hydrogenated vegetable oil that is solid at room temperature.
- Traditional margarines for such uses as spreading on bread, English muffins, and the like. These items contain a relatively high percentage of saturated fats and can be made from either animal or vegetable oils.
- Margarines high in mono- or poly-unsaturated fats, which are made from safflower, sunflower, soybean, cottonseed, or olive oil and are often considered to be healthier than butter or other types of margarine.

Liquids

In contrast to solid fats, oils are fats that are liquid at room temperature. Oils can come from many different plants as well as fish. For purposes of buying foodservice oils, they can best be considered as either cooking oils or flavoring oils.

COOKING OILS Many oils used for cooking, baking, or as an ingredient in other recipes are obtained from plants and have characteristics and attributes that make them appropriate for specific recipes or cooking styles. These include quality oils made from:

- canola
- corn
- peanut
- safflower
- soybean
- sunflower
- coconut

Olive oil is a popular product that is so widely used for cooking (and other purposes) in commercial kitchens that it deserves the special attention of professional food buyers. The olive (*Olea europaea*) is a species of small tree native to coastal areas of the Eastern Mediterranean. Olives and oil are so closely associated that "oil" is actually a variation of the tree's name (*Olea*). Olive oil is the only oil that is extracted from a fruit rather than a seed, nut, or grain. Extra virgin, virgin,

---

On-the-Job Challenges in Purchasing (15.1)

Jean Tye is the owner of the Old World Family Buffet. The clientele of the Old World are primarily older citizens and families. Old World is known for its quality vegetables, varied menu, and made-on-premises cakes, pies, cobblers, and other desserts. One Tuesday, Jean arrived at work to find two messages. One was from the City Restaurant Association's president asking if she had heard that, at the prior evening's City Council meeting, a proposal was made to ban trans fats in all restaurant foods starting in six months. The president seeks Jean's support in publicly opposing the measure. The second call was from a reporter at the local paper asking Jean to comment on the City Council's ruling. Many of the dessert crusts Jean's restaurant produces are made with recipes that include lard, and she uses peanut oil for all of the Old World's fried food products.

Case Study Questions

Assume you were Jean:

1. What would be your response to the Association's president?
2. What would be your response to the newspaper reporter?
3. What and how would you communicate to your customers about this issue?

PURCHASING PROS NEED TO KNOW (15.1)

The International Olive Oil Council (IOOC) is an intergovernmental organization based in Spain. The IOOC promotes olive oil use around the world by tracking production, defining quality standards, and monitoring authenticity. More than 85 percent of the world's olives are grown in IOOC member nations. Twenty-three countries are members. However, the United States is not, and the United States does not recognize the international olive oil labeling standards mandated by IOOC.

As a result, olive oil purveyors selling to the U.S. market choose label wording differently than they do when selling to better-regulated IOOC countries, as a few examples will help make clear:

"*Imported from Italy*" creates an impression that the olives were grown in Italy, although it only means that the oil was bottled there.

"*100% Pure Olive Oil*" is often touted as "good" quality, although it is actually the lowest quality commercially available. (Better grades would have "virgin" or "extra virgin" on the label.)

"*Light olive oil*" refers only to a lighter color, not a lower fat content. All olive oil, which is all fat, has 120 calories per tablespoon.

Although the USDA is considering adopting labeling rules that parallel the IOOC standards, until this occurs terms such as "extra virgin" may be applied to *any* grade of oil, making the term of dubious usefulness. Thus, when it comes to quality olive oils, it is easy to see why U.S. foodservice buyers should definitely have as much (or more) product knowledge as their suppliers.

---

and pure, the label designations of olive oil, refer to the acidity levels of the oil. Low acidity oils labeled Extra Virgin (maximum 1 percent acidity), or Virgin (maximum 3 percent acidity) are best, and the most expensive.

FLAVORING OILS   By themselves, most oils add flavor to foods. Also, other ingredients such as garlic, spices, and herbs may be steeped in oils to add a more complex flavor. Other oils, such as those from nuts (almonds) and seeds (sesame), provide a strong flavor and the aroma of the item from which they are taken. Some specially produced flavored oils are also known as **infused oils.**

Because of their unique source and nonstandardized labeling, olive oils are among the most complex oils purchased by professional foodservice buyers.
Charles Schiller © Dorling Kindersley

Key Term

Infused oils   Products prepared by extracting aromatic oils from other sources and emulsifying them with high-grade olive or canola oils. Commonly produced infused oils include those made with garlic, basil, citrus, and other spices.

Internet Purchasing Assistant (15.2)

There are actually four types of fats: (1) monounsaturated fat, (2) polyunsaturated fat, (3) saturated fat, and (4) trans fat.

Monounsaturated fat and polyunsaturated fat are the "good" fats. It is generally accepted that consumption of saturated fat should be kept low, especially for adults. Trans fats are recognized as particularly unhealthy, and their use in commercial foodservice operations is increasingly prohibited. As a result, it is wise for food service buyers to better understand the composition of the fats widely used in their own operations.

To learn more about the composition of fats and oils commonly purchased for foodservice use, go to: www.hsph.harvard.edu/nutritionsource/fats.html

At the home page:

Enter "Dietary Fats" in the search box to find articles about the relationship between cholesterol and fats.

FLAVORINGS

Regardless of the cuisine, food flavorings are an important part of what makes food taste good and, in many cases, authentic. Thus, for example, many diners expect to taste cumin (a spice) when eating Southwestern-style and Mexican foods. In a similar manner, toasted pecans will top praline-style desserts. In all of these cases, selected foods are used to enhance or augment the flavor of other foods.

HI-TECH PURCHASING (15.1)

The Search for the Perfect Fat (Replacement)?

Many Americans and others worldwide love the taste of fats. Unfortunately, some consumers eat too much of them. Thus, euphoria is the only word that could adequately describe the interest that occurred in the early 1990s when it was announced that products made with olestra, a fat substitute, would go on sale nationwide. In 1968, Procter & Gamble researchers had synthesized a fat substitute called sucrose polyester. They named the product "olestra." Despite objections from The Center for Science in the Public Interest, in 1996 the FDA approved olestra for use in savory snacks such as chips, crackers, and tortilla chips. The products, however, were required to carry warning labels that stated:

This Product Contains Olestra. Olestra may cause abdominal cramping and loose stools. Olestra inhibits the absorption of some vitamins and other nutrients.

Vitamins A, D, E, and K have been added.

Obviously, such wording did not endear Olestra products to American consumers, and the sale of products made with Olestra, although initially strong, steadily declined.

Today, a new fat substitute is creating great interest, and its future seems more secure than that of olestra. "Z Trim," which has no fat, is made from the hulls of corn, oats, soy, rice, and barley. It was developed by scientists at the U.S. Department of Agriculture. Unlike olestra, which raised concerns about diarrhea and stomach cramping, Z Trim has no side effects. Z Trim has zero calories, so its use in foods lowers calories by replacing fats. Because it is an all-natural product made from grains, it supplements foods with dietary fiber, is not known to cause gastrointestinal or other side effects, is gluten free, and can reduce the use of fats in many recipes with no discernible loss of product quality or flavor. Although it cannot be used for frying, its potential to drastically reduce calories in products such as cheese, baked goods, meat products, dressings, and candies is significant. To learn more about this "home grown," hi-tech fat replacement product, go to: www.ztrim.com

In this section, we will examine three broad categories of important food flavorings: sweeteners, spices, and **nutmeats.**

Sweeteners

Sweet (sugary) foods are favorites among foodservice guests. Although some naturally sweet foods are eaten essentially as they occur in nature (e.g., honey and maple syrup), in most cases, sweeteners are used to enhance other foods. When used in combination with other foods, they provide flavor and color. In baked goods, sugars and other sweeteners enhance tenderness because they weaken gluten strands, provide food for yeast, assist in the leavening process, and serve as a preservative.

SUGARS   Chemically, sugars are carbohydrates. They may be classified as either single (simple) sugars such as glucose and fructose, which occur naturally in honey and fruits, or more complex sugars such as sucrose and lactose (milk sugar). Sucrose is the most commonly purchased sugar in the foodservice industry. It may be **refined** from either sugar cane or sugar beet roots. Either is equally suitable for foodservice use because they are chemically identical.

Pure, refined sucrose is most often purchased in granulated (table sugar) or powdered forms. Powdered (confectioners') sugars are available in varying degrees of fineness. For example, 10X is the most common (lower numbers indicate greater coarseness). Bar sugars are superfine granulated sugars (not powdered sugar) that are popular with bartenders because they instantly dissolve in liquids. Brown sugar is simply refined cane sugar with some **molasses** added back to it. Light brown sugar contains approximately 3.5 percent molasses, whereas dark brown sugar contains about 6.5 percent molasses.

LIQUID SWEETENERS   Except for leavening-baked products, liquid sweeteners can be used in the same manner as sugar. Some liquid sweeteners can, just like crystallized sugar, be made from sugar cane. Others are made from plants, grains, or by bees. The most common of these **syrups** are

Corn syrup: This product is made by extracting starch from corn kernels and treating it with acid or an enzyme to develop a sweet syrup. Corn syrup is very thick, but is less sweet than refined sugar or honey. It is, by far, the liquid sweetener most commonly used in commercial food production.

Honey: Honey is made by bees and is a strong sweetener consisting of fructose and glucose. Its flavor and color vary depending upon the season, type of flower or plant from which the nectar used to make it is extracted, and its age. Depending upon the source and its quality, variation in the price of different honeys can be large.

Maple syrup: This distinctive syrup is made from the sap of sugar maple trees. One sugar maple tree produces about 12 gallons of maple sap each year, and it takes 30–40 gallons of sap to produce one gallon of maple syrup. As a result, pure maple syrup (USDA Grades AA and A are best) is quite

---

Key Terms

Nutmeat   The edible portion of nuts.

Refined (sugar)   The process of converting plant sugars into concentrated sugar forms.

Molasses   The thick, dark-to-light brown syrup that is separated from raw sugar in the manufacture of refined sugar.

Syrup   A thick, sticky solution of sugar and water that is often flavored.

Internet Purchasing Assistant (15.3)

The definition of "honey" stipulates a pure product that does not allow for the addition of any other substance. This includes water or other sweeteners, according to the National Honey Board. Honey, a USDA-graded product, is truly an amazing item. One of its defining characteristics is the fact that it cannot spoil. To learn why, as well as to investigate other aspects of honey, go to the National Honey Board's Web site at: www.honey.com

At the home page:

1. Click on "Honey Industry."
2. Review the material in "Honey Quality."
3. Follow the thread to USDA grade standards for extracted honey.

expensive. Maple syrup is often blended with other, less costly syrups, such as corn syrup, to produce maple "flavored" syrup. It is important for foodservice buyers to note, however, that some "maple-flavored" syrups may contain only artificial maple flavoring and coloring, and thus no maple syrup at all.

Molasses: True molasses is a by-product of cane sugar refinery. Some molasses, however, is made from corn syrup and is popular because of its lighter color and milder flavor. Blackstrap molasses is a very dark, distinctively flavored molasses favored in the American South. Sorghum molasses is actually the product that results when the sweet sap of a brown corn plant (sorghum), normally grown as cattle feed, is boiled down to a syrup consistency.

Herbs and Spices

Herbs and spices have, for centuries, been used to augment and complement the taste of foods. The use of quality herbs and spices enhances both the flavor of food

---

PURCHASING PROS NEED TO KNOW (15.2)

Due to a variety of health-related concerns expressed by guests, the foodservice industry's use of artificial sweeteners has increased dramatically in recent years. Artificial sweeteners are chemicals that offer the sweetness of sugar without the calories. Because the substitutes are much sweeter than sugar, it takes a much smaller quantity to create the same sweetness. As a result, menu items made with artificial sweeteners can have a much lower calorie count than do those made with sugar. Artificial sweeteners are often used as part of a weight-loss plan or as a means to control weight gain. People with diabetes may also prefer artificial sweeteners because they make food taste sweet without raising blood sugar levels. Foodservice buyers will find the following artificial sweeteners to be the most commonly requested by guests and popular with chefs:

Aspartame (sold as "NutraSweet" or "Equal")

Saccharin (sold as "Sweet and Low" or "Sugar Twin")

Acesulfame potassium (sold as "Sunsette" or "Sweet One")

Sucralose (sold as "Splenda")

Of course, simply removing sugar from items like cookies, cakes, and chocolate candy will not make them low-calorie, low-fat foods. If too many are eaten, customers and patients will still get more calories than needed and may be encouraged not to try other, more nutritious foods like fruits, vegetables, and whole grains. As a result, the extensive use of these products in noncommercial foodservice settings must be carefully assessed.

Sugar substitutes are so widely used today they are an essential part of any style coffee, or hot beverage, service offered to guests.

Joe Cornish © Dorling Kindersley

and the reputation of the operation using them. As a result, professional buyers should have a thorough knowledge of the use and quality levels of each herb and spice most used by their own operations.

An herb refers to a large group of **aromatic** plants whose flowers, leaves, or stems are used to enhance food flavors.

Most herbs may be purchased fresh or dried. Fresh products tend to have a milder flavor and are more expensive. Dried herbs have greater shelf lives and are typically less expensive. Fresh herbs are generally preferred by those operations where food quality standards are extremely high.

Spices are strongly flavored or aromatic portions of plants. Spices can include bark, roots, seeds, bulbs, or berries. Most, but not all, spices grow in tropical or warmer climates. Spices are almost always used in their dried (not fresh) forms and can typically be purchased either whole or ground.

The skillful use of herbs and spices give many foods and, in some cases, entire food operations and cuisines, their distinctive reputations. Consider, for example, the influence of curry (a spice blend), on Indian foods, Cajun seasonings on foods of that style, and tarragon (an herb) on such classics dishes as béarnaise sauce.

The knowledge needed to effectively purchase herbs and spices is significant. This is made even more apparent when it is considered that some plants (e.g., dill) can be classified as both an herb (its leaves) and a spice (its seeds), and that the quality of available herbs and spices can vary tremendously. Although it is by no means intended to be exhaustive, Figure 15.4 lists 40 of the herbs and spices most commonly used in commercial foodservice, and thus those most likely encountered by professional foodservice buyers.

Nutmeats

Nutmeats play an important role in many foodservice operations. Interestingly, not every one agrees about the definition of a "nut" (technically, a nut is a seed, but not all seeds are nuts). Fortunately, however, foodservice buyers need not

---

Key Term

Aromatic   A food used to enhance the natural aromas of another food. Aromatics include herbs, spices, and some vegetables.

Allspice	Chipotle	Mace	Pepper, White
Anise	Chives	Marjoram	Poppy Seed
Basil	Cilantro	Mint Leaves	Rosemary
Bay Leaf	Cinnamon	Mustard	Saffron
Caraway seed	Cloves	Nutmeg	Sage
Cardamom	Coriander	Oregano	Savory
Celery Seed	Cumin	Paprika	Sesame Seed
Chervil	Dill	Parsley	Tarragon
Chile Pepper,	Fennel	Pepper, Black	Thyme
Ancho Chile Pepper	Ginger	Pepper, Red	Turmeric

FIGURE 15.4 Popular Foodservice Herbs and Spices

concern themselves with a definition that would be acceptable to a botanist. In the kitchen, the term "nut" may be applied to many seeds and pods that are not true nuts. Because nuts generally have a high oil content, they are popular as a food flavoring as well as when **shelled** for eating by themselves.

Popular fruits and seeds that are considered "nuts" in the kitchen include

Pine nuts; Korean pine nuts: Purchased shelled and unshelled, used for pesto and as a salad topping.

Almonds: An edible seed used in making nougat and almond spreads, as well as in baking.

Cashews: A high-fat content and flavorful nut used in Asian cooking as well as spreads, candies, and snacks.

Coconut: Used in making desserts, some entrées, and drinks.

Internet Purchasing Assistant (15.4)

Few foods have played such an important role in the history of humankind, as have spices. Spices were some of the most valuable items of trade in the ancient and medieval world. Spices were the primary reason that the Portuguese navigator Vasco Da Gama sailed to India and (around the same time) that Christopher Columbus first sailed to the Americas (where he quickly described to his sponsors the many new spices available there). The spice trade has influenced the United States in ways unknown by many.

For example, did you know that, in 1672, Elihu Yale, an American-born former employee of the British East India (spice) Company began his own spice business? He became rich by doing so and in the early 1700s supplied the resources used to support the university (Yale) that would eventually bear his name.

To learn more about the history, lore, and culinary uses of a variety of internationally popular spices and herbs, go to: www.mccormick.com

At the home page:

1. Click on "Products," then click on "Herbs & Spices."
2. Click on "Spices A to Z" to learn more about the characteristics and history of many spices and dried herbs offered by this long-established foodservice supplier.

Key Term

Shelled (nut)   The food term used to describe a nut in its ready-to-eat form.

On-the-Job Challenges in Purchasing (15.2)

"That's what I'm trying to tell him," said Sara, the director of central foods purchasing for Middle State University (MSU).

Sara was in the office of Dr. Harriet Haley, director of housing and foodservice for MSU. Sara was meeting with Dr. Haley and Ronald Beecher, the university's newly hired director of foodservice. Both Sara and Ronald reported directly to Harriet. The meeting was held because Ronald had informed Sara that, for the coming school year, he had decided they would be switching to fresh herbs for all pizza, spaghetti, and related tomato-based product sauces used in all five of MSU's dining halls. Although the change was proposed to increase product quality, Sara opposed it.

Sara was concerned about cost and year-around product availability. Because MSU was located in the upper northeastern part of the United States, there would be a limited (if any) supply of fresh herbs such as oregano, basil, and garlic grown locally for much of the year. It was this topic about which Harriet had just inquired.

"Let's get down to business" said Harriet, "I know fresh herbs will improve the taste, but how much will this change cost us per meal served?

"I don't really know," said Ronald.

"Plenty" said Sara.

"But it will be worth it" said Ronald. "The students will taste the difference."

"Yes," replied Sara, "but if we do this, where will we cut to stay within our cost-per-meal budget?

Case Study Questions

Assume you were Harriet:

1. What further questions would you ask of Ronald?
2. What further questions would you ask of Sara?
3. What criteria would you use to make a final decision about this proposed product change?

> *Corn nut:* A roasted maize (corn) seed.
>
> *Peanuts:* Used whole or in pieces for baking and as a spread in myriad recipes.
>
> *Pistachio:* Used for ice cream and candies.

Additional popular nuts include beechnuts, Brazil nuts, chestnuts, filberts, hazelnuts, hickory, and macadamia nuts. Grade standards have been established by the USDA for a number of kinds of nuts; however, use of the standards by suppliers is not mandatory. Nut prices alone are not a reliable basis for judging the quality of shelled, unshelled, or roasted nuts. The best aid to professional buyers is a statement on the label, which shows the nuts are of a certain U.S. grade, that they have been subjected to USDA inspection, or both.

CONVENIENCE FOODS

In Chapter 5, you learned about the "make or buy" decisions routinely faced by professional foodservice buyers. Complementary foods is one category in which buyers commonly find that "buying" is preferable to "making." Consider, for example, an item such as mayonnaise. For some foodservice operations, making classic mayonnaise on site, and from scratch, is important. For most operations, however, mayonnaise is one of those items that, because of the costs of production and importance of product consistency, the purchase of a ready-to-use, high-quality product simply makes most sense.

Interestingly, in some segments of foodservice, the word "convenience," when attached to foods, carries a negative connotation and implication that "made from scratch" foods are superior to convenience items. Knowledgeable buyers know that this perception often reflects a lack of understanding of both history and today's professional food industry. In fact, nearly all foods eaten are made from scratch; some are simply made from scratch in one location and then transported to another. Historically, that has worked well for all members of the foodservice distribution chain. Considered from that viewpoint, purchasing a high-quality convenience item is no different than a restaurant owner–operator who purchases maple smoked hams from a talented charcuterie, freshly made cheeses from a local dairy farm, and daily baked breads from the neighborhood bakery to make, from scratch and on-site, an extraordinary ham and cheese sandwich. What if that same owner–operator disdained convenience foods and attempted to smoke hams, make cheese, and bake bread in the restaurant's own kitchen? Would a quality product result at a price the restaurant's guests could readily afford? Not likely.

Of course, not all convenience items (nor all made-from-scratch items) are of good quality. Just as food production managers should avoid poor quality items made on-site, professional buyers should avoid bringing poor quality convenience items into the kitchen. Dedicated buyers can learn to do just that.

Although the number of quality convenience items available for purchase continues to increase each year, for many foodservice buyers, the majority of convenience items purchased will fall into one of the following categories:

- entrées
- baked goods
- soups and bases
- dressings and condiments

It is good for buyers to know about each of these convenience item categories.

Entrées

Convenience entrées are popular with some foodservice operators because they save labor, reduce spoilage costs, and ensure product consistency. These frozen and, increasingly, modified atmosphere-packaged (see Chapter 14) center-of-the-plate items require minimum preparation and, in many cases, are simply heated before they are served.

Despite the advantages and tremendous increases in product quality related to convenience entrées, professional foodservice buyers must be vigilant on several fronts when they purchase them. These include

- Assurance that the item is made from high-quality products, not substandard ingredients.
- Concern regarding the item's fat and trans fat content, as well as sodium (salt) levels.
- Detailed labeling, including the inclusion of ingredients that could result in the operation's legal liability if not disclosed to guests prior to service (e.g., monosodium glutamate [MSG] or peanut products).
- Disclosure of the use of any **genetically engineered food** ingredients used in the item's preparation.
- The type and amount of preservative used in the product's manufacture.

Key Term

Genetically engineered food   An item produced from crops or animals whose genetic makeup has been altered through a process called recombinant DNA (gene splicing) to give the food a desirable trait.

Baked Goods

One of the largest categories of convenience foods purchased is that of breads, pastries, and desserts. It makes little sense for most food service operations to make their own donuts, bake their own breads, and increasingly, bake their own pies, cakes, and pastries on site. Several factors have contributed to this. Chief among them is the lack of skilled labor capable of producing high-quality baked goods. Paradoxically, there are few professional schools in the United States training individuals for careers as a **patissier.**

In addition, the scale on which quality baked goods are currently produced, and the cost of labor, yields many cases in which convenience items such as **"scoop and bake"** products can be purchased and served at a lower cost than many similar "made from scratch" items.

BREADS AND ROLLS   Quality breads and rolls are important to the success of many foodservice operations. The variation of available products is tremendous, as is cost variation. Professional buyers can typically choose from ready-to-bake, partially baked, fully prebaked, and refrigerated or frozen or fresh-delivered products. The choice of those should be carefully coordinated with kitchen production managers to ensure the proper product, in the proper prebaked or baked state, is selected.

DESSERTS   Some of the most recent advances in high-quality foodservice convenience items are in the frozen gourmet dessert industry. Products in this category include cakes, torts, cheesecakes, petite fours, Bundts, tarts, and the like. Although somewhat costly on a per portion basis, the regular offering of these products can easily raise guests' perceptions of a foodservice operation's quality, while their

Frozen gourmet desserts now on the market allow any foodservice operation to offer extravagant selections that can appeal to a wide variety of guests.

David Murray and Jules Selmes
© Dorling Kindersley

Key Terms

Patissier   Pastry chef. An individual capable of producing a wide range of high-quality baked products.

Scoop and bake   A generic term used to describe a variety of baked goods batters and mixes that are purchased in final form, but are portioned (scooped) and baked on site. Examples of scoop and bake products include muffins, brownies, and cookies.

Internet Purchasing Assistant (15.5)

A wide variety of companies make and sell commercial food bases. However, there is virtual universal agreement in the foodservice industry about who does it best. What genuine Rolex is to watches, and Waterford to crystal, L. J. Minor is to food bases. To learn more about this top-quality company and its product offerings, go to: www.soupbase.com

At the home page:

1. Click on "Minor's Soup Bases," then
2. Click on "Minor's Classic Sauces" to review more of this company's foodservice offerings.

strategic use can elevate selected days and distinctive gatherings to true "special event" status.

Soups and Bases

The foodservice industry has come a long way from the days when convenience soup products essentially meant canned chicken noodle or beef vegetable soup with ingredients of dubious origin and quality. Those foodservice operations that serve significant amounts of soups, or sauce-based products, are among the biggest beneficiaries of the improvement in today's convenience items of this type.

Now available in fresh, canned, frozen, dried, or concentrates, soups are popular with guests. Product consistency, as well as cost, can be maintained properly with the quality convenience products now on the market and from a variety of vendors. For those operations that prefer to make their own soups and sauces, the variety and quality of food **bases** on the market has never been greater; however, the fat contents of convenience soups and the sodium contents of both soups and bases are areas where professional food buyers must pay careful attention before selecting products.

Dressings and Condiments

Some food production managers and buyers use the term "dressing" when referring to any sauce added to a dish before it is served. Of course, the term is also used when describing a popular accompaniment to poultry. Most guests, however, associate the term "dressing" with salads. Although some operations take great pride in producing their own salad dressings on-site, the majority of operations purchase premade salad dressings or dressing mixes.

Similarly, the term **condiment** can be widely interpreted. Strictly speaking, a condiment can be defined as any food that enhances another food.

From the perspectives of most foodservice guests, however, condiments are those items routinely expected to be made available as accompaniments to the foods they are served. Some of these (e.g., salt and pepper) are so popular they are left on diners' tables at all times in most operations. Others, like ketchup (catsup)

Key Terms

Base (food)   Stock concentrates of freshly cooked meat, poultry, seafood, or vegetables.

Condiment   Any food added to a dish to enhance flavor. Examples include herbs, spices, vinegars, and dressings.

Ketchup (catsup) Chutney	"Louisiana style" hot sauce Tabasco sauce*	Bacon bits A-1 Steak Sauce* Heinz 57* Barbeque sauce	Soy sauce Hoisin sauce Plum sauce Teriyaki Tahini
Mustard (yellow) Mustard (brown) Mustard (Dijon)	Relish (pickle) Relish (corn) Relish (mango)	Worcestershire sauce Lea and Perrins*	Picante sauce Taco sauce Salsa
Cocktail sauce Tartar sauce Oyster sauce	Chile sauce Wasabi Horseradish sauce	Sauerkraut Pickles Onion	Jams Jellies Honeys Honey mustards
Mayonnaise-based salad dressings Vinegar-based salad dressings	Malt vinegar Vinegar-based salad dressings	Mayonnaise Hellmann's* Salad dressing Miracle Whip*	Salt Pepper (black) Pepper (flakes) Sugar/sweeteners

and mustard and pickle **relish,** may remain on the table based upon the style of foodservice operation. Other popular condiments are frequently available, but are typically served only "upon request."

Figure 15.5 lists some of the condiments most popular in commercial foodservice operations. The list is not intended to be exhaustive, but instructive, as it lists many (but not all) of the items that buyers may routinely purchase in individual serving-size packets, bottles of various sizes, or even gallon and five-gallon containers. Note that, in some cases, the condiment name in Figure 15.5 is generic (e.g., ketchup), whereas in other cases, a very popular condiment refers specifically to a particular branded item (e.g., A-1 Steak Sauce). When purchasing condiments, one of a buyer's greatest challenges is to determine whether guests will change their perception of an operation based upon the use of generically branded versus name-branded condiment offerings.

Internet Purchasing Assistant (15.6)

Sometimes a condiment is so popular its presence is virtually demanded by guests. Certainly, in the United States, that is true of ketchup and mustard. Most recently, however, "Ranch" dressing has become an essential condiment.

Easily the most popular new dressing/dip to be introduced to foodservice operators in recent decades, Ranch dressing (originally developed by Steve and Gayle Henson to be served to guests at their Hidden Valley Guest Ranch near Santa Barbara, California) sales continue to increase yearly. Although many manufacturers now produce "Ranch" dressings, to learn more about the original, and best known, go to: www.hiddenvalley.com

At the home page:

1. Click on "Products," then
2. Click on "Dry Dressings & Dips" to review more of this company's foodservice offerings.

Key Term

Relish   A condiment containing vinegar, salt, and sugar as well as chopped fruits or vegetables. Examples include products made from pickles, corn, and onions.

Condiments in quick-service restaurants must be offered in PC containers to satisfy the requests of take out and drive-through customers.

Laima Druskis/Pearson Education/PH College

THE SUPPLIER'S SIDE (15.1)

"Insider" Tips on Purchasing: From the Supplier's Perspective

Buyer's Question: Why do so many large companies such as McDonald's, Arby's, and Chic-fil-A put their own restaurant's name on items such as individual packets of mayonnaise, catsup, mustard, and other sauces? Are these special condiment formulations or maybe secret recipes?

Supplier's Answer: They can be, but in other cases, the operator's name on the packet is simply used as a marketing device to help promote the restaurant's brand. Typically, these products are of very high quality. The product itself may have a formulation identical to that of a well-known name brand product and, in fact, may actually be made and packaged by the name brand food manufacturer.

Buyer's Question: I also notice that some large operators have their own names on back-of-house products, such as bulk dressings and sauces, whose containers guests would never see. Why would companies choose to private label items like that?

Supplier's Answer: Again, they may have a special formulation, but it more likely has to do with the food manufacturer's product-marketing dollars.

Buyer's Question: What are product-marketing dollars, and how are they affected by private labeling?

Supplier's Answer: In most cases, large food manufacturers pay food distributors a predetermined dollar amount for each case of their "brand name" product sold. Thus, when companies such as Oscar Mayer, Hormel, Campbell's, Heinz, and others' products are sold to a food distributor's customers, the manufacturer will pay (or rebate) to the distributor an amount per case sold agreeable to both. These payments (or invoice reductions) are known in the food distribution industry by the term "marketing-dollars."

Of course, marketing-dollars are a real cost that food manufacturers must ultimately pass on to their customers in the price of the products they sell. When a product is private labeled, however, the food manufacturer pays no brand name-related marketing-dollars to the distributor. As a result, the user's cost per unit is lower, and the distributor's costs remain the same. Those who buy for large foodservice companies know this and pursue private label options anytime they believe the marketing-dollar costs savings they will achieve are greater than any additional costs they incur by private labeling.

SPECIALIZED FOOD PRODUCTS

Some products purchased for use in foodservice are not special foods, but rather are foods processed in special ways. For foodservice buyers, two of the most important of these food types are **Kosher** and **Halal.**

Kosher

The market for Kosher foods in the United States is large, with more than 23,000 certified Kosher foods available. When a food is labeled as Kosher, this means it has been prepared according to strict rules of food preparation noted in the Bible and formalized in Jewish law. These foods are often labeled with a symbol of a U surrounded by a circle. The practice of Kosher does not allow the mixing of meat and milk in the same meal. Food labeled "Pareve" does not contain either meat or milk and, therefore, can be combined with most other foods during a meal.

Halal

Halal, for Muslims, means "allowed" or "lawful" foods. Halal foods are increasingly in demand and are regularly purchased by some foodservice operators. A simple and effective means of guaranteeing Halal status of all foods purchased is to insist on Halal Certification. The Islamic Food and Nutritional Council of America (IFANCA) has a Halal Certification program, and their approved items contain a "Halal M" stamp on the package. Other genuine Halal foods may be designated as such by a seal with a capital "H" inside a triangle.

It is important for foodservice buyers to note that, even if purchased as genuine Kosher or Halal, these foods must be properly handled after they are delivered to the foodservice operation to maintain their status. In addition to proper handling, special concerns relate to cross-contamination; in this case, the exposure to, or mixing of, Kosher or Halal foods with those that are not so designated.

PRODUCT RECEIVING AND STORAGE

Because complementary foods cover such a wide range of products, some will be delivered fresh, whereas others will arrive frozen, refrigerated, or packaged for holding in dry storage areas.

Receiving

Personnel assigned the task of receiving all grocery products must be vigilant. This is true with complementary foods as well. Frozen foods must immediately be placed in frozen food holding units, and refrigerated foods must be promptly put away. Also, for nearly all complementary food items, a **FIFO** storage system should be used.

In a first in–first out (FIFO) system, receiving clerks rotate stock in such a way that products already on hand are used prior to more recently delivered products. To do so, receiving clerks must take care to place new stock behind, or at

---

Key Terms

Kosher   The name of the Jewish dietary laws. Food prepared in accordance with these laws is considered "Kosher."

Halal   An Arabic term meaning "permissible." In English, it is used most frequently to refer to foods that are permissible according to Islamic dietary laws.

FIFO (First In–First Out)   Short for "First In First Out"; a storage system that seeks to issue products already in storage prior to the issuing of more recently delivered products.

the bottom of, old stock. Sometimes, however, employees do not do this. Consider, for example, the storeroom clerk who receives six 80-pound bags of all-purpose flour. The FIFO method dictates that these six bags be placed *under, or behind,* the five bags already in the storeroom. Will receiving clerks place the six newly delivered bags underneath, or behind, the five older bags when it means moving the five older bags, as well as the six that have newly arrived? They will, but only if proper receiving procedures are enforced. If they are not, employees may be tempted to take the easy way out and simply place newer products on top of, or in front of, previously received products.

Storage

Frozen and refrigerated complementary food products should be held at temperatures consistent with other frozen and refrigerated food products. In many cases, however, buyers will find that complementary food products are stored in dry-storage areas. Dry-storage areas should generally be maintained at a temperature ranging between 65°F and 75°F. Temperatures lower than those recommended can be harmful to food products.

Excessively high temperatures must be avoided as well. In many cases, dry-storage areas can be very warm, especially when they are poorly ventilated and/or located near cooking and baking equipment that generates significant heat. In addition, because many dry-storage areas are not air-conditioned or are poorly air-conditioned, it is a good idea to continually monitor temperatures with a wall thermometer.

Shelving in dry-storage areas must be easily cleanable and spaced properly. Local health codes vary, but shelving should generally be placed at least six inches above the ground to allow for proper cleaning beneath the shelving and to ensure proper ventilation. Dry-goods products should never be stored directly on the ground. Product labels should face out for easy identification. For items such as flours and grains stored in bins or large containers, mobile storage and transport equipment should be used whenever possible to minimize heavy lifting and resulting employee injuries. If possible, grains should be dry-stored in a cool, dark place. For flour products, airtight containers are a must to prevent insect infestation. Whole grains containing the grain oil (germ) must be refrigerated to prevent rancidity.

Purchasing Resources on the Internet

In addition to the Web sites referenced in this chapter's "Internet Purchasing Assistant" feature, the following sites provide detailed information to enhance your purchasing knowledge and skills.

Purchasing Resources on the Internet

Site	Information About
www.wholegraincouncil.org	Benefits and use of whole grain foods
www.oliversbreads.com	Artisan bread shapes
www.barillaus.com	Dried pasta forms and shapes
www.anythingspastable.com	Fresh pasta products
www.italgi.it	Commercial pasta-making equipment
www.zerotranssoy.com	Trans fat-free cooking oils
www.internationaloliveoil.org	The International Olive Oil Council
www.aboutoliveoil.org	North American olive oil consortium
www.boyajianinc.com	Infused olive and Asian oils

(continued)

Site	Information About
www.honey.com/downloads/exhoney.pdf	USDA honey grades
www.freshherbs.com	Fresh herbs and their use
www.spiceadvice.com	Herbs, spices, and condiments
www.thenutfactory.com	Nutmeats and their uses
www.dressings-sauces.org	Dressings and sauces popularity
www.bridgeford.com	Frozen bread doughs
www.richs.com/foodservice	Convenience desserts and toppings
www.stockpot.com	High-quality frozen soups
www.koshertoday.com	Kosher foods
www.ifanca.org	Halal foods

Key Terms

pasta *365*
cereal *366*
flour *366*
whole grain *366*
self-rising (flour) *367*
masa harina *367*
rolled oats *368*
quick-cooking oats *368*

instant oats *368*
muesli *369*
granola *369*
semolina *369*
al dente *371*
fat *371*
emulsion *371*
infused oils *374*

nutmeat *376*
refined (sugar) *376*
molasses *376*
syrup *376*
aromatic *378*
shelled (nut) *379*
genetically engineered
  food *381*

patissier *382*
scoop and bake *382*
base (food) *383*
condiment *383*
relish *384*
Kosher *386*
Halal *386*
FIFO (First In–First Out) *387*

Think It Through

1. Some food products are offered in fresh, frozen, canned, and other forms. Consider such a product. When do you think it is appropriate for a buyer to select one of these forms rather than another? What physical facility factors should buyers consider before doing so?

2. Trans fat-containing foods are only the most recent example of public policy makers seeking to dictate the kinds of products foodservice operators may serve their guests. Many restaurateurs strongly oppose such intervention. Do you believe these same operators would favor the service of trans fat-laden foods in the school foodservice districts in which their own children were enrolled? Explain your answer.

3. Bulk-shipped breakfast cereals reduce manufacturers' packaging costs and are increasingly popular in large-scale feeding operations. Assume the large-scale operation in which you are responsible for buying ready-to-eat cereals instructs you to select the five specific products that will be offered next year. How would you determine the factors you would use to choose the five cereals?

4. Assume that you are the new buyer for a 25-unit group of "Soup and Sandwich" shops noted for their "Made On Site" soups and sandwiches. Assume also that you have just been instructed to purchase dried "Ready-to-Simmer" soup mixtures sold in 5-pound bags. The instructions on the bags instruct direct production staff to simply boil the bag's contents for 10 minutes to rehydrate the ingredients and complete the soup. Is this soup still "Made On Site"? How would you decide? Are any ethical issues in play in this scenario?

5. Some of the hottest food trends of today relate to complementary (as well as other) food categories. Health-related concerns about the fat and caloric contents of foods, as well as the increasing demand for menu items labeled, for example, organic, grass-fed, free-range, and "bite-size," are increasingly prevalent. What specific techniques can professional food buyers use to stay abreast of key consumer demands and expectations that will directly affect what is purchased and served on their menus?

Team Fun

For this exercise, assume that each team consists of members of the food management team at a large military base. More than 5,000 individuals are served three meals daily. The individuals served are split approximately 50/50 between men and women.

One of the most popular items served is breakfast muffins, with more than 150 dozen served per day. The base's food management team is considering how these items should be purchased. The decision has already been made that these products will be baked on-site and made fresh daily.

1. The assignment of the first team is to research and make recommendations regarding a "scoop and bake" muffin product. Include advantages and disadvantages of using this product form.

2. The assignment of the second team is to research and make recommendations regarding a "made from scratch" muffin product. Include advantages and disadvantages of using this product form.

3. The assignment of the third team is to develop a set of detailed criteria, in addition to price, that will be used to evaluate the two alternative product-production approaches that will be presented. Assume that the equipment and production staff needed for either alternative is readily available.

Each team should be prepared to present and discuss their findings and conclusions and comment on how the criteria identified by the evaluation team were, or were not, significant considerations of the product production teams.

16

Beverages

In This Chapter

Drinking and eating go hand in hand. In fact, the first menu item served to most guests visiting a foodservice operation is a beverage. In some facilities, such as the increasingly popular gourmet coffee houses, a beverage may be the primary reason guests choose to visit. This can also be the case in cocktail lounges, bars, pubs, and other facilities that serve alcoholic beverages alone, or in conjunction with food. It is surprising then, that some buyers and foodservice managers take beverages for granted. Because nearly all foodservice guests order a beverage, ensuring that the quality of these products is outstanding, their service temperatures are correct, and they are served in a manner that reflects positively on the facility's image are important dimensions of any professional buyer's responsibilities.

The number and type of beverages offered by even the smallest foodservice operation can be extensive, thus there is much to know about beverages. One way to more easily study beverages is by first categorizing them as either nonalcoholic or alcoholic. Most foodservice operators serve far more nonalcoholic beverages than they do alcoholic beverages. In all foodservice operations, coffee is one of the most-often served beverages, and in this chapter various roasts, grinds, and packaging alternatives of coffee will be examined. Although less popular in the United States, tea drinkers are steadfast in their preference for this beverage, so information on teas and ice teas are included in this chapter, as is information about chocolate beverages.

Carbonated soft drinks are the single most popular beverage category in the United States; however, bottled waters are the fastest growing beverage category. Therefore, information about both of these well-liked and increasingly consumed nonalcoholic beverage groups are presented in this chapter.

Alcoholic beverages are very important to many types of hospitality operations. Restaurants that offer alcoholic beverages are maintaining a hospitality tradition that stretches back to the beginning of the enjoyment of food. People in nearly all cultures have traditionally enjoyed drinking beer, wine, or spirits as they dine or gather to socialize. Beer is probably the oldest alcoholic beverage produced, and it is sold in a variety of styles and packaging types, each of which can be important to foodservice buyers. Beer is the first alcoholic beverage examined in this chapter.

The study of wines can be lifelong. So popular is wine to many foodservice customers, that the terms "wine" and "dining" are nearly synonymous. This chapter presents key information about wine types, the wine containers typically available to foodservice buyers, and the special storage techniques important for maintaining quality in these excellent beverages.

The final alcoholic beverage examined in this chapter is grouped under the broad classification of "spirits." Spirits are differentiated by their flavors, the food product used to make the beverage, the amount of alcohol they contain, and the specific way these beverages are aged, blended, and bottled. Although the total number of different spirits produced worldwide is large, this chapter presents information on those main products most often purchased by food service buyers.

The range of beverages available for purchase is large. As a result, specialized knowledge is required to properly select these products. Also, essential procedures related to receiving and storing beverage products are important. Learning about all of these topics is the overall purpose of this chapter.

■ ■ ■

Outline

NONALCOHOLIC BEVERAGES

The great majority of beverages served in the hospitality industry do not contain alcohol. According to the American Beverage Association (the nonprofit industry group of nonalcoholic beverage manufacturers and suppliers), carbonated soft drinks, bottled water, coffee, and milk (examined in Chapter 14) account for approximately 60 percent of the beverages consumed by the average American. Fruit beverages (such as juice), **sports drinks,** tea, and other nonalcoholic drinks account for another 25 percent.

Key Term

Sports drink   A beverage designed to rehydrate, as well as replenish, the drinker's electrolyte, sugar, and other nutrient levels.

Beer, wine, and spirits, as important as they are to the hospitality industry, account for only about 15 percent of the beverages consumed. It is also important for professional buyers to understand that nearly 100 percent of their operation's guests who purchase food will purchase a beverage as an accompaniment. Not all customers who purchase beverages, however, will purchase food. A few examples of this include customers at bars, lounges, and pubs, as well as those frequenting the increasingly popular upscale coffee shops, or simply stopping at a foodservice operation for a **"to go"** beverage.

Because the presence (and importance) of quality nonalcoholic beverages in hospitality is so prominent, professional buyers should have a good understanding of coffee, tea, soft drinks, and bottled water products.

Coffee

Tradition has it that the first coffee trees were discovered in Ethiopia. Today, coffee is grown in many parts of the world (Brazil, Vietnam, and Colombia are the largest producers) and is enjoyed by foodservice guests in virtually all settings. Every foodservice buyer should have a thorough understanding of the procedures required to make a good cup of coffee. This starts with the selection of a quality coffee bean ground at the restaurant, or the purchase of vacuum-packed, pre-ground coffee from a reputable coffee supplier. The number of choices (roasts, grinds, brands, and price levels) is large, and the serious buyer should become familiar, at least to some degree, with the history, production process, and service of both regular and **decaffeinated** coffee.

The original version of roasted, brewed coffee is that of the Arabs. In fact, in the Middle East, Turkey, and Greece, the original style still thrives. To make coffee, the Arabs ground roasted coffee beans to a fine powder, added sugar and water, and then boiled the mixture one or more times until it foamed. The resulting beverage was decanted into very small cups and drunk immediately (before the sediment it contained increased its already-considerable bitterness).

Significant European modifications of coffee drinking included the invention (by French cooks) of the drip pot, a device used to isolate, or filter, the ground beans from the water used for coffee making. Essentially, with a drip pot, hot water is passed over ground coffee beans, and the resulting liquid is then filtered and allowed to collect in a separate container. This procedure did three important things: It allowed the use of water below the boiling point, limited the contact time between water and ground beans, and produced a brew without sentiments that could be held for a period of time without becoming bitter.

The Paris Exhibition of 1855 would mark the next major advancement in coffee production. It was at that event that **espresso** was introduced.

Using specially designed machines, water is forced through ground coffee at a very high pressure, causing maximum extraction of the ground coffee's oil, which it emulsifies into tiny droplets that create a velvety texture and a pleasant rich taste that lingers on the tongue. Today, made-on-premise fresh-brewed coffee

---

Key Terms

To go (menu item)   The hospitality industry term for menu items intended to be consumed "off premise."

Decaffeinated   A beverage product in which its naturally occurring caffeine has been significantly reduced or eliminated entirely.

Espresso   Roughly, Latin for "to press out at the moment," the term now refers to machine-produced coffee.

Internet Purchasing Assistant (16.1)

The National Coffee Association provides free information about coffee selection, storage, and brewing (including best coffee/water ratios, brewing temperatures, and extraction times). To view their site, go to: www.ncausa.org

At the home page, click on "All About Coffee" to learn more about this foodservice menu standard.

is still produced using either a variation of the drip pot production system or the espresso method.

ROASTS Raw, green coffee beans are hard as popcorn kernels and just as tasteless. Roasting transforms these hard beans into fragile, easily opened flavor packs. Proper roasting releases and enhances the flavors in coffee. Continued roasting darkens the beans and causes a distinct visible gloss as increased oils come to the beans' surface. Coffee beans can be roasted until they are only a very light brown color or they can be further roasted until they are almost solid black.

The skill of the coffee bean roaster, the degree to which a coffee bean is roasted, and how the bean is cooled and handled after roasting can have as great an effect on the end-quality of coffee as does the original bean. Poor roasting techniques can damage the best coffee beans, and thoughtful roasting can minimize the deficiencies of lower-quality beans.

Professionals buying coffee for foodservice use can typically choose from a variety of different roasting styles. Unfortunately, there are no international standards for roasting levels, thus individual roasters are free, when it comes to roasting styles, to label the beans they sell as they see fit. The most commonly used terminology for coffee bean roasting, however, includes

City roast: Also known as "American" roast, this roasting style is the one used for most of the coffee sold in the United States. (Most canned coffee sold in grocery stores is City roasted.) Although it is the most common, it is not particularly the most distinctive, nor would most serious coffee drinkers feel it produces the "best" cup of coffee. In fact, perhaps the greatest advantage of this roast level is that most American coffee drinkers do not find it objectionable. Thus, it consistently produces a "safe," if not noteworthy, cup of coffee.

Brazilian: This roast is darker than City roast. When this roast is used, the beans will just begin to show surface oils. It is also important to know that, in this context, the term "Brazilian" refers only to a roasting style, and not to coffee beans grown in Brazil.

Viennese: Also known as medium-brown roast, this style typically falls between a City roast and a French roast.

French: This roast, also known as a "New Orleans" roast, or "dark" roast, approaches espresso in flavor without sacrificing smoothness. Beans roasted French style will be the color of semisweet chocolate with visible oil on the surface.

Espresso: Espresso, or Italian roast, is the darkest roast. Beans roasted in this style will look almost burnt. The beans will be black with very visible shiny oils on their surface.

GRINDS Although few foodservice operators roast their own coffee beans, many do choose to grind their own beans. The aroma the process produces is unmistakable, and the quality implications are definitely appreciated by serious coffee drinkers.

Foodservice operators who decide to grind their own coffee should seek consistency in their grinding methods.

Reuben Paris © Dorling Kindersley

There is no best grind for a coffee bean. The key to a quality ground coffee is to create consistent particular sizes appropriate to the brewing method used in the foodservice operation. Too much variation in ground particle size makes it hard to control flavor extraction during the brewing process. When not consistent in size, smaller particles may be overextracted (which leads to bitterness), and larger ones will be underextracted (which leads to weakness). As a result, the product produced from inconsistently ground coffee beans is most often bitter and weak.

Many foodservice operators feel the product they brew will be superior if the beans from which it is made are ground just before they are used for brewing. Sometimes that is true, but it is most dependent upon the type of grinder used. Typical propeller grinders (such as those found in most homes) smash all coffee

THE SUPPLIER'S SIDE (16.1)

"Insider" Tips on Purchasing: From the Supplier's Perspective

Buyer's Question: I buy ground coffee, but how do I know what "grind" I should buy? My supplier offers several.

Supplier's Answer: It's important to understand that you could make coffee from whole roasted beans, but it would take hours and not taste very good. You could also make coffee from pulverized beans (some specially built coffee vending machines do it) but it would likely taste bitter using the coffee equipment in your foodservice operation. You want ground coffee of consistent particle size, with no powder.

Buyer's Question: So what's the best particle size?

Supplier's Answer: The best size is the size that works best in your operation. Most suppliers will carry three sizes, so you can choose the best one for you. These are Regular, Drip, and Fine. Any of these grinds contain particles of many sizes. The difference is in the proportion of each size particle they contain. Regular grind is the coarsest, followed by Drip and then Fine.

Buyer's Question: Would "Fine" be best, because I would get the most extraction, because it has the maximum surface area?

Supplier's Answer: No. For most foodservice operations, "Drip" is likely best because it is ground to match the way those operations' coffee makers work. A Fine grind is usually used for making Espresso. For those operations grinding their own beans, the general rule is that if your coffee tastes weak you may need to grind finer, and if the coffee tastes bitter, experiment with a slightly coarser grind.

particles until the machine blades are stopped, regardless of how small the pieces become, so coarse and medium ground coffees end up containing some finely ground powder. More expensive burr grinders (used by commercial coffee suppliers) allow smaller pieces to escape through grooves built into the grinding surface, resulting in a more even, and desirable, particle size.

PACKAGING   Coffee beans for grinding are sold by the pound. Preground coffees can be purchased in individual packages designed to produce from two cups to several gallons at a time. Although there are some industry guidelines, the strength at which consumers prefer their coffees will vary based upon geographic area, brewing style employed, equipment used, and even the time of day the coffee is to be consumed. Many foodservice operators offer more intense coffees for "after dinner" consumption than those they serve before meals. Despite variations of these types, many operators find that, when using a drip method, a ratio of two level tablespoons of coffee to six fluid ounces of water (one "coffee" cup) makes a good cup of coffee. Because a pound of coffee contains approximately 80 level tablespoons, one pound of ground coffee used in a drip coffee maker will produce 40 cups of coffee; however, many buyers find that their consumers prefer a milder brew.

Espresso machines use a ratio of ¼ ounce of coffee to approximately 1.5 to 3 ounces of water, depending upon the strength desired. Foodservice operators who attempt to "stretch" their coffee budgets by reducing the amount of coffee used to produce each cup brewed risk creating coffees that, although less costly, are significantly less tasty as well.

Premade (prebrewed) coffees are sold in powdered form (instant coffee), frozen or room temperature concentrates (for machine dispensing), and in bottles as well as cans. Many times these products are convenient, and may, for a variety of reasons, have a role to play in a foodservice operation. They simply will not, however, produce a drinkable beverage of the same level of excellence as that obtained by freshly brewing high-quality, well-roasted, ground coffees. How important is high-quality, fresh-made coffee to the success of a foodservice operation and, equally important, will coffee drinkers pay a premium for superior coffee products? Just ask "Starbucks"!

Tea

The use of tea to flavor beverages is a technique nearly 5,000 years old and was discovered, according to Chinese legend, in 2737 B.C. by a Chinese emperor when some tea leaves accidentally blew into a pot of water he was boiling. The credibility of such a story is enhanced when you realize that, in many areas of the world, boiling water before drinking it was (and still is) an essential act for ensuring good health.

In the 1600s, tea became popular throughout Europe and the American colonies. Interestingly, the United States has made two significant contributions to the tea industry: In 1904, iced tea was created and served at the World's Fair in St. Louis, and in 1908, Thomas Sullivan of New York developed the concept of tea in

Internet Purchasing Assistant (16.2)

A variety of companies produce excellent coffee grinding and brewing equipment. One of the best is Bunn-O-Matic. To see the Web site, go to: www.bunnomatic.com

At the home page, click on "Commercial" to view the grinding and brewing equipment available to commercial foodservice operators.

PURCHASING PROS NEED TO KNOW (16.1)

Serving a great tasting cup of coffee is important to foodservice operations of all types. In most cases, brewed coffee of poor quality is the result of mistakes made in brewing, holding, and service, not in the purchasing process. To ensure only quality coffee is served to guests, foodservice buyers should work with those responsible for making the coffee to ensure they follow the "Ten Steps to Serving Great Coffee":

1. Ensure purchased coffee is stored in a cool and dry storage area.
2. Keep coffee-brewing equipment meticulously clean.
3. Use fresh water for brewing, as free of impurities and alkalines as possible, and avoid using "softened" water.
4. Use a clean/new filter each time coffee is brewed.
5. When using drip-type brewers (the most common type used in foodservice), ensure water-brewing temperatures are as close to 200°F (93°C) as possible.
6. Remove and dispose of used grounds as quickly as possible to avoid increasing bitterness during holding times.
7. Hold coffee at 175°F to 185°F (80°C to 85°C).
8. Discard brewed coffee after holding 20–30 minutes in open-top containers, or two hours in closed-top containers (vacuum pots).
9. Never mix old brewed coffee with new coffee.
10. Serve coffee at 155°F to 175°F (70°C to 80°C); deliver prepoured coffee immediately to guests to ensure proper serving temperatures are maintained.

Most of the coffee consumed in the United States is brewed with paper filters, a method that produces coffee in the classic "American style": clear, light-bodied, with little sediment or oil. Other brewing methods produce coffee richer in flavor, oils, and sediments. Foodservice buyers whose operations use nonpaper filter brewing methods do need to keep this difference in mind!

---

a bag (tea bags). Today, more coffee than tea is consumed in the United States; however, tea drinkers constitute a committed and sizable consumer group.

VARIETIES   Beverage teas are of three basic types: black, green, and oolong. In the United States, over 90 percent of the tea consumed is black tea. This type of tea has been fully oxidized (fermented), which results in a hearty flavor and an amber color.

On-the-Job Challenges in Purchasing (16.1)

"It will be terrible," said Bill Zollars, the general manager of the 105-room limited-service Sleep Well Inn.

"I'm just telling you what the franchisor's e-mail said," replied Marisha, the hotel's front office manager.

"So now we are required to have coffee available in the lobby 24/7? Do you know what that's going to taste like at 3:00 a.m. after it's been sitting for two hours? And who's supposed to make it?

I don't drink coffee, so I don't know," said Marisha, "but I do know the e-mail said we had to have a 24/7 hot coffee service in place by the first of next month or we'll lose points on our next property inspection."

Assume you were Bill and were responsible for implementing this new brand requirement.

Case Study Questions

1. What coffee service options would be available to you?
2. How would you ensure the coffee you elected to serve is of good quality?
3. What guest service challenges would you face as you implement this new franchisor requirement? How can effective procurement procedures help address these new challenges?

Some popular black teas include English Breakfast (a good breakfast choice because its hearty flavor mixes well with milk), Darjeeling (a blend of Himalayan teas suited for drinking with most meals), and Orange Pekoe (a blend of Ceylon teas that is the most widely used of the tea blends).

Green teas are also popular. Green tea is not oxidized. It has a more delicate taste and is light green or gold in color. Green tea, a staple in the Orient, is gaining popularity in the United States due, in part, to recent scientific studies linking its consumption with reduced cancer risk. It is often served as a complimentary beverage in Chinese or other Oriental-style restaurants.

Oolong tea, popular in China, is partly oxidized and is a cross between black and green tea in color and taste. Most recently, tea manufacturers have begun to offer flavored varieties of black, green, and oolong teas. These are increasingly popular. Also, a significant number of foodservice guests now request **herbal teas.**

Although flavored teas evolve from these three basic teas, "herbal" tea contains no true tea leaves but is popular because, like regular tea, it is considered healthy and contains no calories.

Hot tea drinkers make up a small, but significant, number of foodservice guests. The popularity of iced tea, however, is much greater because approximately 85 percent of the tea consumed in the United States is iced tea. In fact, iced teas are so popular that they are typically one of the beverage choices at quick-service restaurants, as well as nearly all other types of foodservice operations (although **Chai** teas are gaining in popularity).

Quality iced tea begins with quality teas. It should taste fresh, clean, and be sparkling clear (unclouded). Any variety of dry tea may be used to make iced tea. The best iced teas, once made, are allowed to slowly cool to room temperature before refrigerating to prevent the tea from acquiring a cloudy appearance (although prolonged storage in a refrigerator may still render the tea cloudy).

PACKAGING The methods buyers use to purchase dry tea leaves and iced tea products are significantly different. Dry teas may be purchased in bulk, loose-leaf form, but are more commonly purchased in a variety of package sizes, each containing individual, and single-service, tea bags. Because tea that is steeped in boiling water expands, many tea purists prefer not to make it from tea bags (insisting that such bags restrict the tea's ability to expand and thus do not allow for maximum flavor extraction). Despite the potential effects on product quality, however, the overwhelming majority of foodservice operations serving tea in individual portions offer guests tea bags. Professional foodservice buyers purchase these either as single-service tea bags wrapped in paper, or as single-service tea bags sealed in foil pouches to minimize excessive drying of the tea bag's contents.

Iced teas are served either sweetened (popular in the Southern and Southwestern parts of the United States), or unsweetened (more popular in the remaining regions). As a result, foodservice operators may choose to offer one or both of these products on their menus. Of course, those who offer unsweetened teas will also offer one or more types of sugars or sweeteners for those guests who prefer sweetened ice tea (see Chapter 15).

Key Terms

Herbal tea　A beverage that is prepared in the same manner as tea but that contains no actual tea leaves. Instead, these teas are made by steeping the flowers, berries, peels, seeds, leaves, or roots of plants in boiling water. Examples of herbal teas include Lemon, Blackberry, Peach, Peppermint, and Apple/Cinnamon.

Chai (tea)　The Chinese word for "tea"; it is made from brewed tea and milk.

Internet Purchasing Assistant (16.3)

Worldwide, tea is second only to water as the most-often consumed beverage. In the United States, however, teas have historically been less popular than many other drinks. Today, the number of tea products offered to U.S. consumers is expanding greatly. To learn more about why increasing numbers of Americans are choosing tea, go to: www.teausa.org

At the home page:

1. Click on "About Tea."
2. Next, click on "Tea & Health" to read about the health benefits of teas.

When selling ice tea, foodservice operators may purchase loose-leaf teas and make their own product. They may also choose from specially sized "ice tea bags" that contain enough tea leaves to make ice tea in large quantities, concentrates or powders that must simply be mixed with water, or a variety of premade, or ready-to-drink, tea forms. The most popular ready-to-drink teas currently available are sold in cans and/or bottles. These typically are purchased in cases of varying unit counts, with individual product serving sizes ranging from 8 to 24 ounces each. Ready-to-drink iced tea is sold in several flavored varieties, the most popular of which are lemon, raspberry, and peach.

Because of its wide popularity and low cost, foodservice operators who provide guests with machine-dispensed beverages often include ice tea as one of the product offerings. When they do, iced tea concentrates will be purchased and dispensed in the same manner as are the operation's soft drinks.

Chocolate

Chocolate is one of the most remarkable foods purchased by professional foodservice buyers. Like many other foods, the variation in quality and price among chocolate products is significant. Unlike other foods, however, chocolate's flavor is exceptionally rich, complex, and versatile. It is arguably the single-most popular flavor in the world. Chocolate is highly prized for making candies, cookies, cakes, and pastries, but is also popular as a flavoring for milk and as a hot beverage. Chocolate is made by drying, fermenting, and roasting the **cocoa bean** from which it is produced.

Cocoa beans are harvested from the cocoa tree (called *Theobroma cacao*, or "food of the gods"), which originated in South America. Today, Africa grows the majority of the world's cocoa.

Cocoa seeds, and chocolate as a drink, can best be understood by considering the seed's fat and nonfat contents. When the fat (called cocoa "butter") is removed from cocoa seeds, a bitter powder remains. This **cocoa powder** is the product most often used to make **hot chocolate,** a drink popular in cold and warm

Key Terms

Cocoa bean   The seed of the cacao tree. When dried and ground, it is further refined to produce a variety of chocolate forms.

Cocoa powder   The dry powder made by grinding cocoa seeds and removing most of the cocoa butter from the dark, bitter cocoa solids. Cocoa powder has a bitter flavor and is often simply called "cocoa."

Hot chocolate   The sweet drink made from mixing cocoa powder, sugar, and milk. In some areas of the country, it is also known as "hot cocoa" or even more simply, "cocoa."

Raw cocoa beans produced from the *Theobroma cacao* tree take several days to ferment.

Mauritius, GMBH/Phototake NYC

climates. Standard cocoa powder has a cocoa butter content of 10 to 12 percent (USDA standard).

Although it can be made from a variety of chocolate products melted into milk, for most foodservice purchasing professionals, the typical manner in which "hot cocoa" or "hot chocolate" is purchased is in its dry powdered form. It is available in regular and sugar-free formulas. Some manufacturers offer a product that includes dried marshmallows. Most often, it is packaged in various carton sizes containing single-service units, each weighing from approximately .75 to 1.5 ounces each, and producing one 8- to 10-ounce cup of hot chocolate beverage.

The mixture of cocoa powder, sugar, and dried milk solids used for hot chocolate production has a relatively long shelf life. It can easily be prepared by guests (who simply stir the powdered mix into very hot water). It is relatively inexpensive because it does not contain significant amounts of the highly valued cocoa butter needed by chocolatiers for making other superior quality chocolate products such as fine candies and gourmet pastries.

Soft Drinks

Soft drinks are widely served in nearly all restaurants. More foodservice guests elect these products as their beverage of choice than either coffee or tea.

Internet Purchasing Assistant (16.4)

Several companies produce high-quality "hot chocolate" or "cocoa" mixes. One of the most popular is sold under the name "Swiss Miss," a product marketed by ConAgra Foods. To learn more about the origins of this "made in the U.S." beverage mix, go to: www.conagra.com

At the home page:

1. Click on "Brand and product information."
2. Then, click on "Swiss Miss" and read the story of Anthony Sanna, the product's originator.

Key Term

Soft drink   A carbonated beverage produced by combining CO_2 gas, purified water, and flavored sugar syrups. Also known as "soda" or "pop" in some parts of the United States.

Internet Purchasing Assistant (16.5)

PepsiCo and Coca-Cola are the world's largest beverage vendors. Each sells soft drinks, bottled water, and juices, among other products.

To view the PepsiCo site, go to: www.Pepsico.com

To view the Coca-Cola site, go to: www.Cocacola.com

While visiting each site, see the diversity of soft drink (as well as other) products each of these two giant companies sell.

In fact, soft drinks are the single most popular U.S. beverage category. For purposes of this discussion, the term "soft drink" is restricted to flavored, CO_2-carbonated beverages. It should be noted, however, that some foodservice buyers also consider sparkling waters, lemonade, and fruit punch to be soft drinks.

Soft drinks are so popular that some nutritionists have recently questioned the wisdom of their unrestricted service. Soft drinks obtain nearly all of their calories from the addition of refined cane sugar or, increasingly, from corn syrup. One serving of nondiet soft drink contains more sugar than the USDA's recommended daily allowance of 10 teaspoons of "added sugar." (Diet soft drinks do not contain these levels of sugars). Also, soft drinks contain few, if any, vitamins, few minerals, no fiber, no protein and, in most cases, no other essential nutrients. So popular are these beverages that some nutritionists believe the drinks are a significant factor in the increase in obesity in the United States. This is so because their excessive consumption may displace healthier beverage choices such as water, milk, and fruit juices. As a result, soft drink availability in school foodservice and other health-care settings is increasingly restricted.

PRODUCT TYPES Foodservice buyers selecting soft drinks do not have the luxury of choosing from a large number of suppliers. In fact, just two companies account for over 75 percent of the U.S. soft drink market: Coca-Cola and PepsiCo. When the London-based Cadbury Schweppes company is included, the three companies account for over 90 percent of all soft drink sales.

Soft drinks may be purchased in a variety of flavors, with cola, by far, being the best selling. Other popular flavors include citrus, root beer, strawberry, cherry, and variations of Mountain Dew (a PepsiCo product) and Dr. Pepper (a Cadbury Schweppes product). In the United States, prepackaged soft drinks may be purchased in one- and two-liter plastic bottles, glass or plastic bottles that range in size from 8–24 ounces, and in 12–ounce cans. They are typically packaged in 12- to 24-unit cases, depending upon the size of the individual unit size purchased. Because of lower costs per serving that are achieved, however, many foodservice operations choose to produce the carbonated beverages they sell via the use of on-premise production systems.

SERVICE SYSTEMS Soft drinks are made by injecting CO_2 gas into purified water and flavored sugar syrups. Soft drinks are inexpensive to produce if the restaurant

Key Term

CO_2 Carbon dioxide; the colorless, odorless gas used to carbonate water in soft drinks and beer. In its solid form, CO_2 is known as "dry ice."

> ## PURCHASING PROS NEED TO KNOW (16.2)
>
> Most buyers know that 7-UP and Sprite both refer to citrus-flavored soft drinks, and the Coke and Pepsi "cola wars" are legendary, but as a beverage category, the question often arises: What's in a name?
>
> When it comes to soft drinks, the answer is often "geography."
>
> Soft drinks are called "pop" in most of the upper Midwestern parts of the United States.
>
> In the lower Midwest, the term "soft drink" is predominant.
>
> "Soda" is the name of choice in the Northeast, the Southwest, and most of Florida.
>
> "Soda pop" is used by some consumers, especially in the mountain west.
>
> Other common names include "drink" or "cold drink," which are commonly used in some parts of the South (especially Louisiana), whereas "*Coke*," the name of a specific Coca-Cola Company product, is the generic term for soft drinks used in much of the Southern United States. Thus, it is common to hear Southern restaurant guests ask their servers the very sensible question: *"What kinds of Coke do you serve?"*

has the equipment required to create the drinks. This equipment, typically provided and maintained by soft drink manufacturers, requires the purchase of **bag in box** soft drink syrups and mixes.

When using an on-site beverage production system, selecting the soft drinks to be sold usually depends upon the vendor that provides and/or services the dispensing equipment used by the property. Like all machines, soft drink production equipment must be maintained and, because of its function, calibrated on a regular basis to ensure that the proper amount of syrup is mixed with the proper amount of water. Improper calibration can result in excessive product usage and cost (from using too much syrup), or a poor-tasting product (from using too little syrup).

Bottled Waters

Water is the world's most important, and most consumed, beverage. It is a uniquely American custom that, in most restaurants, complimentary iced water is immediately offered to guests when they are seated. Increasingly, however, some American restaurants offer both "still" (noncarbonated) and carbonated bottled water to guests to meet the increased demand for these products. Today, a foodservice operation that offers its guests a choice of coffee, tea, and/or soft drinks should also plan to sell one or more brands of domestic and/or imported bottled water.

CLASSIFICATIONS   The FDA regulates bottled water as a food product. Bottled water companies must adhere to the FDA's standards of labeling, which mandates that beverage companies label their waters to define where the water came from and if it has been purified or carbonated.

Bottled waters are classified with tightly defined terms such as "purified," "spring," and "artesian." All bottled water sold in the United States, whether imported or domestic, must meet the same regulations. The most popular of the

Key Term

Bag in box   The term used to describe the five-gallon syrup containers used in most modern soft drink dispensing systems. It is so named because the soft drink syrup is sealed in a plastic bag that is then placed in a cardboard box for easy transporting.

bottled waters used by foodservice operations are classified by the FDA as one of the following:

Artesian: Bottled water may be labeled as Artesian if it comes from a well that taps a confined aquifer (a water-bearing underground layer of rock or sand) in which the water level stands at a height above the top of the aquifer.

Purified water: Water that has been produced by distillation, deionization, reverse osmosis, or other suitable processes and that meets the U.S. definition of purified water may be labeled as purified bottled water. These waters are taken primarily from metropolitan water sources, run through commercial filters, and purified of chlorines and other items inappropriate for drinking water. These are typically sold in large (5-gallon) containers.

Mineral water: Waters containing not less than 250 parts per million total dissolved solids may be labeled as mineral water. Mineral water is distinguished from other types of bottled water by its constant level and relative proportions of mineral and trace elements, but no additional minerals can be added.

Spring water: These waters originate from an underground formation from which water flows naturally to the surface of the earth. Spring water must be collected only at the spring or through a well drilled directly into the spring.

Sparkling water: Sparkling waters are those that, when bottled, contain the same amount of carbon dioxide that they had at emergence from their source. Soda waters, seltzer waters, and tonic water customarily used in the preparation of alcoholic drinks are not considered bottled waters. These are regulated separately, may contain added sugars, and, by law, are considered soft drinks.

Most of the bottled water sold in the United States is noncarbonated (still), but "sparkling" (carbonated) waters are also popular. In theory, any type of bottled water that is sold may first be carbonated. Some of these products are also flavored with ingredients such as citrus or other fruits. Flavored carbonated waters are similar to soft drinks (sodas) but are lighter in flavor and contain less sugar. They are not likely to be completely calorie-free, but are lower in carbohydrates and calories than traditional soda-type soft drinks.

As with soft drinks, bottled water products from PepsiCo (Aquafina) and Coca-Cola (Dasani) sell best. When combined, however, the Nestles Waters company's brands of Poland Springs, Arrowhead, Ozarka, Deer Park, Zephyr Hills, Ice Mountain, and others outsell both the PepsiCo and Coca-Cola products. Professional foodservice buyers know that local consumer preferences are very important when choosing bottled waters that will be highly accepted by guests.

Internet Purchasing Assistant (16.6)

San Pellegrino (also known as S.Pellegrino) is a carbonated mineral spring water produced and bottled near Milan, Italy.

San Pellegrino's sources are three deep springs that emerge at about 70°F (22°C). The waters come from a layer of rock 1,300 feet below the surface, where limestone and volcanic rocks impart unique minerals and trace elements. San Pellegrino is owned by Nestle and is an extremely popular sparkling bottled mineral water sold in many fine dining establishments in the United States.

To view the Pellegrino site, go to: www.sanpellegrino.com

ALCOHOLIC BEVERAGES

Throughout history, alcoholic beverages have had many uses and played many roles. In some societies, they were thought to possess magical or holy powers. They were an important part of medical treatment well into the 1800s. In many cultures, alcoholic beverages were considered a basic and essential food. Because beers, ale, and wine were not associated with the diseases caused by drinking contaminated water, they became an accepted part of everyday meals. They were particularly important for travelers, who had to be especially cautious about acquiring strange diseases and maladies to which their bodies had not been previously exposed and thus to which they were especially vulnerable. In fact, beer was a determining factor in the early history of the United States. Originally, the Pilgrims were heading for a destination farther south. Before they got there, however, the Mayflower ran out of beer, considered by the crew to be a basic necessity. The captain ordered the ship to land at Plymouth Rock so that they could take on fresh water for the passengers, thereby conserving the beer for the crew. Once on land, the passengers decided to stay where they were, rather than continue to their original destination.

Until the early seventeenth century, the only alcoholic beverages were those made by fermentation (various beers, ales, and wines). Scottish and Irish people first distilled (removed water from) beer and created the first whiskey. The new product was called "usquebaugh," which meant "water of life." From the 1600s to the 1800s, the use of the stronger distilled alcoholic beverages spread throughout the world. Corn and malt, flavored with juniper berries, were distilled to produce gin, which became popular in England and Holland. Vodka, distilled from various grains including potatoes, became a national drink in Russia and Poland; and rum, made from molasses or sugar cane juices, was produced throughout the Caribbean.

Alcohol itself is a colorless product created by fermenting a liquid containing sugar. Fermentation is a chemical reaction that splits a molecule of sugar into equal parts of ethyl alcohol and carbon dioxide. The carbon dioxide escapes into the air and the ethyl alcohol remains. This chemical reaction is caused by yeast. The yeast may occur naturally, or be introduced into the process by the beverage maker. Ethyl alcohol, or ethanol, is in itself neither poisonous nor harmful to one's health. From a buyer's perspective, any drinkable liquid that contains ethyl alcohol can be considered an **alcoholic beverage.**

Government regulations set minimum and maximum amounts of alcohol for various types of alcoholic beverages. Generally speaking, alcoholic beverages can contain as little as 2 percent alcohol (some beers), or as much as 75.5 percent (151-rum) or more. As a group of products, alcoholic beverages may be further classified as a **beer, wine,** or **spirit.**

Some foodservice operations have licenses that allow them to serve all three types of alcoholic beverages, whereas others may serve only beer, wine, or both. For professional foodservice buyers, it is important to have a basic understanding of these three widely popular adult beverages.

Key Terms

Alcoholic beverage   A drinkable liquid containing ethyl alcohol.

Beer   An alcoholic beverage fermented from cereals and malts and flavored with hops.

Wine   An alcoholic beverage produced from fermented grapes.

Spirit (alcohol)   An alcoholic beverage produced by distilling (removing water from) a liquid that contains alcohol. Sometimes referred to as "hard liquor" or "liquor" because of the large proportion of alcohol they contain.

Beer

Beer is generally recognized to be the world's oldest and most popular alcoholic beverage because it is a very versatile product. In ancient times, the Egyptians made it from barley, the Babylonians made it from wheat, and the Incas made it from corn. In fact, barley for brewing was so important to the early Romans that they pictured the grain on their gold and silver coins.

Today, beer is most often produced by fermenting grain starch (commonly barley). The type of grain or other starch used for malting (fermentation), any flavorings (commonly hops) added, and the specific production techniques used by the beer's brewer cause these products to have varying characteristics, colors, and flavor.

Beverage buyers today can choose from many hundreds (or more) of brands of beer. According to data compiled by the Beer Institute (an industry trade association), more than 1,200 breweries and **microbreweries** are currently producing beers in the United States.

STYLES   Two general styles or classifications of beer can be purchased for use in foodservice operations: **lagers** and **ales.**

The lager beers sold include bock, dark lager, light lager, light beer, dry beer, ice beer, malt liquor, and the very popular pilsner. Ales include light ale, brown ale, porter, and stout.

Lagers and ales are basically brewed in the same way, but different types of yeasts and different methods of fermentation yield different bodies and tastes. When guests order a "beer" in the United States, they are usually ordering a lager product. In this country, ale is typically ordered by brand name. Most ale has a higher alcohol content, more body, and a more intense flavor than lager beer.

Most of the lager-style beers sold in the United States are **pilsners.**

All pilsners are characteristically amber colored, light flavored, and contain less alcohol than malt and bock beers. Although not true worldwide, the preference of American drinkers and diners is overwhelmingly for extremely mild pilsner-style beers. These "American-style" lagers are often the subject of disdain among "true" beer drinkers because lighter beers are considered to have less character than most European styles of beer. Although it is true that these beers are different from their heavier bodied counterparts, in fact, American-style beers are increasingly popular worldwide.

A very light color and body and the frequent use of rice or corn in their brewing are the factors that characterize American-style beers. So popular are they that the top five selling beer brands in the United States (Bud Light, Budweiser, Miller Light, Coors Light, and Corona Extra) are all of this type. Of course, the popularity of beer brands can vary greatly based upon the location of a foodservice operation, so buyers should look to their beverage suppliers and conduct market studies to determine beer brands to purchase.

Key Terms

Microbrewery   A very small commercial brewery.

Lager   A bright, clear, light-bodied beer brewed from malt, hops, and water. The mixture is then fermented, lagered (stored) to develop flavor, and then carbonated.

Ale   A heavier brew than lager made from malt or malt and cereals. It is fermented at a high temperature. The resulting beer is full bodied and more bitter than a lager.

Pilsner   Beers of the style made popular by the Pilsner Urquell brewery in Plzen Bohemia (now the Czech Republic).

Internet Purchasing Assistant (16.7)

One of the largest beer manufacturers in the world is Anheuser Busch Inc., located in St. Louis, Missouri (and purchased in 2008 by Belgian brewer InBev). Those 21 and older can enter one of the sites devoted to their most popular beer brand at: www.budweiser.com

At the home page:

1. Click on "American Lagers."
2. Then, click on "Origination of Lager in the U.S." to learn more about how popular American-style lagers are produced.

Less popular in the United States, but more popular worldwide, are the dark varieties of ales such as porter and stout. Porter originated in England in the eighteenth century. Dark brown, heavy bodied and malty flavored, they have a slightly less sweet taste and reduced hop flavor than light ales.

Stout is a heavy beer made with roasted malted barley. The traditional English stouts are "sweet" because they use lactose (milk sugar) in their production and are sometimes called cream stouts. Porter, stouts, and ales are gaining in popularity in the United States as microbreweries broaden the taste preferences of American beer drinkers.

SERVICE   The two primary issues beverage buyers must consider before purchasing beer, as well as many other alcoholic beverage products, are

• What should be purchased?
• How should it be purchased?

Many beverage buyers are challenged when selecting the proper mix of traditional and lower-calorie (light), as well as low-carbohydrate, pilsners, ales, and other beer products. After the decision about which products to purchase has been resolved, the issue of how they should be purchased can be addressed. In many cases, beer can be purchased by the **keg,** in bottles, or in cans.

Draft beer may be served in a variety of glass styles.
© Dorling Kindersley

Key Term

Keg   A container for beer. Kegs vary in size but nearly always contain unpasteurized beer. Beer served from kegs is called "draft" or "draught" beer.

	CAPACITY
Contents in ounces	1,984.0 ounces
Contents in gallons	15.5 gallons
Contents in liters	58.7 liters
Full keg weight	160.5 pounds
Empty keg weight	29.7 pounds
Beer weight	130.8 pounds
	SERVINGS*
Number of 10-oz. servings	198
Number of 12-oz. cases equivalent	6.8 cases
Number of 12-oz. servings	165
Number of 16-oz. servings	124

*The number of servings contained in a keg may be affected by the quality of the beer-dispensing lines, product temperature, CO_2 levels, and bartender's skill.

FIGURE 16.1 Keg Specifications for U.S. ½-Barrel

Bottles and cans of beer are pasteurized and have a longer shelf life than does keg beer (which has not undergone pasteurization). Keg, or draft, beer is typically significantly less costly per ounce to buy, and profit levels for its sale are higher than for canned or bottled beer. Spoilage, however, can be a problem, and there must be adequate refrigeration space for holding and serving from kegs. In addition, beer lines and taps must be cleaned frequently. Although keg sizes can vary, the most popular keg sold in the United States is the ½-barrel (see Figure 16.1).

If keg beer is purchased, it should be in response to a demand that ensures sufficient turnover to warrant the required investment in equipment and maintenance.

Wine

The history of man is intertwined with the history of wine. Although no one knows when wine was first made, even the earliest uncovered literature makes reference to its production. Although wine has been made since the beginning of time, it was not until the mid-1800s that the science of wine production became

HI-TECH PURCHASING (16.1)

A "Sound" Way to Ensure Quality Draft Beer

Professional buyers want to maximize the quality of the keg beer products they buy. Inside a keg, beer exists in a sterile environment that optimizes product quality. The moment the beer leaves the keg, however, it enters a nonsterile environment of supply lines, valves, joints, and taps. These individual components making up the beer lines used to deliver draft beer are not sterile, and thus provide a haven for yeast and bacteria to thrive and reproduce, feeding on the nutrients found in beer. Biweekly use of chemicals of the correct strength can remove built-up contamination, but at a significant cost to the bar owner.

The Perlick company's Beer Line Maintenance System (BLM 2000) is a device that generates an audio signal that is introduced to the interior of the beer line via a transponder. The audio signal used varies in frequency and amplitude, and creates an unfriendly environment for yeast and bacteria cells trying to multiply within the lines. As the signal travels the length of the beer line, it prevents yeast and bacteria bio-film from forming on the inside beer line's parts and surfaces. Without a bio-film growing on the inside of the line, the beer, as it flows from the keg to the guest's glass, takes a contamination-free journey, resulting in a quality product. Tests on the BLM 2000 reveal chemical cleaning need occur only every 8 to 12 weeks, resulting in dramatic cost savings to the bar owner by minimizing beer waste, chemical usage, and labor. The system has been extensively tested and is approved by Coors Brewing Company for use with its beer products.

Internet Purchasing Assistant (16.8)

Maintaining quality draft beer is somewhat of an art. For a Web site that helps solve buyers' potential difficulties with draft beer lines and provides tips on how to correct common draft beer dispensing problems, go to: www.probrewer.com

At the home page:

1. Click on "Resources," then select "Library."
2. Next, click on "Troubleshooting draft problems" to learn more about the ways equipment and service methods can affect the quality levels of keg beer products.

known. Louis Pasteur, the famous scientist, was the first to discover and prove that fermentation was caused by yeasts in the air. The knowledge of "why" fermentation started helped wine producers improve their products greatly.

Some areas of the world produce spectacular wines, whereas other areas produce either no wine or poor wines. Many countries, however, produce good solid wines. Wine is particularly fascinating to people because no two wines are ever exactly identical. There are subtle differences in wines, even those made from the same grapes. Location, climate, soil, wine maker, and product age are but a few of the characteristics that influence the taste of wine.

Good wine appeals to the eye, nose, and mouth. To the eye, the wine should appear clear and brilliant. Red wine should appear rich, and white wines should sparkle. To the nose, the wine should be pleasant, with a hint of flowers, spice, or other characteristics common to the wine type. The aroma, or **bouquet,** should linger, and above all be an indicator of the taste to come.

Finally, the flavor of the wine should be appealing to the drinker. Diners can easily enjoy a variety of wines despite their price or place of origin. From inexpensive to the very highest price, wines are available for every taste and preference. Some foodservice buyers are intimidated by the great variety and seemingly complex information associated with wine. They need not be. Most buyers can do quite well if a few wine basics are well understood and preferences of their own customers are taken into account.

Wines can be classified in a variety of ways. Country of origin, grape variety, and alcohol content are just a few of these methods. Wines can also be grouped based on their sugar content: Wines are often classified as dry, semidry, and sweet. These terms are used to describe the sweetness of a wine and refer to the residual sugar content, or the amount of grape sugar remaining in the wine after fermentation has occurred. Dry wines are the least sweet and have a sugar content below 0.8 percent, whereas semidry wines have 0.8–2.2 percent grape sugar and sweet wines have more than 2.2 percent sugar. Although there are a variety of ways to group wines, for the professional buyer, color is probably the most common method of classification.

A wine's color depends on how long the grape skins remained in the beverage during fermentation. Because all grape juice is clear in color, any juice can be used to make white wine. If grape skins are allowed to stay in contact with the

Key Term

Bouquet The aroma of wine.

juice during production, the juice will take on the color of the grape skins. If the red grape skins stay in contact for a long time, red wine will result. If they are allowed to stay in contact for only a short time, a light red, or **rosé** wine, will result.

Although the study of wine can be a lifelong endeavor (and passion), professional buyers who understand the basics of red and white wines are in a good position to make well-informed buying decisions for their own foodservice operations.

RED WINES   Red wines have traditionally been associated with hearty, full-bodied flavor. The classic red wines are made from the cabernet sauvignon (pronounced cab-er-nay so-veen-yohn) grape. This is the red wine made famous by the Bordeaux region of France. These wines are complex, outstanding products that make excellent food accompaniments and are fine for drinking by themselves. They are typical of the red wines sold to accompany beef, wild game, and dark meat entrées that require a bold, hearty flavor.

A second outstanding grape used for making red wines is the pinot noir (pronounced peeno nwar). It is from this grape that the famous French burgundies are made. Interestingly, this is the same grape used to make champagne (a sparkling wine discussed later in this chapter).

Other important grapes used for making red wine include the merlot (pronounced mer low); the gamay, or napa gamay, grown in France and California; and the zinfandel (pronounced zin-fand-el), a grape grown in California and popular for making a very light red, or blush, wine. These light red wines can range from just barely pink to nearly red. They are called white zinfandels (if they are made from that type of grape), blush, or rosé wines. They are especially popular for drinking in warm weather climates. In addition, these light red wines are frequently drunk when eating light foods such as fish and poultry. Most rosés taste light and fresh, with sweet fruity flavors. These wines are increasing in popularity as white wine drinkers search for wines that have the complex taste of red wines but are not as heavy in body. The most popular of these are zinfandels, named for the grape used to produce them. Zinfandel grapes, the most widely planted grape in California, can be used to produce rich, red wine, but is most often used to create the blush wines associated with its name. Red wines that are made from a blend of different grapes may be labeled as simply "Red" or "Table Red." These wines are less expensive and are often exactly what should be served. The most important thing for the professional buyer to remember is that wines selected for sale should match the tastes and price range of the intended consumer.

WHITE WINES   Although red wines have traditionally been associated with robust food, white wines, with their more delicate taste, have become by far the most popular wine for drinking by the glass in bars, at receptions, and with light foods. White wines do complement delicate foods, such as fish, poultry, and pork, and are often served as a meal accompaniment to these dishes.

White wines are typically served chilled. They range in flavor from those that are dry and tart to others that are sweet and mellow. Their colors range from pale yellow to very deep gold. White wines have a more delicate flavor than red wines. They range in alcohol content from a low of 10 percent to as much as 14 percent. Most of the white wines served in the United States come from Italy, Germany, France, Chile, Australia, and, of course, California and other domestic sources.

Key Term

Rosé   A very light red-colored wine. Sometimes called a "blush" wine.

Grapes used to produce fine white wines vary according to the country that makes the wine. In the Rhine and Moselle valleys of Europe, the riesling grape is most often used to produce the sweet, flavorful wines associated with German whites. The trebbiano grape of Italy produces soave and is even used in chianti, a fruity, Italian, flavored wine. Pinot bianco, pinot grigio, and traminer are other popular Italian grapes used for making white wine.

By far the most popular white wine in the United States today is the chardonnay. This complex wine is aged in oak. Although many white wines are fermented in stainless steel tanks, fermenting and aging in oak and other woods give wines unique and quite complex flavor, color, and aroma characteristics. Like many red wines, chardonnay wine will improve with age prior to its bottling. Chardonnay is made from the same grape used in the Burgundy and Champagne regions of France. It is, however, truly an international sensation, and excellent chardonnay wine is produced in France, the United States, Argentina, Australia, Bulgaria, Romania, Mexico, and even Japan.

OTHER WINES   Although classifying wines as red or white is very helpful to buyers, variations of these wine types do exist and must be understood. For example, **sparkling wines** are characterized by the presence of carbonic acid, in solution, in the wine.

Sparkling wine is generally white, but can be light red (rosé) to dark red. Champagne, a type of sparkling white wine, is actually made from grapes that are bluish-black on the outside and red on the inside. Their juice, however, is white and produces white sparkling wine if it is not allowed to be colored by the dark skins of the grapes. Sparkling wines are those that have been made effervescent (bubbly). Their alcohol content is the same as that of regular wine. Champagne is the most popular sparkling wine and is the standard celebration drink. The name "champagne" legally applies only to a specific sparkling wine made in France.

Some wines are considered neither red, white, nor sparkling, but are still important wine products. These include

Vermouth: Vermouth can be either sweet (Italian) or dry (French). These are fortified wines: those whose alcohol levels have been increased after fermentation is complete. In the case of vermouth, the alcohol level is increased to around 18 percent (36 **proof**).

Vermouths are flavored with products other than the grapes used for its production. French vermouth is steeped in a combination of nutmeg, coriander, orange peel, tea, and other spices and flavorings. Italian vermouth, which is often colored red, is flavored with quinine, as well as a variety of herbs and spices. The most common use of vermouth in the United States is as an ingredient in the martini, a mixture of gin or vodka and dry vermouth, or the manhattan, a combination of whiskey, bitters, and sweet vermouth.

Sake: Sake is often called rice wine, because the term, "sake," means "essence of rice spirit." In fact, sake is a product made from rice, but it is made more like a beer than a wine. Sake is served warm to release its entire aroma. At 14 to 16 percent alcohol content, it has the strength of a wine and can be enjoyed straight, or mixed with vodka or gin in place of vermouth in a martini.

Key Terms

Sparkling wine   A naturally or artificially carbonated wine.

Proof (alcohol)   A measure of the alcoholic strength of a beverage. Proof is equal to two times the alcohol present in the beverage. For example, a beverage containing 2 percent alcohol would have a proof of 50 percent (25 percent alcohol content × 2 = 50 proof).

Sherry: Sherry is a blended wine, made famous by the sherries originally produced in Spain. There are a great number of varieties, from the very dry varieties to the sweet, deep golden cream varieties. Sherries contain from 13 to 20 percent alcohol and are drunk both before and after dinner.

Port: Port is a variety of wine produced in Portugal. It became widely distributed and popular in English-speaking countries during the early 1700s. All port bottled in Portugal is certified as "Porto" by the Portuguese government. The rest of the port made outside Portugal is called port or port wine. Port is a rich, popular after-dinner drink.

Wine coolers: The term "wine cooler" has come to mean a variety of flavored wines. Typically a mixture of wine and fruit juices, these "easy-to-drink" wines are sweet and appeal to many guests who would not ordinarily order wine. Wine coolers have about half the alcohol content of table wines (about 6 percent) and are available in many flavors, including citrus, orange, strawberry, peach, and raspberry. They are typically served well chilled or over ice.

Like many foods, wine labels carry a great deal of information about a wine that can be helpful to buyers. Some labels, like those found on German wines, can be very detailed. Other wine labels carry less information. Among the information that can generally be found on wine labels is

- **Vintage,** the year the grapes used to make the wine were grown
- Where the majority of grapes used to produce the wine were grown
- Type of grape used
- Vineyard owner's name and address
- Bottler's name and address
- Shipper's name and address
- Governmental inspection/authorization information

Although it is well beyond the scope of this book, it is important to understand that an in-depth knowledge of wine is truly essential to the professional

Buyers can find valuable information on wine labels if they are knowledgeable about legally mandated labeling standards.

Demetrio Carrasco © Dorling Kindersley

Key Term

Vintage The year in which the majority of grapes used to make a wine was grown. In the United States, 85 percent of the contents of a wine bottle must have been grown in the year stated on the wine's label.

Internet Purchasing Assistant (16.9)

Learning about wine can be fun. Professional buyers who are serious about improving their product knowledge skills can choose from a variety of free online resources. To review one of the best wine books on the market, however, go to: www.amazon.com

At the home page:

1. Click on "Books" under the "Search" drop-down menu.
2. Next, enter "Tom Stevenson" in the search window, to retrieve and review his excellent book, "*The New Sotheby's Wine Encyclopedia, 4th Edition*" (ISBN 978-0756613242).

wine buyer. Guests expect these buyers to choose wines that are pleasant when served on their own or as a complement to the menu choices offered them. In most food operations serving alcohol, wine is consistently popular with guests and is important to them.

SERVICE   Most foodservice operators will offer guests wine menus (lists) consisting of wines sold to guests by the bottle or **by the glass.**

Because wines are frequently purchased and sold to diners "by the bottle," wine buyers should be well acquainted with the most common bottle sizes used by wine suppliers. These are listed in Figure 16.2.

Increasingly, some wines are sold to foodservice operators in boxes rather than bottles. The box containers sold to foodservice operators typically contain two to five liters of wine. Boxed wines are actually "bagged" wines, because wineries selling boxed wines package their products in vacuum-sealed bags. These are designed to minimize the presence of oxygen and prevent oxidation that can cause wines (as well as other foods) to deteriorate. Well-designed bag-in-box wine containers can keep wines at top quality for up to four weeks after they are opened.

Wines are sold in sealed boxes for the purpose of reducing storage, packaging, and shipping costs. Historically, most of this alternative packaging was associated with lower-quality "bulk" wines intended only to be sold to guests "by the glass." More frequently, however, quality wines are being sold in boxed containers as foodservice operators seek to increase the quality of the wines they sell "by the glass."

Bottle Size (Capacity)	Name	Description
.100 Liters	Miniature (mini)	A single serving bottle
.187 Liters	Split	1/4 a standard bottle
.375 Liters	Half-Bottle	1/2 a standard bottle
.750 Liters	Bottle	Standard wine bottle
1.5 Liters	Magnum	Two bottles in one
3.0 Liters	Double-Magnum	Four bottles in one

Note: 1 U.S. quart = 0.946 liters
1 U.S. gallon = 3.785 liters

FIGURE 16.2   Common Wine Bottle Sizes

Key Term

By the glass (wine)   Wine priced for, and sold to, guests by the single serving (rather than by the bottle).

PURCHASING PROS NEED TO KNOW (16.3)

Wine buyers can be challenged by the vast number of products available to them. Their job can be made easier when they remember the following wine-buying principles.

Always select wines that complement the menu items served in the food service operation (e.g., Italian wines with Italian food).

Select wines that are primarily modestly priced in relation to the menu prices, but consider some higher-priced wines for guests who know about and prefer a higher-quality wine.

Select some popular-priced wines that can be sold "by the glass."

Include light and dry red wines when the menu features beef. Include full-bodied dry red wines when the menu features game and game birds.

Include dry white wines when the menu features poultry, pork, veal, or seafood.

Include semisweet or sweet wines to complement desserts and at all times in the meal for those who simply prefer them.

Include, for a reasonable price, one sparkling (carbonated) wine to be sold with dessert or at any time during the meal for guests celebrating (or creating) a special occasion.

Select wines that are readily available in quantities consistent with the restaurant's anticipated sales volume of that wine.

Always remember: The guest's preference for any wine with any food at any time during the meal is a better "rule" than one dictated by any expert's mandated food and wine pairing.

Spirits

Spirits are the most potent of alcoholic beverages. The reason: Water and alcohol boil at different temperatures, so **distillation** allows the concentration of alcohol in the beverage to increase.

The boiling point of water is 212°F (100°C), whereas alcohol boils at 173°F (78°C). When distillers boil a liquid mixture containing alcohol at a temperature

---

On-the-Job Challenges in Purchasing (16.2)

"You see, Shashank," said Dave Seguola, the salesperson for Classico Wines, "The key to increased wine sales is guest choice. People love wine with their meals . . . you just have to offer them the choice of the products they already know and like. Do that, and you'll see your wine sales increase, I'll promise you that!"

Dave was attempting to convince Shashank Abhyankar, manager of the Fifty Yard Line Steakhouse, that he should significantly increase the number of wines offered to the guests of the restaurant.

"I don't know, Dave," replied Shashank, "We have six good reds, five whites, and three blush wines on the menu now. Additional choices may simply result in guests switching from their current wine selection to a different alternative. That doesn't mean increased sales . . . just increased inventory."

Case Study Questions

Assume that you were Shashank:

1. What signs would indicate to you that the number of wines offered on your menu is insufficient and thus should be expanded?
2. What role would you want your salesperson, and Classico Wines, to play in this assessment?

Key Term

Distillation (alcohol) A method of separating chemical substances based upon differences in their boiling points.

above the boiling point of alcohol, but below the boiling point of water, the alcohol will vaporize, but the water in the mixture will not. If they can then capture the alcohol and convert it back to a liquid before the vapor escapes into the air, they will have created the basis for a distilled beverage.

The Arabs are generally credited for the term "alcohol," a discovery they made when using the alembic still, the heating device first used to distill alcohol. Whereas beer is the result of the fermentation of grain, and wine is the result of the fermentation of grape juice, spirits are the distillation of these and other fermented sugar products. For example, vodka is a spirit made from grain, rum is made from sugar cane, and brandy is the result of distilling grape juice. Other spirits include whisky, gin, tequila, and liqueurs.

Most spirits are approximately one-half water and one-half alcohol (80 to 100 proof). Taste differences occur among types of spirits (e.g., gin versus vodka), within product categories (Irish whiskey versus Scotch whisky), and among different brands of the same product (one brand of vodka versus another). In most cases, the manager's first purchasing decision relates to which liquors will be the restaurant's **well brands** and which will be its **call brands.** The former typically cost less and are sold for less than their call brand counterparts.

The very best of the call brands are sometimes referred to as "premium" or "super premium," depending upon the product's cost and selling price potential. In most operations that serve spirits, buyers offer guests their choice of well, call, and selected premium products.

Specific well brands may be selected because they cost the operation less than better-known and more popular call brands. If, however, the well brands selected are viewed by guests as too "cheap," the operation's reputation may suffer. Guests who do not specify a brand generally do not care which is used as long as the quality of the beverage is acceptable. In practice, a buyer's liquor distributor can advise about well brands in keeping with the quality image desired by an operation, as well as appropriate call and premium products that could be offered.

Internet Purchasing Assistant (16.10)

One of the best ways to learn about spirits is to visit the Web sites of the companies that make and/or distribute them. One of the largest of these is the Diageo Company. Their brands include Smirnoff vodka, Johnnie Walker scotch, Cuervo tequila, and Tanqueray gin, among others. To view a list of all brands they carry, go to: www.diageo.com

At the home page, use the "Our brands" drop-down menu to learn about the characteristics of these spirit products (as well as wines and beers).

Key Terms

Well brand   The brand of liquor that is served when the guest does not indicate a preference for a specific brand. Sometimes called the "house" or "pour" brand. For example, a guest ordering a "vodka tonic" would be served the operation's well vodka in the drink.

Call brand   The brand of liquor that is served when the guest indicates (calls for) a specific spirit brand. For example, a guest ordering a "Tanqueray and Tonic" would be served Tanqueray brand gin and tonic water.

PRODUCTS   As is true with beer and wines, the amount of product knowledge buyers can obtain about spirits is vast. There is, however, some basic information all potential buyers should know about the most popular spirits.

Vodka: Vodka is the largest selling spirit in the U.S. market today, accounting for approximately 25 percent of all the spirit beverages sold. It is distinguished by its aroma, texture, weight, and smooth, silky character. It is also noted for its bite, which makes it a good accompaniment to oily and smoked foods such as caviar and salmon. It is also famous for the warming sensation it provides the body as it is drunk, perhaps a reason for its popularity in cold climates. Vodka was invented in Poland, but was adopted by the Russians as their official drink. In fact, the word vodka is a variation of "voda," the Russian word for water. Contrary to popular opinion, the best vodka is made not from potatoes but rather is distilled from fermented grain. Unlike whiskey or gin, which are lightly flavored by the distiller, vodka is produced with the objective of creating a tasteless, colorless, odorless product. To achieve this result, the vodka is filtered through charcoal. It requires no aging and mixes easily with other beverages because of its neutral qualities. Most recently, flavored vodkas have appeared on the market. These products are flavored with a variety of ingredients including berries, oak, chocolate, honey, pepper, currants, pineapple, and citrus.

Gin: In the 1950s, gin outsold vodka in the United States by nearly a three-to-one margin. Today it is less popular but it is still favored by many older drinkers as well as those who enjoy the simplicity of the gin martini, a popular **mixed drink.**

The flavor of gin comes from juniper berries. The beverage was invented in Holland in the 1600s. Today, gin is available in two basic types: Dutch and English. Dutch gin is meant to be drunk straight and cold and is not typically mixed. English (dry) gin is made in both England and the United States and is used most often in mixed drinks.

Typically, manufacturers choose copper as the preferred metal for distilling liquor. When using this metal, they must distill their products twice to remove any harmful chemicals the copper contains.

Chad Ehlers/Stock Connection

Key Term

Mixed drink   A beverage created by combining one or more spirits with various other beverages and/or flavorings. Sometimes called (erroneously) "cocktails."

Rum: Rum is a spirit with a significant history in the development of the New World. It is said that Columbus brought sugar cane cuttings to the West Indies from the Caribbean islands in the early 1500s. Molasses, which is produced when sugar is refined, became to Caribbean countries what malted barley was to the Scots and grape juice was for the French and Italians: the essence of a unique and flavorful distilled spirit. Rums of many flavors and color are produced throughout the Caribbean, as well as Central and South America. They can be either light or full-bodied. The great majority of rum sold in the United States is of the light variety. Darker rums tend to be fuller flavored than the lighter varieties. Spiced and fruit-flavored rums are also popular. The two most often requested are Captain Morgan's (flavored with apricot, fig, vanilla, and other ingredients) and Malibu Rum, flavored with coconut.

Tequila: Tequila is a spirit product produced in Mexico. Tequila is aged in oak and can be produced only in a very tightly controlled area of the country—Tequilas—the official district surrounding the town of Tequila, Mexico. Tequila is made from the blue agave plant and, to earn its name, must contain at least 51 percent fermented agave juice. Tequila is the principle ingredient in the very popular margarita, a fruit juice and tequila mixed drink that can be served frozen or over ice.

Whiskey: Whiskey is a "brown" (colored) spirit, rather than a "white" (clear) spirit such as those discussed above. Currently, the sale of brown spirits is declining as the sale of white spirits (vodka, rum, and tequila) is increasing. For professional spirit buyers, however, a basic understanding of whiskey is still essential. Scottish and Canadian distillers spell whisky without an "e," whereas Irish and American distillers include the "e" (whiskey).

There are two general types of whiskey: straight and blended. Straight whiskies are unmixed or mixed with whiskey from the same distiller or distillation period. Blended whiskies are a mixture of similar straight whiskies from different distillers or distillation periods. By government standards, an American whiskey can be labeled as straight if it contains at least 51 percent of a single grain (e.g., corn, rye, or other grain). Whiskies are typically categorized according to country of origin. These include

- *Scotch Whisky.*   This is the whisky of Scotland, and it is light bodied and smoky flavored. Barley, and sometimes corn, is the grain used to produce it. Most Scotch whisky is blended rather than straight and is bottled at 80 to 86 proof. The base grain is dried over open, peat fires that give the product its smoky taste. The grain is then combined with water (mash), fermented, distilled, and aged at least four years.
- *Canadian Whisky.*   This is a blended whisky and is light in body. It may contain corn, rye, wheat, and barley as base grains. It is aged six years or more and bottled at 80 to 90 proof.
- *Irish Whiskey.*   This uses the same ingredients and is made the same way as Scotch whisky. The main difference is that the malted barley is not exposed to peat smoke when it is dried, so there is no smoky taste. The product also goes through a triple distillation process and uses several grains in addition to malted barley. The result is a very smooth high-quality whiskey that is offered for sale after aging a minimum of seven years.
- *United States Whiskey.*   These include bourbon, rye, corn, bottled-in-bond, blended, and light whiskey. Bourbon is the most popular and is a straight whiskey distilled from a fermented mash containing a minimum of 51 percent corn. It is aged in charred oak barrels from two to twelve years. Bourbon has a strong flavor and a full body. It is generally bottled at 80 to 90 proof. Blended whiskey is a combination of straight whiskies. Nearly one half of the United States whiskies consumed are blends. These are designated by the words "American Whiskey" on their labels.

- *Brandy.* Brandy is a distilled spirit made from a fermented mash of fruit, generally grapes, but also apples, cherries, apricots, and plums. The word itself has its origins in Holland, where it is derived from "brandewijn," or burned wine, a reference to the fact that the wine product from which the brandy was made was heated when distilled. If brandy is made from grape juice, the term "Brandy" stands alone on the label. If it is made from other fruits, the name of the fruit appears with the term "Brandy" (e.g., Apricot Brandy). Brandies must be bottled at 80 proof or more. Different types of brandies include
    - Cognac: Considered the finest of brandies. It is produced in the Cognac region of France. Cognac is the distillation of grape juice only.
    - Apple brandy: The American name, or Calvados—the French equivalent of apple brandy.
    - Kirsch or Kirschwasser: German brandy made from a wild black cherry.
    - Ouzo: Greek brandy that is colorless and has a licorice-like taste.
    - Per William: Made from Swiss or French pears.
    - Elderberry: Made from the elderberry.
    - Fraise: Made from strawberries.
    - Framboise: Made from raspberries.
    - Slivovitz: Made from plums.
- *Liqueurs.* Liqueurs (sometimes called cordials) are spirits that have been redistilled or steeped with fruits, plants, flowers, or other natural flavorings, and then sweetened with sugar. When the sugar content is high, the liqueur has a creamy quality and is designated "creme de" (as in creme de cacao). Some popular liqueurs include
    - Anisette: Red or clear color with an anise or licorice flavor.
    - Amaretto: Almond flavor, but made from apricot stones.
    - Coffee liqueur: Made from coffee beans.
    - Creme de Bananes: Yellow color; banana flavored.
    - Creme de Cacao: Brown or clear color with a chocolate–vanilla flavor.
    - Creme de Menthe: Green or clear color with a mint flavor.
    - Creme de Cassis: Deep red color with a red currant flavor.
    - Curacao: Orange, blue, or clear color with an orange peel flavor.
    - Triple Sec: A white Curacao (orange flavor).
    - Kummel: Clear color with a caraway seed flavor.
    - Maraschino: Clear color with a nutty, cherry flavor.
    - Sambuca: Licorice flavored, usually clear in color.
    - Sloe Gin: Red color with a plum flavor, made from the sloe berry.
    - Schnapps: In the United States, the term "schnapps" was traditionally used only to describe a peppermint-flavored liqueur. Schnapps in Germany, however, is a generic term for distilled spirits. Today, popular schnapps flavors still include peppermint and spearmint; however, cinnamon, banana, peach, strawberry, apple, raspberry, root beer, licorice, cola, and even a peppermint-flavored product that contains real 23-carat-gold flakes are also popular.

SERVICE Professional spirits buyers may choose from a variety of container sizes when purchasing products. In the United States, spirits may be purchased in any of the bottle sizes listed in Figure 16.3 below (spirit bottle sizes and capacities). The common, but now very inaccurate, names for these bottles predate the U.S. beverage industry's 1980s conversion to a complete metric measurement system.

Some beverage operations, especially those with very high volume, automate all or part of their drink production processes. In these systems, the production of drinks such as scotch and water, gin and tonic, rum and cola, beer, and even wine may be dispensed, in a pre-determined amount, by a machine that is activated by the bartender or a wait staff member. Ideally, the automated

Common Bottle Name	Metric Capacity	Fluid Ounce Capacity
Miniature	50 ml	1.7
Half-Pint	200 ml	6.8
Pint	500 ml	16.9
Fifth	750 ml	25.4
Quart	1.0 liter	33.8
Half-Gallon	1.75 liters	59.2

Note: 1 liter equals 1,000 milliliters; 1 fluid ounce equals 29.4 ml.

FIGURE 16.3 Spirit Bottle Sizes and Capacities

dispensing system is interfaced (connected to) the bar area's POS system. This ensures that the charge for each drink produced by the system is automatically assigned to the proper guest, the opportunity for bartenders to give away free drinks is reduced, and the amount of revenue that should be generated is known.

When buying for automated systems, the type of liquor that may be dispensed is not typically restricted; however, the number and kinds of products that may be dispensed often confine spirit buyers to specific bottle sizes. Despite some shortcomings, buyers should expect to see increasing use of these automated systems in the future because they yield the following advantages:

- Elimination of bartender's over or under pouring.
- Reduced spillage.
- Elimination of drink pricing errors.
- Accurate record keeping of all products sold.
- Reduced incident of bartender production errors.
- Less required bartender supervision.
- Lower and more consistent product costs.
- Reduced cost per product ounce when purchasing (because liquor may be purchased in larger containers for dispensing).
- Reduced liability potential that could result from not strictly controlling the amount of alcohol in each drink.

For those operations achieving high-volume sales levels, it is advisable for buyers to investigate the advantages (as well as the potential disadvantages) of automating all or part of their facility's beverage production system.

PRODUCT RECEIVING AND STORAGE

Unlike many other foodservice products, the quality variation of beverage products is small. In most cases, although the product purchased determines product quality, quality will not vary from one supplier to another. For example, a case of tea bags purchased from one supplier will (if the product has been properly stored) be identical in quality to the same tea brand purchased from any other source.

Internet Purchasing Assistant (16.11)

A variety of companies sell advanced automatic beverage dispensing systems. The Web site of one such company, located in Madison, Wisconsin, can be found at: http://www.berg-controls.com
At the home page, click on "Products" to review their automated systems.

When buying alcoholic beverage products, government regulations often affect supply and delivery. States can be either **control states** or **license states.** In control, or monopoly, states, the state is the sole purveyor of liquor. All liquor must be purchased directly from state stores by individuals and retail establishments alike. In license states, the state frequently licenses wholesalers, distributors, and sometimes manufacturers. The specifics vary by state but all serve to enhance product consistency and reduce questionable supplier behavior.

Receiving

After beverages have been properly received, they should be appropriately stored, and in a timely manner. When receiving alcoholic beverages, special considerations apply to procedures needed after the products received are checked against the products ordered. These include ensuring that beverage employees, not delivery personnel, move products to inventory areas. There is an increased chance of theft when nonbeverage operation staff members are allowed into storage areas containing large quantities of expensive and theft-prone products. In addition, prompt placement into storage areas reduces the chance for employee theft when products are left in unprotected areas.

Storage

In most cases, the storage of nonalcoholic beverage products is relatively uncomplicated. Coffees and teas are most susceptible to deterioration during storage. Those items, as well as canned and bottled beverage products, should be stored in a well-ventilated, clean, and dry or refrigerated storage area. Received product should be properly rotated when stored, and special attention must be paid to the expiration dates (if any) on the beverages' containers.

Most wines and spirits are relatively nonperishable, and the shelf life of canned and bottled beer products is relatively long. However, it is always important to manage the storage of these products to ensure maximum product quality. The following are recommended storage procedures for alcoholic beverages.

For Beer:
- Store keg beer between 36°F and 38°F (2.2°C–3.3°C).
- Store canned and bottled beer at 70°F (21.1°C) or lower, and rotate stock as it is delivered
- In all cases, expiration **(pull dates)** on beer products should be carefully monitored.

For Wine:
- Store bottled wine on its side.
- Store red wines at temperatures between 50°F and 70°F (10°C–21.1°C) and, if at all possible, at **cellar temperature.**

Key Terms

Control state   A state in which the right to sell alcohol is restricted exclusively to a state governmental entity. Sometimes called a "monopoly" state.

License state   A state that grants private distributors the right to sell wholesale alcoholic beverages within its borders.

Pull date   The date after which a packaged alcoholic beverage should not be served to guests. Also known as the package's "expiration" date.

Cellar temperature   A constant storage temperature between 55°F and 60°F (12.8°C–15.6°C).

- Store white and sparkling wines in refrigerators if they are to be used within a few months of purchase, or between 50°F and 70°F (10°C–21.1°C) if they are to be held longer.
- Avoid excessive light, humidity, and heat in wine storage areas because these can damage wines and their containers.

For Spirits:

- Store spirits in clean, dry, and well-ventilated storage areas.
- Store sealed cases with the date of receipt marked on the case to allow for easy rotation.
- Store individual bottles with the date of receipt upright on shelving that allows for easy rotation.
- Despite the relative nonperishability of spirits, avoid excessive heat in the dry storage area because this can harm the beverages.

Purchasing Resources on the Internet

In addition to the Web sites referenced in this chapter's "Internet Purchasing Assistant" feature, the following sites provide detailed information to enhance your purchasing knowledge and skills.

Purchasing Resources on the Internet

Site	Information About
www.beveragemarketing.com	Beverage consumption trends
www.coffeereview.com	Coffee buying tips
www.coffeetea.about.com/cs/grinding/tp/grinders	Coffee grinders
www.empiretea.com	Teas and hot tea brewing
www.buyteawholesale.com	Loose leaf iced tea recipes
www.worldcocoafoundation.org	Cocoa and chocolate products
www.ameribev.org	Nonalcoholic beverages
www.bottledwaterweb.com	Bottled waters and their service
www.evian.com	A high-end bottled water
www.brewpubzone.com/Microbrews.html	U.S. brewpubs and microbreweries
www.samualadams.com	A very unique American-style beer
www.winespectator.com	Fine wine products
www.winepros.org	Wines and wine basics
www.globalwinespirits.com	International wines
www.wineandspiritsmagazine.com	Spirits and wines
www.cognac-world.com	Cognacs
www.webtender.com	Bartending and mixed drink recipes
www.accubar.com	Automated liquor inventory systems
www.libby.com	Bar glassware

Key Terms

sports drink *391*
to go (menu item) *392*
decaffeinated *392*
espresso *392*
herbal tea *397*
Chai (tea) *397*

cocoa bean *398*
cocoa powder *398*
hot chocolate *398*
soft drink *399*
CO_2 *400*
bag in box *401*

alcoholic beverage *403*
beer *403*
wine *403*
spirit (alcohol) *403*
microbrewery *404*
lager *404*

ale *404*
pilsner *404*
keg *405*
bouquet *407*
rosé *408*
sparkling wine *409*

Think It Through

1. The "gourmet" coffee segment of the foodservice industry is expanding rapidly with the continued proliferation of stand-alone coffee shops and even quick-service restaurant operations adding premium-priced coffees. As a foodservice professional, what do you think is driving consumer interest in premium coffee products? Would that interest remain in troubled economic times? As a professional buyer, how would you stay abreast of consumer beverage consumption trends such as this one?

2. The current methods used to produce cocoa in some countries (especially those in Africa) cause many professional foodservice buyers to question the wisdom of purchasing chocolate products produced from cocoa grown in these countries. To better understand the issue, enter "cocoa production exploitation" in the search engine of your favorite browser. Read a minimum of two articles on the issue. Would you buy, for your own operations, chocolate products produced from African cocoa? Why or why not?

3. Many health professionals question the wisdom of offering guests soft drinks in the "mega sizes" popular today. What, if any, responsibility do those in the hospitality industry have to restrict the soft drink consumption of those they serve? Would your answer vary if you purchased food and beverages for a school foodservice program?

4. Convenience stores (C-stores), vending operators, and sports stadiums are just three of the many segments of foodservice that sell standard bottled waters for prices equal to that of soft drinks. Sit-down restaurants typically do not do so. In many cases, these water products are not even offered for sale. Why do you believe that to be the case?

5. As increased attention has been placed upon the dangers of drinking and driving, what affect will that have on foodservice operations that serve alcohol? Do you think foodservice buyers could address this issue by insisting that alcoholic beverage manufacturers offer their products in smaller-size containers (i.e., smaller wine bottles and beer cans/bottles)? Why or why not?

Team Fun

For this exercise, assume that each team consists of those individuals who will be selecting the carbonated beverage products to be sold in an extremely high-volume quick-service restaurant. The operation features ¼-pound burgers and fries. The total sales volume for the unit is $ 4,000,000 per year.

Soft drink sales account for $1,000,000 of the revenue. Soft drinks for dine-in customers are self-dispensed. Drive-thru and take-out customers are served their soft drinks in paper "to go" cups. Soft drink purchases from suppliers last year were 20 percent of soft drink revenue, or $200,000.

Divide into three teams.

1. The assignment of the first team is to defend the decision to maintain the soft drink contract with the current vendor. That vendor sells the single most popular soft drink in your area.

2. The assignment of the second team is to recommend switching to an alternative vendor. That vendor sells the number two and three most popular soft drinks in your area, and is prepared to sell all its products for 10 percent less than the current vendor.

3. The assignment of the third team is to identify those specific factors that would:
   A. Cause the operation to remain with its current vendor.
   B. Persuade the operation to switch to the newer, less-expensive vendor.

Each team should be prepared to present and discuss their findings, conclusions, and recommendations.

17

Food Service Purchases: Nonfood Items

In This Chapter

In the previous four chapters, you learned much about many of the food and beverage products purchased by foodservice buyers. In addition to the menu items served to guests, buyers must know a great deal about the products needed to serve those menu items. For example, choosing the quality ingredients required to produce an outstanding soup is important, but so is choosing the container the soup will be served in as well as the spoon used by the guest to eat the soup.

In this chapter, you will learn about four major categories of nonfood products, which are critical for the successful operation of a food facility: dining room supplies, takeout supplies, back-of-house supplies, and cleaning supplies.

The dining room supplies chosen by a foodservice buyer do much more than merely provide the utensils guests need to consume their food. The number and quality of service items provided with meals communicates a great deal to customers about an operation's quality level. Because that is true, the thoughtful selection of china (dishes), glassware, flatware (silverware) and, where applicable, table linens in concert with the guests' expectations is very important. If the quality levels of these or other products are inappropriate, the guests' image of the operation may suffer (if the quality is too low) or excessive costs will be incurred (if quality is higher than planned for).

For many professionals in the foodservice industry, the vision of foodservice customers enjoying their food and beverage purchases conjures up images of a comfortable on-site dining area. The reality of today's foodservice clients is that many of their purchases are eaten away from the place of purchase. "Takeout" foods and beverages are those purchased by customers for consumption at their homes, or to be eaten in their cars, commuter trains, offices, or myriad other settings. As this segment of the foodservice industry continues its rapid growth, professional buyers face a series of decisions about the items that must be supplied to "go along" with the "takeout" foods. In this chapter, you will learn about the most important of these items.

Every kitchen requires specific nonfood items if quality products are to be produced and served cost effectively. These include small wares such as portion-controlling scoops and ladles, storage containers, and cooking pots and pans. Also, hand tools, including various spoons, measuring tools and, of course, knives must be provided in sufficient quality and quantities to ensure workers have the tools they need to do their jobs.

Any foodservice professional who has been unfortunate enough to work in a facility that experienced an outbreak of food-borne illness knows the importance of the final category of nonfood items presented in this chapter. The proper selection and use of foodservice cleaning supplies helps ensure the service of high-quality and safe-to-consume foods and beverages. Just as importantly, proper selection and use of cleaning supplies helps ensure healthful working conditions for all employees.

■ ■ ■

Outline

DINING ROOM SUPPLIES

Just as a foodservice production area requires the products and tools necessary to produce menu items, so too does the dining room area need the resources required to serve those items. Although there are many ways to categorize nonfood items, one convenient way is by segmenting these products into those served to the guests and those used by the staff who actually serve guests.

In many foodservice operations, the items supplied to guests will include **table top** items as well as, in many operations, **single service** (disposable) items.

Key Terms

Table top (items)   Reusable products used to serve menu items to customers including china, glassware, flatware, and linens.

Single service (items)   Also commonly called "disposable" items, these are non-reusable products used to serve menu items to customers. These items typically include dishes, cups, flatware, and napkins made of plastic, foam, aluminum, and/or paper.

In addition to the table top and single service items provided, many food service operations supply guests with a limited number of "on the table" items that have come to be expected. For example, in many foodservice operations, salt and pepper shakers may be continually left on the dining tables for the use of all guests.

In addition to the items guests use when dining, there are nonfood items used by those who serve guests. For example, in many facilities, those who serve guests will be required to wear a uniform that may be provided, in all or part, by the employer. As a result, professional hospitality buyers must understand the basics of uniform selection and procurement. Other nonfood items routinely used by dining room staff vary based upon the service levels provided. However, they frequently include minor service items such as corkscrews, and writing utensils or other devices required for guest order taking.

Guest Directed

It is as difficult to describe the "typical" nonfood items supplied to guests as it is to describe the typical foodservice guest. The nonfood items needed to provide a guest with a "takeout" bagel and cup of coffee vastly differ from those required to serve the same guest an elegant four-course dinner. Despite the variations, however, it is convenient to place guest-directed nonfood products into the following groups:

- Table top items
- Single service items
- Condiments

TABLE TOP ITEMS   The number and type of table top items used in the foodservice industry is vast and can range from the inexpensive metal buckets used by some casual operations for the service of bottled beer on ice to the most elegant (and costly) fine porcelain china.

Essentially, table top items can be classified as one of the following:

- Dishware
- Glassware
- Flatware
- Linen

The distinguishing characteristic of these nonfood items is the intention of the foodservice operator to reuse them. As a result, **cost per use** is an important consideration. To illustrate, consider the buyer who is faced with the choice of purchasing two different brands of glassware.

The less expensive of the two alternatives costs $3.00 per unit and has an expected life of 400 uses. The cost per use in this case would be computed as:

$$\frac{\$3.00 \text{ per unit}}{400 \text{ uses}} = \$0.00750 \text{ cost per use}$$

The more expensive item is more durable and has an expected life of 800 uses, but costs $5.00 per unit. The cost per use in this case would be computed as:

$$\frac{\$5.00 \text{ per unit}}{800 \text{ uses}} = \$0.00625 \text{ cost per use}$$

Key Term

Cost per use   The average purchase expense incurred when using a table top item one time.

Although cost per use is only one of several factors that likely would be important to the buyer making this decision, it is clear that the more expensive (purchase cost) item would, in this specific case, be least costly to the operation!

Dishware   Dishware (dinnerware) refers to reusable foodservice dishes most often made of plastic, metal, **ceramics,** glass or, in some cases, ceramics and glass. These include guest use items such as plates, bowls, cups, saucers, and so on.

Porcelain, in its many forms, is an extremely popular material used for making dishes; however, many other types of ceramics can also be used. In the hospitality industry, "china," a type of porcelain, is so popular that it is a term often used synonymously with the word "dish."

Although porcelain is frequently referred to as china, the two are not identical. They resemble one another in that both can be **glazed** or unglazed.

However, china is softer than porcelain. This difference is due to the higher temperatures at which true porcelain is heated (2,650°F, 1,454°C for porcelain versus 2,250°F, 1,232°C for china). Due to its resulting greater hardness, porcelain has some medical, dental, and industrial applications that china, limited to domestic and artistic use, does not. Moreover, whereas porcelain is always translucent, china is opaque. Although the terminology used to describe various ceramic dishes can vary somewhat, the most popular categories of ceramic dishes include

China: A high-quality clay that may contain bone (calcium phosphate) and is heated to 2,250°F (1,232°C) or above. Porcelain (china) was indeed first made in China, and it is a measure of the esteem in which the exported Chinese porcelains of the seventeenth and eighteenth centuries were held in Europe that in English "China" became a commonly used synonym for the Franco-Italian term *"porcelain."*

Stoneware: Made from clay of a less fine quality than China. It is heated to about 2,200°F (1,205°C) or above.

Pottery: Clay baked at approximately 1,500°F (816°C) or above.

Terra Cotta: Clay baked at approximately 1,000°F (538°C) or above.

Bone china (first developed in Great Britain) is an extremely popular foodservice form of china and is characterized by its whiteness, translucency, and strength. Production of bone and other types of china usually involves a two-stage firing where the material is first heated to a temperature of 2,336°F (1,280°C), glazed, and then fired (heated) to a lower temperature (below 1,976°F, or 1,080°C).

Although china is popular as a dish-making material, other materials are also used. Glass dishes are made from glass material containing boric oxide, soda, and silica (sand). Glass dish variations developed by manufacturers such as Corning and others have proved durable and are commonly purchased under a variety of trademark names. In addition, many foodservice operators find that various formulas using plastic (or metal) serve their dish needs as well. In all cases, buyers should look for dishware of appropriate quality, price, and durability.

Key Terms

Ceramic   Inorganic, nonmetallic materials whose formation is caused by heat. Foodservice examples include bone china, porcelain, clay, and stoneware.

Porcelain   A clay-based ceramic made by heating selected and refined materials to a very high temperature. Porcelain is very popular for its use as a material in dish making.

Glaze   When used in conjunction with ceramic dishes, a shiny material coating the outside of the dish.

Internet Purchasing Assistant (17.1)

Foodservice buyers can choose from a variety of quality dishware companies. Oneida Ltd. is one of the world's largest. It offers a complete range of tabletop items, including flatware, china dinnerware, and crystal and glassware items. To view their site, go to: www.oneida.com

At the home page:

1. Click on "Oneida Foodservice."
2. Then, click on "Dinnerware" to view their dishware offerings.

Glassware   Glassware, as the term is used in the hospitality industry, refers to drinking vessels. Actually, these items may be made of materials other than glass. Thus, Styrofoam, plastic, and metal are popular materials for making "glassware." Glass is such an extremely popular material for making drinking vessels, however, that the term "glass" is used to refer to these items regardless of the material from which they are made.

True glass is a biologically inactive material that can be formed into a variety of smooth shapes. Some glass is brittle and will break into sharp shards. When compressed, however, pure glass can withstand a great amount of force. The properties of glass can be modified or changed with heat treatments and the addition of various chemicals and materials.

For glassware used in foodservice, glass is made by fusing (heating) sand (silica) in combination with soda and lime. Additions of metals (such as lead) change the properties of glass. Lead crystal (also called **crystal**) is glass that has been hand or machine cut with facets. Lead oxide added to the molten glass gives lead crystal a much higher index of refraction than normal glass, and consequently a much greater "sparkle." The presence of lead also makes the glass softer and easier to cut. Crystal can consist of up to 33 percent lead, at which point it has the most sparkle. True crystal, however, is fragile and expensive. Most foodservice operators find that a lower cost, more durable type of glassware is sufficient to meet their needs.

Flatware   Knives, spoons, forks, and their variations are known, collectively, as flatware. Internationally, flatware is more commonly referred to as **cutlery**, the term used to identify any hand utensil used for serving or eating food.

Internet Purchasing Assistant (17.2)

Hospitality buyers can choose from a huge number of different styles of glassware for use in their guestrooms, restaurants, and bars. The Libbey Company offers more than 1,000 different products to hospitality users. To view their site, go to: www.libbey.com

At the home page, click on "Foodservice Operators."

Key Terms

Crystal   Glass of fine quality and a high degree of brilliance.

Cutlery   Various utensils, such as knives, forks, and spoons, used at the table for serving and eating food.

Distinctive glassware can enhance the image of any foodservice operation.

Russell Sadur © Dorling Kindersley

Interestingly, in the United States, cutlery is used most often to identify knives, whereas the term "silverware" or "silver" is often used as a synonym for flatware. This is so because, traditionally, good quality flatware was made from silver. Because of silver's expense, however, beginning in the mid-1800s electroplated nickel silver (EPNS) was used to fuse a thin silver coating on nonsilver utensils (a process commonly known as silver plating).

Today, most foodservice cutlery, including very high-quality designs, is made from stainless steel. In this process, the individual flatware items are punched out of sheets of rolled stainless steel.

Flatware that is not punched out of sheets is made from stainless steel that that has been rolled to various thicknesses. The thickness of the flatware is measured by its **gauge.**

Good quality flatware will be at least 12 gauge (.1094 inches thick).

The best stainless steel flatware is made in a process that includes the addition of chrome nickel. Higher chrome contents increase an item's lightness of color and brightness or sheen; however, flatware with very high chrome contents are also prone to rust and pitting. Stainless steel can be finished to give flatware either a shiny or dull (pewter-like) appearance.

The number of types of flatware pieces used by an operation can be significant. For example, a buyer selecting spoons may choose from a manufacturer's selection of soup, table, tea, dessert, demitasse, bouillon, grapefruit, egg, and caviar spoons. In addition to knives, spoons, and forks, some foodservice operators purchase sporks (a combination spoon and fork) and splades, or knorks (words used to describe a fork with a cutting blade on one side).

Linens   Linen is so important to some foodservice operations that, in the minds of many customers, the finest dining experiences are to be had at "white tablecloth" restaurants. With their crisp white linens and clean elegant look, these establishments project an upscale image that complements great food and justifies higher menu prices. Table linens (tablecloths and napkins), however, can establish a mood and enhance the decor at any restaurant, from casual cafés to formal fine-dining rooms.

In most cases, restaurants rent the linen products they select, whereas some large hotels and other facilities may have on-premise laundry operations that

---

Key Term

Gauge (stainless steel)   In stainless steel flatware, a measure of thickness.

Dining Table Size	Select Tablecloth Size
24" × 24"	42" × 42"
30" × 30"	52" × 52"
36" × 36"	62" × 62"
42" × 42" square or round	62" × 62"
48" × 48" square or round	71" × 71"
60" round	85" × 85" square or 90" round
	120" round (to the floor)
72" round	85" × 85" square or 90" round
	132" round (to the floor)
30" × 48"	52" × 72"
30" × 72"	52" × 96"
30" × 96"	52" × 114"

FIGURE 17.1 Table Size/
Tablecloth Size Guide

allow them to purchase their linens. From a buyer's perspective, the two most important characteristics of linen are the fiber(s) from which it is made and its size.

Traditionally, the best food service linens were believed to be made from cotton or cotton blended with other fibers. High-quality cotton products will have about 200 threads per square inch of fabric and, when washed, will shrink less than 10 percent from their original size. Today, because of their resistance to wrinkles and ease of care, nylon, rayon, acrylic (for flame resistance), and polyester are popular linen fibers. Although often not as absorbent as cotton, these man-made fibers are more durable and often more stain resistant.

Size is the second major consideration when selecting linens. Figure 17.1 indicates the size of tablecloth that should be purchased or rented based upon an operation's dining table size.

Napkins can be procured in a variety of sizes; however, standard rental sizes are 12-, 14-, and 16-inch squares. They should be made from fabric material that weighs at least four ounces per square yard. White napkins are, by far, the most popular color chosen, due in part to the color variations that frequently result from the repeated washing of colored napkins.

SINGLE-SERVICE ITEMS   As more foodservice customers consume their foods away from the facility in which they are purchased (or due to the casualness of the operation itself), professional buyers are purchasing increasing numbers of single service (disposable) dishware, flatware, and glassware items, as well as napkins.

Items such as dishware may be made from paper, plastic, aluminum, or foam. Flatware is typically made from plastics and may be purchased in bulk cartons, wrapped in a grouping (e.g., a knife, spoon, and fork and, often, a napkin), or individually wrapped. Glassware may be made from Styrofoam or from waxed or unwaxed paper. Napkins are, of course, produced from newly made or, increasingly, recycled paper.

In all cases, foodservice operators should recall that quality disposable products, like reusable products, can be purchased at a variety of quality levels. The level chosen will, in many respects, dictate the value perceived by the operation's clientele. For example, paper napkins of increasing thickness (ply) can be perceived by guests as an indication of increased operational quality.

CONDIMENTS   As you learned in Chapter 15, a condiment is any food added to a dish to enhance flavor. Examples include spices, herbs, vinegars, and dressings. Thus, technically, condiments are edible food items, yet they are included here as a category because they also are "table top" items. Thus, for example, salt and pepper (the two most popular condiments) consist both of the products and their serving containers. These can range from the simple (and disposable) used by quick-service restaurants, to the very ornate grinders used in fine dining restaurants.

Internet Purchasing Assistant (17.3)

Most full-service foodservice suppliers carry a wide range of disposable (single-use) items. To see one large purveyor's product offerings of this type, go to: www.sysco.com

At the home page:

1. Click on "Products."
2. Then click on "Disposables" to view their offerings.

Buyers of these items need to recognize that their purchase can be critical to guest satisfaction. For example, consider the quick-service restaurant that elects to offer portion controlled (PC) ketchup "on request" for takeout orders. The size of packet or container, the brand (or private label), and even the ease of package opening will all send a message to customers that can reinforce, or significantly detract from, a desired customer perception of value. Ketchup, mustard, salt, pepper, soy sauce, salsa, salad dressings, and a variety of other condiments are important to many operations, and their purchase according to carefully established specifications is no less important than that of the ingredients used to make the operation's main menu items.

Staff Directed

As important as table top, single service, and condiment items are to the image portrayed by a foodservice operation, the nonfood items provided for staff use are

HI-TECH PURCHASING (17.1)

Low-Tech, Hi-Tech, and Environmentally Friendly

The hospitality industry has many creative and responsible members. In March 2006, Starbucks introduced a new disposable cup containing 10 percent postconsumer recycled content. After much research, tests, and a series of focus groups, two different environmental and economic improvements were implemented: the use of reusable cups (low-tech), and the development of a new, environmentally preferable single-use cup (high-tech).

As a result of these initiatives, Starbucks customers who bring in their own reusable cups get a discount. To address the problem of the paper cup, Starbucks challenged its suppliers to find better materials and designs for its disposable cups. A major obstacle toward a more eco-friendly paper cup was that recycled content had never before been used in direct contact with food—especially not with steaming hot beverages. In 2004, however, the suppliers won FDA approval for a new cup using 10 percent recycled paper, a first for the industry.

As the country's number-one specialty coffee retailer, Starbucks goes through a lot of cups—1.9 billion of them per year. EnvironmentalDefense.org calculates that Starbucks' move to use the new cups (with 10 percent postconsumer recycled paper) achieved the following annual environmental improvements:

Resource Savings	Equivalent to
11,300 fewer tons of wood	78,000 trees
58 billion BTUs of energy	Enough to supply 650 homes for one year
47 million gallons of wastewater	Enough to fill 70 Olympic-sized pools
3 million pounds of solid waste avoided	Enough to fill 110 garbage trucks*

Source: www.papercalculator.org

The thoughtful selection of appropriate condiments and their containers are important to all foodservice operations.

Doug Scott/AGE Fotostock America, Inc.

also instrumental in reinforcing an operation's quality and value message. The uniforms supplied to staff, as well as other front-of-the-house tools and supplies, affect guest and employee attitudes as well.

UNIFORMS   Those who understand consumer behavior would agree that a critical component for success in today's highly competitive hospitality environment is to implement a well-conceived uniform program. Doing so ensures that each employee projects an identically inviting public image. Uniform programs help to ensure that a company's employees support its desired business image. When employees wear professional uniforms, they reflect an image, or brand, that can project instant credibility to consumers.

The importance of uniforms can be easily illustrated by examining professional sports teams. Consider the loyal fans of your favorite team. Individual players on the team are traded, change teams, and eventually retire; meanwhile, fan loyalty toward "the team" remains a constant over years. Why? Because the loyalty is linked to the team's image, and a big part of the image is the team uniform, regardless of who is wearing it. In a similar manner, guests frequenting a foodservice operation come to associate the uniform with the operation, an important factor to recall in an industry where employee turnover rates can be quite high. A business' employees can change, but its uniforms can keep its customers coming back time and time again.

Few topics generate more front-of-house employee interest and concern than the uniforms they are required to wear. Uniform standards generally vary by company. In some cases, employees may be required to provide one or more uniform items (e.g., dark shoes, or khaki slacks). In other cases, employees will be supplied uniforms and are responsible for their maintenance. In still other cases, uniforms may be supplied and maintained by the employer. Regardless of the option chosen, it is important for professional buyers in hospitality to understand the laws that relate to uniform standards.

For example, under California law, an employer that requires its employees to wear uniforms is responsible for providing those uniforms and maintaining them in good repair. This means, of course, that the uniforms belong to the employer, and the company can charge the employee a reasonable deposit while the uniform is in the employee's hands.

An employee who does not return the uniform when asked will find that his employer can legally keep the deposit or deduct the cost of the uniform from the employee's last paycheck. Other state do not have similar laws, so it is best for professional buyers to understand applicable laws in each state in which their organization has operating units.

PURCHASING PROS NEED TO KNOW (17.1)

In the hospitality industry, the selection and purchase of employee uniforms can be a complex issue. In addition to evaluations of the price and quality of selected items, some additional purchase-related factors that experienced buyers must consider include:

1. **Compliance with company policies.** Company-mandated dress requirements, and thus the uniforms selected for employees, must not illegally discriminate. Issues related to male versus female dress requirements, and even company-permitted uniform variations intended to accommodate diverse religious beliefs, are among the compliance issues to be considered by buyers prior to their selection of specific employee uniforms.

2. **Guest impressions and expectations.** The employee uniform selected by buyers sends an important and distinct message about the image of the operation. Consider, for example, the different dining expectations you would have as a customer if you were greeted by a hostess dressed in a tuxedo shirt and formal jacket versus being greeted by the same employee dressed in a polo-type shirt and khaki pants.

3. **Modesty.** A professional image extends to issues of conservatism in dress. Because of differences in employees' height, weight, and even body shape, buyers must carefully consider potential employee concerns regarding the appropriateness of selected uniform components.

4. **Safety.** Uniforms that look good on employees are certainly desirable, but the uniforms must be functional as well. All uniform selections must be considered for their ability to contribute to worker safety. This means avoiding uniform components that restrict movement, consist of materials that could get caught in operating equipment or machinery, or could constitute a hazard.

5. **Ease of Care.** Where employees will be responsible for the cleaning and maintenance of their own uniforms, careful consideration must be given to the issue of fabric care. Not all employees possess the knowledge or laundering equipment necessary to properly care for some uniform fabrics, and this limitation is always considered by experienced buyers. In cases where employees will maintain their own uniforms, easy-care fabrics, such as those that are easily washable and resist wrinkling, are highly desirable materials for uniform construction.

On-the-Job Challenges in Purchasing (17.1)

"I'm just telling you, if you want a mutiny on your hands, go ahead and pick JR3501," said Jenny Lopez.

Jenny was talking to Max Schnelling, the new manager of the 50 Yard Line Steak House restaurant. Max had been recently hired by the restaurant's owners to update the successful operation's menu and dining room "feel." As part of that process, Max had asked Jenny, the restaurant's dining room manager, her thoughts about his choice of new staff uniforms. Max liked item JR3501, featured prominently in his chosen uniform vendor's new spring catalogue.

Jenny, however, truly hated the "look" Max was proposing and was convinced her dining room staff would hate it as well.

Case Study Questions

Assume that you are Max:

1. What input do you feel staff should have in decisions such as the uniforms they will wear?

2. How important do you feel Jenny's support would be in the successful implementation of a change in employee uniforms?

3. What steps could you take to help enlist Jenny's support yet still implement the changes you feel are best for the restaurant?

Professional uniforms help enhance the image of an entire operation.

© Dave Bartruff/Corbis

Ashtrays	Ramekins	Salsa bowls
Sauce cups	Bread baskets	Bud vases
Tabletop butter warmers	Individual coffee and tea pots	Condiment holders
Cream pitchers	Tabletop napkin dispensers	Syrup dispensers
Tortilla servers	Wine service items (buckets and stands)	Menu holders

FIGURE 17.2 Miscellaneous Front-of-House Service-Related Items

OTHER STAFF SUPPLIES   In addition to uniforms, the other significant items provided to front-of-house employees are those related to one or more of the following activities:

- *Recording guest orders.*   These include guest checks, paper, and pens or pencils and, increasingly, handheld recording order devices.
- *Serving guests.*   These supplies include such items as serving trays, jack stands, and miscellaneous dishware and meal service items (see Figure 17.2).
- *Collection of payment.*   These typically include small trays or payment folders for the presentation of customer bills and the return of payment cards or change.

Some foodservice operations elect to place their facility or company logo on staff supply items. Although small, and often overlooked, these staff supplies are critical for the effective service of guests.

PURCHASING PROS NEED TO KNOW (17.2)

In the hospitality industry, big changes are taking place in the recording of guest orders and collection of guest payments. One of the most rapidly advancing areas is that of "pay-at-the-table" systems, which allow guests to pay for their meals in a manner similar to that of self-check grocery store lines. In these systems, cards are swiped, data entered, and receipts printed, all at the table.

Pay-at-the-table systems have many advantages. When guests are provided POS-interfaced devices that allow them to pay for their meals at their dining table, those tables can be turned faster. Transaction times are reduced (because servers need not make multiple trips to the table), and guests' feelings of security are enhanced (because only they are handling their payment card and/or entering their PIN number). In addition, with these systems, end-of-shift closings and tip reconciliations can be performed more quickly and payment card transaction (discount) fees may be reduced.

When combined with handheld order-taking devices, pay-at-the-table systems may quickly make servers' paper guest checks, pens, and pencils as obsolete as mechanical cash registers.

TAKEOUT PACKAGING

For most professional foodservice buyers, an understanding of the purchasing requirements for food served to diners who will eat away from the operation are crucial. This is so because of the sheer size of the **takeout** market.

The National Restaurant Association estimates that more than half of the food sold by its members is either takeout or delivery. Annual growth in the takeout market yearly exceeds that of the foodservice industry overall. The importance of this market is easy to recognize when you consider that the total takeout sales for the top five quick-service restaurants (McDonald's, Burger King, Wendy's, Subway, and Taco Bell) far exceed their dine-in sales.

It is also important that buyers recognize that takeout foods are often (but not always) sold in restaurants that offer table-service options as well. Increasingly time-pressed consumers have expanded the number of foodservice operations in which they have an interest in buying takeout products. As a result, even high-end steak and seafood houses report increased interest in takeout options related to their products. Thus, buyers may be assigned the task of selecting appropriate packaging and condiment items for takeout sold in facilities offering extensive dine-in options, as well as for the specialized and popular takeout option known in the hospitality industry as **drive-thru.**

Traditional Takeout Packaging

Takeout food is often "fast food," but not always so. Whereas fast food often implies standardized products from a chain or franchise, takeout outlets can also be small businesses serving traditional food, which can be of extremely high quality. Examples include the sandwiches sold by high-end delicatessens, home replacement meals sold by full-service restaurants, Chinese and other Asian foods, and pizza.

Takeout foods may be delivered by a restaurant to its customers. In some cases, operations are so geared to takeout and delivery customers that they provide no facilities for dining on-site. Then foodservice buyers must concern themselves with both the packaging materials in which food will be held (e.g., pizza boxes and sandwich wrapping materials), and the heating/holding devices to keep foods at the proper temperature until they are delivered. Also, certain types of food that are normally and predominately served in sit-down settings can still be packaged "to go" (based upon orders taken by telephone, fax, or Internet). In such circumstances, the nonfood packaging materials needed to ensure high-quality product delivery is of great importance.

Drive-Thru Takeout Packaging

Takeout operators are making prepared food fresher, cheaper, faster, tastier, and more convenient than ever. As a result, more consumers are asking themselves: Why do it myself? The time required for shopping, cooking, and washing dishes at home is rapidly disappearing, thus more customers elect to simply "drive-thru" and pick up their meals. As those in this industry segment know well, the drive-

---

Key Terms

Takeout   Food and beverages sold with the intent that guests will not consume them at the point of purchase. Also known as "carryout" and "grab and go."

Drive-thru   Food and beverages sold to customers who do not leave their vehicle to enter the restaurant, but rather place their orders, receive, and pay for their items at specially designated drive-thru "windows."

Internet Purchasing Assistant (17.4)

The number of paper, plastic, foam, and metal service products available to support carryout food and beverage food sales is nothing less than astounding. To view a sample of the wide variety of products developed to assist operators in serving quality takeout sandwiches, pizzas, burgers, and chicken, go to: www.foodservicedirect.com

At the home page, click on "Takeout & Pizza supplies."

Internet Purchasing Assistant (17.5)

Those foodservice buyers working in operations that do significant amounts of drive-thru or other takeout business can help themselves stay on top of major product packaging and sales trends by subscribing to *Quick Service Restaurant (QSR)* magazine. You can view its online version free at: www.qsrmagazine.com

thru segment flourishes or suffers based upon the operation's ability to fill orders accurately and, most importantly, rapidly.

By outfitting their employees with headphones, developing advanced point-of-sale systems, and installing speakers in their kitchens to improve communications, operations can dramatically improve their speed of service. Packaging materials that hold foods in top condition until customers consume them are a critical part of this segment's success or failure. In most cases, this results in the need to design menu items and select packaging materials that allow guests to eat their meals in their vehicles, and often with only one hand.

BACK-OF-HOUSE SUPPLIES

Just as professional buyers must supply front-of-house employees with the tools they need to serve products to guests, back-of-house employees, too, must be supplied the items needed to prepare products for service. The purchase of large pieces of stationary equipment is addressed in this text in Chapter 20. In this chapter, you will learn about the kitchen supplies (**small wares** and kitchen hand tools) purchased by foodservice buyers, as well as briefly examine the office supplies necessary to support an operation's basic administrative needs.

Kitchen Supplies

The kitchen and bar-related items that professional foodservice buyers must purchase to support production of their food and beverage products will depend entirely upon the needs of the operation. Clearly, the kitchen supplies needed by a

Key Term

Small wares   The collective term used to identify the pots, pans, storage, and related products used to prepare and serve foods.

Internet Purchasing Assistant (17.6)

Lincoln Wear-ever is a manufacturer of a wide range of small wear items designed exclusively for foodservice professionals. The items they make are well known and well respected. In fact, it is the rare food production facility that does not possess one or more of their many products. To see a complete listing of their offerings, go to: www.lincolnsmallwares.com

At the home page, click on the links listed under "Product Menu."

takeout pizza parlor differ from those needed by a large hospital's foodservice department. However, all buyers must be concerned with selecting quality products that enhance (not detract from) their intended use. For example, sharp knives work better, and are safer to use, than dull knives. Also, quantity concerns are important. Another example is a shortage of proper storage containers, which will increase food costs because of product deterioration from improper storage.

SMALL WARES   Small wares purchasing can be challenging simply because of the wide price range related to many items. For example, from some manufacturers, a ten-inch sauté pan could be purchased for as little as $15. Alternatively, the French-made Mauviel Cuprinox 2.5 mm 10-inch Copper Fry Pan sells, in quantity, for $189 each. Which is best? The answer, of course, is that "it depends." The point for professional buyers to remember is that the price and quality variations they will encounter when buying small wares are extremely significant. As a result, great care must be taken to carefully specify the precise quality desired before selecting product vendors for these items.

The number of small ware items available to foodservice professionals is as varied as the foods they prepare, however, and Figure 17.3 lists some broad categories of the most commonly purchased cookware and bakeware items.

KITCHEN HAND TOOLS   Like small wares, the price and quality variations when purchasing kitchen hand tools can be great, especially relative to knives, the kitchen hand tool of most importance to chefs and many other production workers.

The total number of different and specialized foodservice hand tools is extensive and ranges from the common (vegetable peelers) to the unique **(mandolines).**

FIGURE 17.3   Common Cookware/Bakeware Categories

Bain Marie pots
Frying pans
Sauté pans
Sauce pans
Stock pots
Double boilers
Baking pans
Roasting pans
Pie pans
Cake pans
Loaf pans
Sheet trays
Display pans (line/hotel/steamtable)

Key Term

Mandoline   A device used for safely and rapidly cutting vegetables such as roots, onions, potatoes, cucumbers, and the like into uniform slices of various thickness.

Bag squeezers	Garnishing tools	Meat tenderizers	Scoops	Strainers
Can openers	Ice cream dippers	Measuring tools and devices	Serving spoons	Tongs
Coring tools (vegetable)	Ladles	Mixing spoons	Skimmers	Turners/spatulas
Dishers	Mashers	Rubber spatulas	Spreaders	Whips

FIGURE 17.4   Selected Kitchen Hand Tools

Figure 17.4 lists twenty of the most popular categories of kitchen hand tools.

Experienced foodservice buyers know that, in addition to the categories listed in Figure 17.4, kitchen knives are, by far, one of the most important of kitchen hand tools. It is essential that foodservice buyers understand the construction materials and techniques used to produce quality hand knives.

KNIVES   Technically, any sharpened blade with a handle can be considered a knife. Kitchen knives come in a variety of shapes and sizes. Quality knives are forged, not stamped. A fully forged knife is a single piece of metal beaten and ground into shape in several stages involving high heat and many tons of pressure, whereas stamped knives are cut out of sheet metal.

Most good-quality knives are forged. These are more expensive than stamped items, but considered by professionals to be well worth the price. Forged knives are stronger tools because forged metal is worked more than stamped is; this means the metal is finer-grained and sturdier. Quality knives have a sharp blade; however, other parts of the knife are equally important. Figure 17.5 shows the main parts of a typical "chef's" knife.

A. The "tip," or "point," of the knife is helpful for scoring shallow cuts and is used for piercing. Care must be taken, however, because abuse can result in breakage of this somewhat delicate part.
B. The "spine" is the opposite part of the blade, or the un top. The spine, tapered thicker than the blade, adds heft. It is used primarily to push chopped items around a cutting surface.
C. The "bolster" gives the blade weight, balance, and (most importantly!) keeps fingers from slipping onto the blade. Bolsters are found only on forged knives, not on stamped knives. It is one of the important elements designating a quality knife. Bolsters that extend the full length of the blade are best.
D. The "heel" is used for chopping small bones and for cutting through tough items that involve using weight or force.
E. The "rivets" (binding posts) affix and secure the handle to the blade. If visible, they should be completely flush with the handle's surface so that food cannot be trapped and create a food-borne illness hazard.
F. The handle should be sturdy and easy to grip. Handles can be made of wood, metal, or synthetic material. Some synthetic materials are a better choice than wood or metal because they can withstand high temperatures,

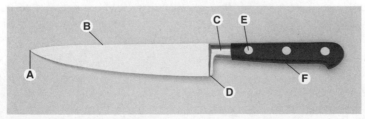

FIGURE 17.5   Basic Knife Parts
Dave King © Dorling Kindersley

Quality knives allow staff to work safer and more productively.

Ian O'Leary © Dorling Kindersley

are dishwasher safe, and can provide better friction for grip. For commercial use, water-resistant handles are best. If used, wood handles must be well sealed and may require periodic oiling.

In addition to the knife parts listed in Figure 17.5, the **tang** should also be mentioned.

In cheaper, lower-quality knives, this part of the knife is often a cost shortcut because it is not always visible. In quality knives, the tang usually extends all, or nearly all, the way to the butt (end) of the handle. The tang is important for knife balance and to ensure that the blade will not break off the handle during heavy or prolonged use.

As important as how knives are made is the material from which they are made. High-carbon steel (also called cutlery steel) is considered to be the best steel from which to make knife blades, but is not widely available. Professionals generally agree that this is the best metal used for cutlery because it holds an excellent edge and is quite easy to sharpen. It is somewhat brittle, however, and can break when dropped. Also, it has a tendency to rust if it is not dried thoroughly after use. Lastly, because of steel's reaction to acids and alkalis in foods such as tomatoes and citrus fruits, the knives discolor easily (although this does not affect the other good qualities of this type of knife).

Unlike carbon steel, stainless steel blades do not discolor or rust. This metal alloy is so hard that it strongly resists sharpening. Although it remains sharp longer, once it loses its edge it is no longer useful. Recent advances in technology have produced some never-need-sharpening knives that do hold up for many years. Knives in this class almost always lack the quality, balance, and feel of good quality knives. They remain a viable alternative, however, for those operators who do not wish to care for, or sharpen, their cutlery.

High-carbon stainless steel knives combine the best attributes of carbon steel and stainless steel blades. They have the toughness and ability to hold an edge and do not discolor. This alloy has become the most popular of metals used in knife construction because of its rust and stain-resistant quality. It does not hold its edge quite as well as high-carbon steel and is not quite as easy to sharpen; nevertheless, its convenience and ready availability make it the most frequently chosen knife material.

Key Term

Tang (knife)   The portion of a knife's blade that extends into the handle.

Titanium blades are made from a mold of titanium and carbides. When compared to steel, titanium is lighter, is more wear resistant, and holds its edge longer. The titanium blade is more flexible than steel and works best for knives used for tasks such as boning and filleting. Titanium-coated, or titanium-edged, knives do not have the same quality as those made wholly of titanium or titanium and alloys and have a relatively short useful life span, because the edge hardness is usually lost after only a few sharpenings.

Ceramic knife blades are both strong and brittle. They are stronger than steel and have an edge that can be significantly thinner than steel. This makes cutting easier, and the edge can last significantly longer with proper care. Because of their brittleness relative to steel, ceramic knives are best used for slicing (not chopping) because they can be made very thin and with a very sharp edge. Because of the lightness of ceramics, they do not have the heft expected of a metal knife. Sharpening of this knife blade is done using diamond hones. Although much more delicate than steel knives, they tend to hold their edge up to 10 times longer. Once the blades have dulled, however, they must be sharpened by a professional.

Because steel-bladed knives are the most commonly encountered by foodservice buyers, it is important to know the difference between **hollow ground** and **taper ground** knives.

Hollow ground blades are manufactured using a process that fuses two separate pieces of metal together. After the pieces are fused, a beveled blade edge is created. Although these blades often have very sharp edges, the blade lacks the balance and longevity of a taper ground blade. Hollow ground blades are most often found on knives that are used less frequently.

Taper ground knife blades are manufactured with a single sheet of metal and have been ground so that they taper smoothly from the spine to the cutting edge. The taper ground knife is a more stable item due to the rigid structure of a finely tapered, single sheet of metal. Thus, the taper ground blade is made to withstand

Internet Purchasing Assistant (17.7)

Few items elicit the passion among food production professionals as do knives. From the chefs who bring their own knives to work daily, to the commercial restaurant employee who has a favorite knife "hidden" in the kitchen, there is no doubt production personnel understand the importance of working with quality knives. Although several companies produce outstanding knives, one of the most respected and well known is J. A. Henckels. The history of the Zwilling/J. A. Henckels brand began in 1731 (under the Gemini star sign). It was in that year that knife-maker Peter Henckels from Solingen (Germany) registered the "Twin" symbol as his trademark with the Cutlers' Guild of Solingen. This symbol, which is now well known by foodservice workers all over the globe, is thus one of the oldest trademarks in the world. To view their quality cutlery online, go to: www.zwilling.com

Key Terms

Hollow ground (knife)   A knife blade that is made using a process that fuses two separate pieces of stamped metal together, which is then ground to create a beveled edge.

Taper ground (knife)   A knife blade that is manufactured with a single sheet of metal that is ground (tapered) from spine to cutting edge.

more cutting action as it cuts cleanly through a variety of foods and food textures when slicing or chopping. This type of blade is most often desired on knives that are intended for heavy usage.

The purchase of cutting boards is closely related to that of knives. Wooden or polyethylene cutting boards minimize resistance against the edge of a knife and thus help maintain its sharpness. Ceramic, stone, metal, or other too-hard plastic surfaces can quickly dull a knife's sharp edge. Regardless of the cutting board material chosen, it must be approved by local health inspection authorities and be easy to sanitize. Plastic cutting boards can go in the dishwasher; wood boards should be carefully washed by hand, because thorough washing and air-drying diminish the likelihood of germs remaining on the surface. Controversies around which is better (wood or plastic) have been somewhat inconclusive. In all cases, users should clean the boards well after use, let them air-dry thoroughly, and store them in a well-ventilated area.

Office Supplies

Most hospitality buyers tend to minimize the importance of office supplies. In the past, that certainly made sense. If a facility could secure pads of paper, pens, or pencils and, perhaps, adding machine tape, the needs of the "office" were essentially met. Contrast that to today's situation, however, and you can readily see the importance of securing a steady and cost-effective supply of printer ink cartridges, paper, miscellaneous writing supplies, furniture, copy services, and even computer terminals (to name only a few items). Although small in the dollar amount needed to create them, foodservice activities generate a tremendous

---

THE SUPPLIER'S SIDE (17.1)

"Insider" Tips on Purchasing: From the Supplier's Perspective

Buyer's Question: Our production people always complain about dull knives, but won't sharpening knives too frequently wear them out early?

Supplier's Answer: Knife edges should be regularly realigned using a butcher's steel, or a device similar to it, to keep the knife sharp and safe. A sharp knife is safer because of the effortless way in which it does your bidding; accidents can occur with dull knives because of the extra effort that it takes to push the blade through the food and the slipping that can occur. Sharp knifes will actually last longer than dull ones.

Buyer's Question: Should we sharpen our knives in-house?

Supplier's Answer: Sharpen? Probably not. It really takes an expert to do it right. But "steeling" your knives? Absolutely. All that takes is a few slow, easy strokes, alternating sides of the blade while holding the edge at about a 20-degree angle from the steel. The secret is to be gentle; don't push too hard.

Buyer's Question: If knives are "steeled" regularly, do they ever need sharpening?

Supplier's Answer: Yes, they will. A steel ideally removes only a minimal amount of metal from the edge. Over a period of time, however, perhaps six months or so, enough metal is removed that the edge requires sharpening by grinding.

Buyer's Question: When that happens, can we just use one of those electric knife-sharpening grinding wheels sold in home kitchen supply shops?

Supplier's Answer: Don't even think about it! Electronic sharpeners at preset angles, and "rolling" sharpeners, should not be used because they usually are made of ceramic or other hard substances that will remove too much metal. They shorten the life of your knife and may create hot spots, indicated by bluing marks, that remove the temper from the blade, making it difficult to keep sharp. Find a reputable sharpening service that can sharpen and repair your knives as needed.

Internet Purchasing Assistant (17.8)

Even fairly small hospitality operations can use significant dollar amounts of office-related supplies and take advantage of discount programs offered to businesses. Most national purveyors of office supplies offer these programs. To review one such program, go to: www.staples.com
    At the home page:

1. Scroll down and click on "20 or More Employees."
2. Then click on "Staples Business Advantage."

amount of paper and reports, and an appropriate source of the supplies and tools needed to support those activities must be ensured. In most cases, this can be easily accomplished by establishing an account with one or more local office supply vendors.

CLEANING SUPPLIES

In many respects the purchasing of appropriate cleaning supplies, including the tools employees use for cleaning and the chemicals that help them do their jobs more effectively, would seem to be very straightforward. In many regards, that is the case. As you learned in Chapter 3, however, those laws enacted at the federal, state, and local levels directly affect many aspects of hospitality purchasing. When making purchasing decisions in the area of cleaning supplies, professional buyers must be aware of the Occupational Safety and Health Act (OSHA) requirements that affect those decisions.

It is important to understand that the main purpose of the OSHA is to help ensure safe and healthful working conditions. As a result, OSHA is very aggressive in enforcing the rights of workers. Every hospitality operation is legally required to comply with the extensive safety practices, equipment specifications, and employee communication procedures mandated by OSHA. As a buyer, your interaction with OSHA can best be viewed as that of two partners working toward the same goal.

Thus, OSHA activities will help ensure that you:

• Provide a safe workplace for employees by complying with OSHA safety and health standards.
• Provide workers only with tools and equipment to do their jobs that meet OSHA specifications for health and safety.
• Establish training programs for employees who use hazardous chemicals.

Although there are other OSHA requirements (e.g., businesses must report to OSHA within 48 hours any work site accident that results in a fatality or requires the hospitalization of five or more employees, and must maintain on-site records of work-related injuries or illnesses), a buyer's most significant concerns relate to OSHA-approved tools and chemicals.

Before we examine cleaning tools and chemicals in detail, however, it is important for all managers to understand that OSHA has inspectors assigned to monitor the safety-related efforts of businesses. These inspectors are allowed to visit your business to ensure your compliance with their regulations. When initially developed, few businesses viewed OSHA as a partner in their worker safety efforts. Today, astute managers recognize that compliance with OSHA standards results in fewer accidents, lower insurance costs, and a healthier workforce.

FIGURE 17.6 OSHA Recommendations for Garbage Removal

Source: www.osha.gov/SLTC/ youth/restaurant/ cleanup_strains.html

- **Reduce** lifting during garbage-removal tasks by using garbage-handling bags with wheels or garbage cans with wheels for garbage collection whenever possible.
- **Handling carts** have a frame with one side open to allow for easy disposal of garbage without reaching into and pulling bags up and out. The bags should be able to slide off the cart without lifting.
- **Limit** the size and weight of these bags and provide handles to further decrease lifting hazards.
- **Use** garbage cans that have a frame versus a solid can to promote ease of emptying. This will prevent plastic bag liners from sticking to the inside of the can. If the garbage bag gets stuck in the can, you must lift a lot more weight to release the vacuum than just the weight of the garbage.
- **Use** anticling products that can be applied to the inside of your garbage can to prevent the plastic bag from sticking to the inside of the can.
- **Limit** the size of garbage containers to limit the weight of the load employees must lift and dump.
- **Place** receptacles in unobstructed and easy-to-reach places.
- **Install** dumpsters at or below grade level to minimize required lifting.

Tools

In many cases, the cleaning tools needed by back-of (and front-of) house employees are readily available from a variety of vendors and may be purchased alongside various food products offered by those vendors. Thus, for example, scrub brushes, mops, mop buckets, griddle bricks, scrapers, and cleaning cloths of all types are simply "specified" in the same manner as any other item and then purchased as needed. In other cases, however, consideration of OSHA requirements regarding cleaning tools and equipment is very important. For example, consider Figure 17.6, which details the OSHA recommendations for the task of garbage removal. As you review the following information, consider the number of areas in which the recommendation would likely influence a professional buyer's decision to select one cleaning tool or product rather than another.

Suppliers may (or may not) provide adequate information when advertising their items. When in doubt, however, it is the job of a professional buyer to ensure that, if an OSHA standard exists for it, any cleaning tool purchased meets or exceeds the standard or recommendation.

Chemicals

The number of chemical compounds needed to ensure clean and healthful kitchen facilities are significant, and these may be purchased from full-service food vendors or companies that specialize in chemical supply. In either case, buyers should recognize that this is another area of purchasing that OSHA heavily influences. This is so primarily because of the requirement that **Material Safety Data Sheets (MSDS)** for each chemical product encountered be made readily available to all workers prior to their exposure to, or use of, the chemical.

Key Term

Material Safety Data Sheet (MSDS)   A written statement describing the potential hazards of, and best ways to handle, a chemical or toxic substance. An MSDS is provided by the manufacturer of the chemical or toxic substance to the buyer of the product and must be made available in a place where it is easily accessible to those who will actually use the product.

Acquiring an OSHA-approved MSDS for each cleaning product purchased is an important responsibility of all professional hospitality buyers.

Vincent P. Walter/Pearson Education/PH College

Currently, OSHA's requirements regarding MSDSs are that, for each chemical sold, its MSDS must address:

- The material's identity, including its chemical and common names.
- Hazardous ingredients contained in the product (even in parts as small as 1 percent).
- Cancer-causing ingredients (even in parts as small as 0.1 percent).
- A list of physical and chemical hazards and product characteristics (e.g., if the product is flammable, explosive, or corrosive).
- A list of known health hazards, including:
    Acute effects, such as burns or unconsciousness, that occur immediately.
    Chronic effects, such as allergic sensitization, skin problems, or respiratory disease, which build up over a period of time.
- If the material is a known carcinogen.
- Limits to which a worker can be exposed, specific target organs likely to sustain damage, and medical problems that can be aggravated by exposure.
- Precautions and safety equipment and emergency and first aid procedures.
- Specific fire-fighting information.
- Precautions for safe handling and use, including personal hygiene.
- Identity of the organization responsible for creating the MSDS, date of its issue, and emergency contact phone number.

It is important for buyers to recognize that it is part of their professional responsibility to ensure that employees who may be exposed to hazardous chemi-

On-the-Job Challenges in Purchasing (17.2)

Carlos Magana is a newly hired Portuguese-speaking custodian working in a health-care facility kitchen. Carlos is from Brazil and is an outstanding worker. Bert LaColle, the facilities purchasing director, is quite upset. "If you are going to hire non-English-speaking staff, I need to know about it," said Bert to Thomas, the facility's director of human resources.

"Why are you so upset?" asked Thomas, "Carlos is a great worker. He'll do fine."

Assume that Bert knew part of Carlos' job included cleaning kitchen floor tiles with a powerful grout cleaner.

Case Study Questions

1. What is one OSHA-related concern Bert might have related to the hiring of Carlos? How could that concern be adequately addressed?
2. Whose responsibility do you believe it is to ensure that Carlos gets the information and training he needs prior to using the powerful grout cleaning chemical that is a necessary part of his cleaning tasks?

cals have access to the protective information they need prior to using the chemical. This can be a challenge when buying for facilities that employ large numbers of employees, many of whom do not speak or read English. Despite the challenges, however, providing such information is both the right thing to do and the legal thing to do. In this regard, experienced professional buyers know that their chemical suppliers can be a great asset in complying with the letter and spirit of the law.

Purchasing Resources on the Internet

In addition to the Web sites referenced in this chapter's "Internet Purchasing Assistant" feature, the following sites provide detailed information to enhance your purchasing knowledge and skills.

Purchasing Resources on the Internet

Site	Information About
www.bryanchina.com	Dinnerware
www.baccarat.com	French crystal
www.waterford.com	Irish crystal
www.onlinestainless.com	Flatware
www.dartcontainer.com	Single-use foodservice products
www.nationalmenuboard.com	Drive-thru and other menu boards
www.ntnwireless.com	Electronic ordering systems
www.don.com	Small wares and cookware
www.vollrathco.com	Cookware
www.mauviel.com	Copper-clad cookware
www.kikuichi.net	Carbon steel knives (Japanese)
www.cadcutlery.com	Forschner brand stamped blade knives
www.gunterwilhelm.com	Innovative chef's knives
www.officemax.com	Office supplies, furniture, and technology
www.3mfoodservice.com	Cleaning and other supplies
www.ecolab.com	Cleaning and sanitizing chemicals

Key Terms

table top (items) 422	glaze 424	drive-thru 432	taper ground
single service	crystal 425	small wares 433	(knife) 437
(items) 422	cutlery 425	mandoline 434	Material Safety Data
cost per use 423	gauge (stainless	tang (knife) 436	Sheet (MSDS) 440
ceramic 424	steel) 426	hollow ground	
porcelain 424	takeout 432	(knife) 437	

Think It Through

1. Some foodservice operations purchase logo items such as flatware and dishware despite the additional costs of doing so. As a professional buyer, what might be other drawbacks to purchasing such items? What might be some purchasing advantages to doing so?

2. Although buying one standard glass size in large quantity is most often the least costly approach, bartenders and bar managers tend to want many different glass shapes and sizes to best market the products they sell. Assume you were the individual responsible for making glass-purchasing deci-

sions for a very large, and busy, foodservice operation that sold a significant amount of alcoholic beverages. What factors would you consider as you sought to determine the "optimum" number of different glass types to use when serving beverages to your customers?

3. Food service operations that rely on carryout sales for a large portion of their business can face difficult decisions when developing service standards for their dine-in customers. As a professional buyer, what specific challenges exist in seeking service items (dishware, glassware, and flatware) that can cost-effectively service both takeout and dine-in guests?

4. Assume you were responsible for making the cutlery (knives) purchasing decision for a ten-unit steakhouse chain. The units will need twenty to forty back-of-house production knives of various sizes and purposes per facility. Assume you must choose between a vendor that offers inexpensive stainless steel products and one that sells more expensive high-carbon stainless steel alternatives. What key factors would affect your decision to select one vendor over the other?

5. Buyers in hospitality can play an important part in ensuring that workers using chemicals and other cleaning supplies understand the hazards associated with using those products. Assume you were one of the buyers in a large hotel franchised by a company such as Hilton or Marriott. Assume also that you knew there were many employees of different nationalities working for your company (in a cleaning capacity), many of whom you believe cannot read English. In such a case, what do you believe would be your responsibility to communicate to them the information contained in a MSDS? How could that be done?

Team Fun

For this exercise, assume that each team consists of individuals responsible for helping to open the *Wok on the Wild Side*, an Asian-themed restaurant. Although the restaurant will have a small dining room, it is estimated that 75 percent of the business will consist of "takeout" orders to be consumed away from the facility.

At *Wok on the Wild Side*, customers will proceed through a "cafeteria-style" line, making their selections from a wide range of freshly prepared foods and soups. The items are portioned into takeout-style containers by uniformed servers and are then paid for at a cashier's station located at the line's end.

Because the majority of diners will be taking their food out of the facility, the decision has been made to use plastic flatware for all customers.

1. The assignment of the first team is to research plastic flatware options with a focus on which specific flatware items (utensils) should be made available, in which color, and at what quality level.

2. The assignment of the second team is to consider the alternative of "prepacking" items in groups rather than individually, and what those packages should consist of.

3. The assignment of the third team is to consider what, if any, differences should exist in the number, type, and packaging of flatware items provided to in-facility diners versus those who carry out their selections.

Each team should be prepared to present and discuss their findings and conclusions.

18

Procurement for Lodging Facilities

In This Chapter

Selecting the specific information needed by buyers who purchase products and services in the lodging segment of the hospitality industry is difficult simply because of the wide variation in lodging facilities. The inexpensive, select-service motel located at the intersection of an interstate highway bears, in many ways, little resemblance to the four- or five-star resort hotel. Despite the significant differences, however, there are common elements to most lodging facilities, and those elements will be examined in this chapter.

Regardless of their property's style, price, or location, all buyers for lodging facilities must select those room supplies provided to overnight guests. For example, all lodging facilities provide bedding items for guest rooms. In addition, the bath area of a guest room will contain items consistent with the type of lodging product offered. Depending upon the size and features offered by the hotel, additional areas of a guest room might include whirlpool tubs, parlors, and patios. In many cases, these additional areas will require the purchase of special guest supplies.

In addition to the products buyers select, in most lodging facilities, guest rooms will also require services. Some of these services, such as heat, power, water, and communication services, are addressed elsewhere in this book. Those guest services that will be examined in this chapter include in-room entertainment, Internet connections, and valet (laundry/dry cleaning) services.

Many, hotels provide extensive public areas for their guests' enjoyment. Typically, these include open-to-all-guests areas such as swimming pools, spas or hot tubs, fitness centers, and more recently, business centers. Some of the unique aspects of purchasing for these areas are included in this chapter.

In Chapter 17, you learned that hospitality buyers often must select items that allow staff members to better do their jobs. The same is true of those who purchase for lodging facilities. All hotel departments purchase department-specific goods and services, but staff members in the major hotel departments of Sales and Marketing, Convention Services, and the Front Desk all have very special purchasing needs that must be addressed. Sales and Marketing staff must maintain records of what, and to whom, sales have been made. Today's Convention Services staff assists guests with very sophisticated equipment needs, and Front Desk staff require specialized items for guests as well as for themselves. Thus, the unique purchasing needs of these three important areas conclude this chapter.

■ ■ ■

Outline

Guest Room Supplies
   Sleeping Area
      Beds
      Bedding

GUEST ROOM SUPPLIES

In the hospitality industry, it has been said that, "when the guest is sleeping, all hotel rooms look the same." This tongue-in-cheek comment is true. However, it reinforces the need to enhance guest value by ensuring that those items the guest looks at, touches, and smells when in a guest room help enhance the overall value perception of that guest's lodging experience.

One characteristic all quality lodging facilities should share is that of providing a safe and comfortable bed to their guests. From very modest bedding to the "Heavenly Bed" that has become a large part of the Westin hotel's marketing program, buyers for lodging facilities would agree that a comfortable bed is critical to guest satisfaction. As a result, the beds (mattresses) and bedding (sheets, blankets, and pillows) chosen by a hotel are of critical importance.

In a guest room's bath area, two major categories of supplies are purchased: (1) towels, hand cloths, washcloths, and related items used for bathing (**terry cloth** products); and (2) single-use items (**in-room amenities**) provided to guests. Typically, these amenities include items such as soaps, shampoos, and lotions.

In addition to those items in sleeping and bath areas, a wide variety of additional in-room items are commonly provided to guests. These will vary based upon the service levels of the hotel and the average prices charged per room. Those who buy for lodging facilities must know as much about their special products as do those buyers who purchase food. Manufacturers of products can often name or define their product offerings in ways that can be confusing to unsophisticated buyers. Thus, knowledgeable purchasing professionals know they must take the time to fully understand the industry terminology and standards used when buying guest room supplies.

Sleeping Area

In most hotel guest rooms, the bed is not only the most important item provided to guests; it is the focal point for the entire room. To examine this important guest room feature, it is helpful to distinguish between a bed's major components (box spring and mattress) and the "bedding" (sheets, pillows, and coverings) that, together, comprise the item guests commonly refer to as the "bed."

BEDS The typical hotel bed consists of a metal or wooden frame holding a **box spring.** A mattress is then placed on top of the box spring to form the bed.

In the U.S. hospitality industry, many companies manufacture box springs and mattresses; however, the Big S's—Simmons, Serta, and Sealy—dominate the market.

Regardless of manufacturer, it is important to understand that coils form the heart, or center, of most box springs and mattresses purchased by lodging facility buyers. The manufacturing of bedding coils is a highly specialized process. Interestingly, the overwhelming majority of mattress manufacturers (including, with only a few product exceptions, the Big S's) buy their coils from the same company (Leggett and Platt). Mattresses have components in addition to coils. Experienced buyers know that each component adds to (or detracts from!) the quality of the final mattress product.

These components include

Wires and coils: Coil counts (the number of coils used to build the mattress), and the gauge (thickness) of the metal used to make the coils can vary greatly between different mattress products. The specifications of these items are one important quality consideration. The traditional coil design used in hotel mattresses is a wire-tied inner spring mattress (basically one continuous coil). A second, more expensive type is a pocketed coil, in which each coil, wrapped in a resilient fabric, reacts to pressure independently. Coils will be tied (connected) to each other with a border wire that keeps the

---

Key Terms

Terry cloth A cotton or cotton blend fabric with loops designed to be soft and absorb large amounts of water. It is manufactured by weaving or knitting the fabric. Also known as terrycloth, looped terry, or toweling.

In-room amenities Hotel industry jargon for the single-use items such as soaps, shampoos, conditioners, sewing kits, and so on intended for guest use and provided in the room for no additional charge.

Box spring A supporting device for a bed's mattress typically built of wood and metal coils and covered with fabric.

coils in place and forms a firm edge on the side of the mattress. In many (but not all) cases, increased coil counts indicate increased mattress quality. Coil counts in the range of 600–800 for a queen-size bed would be considered common for a hotel industry mattress of that size.

Pillow tops: Pillow tops are soft layers of foam (or cotton, or wool) sewn to the top of the mattress (but not the box spring). Although they are popular in upscale properties, they can add hundreds of dollars to the purchase price of mattresses. Experienced buyers understand that they consist of little more than sewn-on foam or cotton. They do add to the perceived "thickness" of a mattress, as well as to its weight.

Thickness: Increased mattress thickness is a relatively recent hotel industry fad. In fact, some Stearns and Foster mattresses (a brand owned by Sealy) measure nearly 2 feet (24 inches) thick. Most experts would agree, however, that increased thickness alone does not equal increased comfort. Common mattress thickness is in the range of 6–14 inches per unit (box spring or mattress).

Covering material: Although it may look impressive and be brightly colored, the appearance of the material used to cover a mattress (called the ticking) is actually of little importance. In a hotel setting, this material is likely to be completely covered.

Other mattress materials: Although not frequently encountered, there are different materials from which mattresses can be made. Among the most common of these are

Memory foam: These mattress brands (e.g., Tempur-Pedic) are made from viscoelastic foam and thus "form" to the body shape of the individual lying on the bed. These are comfortable, but still considered too expensive for widespread deployment in most hotels (prices in the range of $1,500 per mattress are common). This material is increasingly used as one component in thicker pillow top mattress products.

Air: Firmness in air mattresses can be controlled by a remote control operated pump, and thus theoretically by the desires of each hotel guest. When air is compressed by the weight of the individual lying on the mattress, however, the comfort levels reported are not as high as those associated with coil and foam mattresses.

Water: Waterbeds have been around for some time and have strong advocates; however, due to concerns about durability, these are rarely used in the hospitality industry.

After considering the needs of the individual property, and the quality considerations important to them, buyers can produce box spring and mattress specifications to effectively solicit vendor bids on identical products. Figure 18.1 is an example of one such hotel's specification.

In the case of franchise-affiliated hotels and those operated by a chain, specifications for guest room mattresses will likely be determined by that hotel brand's managers (the franchisor).

Although most beds in guest rooms are placed on stationary frames, many hotels offer guests the option of fold-up **rollaway** beds, or beds built into pull-out sofas.

Key Term

Rollaway A bed designed to be easily moved from one location (guest room) to another.

FIGURE 18.1 Typical Box Spring and Mattress Specification

Box Spring: Specification
1. Minimum of 7" deep, within a 1/4" tolerance 2. Coil count: King—672, Queen—532 3. Coil wire: 9.5 gauge 4. Border wire: 3 gauge 5. Frame: Double wood frame 6. Insulator: 3 fiber pads 7. Cover: Nonskid top-ticking must match mattress
Mattress: Specification
1. Minimum of 9" deep, within a 1/4" tolerance 2. Coil count: King—992, Queen—800 3. Coil wire: 15 gauge 4. Border wire: 6 gauge 5. Insulator: 1/4" synthetic fiber 6. Cover: 3/8" synthetic fiber insulator + 1/2" foam + 3/8" foam + 1/4" synthetic fiber + 1/2" foam layers to achieve required height

Mattresses for these products must be built differently (from foam and fabric only, no coils) because they are designed to be folded between uses.

BEDDING Like box springs and mattresses, the bedding used by a lodging facility will be determined in large part by the quality level the lodging property wishes to provide for its guests. Bedding in use in the industry is varied, but consists of the following layers, starting from the top surface of the mattress:

1. Mattress pads
2. Sheets and pillowcases
3. Blankets
4. Bedspreads or variations
5. Pillows

Internet Purchasing Assistant (18.1)

Although there are many box spring and mattress manufacturers, Serta is one of the largest. To learn more about this company and their product lines, go to: www.serta.com

Mattress Pads The purpose of a mattress pad is to provide a moisture barrier between the outer fabric cover of the mattress and its interior fillings. Mattress pads are in use at most lodging facilities to minimize the potential damage to mattress fabric from liquid absorption (e.g., from spilled beverages, vomit, or urine), as well as the stains and odor that could result from these accidents.

The best quality mattress pads consist of one-piece construction (seams could allow liquid to leak through the pad material and onto the mattress). The pads should be machine washable and dryable. Fillers for mattress pads should be of high quality materials with the top surface being absorbent and the bottom surface (that touching the mattress) being moisture resistant. Foam mattress pads should never be selected for commercial use.

Sheets and Pillowcases   Hotel sheets are used to provide guests with a "next to body" fabric that is easily cleaned. Typically, one sheet (called the "bottom" sheet) is placed directly over the mattress pad. This sheet may be manufactured to fit tightly to the mattress (if so, it is known as a "fitted" sheet), or simply to lie flat on the mattress (a "flat" sheet). In addition to the bottom sheet, and as directed by the facility's housekeeping managers, room attendants place one or more additional "top" sheets on the bed to separate the guest's body from the bed's blankets and/or bedspreads (which most often are not washed between each guest's use).

Because they come in direct contact with the guest's body, hotels consider the quality of the sheets they purchase to be of high importance. Most sheets are made from cotton or cotton/polyester blends, although satin and silk sheets are also common.

In all cases, however, sheets that are soft to the touch yet durable are considered to be of best quality. Inexperienced buyers often believe that **thread count** is a direct indicator of sheet quality.

Some sheet manufacturers actually take advantage of this misconception by advertising sheet thread count numbers as if they were directly related to product quality. They do so because the perception of some buyers is that the higher the thread count, the higher the quality and softer the sheet. In reality, this is not always the case. Many factors, including origin, weave, and cotton quality, add to the superiority (and cost) of a sheet. As a result, experienced buyers look for particular sheet features, know which features they can afford, and then make the smart buy by getting the most sheet for their money.

For lodging facility buyers, sheet quality will be determined, in part, by each of the following characteristics:

Size: Sheets that are too small for the beds upon which they are used may cost less per unit, but will likely frustrate both room attendants who must make the beds and guests. As a result, buyers for lodging facilities must specify sheet size carefully (because one of the most evident indicators that a manufacturer is cutting costs is the size of the sheet). Although some variance is allowable, a flat sheet for a king-size bed should be 118 inches wide and 118 inches long. A generous queen-size flat sheet will be 98 inches wide by 118 long. These dimensions allow for a good-size drop on all three sides (so the sheet stays tucked into the space between the mattress and box spring).

Yarn size and ply: Yarn size refers to the thickness of the yarn used to make the sheet fabric. The finer the yarn, the more of them that will fit into a square inch, thus increasing the material's thread count. Ply refers to the number of individual yarns used to make a strand. Some single-ply yarn can feel scratchy. If two-ply yarn is used, the finished sheet will have twice the thread count and will be softer.

Cotton: Experienced lodging facility buyers agree that Egyptian cotton is the standard against which all cotton sheets are measured. Yet, there are up

---

Key Term

Thread count   The number of horizontal (weft) and vertical threads (warp) in a single square inch of sheet material.

to thirty grades of Egyptian cotton. Also, not all sheets with Egyptian cotton actually contain 100 percent of it. The best sheets are 100 percent cotton. The very best are 100 percent Egyptian cotton. Cotton wicks away moisture from the body, keeping the sleeper comfortable and not clammy. Although polyester and polyester/cotton blended sheets will wear like iron, and never need to be ironed, they often can feel as hard as iron!

Experts generally classify cottons into four main types with many categories in each type. These classifications are based on appearance and staple length (extra-long, long, medium, and short): the longer the staple, the finer the fabric. Approximately 90 percent of the world's cotton crop is American Upland cotton. This medium-to-long fiber cotton is grown in most cotton-producing countries. With fibers 7/8-inch to 1 1/4-inch long, however, it is not suited for "exceptional" sheets. Egyptian cotton, in contrast, is a long staple variety. It has extra-long and fine silky fibers about 1 1/2-inch long. Growers in the United States have developed Egyptian varieties known as Pima cottons. These are preferable for sheets, both for their silky softness and durability.

Origin: Most experts agree that for the very best quality, **linen** buyers choose linens that are made in European countries such as Italy, Germany, and Sweden. European makers typically use the highest-grade Egyptian cotton and take other quality steps developed over centuries of making linen goods.

Dye: How a sheet is dyed has a greater effect on softness than many buyers believe. For example, pigment dyes are sprayed on the surface and can give the sheet a scratchy feel. Fiber-reactive dyes are considered the best.

Combing: The combing process removes the dirt and debris that may be in the cotton fiber. When well combed, the cotton can produce a cleaner, more uniform yarn (double combing is even better).

Weave: Fabric may be weaved in a variety of styles. For sheets, percale and sateen are equally good. Percale is a closely woven, plain-weave fabric. Its high thread count gives it a soft, silk-like feel. Sateen is a weave construction that has more yarn surface on the face of the cloth than other basic weaves, giving it a softer feel and more lustrous look.

Thread Count: If each of the seven previously mentioned characteristics is identical, the higher the single ply (fiber strand) thread counts, the finer the quality of the sheet. It takes long fibers of cotton to make strong but thin threads, and it takes these silky thin threads to make high thread count fabrics. ("Burlap" would be at the other end of the spectrum, with fat fuzzy threads that can be counted with the naked eye.) The highest thread count sheets made in the United States range from 310–350, whereas European and some other sheets can go much higher (to 1,500). "Good" quality sheets start at about a 200-thread count. A high thread-count sheet, made from high-quality cotton, will noticeably increase in softness and luster after it is washed a number of times.

Blankets Blankets are an essential bedding component for hotels because they increase heat retention of those sleeping in the bed, thus resulting in lower energy expenses for heating guest rooms. In addition, blankets (like linens) serve

Key Term

Linen Technically, the products made from flax fibers; it is the commonly used and collective term for bottom sheets, top sheets, and pillowcases.

PURCHASING PROS NEED TO KNOW (18.1)

Egyptian cotton has not gained its outstanding reputation without reason. Egyptian cotton is considered the world's finest, and the following characteristics are what set Egyptian cotton apart from other natural fibers:

- The length of the fiber makes it possible to make the finest (thinnest) of yarns without sacrificing the strength of the yarn.
- The strength of the fiber makes fabrics more solid and more resistant to stress.
- Its ability to absorb liquid dyes gives fabrics made of Egyptian cotton deeper, brighter, and more resistant colors.
- It is the softest of natural fibers, truly like nothing else in the world.
- Egyptian cotton is hand picked, which guarantees the highest levels of purity.
- In addition, hand picking puts no stress on the fibers—as opposed to mechanical picking—leaving the fibers straight and intact.

These factors have resulted in Egyptian cotton being considered the best cotton in the world for sheets. Linens made of Egyptian cotton are softer, finer, and will last longer than those made from any other cotton. Also, their softness is enhanced with each washing.

---

to communicate the hotel's quality standards. Buyers can choose from a variety of blanket materials, colors, and sizes. The quality of blankets can range from those made of 100 percent Mongolian Cashmere (extremely high quality) to very low-cost polyester blend fabrics (lower quality). As is true with box springs, mattresses, and other bedding items, franchisors most often dictate blanket specifications (both the number to be supplied per room and the type) for their franchisees.

Bedspreads or Variations   The bed covering in a guest room serves a variety of purposes. It is, first and foremost, a décor item. Because it covers the bed, and because the bed is the focal point of most hotel rooms, the appearance of the bed's cover (bedspread) is of prime importance. Also, the weight and feel of a bedspread is important, because most guests believe that a bedspread that is heavier and softer reflects the best quality. Because of the importance of weight, bedspreads are sold at designated **fill** levels ranging from 4 ounces (lower quality) to 12 ounces (higher quality).

Increasingly, some lodging facilities are replacing their traditional guest room bedspreads with comforters or **duvets.**

Duvets reduce the complexity of making a bed, because they may be used to replace both the blankets and bedspread. In many cases, the cover of the duvet can be removed for ease in cleaning because they are typically constructed with three closed sides and one open side for the removal of the filler. A duvet also offers expanded decorating options because it allows the hotel to change the look of a room without the expense of purchasing a new bedspread.

Pillows   Pillows, from a guest's perspective, are perhaps the single most important bedding item. Soft, fluffy, and numerous pillows yield positive comments;

Key Terms

Fill   A measure of the density of filling in bedding such as bedspreads and comforters; usually defined as ounces per square inch or foot of goods.

Duvet   A soft, flat bag filled with down, feathers, silk, wool, or foam (in Spanish: an edredón), used as a substitute for a bedspread.

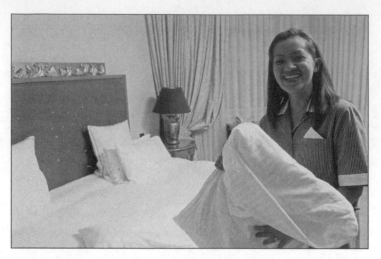

Quality bedding materials serve to enhance guests' perceptions of hotel quality.

David De Lossy/Getty Images-Photodisc

THE SUPPLIER'S SIDE (18.1)

"Insider" Tips on Purchasing: From the Supplier's Perspective

Buyer's Question: What is a "down" pillow?

Supplier's Answer: A true down pillow is made from the soft inner plumage of waterfowl such as ducks and geese. Down has numerous light, fluffy filaments extending in all directions, without a feather's quill shaft. In a pillow, down is soft yet provides support due to its ability to spring back to its original shape (known as lofting). Down is more comfortable than synthetic filling due to its ability to let moisture such as perspiration escape in a process known as wicking. Simply put, a down pillow is more comfortable than one made from any other materials.

Buyer's Question: What is a "feather" pillow?

Supplier's Answer: Feather pillows are made from feathers, the flat, two-dimensional covering of birds characterized by a pointy central shaft. Because feathers are harder than down and provide support and resilience, they are also used in items like pillows and featherbeds where additional support is preferred by some. But, if too low a "thread count" is used in a feather pillow's construction, the pointed shafts can sometimes penetrate the pillow's outer covering, causing discomfort to guests.

Buyer's Question: Why is thread count important?

Supplier's Answer: Thread count equals the number of threads per square inch of fabric. Higher thread count means a tighter weave and a softer and silkier feel to the fabric. For down and feather pillows, higher thread counts also keep the pillow's fill from getting out (or poking through) the pillow. Minimum thread counts for quality pillow coverings are 250 and higher.

Buyer's Question: What exactly is a "fill" as it relates to pillows?

Supplier's Answer: Fill can refer to two things: either fill "power" or fill "weight." Fill power is a measure of the quality of down. Once down has been sorted, cleaned, and sterilized, it's measured for fill power rating. Fill power is the number of cubic inches that a single ounce of down occupies. The very finest down has a fill power of at least 750 cubic inches per ounce, and the lowest is around 300 per ounce. Average department store comforters are often 500–550 fill power. Higher fill power ratings indicate that a single ounce of down occupies more space and is of higher quality. Higher fill power means more warmth with less weight. Higher fill power down is also fluffier in appearance. Alternatively, fill "weight" measures the *quantity* of down (not *quality*) used in a product.

	Bath towels	Hand towels	Washcloths	Bathmats
One bed	3	3	3	1
Two beds	4	4	4	1
Color	Ivory	Ivory	Ivory	Ivory
Minimum terry content	100%	100%	100%	93%
Maximum polyester	0%	0%	0%	7%
Minimum size	27" × 54"	16" × 30"	13" × 13"	20" × 30"
Minimum weight per dozen	15.0 lbs.	4.5 lbs.	1.5 lbs.	6.9 lbs.

FIGURE 18.2 Typical Terry Product Specifications

small, flat, and sparse pillows yield the opposite. Pillows may be purchased at a variety of quality levels and from a variety of construction materials. The best pillows are made from goose down and/or feathers. Polyester fiber-filled pillows are popular, as are those made from polyurethane. Pillow coverings are typically made from cotton or cotton/polyester blends. Unlike the ticking on a mattress (which is not seen by guests), the ticking on a pillow may be important to guests and thus should be reasonably attractive. Lodging industry pillows must be washable and dryable.

Bath Areas

For many travelers, their bath area is even more important than their bed. Of course, bathrooms must be kept meticulously clean. In addition, however, most hoteliers understand that the quality of terry cloth used in the bath area of their guest rooms sends an unmistakable (positive or negative!) quality message to guests.

TERRY   Terry products commonly supplied in the bath area of guest rooms include bath towels, hand towels, washcloths, bathmats, and robes. When purchasing terry products, quality levels are important, but so are the number and size of products supplied. Figure 18.2 details the terry specifications that might be established for a midpriced hotel. The number, size, and quality of the products are all factors related to the purchase specification.

Terry products are produced with two distinctive border styles: cam borders feature a plain, flat edge around the towel; dobby borders feature a terry-texture trim around the towel and may be made in a variety of patterns. Dobby borders, when used, make the towel "seem" different to guests because they are not commonly used in homes and because they take away the institutional or commercial look and feel of the item.

In the lodging industry, the most widely used, economically priced terry products are approximately 86 percent cotton and 14 percent polyester. This is a good combination because it allows the terry loops to be 100 percent cotton (for absorbency) but permits the borders to be polyester (to minimize shrinkage).

Internet Purchasing Assistant (18.2)

Although Egyptian cotton is the standard by which sheets are judged, the Turkish towel is considered the best in the world. Of course, the best Turkish towels are made from Egyptian cotton. To learn more about these unique products, go to: www.turkeyforyou.com

At the home page, click on "Culture and History," then click on "Turkish Towels."

On-the-Job Challenges in Purchasing (18.1)

I'm telling you," said Jona Walbert, executive housekeeper at the Plaza Grand Hotel, "Our robes are just too nice. I'm losing 6 to 10 dozen per week. That's costing us a lot."

"Certainly, we could buy cheaper robes . . . if you think that would be better," replied Thomas Lytle, the hotel's director of purchasing.

"I think it's because they have the Plaza Grand logo embroidered on them," offered Gail Hudgens, the hotel's rooms manager. "Take the logo off, and the guests won't take as many. I worked at another hotel and we used to have really nice lightweight cotton bathrobes in the rooms but people took them because they were lightweight and had the hotel's logo sewn into them. It cost us a fortune on an annual basis, so we changed them to heavy terry-cloth robes without the logo, and the theft dropped by 90 percent," she continued.

Case Study Questions

Assume that you are Thomas:

1. What specific guest image perception issues are in play in this situation?
2. What specific guest-relation issues and cost-related issues are in play in this situation?
3. What do you believe is the purchasing-related problem described in this scenario? How can it be solved?

SINGLE-USE ITEMS   For the majority of guest room supplies examined above, durability is an important characteristic. Most guest room **amenities,** however, are different because they are designed to be single-use items.

Guest room amenities are similar to other guest room supplies because the quality and number of such items provided conveys to guests a great deal about the quality of hotel. As a result, hoteliers and buyers must make important decisions regarding the:

- Number of guest room amenities to be supplied
- Quality of guest room amenities to be supplied

Number of Amenities   Assume that you are a guest at a hotel. When you check into your room, you survey the amenities provided in the bath area and find one very small bottle of shampoo/conditioner and one extremely small bar of soap. Although it is unlikely that you would complain about these items, contrast your experience to that of staying in another property in which, upon checking into your room, in the bath area you found the following:

- One large bar of deodorant soap (for use in the tub/shower area)
- One bar of facial soap (for use at the sink area)
- One bottle of shampoo
- One bottle of conditioner
- One bottle of body lotion
- One bottle of mouthwash
- One single-use toothbrush
- A medium-size comb (with hotel logo)
- Personal shower cap
- Sewing kit

Key Term

Amenity   Technically, any hotel feature that provides comfort, convenience, or pleasure to guests. The term, as most commonly used, refers to personal, single-use, in-room guest items. Examples include soaps, shampoos, mouthwash, shoe mitts, and sewing kits.

Internet Purchasing Assistant (18.3)

An extensive number of in-room, single-use guest amenities are available to hotel buyers. At least 100 different items are commonly available and, to view one company's very large supply of amenity products (as well as the wholesale list prices per unit of these items), go to: www.hotelsupplies-online.com

At the home page, click on "Guest Room Amenities!" to review the variety of products they offer.

- Sanitary-wrapped nail file/emery board
- Cotton shoe polish mitt
- Six-ball, sealed cotton ball package

If you are like most guests, your perception of the hotel's value would be positively affected by the sheer number of items the hotel has offered you for "free." Of course, like all amenities offered, "free" to guests does not mean "free" to the hotel. As the number of amenities offered increases, so does the cost of supplying them. As a result, the total cost of providing in-room amenities is a function of both the number of items offered, and the quality of those items.

Quality of Amenities   In some cases, the quality of a guest room amenity is established simply by its presence. Thus, for example, merely placing a bottle of single-use mouthwash in the bath area of a guest room should have a positive effect on the guest's perception of value. In other cases, however, it is the size and/or brand name of the amenity item provided that most influences guest perceptions. For example, a 2.5-ounce bar of soap will likely have a greater positive effect on guest perceptions of quality than will a ¾-ounce bar of the same brand.

In a similar manner, a bar of soap manufactured by a brand-name company (especially if the brand is perceived very highly by guests) will likely make a greater impact on guests' perceptions of value than will a bar of soap manufactured by a company with lesser perceived prestige.

Other Guest Room Supplies

In addition to beds, bedding, and single-use guest amenities, numerous other items must be purchased to maintain a hotel guest room. The actual number and desired quality levels vary by hotel brand and by the image the hotel's managers seek to project. As a result, buyers of hotel guest room supplies must become knowledgeable about a wide range of products. Figure 18.3 lists thirty of the most common in-room products and supplies hotel buyers are responsible for procuring.

Alarm clocks/radios	Condiments (coffee)	Ironing board
Ashtrays	"Do Not Disturb" door hanger	Laundry bags
Baskets/trays	Evacuation map	Matches
Blow-dryers	Glasses	Microwave ovens
Coffee cups	Guest stationary	Notepads
Coffeemaker	Hangers (skirt clip)	Pens
Coffee packets (decaffeinated)	Hangers (wooden)	Room service menus
Coffee packets (regular)	Ice buckets	Safes
Coffee trays	In-room directories	Shower curtains
Comment cards	Iron	Wastebaskets

FIGURE 18.3   Thirty Common Guest Room Supplies

Internet Purchasing Assistant (18.4)

In many respects, American manufacturers are behind their European counterparts when it comes to applying advanced technology to minibar design. American hotel companies, such as Hilton, Hyatt, and Radisson, however, are no strangers to the innovative products these companies sell. To view the offerings of one of the international leaders in minibars, go to: www.bartech.fr

At the home page:

1. Click on "International."
2. Then, click on "Products" to begin viewing this progressive company's line of electronic-scan minibar products.

In addition to the guest room supplies previously described, at least two additional guest room products must be well understood by hotel supply buyers: minibars and beverage stations.

Minibars   Hotels have long provided in-room **minibars** that allow guests the convenience of selecting alcoholic beverages, soft drinks, and snacks from in-room storage units (minibars).

Only recently, however, have advances in bar coding technology created a situation in which in-room minibar charges can be automatically added to the guest's bill. In advanced systems, the time of the transaction, as well as the selling price of the item removed, is automatically posted to the guest's **folio.**

Beverage Stations   In most cases, when hoteliers speak of in-room beverage stations, they are actually referring to their complimentary in-room coffee programs. In all but the least expensive hotel rooms, coffeemakers, regular and decaffeinated coffee (and sometimes tea), as well as the condiment packets of cream, sugar, stir sticks, and so on associated with coffee making, have become commonplace. Beverage stations can range from those that are low in cost; consisting of only a small coffeemaker and minimal coffee supplies, to very extensive coffee and other beverage product offerings. Due to the proliferation of beverage stations, those who buy hotel guest supplies should become familiar with the options and costs associated with this very popular guest room amenity.

GUEST ROOM SERVICES

In addition to the guest supplies, hotel buyers must choose some unique in-room services. Although the specific number of services and quality levels associated with each vary, most hotels commonly offer the following services:

✓ In-room entertainment
✓ Internet connection
✓ Valet

Key Terms

Minibar   Small, in-room refrigerated or unrefrigerated cabinets used to store beverages, snacks, and other items the hotel wishes to offer for sale to guests.

Folio   A detailed list of a hotel guest's room charges, as well as other charges authorized by the guest or legally imposed by the hotel.

Internet Purchasing Assistant (18.5)

American Hotel Register is the single largest supplier of products to the hotel industry. Literally, they sell almost everything. Thus, they are a quick and easy source of product information. For example, assume you wished to know about the condiment (sugar, creamer, sweeteners, and so on) packets available as you develop your own in-room coffee service program. You could quickly review a large number of alternative condiment options and prices by visiting the American Hotel Register Web site. To illustrate, go to: www.americanhotel.com

1. At the home page, click on "All 24 Product Departments."
2. Then, click on "Guest Room Supplies."
3. Next, click on "Coffee, Snacks & Beverages."
4. Next, click on "Coffee and Condiment Kits" to view this company's line of coffee condiment products.

In-Room Entertainment

On-demand, pay-per-view movie systems have long been a popular feature offered to hotel guests. Essentially, these systems offer guests the opportunity to view, at their own time preference, recently released movies. In addition, most pay-per-view providers also offer a variety of adult-oriented movies. The demand for these current and popular movies can be quite strong. Guests pay the hotel for viewing the movies. Then, at month's end, the movie provider charges the hotel based on the number of movies viewed, as well as for any equipment charges included in the hotel's pay-per-view contract.

Originally devised as video tape-based systems, today's in-room movie services are more likely to be delivered to the hotel by satellite. Additional satellite (or cable) services that can be purchased by a hotel for offering to in-room guests include

- Video-on-demand
- Music-on-demand
- Games-on-demand
- Internet access

Music, music videos, and interactive "video" games are typically accessed in the same manner as pay-per-view movies. Although games-on-demand services are very similar to pay-per-view movies (they are pay-per-play), the significant difference is the requirement for an in-room joystick, mouse, or keyboard to actually play the game. This means that the hotel must provide these electronic

Internet Purchasing Assistant (18.6)

LodgeNet is the lodging industry's largest supplier of in-room entertainment services. Founded in 1980, its customer base now includes more than 10,000 lodging properties representing more than 1.9 million hotel rooms. Clients include Best Western International, Hampton Inn, Hilton, Holiday Inn, Inter-Continental, Radisson, Ritz-Carlton, Sheraton, W Hotels, Westin, and others. For a sample of the type of movies shown to guests on a pay-per–view system, review their current movie offerings at: www.lodgenet.com

At the home page, under "Now Playing," click on "View all Videos."

High Speed Internet Access
(HSIA) is now an essential
in-room amenity at most
U.S. hotel properties.
Ryan McVay/Getty Images, Inc.-
Photodisc

devices and keep them secure in the rooms. The logistics and difficulty of doing so has made some hotels reluctant to actively offer games as an in-room amenity. As a result, buyers responsible for securing these game-activation devices must be concerned about their cost and the manner in which they will be secured.

Internet Connection

Beginning in the late 1990s, some business traveler-oriented hotels began to aggressively market in-room Internet services. The intent was to capitalize on the increasing use of the Internet by travelers of all types. Some of these efforts met with success, whereas others, the victim of the famous "dot.com" bust of 2001, were cancelled or delayed when companies offering the services failed to deliver because of defective business models. In many cases, these failures resulted because the Internet connections were designed to be delivered to hotel rooms via coaxial cable. This system of delivery was slow to catch on due to the very high cost of "rewiring" existing rooms with the proper cable type. Use of existing telephone lines to deliver the service offered some improvement; however, the explosion in the service offering began in the mid-2000s when the technology for service delivery changed to satellite. This allowed some existing in-room entertainment companies to provide Internet service, as well as many companies that already had satellite delivery experience and capacity. Today, those who purchase Internet services for hotels can choose from a large number of qualified vendors, most of whom are quite capable of providing dependable high-speed wireless Internet service to guest rooms and other areas of a hotel.

Interestingly, despite its great popularity, from the beginning, most hotel guests are reluctant to pay an extra fee for the ability to connect to the Internet. As a result, today's hotel services buyer must carefully select a vendor who will be dependable and provide Internet connectivity at a price that recognizes Internet connectivity has, in most hotels, become a "free-to-guest" amenity.

Valet

In the hotel business, the term **valet** has a dual meaning: It is used to indicate staff who, for example, park vehicles and assist guests with luggage.

Key Term

Valet A traditional term used to identify an individual who cared for the clothes of wealthy travelers.

Today the term is also used to indicate the clothes-care services offered by a hotel. Most hotel franchisors mandate that the properties in their chain offer guests 24-hour turnaround laundry and dry cleaning services. In some hotels, guest laundry and dry cleaning requests will be processed in-house, using the hotel's own laundry equipment and staff. In most cases, however, the dry cleaning and laundering of clothes is a specialized service that professional buyers out-source to an external vendor (see Chapter 19).

From the perspective of the professional buyer, although the price charged is important, it is more important that the valet service provider chosen be dependable (to return guest clothes within the necessary time period) and highly qualified (to avoid upsetting guests by damaging or losing clothes entrusted to the hotel for cleaning).

PUBLIC AREA GUEST SERVICES

In addition to those items purchased for use in guest rooms, professional hotel buyers are responsible for selecting items used in a hotel's nonguest restricted areas and **public areas.**

Restricted areas within a hotel are typically reserved for the exclusive use of guests. Examples include pools and whirlpools, fitness centers, and business centers. Public areas must be cleaned and furnished (in some cases), but restricted areas have specific purchase-related needs. As a professional hotel buyer, you should be aware of the specific needs related to:

Pools and whirlpools

Fitness centers

Business centers

Pools/Whirlpools

Hotel swimming pools are exceptionally popular despite the fact that they are typically used by only a small percentage of hotel guests. Consistently, in opinion polls regarding desirable services, travelers rank the mere presence of a swimming pool near the top of hotel amenities that influence their hotel selection decision. The legal liability resulting from accidental slipping, diving, or even drowning, however, requires that hotels address their pool (and whirlpool) area purchases with extra prudence. Hotels that have whirlpool, hot tub, or spa areas face special safety and liability concerns. Although these areas are also popular, they can be dangerous to young children, the elderly, intoxicated individuals, and those on special medications. Potential injury and accidents in pool areas include those related to:

- Falls on the pool deck due to slippery conditions or from running.
- Diving accidents caused by misjudging the pool depth.
- Drain entrapment caused by malfunctioning pumps or broken drain covers.
- Illnesses from waterborne bacteria and parasites.

As a result, buyers must take extra care when purchasing the following products related to maintaining their pool and whirlpool areas:

Chemicals: Making available the proper chemicals in the proper quantities is an important part of buyer's responsibilities. Cloudy, murky pools are

---

Key Term

Public area (hotel)   The space within a hotel that can be freely accessed by guests and visitors. Examples include lobby areas, public restrooms, corridors, and stairwells.

Swimming pools are an extremely important amenity to many travelers. Buyers play an important role in the critical task of maintaining pools properly.

Philippe Giraud © Dorling Kindersley

unattractive, are dangerous, and increase a hotel owner's potential liability in case of accident. Pools with too high a concentration of chemicals can cause burning of the swimmer's skin.

Equipment: Although the initial purchase of pool pumping and filtering equipment is likely the responsibility of a well-trained engineering technician, in many small-to-medium-size hotels, the general manager is responsible for authorizing the purchase of additional or replacement pumps, filters, drain covers, skimmers, and so on. It is critical that they understand the importance to guest safety of maintaining pool and spa pumping and filtering equipment in the very best of operating condition.

Signage: Pool and spa signage requirements may be dictated in large measure by a hotel's insurer; however, the presence of the signs must be ensured by an individual who is on the property and can monitor sign placement. Missing or poorly placed signs, or those not easily read, are potential problems that must be directly addressed by the buyer.

Safety equipment: The presence of life-saving equipment such as hooks, poles, carry boards (for use in transporting injured persons), pool divider ropes, and so on will vary based upon a pool's location, standards imposed by the hotel's franchisor, and the requirements of the hotel's liability insurance carrier. What will not vary, however, is the responsibility of the hotel's pool products buyer to ensure that these items are in place, in good repair, and readily accessible to those who will need to use them.

Internet Purchasing Assistant (18.7)

Pool and spa area signage is important in helping to reduce a hotel's legal liability in case of accidents. This remains true despite the mixed response of juries to their value (i.e., "CAUTION! NO LIFEGUARD ON DUTY and SWIM AT YOUR OWN RISK" signs are of questionable value to the high-risk toddler who is still a little fuzzy about the difference between the letter "A" and the color "blue"!).

Despite their limitations, exculpatory signs (those that indicate management does not accept responsibility) are highly recommended in pool and spa areas. To see recommendations about signage and other pool-related safety issues, go to: www.swimmingpools101.com

At the home page, click on "Pool Safety."

Furnishings: Pool furnishings such as chairs, tables, umbrellas, and benches should be made of materials that can withstand high humidity levels (indoor pools) and/or intense direct sunlight (outdoor pools) without excessive deterioration. Despite the importance of durability, however, structural sturdiness and safety must be a buyer's primary concern when purchasing pool furnishings.

Fitness Centers

Fitness or exercise centers are also a popular hotel amenity. These can range from very small workout areas to extensive spa/gym combinations. In all cases, however, those who are responsible for purchasing items to furnish these facilities must address quality and safety concerns. Purchases made for a typical fitness center include one of more of the following items:

- Treadmills
- Stair steppers
- Stationary bikes
- Free or controlled weights
- Stretching and workout accessories

Exercise rooms should also contain a towel rack for clean terry and a bin for soiled terry. Access to television or music systems is also commonly provided. In addition, a system must be in place to ensure controlled access to the fitness area. Typically this is done via the use of a functioning card reader system similar to, or the same as, that used by guests to access their guest rooms.

Business Centers

In the recent past, it was widely believed that a hotel's business center could be a significant factor in the satisfaction levels of business travelers. Although that was true, leisure travelers also seek out business centers to check their own incoming e-mails, e-mail friends and relatives about their travels, and even send their vacation snapshots and video clips home via the Internet to free up storage space on their digital cameras and telephones (for even more photos and videos!).

Like fitness centers, the furnishings of an individual hotel's business center will vary based upon the type of guests served and the number of rooms in the hotel. In most cases, however, in addition to a pleasing aesthetic design, a business center will consist of one or more:

- Personal computers (PCs) consisting of an appropriately powerful CPU (central processing unit), monitor, keyboard, and mouse. Thoughtful operators increasingly should consider making an Apple computer available as well.
- Laser quality printer
- Copy machine (a color copier is generally preferred by guests)
- Fax machine
- High-speed Internet access points (hard wired or wireless)
- Office supplies (e.g., paper, stapler, binder clips, tape, and Post-it notes).
- Wastebaskets
- Chairs and work surfaces (desks and/or tables)

LODGING STAFF SUPPLIES

You have learned about many products and services purchased for use by hotel guests. Buyers must also purchase supplies and services needed by hotel staff. A hotel's housekeeping, laundry, and maintenance departments will routinely buy literally hundreds of supply and replacement items. Also, members of the hotel's sales team and those working at its front desk area require specialized tools and supplies. Although many specialized items are used by employees in a hotel's various departments, those in the following areas merit the special attention of professional hotel buyers:

- Sales and marketing
- Convention services
- Front desk

Sales and Marketing

Employees working in a hotel's sales and marketing department use the same types of office supplies (e.g., computers, copiers, and fax machines) one would expect in any professional sales office setting. Fundamentally, the job of a hotel sales staff is to sell the property's guest rooms, meeting spaces, and food and beverage services. To do their jobs well, however, they must carefully monitor what has been sold and to whom it has been (or could be) sold. As a result, lodging facility buyers must supply sales staff with the tools they need to effectively manage the sales efforts. A variety of specialized resources are available to assist hotel professionals to do that. Essentially, these can be classified as tools that either manage sales or manage clients.

SALES MANAGEMENT   If given only a cursory examination, the process of recording who is buying a hotel's guest rooms, meeting space, and food and beverage services might appear to be a relatively easy task. As experienced hotel sales professionals know, however, in a large hotel, with many sales staff members, hundreds of guest rooms, dozens of meeting rooms, and multiple food and beverage venues, simply keeping track of who is coming to the hotel, what these guests are buying, as well as the myriad details of their stay, can be overwhelmingly complex. Fortunately, there are software tools available to help manage the process. Some such tools are built into a hotel's existing property management system (PMS), whereas in other cases, these tools must be purchased separately. Advances in this area take place rapidly; thus, it is important for professional buyers and sales and marketing department personnel to stay abreast of the technological advances that permit increased accuracy and efficiency in managing a hotel's space and guest calendars.

CLIENT MANAGEMENT   To easily understand the importance of **contact management** and the tools needed to effectively administer a hotel's sales effort, consider the case of a hotel whose largest client purchases thousands of guest room nights per year.

The company holds dozens of meetings per month at the hotel, and each year in December, it rents the hotel's ballroom on the Saturday before Christmas to hold its annual holiday party. Now, consider the surprise that would occur if it was later discovered that a new member of the hotel's sales staff had "sold" the ballroom on the Saturday before Christmas to a young couple holding their wedding reception at the hotel. The existing client will not be pleased about that sale, nor will the hotel's general manager when the client calls to complain. The cause of this problem? No one on the sales staff remembered to send a confirming contract to the existing client in time to reserve the needed space. This common example, multiplied by the number of new and returning clients that a hotel serves, illustrates the importance of contact management (and space management) software to a hotel's sales effort.

Key Term

Contact management   The process of documenting the efforts of an organization in communicating with its current and potential customers (contacts).

Internet Purchasing Assistant (18.8)

Although there are a variety of client tracking programs on the market, ACT! is, for small businesses and workgroups or divisions of larger organizations, perhaps the best known and most widely used contact and customer management program.

ACT! enables access to detailed contact and customer information. It also allows users to manage calendars and activities and to capture all customer communications. To learn about their different products designed to assist in contact (client) management, go to: www. act.com/index.cfm

At the home page, click on "Products & Solutions."

Convention Services

The convention services department in a hotel is charged with the responsibility of fulfilling the meeting space requirements of a hotel's clients. In years past, a hotel's convention services department was called upon to do little more than set up tables and chairs, place an overhead projector in a room, and perhaps adjust the sound on a portable microphone stand. Contrast that to today's convention service staff which can be called upon to provide the equipment needed to allow a client to participate in a satellite-delivered international video conference, and you can readily understand that the sophistication of audiovisual equipment that must be maintained by a hotel's convention services staff is simply remarkable. The result is a need for dependable graphic display and audio equipment, as well as advanced training programs sufficient to meet the needs of those staff who will operate this equipment.

Front Desk

For many hotel guests, the only employee encountered during their stay will be a staff member in the hotel's Front Desk area. For those employees whose primary role is checking guests in, dealing with guest questions and needs during their stays, and then checking guests out of the hotel, purchasing agents play a critical role. They must supply Front Desk staff with essential supplies related to guests and needed by the department's own staff members.

Advances in image projection and graphic display technology have greatly increased the training required of hotel Convention Services staff members.

AP Wide World Photos

On-the-Job Challenges in Purchasing (18.2)

"Don't you know how to hook it up?" asked Melissa Tobal, the hotel's convention service manager.

"Are you kidding me?", replied Mike Edgar, the hotel maintenance person on duty when Melissa called from the ballroom to report that a guest was having trouble hooking her laptop to the Liquid Crystal Display (LCD) projector the hotel convention services department (through Melissa) had rented to the group for $400 a day. "I just don't know anything about these things," he said, shaking his head while looking at the projector's blank screen.

It was clear the group leader who had rented the projector was not amused. Neither was Melissa. "Well, who here can get it to work?" she asked Mike.

Case Study Questions

Assume the hotel owned this piece of equipment:

1. What should have happened (but did not) before the piece of equipment was put into service?
2. Who should have been responsible for ensuring the hotel's staff was properly trained in the use of this piece of equipment?
3. Assume further that you were responsible for the equipment's purchase. What sources could you likely have used to ensure proper staff training prior to the rental of this guest service equipment?

GUEST-RELATED SUPPLIES As experienced Front Desk agents know, travelers often forget, or run out of, personal toiletry items that are critical to their comfort. Thus, for example, guests frequently call Front Desk staff to inquire if selected items such as toothpaste, razors, or deodorants are available within the hotel. As a result, many upper-scale hotels operate **forgotten items** programs.

Forgotten items are similar to the in-room amenities offered to guests in their rooms. In the case of forgotten items, however, guests are issued these products, upon request, directly from Front Desk staff or, in some cases, the staff of the Housekeeping department. In either case, it is critically important that the quality and quantity of the forgotten item supplied reflects positively on the hotel and the staff member dispensing the item to the guest. As a result, buyers must choose these guest supplies very carefully.

Typical forgotten item amenities made available to guests on a complimentary basis and upon request include

- Razor
- Shaving cream
- Toothbrush
- Toothpaste
- Deodorant
- Sewing kit
- Shower cap
- Mouthwash

STAFF-RELATED SUPPLIES A hotel's Front Desk (Front Office) staff require the same types of office supplies and technology equipment needed by other hotel

Key Term

Forgotten items Personal toiletry items provided at no cost, but only upon request, to a hotel's guests.

Thoughtfully designed forgotten-items programs can significantly enhance the quality and value perception of a guest's stay.
AP Wide World Photos

departments; however, they also have a supply need that is unique to them and critically important to the successful completion of their jobs. In many respects, the Front Desk is the heart of the hotel. Front Desk agents must maintain information about guest room status (e.g., information related to which rooms are clean, dirty, occupied, ready to rent, and so on), announce the arrival of large groups, and communicate guest complaints or concern to peers who can address them. Therefore, it is often critical that members of a hotel's Front Desk staff communicate (and do so quickly) with other members of the hotel's operating team.

The difficulty with such communication, however, is the inability of Front Desk staff to physically leave that area, and staff members with whom they must communicate may be located in many different parts of the hotel. The result is the need for a dependable, rapid, and clear mobile communication system. It is the purchaser's responsibility to provide a dependable system to those members of the Front Desk staff who must effectively communicate guest requests and information.

HI-TECH PURCHASING (18.1)

"Front Desk Calling Maintenance: Do You Copy?"

Rapid communications in hotels are among lodging employees' greatest challenges. When the front desk receives a call from a guest room reporting an overflowing toilet, burned-out light bulb, or T.V. remote with a depleted battery (to name just a few incidents), it is important to notify the maintenance staff on duty to quickly correct the problem. The difficulty, of course, is that the exact location of the needed individual is likely unknown. Other concerns require Housekeeping and the Front Desk, Food and Beverage and Convention Services, and Housekeeping and Maintenance personnel to immediately communicate with each other.

In years' past, walkie-talkies, the low-frequency radio devices developed by Motorola for use during World War II, were commonly used by hotel staff. Today, cell phones with Push-to-Talk (PTT) or "Direct Connect" features are more common. Interestingly, the cellular network required to support this cell phone feature was also developed by the Motorola Company. Their Integrated Digital Enhanced Network (iDEN) makes direct connect possible through the use of the 800-MHz portion of the radio wave spectrum. Like a walkie-talkie, PTT requires the person speaking to press a button while talking and then release it when they are done. The listener then presses his or her button to respond. This way, the system knows in which direction the radio signal should be traveling. PTT relies on cellular technology to connect to the recipient(s). PTT is a much improved system because a normal "Walkie-Talkie" style two-way radio will operate only if the radios are within relatively close proximity. Systems using the iDEN can communicate anywhere within the service area covered by the cell phone carrier, including a large urban area, state, or even the entire country!

Purchasing Resources on the Internet

In addition to the Web sites referenced in this chapter's "Internet Purchasing Assistant" feature, the following sites provide detailed information to enhance your purchasing knowledge and skills.

Purchasing Resources on the Internet	
Site	**Information About**
www.stearnsandfoster.com	Bedding terms glossary
www.valiantproducts.com	Mattresses
www.starlinen.com	Sheets and other amenities
www.hotelblankets.com	Blankets
www.downandfeathercompany.com	Feather and down pillow products
www.hdsupply.com	Terry products
www.A1textiles.com	Terry and bedding products
www.casswell-massey.com	Shampoos/soaps
www.polarbar.com	Minibars
www.classiccoffeeconcepts.com	In-room beverage stations
www.comcastcommercial.com	Cable/Internet vendor
www.poolproducts.com	Pool chemicals
www.promaximamfg.com	Fitness equipment
www.walkwire.com	Business centers
www.nfs-hospitality.com	Facility space reservations
www.salesforce.com	Web-based contact management
www.avservicescorp.com	AV and convention services equipment
www.nationalsatellitecorp.com	Satellite-delivered AV
www.americanhotel.com	Single-use guest supply items
www.techwholesale.com	Traditional walkie-talkie systems

Key Terms

Think It Through

1. One potential vendor would like to sell you box spring and mattress sets with high coil counts, but thinner gauge coils. Its competitor would like to sell you bed sets made with higher gauge coils, but fewer of them. Each extols the virtue of their manufacturing approach. The costs of the mattresses are similar. As a professional buyer, what process would you use to determine which product would be best for you?

2. A hotel is experiencing significant numbers of guest complaints regarding the "scratchiness" of its new sheets. When confronted by the general manager, the executive housekeeper maintains that only sheets of 210-thread count or higher have been purchased, thus the sheets are "fine," and the guests are unjustified in their complaints. As the general manager, what additional information about the new sheets would you want from your executive housekeeper?

3. Two laundry companies are bidding for your 500-room hotel's valet service (dry cleaning and laundry) business. Deluxe Cleaners offers same day service; they state that clothes picked up by noon will be returned to the hotel by 5:00 p.m. the same day. Clauson Cleaners, the second potential vendor, states that any clothes picked up by noon will

be delivered back to the hotel the next morning by 9:00 a.m. Clauson's services cost 20 percent less per item cleaned. What factors would you consider before selecting your preferred valet services vendor?

4. Assume you are outfitting a hotel's 10 × 10 foot fitness facility. What pieces of exercise equipment do you think are "must-haves" if you were buying for a business traveler's hotel? What would you recommend if the space were increased to 20 × 20 feet?

5. Assume that you are the general manager of a hotel and have recently hired a new director of sales and marketing (DOSM). That individual was trained in the use of a Contact Management program that is different from the one currently used in your property. The DOSM approaches you to request the hotel purchase the alternative software program. What factors would be important for you to consider prior to responding to the DOSM's request?

Team Fun

For this exercise, assume that each team consists of an operating division of a large hotel franchise company. This franchisor licenses the "Sleep Good" chain. That chain has an average daily rate (ADR) of $60 per night, and it is designed to appeal to budget-minded travelers.

The company also franchises the "Homestead Express" chain, a mid-priced product with an ADR of $100. Finally, the company franchises the "Waterford Resorts" brand, a lodging product geared to upscale travelers and currently achieving a $200 per night ADR.

Your company CEO has instructed each brand's managers to search the Internet and make specific recommendations for the items to be included in the brand's compulsory, in-bath personal amenity package. The only amenity item mandated by the CEO for each brand is bath soap.

1. The assignment of the first team (Sleep Good) is to select in-bath guest amenities with a total cost of $1.00 per occupied room.
2. The assignment of the second team (Homestead Express) is to select in-bath guest amenities with a total cost of $ 2.50 per occupied room.
3. The assignment of the third team (Waterford Resorts) is to select in-bath guest amenities with a total cost of $ 5.00 per occupied room.

Each team should be prepared to present and discuss their recommendations, as well as describe the source of their recommended in-bath items' prices.

19

Procurement of Hospitality Services

In This Chapter

In previous chapters, you learned about many of the products that restaurant, hotel, and noncommercial facility buyers and managers select when determining how to best serve their guests. In some cases, however, items must be purchased simply because they are a necessity. In many of these cases few, if any, alternative options may be available to buyers. For example, all hospitality businesses must have fresh water to serve guests, cook foods, and clean their facilities. In most cases, water will be supplied by a local or regional water company. In a situation such as this, it is unlikely the buyer will be allowed to "choose" from alternative water supply sources. A similar situation is likely to exist in the case of electrical supply, energy sources, and in some cases, waste removal. In such cases, it might appear that the role of the buyer is diminished because purchase alternatives do not exist. In fact, in cases such as these, buyers must become even more vigilant than normal. This is so because, historically, in situations where a supplier has a monopoly on a service or product, the normal market conditions (competition) that help control price increases and ensure the quality of services may be absent. As a result, buyers faced with buying from a single-source (monopoly) supplier must be especially aware of potential service, billing, and payment issues.

In addition to the essential services that must be purchased by their businesses, hospitality buyers face many instances in which they will voluntarily decide if a specific service will be performed in-house (by the operation's own staff), or if the service will be purchased from an outside vendor. For example, the manager of a restaurant housed in a single-story building might determine that the restaurant's own staff could perform window-washing tasks. If, however, the restaurant were two or more stories tall, the determination might be made to outsource the required cleaning activities to a professional window-washing company.

The ability to properly choose the tasks that should be outsourced by a business is a critical one. Also, when determining those services that should be outsourced, the manner in which bids for the needed services will be secured, and how final vendor selection will be made, are important considerations, and you will learn about these in this chapter.

Buying professional services can be very different from buying products. When hospitality buyers select, for example, an apple or bed sheet for use by their business, it is a fairly straightforward process to assess the quality of the product received. This is so because known quality characteristics can be developed, and the products received can be objectively measured against those previously identified characteristics. When purchasing services, however, determining if the actual service provided was exactly the service the buyer intended to purchase can become a much less objective process. In such cases, the vendor's adherence to the service contract's specific terms is critical. In addition, the vendor may be assessed on one or more subjective factors. Both of these approaches will be examined in the concluding portion of this chapter.

■ ■ ■

Outline

PURCHASING ESSENTIAL SERVICES

One important task faced by all professional hospitality buyers is that of procuring those essential services that are needed simply to open the doors of the business. One such group of essential services relates to the utilities consumed by the operation. For example, a supply of electricity sufficient to operate the business is fundamental to serving customers. Without electricity, the business could not open, and guests would not be served. Similarly, water supplies and the fuels needed to operate the business's **HVAC** system are essential.

In addition to the essential utilities they consume, hospitality businesses generate waste products. These wastes must be removed from the business, and

---

Key Term

HVAC Industry jargon for a building's "heating, ventilation, and air-conditioning" equipment and systems.

doing so can represent a significant cost. As a result, waste removal services are also essential business services about which professional buyers should be very familiar.

Utilities

Utility management is a tremendously important part of a hospitality business's overall operation. Utility costs include expenses for water bills, gas, electricity, or fossil fuel for heating and cooling the building housing the business, fuel for heating water, and, in some cases, the purchase of steam or chilled water for heating and cooling.

Energy-related expenses, which had been taken for granted by most businesses, became very important and costly during the energy crisis of the early 1970s and again in early 2008. Since then, however, these costs have moderated somewhat. When the cost of utilities is relatively low, few Americans, including those in the hospitality industry, take strong measures to conserve resources and to implement energy management programs. Alternatively, when energy costs are high, managers have a heightened sense of awareness about these costs.

It is important to remember that, in most cases, the utility costs involved in lighting, heating, and operating the equipment required to run a hospitality business will be incurred regardless of revenue levels. Although it is true that higher sales levels will result in some incremental increase in utility costs, as much as 80 percent of total utility costs for hospitality businesses are fixed. A building's original design and construction, the age of its utility-consuming equipment, its regular maintenance, and the energy conservation techniques used by a business are all factors that affect utility purchase and usage.

Although the utility needs of a business are determined in part by the products and services they sell, as well as the location of the building, most hospitality buyers will find that they are responsible for ensuring adequate supplies of the following essential utilities:

Electricity

Water (including hot water)

HVAC-related utilities

ELECTRICITY   Electricity is the most common and usually the most expensive form of energy used in hospitality businesses. Although some operations (e.g., resort hotels) can generate their own electricity in an emergency outage situation through the use of one or more backup generators, most businesses will rely on one or more local power providers to deliver electricity to the operation. As with any other item required by their operations, professional purchasers should strive to buy only the amount of this essential service that is actually needed by their business, but never more than is truly needed.

Electricity is expensive. In some areas, electric bills account for well over 50 percent (and sometimes as much as 80 percent) of a hospitality businesses' total utility costs. Electricity is used everywhere in the hospitality industry: It powers the business's administrative computers, operates fire safety systems, keeps food cold in freezers and refrigerators, and provides power for security systems, to name but a few uses.

In many cases, electrical usage is also tied directly to water and HVAC energy use. In a typical foodservice operation, electrical pumps move water from one area within the business to another. Electricity is also used to power food production equipment and may heat the water used in dishwashing and for general cleaning.

In hotels, electricity also influences water consumption and HVAC operations. For example, electricity is used to operate the pumps moving water to guest room shower areas and through pool filter systems, is integral to washing linens in electric motor washing machines, and is likely used to power one or more parts of a hotel's heating and cooling system. Of course, electricity also allows guests to operate a wide variety of in-room amenities such as televisions, blow-driers, microwaves, and so on. Even the lights illuminating hotel parking areas that welcome guests operate on electricity. Clearly, electricity serves many roles in a hospitality business. It is no wonder, then, that its purchase should not be taken for granted. This is especially true regarding electricity as the primary source of facility lighting.

The lighting in a hospitality business is tremendously important to **curb appeal,** guest comfort, worker efficiency, and property security.

Lighting is sometimes referred to as illumination, and light levels are measured in **foot-candles.** The electrical power required to generate various illumination levels varies by the type of light fixture used. Hospitality businesses require varying degrees of illumination in different locations, and the type of light fixtures and lightbulbs used play a large role in producing the most appropriate, cost-effective light for each setting.

In many cases, artificial light is produced to supplement natural (sun) light. Natural light is, of course, free and when used can have a very positive effect on utility costs by limiting the amount of artificial light that must be produced. Most businesses must supplement natural light, however, and when they do so they choose from two basic lighting options. The first of these is **incandescent** lamps.

Incandescent lights are the type most people think of when they think of the lightbulbs used in their homes. Incandescent bulbs have relatively short life spans (2,000 operating hours or less) and must be frequently changed. They are also fairly inefficient producers of foot-candles.

Incandescent bulbs are popular with guests, however, because they produce a soft and pleasing light that is less harsh than other alternatives. Hoteliers like incandescent lights because they are easy to install, easy to move, inexpensive to purchase, and have the characteristic of starting and restarting instantly. Incandescent lamp bulbs can also be manufactured in such a way as to concentrate light in one area (these are known as spot or floodlights).

In cases where an incandescent light source is not the best for a specific lighting need, businesses can select an **electric discharge** lamp as a second lighting option.

Electric discharge lamps are characterized by longer lives (5,000–25,000 operating hours) and higher foot-candle producing efficiency. The most common of this lamp type is the fluorescent, and it is frequently used where high light levels and low operating costs are a consideration. Other types of electric discharge lamps used include those for parking areas or security lighting. In cases such as these, sodium lamps are a popular choice because they are extremely efficient

Key Terms

Curb appeal   The term used to indicate the initial visual impression a business's parking areas, grounds, and external building aesthetics create for an arriving customer.

Foot-candle   A measure of illumination. The greater the illumination level, the greater the measured number of foot-candles.

Incandescent (lamp)   A lamp type in which a filament inside the lamp's bulb is heated by electrical current to produce light.

Electric discharge (lamp)   A lamp in which light is generated by passing electrical current through a space filled with a special combination of gases. Examples include fluorescent, mercury vapor, metal halide, and sodium.

foot-candle producers and have very long lives (of course, the cost to purchase and install these lights is usually greater also).

In the late 1980s, compact versions of fluorescent lights—compact fluorescent lights (CFLs)—became popular in many businesses and especially hotels. These bulbs use at least two-thirds less energy than standard incandescent bulbs to provide the same amount of light, and last up to ten times longer. These lights were designed to combine the energy efficiency and long life of a traditional fluorescent light with the convenience of an incandescent light. In many cases, buyers have found that these lamps provide an excellent blend between operational efficiency (energy savings) and convenience.

WATER While some hospitality businesses may own and utilize their own water wells, in most cases, restaurants, hotels and institutional facilities must purchase the water they use. Typically, local water utilities sell water to commercial accounts in 100 or 1,000-gallon increments. Water prices vary nationally based upon the scarcity of water in an area, seasonality, and the total quantity of water purchased per month by the business. In some communities, larger volume users are given a discount for quantity purchases, but in other communities, volume users are penalized with increases in per gallon prices as their water usage increases.

Regardless of the pricing method the local water supplier uses, carefully controlling a business's water purchases is very cost-effective because it pays three ways. Conserving water:

1. Reduces the number of gallons of water purchased.
2. Reduces the amount the business will pay for sewage (waste water disposal).
3. In the case of hot water, reduces water-heating costs because less hot water must be produced.

Water purchases can be significantly reduced if all members of a hospitality operation conscientiously monitor water usage (actions businesses can take to reduce water usage, and thus water purchases, will be examined later in this chapter).

HVAC-RELATED UTILITIES Another significant consumer of electrical or other utilities is the business's HVAC system. Heating, ventilation, and air conditioning are considered together because they all utilize the operation's air treatment, thermostats, duct, and air handler systems. While it is not realistic to assume that buyers of hospitality products and services will also be experts in HVAC operations, it is

---

PURCHASING PROS KNOW (19.1)

Compact fluorescent lights (CFLs) are extremely efficient. Since CFLs use about a quarter of the energy of incandescent bulbs they are a key part of efforts to fight pollution. However, CFLs contain trace amounts of mercury. The amount is not large enough to pose a hazard to users (it is about 1/5 the amount in a typical digital watch battery), but it can become a concern at landfills and trash incinerators where the mercury from many bulbs can escape and contribute to air and water pollution. As a result, local ordinances may require users of CFLs to:

1. Take used CFLs back to where they were purchased so the supplier can recycle them correctly; or
2. Take used CFLs to a local recycling facility.

To find out about the presence (if any) of local ordinances related to CFL disposal, purchasing professionals always check with local environmental protection officials in their own operating areas.

realistic to point out that a basic understanding of such systems is essential if the buyer is to fully understand the impact HVAC operations will have on utility purchases.

A properly operating HVAC system delivers air to various parts of a building at a desired temperature. The efficiency at which an HVAC system operates, and thus the energy that must be purchased to heat or cool the operation's air space, is affected by a variety of factors, including

- The original temperature of the room.
- The temperature of the new air delivered to the room.
- The relative humidity of the new air delivered.
- Air movement in the room.
- Temperature-absorbing surfaces in the room.

HVAC systems can be simple or very complex, but in most locations will consist of components responsible for both heating and cooling. Therefore, professional utility buyers should understand both of these major component groups.

Heating Components   An effective HVAC system heats air and water. Although it is possible that all of a business's HVAC heating components are operated by electricity, this is not normally the case. Heating by electricity, especially in cold climates, is not generally cost-effective. Because of this, businesses generally heat the air for at least some parts of their buildings using natural gas, liquefied petroleum gas (LPG), steam, or fuel oil (although electricity can be used to heat small areas).

In most businesses, the heating of hot water is second in cost only to the heating of air. As a result, most hospitality operations require an effective furnace (or heat pump system) for heating air and a properly sized **boiler** for heating water.

Like furnaces, boilers may be powered by electricity, natural gas, liquefied petroleum gas (LPG), or fuel oil. Regardless of the energy source(s) used, electricity will be used by fans or pumps to move warm air produced by an operation's furnace, or hot water produced by the boiler, to the appropriate parts of the building.

Cooling Components   Just as an operation must heat air and water, in many locations one or more parts of the building must be cooled. In most cases, the major cost of operating air-cooling or conditioning systems is related to electricity usage. Essentially, in an air-conditioning system, electrically operated equipment extracts heat from either air or water and then uses the remaining cooled air or water to absorb and remove more heat from the building. The effectiveness of a cooling system, and thus the energy that must be purchased to operate it, depends on several factors, including the:

- Original air temperature and humidity of the room to be cooled.
- Temperature and humidity of the chilled air entering the room from the HVAC system.
- Quantity of chilled air entering the room.
- Operational efficiency of the air-conditioning equipment.

Some cooling systems are designed to produce small quantities of very cold air that are then pumped or blown into a room to reduce its temperature; other systems supply larger quantities of air that are not as cold, but because the quantity

---

Key Term

Boiler   A large tank in which water is heated and stored, either as hot water or as steam. If relatively small, a boiler may be referred to as a "hot water heater."

supplied is greater, have the same room cooling effect. The ability of a cooling system to deliver cold air or water of a specified temperature and in the quantity required determines the effectiveness of a cooling system. Many times, especially in hot humid weather, the demands placed upon a facility's cooling system are intense. Effective and continual maintenance on cooling equipment plays a crucial part in minimizing the energy purchases required to operate an air conditioning system.

Waste Removal

The operation of a hospitality business inevitably results in the generation of waste materials. These waste products may be in liquid form, solid form, or a combination of both. Because liquid waste removal (sewage) costs have, historically, been reported by hospitality businesses as part of their utility (water) bills, liquid waste removal is generally considered a utility cost and accounted for accordingly.

Solid waste (garbage and trash) removal, however, has not generally been considered a utility cost from a hospitality accountant's perspective (rather, it is considered an operations cost). Nevertheless, waste removal expense is examined here because, like utility costs, these expenses are related to an essential service, and their total costs should also be properly controlled.

In some cases, the liquid waste (including that from sinks, floor drains, and toilets) generated by a hospitality business will be processed in the business's own on-site (septic) sewage disposal system. A septic system is simply a small-scale sewage treatment system commonly used in areas with no connection to main sewerage pipes. In most cases, however, the liquid waste generated by a hospitality business will be pumped (or fed by gravity) into a larger municipally operated waste water treatment (sewage) system. In either case, there will be expenses associated with disposing of liquid waste.

In addition to liquid wastes, foodservice operations and lodging facilities generate a tremendous amount of solid waste or trash. Sources of waste include packaging materials such as cardboard boxes, crates, and bags that were used in the shipping of hotel supplies, kitchen garbage, guest room trash, and even yard waste generated from the business's landscaping efforts.

Increasingly, hospitality industry professionals, including buyers, have come to realize that excessive waste and poorly conceived waste disposal methods are detrimental to the environment and represent a poor use of natural resources. In addition, as landfills become scarce, the cost of solid waste disposal has risen. As a result, all hospitality professionals have a heightened interest in minimizing their essential service (utilities) costs, as well as properly controlling costs associated with waste disposal. Consequently, conservation of essential services is a critical topic, and it is to that topic we will now turn our attention.

CONTROL OF ESSENTIAL SERVICES COSTS

Assume that a buyer for a foodservice operation purchased a large bag of carrots for eventual service to the operation's guests. Assume also that the carrots were not stored properly, resulting in a loss of 20 percent of the bag's contents. Further, assume that through poor preparation and cooking techniques, another 20 percent of the product was lost. Finally, assume that because of poor postproduction storage techniques, yet another 20 percent of the product was lost. In this example, more than half of the carrots purchased did not make it onto plates of the operation's guests. If such a food production situation actually existed, it would clearly be the job of management to correct the problem. In a similar manner, if a business's financial resources are being needlessly expended on essential services such as utilities and waste removal, corrective action must be taken. In the hospitality industry, essential services costs can, to a large degree, be controlled on-site. Through **source reduction,** however, these costs can be controlled even prior to the arrival of needed products.

Thus, a complete understanding of essential services cost control involves encouraging both source reduction and effective on-site conservation efforts.

Source Reduction

The removal of solid wastes is expensive. Therefore, many hospitality businesses have encouraged manufacturers who ship products to them to practice source reduction and have aggressively implemented creative programs to reduce the generation of their own solid waste. Source reduction decreases the amount of materials or energy used during the manufacturing or distribution of products and packages. Because it stops waste before it starts, source reduction is the top solid waste priority of the U.S. Environmental Protection Agency (EPA).

Source reduction is not the same as recycling. Recycling is collecting already used materials and making them into another product. Recycling begins at the end of a product's life, whereas source reduction takes place when the product and its packaging are being designed. Perhaps the best way to think about source reduction and recycling is as complementary activities: Combined, source reduction and recycling have a significant influence on preventing solid waste and saving resources.

Source reduction conserves raw material and energy resources. Smaller packages and concentrated products typically use fewer materials and less energy to manufacture and ship. The result is lower purchase prices for products. Source reduction also cuts back on what has to be thrown away, which helps keep solid waste disposal costs down.

Specific source reduction strategies that can be implemented by hospitality buyers include:

- *Purchasing concentrated products.*   Many cleaning products, for example, have been reformulated to use less product to do the same job.

Internet Purchasing Assistant (19.1)

The focus of this text is the skills and knowledge needed by professionals buying items for use in the hospitality industry. Strictly speaking, all such professional buyers should be "conservationists" because they should want to buy no more (of any product or service) than that absolutely needed by their businesses. This includes natural resources.

"Green" is the generic term used for those individuals in many areas of society who are also concerned with conserving natural resources. Thus, in the hospitality industry, there is a "Green Hotels" association.

To learn more about this group's philosophy and its goals, go to: www.greenhotels.com
At the home page, read the information under "What Are 'Green' Hotels?"

Key Term

Source reduction   The effort by product manufacturers to design and ship products to minimize waste resulting from the products' shipping and delivery.

- *Buying the largest size container that can be used efficiently.* Purchase prices for larger quantity items are typically lower, as will be packaging disposal costs.
- *Buying refill systems whenever possible.* These systems eliminate the shipping of duplicate dispensing products (e.g., self-dispensed shampoos and conditioners located in guestroom shower areas).

On-Site Efforts

Getting plugged into energy conservation is important to profits, the environment, and your customers. According to the U.S. Environmental Protection Agency (EPA), saving 20 percent a year on energy operating costs can increase the profits shown on a restaurant's **income statement** by as much as one-third.

In most cases, using simple preventive maintenance programs for equipment and remembering to turn off equipment and lights when they are not in use can shave dollars off utility bills. Although those professional purchasers seeking specific recommendations on how to conserve energy and thus reduce utility purchases should have no difficulty locating them (just enter "hospitality energy savings" in your favorite search engine), the following are specific utility conservation steps many foodservice facility and lodging facility managers can easily implement.

FOODSERVICE FACILITIES Specific utility-related cost reduction techniques that can be used in foodservice facilities vary based upon the operation's size and menu offered. However, cost reduction tactics related to the following major expense categories can often be helpful and should be considered by professional buyers:

Reducing the idle temperatures of foodservice equipment between peak usage periods is an easy way to help conserve energy.
Eddie Gerald © Rough Guides

Key Term

Income statement   The itemized record of a business's income, expense, and profit (or loss) during a specifically defined time period. Also known as a Profit and Loss (P&L) statement.

On-the-Job Challenges in Purchasing (19.1)

"What are you reading, Tina?" asked Larry.

Larry was one of the night foodservice supervisors at Cary Quadrangle, the largest dormitory at State University. The Quad's four separate dining rooms, connected to a common kitchen, served more than 3,000 students during each meal period. Tina was a morning foodservice supervisor at Cary and, although they worked different shifts, she and Larry were professional friends.

"Well," replied Tina, as she put down her copy of *Foodservice Director*, a monthly trade magazine for institutional foodservice professionals. "It's a fascinating article about energy loss due to worn or faulty refrigerator and freezer gaskets. The amount of energy that can be lost when doors don't fit tightly is incredible. Fixing them can save a lot of money."

"Who cares," replied Larry, "We don't pay for energy. There isn't even a line on our monthly Operating Income Statement for it. The University pays."

Case Study Questions

Consider Larry's response, and assume that he was correct about his unit's income statement.

1. What would be your reply to Larry if you were Tina?
2. What would be your reply to Larry if you were the individual responsible for the budget used to heat, cool, and power all University buildings?
3. What would be your reply to Larry if you were the president of the University?

Electricity:

✓ Replace old incandescent-bulb fixtures with ones that use fluorescent bulbs, which last longer and use less energy.
✓ Replace electrical cooking equipment and water heaters with gas units.
✓ Replace air (fan)-cooled ice machines with water-cooled units.
✓ Clean refrigerator and freezer condenser coils at least once every three months.

Water:

✓ Serve water to guests only upon request.
✓ Install low-pressure prerinse spray valves in dish areas.
✓ Thaw foods in the refrigerator rather than under running water.
✓ Install water-efficient (low-water usage) toilets in guest-area and employee restrooms.

HVAC-related utilities:

✓ Professionally service all HVAC equipment at least twice per year.
✓ Replace electric water heaters in dishwashers with gas heaters.
✓ Ensure walls, windows, ceilings, and foundations are properly insulated to avoid heat or cooling loss.
✓ Consider the installation of energy-management systems that automatically reduce thermostat settings when the operation is closed.

LODGING FACILITIES   Like foodservice facilities, specific utility-related cost reduction techniques in lodging facilities will vary based upon the operation's size and services offered. The following dozen cost-reduction tactics, however, are examples of the type that often are effective and should be considered by all lodging facility operators:

Electricity:

✓ Replace incandescent guest room lightbulbs with compact fluorescent lights (CFLs).

HI-TECH PURCHASING (19.1)

Table for Two by the (Low-E) Window? Right This Way

In some climates, windows are attractive, but can significantly increase the heat build-up in a building. Low-emittance (Low-E) coatings are microscopically thin, virtually invisible, metal or metallic oxide layers deposited on a window or skylight glazing surface primarily to suppress radiant heat flow.

The principal mechanism of heat transfer in multilayer glass is thermal radiation from a warm pane of glass (outside) to a cooler pane (inside). Coating a glass surface with a low-emittance material and facing that coating into the gap between the glass layers blocks a significant amount of this radiant heat transfer, thus lowering the total heat flow through the window (and into the building). Low-E coatings are transparent in normal light and thus can often be an excellent resource for hospitality operators seeking to minimize facility utility costs while maximizing the use of natural lighting.

- ✓ Provide nightlights near bathrooms (to prevent guests from leaving lights on all night).
- ✓ Inspect the cooling (heat discharge) areas of electric equipment (ice machines, vending machines, and the like) to ensure the removal of anything that would obstruct free air movement.
- ✓ Calibrate thermostats on electrical heating equipment on a regular basis.

Water:

- ✓ Implement voluntary linen reuse programs for guests. According to Project Planet, a hospitality industry leader in environmental programs, a 100-guestroom property with 75 percent occupancy will save, conservatively, an estimated $25,000 per year through a linen and towel reuse program. These cost savings are derived from an 81,000-gallon reduction in water consumption plus a 540-gallon reduction in detergent.
- ✓ Install faucet aerators and high-efficiency (2–3 gallon per minute) showerheads.
- ✓ Install ultralow-flow toilets, or adjust flush valves on current guest room toilets.
- ✓ Wash only full loads of laundry.

Many of today's hotel guests appreciate the opportunity to participate in linen reuse programs because guests are themselves environmentally conscious.

Rob Melnychuk/Getty Images, Inc.-Taxi

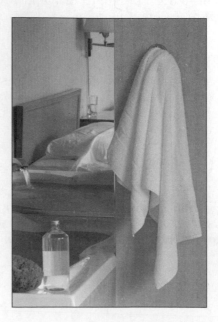

Internet Purchasing Assistant (19.2)

ENERGY STAR is a joint program of the U.S. Environmental Protection Agency (EPA) and the U.S. Department of Energy designed to help save money and protect the environment through energy-efficient products and practices. In 1992, the EPA introduced ENERGY STAR as a voluntary labeling program designed to identify and promote energy-efficient products. Computers and monitors were the first labeled products. Through 1995, the EPA expanded the label to additional office equipment products and residential heating and cooling equipment. In 1996, the EPA partnered with the U.S. Department of Energy for particular product categories. The ENERGY STAR label is now on major appliances, office equipment, lighting, home electronics, and more. The EPA has also extended the label to cover new homes and commercial and industrial buildings. To learn more about specific ideas related to energy conservation, go to: www.energystar.gov

At the home page, click on "Partner Resources" and then "Retailers" to review their lists of specific recommendations (by category) for saving money through energy conservation.

HVAC-related utilities:

✓ Install energy-efficient air-conditioning units in guest rooms.
✓ Replace electric pool water heaters with gas units.
✓ Bimonthly, inspect utility fittings (for leaks) on all equipment.
✓ Clean and/or lubricate all HVAC system filters, fans, motors, pumps, pulleys, and shafts twice annually.

ESSENTIAL SERVICES BILLING

Like any other product or service, when professional buyers purchase essential services such as electricity, water, and HVAC fuels, they would like to pay what they owe, but no more. Unfortunately, for several reasons, purchasing an item such as electricity is not as easy as buying a case of lettuce or a dozen bed sheets. For example, those who buy electricity do not actually see what they have purchased. The results of electricity consumption may be easy to see, but the product itself is invisible, so it is not always easy to "know" how much of the product was purchased. Second, although hospitality buyers are familiar with terms such as cases, pounds, ounces, and dozens, fewer buyers would immediately recognize the terms **KwH, CCF,** or **decatherm,** yet these are the most common (but not only) purchase units for, respectively, electricity, water, and natural gas.

Key Terms

KwH Short for kilowatt hour. It is the measurement used to calculate electricity usage. It may also be abbreviated as "kW·h" or "kWh."

CCF Short for "one hundred cubic feet." It is one measurement used to calculate water usage.

Decatherm The measurement used to calculate natural gas usage. One decatherm is equal to 1,000,000 British thermal units (BTUs).

It is also important to understand that utilities are one item in which total consumption (and thus the amount purchased) is not completely in the hands of the buyer. Consider, for example, the hotel guest who elects to let run, for one hour, a hot water shower in a bath area of a guest room in an effort to "steam" the wrinkles out of a too-tightly packed business suit. In this case, the essential services consumption (electricity to operate the water pump, the water itself, gas to heat the water, and sewage charges) will rise dramatically for that room. In a similar manner, in both foodservice operations and lodging facilities, employees who do (or do not) practice sound energy conservation techniques will dramatically affect the quantity of essential services that buyers must purchase.

Lastly, utilities such as electricity, water (and sewage services), and natural gas are typically metered products. Thus, the amount consumed is determined based upon beginning and ending time period meter readings. In this chapter, you will learn how meter readings (or meter estimates) are used to compute utility payments due. It is important to recognize, however, that it is the meter reading (not actual product usage) that will determine the amount to be charged to the hospitality operation. Therefore, and because the cost of essential services is significant, buyers must understand how they will be billed and pay for electricity, water (and sewage), HVAC fuels such as natural or propane gas, and solid waste removal.

Electricity

The electric bills assessed to a hospitality business are determined by two main factors: (1) the amount of electrical usage, and (2) the time the electricity was used. Electricity usage is measured by the kilowatt hour (number of watts generated times the number of hours generated). To illustrate, consider a restaurant with an "Exit" sign. The sign is set up with two 50-watt lightbulbs (100 watts total) and left on for 10 hours per day. The exit sign will consume 1,000 "watt-hours" (1 kilowatt-hour) per day. If a power company charges $0.10 per KwH, then those two lightbulbs will cost the operation $0.70 over the course of a week. It is easy to see why those products that are efficient users of energy (watts), and thus result in lower operational electrical bills, are highly desirable.

Electric bills are also affected by time. Unlike some other energy sources, electricity cannot easily be stored, and so it must be produced as it is needed. As a result, most electricity providers penalize users who consume large amounts of electricity during peak consumption periods. Rates tend to be lower during non-peak consumption periods.

Like most utility services, electricity is a metered product. Therefore, the actual electricity bill received by a business will include the following information, all of which is important to the buyer responsible for billing accuracy and thus must be carefully examined:

Customer name: Just like other vendors, utility companies can make billing errors, including sending the wrong invoice to the wrong business, so this information should be carefully examined.

Billing date: The date this bill was printed.

Due date: The date your bill for the month is due. This is important because significant late payment charges will likely be added to overdue bills.

Type of service: Typically, a code that indicates the type of service (commercial, home, etc.) provided. An explanation of your code(s) will likely be found on the back of your bill.

Reading date: The date your meter was read (or estimated).

THE SUPPLIER'S SIDE (19.1)

"Insider" Tips on Purchasing: From the Supplier's Perspective

Buyer's Question: My electric, gas, and water bills seem really high. How do I know the meters outside my building are accurate?

Supplier's Answer: Most utility rules require that meters not be more than two percent fast or two percent slow. Moreover, every utility is required to randomly test a series of meters annually to ensure that they are accurate. If you have serious questions, ask for a meter accuracy test. In most cases (if you do not request them too frequently), such verification tests are offered at no charge.

Buyer's Question: It says on my bill that the meter reading is an "estimate." Do I still have to pay the entire bill?

Supplier's Answer: In most cases, customers must pay their bills whether they were based on an actual or estimated reading. However, if the estimated reading appears to be out of line with what you normally use during the same time of year, you are justified in requesting that the utility investigate the accuracy of your bill. Under most state's laws, you do not have to pay the amount *in dispute* pending an investigation by the utility. You still must pay the amount you are not disputing.

Buyer's Question: My meter readings are estimated much of the time. A high estimated bill means I overpay, whereas a low estimate requires a large "catch up" bill later. What can I do?

Supplier's Answer: Most utility companies strive to obtain regular monthly meter readings. If the utility is unable to read the meter, however, the customer will receive a bill based on an estimated reading. Utilities may estimate a bill when certain conditions exist, such as extreme weather conditions, emergencies, work stoppages, or if other circumstances exist beyond the control of the utility. If your meter reading is frequently an estimate, contact your utility company. In many cases, the utility can supply meter-reading cards that you can use to record and submit your own meter reading information. Don't forget, however, that under such programs, at least once every twelve months the utility will obtain an actual meter reading to verify the accuracy of the readings you report.

Number of days: The number of days between your present and previous meter readings. It shows the number of days of service covered by this bill and may vary by as many as two to seven days from the number of days in the prior billing period or that of the previous year.

Meter readings: These numbers are the dial readings, which appear on the face of your meter. If this number has been estimated (because the meter was not actually read), the fact that it is an estimate will be noted by the utility provider.

Difference: The amount of electricity consumed. It is derived by subtracting the previous period meter reading from the present period meter reading.

Temperature differences (optional): This entry, when present, compares the average outdoor temperature of the current billing period to the average temperature of the previous month and year.

Usage differences (optional): This entry, when present, compares the actual usage by the operation during the current billing period to the average usage last month as well as last year.

The electric bills generated by local utility companies are often difficult to decipher, yet it is critical that those responsible for ensuring their accuracy understand them well. A good place to begin is in the customer service department of the local

Severe weather, such as significant snowstorms, may result in an estimated utility meter reading. For bill payment purposes, such estimates should, in most cases, be treated just like a normal meter reading.

George Mobley/NGS Image Collection

utility, where a line-by-line examination of a "typical" monthly bill should be carefully undertaken between the utility provider's representative and the operation's utility buyer.

Water/Sewage

Water billings for hospitality operations typically consist of two main parts: (1) the purchase unit, and (2) the price per unit. Hospitality buyers are likely to encounter one of two purchase units depending upon the preference of the entity supplying their water. Some buyers purchase water by the 100 cubic foot (CCF). One CCF equals 748 gallons of water so, for example, a water bill for usage of 1,525 CCF would be 1,140,770 gallons of water (1,525 CCF × 748 gallons per CCF = 1,140,770).

Alternatively, a local water provider may bill businesses based upon the **Cgal.** In the previous example of an operation using 1,140,770 gallons of water, the billing for that quantity would be 11,408 Cgals (1,140,770 gallons used / 100 gallons per Cgal = 11,408 (rounded) Cgals used).

Like electricity, water is a metered product, so it is important that buyers periodically test the accuracy of water meters, replacing them if any questions arise about their precision. In most utility districts, sewage charges (because sewage usage is not typically metered) are tied to water usage. The rationale for doing so is that, in a home or business, all water entering the building is likely to end up, at some point, going "down the drain." Thus, sewage billings typically include a flat charge for sewage access and a sewage use unit charge tied directly to water usage. Due to the nature of billing sewage charges, it is easy to see why it is imperative that water used for landscaping purposes, or for any other purpose that will not require use of the utility entity's sewage treatment system, be metered separately when the business is permitted to do so.

Key Term

Cgal Short for "hundred gallons"; a measurement to calculate water usage.

HVAC Fuels

In many geographic areas, natural gas or liquefied petroleum gas (also known as LP-gas, or even more commonly, propane) may be used to heat water and air. In hotels, gas may be used to heat water for guest rooms and to power laundry clothes dryers. In addition, natural gas is used in many hotel power plants to directly or indirectly provide heat to guest rooms and public spaces. In foodservice operations, the overwhelming majority of chefs and cooks also prefer natural gas when cooking because of its rapid heat production and the degree of temperature control it allows. Managed properly, gas is an extremely safe and cost-effective source of energy.

Hospitality buyers purchasing natural gas may also encounter one of two different purchase units depending upon the preference of their gas provider. Like electricity and water, gas is a metered product. On some meters, gas usage is measured, by volume, in **Mcf** (1,000 cubic foot) units.

Increasingly, however, gas consumers are demanding (and gas vendors are responding by supplying) gas bills metered in decatherms. This is important because:

- The energy-producing ability of gas varies based upon many product characteristics including quality, origin, and purity.
- The volume of gas delivered to a business is affected by the altitude at which it is delivered.
- The volume of gas delivered to a business is affected by the temperature at which it is delivered.

As a result, gas bills measured in decatherms are a better indication of product usage for many hospitality operations than are those generated using Mcf.

Solid Waste

Solid waste removal charges (garbage, trash, and recycled materials) are generally dictated by at least three independent factors:

- Number of waste containers supplied by the vendor.
- Size of waste containers supplied by the vendor.
- Frequency (number of times per period) waste containers are emptied.

Effective buyers of waste removal services work with their vendors to manipulate these three factors in such a manner as to minimize costs while optimizing service levels.

PURCHASING ADDITIONAL SERVICES

Services such as electrical power, water, and other utilities simply must be purchased. Buyers have no choice. The purchase of some other services, however, can be viewed as optional. Consider, for example, the buyer for a restaurant located in the suburbs of a large Midwestern city in the United States. It is certainly not mandatory for such a buyer to select and employ a snow removal service. A decision not to secure such a service, however, is likely to meet with disaster the sev-

---

Key Term

Mcf   Short for "1,000 cubic feet"; a measurement used to calculate gas usage. The price of natural gas varies greatly depending on the geographic location and type of consumer but, in 2009, a price of less than $10 per 1,000 cubic feet was typical in the United States.

eral times per winter when the restaurant's large parking area will be impassable due to significant snowfall. In a similar manner, a hotel need not contract with a plumbing/sewage company to periodically service (clean) its guestroom tub/shower drains. Failure to do so (or to perform the same service with its own hotel employees), however, will inevitably result in slow drains and, as a direct consequence, unhappy hotel guests.

As these two examples illustrate, professional hospitality buyers will, of necessity, identify a variety of services that must be performed for or provided to their operations. Some additional examples include payroll processing, valet services, laundry, pest control, ventilation hood cleaning, window washing, exterior building maintenance, landscaping and/or lawn care, as well as parking lot lighting and maintenance (to name but a few such services commonly required). For buyers responsible for securing services such as these, two issues are paramount. The first is the initial decision of whether to perform the service **in-house** or to outsource the same activity.

Second, if the decision is made to outsource the service activity, buyers must then use a vendor identification process that culminates in the selection of a supplier who can consistently provide the needed service at required quality levels.

Considerations in Source Selection

When buyers consider the desirability of performing a required service in-house or, alternatively, contracting for that service with an outside vendor, three major factors must be evaluated:

- Timing
- Skill level requirements
- Continuity requirements

TIMING   The quality of some required services is very dependent upon the timing of service delivery. In the example of the Midwestern restaurateur securing snowplowing services, a delay of several hours (or days!) in providing the plow service will make a significant difference in its quality. This is so because the "need" for plowing is immediate and cannot be delayed. Alternatively, however, if the same restaurant determined that its plants, shrubs, and trees required once-per-year fertilization, a service-delivery delay of days or even weeks may not be considered significant. Buyers evaluating the importance of service timing must firmly establish just how important the timing of delivery will be to their ultimate evaluation of service quality.

SKILL LEVEL REQUIREMENTS   In many cases, the delivery of a service requires highly skilled individuals and very specialized tools or equipment. Thus, for example, the tools and equipment needed to clean a kitchen's vent hoods may, in one geographic area, be owned and properly operated by only a few service providers. Because the service is needed only infrequently, it simply may not be in the best interest of the restaurant to invest in the equipment and training needed to perform this service in-house. Additional examples of areas in which technical complexity is so advanced that (in all but the largest of operations) services would likely be outsourced include computer and telephone systems repair, HVAC component repair and replacement, servicing of kitchen equipment, cleaning of draft

---

Key Term

In-house (service)   The situation that exists when a hotel's employees are directly responsible for providing a needed service.

beer lines, and masonry, carpentry, and electrical work. Other outsourced services commonly include specialized tasks such management recruitment, payroll processing, and legal and tax services.

CONTINUITY REQUIREMENTS   In some cases, a hospitality buyer can move easily between performing a service in-house and using an outside vendor. Thus, for example, a hotel may determine that in-house maintenance staff will perform minor guest room wall vinyl repair and replacement. The concurrent replacement of wall vinyl in several floors of guest rooms, however, may be subcontracted to an outside vendor. Both of these activities could be undertaken without conflict. In cases such as payroll processing, however, frequently moving back and forth between in-house service delivery and the use of an outside vendor would be impractical.

In general, when an operation must make a significant investment in staff training and equipment acquisition to provide a service in-house, it will likely be most cost-effective to continue providing the service in-house. When timing, skill level, and continuity requirements point to the use of an outside vendor, professional buyers must purchase those services. In these situations, they must turn their attention to securing appropriate supplier bids followed by the selection of their preferred vendor.

Securing Vendor Bids

As you have learned in previous chapters, two critical factors that must be considered if the procurement process is to be effective are purchase specifications (see Chapter 4) and supplier relations (see Chapter 8). These factors are also essential when selecting service providers, and, it is important to recognize, they are interrelated. Service providers can hope to fulfill buyers' expectations only if they understand fully the work that they are expected to accomplish. Thus, a service specification that details precisely the service required, as well as any critical contract terms related to the service, is crucial if a positive supplier relationship is to be developed and maintained.

On-the-Job Challenges in Purchasing (19.2)

In response to a telephone inquiry, McClean's Tree Service offered to trim the damaged branches from a large apple tree on the lawn outside the entrance to the Prime Rib Roaster restaurant, for a fee of $1,000. The service was needed because a recent storm had damaged the tree, and Steve Wilbert, the restaurant's manager, was afraid the damaged branches might fall and hit a guest, employee, or another person entering the restaurant.

Mr. Wilbert, again by telephone, agreed to the price and to a start date of Monday. At noon on Monday, McClean's informed Mr. Wilbert that the job was completed. The tree trimming went fine, but a large amount of branches and leaves from the tree were left neatly piled near the tree's base. When Mr. Wilbert inquired about the removal of the debris, McClean has stated that removing it had never been discussed and was not included in the quoted price. Mr. Wilbert agreed that the topic of removal was never discussed, but stated that it is generally assumed that when a company trims a tree, it will remove the brush it generates; therefore, he refused to pay until the brush was removed.

Case Study Questions

1. Assume that you are a small claims court judge and this case appeared before you. In your opinion, which party to this service contract has the more valid argument? How would you resolve their issue?
2. Based upon your knowledge of procurement principles, what specific errors did Steve Wilbert make when entering into this service contract?

In an open bid system, initial supplier bids may be received via telephone. These should, however, be followed by confirmation, in writing, of the selected vendor's final bid.

© Dorling Kindersley

When professional buyers have thoroughly defined (specified) the services they need to have performed, it is appropriate to ask potential vendors to submit a written bid for supplying those services. A bid is simply an opportunity for potential suppliers to submit their charge for supplying a particular service. In most cases, buyers requesting bids will use one of two alternative bid systems.

A **closed bid** system is one in which a potential supplier submits a formal, written, and confidential pricing document to the buyer. Usually all closed bids are opened and reviewed by the buyer at the same time, with the job awarded to the lowest bidder who meets fully the bid's specifications.

An **open bid** system is more informal and is often used when time is a critical factor.

For example, assume that a hotel guest with a room on the fourth floor checks out of his room at 5:30 a.m. one morning and inadvertently leaves the shower in his room turned on, with the tub stopper engaged. The tub overflows, but it is nearly two hours before the hotel's maintenance department is alerted to flooding on the third floor. In such a case, the hotel will likely seek the services of a water extraction services company. Time will likely be of the essence because the longer the water is in contact with walls, carpets, carpet pads, and furnishings, the greater the damage to the hotel. In such a case, the development of bid requirements followed by a formal closed bid system is unrealistic. In this scenario, open bids, characterized by immediate response to the bid request, as well as immediate bidder selection, is the rule.

Key Terms

Closed bid   A method of price solicitation in which confidential bids are submitted to be opened at a predetermined place and time. Also known as a "sealed bid" or "confidential bid."

Open bid   A method of pricing solicitation in which bids are submitted and evaluated as they are received. In this system, the buyer may evaluate price as well as speed of response when awarding the bid.

Selecting Vendors

As is true in the purchase of products, professional buyers understand that, when selecting a service provider, price is an important factor to consider. Price is, however, only one factor among many, and in the case of a service provider, price is rarely, if ever, the most critical factor. More important is the quality of service provided, the reputation of the vendor, and the willingness of service suppliers to stand behind their work.

As you learned in Chapter 3, warranties specify the conditions under which the service provider will make repairs or remedy other problems that may arise, at no additional cost to the buyer. A written warranty typically describes how long the warranty remains in effect, as well as which specific repairs will be made, or services provided, at no extra charge. Warranties generally cover workmanship or the failure of the product if used normally, but not negligence or abuse on the part of the buyer. In most situations, quality suppliers of services routinely warranty their work as part of their service price. Experienced buyers, however, always ensure (in writing whenever possible) that this is the case.

EVALUATION OF VENDOR SERVICES

Buyers generally evaluate the quality of products they buy when the purchased items are delivered. In a similar manner, when vendors provide services, the quality of service provided must be evaluated. The reason for doing so is twofold. First, before authorizing payment for vendor services, buyers must be assured the service purchased has in fact been performed. Second, when a purchased service will likely be purchased again in the future (e.g., lawn care service, equipment repair, pest control, or tax preparation service), the quality of service provided should be assessed to determine the suitability of reusing the same service provider.

Although professional buyers would agree upon the necessity of evaluating service providers, they would also agree about the complexity of doing so. This is because the evaluation of services is more complex than the evaluation of products. The reasons why this is true are many, but include

Intangibility: The quality of a service cannot be easily measured, seen, or touched. Consequently, honest differences of opinion regarding quality level can exist between service providers and those who receive the services. In the final analysis, however, the buyer, not the service provider, ultimately determines quality levels because only buyers make the final quality assessment. Thus, it is important for hospitality service providers to remember that quality is ultimately determined by the consumer. Also, hospitality buyers should fully and carefully define their service expectations to best ensure that differences in service expectations are minimized. Quality in service delivery is not about achieving zero defects, but meeting or exceeding client expectations.

Inseparability: In most cases, the *production* of a service cannot be separated from its *consumption*. For example, the production and consumption of a window washer's service happen together. This means that the buyer may expect the service to be provided in a specific way or by a specific individual. Quality inspection, in such cases, happens after the vendor has performed the service and thus believes they are "finished." In such situations, it is not surprising that the vendor and service provider may differ on whether the service has indeed been fully delivered.

Variability: Service quality and consistency is subject to great variability simply because they are delivered by *people,* and human behavior is difficult to control. Because services are people based, quality can vary by time of day (people get tired), experience, attitude, knowledge, style, and friendliness. Consider two window-washing companies. The first has well-groomed, friendly, and

Even the grooming and attire of service providers will affect client perceptions of service *quality*, a point that should be well recognized by those managing in the hospitality industry.

Getty Images, Inc.

professionally dressed employees whose window-washing abilities are average. Employees of the second company are surly, slovenly in appearance, and often arrive one or two days later than their scheduled time. These employees, however, are not merely good at what they do, they are spectacular. For days after they clean the operation's windows, incoming customers make positive comments about how "clean and bright" it is in the restaurant. Which company provides quality window washing service? It is for the buyer to decide.

Despite the inherent challenges, buyers must evaluate service levels as part of their overall vendor assessment process (you will learn more about evaluating the entire procurement process in Chapter 23). In all cases, those who choose service vendors must ensure these suppliers have fully complied with the specifications (contract terms) established by the operation and that this compliance meets or exceeds established quality levels.

Purchasing Resources on the Internet

In addition to the Web sites referenced in this chapter's "Internet Purchasing Assistant" feature, the following sites provide detailed information to enhance your purchasing knowledge and skills.

Purchasing Resources on the Internet

Site	Information About
www.energy-eye.com	Guest room utility management systems
www.ecomagination.com	Manufacturer's conservation site
www.aga.org	Advantages of gas use (American Gas Association)
www.sdge.com	Energy-saving tips for offices (At the home page, click on "Energy Savings Center")
www.hospitalitynet.org	Hospitality-specific energy saving ideas
www.4hoteliers.com	Water conservation
www.ase.org	Energy efficiency activities worldwide
www.dulley.com	Practical energy-saving ideas
www.perfect.com	E-procurement systems
www.amazon.com	Books about evaluating service levels

Key Terms

HVAC *469*	electric discharge	KwH *479*	in-house (service) *484*
curb appeal *471*	(lamp) *471*	CCF *479*	closed bid *486*
foot-candle *471*	boiler *473*	decatherm *479*	open bid *486*
incandescent	source reduction *475*	Cgal *482*	
(lamp) *471*	income statement *476*	Mcf *483*	

Think It Through

1. It has been estimated that, for each hotel guest room sold in the United States, the hotel will use between 100 and 200 gallons of water per day. Search the Internet and identify at least three specific and ongoing sources of information hoteliers can use for water-saving ideas and suggested conservation activities.

2. Older foodservice facilities are often less energy efficient than newer ones. Identify five specific energy-saving strategies that you, as a buyer of utilities, might recommend to the owners of a foodservice facility that is several decades old.

3. Some hospitality operators feel the implementation of energy-saving activities are justified only when the payback (in savings) for such activities exceed their cost. Others believe conservation is the responsibility of businesses even if the amount spent on conservation activities exceeds potential savings. What is your position?

4. Some hospitality buyers feel it is appropriate to share one service vendor's open bid with another potential vendor who has yet to bid. Do you feel that position is ethical? Why or why not?

5. As a consumer, would you rather go to a restaurant that provided average food and outstanding service, or one that offered outstanding food but only average service? In which setting would you feel you received the most value for your money?

Team Fun

For this exercise, assume that each team works for a 1,000-room resort hotel located on 25 landscaped acres. Its water utility company charges for water by the Cgal, and sewage costs are tied directly to water usage based upon the theory that each gallon of water used by its customers will inevitably end up being treated in its sewage treatment facility.

The resort's general manager would like to make the case that this approach is inappropriate for the resort because so much of the water it uses will *not* be treated by the wastewater treatment facility.

1. The assignment of the first team is to build a case for the fact that a large amount of water used in the resort's laundry facility will not go "down the drain" but rather will be removed by the facility's dryers, and to provide detailed data backup for that position.

2. The assignment of the second team is to build a case for the fact that a large amount of water used for the hotel's large indoor and outdoor pools will not go "down the drain" but rather will be lost to evaporation, and to provide detailed data backup for that position.

3. The assignment of the third team is to build a case for the fact that a large amount of water used for the hotel's landscaping needs will not go "down the drain" but rather will be absorbed by plants or lost to ground water, and to provide detailed data backup for that position.

Each team should be prepared to present and discuss their findings and conclusions.

20

Procurement of Capital Equipment

In This Chapter

For most hospitality buyers, routine purchases involve buying supply items required to operate their businesses on a daily basis. For example, food service buyers purchase food and beverage items such as those described in Chapters 13–17. Other hospitality buyers, such as those working in the areas of lodging, health care, and clubs, also select products and services used daily in their operations. All hospitality buyers will, however, from time to time, be confronted with the task of purchasing capital equipment.

In this chapter, "capital equipment" will refer to business resources used to generate income and with an expected life of more than one year. Examples in the food service industry include items such as tables, chairs, and kitchen equipment. Examples in the lodging industry include carpets, sinks, bedding, in-room televisions, and lobby furniture. If you find it somewhat odd to think of carpet or a bed as a piece of "equipment," you are not alone. The types of capital equipment purchased are diverse, and many buyers simply use the term "capital" or "capital expenditure" when referring to any of these purchases. Other buyers prefer the industry shorthand term of FF&E (furniture, fixtures, and equipment) when referring to their capital purchases. Regardless of the term used, however, the buying of capital items is very different from that of buying normal operating supplies, and in this chapter you will learn about some of these important differences.

Hospitality buyers making capital purchase decisions are influenced by a variety of unique factors, and these are examined in the chapter. How capital items are purchased varies, and the specific items food service, lodging, and other industry segments buy differ as well. In this chapter, you will learn about some of the most important of these segment-specific capital items.

Because capital items are generally more expensive than normal operating supplies, the manner in which they are financed can have a big influence on what (and how) buyers make their selections. For example, in some cases, the decision will be made to pay cash for a capital item. In other situations, a long- or short-term loan may be used to pay for the item. In still other cases, buyers may elect to lease, rather than purchase, a capital item. The chapter examines these strategies and the effect they have on the financial reporting of the business.

Finally, government entities write tax codes that change often, but always affect business investment, and the tax considerations often determine the wisdom of a capital purchase decision. Taxes are not voluntary contributions. Most businesspersons want to pay the taxes they owe, but no more than they owe. To better understand the tax consequences of capital expenditures, this chapter concludes with an examination of the effect that alternative capital purchase strategies have upon a business's total tax liabilities.

■ ■ ■

Outline

Capital Expense Purchases and Operating Expense Purchases
Capital Purchase Needs Assessment
   Input on Decision Making
   Assessment of Replacement Needs

CAPITAL EXPENSE PURCHASES AND OPERATING EXPENSE PURCHASES

In Chapter 1, you learned that a "capital equipment" purchase referred to an item that was expected to benefit the hospitality operation for more than one year. Thus, furniture, **fixtures,** and equipment (FF&E) are all considered capital purchases.

Although "land" and "buildings" are also considered capital purchases, in this chapter we will examine only the types of capital purchases typically made by hospitality buyers in the course of their normal procurement activities: FF&E items.

Thus far, you have learned primarily about purchasing items such as foods, beverages, and guest room amenities that are considered "normal" operating expenses. Items purchased as a capital expense are in many ways, however, treated differently from those purchased as a normal operating expense. Because capital expense items will be used by an operation for more than one year (and perhaps for as many as twenty or thirty years), these items are depreciated over several years (rather than expensed in the year in which they are purchased). The result of this generally accepted accounting principle (**GAAP**) is that capital expenditures have a different effect on an operation's financial statements and tax liabilities than do normal operating expenses.

In addition to how they are treated for accounting purposes, there are other significant differences between capital expenditures and the purchase of normal operating supplies. For example, if a buyer selects a vendor and buys a 50-pound bag of onions, and later finds the flavor of the onions was inferior, it is not a big problem to change vendors to improve the quality of product. Consider, however,

Key Terms

Fixture　Something that is permanently attached to a building as an essential or structural part (e.g., plumbing or lighting fixture).

GAAP　Short for "Generally Accepted Accounting Principle"; a set of accounting rules used to standardize financial reporting.

In most cases, capital purchases result in equipment that is expected to have a useful life of many years.

Brady/Pearson Education/PH College

if the purchase involved an expensive machine to slice or chop the onions. Then this inferior piece of capital equipment will have to be used for many years or replaced at great expense to the hospitality operation. Thus, the importance of effective capital purchasing relates to the fact that decisions made in this area will often have very long lasting positive or negative effects on the buyer's operation.

In business, capital is a term synonymous with "money." Those who invest their capital understand that, in most industries including hospitality, investing money can be risky. Thus, effective capital purchasing seeks not only to secure quality products, but also to minimize business risk.

As you learned previously, capital expenditures are recorded on a business's Balance Sheet, whereas operating expenses are normally recorded on the Statement

PURCHASING PROS NEED TO KNOW (20.1)

Most hospitality managers spend a good deal of time developing budgets. They are important because the management of a business's cash and other financial resources must be planned. If, for example, a food service manager knows that revenues will be high next month, he or she knows they must budget for more labor to serve higher guest counts. Similarly, that manager will need to purchase additional food and beverage products to ensure the operation does not run out of its menu items. It is easy to see why the ability to effectively budget revenue and operating expenses is a critical skill.

Capital budgets are a special form of budget that managers and buyers must also understand. A capital budget is a long-range plan that identifies capital expenditures that should be undertaken, as well as when these expenses should be incurred. For example, a hospitality buyer working in a hotel may be required to provide the hotel's owners with answers to the following types of questions:

When should the parking lot be repaved?

When should guestroom bathrooms be remodeled?

How old should our mattresses and box springs be before they are replaced?

How often should the lobby be remodeled and the corridor carpets replaced?

When should we purchase new tables and chairs for the restaurant?

Note that questions of this nature require buyers to understand product quality issues as well as issues of useful product life. For owners, too little investment of capital (too small a capital budget) can result in reduced sales and negative customer perceptions of the property. Insufficient capital investment may also result in the inefficient use of labor (as, for example, when there is inadequate investment in labor-saving machinery).

Too much capital investment (too large a capital budget), however, can mean fewer profits are generated relative to the amount of money invested. To become truly valued advisors, professional hospitality buyers must learn to identify quality capital items, and they must also be able to advise owners about the optimal times to buy them.

of Income and Expense. Capital expenditures typically are more costly than those related to daily operating expenses, and the owners of a business pay particularly close attention to them. In fact, because of their critical nature, in most cases only a company's owners can approve capital expenditures. As a result, even those buyers with a good deal of responsibility and authority will likely find their capital purchase expenditures closely scrutinized.

CAPITAL PURCHASE NEEDS ASSESSMENT

Now that you know about capital expenditures, their importance, and how they vary from operational expenses, it is important to understand why assessing the need for capital purchases is much more complex than assessing noncapital purchasing needs. The critical factors affecting capital purchases decision making are, in very significant ways, different from those required for normal operating expenses.

Buyers directly involved in selecting capital equipment will find the process heavily influenced by several unique factors. Among the most important of these are

- Input on decision making
- Assessment of replacement needs
- Assessment of future needs
- Competitive influences
- Payback periods

Input on Decision Making

When hospitality buyers purchase items such as fresh produce normally used in their foodservice operations or individual shampoo bottles routinely placed in guest rooms, few preapprovals are likely necessary. In fact, after purchase specifications have been established for products such as these, only the buyer may need to authorize their purchase. When purchasing capital items, however, the individuals and groups that provide input can be diverse in perspective and in influence. The most important of these include the following:

Owners: You have learned that a business's owners are the ultimate providers of investment funds, and thus the money required for capital expenditures. Because they must take ultimate responsibility for any capital purchase, it is logical that these individuals have a significant voice in the selection and approval of FF&E items. Buyers must understand that there are always pressures from various constituencies (managers, employees, customers, and potential vendors) to "improve or upgrade" capital items. What manager, for example, would not want to have newer equipment, furnishings, and the latest in technological advancements? In the final analysis, however, the purchase of these items must be cost justified, and the individuals to whom they must be justified are the owners of the business.

Buyers: Professional buyers who are respected by a business's owners will have a significant voice in the selection of capital items. They must be knowledgeable about product quality and product life cycles and, when they demonstrate understanding about these factors, their opinions about capital purchase advisability will be strongly considered.

End users: In most cases, it is highly advisable to seek the input of end users when contemplating a capital purchase. Consider, for example, the hotel owner/operator who will be selecting a new riding lawnmower for use in maintaining the hotel's landscaped areas. The purchase price of the new commercial-grade mower will be between $4,000 and $7,000. It would make sense to seek input about the machine's size, desirable features, and ease of use from those who will be operating the machine. This is not to imply that end users will ultimately determine capital expenditures and items to be purchased, but professional buyers should seek, whenever possible, helpful input from those workers who will be most affected by the capital purchase.

FF&E vendors: It might seem unusual for vendors to be listed in a group of individuals from whom capital expenditure advice should be sought. Information they provide can be important, for example, when buyers consider options related to warranties, service and repair availability, compatibility with current equipment, and even "style" issues. Of course, professional buyers understand that the natural bias of FF&E vendors will be toward increased, not decreased, capital expenditures. Despite that bias, knowledgeable buyers can mine this valuable source of information and use what they learn to make improved buying decisions.

Financial managers: Because capital purchases typically involve large sums of money, the input of a business's financial managers or controllers is often sought prior to making an FF&E purchase decision. Many hospitality businesses experience differences in cash flow (see Chapter 1) that make funds more available in some time periods than in others. When the timing of a capital expenditure significantly affects the amount of cash a business has to pay its other expenses such as payroll, utilities, taxes, and vendor invoices, the input of financial managers can be critical.

In addition to cash flow management, financial managers may be more experienced in negotiating with vendors about payment schedules, financing, and related payment terms. These can have a significant effect on the ease with which a capital expenditure can be paid for, as well as the "total" cost (principal plus interest) charged by vendors when a capital purchase is financed by the vendor.

Assessment of Replacement Needs

Because furnishings and equipment wear out, some FF&E purchases must be made simply to maintain predetermined quality levels. As a result, professional buyers must be aware of the condition of all their operations' FF&E items. Carpets, tables, chairs, booths, stools and bar tops, and kitchen equipment are examples of the type of hospitality products that must periodically be replaced simply to maintain quality standards.

In hotels, carpets, mattresses, box springs, **case goods,** sofas, desks, and chairs must be replaced regularly to maintain a fresh look and to comply, where applicable, with franchisor-mandated quality standards.

Due to normal wear and tear, all hospitality buyers encounter the need to purchase FF&E products simply to replace and maintain their existing capital items.

Assessment of Future Needs

Often, when foodservice operations undertake significant FF&E renovations, it is because the operation is changing its concept (e.g., from one theme to another), or when a building is converted from a prior use to one involving the service of food and beverages. In such cases, buyers are not replacing current FF&E items but rather purchasing the operation's future FF&E needs. This is a more challenging activity because much can be unknown about the actual FF&E needs of the business before it begins to operate.

Key Term

Case goods Pieces of furniture, such as dressers, nightstands, chests of drawers, and so on that provide storage in guest rooms.

Normal wear and tear require that most guest room FF&E items be replaced on a regular schedule that ranges between 5–10 years, depending upon the hotel's clientele and its business volume.

Rob Reichenfeld © Dorling Kindersley

In a similar manner, if a hotel's owners elect to **re-flag** their properties, the new franchisor will likely require a significant **product improvement plan (PIP)** prior to allowing the hotel the right to operate under the new brand.

Because PIPs routinely call for the extensive replacement of FF&E items, when hotels are operated under a franchise agreement, the franchisor often becomes a "partner" in the FF&E procurement process. Of course, even a hotel that is not in the process of re-flagging can, based upon the goals of its owners, undertake extensive FF&E enhancements.

Current and pending legislation may also affect future capital expenditure decisions. When considering remodeling and refurbishing costs, hospitality managers must consider the effect of changing building codes, laws such as the Americans with Disabilities Act (ADA), and other legislation that can directly influence what, and when, capital items must be purchased. The ADA has mandated many changes, including those related to the physical facilities of restaurants, hotels, and clubs. Title III of the ADA covers public accommodations (private entities that own, operate, rent, or lease to places of public accommodation) such as restaurants, hotels, theaters, convention centers, retail stores, shopping centers, hospitals, zoos, amusement parks, private schools, day care centers, health spas, and bowling alleys. Many hospitality operators found that capital investment in parking lots and spaces, entranceways, and seating facilities were required because of ADA mandates.

COMPETITIVE INFLUENCES One of the most significant reasons for investing in FF&E items is because other businesses do so. The hospitality business is competitive, and organizations that do not invest and reinvest in their physical facilities can discover that their products are perceived by consumers to be "out of style" or worn out. Business owners must avoid such consumer perceptions of their products.

Even when a business's FF&E items are not out of date or worn, they may still need to be replaced, updated, or complemented. Consider, for example, the lodging industry's rush to replace perfectly functional bedding products when Starwood Hotels introduced its "Heavenly Bed." This item consists of a custom-designed

Key Terms

Re-flag The conversion of a hotel from one brand to another.

Product improvement plan (PIP) A detailed plan for enhancing a hotel property. Most often undertaken in conjunction with a re-flag effort. Often referred to as a "PIP."

pillow, top mattress set by Simmons with 900 individual coils, three sheets (in the triple-sheet bed-making method, one sheet is spread over the top mattress; the other two sheets sandwich a thin, often down-filled blanket [or down alternative for those with allergies] to ensure that guests make contact only with the bedsheet, not the blanket), ranging in thread count from 180 to 250, additional down blanket, comforter, and white duvet with five goose down/goose feather pillows. This roll-out with accompanying publicity caused that company's competitors to reassess their own capital purchase priorities to effectively compete against this new guest room amenity. In a similar manner, most industry observers believe the decision by McDonald's to invest in the coffee-making equipment needed to produce its own line of "gourmet" coffees was a direct result of the competitive pressures they felt from other high-end coffee sellers such as Starbucks, Caribou, and Big B's.

Unless they are the business's owner/manager as well as the buyer, a purchaser may not have the responsibility to monitor the competition for improvements that may result in the need for capital expenditures. However, monitoring competitive forces is a task that must be addressed by someone within the hospitality organization. In a large number of cases, it may be the professional hospitality buyer.

PAYBACK PERIODS   **Payback period** refers to the length of time it will take to recover 100 percent of the amount invested. Generally, the shorter the time period required to recover all of an investment amount, the more desirable it is.

The formula that managerial accountants use to compute payback period is

$$\frac{\text{Capital Invested}}{\text{Annual Income (or Savings)}} = \text{Payback Period}$$

To illustrate a payback period based upon annual income achieved, assume that the purchase of a frozen drink-making machine in a high-volume bar will cost the bar's owner $5,000. Management estimates that the drink machine will generate $300 in after-cost revenues per month, or $3,600 per year ($300 month $\times$ 12 months = $3,600/year). The payback period in such a case would be computed as:

$$\frac{\$5,000}{\$3,600} = 1.4 \text{ years (approximately 17 months)}$$

To illustrate a payback period based upon annual savings achieved, assume that a restaurant can, for $1,500, purchase a new, energy-efficient water heater powered by gas, rather than by electricity (which is used by the current hot water heater). Based upon an assessment of current utility bills, and information provided by the unit's manufacturer, the purchaser estimates the restaurant will save $75 per month in reduced energy costs or $900 per year ($75 month $\times$ 12 months = $900/year). The payback period in this case would be computed as:

$$\frac{\$1,500}{\$900} = 1.7 \text{ years (approximately 20 months)}$$

Owners and purchasers use the payback period formula to evaluate different investment alternatives. In nearly all cases, shorter payback periods are preferable to longer ones. The question of the "appropriate" minimum length of payback period required to justify an owner's investment, however, ultimately depends upon the goals set for the business.

Key Term

Payback period   The amount of time required to fully recover an investment amount. Payback periods are typically computed in years and months.

PURCHASING FURNISHINGS, FIXTURES, AND EQUIPMENT

Professional buyers in the hospitality industry routinely purchase some FF&E items. The specific items purchased depend upon a variety of factors, including the segment of the industry in which the buyer works. In all cases, however, effective FF&E purchasing has four main goals:

1. *A better-looking property:* In many cases, FF&E items are purchased "for show"; that is, they are quite visible to guests. Entrance or lobby areas in hotels, hospital dining rooms, hostess stations in restaurants (as well as dining rooms and bar areas), and club houses in private clubs are all examples of industry segments in which FF&E items make a significant visual impact on guests. As a result, these areas must reflect a level of style, quality, and cleanliness that is in keeping with the image the business seeks to project.

2. *A more efficiently operating property:* In many cases, FF&E upgrades improve business efficiency. This can occur because of changes in the design of FF&E products themselves (such as when standard toilets are replaced with those that make more efficient use of water that reduces utility bills), or when significant labor savings result. Professional buyers know that, in the final analysis, an FF&E purchase is a business investment. Business owners look more favorably upon those investments that reduce costs, increase efficiency, and improve labor productivity than those that do not.

3. *Maximize the impact of FF&E expenditures:* Experienced hospitality managers agree that there never seems to be enough money in their annual FF&E budgets. Owners invest in businesses wisely. In most cases, that means that FF&E resources will be expended only when there is a compelling reason to do so. Each dollar dedicated to FF&E replacement must be wisely spent to maximize its effect on the business.

4. *Increased business and more satisfied guests:* Businesses desire growth, and in the hospitality industry that means serving more guests and serving them more frequently. Word-of-mouth, the process of one customer recommending a facility to other customers, has long been recognized as one of the most powerful sources of new business. When FF&E items reflect positively on a business, constructive word-of-mouth is maximized. Unfortunately, when the appearance of FF&E items results in damaged customer perceptions, negative word-of-mouth can also be maximized.

Visually stunning architectural design can impress guests, but the FF&E items that complement the design are just as important.

Bernardo Grijalva / Shutterstock

Regardless of the industry segment in which they work, professional buyers must have detailed knowledge of the FF&E requirements unique to their area of specialization. These include food service, lodging, and other industry segments.

Food Service

In food service, FF&E expenditures can be viewed most easily in terms of their **front of house** or **back of house** placement.

Front of house FF&E include those items found in public restrooms, dining room tables, chairs, and lighting fixtures, and the décor pieces that give a food service its unique style or ambiance. FF&E items in these areas must be kept fresh looking, clean, and in good repair.

Back-of-house FF&E items include food production, cooking, and holding equipment as well as cleaning equipment. In many cases, specialized equipment will be needed to support the menu. These specialized equipment items (e.g., items such as bar-b-que meat smokers, rotisseries, and pizza ovens) must then be carefully maintained if the restaurant is to execute its menu properly.

Hotels

Besides the obvious signs of wear and tear, sometimes the decision to replace FF&E is essentially already made for the hotelier. That is the case, for example, if owners seek to reposition their property, place it in a higher average daily rate (ADR) tier, or even give it a different character or feel.

Although there are some informal industry "standards" about the frequency with which FF&E in hotels should be replaced, higher-volume hotels such as airport properties and resort hotels may need earlier refurbishment. Also, the quality of any previous FF&E replacements will directly influence the frequency of future updating required by a lodging facility. Theoretically, the higher the quality of previous updates, the longer FF&E items should last. As a result, experienced buyers in the hotel industry recognize that FF&E purchase decisions often require them to balance "cost" and "durability." Technological advances can also create challenging lodging-related FF&E decisions.

In addition to cost, durability, and technology, hotel FF&E buyers face significant "fashion" issues. To illustrate, consider that a restaurant FF&E buyer might buy a back of house item such as a food mixer knowing it will last twenty-five years or more, and as a result, he or she would be willing to pay more for it. Hotel operators, however, want their guests to feel everything in their rooms is fresh, new, and in style, all of the time. The result: more frequent capital replacements (of admittedly lower-cost FF&E products) are a common practice among many hoteliers.

Other Hospitality Segments

The types and kinds of FF&E items purchased by professional hospitality buyers are as varied as the industry segments in which they work. Purchasers in private clubs will require knowledge about golf carts, whereas information about slot

---

Key Terms

Front of house   Those areas within a food and beverage operation that are readily accessible to guests. Front of house areas include public restrooms, lobbies, dining rooms, and bar areas.

Back of house   Those areas within a hospitality operation that are not typically accessible to guests. Back-of-house areas include employee locker rooms, kitchens, production areas, and offices. Sometimes called "heart of house."

HI-TECH PURCHASING (20.1)

Buying Video Display Units (or Are They TVs?)

Capital equipment purchases require buyers to stay current with technological advancements, and this can be challenging. For example, buying today's video display units (called TVs by those who are less technologically advanced!) for hotel guest rooms or for use in a food service or bar operation is a lot more complicated than it used to be. Where in the past, buyers concerned themselves primarily with screen "size" (measured in inches diagonally across the face of the screen), today's hospitality buyers need to understand size as well as the answers to entirely new purchasing questions:

Plasma or LCD? Plasma flat-screen technology consists of hundreds of thousands of individual pixel cells, which allow electric pulses (stemming from electrodes) to excite natural gases, causing them to glow and produce light. This light illuminates the proper balance of red, green, or blue sensors contained in each cell to display the proper color sequence. Each pixel cell is essentially an individual microscopic fluorescent lightbulb, receiving instructions from software contained on the rear electrostatic silicon board.

     Whether spread across a flat-panel screen or placed in the heart of a projector, all LCD displays come from the same technological background. A matrix of thin-film transistors supplies voltage to liquid-crystal-filled cells sandwiched between two sheets of glass. When hit with an electrical charge, the crystals untwist to an exact degree to filter white light generated by a lamp behind the screen (for flat-panel TVs). LCD monitors reproduce colors through a process of subtraction: They block out particular color wave lengths from the spectrum of white light until they are left with just the right color. With costs lower than for plasma units, LCDs make a good choice for most hospitality buyers.

What about HDTV? HDTV (High Definition TV) is a must. Eventually, all cable, satellite, and over-the-air television will broadcast in HD. "HD-ready" is a less expensive alternative, but this requires the addition of an external HD tuner, cable, or satellite box.

How about contrast ratio and response time? The higher the contrast ratio, the better the picture. A 1200:1 contrast ratio is better than a 500:1. Faster response times are better. Thus, an 8 ms response time is an improvement over a 12 ms response time.

What do all those other numbers mean? 1080p and 720p refer to lines of resolution. Regular TVs go up to 480p. 1080 is top of the line. Buy 720p or higher.

Why do purchasers need to know all this? So they can easily read and understand the "specs" for today's typical TV set, like the Vizio VX32L (www.vizio.com). This particular video display unit is a 32-inch HDTV LCD with a 1200:1 contrast ratio, 1080 resolution, and 8 ms response time. Got it?

Internet Purchasing Assistant (20.1)

Extensive FF&E purchases required for major property updates typically occur every six to ten years in the hotel business. In restaurants, the times between major facility renovations may be even longer. As a result, professional buyers may not have significant experience overseeing the purchasing process involved in such a major renovation.

     To assist these buyers, professional design and FF&E procurement companies offer their specialized services. To view the Web site of one such company, and to review their service offerings, go to: www.innvisionsupply.com

     At the home page, surf their site, and then click on "Portfolio" to see a list of their completed projects.

Buyers in specialized areas of hospitality must become experts on purchasing a wide variety of specialty items, such as golf carts and watering systems for those working in country and private golf clubs.

Francesca Yorke © Dorling Kindersley

machines is needed by those working in the casino industry. Cruise lines, health care, bed and breakfast, college and university feeding, school food service, and airline feeding are just a few of the industry segments in which FF&E buying is highly specialized.

CAPITAL PURCHASE FINANCING

When a hospitality buyer purchases a normal operating supply, it is typically assumed that the supply will be paid for shortly after it is delivered. Payment is typically made in the form of cash or check and is generally for the full amount of the item's cost.

When purchasing capital items, however, owners can choose from a variety of payment or financing methods. Used in this manner, the word "financing" simply refers to the method of securing (funding) the money needed to purchase the capital item. A variety of issues can affect decisions regarding the "best" financing alternative for capital items. These include a fundamental understanding of the **time value of money** and earnings made on investments.

Financing alternatives available to investors include paying cash for their purchases. Significant financing alternatives to full cash payments are available, however, and these will be examined in this section as will the effect of various financing alternatives on a business's financial statements and the taxes it must pay.

Time Value of Money

If you talk about prices paid by consumers for goods and services with older persons, you will likely discover that many of them are "shocked" over the prices of today's products. Often they shake their heads disbelievingly at their own children's or grandchildren's college tuition bills, the price of gasoline, or the cost of a restaurant meal or hotel guest room rental. These examples illustrate how the passage of time truly does change people's view of the worth of a "dollar," and they are one key to understanding the time value of money.

Key Term
Time value (of money)   The concept that money available now is worth more than the same amount in the future, due to its potential earning capacity.

To illustrate, assume that you just won $100,000 in a multistate lottery. As a winner, your options for collecting the money are

A. Receive $100,000 now

or

B. Receive $100,000 in three years

If you are like most people, you would choose to receive the $100,000 now. This is because most people instinctively understand that it makes little sense to defer a payment into the future when they could have the exact same amount of money now. At its most basic level, the time value of money demonstrates that, all things being equal, it is better to have money now rather than later. From an investment perspective, those in business also know they can "do" more with their money if they have it now because they can use it to earn even more money through wise investments. Thus, as a general rule, "today" dollars are worth more than "tomorrow" dollars both from a control aspect and from a potential earnings perspective.

Earlier in this chapter, you learned about payback periods and how these affect capital expenditure decisions. Closely related to payback periods and the time value of money is the concept of **return on investment (ROI).**

To illustrate, assume a buyer is considering the purchase of a piece of capital equipment for $5,000. Assume also that this equipment will save the business $1,000 per year for a five-year period. As you learned earlier, the payback period on this purchase would be five years ($5,000 invested/$1,000 savings per year). The ROI for the piece of equipment would be computed using the following ROI formula:

$$\frac{\text{Money earned on funds invested}}{\text{Funds invested}} = \text{ROI}$$

In this simplified example, the ROI for the piece of capital equipment would be computed as:

$$\frac{\$5,000 \text{ earned}}{\$5,000 \text{ invested}} = 1.00 \text{ or } 100\% \text{ over five years}$$

On an annual basis, the ROI realized would be:

$$100\%/5 \text{ years} = 20\% \text{ per year}$$

Different business owners establish their own ROI requirements for capital investment based upon their specific investment goals, and buyers should know these ROI minimums and the long-term goals owners have for their businesses. This is especially important when buyers realize that operating profits are not the same as return on investment. For example, sometimes, a restaurant that achieves a very good profit percentage (of revenues) is still not a good investment for the restaurant's owner. In other cases, a restaurant that achieves a less spectacular net income is a better investment. To illustrate, assume two restaurant owners have generated $200,000 in profits after a year of operating their respective restaurants. The first owner invested $2,000,000 in the operation; the second owner invested $4,000,000. The first owner achieved a ROI of 10% ($200,000 ÷ $2,000,000 = 10%), whereas the second owner achieved an ROI of 5% ($200,000 ÷ $4,000,000 = 5%). Actual returns on investment can vary greatly, but few, if any, investors will continue

Key Term

Return on investment (ROI)   A ratio that describes the amount of money earned or saved by an investment, when compared to the amount of money originally invested.

Internet Purchasing Assistant (20.2)

The manner in which investors compute ROI can vary by the industry in which they invest. Also, ROI calculations can become more complex when, for example, investors seek to compare two different investment options, or include an assessment that considers the differing costs of acquiring capital. To view the product offerings of a company that creates calculators designed to address these (and many more) investor concerns, go to: www.pine-grove.com

At the home page:

1. Click on "Windows Calculators."
2. Next, scroll down the alphabetical listing to explore investment return calculators of interest to you.

to invest in a hospitality operation if their ROI is less than what they could achieve with other investment opportunities offering the same or even lesser risk.

Financing Alternatives

Professional buyers understand that most business owners seek to maximize the returns on their investments. In the majority of cases, it is only after investors determine that a capital purchase should be made that they must determine the best way to **finance** the investment.

On-the-Job Challenges in Purchasing (20.1)

"I don't understand why they can't just buy a new one," said Sara. "This machine is old, and I think it's dangerous, too!" she added.

Sara was talking to Tim Rydell, her coworker at Pollo Plus, an independently owned and managed restaurant whose menu featured fried and roasted chicken products.

Sara and Tim were "closers"; their jobs required that they close the restaurant kitchen each day and, in doing so, perform a variety of cleaning tasks. One of those tasks was straining the oil in the restaurant's deep-fat fryer. Because the oil was usually hot, the mechanical filtering system used by the fryer needed to be put in place and operated very carefully.

"I don't see why the owner doesn't buy a new machine," continued Sara, "They make them with automatic filter systems now."

"Well," replied Tim, "Maybe you should suggest that. If you do, maybe we'll get a new one!"

Case Study Questions

Assume that you are the owner/manager of this restaurant.

1. Do you think a new fryer would increase revenue levels in your business?
2. Assume also that your fryer was only two years old. What would you say to Sara if she asked you about buying the new piece of equipment?
3. Assume, alternatively, that your fryer was near the end of its useful life. What would you now say to Sara if she asked you about buying the new piece of equipment?
4. Identify at least three capital equipment-related purchasing issues that are evident from this on-the-job challenge.

Key Term

Finance   To provide the money required to make a purchase.

To illustrate the process, assume that you are shopping for a new car. Your first task is to find the vehicle that suits your purpose and is offered for sale at a price you believe is reasonable. After you have done so, you could then determine the best way to finance it.

Theoretically, financing alternatives for your car purchase could range from paying cash for the full purchase price to borrowing 100 percent of the purchase price. Paying all cash at the time of purchase is known as 100 percent **equity** funding because, when used, buyers have 100 percent free and clear ownership of the item.

Borrowing the full purchase price (100 percent debt financing) could be another alternative, as is the option of partial equity and partial debt financing. If you wished, you could even investigate and ultimately choose to **lease,** rather than purchase, your new car.

In the hospitality industry, large FF&E purchases are often financed with both equity and debt. The precise manner in which financing is secured will have a major influence on the ROI investors ultimately achieve, so buyers must understand the effects of alternative approaches to FF&E financing.

When a person or company makes a capital investment, they typically do so with the intention of increasing (not decreasing) the monetary value of their investment. In most cases, investors can choose from a wide variety of investment options. In fact, in today's complex financial world, buyers acting on behalf of owners can choose from literally hundreds of investment options.

In most cases, the greater the **leverage,** or funding supplied by debt, the greater the investment risk and the greater the typical ROI achieved by the investor.

Recall that, in our car purchase example, you may have the option of leasing, rather than purchasing, your vehicle. For a business, the decision to lease, rather than purchase, a capital asset greatly affects ROI as well. Also, a lease decision affects, in some cases, the taxes that will be paid by the business. In this section, you will learn about the effect on ROI of debt/equity funding decisions, as well as the effect on ROI of alternative lease/purchase decisions.

DEBT OR EQUITY FINANCING   Investors seeking to finance FF&E projects choose between debt and equity funding. Loans are debt financing. Essentially, the investor borrows money and must pay it back, with interest, within a certain timeframe. When equity funding is used, investors raise money by selling a portion of ownership in the company (or specific asset purchased). When investors use their own money for equity funding, they are, in effect, selling the ownership in the business or asset to themselves.

Debt financing can be supplied by banks, finance companies, credit unions, credit card companies, and private investors. Equity funding typically means using cash on hand or taking on business partners. In many small hospitality businesses, owners secure their equity funds from relatives, friends, colleagues, or customers who hope to see their businesses succeed and obtain a return on their investment. Other sources of equity financing can include venture capitalists willing to take risks on promising new businesses.

Key Terms

Equity   Free and clear ownership of an asset (the difference between the value of an item and the amount owed on the item).

Lease   A legal contract allowing for the exclusive possession of another's property for a specific time in exchange for a payment.

Leverage   Investing with borrowed money.

When an owner/investor funds an FF&E purchase with a combination of equity and debt, their ROI on equity funds is achieved only after those who have supplied debt funding have first earned their own ROIs. Stated another way, equity ROIs are subordinate (secondary) to debt ROIs.

The amount of ROI generated by an investment is greatly affected by the ratio of debt to equity financing in that investment. To illustrate, consider the case of Penny Vincent, the manager of the Great Fox Water Park. Penny proposes to add a new snack bar area inside the park's large indoor pool area. The total project is estimated to cost $270,000. The money earned on funds invested (**net operating income**) is estimated to be $51,500 per year. Assume Penny approaches the park's owners to finance the FF&E required to create the snack bar.

If the park's owners provided 100% equity financing, their annual ROI would be computed as:

$$\frac{\text{Money earned on funds invested}}{\text{Funds invested}} = \text{ROI}$$

or

$$\frac{\$51,500}{\$270,000} = 19.1\%$$

Although many investors would consider a 19% ROI to be very good, assume that Penny's owners seek a higher ROI. Assume also that they are able to secure debt financing at an annual percentage rate of 8%. Figure 20.1 illustrates the effect on their equity ROI of funding the snack bar FF&E purchases with varying levels of debt and equity.

As you can see from the data in Figure 20.1, if Penny's owners elect to fund 50% (rather than 100%) of the project's cost with equity, the ROI achieved is 30.1% (rounded), an ROI much higher than the 19% ROI that would be achieved if they did not leverage their investment at all. With even greater leverage (only 20% equity funding and 80% debt funding), even greater investment returns (63.4% (rounded) ROI) on equity are achieved. Given the data presented in Figure 20.1,

Great Fox Water Park Snack Bar

		Project Cost	% Return	Net Operating Income (NOI)
Total	100%	$270,000		$51,500
Debt	50%	135,000	8.0%	10,800
Equity	50%	135,000	30.1%	40,700
Debt	60%	162,000	8.0%	12,960
Equity	40%	108,000	35.7%	38,540
Debt	70%	189,000	8.0%	15,120
Equity	30%	81,000	44.9%	36,380
Debt	80%	216,000	8.0%	17,280
Equity	20%	54,000	63.4%	34,220

Rate of return based upon $270,000 project cost; 8% interest rate on debt financing.
FIGURE 20.1 Effect of Debt on Equity Investment Returns

Key Term

Net operating income (NOI) An accounting term referring to the amount by which operating revenues in a defined period exceed operating expenses.

buyers might ask, "Why not fund nearly 100% of every investment with debt?" The answer, of course, is that lenders also have their investment goals. The experience of most lenders is that, to maximize the chances of having money they lend paid back, they require borrowers to "risk" a portion of their own funds as well as those of the lenders. This is necessary because, although Penny has "estimated" a $51,500 profit, if no actual profit materializes, lenders will still expect (and demand!) full payment for their invested funds.

In many cases, as the percentage of money lent for a project increases, so too does a lender's risk that their loans will not be repaid. Because many lending groups consider businesses in the hospitality industry to be very high risk, some will provide debt financing for no more than 50%–70% (or even less) of an FF&E project's total cost. Those borrowers with excellent credit, however, can sometimes secure higher levels of debt-to-equity funding. As a result, it is easy to see why the credit history of borrowers heavily influences the *future* ROIs they can achieve. This is a concept that buyers who are not the owners of a business must recognize when seeking funding for suggested FF&E purchases and projects.

LEASE OR BUY DECISIONS   Leasing allows a business to use an asset without buying it. Just as a business owner's decision to vary the debt–equity ratio funding of a project directly affects ROI, so will ROI be affected by a decision to lease, rather than to purchase, capital assets. Leasing can provide distinct advantages for **lessors** as well as for the **lessee.**

In a lease arrangement, lessors gain immediate income while still maintaining ownership of their property. Lessees enjoy specific property rights (e.g., they can use, but not sell, the asset), distinct financial and tax advantages, and the right in many cases to buy the property at an agreed-upon price at the end of the lease's term.

Professional purchasers understand that, from a legal as well as a financial perspective, buying a capital asset is much different than leasing it. Figure 20.2 details some significant differences between the legal rights of lessors (the property's owners) and the lessees of that same property.

Despite the significant differences in the legal treatment of owned and leased property, in most cases the decision to lease rather than purchase property is a financial rather than legal one. The financial and tax consequences of leasing assets rather than buying them are significant, and as a result, those buyers considering such decisions should consult with their organization's tax advisors. This is suggested because many factors affect the desirability of leasing, including the purchase price of the item, the cost and length of the lease, and the treatment of the asset at the end of the lease period.

	Owner	Lessee
Right to use the property	Unlimited use in any legal manner they see fit	Use is strictly limited to the terms of the lease
Treatment of cost	Property is depreciable in accordance with federal and state income tax laws	Lease payments are deductible as a business expense, according to federal and state tax laws
Ability to finance	Property can be used as collateral	Property may not generally be used to secure a loan
Nonpayment of lease	Retains rights to the property	Loses right to keep the property

FIGURE 20.2   Select Legal Considerations of Buying versus Leasing Property

Key Terms

Lessor   The entity that owns a leased asset.

Lessee   The entity that leases an asset.

Especially for very large restaurant projects, decisions regarding debt and equity funding will play an important role in determining an owner's overall ROI.

Tobik / Shutterstock

Effect on Financial Statements

The methods used to finance capital acquisitions affect all three of the most important financial statements prepared by businesses. Those three statements are

- Balance Sheet
- Income Statement
- Statement of Cash Flows

As you learned in Chapter 12, the balance sheet is an important financial document. It details the actual value of a business's assets, the total debt (liabilities) owed by the business, and the amount of any equity held by the owners or shareholders of the business.

THE SUPPLIER'S SIDE (20.1)

"Insider" Tips on Purchasing: From the Supplier's Perspective

Buyer's Question: Cash flow is always a potential problem in my operation, so it seems leasing would always be the best way to go for my capital acquisition needs. Right?

Supplier's Answer: Strictly from a short-term cash flow perspective, you may be right. But despite their many advantages, leases can have distinct disadvantages.

Buyer's Question: What kind of disadvantages?

Supplier's Answer: The first is cost. In almost all cases, leasing then buying equipment is more expensive in the long term than buying it in the first place. More importantly, however, with some purchases, changing technology may make leased equipment obsolete before the lease term is expired. In fact, the opportunity to acquire (lease) newer and more advanced technology at the expiration of an existing lease can be an advantage to the leasing alternative.

Buyer's Question: Can't I usually get out of a lease by just returning the equipment?

Supplier's Answer: Not usually. Typically, significant penalties are incurred if a lessee seeks to terminate the lease before its original expiration date.

Buyer's Question: So is leasing ever a good idea?

Supplier's Answer: Sure. An example is a dishwashing machine where service is included as part of the lease. In this case, the operator gets both newer equipment and qualified service technicians as part of the lease. The important point to remember is that each lease situation must be considered separately before you decide if it is the best way to proceed.

The financial effect of a decision to lease, rather than to buy capital assets, has several effects on the balance sheet of a business. The most critical of these is that an agreement to lease a capital asset creates a liability for a business. That is, the business agrees to pay the lease and establishes a debt that will be recorded on the balance sheet.

Also in Chapter 12, you learned that businesses create an income statement that details the organization's revenue, expenses, and profit, for a specified accounting period. It details how much money (revenue) the business brought in during a specific period of time, how much it spent (expense), and finally, how much, if any, money (profit) remained after the expenses were paid. (It is for this reason that many people call the income statement a "profit and loss" or P&L statement).

Various capital asset purchasing strategies affect the income statement of a business, and often these influences are so complex they are best determined by the business's owners, financial managers, tax accountants, and legal advisors. Professional buyers should understand that decisions regarding the acquisition of capital items often have a significant influence on the income statement of a business. They should also recognize that an income statement is, in most cases, used to evaluate the effectiveness of the managers operating a business. As a result, the managers will be very interested in the financing methods used to acquire capital assets.

The third financial statement affected by capital acquisition strategies is typically less well known than either the balance sheet or income statement. It is called a **statement of cash flows.**

There are actually three distinct activities that affect overall cash flow, and the statement of cash flows details each one:

1. *Operating activities:*   These include the revenues generated by sales and the expenses required to generate those sales. When revenues exceed expenses, operating activities will generate cash. When expenses exceed revenues, cash levels are reduced.
2. *Investing activities:*   When assets like land, buildings, or equipment are purchased for cash, cash levels decrease. When assets are sold for cash, cash levels increase.
3. *Loan (financing) activities:*   When loans are received by the business, cash levels increase. As these loans are repaid, cash levels will decline.

Several other activities also affect a restaurant's cash position. Some of these are shown in Figure 20.3.

Activity	Decrease Cash	Increase/Conserve Cash
Equipment or other capital assets are purchased and paid for in cash	X	
Equipment or other capital assets are purchased and paid for by loans to the business		X
Repayments of loans	X	
Equipment or other capital assets are leased		X
Assets are sold		X

FIGURE 20.3   Selected Activities That Impact a Business's Cash Position

Key Term

Statement of cash flows   A summary of the change in cash available to a business during a designated accounting period.

On-the-Job Challenges in Purchasing (20.2)

"But that doesn't make any sense to me. And it will kill our bonus for this month," said T.J., the assistant restaurant manager. He was talking to MaryAnn, the unit manager for Captain Morgan's Seafood, a company-owned quick service restaurant.

"Well, it does make sense actually," replied MaryAnn. "The hot water heater for our store is pretty old. A new unit vented the way we need it done is $3,000. A replacement of the worn-out heating coil is only $1,500, and our service technician tells me if we make that repair it will be good as new."

"Did the technician also mention that equipment repairs are reported on our monthly income statement, and with a $1,500 charge this month, we won't make our bonuses?" asked T.J. angrily.

"I'm sorry T.J., I know it's a big hit to us personally, but what would you do?" asked MaryAnn.

"I would tell the technician to replace the whole unit. Replace, not repair. Then there is no repair bill on this month's P&L, we get our bonuses, and our restaurant gets a new hot water heater that our company can depreciate. Everybody wins."

Case Study Questions

Assume that you are MaryAnn:

1. If the cost of a new hot water heater does not affect the income statement, what financial statement(s) would it affect?
2. Would you be persuaded by T.J.'s rationale? Why or why not.
3. How do you think the president of your company would respond to T.J.'s comment that, under his recommendation, "everybody wins?"

Because so many capital purchase-related decisions affect a business's cash position, and because of the importance of cash management, buyers must understand the effect of their capital purchase recommendations on the statement of cash flows as well as other measures of a business's financial performance. This is especially so because of the favorable laws affecting the depreciation (see Chapter 12) of capital assets.

Impact on Tax Obligations

Those who understand the very complex tax laws under which their businesses operate can make decisions that help ensure taxes paid are exactly the amount owed. This is important because, when the correct amount of tax is paid, the owner's ROIs will be maximized: They (the owners) will reap the benefits of the investment's return.

Taxing entities, such as the federal, state, and local governments, generally assess taxes to individuals and businesses based upon these entities' definitions of "taxable" income. As you have learned, the manner in which capital purchases are made can directly affect taxable income levels, and thus the taxes a business must pay.

Hospitality buyers are not expected to be experts in tax accounting, nor must they have detailed knowledge of all the laws related to the taxes a business must pay. They must, however, understand the effect of their capital purchase decisions on tax obligations, and the information in Figure 20.4 can be helpful to do so. It provides an example of federally imposed business tax rates for corporations. Although the actual rates contained in federal taxation legislation change and thus will vary somewhat from year to year, the important point to notice is that, as business income rises, taxes that are due and payable rise as well.

A business's net income may be subject to tax at the state and even local levels. In addition to income taxes, the federal government (and some states) imposes a tax on gains from the sale of property, which normally includes FF&E items. The

TAXABLE INCOME OVER ($)	NOT OVER ($)	TAX RATE (%)
0	50,000	15
50,000	75,000	25
75,000	100,000	34
100,000	335,000	39
335,000	10,000,000	34
10,000,000	15,000,000	35
15,000,000	18,333,333	38
18,333,333 +		35

FIGURE 20.4 Typical Corporate Income Tax Rates (Federal)

PURCHASING PROS NEED TO KNOW (20.2)

The Effect of Depreciation

Current tax policy in the United States is heavily biased in favor of businesses that invest in capital assets by purchasing them. When they own (rather than lease) their assets, companies are allowed to reduce their taxable incomes by the amount of legally allowable asset depreciation. Lower taxable incomes for businesses mean reduced tax levels.

The laws surrounding allowable depreciation rates are complex, and professional buyers would do well to notify their business's tax advisors when decisions related to capital asset acquisition are to be made. In some cases, the manner in which depreciation rates are calculated will have such a significant effect on capital acquisition decisions that they will be the single most important factor in such decisions.

---

time value of money concept you learned about earlier emphasizes that deferring payment of all taxes is a powerful business advantage.

With literally thousands of federal, state, and local agencies, departments, offices, and individuals charged with setting or enforcing tax policy, it is not possible for a typical hospitality buyer to be completely knowledgeable about all the tax requirements that could significantly affect their capital purchase decisions. Professional buyers selecting capital equipment should confer with the tax specialists employed by their companies (or the owners of the business) before making significant capital equipment acquisition commitments.

Purchasing Resources on the Internet

In addition to the Web sites referenced in this chapter's "Internet Purchasing Assistant" feature, the following sites provide detailed information to enhance your purchasing knowledge and skills.

Purchasing Resources on the Internet

Site	Information About
www.theinteriorgallery.com	Dining room décor items
www.LGCommercial.com	Visual display units (and TVs)
www.andreuworldamerica.com	Restaurant tables and chairs
www.springusa.com	Restaurant serving equipment
www.alto-sham.com	Food holding and cooking equipment
www.wolfrange.com	Restaurant cooking equipment
www.fryerworld.com	Deep-fat fryers
www.subzero.com	Refrigerators and freezers

(continued)

Site	Information About
www.stainlessusa.com	Stainless steel work tables
www.hobart.com	Food production equipment
www.neo-metro.com	Hotel public space restroom fixtures
www.vitalityfurnitiure.com	Hotel guest room furnishings
www.hdsupplysolutions.com	Hotel FF&E
www.modernoutdoor.com	Outdoor patio furniture
www.kiefferdesigngroup.com	Hotel design consultants

Key Terms

Think It Through

1. Based upon the information you learned in this chapter, identify at least three ways in which, from a buyer's perspective, capital expenditures differ from normal operating expenditures.

2. In this chapter you learned about a variety of information sources that buyers can use when considering capital purchases. Which of these sources do you feel is most important? Least important? Explain your answers.

3. Consider the segment of the hospitality industry in which you are most interested. Identify five specific FF&E items about which you must be well informed if you are to serve as a buyer in that segment. How would you stay up-to-date on product changes, improvements, and developments related to those specific items?

4. Leasing FF&E items is more popular in some segments of the hospitality industry than in others. Identify three reasons, however, why you would advise a buyer in any segment to consider leasing a product, rather than buying it.

5. Leased FF&E items affect a business's cash flow. Draft a short paragraph that would clearly explain to a "nonaccountant"-type the net effect on the Statement of Cash Flows of leasing, rather than buying, an expensive piece of equipment.

Team Fun

For this exercise, assume that each team is employed by Mega Health Care, a for-profit company that operates extended-care retirement facilities. Residents of the facility are strongly encouraged to consume their meals in each facility's dining room, but they may dine in their private rooms if they wish to do so. In one facility that houses 150 residents, the decision has been made to replace the single-tank dishwashing machine in the kitchen that services the dining room.

1. The assignment of the first team is to identify all of the interest groups that should be consulted prior to developing the product specifications for the new dishwashing machine.

2. The assignment of the second team is to identify five sources of information about the types and costs of new dishwashing machines currently available on the market.

3. The assignment of the third team is to identify two business advantages and two disadvantages of:
Buying the machine
Leasing the machine

Each team should be prepared to present and discuss their findings and conclusions.

21

Procurement of Technology-Related Products and Services

In This Chapter

Just as advancements in technology have caused rapid change in society, the hospitality business has been, and will continue to be, changed significantly by those same forces of technology. For professional buyers, this means it is critical that they stay abreast of the technology-related product and service advancements that affect their industry segment.

In some ways, buying advanced technology products is more complex than purchasing other hospitality goods and services. Often buyers will know what they want a new product to do, but will not know *how* the product does it. Few people, for example, truly understand how televisions, computers, or cell telephones actually "work"! Fortunately, buyers need not be technology experts to effectively purchase advanced technology products. In this chapter, you will learn about the significant factors these buyers must know and consider when selecting which items to purchase.

It is important to remember that, despite their complexity, technology products are essentially machines that are subject to malfunction, breakdown, or simply wearing out. As a result, vendors who provide technology products-related service and repair must also be selected. The importance of these service providers is easily overlooked until they are needed. When, however, a computer system "crashes," a credit card processing machine "goes down," or a hotel's telephone system "drops" all incoming calls, the need for these technology service providers becomes readily apparent. In this chapter, you will learn how experienced hospitality buyers choose the quality vendors that supply these needed services.

Although some advanced technology items such as telephones, computers, printers, and software programs are not designed especially for the hospitality industry, other products are industry-specific. For example, food service operators must understand the characteristics of quality point of sale (POS) systems if they are to select one that best records and reports their revenues, menu item sales, and product usage. In a similar manner, they must choose electronic beverage-dispensing equipment to ensure the quality service of these products. And, like most other retailers, the majority of foodservice operations accept payment cards (debit, credit, and gift) when guests pay for their meals. The processing of these cards is an essential service that combines Internet technology and banking services. Thus, the quality of the vendor chosen for the processing task is critical.

Hoteliers, too, face technology challenges unique to their industry segment. For example, hoteliers must understand the key features of any property management system (PMS) they are considering before they acquire it. Telephone and security systems are among other important advanced technology products buyers commonly purchase. In this chapter, you will learn about these hospitality industry-specific advanced technology products.

■ ■ ■

Outline

CONSIDERATIONS IN TECHNOLOGY PROCUREMENT

There is little doubt that the future of hospitality management and operations will continue to be heavily influenced by technological advancements. Although it is not expected that most hospitality buyers will become experts in technology, they must become experts in evaluating the appropriateness of purchasing and using advanced technological systems. In most cases, hospitality operators desiring advanced technology to enhance their revenue and cost control systems are interested in one or more of the following goals:

- Enhanced guest satisfaction.
- Increased revenue.
- Reduced costs through improved decision making.

- Increased employee or management productivity.
- Improved communications.
- The creation of a competitive advantage.

Although rapid advances in technology have made many products and services more versatile and flexible, there can be disadvantages as well as advantages in using them. Advanced technology systems can sometimes become so complicated that they can be used by only a few, highly trained individuals. This may be acceptable (as, for example, when a professional sales staff member masters an advanced client tracking software program), or it may lead to great frustration (as, for example, when hotel guests are required to use self-check-in **kiosks** with which they may be unfamiliar and cannot easily navigate).

Technological improvements encompass everything from advancement in a simple electronic cash register to property-specific, networked training delivered via the Internet in a multilanguage format. Although an operation's effectiveness can often be greatly improved by well-designed and integrated technology, there are limitations to the role technology can reasonably be expected to play. An over-reliance on technology or a misapplication of its features can result in frustration and wasted time and money. To avoid such a situation, buyers must carefully consider the following essential elements before selecting and purchasing any technological enhancement designed to enhance their existing operational efforts:

- Cost
- Complexity
- Warranty/maintenance
- Upgradeability
- Vendor reliability
  - o Location and response time
  - o Service quality
  - o Reputation

Let's look at each of these technology selection factors more closely.

Cost

It can be difficult to cost-justify any investment in technology. Consider an item as simple as the telephone. When telephones first appeared, it may have been difficult to prove cost effectiveness even though they were judged an important technological advancement for a hospitality operation. Today, of course, few businesses can be operated without a voice-activated communication device.

Cost, of course, plays an important role in the decision of how much technology a facility can afford. When it is possible to demonstrate that the technological advancement will pay for itself (e.g., reduced labor or increased revenues) relatively quickly, the decision can be an easy one. Often, however, it is difficult to identify actual savings. Technology vendors can be helpful in this area, but their goal is to sell their products, and their advice and cost reduction/savings calculations must be carefully scrutinized.

Complexity

Some technology systems are so advanced that their implementation and routine operation requires very high levels of skills. A recipe conversion software package,

Key Term

Kiosk   A small structure with one or more open sides used to provide or vend merchandise and/or services.

for example, may require knowledge of both computer entry techniques and basic cooking skills. If a production staff does not have advanced skill or language levels to use the technology purchased, difficulties can arise. These may be reduced or eliminated through the implementation of thorough training programs. Again, technology vendors should be more than willing to provide or help buyers secure such programs at little or no cost.

Warranty/Maintenance

Because technology items are essentially highly advanced machines, they need routine maintenance and can break down. When they do, it will be critical that buyers receive quality repair service in a timely manner and at a fair price. Typically, a technology purchase will include a warranty. Buyers should study their warranties carefully. Items of particular importance will be:

- A listing of precisely which items are covered under the terms of the warranty.
- The length of the warranty.
- The hourly rate charged for repair service for nonwarranty-covered items.
- Expected response time of the service/repair technicians.

Note: Many standard warranties specify 24-hour response time to service problems. Consider, however, the very busy restaurant whose POS system (see Chapter 6) goes down on a busy Friday evening. In such a case, the restaurant's manager would certainly want it repaired sooner than 24 hours.

Upgradeability

Although it is difficult to predict what new technological developments may occur in the future, advancements that are compatible with current systems will likely prove to be less expensive than those that require completely new software or hardware. Therefore, many buyers prefer to work with larger, more established technology vendors because these organizations generally ensure that advancements in their products are compatible with those they already have marketed. Smaller and newer technology companies may offer some features that are desirable. However, their systems may be subject to complete obsolescence if newer technology makes the old systems incompatible with newer ones offered by alternative vendors.

Vendor Reliability

Where reliability of advanced technology products is concerned, two areas are of importance: reliability of the product, and service and reliability of the vendor. To help ensure that a vendor's products or services are reliable, buyers should insist that their potential vendors provide a list of current customers who can be contacted for information about the reliability of the products they have purchased.

Vendor reliability is also very important. There is no more important consideration when selecting a new technology than the quality of the vendor supplying it. Although a variety of factors can influence vendor reliability, three essential reliability factors are worthy of close examination:

Location and response time

Quality of service staff

Vendor reputation

LOCATION AND RESPONSE TIME Generally, the closer the location of the vendor to your property, the more successful that vendor will be in providing reliable service. Long-distance vendor relationships certainly can work, but only if the

On-the-Job Challenges in Purchasing (21.1)

"What did they say?" asked Carl Graves, the hotel's general manager. Carl was talking with Mike Freeport, the hotel's chief engineer. It was 2:00 a.m. Both Carl and Mike were on the property, and Mike had just completed a call to "Eagle Eye," the energy management vendor who had installed their in-room energy management system. Essentially, the system used motion sensors to detect when guests were in a guestroom. When guests were detected, the HVAC system allowed guests to set their own preferred room temperature levels.

If the energy management system did not detect anyone in the room, however, the in-room HVAC systems were programmed to revert to a lower cost "idling" temperature preset by management. The system had saved the hotel 30 percent on its utility bills since the day it was installed.

Today, however, the system was costing the hotel its guests' goodwill. And it was doing so in a big way.

"They said it sounded like either our wireless receiver or the mini-relay power pack is bad. They won't know until they get here," replied Mike. "In the meantime, the system actually thinks all of our rooms are unoccupied, and that's why the guests are calling the front desk to say that they are freezing and can't get their heaters to work!"

Case Study Questions

Assume that you are the hotel general manager:

1. At this point in time, how important is this product's "warranty" to your problem? Why?
2. At this point in time, how important is product upgradeability to your problem? Why?
3. At this point in time, how important is "vendor reliability" and "response time" to your problem? Why?

vendor is highly motivated and has **field representatives** who can quickly come to a buyer's site if needed.

Location is important because of its direct effect on response time, which is critical when an advanced technology system is down. Regardless of the warranty in place, service response time, rather than who is to pay for that service, can be of critical importance in a down time emergency.

Buyers should be cautious if the service person, or field representatives provided by a vendor, works as an independent contractor or for a company not directly related to the one from which they are buying. Subcontracted service can be acceptable, but is often a sign that buyers may have difficulty acquiring a prompt response to potential problems. The best advanced technology companies provide their own service representatives and in a timely fashion.

QUALITY OF SERVICE STAFF Experienced buyers know that service interruptions in advanced technology products will occur. When a problem develops, it is the quality of the service/repair department, not the vendor's sales department, that will be of most importance. Before selecting a technology vendor, buyers should insist that they meet with the service person(s) who will be responsible for their account. They should ask the questions needed to ensure that the service provider understands the buyer's operation well enough to be of true assistance when needed.

Many buyers seek to maximize the reliability of the vendor relationships by doing business only with very well established companies. They understand that,

Key Term

Field representative   A vendor's employee assigned to the on-site management and service of the vendor's client accounts.

When purchasing advanced technology products, the quality of repair service provided by the vendor may be just as critical as the product itself.

Mark Hamilton © Dorling Kindersley

for example, even though Microsoft was itself once a start-up company, in general it is best to deal with technology suppliers who have an established record of accomplishment. Technology start-up companies typically experience a high failure rate, perhaps because of further technology advancements for which they are unprepared regardless of the quality of product the company sells.

VENDOR REPUTATION   Perhaps the most important factor in selecting a technology vendor is the same one guests use when evaluating a hospitality operation. The integrity of an advanced technology vendor is as critical as that of the buyer. Honesty, fairness, consistent quality, and a willingness to stand behind their promises are characteristics that buyers should seek in all vendors, but especially those involved in advanced technology products and services. Vendors with solidly positive reputations for integrity maximize a buyer's chances of purchasing a reliable system from a reliable vendor who provides reliable service!

PROCUREMENT OF ADVANCED TECHNOLOGY PRODUCTS

Like buyers in virtually every other business, those in hospitality encounter a seemingly endless variety of new product and service innovations brought about by technological advancements. It would be impossible to describe in one chapter (even briefly!) all of the ways new technologies could affect hospitality operations and professional hospitality buyers. These advancements are recurrent, and they directly affect the assessments purchasers must make about the appropriateness of new technologies for implementation.

Implementation of advanced technology systems generally has a cost, which must be recovered if the purchase is to be economically viable. Also, some implementation costs may be nonmonetary. Consider, for example, the hospitality manager who's thinking about eliminating employee-punched time cards in favor of newly developed laser time clocks that "read" employees' fingerprints (or the iris of their eye) to establish the employee's identity and time they report to work. Because it eliminates "**buddy-punching**," the system may easily be cost justified in labor savings. However, the impact on employee perceptions must also be considered. (Will employees feel that management does not really "trust" them?)

Key Term

Buddy-punching   The usually prohibited practice of one employee punching a time card in (or out) for another employee.

Other costs of hospitality-related technology advancements may come in the form of guest relations. For example, lodging industry vendors have, for several years, offered easy-to-use systems that allow guests to check themselves in and out of a hotel. Some hoteliers have hesitated to implement this technology, however, because of a concern that guests will not appreciate the impersonal service that results (even though the speed of check in/check out may increase). As a result, even those hotels offering kiosk check-in continue to provide traditional (manual) front desk check-in services.

Despite their potential disadvantages and some concerns associated with them, technological advances in hospitality are likely to continue at a fast pace. All buyers must remain current about changes that will affect their own industry segment. (Specific methods for doing so are described later in this chapter.) Although new products and services will inevitably appear, for most hospitality buyers, the most common occurrence of advancements and enhancements relate to the technology systems they currently use. As a result, professional buyers should understand the essential components of those technology systems already in place in both the food service and lodging segments of the industry.

Food and Beverage Service Products

Advanced technology systems used in food and beverage service vary greatly by industry segment. Buyers for quick-service restaurants may be very interested in software and hardware innovations designed to speed the processing of drive-through orders. Buyers for full-service restaurants, however, may be more interested in advancements in handwriting recognition systems that allow servers to write an order at the guest's table and then send it to the kitchen with the touch of a stylus on their handheld order pad.

Buyers in health care food service settings may seek and evaluate advancements in nutritional assessment software that go far beyond calculating nutrients of menu items. Advanced software programs could include automation of ingredient, recipe, and menu functions, resident-specific tracking (e.g. food preferences/allergies, nourishments, room and meal service locations, medical and weight histories), and even the flagging of individual patient or residents' food likes, dislikes and allergies.

Despite the diversity of need, and the variation in speed, of innovation across industry segments, most foodservice buyers will encounter some hospitality-specific and widespread technology-related systems regardless of their industry segment. Three of the most common products, about which most buyers should be aware, are

Point of sale systems

Dispensing systems

Merchant services

POINT OF SALE SYSTEMS   In Chapter 6, you learned that a restaurant's point of sale (POS) system is used to record financial information. In a very basic POS system, the records maintained include customer counts, revenues generated, and menu items sold. More advanced systems may be **interfaced** with product ordering or payroll systems and allow the capabilities of the POS to expand greatly.

Key Term

Interfaced   Electronically connected for the purpose of data sharing.

Internet Purchasing Assistant (21.1)

Some new input devices have been designed to read a server's handwriting and send requested orders directly to the kitchen or bar. To see one such handwriting recognition program, go to: www.actionsystems.com

At the home page, click on "Write On Handheld."

Buyers investigating POS alternatives should consider the technological advancements that relate to each of the hardware and software components of these systems. Hardware advances in POS systems occur rapidly, and those most important to buyers relate to:

Monitors: Monitors can be used as input and/or display devices. In the kitchen, monitors display guest orders in the sequence they are received and highlight order revisions. They must be designed to withstand the extreme heat, smoke, and humidity conditions that exist in many kitchens. In dining areas, monitors are increasingly designed to feature touch screen entry and are designed to maximize server effectiveness through the thoughtful placement of data entry functions, easy-to-view content displays, and efficient print functions.

Input devices: Input devices allow servers to place orders. Traditionally, this has been done by entering orders onto a keypad or touch screen. Recently, however, new input devices have been developed that are handheld for wireless connection to the main POS terminal. This allows servers to enter guest orders without having to return to a central POS station, or to wait in line, whereas other servers manually enter orders into a POS terminal. Typically, these devices use a touch pad for information entry, but some have recently been developed that can be programmed to recognize an individual server's handwriting.

Receipt printers: Receipt printers serve two functions. In the kitchen, dependable dot matrix printers can provide production personnel with hard copy orders even in the extreme conditions of the cook's preparation areas. In the dining room, thermal printers quickly and quietly print guest receipts with speed, accuracy, and reliability.

Payment card readers: Card readers that allow servers to authorize credit, debit, and other types of charge cards have advanced in speed and ease-of-use. They are typically designed as an integral part of the POS system and completely eliminate the sometimes-difficult process of interfacing separate card readers with the POS system.

In the early days of POS system development, software was limited primarily to programs that added revenue totals, maintained guest check totals, and identified the number of guests served. Today, sophisticated software programs either designed as stand-alone personal computer programs or included as part of a larger POS system are readily available.

A buyer's choice of POS and the software it contains will depend greatly upon the type of food service operation using it. For many buyers, however, helpful POS software programs related to revenue collection and cost control include those that:

- Maintain revenue totals from different POS locations within one restaurant.
- Maintain revenue totals from different POS locations within a restaurant chain or group.

HI-TECH PURCHASING (21.1)

"When More *Isn't* Better

Selecting a new POS system will be one of a professional buyer's most important decisions. With virtually hundreds of brands on the market, the features and capabilities available to you can be overwhelming. A common mistake is the selection of a system that offers countless features, despite the fact that only a few selected features are ultimately used. System features are purchased, but not used. As with many advanced technology programs, the many features offered by the system may simply exceed the ability of users to fully understand, appreciate, and then use them. As a result, when selecting a new POS, experienced buyers always:

1. Investigate fully both the initial and ongoing training systems that will be included with the system's purchase.
2. Assess the ability of the operation's current (and future) staff to use the system's most advanced features.
3. Pay only for those system features deemed essential by the business's owners.
4. Recognize that manufacturers of POS systems (to a degree much more than many other technology tools you will purchase) seek to distinguish themselves by the *number* of functions their products can perform. Ease of use and dependability, however, are the POS features most highly prized by experienced hospitality buyers.
5. Seek input about the proposed POS purchase from actual users (e.g., unit managers, supervisors, servers, and bartenders) before a final selection decisionis made.

- Compare products produced (from guest checks) in the kitchen or at the bar to actual inventory reductions.
- Reconcile guest check totals with total revenues collected.
- Identify revenue collection and menu item sales variances by outlet, day, shift, hour, and/or server.
- Reconcile credit card deposits with credit card sales.
- Maintain accounts receivable records.
- Create the revenue portion of the income (P&L) statement after reconciling bank deposits, charge card sales deposits, returned checks, and bank deposits.

Buyers selecting POS-related software programs should remember that interfacing (connecting) the various software programs will be very important. For example, a POS containing a software program that computes total server gratuities (from charge card payments) in a specific payroll period is good. If that program interfaces with an operation's own payroll-generating software, that is even better.

BEVERAGE DISPENSING SYSTEMS   Many restaurants and bars, especially those that are very high-volume operations, automate all or part of their drink production

Internet Purchasing Assistant (21.2)

For most foodservice buyers, the selection of a POS system greatly affects their overall management and financial reporting systems. The features and options available to buyers when choosing POS systems continue to expand. Digital Dining is one company that offers a wide variety of POS options. To view their Web site, go to: http://www.digitaldining.com

At the home page, click on "Products" to learn more about the variety of systems and components now available to you on a modern POS system.

processes. In these systems, the production of drinks such as scotch and water, gin and tonic, rum and cola, beer, and even wine may be dispensed in a predetermined amount by a machine activated by the bartender. Buyers can chose from an array of technology and automation levels, as well as price.

In the best systems, the automated dispensing equipment is interfaced to the bar area's POS system. This helps ensure that each drink produced by the system is correctly priced and automatically charged to the proper guest. This also reduces opportunities for bartenders to give away free drinks. Automated dispensing systems that record the number of drinks produced, the amount of alcohol of each type dispensed, and the revenue value of the drinks prepared increase an operation's ability to effectively control products and revenue. Additional benefits from using an automated beverage dispensing system can include

- Elimination of pouring too little or too much alcohol in a guest's ordered drink.
- Reduced product spillage.
- The elimination of drink pricing errors.
- Accurate record keeping of all products sold.
- Reduced incidents of bartender production errors.
- Less required supervision of bartenders.
- Lower and more consistent product costs.
- Reduced cost per product ounce when buying (because liquor may be purchased in larger containers for dispensing).
- Reduced liability potential resulting from failure to strictly control the amount of alcohol in each drink.

Advances in automatic dispensing equipment have eliminated many of the difficulties associated with these systems when they were first introduced. Equipment breakdowns and malfunctions have been greatly reduced, as have the costs required for system maintenance and upkeep. Buyers for properties with high-volume sales should investigate potential advantages and disadvantages of the differing levels of dispensing equipment technology available to them. As with the automated hotel check-in/check-out technology discussed earlier in this chapter, hospitality managers and purchasers must also consider the guest-relation aspects of these systems. For example, some guests seated at bars where this equipment is used may question the serving size and brand (quality) of alcoholic beverages dispensed through the system.

Many busy beverage operations depend upon automated dispensing systems for both speed and product control.

Nigel Hicks © Dorling Kindersley

THE SUPPLIER'S SIDE (21.1)

"Insider" Tips on Purchasing: From the Supplier's Perspective

Buyer's Question: What do I need to know about buying carbonated beverage (nonalcoholic) dispensing systems?

Supplier's Answer: In most cases, you really don't need to know much.

Buyer's Question: Why?

Supplier's Answer: In the overwhelming majority of cases, carbonated beverage dispensing machines will be supplied (and serviced) by your carbonated beverage product supplier. It is virtually standard in the hospitality industry for product suppliers to provide this equipment.

Buyer's Question: Why do they do that?

Supplier's Answer: The main answer is consistency of product. Companies such as Coca-Cola, Pepsi, and Royal Crown control the quality of their products by carefully maintaining the dispensing equipment they "lend" to their customers.

Buyer's Question: So if I switch vendors my dispensing equipment will be replaced?

Supplier's Answer: In nearly every case, yes.

Buyer's Question: But if I don't own the equipment, how do I ensure quality beverages?

Supplier's Answer: Your carbonated (and noncarbonated) product vendor is just as interested as you are in product quality, so he or she ensures that your dispensing equipment is serviced regularly. Keep records of the service calls. Doing so is the best way to ensure the beverages you serve will be the best they can be.

MERCHANT SERVICES (PAYMENT CARD PROCESSING)   In the United States (as well as worldwide), fewer consumers carry large amounts of cash, and many foodservice operations are reluctant to accept personal checks. Most foodservice operations (including quick-service restaurants) now accept a variety of "plastic" forms of bill payment. Since the 1960s, **credit cards** have been the most common form of payment card accepted at most restaurants. Today, **debit cards** are increasingly used by guests to pay their bills.

Merchants (such as foodservice operations and hotels) accepting credit cards for payment are charged a fee by the banks for the right to allow their customers to pay by credit card. Examples of credit cards are Visa and MasterCard. Travel and Entertainment (T&E) cards are a payment system by which the card issuer collects full payment from the card users on a monthly basis. These card companies do not typically assess their users' interest charges. Instead, they collect fees from merchants accepting the cards to make a profit. Examples of T&E cards are American Express (Amex) and Diners Club. In some cases, the fees charged by T&E card issuers have been raised so high that some foodservice properties no longer accept them.

Increasingly, debit cards are used for guest payment. Funds needed to cover the user's purchase are automatically transferred from the user's bank account to

Key Terms

Credit card   A card used in a payment system in which banks loan money (usually with interest) to the card's user as he or she makes purchases.

Debit card   A card used in a payment system in which the amount of a user's purchases are automatically transferred from the user's bank account to the entity issuing the debit card.

the entity issuing the debit card. As with bank cards and T&E cards, merchants accepting debit cards are assessed a fee for the right to do so.

The collection and payment of fees assessed to merchants accepting payment cards and the transfer of funds to a merchant's account are handled by a food service buyer's **merchant services provider (MSP)**. An MSP plays an important role as the foodservice operation's coordinator/manager of payment card acceptance and funds collection.

Payment card issuers and the MSP charge the food service operation. All businesses that accept cards—credit or debit—are charged fees for every transaction by the card's issuer. The percentage charged is different for various types of businesses. For example, restaurants are charged different fees than are department stores. In most cases, the average charge ranges from 1 percent to about 3 percent of each transaction's value (including charged tips). The rate charged varies depending on whether a credit or debit card is used, whether it is swiped or hand-entered into a system, and if a customer's billing information is provided at the time of purchase.

The MSP also assesses a variety of fees, including those for set-up, individual transactions, programming, statements, and managing the card company's usage assessments and fund transfers (payments). In most cases, foodservice operations have little option but to accept the most popular of payment cards. The quality of MSP selected and the fees it charges, however, can vary greatly. Essentially, the MSP serves as an intermediary for payment card transactions, taking care of the money transfers between the customer's and merchant's banks. Typically, the MSP will keep 10 to 20 percent of all the fees foodservice operators pay for card services, and the card company (Visa, MasterCard, and others) receives the balance. At the end of the month, the foodservice operator receives a statement displaying the total transactions and the various fees paid (because the fees are withdrawn by the MSP before any revenue is deposited in the foodservice operator's account).

As with any vendor, hospitality buyers should select MSPs they can trust and that charge a fair rate for their services. The MSP rate varies based upon the average size bill paid by the operation's guests, the total number of payment card transactions annually processed by the operation, the business's own credit worthiness, and how the foodservice facility will connects its POS system to the MSP. The technology chosen for the interface (manual, dial-up, or high-speed dedicated leased line) has a significant effect on the total fees charged to the restaurant.

Lodging Products

Like their counterparts in foodservice, lodging industry buyers encounter ongoing industry innovation. This is good because guest expectations are continually increasing, and the industry must evolve to keep pace. Although the specific technology-related advancements deemed important by a particular buyer will vary based upon the lodging industry segment in which they work, three important technology-related systems common to most lodging facilities are

Property management systems

Telephone systems and service

Security/surveillance systems

It is vital that lodging industry buyers understand the essential elements of these systems and to monitor continued advancements in them.

Key Term

Merchant services provider (MSP) A business's chosen coordinator/manager of payment card acceptance, fee payments, and funds collection.

On-the-Job Challenges in Purchasing (21.2)

"I don't know," said Carlos Magana, district manager of Lombardi's Pizzeria and Pasta House. "What do you guys think?

Carlos and 20 of his 22 unit managers who had assembled for their quarterly manager's meeting had just heard a presentation given by a vice president of ATP, their payroll processing services company. The vice president introduced a new payroll processing software program that, when purchased for a modest fee, eliminated paper paychecks for employees and, instead, direct deposited their pay into the employees' checking accounts. The new program completely eliminated "lost" or "late" paychecks that sometimes occurred with the "overnight courier" paycheck delivery system currently in place in all the units. The costs savings estimate for the new program was $1 per employee per biweekly pay period.

Michele Austin, one of Carlos's best unit managers, was the first to speak: "I'm not so sure I like it. Many of my employees don't have checking accounts. They can't afford them."

"Some of my employees don't even have bank accounts," added Justin Harper, another manager.

"Well, maybe we should make them all get with the times and get one," said Tom Schafer. "Using this new program could really save us some money!"

Case Study Questions

Assume that you are Carlos and responsible for making this new technology implementation decision:

1. How would you go about assessing the "money savings" aspect of this advanced technology purchase? The human costs?
2. How would you assess the comments of Michele and Justin?
3. Would you agree or disagree with Tom's perspective? Explain your position.

PROPERTY MANAGEMENT SYSTEMS A hotel's **property management system (PMS)** includes the technology used by the hotel to manage its rooms revenue, room rates, reservations and room assignments, guest histories, and accounting information, as well as other selected guest service and management information functions.

In a franchised hotel, the franchisor will likely dictate the type of PMS used in the lodging operation. In most cases, the PMS will actually have been designed by the franchisor. Moreover, system servicing will also be provided by the franchisor. Independent hotels, however, can select a PMS from a variety of alternative vendors.

A simple PMS has limited features, whereas more extensive (and expensive) systems offer a wide range of management information features. Hospitality buyers who help select PMS must know exactly which features the hotel's managers desire because the typical PMS offers many more features than are used by a specific facility. Although it is important to know which features are offered by a specific PMS, it is more important to know which ones are needed by a specific hotel.

It is also important to remember that the PMS, like any other piece of equipment, requires its own care and maintenance. Consider, for example, the difficulties that would occur if, one hour before check-in time on a sold-out night, the PMS indicating reservation information "crashed."

Key Term

Property management system (PMS) The computer hardware and programs used to record guest reservations and to manage the prices charged for rooms and other services. The system can be used to record and store additional sales and financial data as determined by the hotel's management.

Internet Purchasing Assistant (21.3)

The history of the PMS industry is not a long one. The Fidelio Company (based in Germany and named for Beethoven's only opera) was one of the first PMS developers. It was formed in 1987, purchased by Microsoft in 1995, and is now known as Micros-Fidelio. The company has developed a variety of PMS products and services, which you can review at: www.micros.co

At the home page:

1. Under "industries," click on "hotels & resorts."
2. Next, click on "OPERA Enterprise Solution."
3. Review the features of this popular PMS.

Although hardware problems can sometimes occur, most frequently it is a software-related problem that causes PMS difficulties. The PMS is frequently connected by a modem to the PMS's software support organization, so repairs are possible by calling the software support entity. In fact, one of the primary features separating outstanding PMS systems from less effective ones is their level and availability of software and service support. Software support from the PMS vendor is not typically free, so securing service at an affordable price is also an important consideration when selecting a PMS vendor.

Although a hotel's PMS is the focal point of its data management system, the PMS is not the lone provider of information about hotel guests, their activities, and their purchases. Many supplemental data management systems also exist (e.g., POS records of the amount owed by guests for charges made in the restaurant or lounge). In fact, in many cases, data generated from these various subsystems is so important that it also needs to be stored in the hotel's PMS. If it is not, guest purchases must be manually added to a guest's folio (bill), an approach that is time consuming, inefficient, and prone to error.

Unfortunately, not all of the data-gathering systems used in a hotel interface with every PMS brand. As a result, when a buyer is considering the purchase of a specific PMS, the ability of the system to interface its own data with that of other data management systems maintained by the hotel is very important. Some of the crucial PMS interfaces that should be reviewed by buyers prior to system purchase include those connecting it to the hotel's:

- POS system
- Merchant service provider systems
- Electronic locking systems
- Energy management systems
- Telephone systems (including call accounting)
- In-room entertainment (movie) systems
- Credit card payment systems
- Travel agent payment systems
- Back office accounting systems

TELEPHONE SYSTEMS AND SERVICE Second in complexity only to the PMS, a lodging facility's telephone system is an intricate data and voice management device. Today's telephone systems are highly automated because of the significant use of telephones within the typical hotel. Actually, a hotel's telephone system includes several major components, some of which may be manufactured by a variety of vendors but all of which must be interfaced properly if the telephone system is to function with optimal efficiency. In addition to the call switching equipment designed to handle incoming and outgoing calls, hotel buyers commonly supplement their basic telephone systems with one or more of the following system add-ons.

Some PMSs allow room attendants to update room status (cleanliness) reports via an interface between the PMS and guestroom telephones.

Richard D. Wood/Pearson Education/PH College

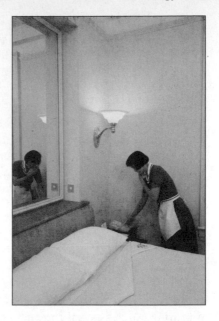

PURCHASING PROS NEED TO KNOW (21.1)

PMS systems continue to evolve. In fact, each year brings innovation and improvement to these systems. Thus, purchasing pros know that this is an area of technological advancement with which they must stay continually updated.

In the near future, for example, look for touch screens at the front desk to become more popular as prices for this hardware decline. Although "point and click" with a mouse was certainly an improvement over older-style keyboard data entry, "point" is much better and faster than "point and click." This advancement, already in use for many years in quick-service restaurants, is long overdue in hotels.

Also, look for concurrent PMS and POS programs on the same workstations. This would be helpful for checking details of a disputed restaurant check at the front desk. Another example involves front desk staff in smaller full-service properties; instead of taking room service calls from guests, they could place the orders directly into the PMS (which they have ready access to), which could serve as an additional Food and Beverage department POS terminal. The result? Faster, more effective, and better guest service.

In the future, wireless PMS terminals will enable guest check-in in nontraditional areas. Combined with portable swipe devices designed to make electronic room keys, guests could be checked in anywhere, including in the airport baggage claim area or during the guest's walk across the hotel's parking lot.

Most importantly, look for PMS developers to move from PC-based systems (with most guest data held on property computers) to an **application service provider** (ASP)-based technology. The use of this technology moves data storage and retrieval off the site of the individual property and onto a managed Internet Web site. Despite some data security issues that must be addressed, ASP technology expands greatly the ability of the data host to provide improved data management services, report generation, and system dependability.

Key Term

Application service provider (ASP)   A third-party entity that manages and distributes software-based services and solutions to customers across a wide area network from a central data management center.

Auto Attendant: If you have ever made a call answered by a recorded voice asking you to push selected numbers on your dial pad to reach the party you *really* wanted, you are familiar with auto attendants. Although frustrating to many, these systems are helpful in guiding large numbers of callers to their intended parties, which, in a hotel setting, may include guests, specific staff members, or various hotel departments.

Call Accounting: When guests use a guestroom telephone to make long-distance calls, the calls should be routed in a way that minimizes the hotel's costs. If a registered guest directly dials a person in another state from his or her hotel room, the hotel will be billed for the call. Therefore, the hotel desires low-cost service while still ensuring that guests have quality long-distance service. The hotel will add a charge including mark-up to the guest's folio to offset the cost of the call. A call accounting system records the time, length, and number called of each telephone call made within each guest room (as well as those made from administrative phones). Some hotels use the call accounting system to charge guests for local calls as well as long distance, whereas other hotels routinely allow guests to make free local calls. The call accounting system, when interfaced with the PMS, posts these charges directly to the guest's folio. System dependability and ease of programming are essential product characteristics of quality call accounting systems.

Wake-up Calls: Traditionally, guests requested a "wake-up" call, and a member of the front office staff would then call the guest at the requested time. Today's telephone systems automate these calls and, in the best systems, they can be programmed either by guests in their own rooms or by staff at the front desk.

Voice Mail: Voice mail is a feature that is now a standard (but often separately interfaced) telephone system component. A properly operating voice mail system is mandatory for those hotels seeking to attract business travelers, and hotels increasingly provide this service to guests. In a modern telephone system interfaced with voice mail, the voice mailbox for the guest is activated by the PMS at check-in and then deactivated by the PMS when the guest checks out. Voice mail is also critical for administrative staff who must have telephone contact with guests or potential guests. This is especially true of the sales and marketing department. As a result, the voice mail systems chosen by buyers must be dependable, easily accessible, and user friendly.

"Message on Hold": This feature allows the hotel to play a "message" on the line when a caller is placed on "hold." For example, a caller to a hotel attempting to make a room reservation may be placed on hold until the next reservationist is available. During this time, the system may play a recorded message that can include features of the hotel, unique services offered, and a general "apology" for placing the caller on hold. Typically, a message-on-hold apparatus interfaces the telephone system with a combination of pleasant music and a well-written marketing script.

Additional telephone system features or add-ons now include **VOIP** (Voice Over Internet Protocol) technology that uses the Internet for transmitting local and long distance calls, Wi-Fi interfaces, and cell telephone connectivity.

Telephones play an important part in a hotel's total guest service offerings because they allow guests to make calls to other guests within the hotel (room-to-room), call the front desk from house phones, and use emergency phones such as those

Key Term

VOIP Short for "Voice Over Internet Protocol": a technology that uses the Internet for sending and receiving local and long distance telephone calls, Wi-Fi interfaces, and cell phone connectivity.

Internet Purchasing Assistant (21.4)

Mitel is one of the most established and highly advanced telephone system vendors. They offer a variety of quality products and services. You can visit their site at: www.mitel.com

At the home page:

1. Under "Solutions," click on "Hospitality."
2. Next, click on "Hospitality Solutions Overviews."
3. Under "Products," click on "Business Telephones."
4. Review the information about Mitel's lodging-related telephone products.

located in elevators, at the pool, or in fitness areas. The uninterrupted operation of a hotel's telephone system is important, and it is the buyer's job to help ensure that the system selected will be dependable and efficient.

Just as dependable telephone equipment is important, so too is dependable service. Prior to the 1974 breakup of American Telephone and Telegraph (AT&T) initiated by a U.S. Department of Justice antitrust lawsuit, hoteliers, like all other business owners, had limited options regarding the company that would provide their local and long distance call service. Today, in most locations, hoteliers can choose from a variety of **LECs** and **LDCs**. Prices for telephone connectivity services vary widely based upon a variety of factors including call volume, average call length, call destinations, and the times at which the largest number of calls are made. The result is that selecting an appropriate LEC and LDC is one of a hotel buyer's most complex, but also most important, decisions.

SECURITY/SURVEILLANCE SYSTEMS Electronic surveillance plays a big role in some hotels' safety and security programs. Buyers choosing these systems generally select from one of two basic systems. The first involves using CD or DVD equipment to record the activity within an area of the hotel. For example, a hotel could set up a security/surveillance camera that records the activity outside a liquor storeroom. Then, if the storeroom were broken into, a video recording would exist that could be useful in identifying the thieves. Recording activity at the front desk, in parking areas, and near cashiers is among the most frequent use of surveillance systems.

The second type of security/surveillance commonly used in hospitality operations involves a **closed-circuit television (CCTV)** system.

The potential uses of CCTV within a hotel are many. It can be used, for example, in a multiple-entry property so activity outside each entrance can be

Key Terms

LEC Short for "Local Exchange Carrier"; the telephone company that provides "local" call service.

LDC Short for "Long Distance Carrier"; the telephone company that provides "long distance" call service.

Closed-circuit television (CCTV) A camera and monitor system that displays, in real time, the activity within the camera's field of vision. A CCTV consisting of several cameras and screens showing the camera's field of vision may be monitored in a single hotel location (often behind the front desk or, in larger properties, in the office of the director of hotel safety and security).

HI-TECH PURCHASING (21.2)

To Record or Not to Record? Is That the Question?

Some hoteliers attempt to give "outsiders" the illusion of having a CCTV system in place when, in fact, the "cameras" are not truly cameras, or the monitors are not constantly monitored. This is typically done in an effort to save the costs of operating the CCTV system. The rationale is that the mere presence of the cameras would be sufficient to deter criminals (including employees!) who would not realize that they were not actually being observed. Courts and juries have found, however, that this approach may not be best because victims of violent crimes may observe the cameras and erroneously think that help is on the way (because they believe their situation is being monitored), and they may base their behavior on that belief. The result may be increased (not decreased) legal liability for the hotel operator.

Hotel managers wishing to operate a CCTV that will not be constantly monitored should consult with both their insurers and their legal counsel before doing so. When considering the use of either a recorded or monitored security/surveillance system, the issues for buyers and management include price, quality, and balancing guest and employee privacy with safety. Buyers should also consider whether visible cameras actually increase or detract from guest security, as well as the cameras' possible effects on legal liability.

monitored. It is important to remember that, to be most effective, a CCTV system must be monitored. Viewing monitors are typically placed in a central location and viewed by an assigned employee who is trained to respond appropriately to activities seen on the monitor. For example, if an outside entrance monitor shows that a break-in is being attempted, the employee will, hopefully, have been trained to summon the local police. Some hotels add an intercom to the area being monitored to extend the effectiveness of the individual monitoring the system. Within casino hotels, states typically mandate the use of CCTV to improve security. As a result, buyers of these CCTV systems must clearly understand management's objectives and requirements when developing purchase specifications for them.

MONITORING ADVANCEMENTS IN HOSPITALITY-ORIENTED TECHNOLOGY PRODUCTS AND SERVICES

Regardless of the level of information a buyer possesses, it can be very difficult to keep up with all of the hardware, software, and services advancement that can directly affect their businesses. However, it is critical that buyers do so. Your own

Some hospitality operations, like this casino, have very specific needs for electronic surveillance.

Jeff Greenberg/Omni-Photo Communications, Inc.

Internet Purchasing Assistant (21.5)

One of the best ways to stay current with technology advancements is to monitor the information at the Web site of the Hospitality Financial and Technology Professionals (HFTP). You can visit their site at: www.hftp.org

At the home page, review their current news releases. Next, look for the location and date of their annual trade show.

choices for continuing education in this area are varied and depend on your own preferences, but most buyers in the hospitality industry can choose from one or more of the following methods:

- Professional associations/trade shows
- Publications
- Current vendors
- Competitive vendors
- Technology-related classes
- Buyer's own organization

Professional Associations/Trade Shows

As a hospitality professional, you will likely elect to join one or more **professional trade associations**.

These associations typically address a variety of certification, educational, social, and legislative goals that its members feel are important. Associations typically hold annual gatherings and invite technology-related exhibitors (and others) who sell products and services that are of interest to their members (see Chapter 8).

Trade shows will generally bring together a variety of vendors, all of whom are interested in exhibiting their latest product offerings. The shows are an extremely efficient way to see the product offerings of a large number of advanced technology vendors in a very short time. Many trade associations also have both state and local chapters, some of which will host their own smaller trade shows.

Local Chambers of Commerce and other professional service organizations often hold meetings and schedule speakers who can update buyers on the newest business applications of technology. Membership in these organizations is generally well worth its modest cost.

Publications

Regular reading about the hospitality industry will also keep you abreast of the latest technological trends. In many cases, technology and its applications have become such a large part of the editorial interest of these publications that a special technology editor is employed to monitor technological changes that could be of interest to the publication's readers. Some printed publications are distributed free to qualified members of the hospitality industry, whereas others are not. Many publications that are available on the Internet (and these are increasing) require only that interested readers supply a valid e-mail address.

Key Term

Professional trade association   Voluntary membership organizations that serve the certification, educational, social, and legislative goals of its members.

Current Vendors

A hospitality operation's current suppliers of software, hardware, or technology services can be a valuable source of free information. Each will inevitably make improvements in their products and services as competition and the desire to grow drive their own development efforts.

An added advantage of working with an operation's current technology suppliers is the fact that any new systems they develop are likely to be compatible with those systems the operation already owns and maintains. This can reduce staff training time and the errors that sometimes arise with new system implementation. In addition, current vendors may be more competitive when pricing their new offerings because, in most cases, they would very much like to expand the business they do with current clients.

Competitive Vendors

Although current technology vendors can inform buyers of their own innovation efforts, competition in technology-related products and services in the hospitality industry is robust and getting stronger. Whether a buyer's interest is software, hardware, or services, identifying his or her current vendor's strongest and best competitors is a good way to monitor advances in technology. Annual contacts, either in person or by telephone, can help buyers quickly identify improvements in procedures and features that their own vendor may have overlooked or dismissed. Experienced buyers also contact small and start-up vendors they see advertised in publications or exhibiting at trade shows. Often, these companies offer the most innovative and cutting-edge products and services available. Remember, however, that their small size may limit their ability to adequately service a very large account. In many cases, however, they can be a source of new information.

Technology-Related Classes

Many community colleges and private training organizations offer instruction about technology that can be applied to the hospitality industry. For example, successfully completing an advanced course in word processing techniques using Microsoft Corporation's "Vista" operating system may allow a food operation to design and print its own "daily special" menu. Similarly, a course in the applications of database programs (those programs designed to manipulate and store information such as street addresses, e-mail addresses, and telephone numbers) may allow the operation to more efficiently develop its own direct-marketing programs.

Current technology vendors may also be a source of free or reduced-cost instruction. Experienced buyers regularly contact the companies that currently provide their software, hardware, and services to see if they do, in fact, offer free or low-cost classes on effectively using their current products or instruction on newer products they are offering.

Buyer's Own Organization

For those buyers employed by an international or national chain (or even a very large company), the parent organization can be an excellent source for information about advanced technology management tools. Often, a large company produces newsletters, conducts in-service training, or holds regularly scheduled conferences that can be a good source of information about rapidly changing technology. All of these resources should be monitored and used if they are available. Sometimes, a direct conversation with a buyer's area or regional supervisor regarding the technological changes affecting their own organization can be of tremendous value. Many times these professionals are in a very good position to see the technology advancements that could work best within the company.

Current vendors can be an excellent source of information about new technology products.

Michael Newman/PhotoEdit Inc.

As competent professionals, hospitality buyers know that they must continually be aware of changes in technology and be committed to implementing the best and most cost-effective of these changes to benefit their organization (and their own careers!). Advances in technology will continue to change society and the hospitality industry as well. When these advances help buyers significantly improve their operations, the business, its employees, and its guests will all benefit.

Purchasing Resources on the Internet

In addition to the Web sites referenced in this chapter's "Internet Purchasing Assistant" feature, the following sites provide detailed information to enhance your purchasing knowledge and skills.

Purchasing Resources on the Internet

Site	Information About
www.posworld.com	POS systems
www.squirrelsystems.com	POS systems
www.ncr.com	POS systems
www.berg-controls.com	Beverage dispensing systems (alcoholic)
www.maintowocfsg.com	Beverage dispensing systems (carbonated)
www.vantagecard.com	Merchant services/card processing
www.etsms.com	International merchant services/card processing
www.execu-tech.com	Hotel PMS products
www.innpoints.com	Hotel PMS products
www.iqwareinc.com	Time-share and condo–hotel PMS products
www.hitel.com	Hitachi telephone systems (large hotels)
www.nortel.com	Hotel telephone systems (smaller hotels)
www.securitysolutions.com	Security systems (including video)
www.eatright.org	American Dietetics Association trade show
www.ahla.com	American Hotel and Lodging Association trade show
www.restaurant.org	National Restaurant Association trade show
www.dmaonline.org	Dietary Managers Association trade show
www.acfchefs.org	American Culinary Federation trade show
www.cmaa.org	Club Managers Association trade show
www.ir-ha.com	International Restaurant and Hotel trade show

Key Terms

kiosk *513*	debit card *521*	application service	closed-circuit television
field representative *515*	merchant services	provider (ASP) *525*	(CCTV) *527*
buddy-punching *516*	provider (MSP) *522*	VOIP *526*	professional trade
interfaced *517*	property management	LEC *527*	association *529*
credit card *521*	system (PMS) *523*	LDC *527*	

Think It Through

1. Some hospitality buyers are disappointed when new technology products they have purchased prove too complex for the employees using them. What are two specific methods that can be used to help ensure that would not happen?
2. Critics often point to POS systems designed with food "photos" on their keyboards (rather than print) as evidence that POS manufacturers encourage quick-service restaurants to have very low hiring standards. How would you reply to such a criticism?
3. Many hotel buyers expended significant organizational resources "hard wiring" their guest rooms for high-speed Internet access only to find that, within a few years, Wi-Fi access allowed them to avoid such costly expenditures. What can buyers do to avoid making expensive technology procurement errors such as this?
4. Some professional buyers in both foodservice and hotels have resisted ASP technology because of concerns that guest credit and debit card numbers would be stored on the Internet (and thus would be subject to hacking). If, as a buyer, you chose a POS or PMS that used ASP technology, do you believe it would be appropriate to inform your guests who use credit or debit cards to pay their bills? Why or why not?
5. Some hospitality buyers want to keep their companies on the "leading edge" of technology advancements. Others fear they will be on the "bleeding edge" if they move too quickly to embrace advancements in technology. What is your own view about the speed at which hospitality organizations should adopt new technologies? What are advantages of being an industry "leader" in this area? What are potential disadvantages?

Team Fun

For this exercise, assume that each team consists of members of the corporate "International Operations Management" department of "Burger Time," a global chain of company-owned quick-service restaurants with a menu featuring gourmet-quality burgers, chicken sandwiches, fries, and milk shakes.

    Like most multi-unit foodservice operators, the company is interested in combining sales and expense data from its 75 international locations to better analyze departmental profitability and to make comparisons with prior period results and budgeted revenue and expense forecasts. Historically, this has been somewhat difficult because the managers of each international unit now manually compile and report (by e-mail) their results to the corporate office on a weekly basis.

    The company has been approached by the sales representative of a U.S.-based company that has developed an Internet-based POS system. With this system, each of the restaurants would be equipped with a machine that would serve as both its POS terminal and an Internet connection to the home office to allow for automatic and daily download of sales and expense data.

1. The assignment of the first team is to assess and report on the advantages that could accrue to the company with the use of such a system.
2. The assignment of the second team is to research the dependability of satellite-delivered Internet connectivity, identifying strengths and weaknesses of such data-delivery systems.
3. The assignment of the third team is to assess the difficulties that could be encountered if the system is purchased and, in the future, the vendor company ceases to remain in business because of insufficient product sales.

Each team should be prepared to present and discuss their findings and conclusions as well as its recommendation regarding the purchase or nonpurchase of the new system.

22

Purchasing in the Global Marketplace*

In This Chapter

Most U.S. hospitality purchasers do not require extensive information about purchasing in the international marketplace. They rely on the manufacturers, processors, growers, and others in domestic and global distribution channels to provide them with needed products. For example, restaurants do not need to purchase and import fine French wines, and hotels do not need to purchase exquisite guestroom furnishings from desired locations throughout the world. Instead, they can purchase these items from domestic suppliers who have knowledge and experience in "navigating" throughout the legal, financial, and contractual requirements of international procurement. However, some hospitality managers and purchasers may purchase from global sources, and others may desire background information to appreciate the activities that precede delivery of international goods to their loading docks. The primary goal of this chapter is to provide information about global procurement and to address significant issues that differentiate domestic from international purchasing.

The chapter begins by discussing instances in which knowledge of international purchasing practices is important. Examples include when managers of domestic-based multi-unit franchise companies have purchasing responsibilities for operations in foreign countries, and when purchasing managers with multi-unit company-owned and managed operations work in foreign countries. In both instances, those with purchasing responsibilities are often concerned about procuring quality products and services that help standardize the brand. Customers at a McDonald's restaurant or Ritz-Carlton Hotel, for example, have minimum expectations that attract them to the brand. These are important regardless of location and can occur only if the products and services offered meet basic standards.

Knowledge of international procurement also becomes important when an **expatriate** manages a hospitality organization on an international assignment. Purchasing practices differ between countries and even between locations within a country. This chapter discusses two significant challenges of international purchasing. The first relates to the need for variations in allowable standards due to local tastes, customs, and the availability of supplies. To what extent should (or can) brand standards be "enforced" in global locations? This is partially a marketing-related issue (do customers desire a dining or lodging experience similar to that in other locations, or one that reflects the local pace and customs?). It can also be a logistics issue; unavoidable

*This chapter was authored by Dr. A. J. Singh, Associate Professor, The School of Hospitality Business, Michigan State University.

Key Term

Expatriate   A person who is a resident of one country and who lives and works in another country.

supply variations may be necessary when some products are unavailable locally and must be imported or replaced with available alternatives.

Foreign sourcing is a second challenge of international purchasers. This can often be managed as U.S.-based organizations partner with individuals and/or companies in foreign locations that are experienced with global sourcing and who are knowledgeable about local procurement practices.

Expatriates managing international properties can experience numerous advantages of selecting local supply sources and, when managed effectively, "buying locally" supports the hospitality business, local economy, and political relationship between the business and host country. As products are purchased within a country, numerous contractual and legal issues and international trade terminology distinctions are avoided or minimized. Financial concerns, including currency exchange and import/export costs, and logistics of cross-border transportation, are also reduced.

Challenges related to selecting local supply sources include those regarding quality and safety. Many countries do not have industry-wide accepted definitions of quality that can be incorporated into specifications, and food inspections relating to wholesomeness may be a problem in some areas.

Expatriate purchasers must know about the numerous communication challenges that can arise as business is conducted in global locations. Also, basic protocols applicable to business and procurement can differ between countries. Expatriate managers must be fully aware of acceptable and unacceptable social and business practices in their host country.

A final section of this chapter provides examples of procurement practices in selected global locations and procurement tactics used by U.S.-based hospitality organizations operating in these areas. Perhaps the most important generalization to be derived from this discussion is that procurement practices may not be consistently "better" in some countries than in others. Instead, they are simply different. To be a successful purchaser, these differences must be known, and the best practices applicable to a specific global location must be consistently practiced.

■ ■ ■

Outline

ROLE OF GLOBAL PURCHASING PROFESSIONALS

Our study of global purchasing begins by considering the need for domestic-based operations to purchase globally and by reviewing global purchasing concerns.

Foreign Sourcing for Domestic Operations

Trade between major nations throughout the world is commonplace, and international purchasing is not an unusual activity for most major manufacturing organizations in the United States. However, domestic hospitality purchasers can typically secure most of their products from organizations in U.S.-based distribution channels. This makes their purchasing task much easier because they do not need to identify foreign sources and import items directly into the United States.

Those that do purchase from foreign sources should recognize that the task is fundamentally the same as when products are obtained from domestic suppliers. Financial objectives will still be important, and basic purchasing principles and processes apply to all decisions. Similar problems also are encountered with the exception that legal and foreign trade concerns create even more challenges that must be addressed.

From an operational perspective, it is easier to purchase products domestically than internationally for many reasons, including:

- More accessible supplier location
- No language problems
- Similar business customs and culture
- Common legal system

Internet Purchasing Assistant (22.1)

U.S. Foodservice is a major U.S.-based distributor that has a special import division with the ability to import a wide variety of specialty items. To view its Web site, go to: www.usfoodservice.com
At the home page, check out the wide range of services and information that are provided.

- Basic understanding of required quality standards
- No currency exchange problems
- Shorter lines of communication
- Faster delivery times
- Fewer delays that require expediting

Given the advantages of domestic purchasing, what are common reasons for foreign sourcing? Primary factors include concerns about product exclusivity (e.g., a fine dining restaurant may wish to offer a French wine not commonly **imported,** and a hotel chain may negotiate a contract for large quantities of specialty bedding products directly with a foreign manufacturer to reduce "middleman" costs). Some U.S.-based food service and lodging organizations are part of international **conglomerates.** Then the **parent company's backward linkages** into global markets may provide a direct source of purchase.

Wise purchasers use several basic steps when buying from international sources. Figure 22.1 provides a checklist of procedures and information sources that are helpful.

As you'll note from even a brief review of the Web sites in Figure 22.1, the process of making direct international purchases is cumbersome, and it requires a significant amount of knowledge and personal contacts. It is for these reasons, among others, that hospitality buyers typically purchase international and specialty products from domestic distributors.

Global Hospitality Purchasing Concerns

Purchasers employed by large domestic multi-unit hospitality organizations may contract with foreign supply sources for numerous products. For example, Starbucks purchases coffee beans and McDonald's Corporation purchases meat products from numerous global locations.

Special concerns become important as global sources are used for domestic operations. For example, **fair trade movement** issues must be addressed to ensure that local producers, including farmers and the communities in which they live, are not exploited. Also, many customers of domestic restaurant chains prefer that purchasers "Buy American," and public relations issues can arise if domestic producers are bypassed for potentially less expensive products purchased in the international marketplace. Furthermore, hospitality organizations importing food products may be confronted with food safety concerns, including those related to "mad cow disease," contaminated products, and avian influenza (that affects poultry). These issues become especially important when, for example, large chains such as McDonald's must look to foreign supply sources to supplement U.S. supplies of lean ground beef.

Key Terms

Import To move (transport) products for sale or use from one country into another country.

Conglomerate A corporation that operates businesses in diversified industries.

Parent company An organization that owns and controls the operations of other companies.

Backward linkage The use of products by one company that are produced by another company that is part of the same organization.

Fair trade movement Efforts to ensure that farmers and other small-volume producers of agricultural products receive a fair price for their harvests and achieve an acceptable wage or income for their efforts.

Step	Detailed Information (Web site examples)

Identify and select the best supplier	• Attend the two largest U.S. hospitality trade shows and meet with exhibitors.
	–National Restaurant Association Show
	  www.restaurant.org/show/
	–International Hotel & Restaurant Show
	  www.ihmrs.com
	• Check with a third-party credit agency (e.g., Alibaba)
	–www.alibaba.com
	• Check out international products (e.g., Global Sources)
	–www.globalsources.com

Request and verify references	American Chambers of Commerce Abroad www.uschamber.com/international
Agree to pricing and payment terms	Foreign Trade Online www.foreign-trade.com
Learn about shipping service alternatives	FedEx www.fedex.com Freightquote www.freightquote.com
Prepare shipment and documentation (e.g., **bills of lading**, **export declarations**, and **certificates of origin**)	UPS www.ups.com DHL. www.dhl.com
Understand custom procedures (import duties and taxes)	Use the membership directory of the National Customs Brokers & Forwarders Association of America www.ncbfaa.org Review information from the U.S. Department of Commerce. www.commerce.gov

FIGURE 22.1 How to Purchase from Overseas Suppliers

Purchasers working for multi-unit hospitality organizations with franchisees in foreign countries, and others with company-owned or managed operations in global locations, also have global purchasing concerns. They must, for example, develop and provide specifications detailing basic quality requirements to foreign operators to help purchase products of similar quality in diverse global locations. They may also have responsibilities to help design procurement systems, train local purchasing personnel, and assist with problem-solving tasks that can arise.

Expatriates living and working in a foreign country must recognize the political, economic, and cultural environments in their locations. These affect their personal lives and, as importantly, their business activities. Rigid standard operating procedures (SOPs) and purchasing policies used by domestic hospitality organizations are likely to be much less useful in many global operations. Customs and business practices used for conducting business in the host location will likely have a significant influence upon purchasing practices and other operating aspects of hospitality organizations.

Key Terms

Bill of lading A document issued by a freight carrier to a shipper that provides contractual terms for transporting the shipment to its final destination.

Export declaration A statement provided to customs officials at the point of exit from a country that specifies details about products being exported.

Certificate of origin A document required by some countries that certifies the country from which products being shipped internationally originated.

CHALLENGES IN INTERNATIONAL PURCHASING

In today's global economy, buyers must increasingly operate in the challenging world of international purchasing. For example, many successful hospitality companies serve customers worldwide and cannot limit their buying to U.S. sources for U.S. consumers. Those organizations must identify and establish sound working relationships with the best **domestic** and **foreign** suppliers.

American hospitality organizations have operated properties in other countries for many years. Conrad Hilton bought his first hotel in Cisco, Texas, in 1919. Thirty years later, Hilton became the first U.S. hotel company operating internationally when it opened the Caribe Hilton, in San Juan, Puerto Rico. McDonald's illustrates the international popularity of American foodservice companies. The first McDonald's restaurant opened in Des Plaines, Illinois, in 1955. Today, McDonald's operates more than 17,000 restaurants in over 115 countries, excluding those in the United States. McDonald's operates or franchises approximately 13,500 restaurants in the United States, so you'll note that it has more international than domestic operations.

Whereas Hilton and McDonald's are well-known examples, the number of hospitality companies now operating in the international market increases each year. Burger King, Wendy's, Holiday Inn, Choice Hotels International, Dave and Busters, Hooters, T.G.I. Friday's, Mrs. Fields, Dunkin' Donuts, Baskin Robbins, Pizza Hut, Marriott, Taco Bell, Aramark, TCBY, and Rainforest Cafe are just a few examples of the increasingly large number of U.S.-based companies expanding internationally. As the hospitality business in the United States becomes saturated, more hospitality companies will look beyond their own country's borders for expansion and growth opportunities.

Variations in Standards

Many domestic hospitality managers work for companies that conduct business internationally. They realize that, although product and service consistency may

Visitors to this resort desire, and will pay for, the best food and beverage products. They are not likely concerned about the significant challenges confronting the resort's purchasing staff who must make these products available.

Linda Whitwam © Dorling Kindersley

Key Terms

Domestic (supplier)   A seller located in the same country as the buyer.

Foreign (supplier)   A seller located in a different country than the buyer.

HOTEL PURCHASING PRACTICES IN TWO PACIFIC ISLAND NATIONS

Purchasers must learn about and function within the restraints imposed by the government and traditions of the local industry when they work within an international setting. Here are two examples:

- *Republic of the Marshall Islands.* The Marshall Islands are located in the North Pacific and are a U.S. protectorate. Purchases are made in U.S. dollars so there are no problems with exchange rates. Also, many items are sourced from the United States. However, importers must pay **duty** taxes and other special fees (e.g., there is a special tax of more than 100 percent of the purchase cost on imported liquors).

  Most nonperishable products are transported in containers on barges. Hospitality buyers must purchase in 28-day cycles and, interestingly, place new orders before their currently placed orders arrive. When incoming barges are sighted in the lagoon, production personnel know that products will likely be available later that day or the next day.

  Containers are off-loaded at dockside, and employees of the hospitality organization travel to the dock, present "paperwork" to clear the shipment, and physically unload the containers for transfer to the hospitality operation. Another anecdote: The barge company serving the islands also provides service to nearby islands with U.S. military installations. When there are "emergencies," shipments bypass the Marshall Islands first to make deliveries to these military bases, and then deliveries are delayed even longer.

  The primary cooking fuel on the island is propane, which, unfortunately, is sometimes unavailable anywhere on the island (e.g., there was a seventeen-day period when propane supplies had been depleted, and kitchens had to operate using wood, coconut husks, and kerosene as fuel for barbeque grills).

- *Fiji (Republic of the Fiji Islands).* This independent nation is comprised of numerous islands in the South Pacific. A large number of resort destinations serve travelers from nearby Australia and New Zealand as well as from throughout the world. Incoming products are charged a value-added tax (VAT) in excess of 12 percent in addition to import duties and other charges associated with its currency exchange costs. Most imported products originate in Australia and New Zealand.

  Buyers, even from the largest hospitality organizations, develop personal relationships with the many local farmers and other suppliers. Meetings to arrange purchases might begin with a cup of tea or kava (a nonalcoholic drink made from the root of a plant) in the supplier's home. Local fishermen are a source of local seafood products, and buyers typically barter with fishermen who sell freshly caught seafood.

be important from the customers' perspectives, in some cases international standards must vary from those used in U.S.-based operations. Although this can result in procurement challenges, sometimes variations in standards are not significant. In fact, when they are recognized, they are often easily integrated into the procurement process.

To what extent should purchasing specifications be standardized for all properties within a hospitality organization without regard to their location?

At first glance, it probably seems natural that U.S. companies doing business internationally would want to offer the same products in their foreign locations as in their domestic locations. The logic: "International patrons of our business must 'like' our products, and that is why they visit our properties when they travel abroad."

Key Term

Duty A tax imposed by a government on imports.

In fact, some international customers do desire and expect a level of consistency in the products and services they purchase. However, others associate a specific brand with a defined level of quality, but also desire a dining and/or lodging experience reflective of the property's unique geographic location. Developers and owners of these international units face numerous, and sometimes conflicting, challenges as they identify their own markets' needs and assess how those needs can affect purchase decisions.

As many U.S.-based companies have learned the hard way, there are often good reasons for variations in products offered and in purchasing standards for items sold in international operations. These may make good sense for a variety of reasons, but they can typically be grouped into variations due to local tastes and customs, or because of supply/availability issues.

LOCAL TASTES AND CUSTOMS CREATE MENU VARIATIONS When professionals in the hospitality industry consider product and service standardization, the McDonald's Corporation is often mentioned. Few organizations have enjoyed the worldwide popularity of this company, and few are as passionate about product consistency. McDonald's, however, understands the need for menu and product purchase specification variations due to local customs and tastes (e.g., in predominantly Muslim countries like Malaysia, pork is not served due to Muslim dietary laws). Similarly, in North African Morocco, as well as other Muslim countries, all meat used must meet Halah standards (see Chapter 15), or it is not accepted for use.

Entrée items sold on the McDonald's menu vary throughout the world and even within the United States. For example, customers visiting a McDonald's in Costa Rica can choose "Gallo Pinto" (painted rooster). This popular dish consisting of rice and beans combined and served with sour cream is enjoyed by Costa Ricans for breakfast, lunch, and dinner. Gallo Pinto is a mainstay menu item of nearly all Costa Rican restaurants, a fact that McDonald's readily recognizes. The beverages served at McDonald's can vary also. Soft drink options feature local brands alongside traditional Coca-Cola Company alternatives. For example, "Irn-Bru" in Scotland and "Guarana" in Brazil are equally as popular as "Coke" and are offered to McDonald's customers in those countries.

Pizza Hut is another example of a company that has made significant menu adaptions as it expanded in international locations. In India, for example, special Indian toppings and vegetarian pizzas were developed, and there are Pizza Hut units selling only vegetarian products. The chain offers a **Jain menu** in India without root-based ingredients such as onions and garlic in consideration of local preferences. Jain bread is served instead of garlic bread, and salad dressings do not contain egg products.

SUPPLY (AVAILABILITY) CREATES MENU VARIATIONS Sometimes decisions to change purchasing standards and product or service offerings are made because of product unavailability. In many regards, hospitality buyers working in the United States enjoy the best of all possible situations. For them, the number of product choices is large, as is the number of vendors willing to supply the products. In many areas of the world, however, desired products simply may be unavailable. Then buyers are forced to choose between incurring the added expense and other challenges incurred to import a product or of substituting alternative products. In many situations, product specifications are altered to fit the realities of the buyer's purchasing environment.

Key Term

═══

Jain menu A very strict vegetarian menu that does not include products grown beneath the ground.

Foreign Sourcing Concerns

Supplier sourcing begins by learning as much as is reasonably possible about potential suppliers. Then buyers can assess which suppliers will most likely meet their needs. Domestically, well-developed tools such as hospitality buyers' guides published by trade publications, Internet listings, and other buyers' directories help purchasers identify potential vendors. Internationally, it is often more difficult to locate and evaluate information about alternative suppliers. Travel can be expensive, and cultural differences can confuse those inexperienced in working with foreign businesses or their agents. Therefore, the selection of foreign vendors and supply sources can be challenging for U.S.- and even foreign-based buyers responsible for purchasing internationally.

CHALLENGES FOR U.S.-BASED BUYERS Learning as much as possible about suppliers based in the United States is difficult enough for most hospitality buyers. Gaining sufficient information about global vendors, especially when the buyer is located in the United States, can be especially complex. The lack of effective communication channels is common. Also, the quality of information received cannot, in many cases, be assumed to be as accurate as that which domestic companies are legally required to provide. The result can be the selection of suppliers about whom a good deal may be unknown.

There are, however, some sources of accurate information (e.g., the government of the country in which the product is grown or manufactured). Buyers seeking information about companies based in other nations can contact the foreign consulates of those countries (located in the United States) for information. Sometimes these consulates can help to supply lists of suppliers engaged in legitimate import/export enterprises in their countries. In addition, trade groups representing product lines often exhibit at hospitality trade shows held in conjunction with the annual conferences of professional associations such as the National Restaurant Association (NRA), American Hotel and Lodging Association (AH&LA), and others.

On-the-Job Challenges in Purchasing (22.1)

"What do they want?" asked Jerry, vice president of purchasing for Sage Food Services, a very large foodservice management company with contracts worldwide. Jerry was talking with Sandy, a regional director with the campus dining division of Sage who was responsible for all dining contracts in the Northeastern United States.

The "*they*" Jerry was referring to were the college students at State University, a campus at which Sage provided dining services.

"Well," explained Sandy, "according to their letter, they want us to issue a statement confirming that we do not buy any product, anywhere we do business, that is grown or manufactured under sweatshop conditions."

"We have thousands of local suppliers who service our accounts worldwide," replied Jerry. "How can we know about the working conditions in all of their businesses?"

"I understand," replied Sandy. "But my own issue is pretty simple. If we don't reply to this letter stating that we oppose organizations characterized by low pay, poor working conditions, safety violations, and generally inhumane employee treatment, and that we do not do business with them, this student group is going to recommend to the University Administration that our contract not be renewed."

Case Study Questions

1. Assume you were the leader of the student group. Do you feel your "demands" are legitimate? Fair?
2. Assume you were Jerry. Would you supply such a letter to Sandy? Defend your response.
3. Assume you were Sandy. What level of knowledge do you feel you have a right to expect from those responsible for the purchasing function in your company?

How are deliveries made to a restaurant located on this busy street?

Normar/Getty Images, Inc.-PhotoDisc

CHALLENGES FOR INTERNATIONALLY BASED BUYERS Internationally based hospitality buyers often must import a large proportion of their consumable products. Items such as furniture, linens, flatware, china, and glassware are often imported either because these items contain the organization's logo, or because the hospitality company's buying power makes importing the items cost-effective, despite additional shipping costs. Some (frequently many) food products must be imported because of quality and/or availability issues. Hospitality buyers sourcing from distant markets are well aware of the longer order–lead times that are needed and the (often) unreliable delivery schedules after shipments reach the host country.

Inevitably, however, even the largest companies discover that some of their purchasing needs must be filled locally. When a hospitality buyer is stationed in a country with which he or she is not familiar, selecting local vendors can be especially difficult. Then wise professionals look to their own employees and colleagues in the industry for assistance.

A successful hospitality purchasing system requires the efforts of many individuals. Invariably, some of them will be local residents familiar with suppliers in their area. Some may also have had experience working in other organizations with similar purchasing needs. Also, local investors, if any, in the operation will likely have knowledge, or can obtain information, about potential suppliers. This is often an important reason why U.S.-based hospitality organizations partner with local businesspersons.

INTERNATIONAL PURCHASING PROCESS

Purchasing products for an international operation is a challenging aspect of any buyer's job. You have learned that variations in product needs and standards, supply limitations, and the presence or location of appropriate vendors are all important factors when making global purchasing decisions.

There are several ways to buy from a foreign supplier in a foreign country. You can purchase from the supplier's wholly owned subsidiary or independent representative in the buyer's country. For example, a multinational foodservice company such as Switzerland-based Nestlé has representatives in many foreign countries (86 different countries at the time of this book's production).

Another method occurs when the purchaser's company establishes a purchasing office in a foreign country. The office may handle purchase orders for international shipping to company units within the country or regional area, and it

> **PURCHASING PROS NEED TO KNOW (22.1)**
>
> Depending upon the country and specific location within it, hospitality buyers may need to import significant or very little food products. For example, let's consider the Middle East: T.G.I. Friday units in this area must import between 40%–60% of required food products and supplies depending upon the country. Chili's properties in the area import a large percentage of fresh items from the United States. By contrast, more than 80% of vegetables, chicken, and fish are purchased from Egyptian suppliers by operators in that country. Most McDonald's potatoes are sourced from the United States, with beef or chicken imported from Australia and New Zealand. However, McDonald's does contract with Middle Eastern dairy, bakery, and packaging producers for its units' needs in the Gulf region.
>
> *Source:* Rick Ramseyer, "Mid East Piece. Market Report: Middle East." *Restaurant Business*, June 15, 2001.

will be active in locating local supply sources. These offices are commonly called **international procurement offices (IPOs),** but may go by a variety of different names.

A third method of buying from a foreign supplier is to deal directly with the supplier in the country without any intermediaries. This is becoming more popular as international procurement becomes easier and more familiar to many hospitality buyers. As you'll learn in the McDonald's case study at the end of the chapter, sometimes expatriate organizations even help the suppliers to develop their business and to operate more professionally.

The local distribution channels in many countries are changing to better meet the needs of the modern hospitality business. For example, in India, China, and many emerging countries, some hotel and restaurant chefs purchase from small distributors. However, many make morning trips to "wet markets" (similar to "farmers' markets" in the United States) to purchase products. An emerging alternative is retail stores that offer competitive prices and even advertise opportunities to shop in an air-conditioned environment and take advantage of "happy hour" food pricing specials.

The link between the tourism industry's demand for food and local agricultural production can stimulate the local economy, which channels benefits to local farmers and increases the amount of money that is spent (and respent) locally. However, numerous factors can work against the local production of foods for tourism purposes:

- Lack of appropriate and consistent quantities.
- Improper quality.
- High prices (in part because of low **economies of scale**).
- Poor growing conditions.
- Lack of capital and investments.
- Technological limitations.
- Inadequate labor because of alternative employment in tourism businesses.
- Buyer preference for processed and imported foods.
- Sanitation/hygiene concerns.

Key Terms

International procurement offices (IPOs)   A purchasing office in a global location established by a domestic company that helps to locate local supply sources and arranges purchases for company affiliates; often abbreviated "IPO."

Economy of scale   The concept that productivity per unit of output can increase as the volume of output increases.

Have you ever wondered how hospitality operations around the world purchase the food, beverage, and numerous other products needed to serve their guests?

Stepahnie Ruet/Corbis/Sygma

- No or inadequate promotion of local foods.
- Poor/inadequate storage, transportation, processing, and marketing capabilities.
- Mistrust between tourism and agricultural personnel.
- Bureaucratic obstacles.
- Marketing networks that limit local access.
- Informal ("unbusinesslike") nature of local agricultural operations.

Other purchasing alternatives can be employed such as using brokers and other sales agents. Regardless of the specific purchase methods used, there can be many advantages associated with buying from foreign companies. There are also a variety of challenges associated with using these supplies, and these should also be well understood by professional buyers.

Advantages of Local Supply Sources

Buyers responsible for procurement in global locations seek high-quality, dependable, and honest suppliers to service their foreign-based units. Doing so helps avoid many supply difficulties. Solid relationships with local suppliers also bring distinct advantages to the business, local economy, and political relationship between the host country and the business.

BUYER/BUSINESS BENEFITS Experienced buyers know that, when quality and price are relatively consistent, local vendors are preferable to distant ones. Supplier relations are critical to long-term effective procurement efforts. Therefore, when hospitality buyers can locate local suppliers who meet their product supply and service requirements, they typically do so for their and the suppliers' benefits.

When positive one-on-one relationships exist, buyers can take action to improve their available product choices. In some locations, purchasers have made concentrated efforts to assist agricultural development by working with local farmers to grow fruits and vegetables or specialty items specifically needed by their foodservice operations. The result is improved supply and quality for the buyer, increased customer satisfaction for the business's guests, and increased revenue for the local producer. In some instances, hotel owners also control the quality of food supply by investing in their own farms and dairies to ensure a reliable supply of goods.

LOCAL ECONOMY BENEFITS Many advantages accrue to the local economy when hospitality buyers purchase locally. Before multinational firms enter foreign (especially emerging countries) markets, they typically analyze supplier quality and if necessary make the investments required to ensure consistent sourcing. This helps preserve their brand equity. They do not want to risk selling their products without ensuring an effective procurement system. All of these "technology transfer" activities result in upgrading the quality of procurement systems in the local economy. Among the other positive economic effects of hospitality businesses are **foreign exchange** earnings, contributions to government revenues, and the generation of employment and business opportunities.

When hospitality buyers purchase locally, employment opportunities expand. Hospitality businesses generate jobs directly through the operation of hotels, restaurants, nightclubs, transportation, and souvenir sales (among others). They can also create jobs indirectly because local suppliers who provide goods and services needed by tourism-related hospitality businesses must employ workers to help them.

Tourism expenditures and the **export** and import of related goods and services generate income for the host economy. That income can stimulate investments necessary to finance growth in other economic sectors. In addition to its positive influence on local merchants, tourism significantly affects the economic positions of local governments. For example, direct contributions to governments are derived from taxes on the incomes of those employed by tourism-related business and from the revenues (sales taxes) they generate. Other governmental revenues are generated from taxes and duties levied on goods and services purchased by tourism-related businesses.

Note: These purchasing-related taxes and fees are among many types of charges levied against the hospitality industry in many countries, including the United States. Government agencies assess hotel occupancy taxes and sales taxes on nonroom sales (including in India, a tax of 100 percent or more on imported liquor after a customs duty tax of almost 250 percent is paid.).[1] Other taxes take the form of fees for tour bus and air travel, and for land, sea, and/or air departures from a country.

POLITICAL BENEFITS   A hospitality organization that operates in a foreign country does so as a guest of that country's government. There are no international business "rights" to operate in a specific country. Therefore, governments that permit international operations must balance the positive effect of the guest company with potential negative effects.

Positive effects include important factors such as those noted above: jobs for local residents, tax revenues, and the financial advantages that occur from local suppliers doing business with the foreign company. Operators who purchase all or most of their supplies from outside a host country can negatively affect the host government's revenues, and that may adversely affect the relationship with the host governments.

Hospitality buyers should understand the real costs incurred by a country that agrees to host an international hospitality company. Although a large hotel in a small community may provide jobs for many local residents, it can also disrupt the traditional balance of product supply and demand. Labor-related problems can also arise when, for example, there are disputes between hospitality managers, licensees, and companies that provide or manufacture products for the hotel or restaurant.

Key Terms

Foreign exchange   The transfer of money from one country to another as a result of business activity.

Export   The movement (transport) of products out of one country for sale or consumption in another country.

The consumption of large amounts of essential services such as power and water can strain local capacity and raise prices or reduce availability to local residents. Consequently, there is potential for an actual decline in the community's standard of living. The governmental entity approving an international business must recognize counterbalancing contributions to the local economy and companies purchasing the maximum amount of goods and services locally help them to do so. Without a positive synergistic relationship, internationally operated companies may encounter local governments that are slow to respond to requests for needed permits, services, security, and **tax waivers** or **tax credits.**

Challenges When Using Local Supply Sources

Despite the advantages detailed above, experienced hospitality buyers understand there are challenges in doing business with local vendors in international settings. This is true with a variety of products and services, but most often with food supplies.

Numerous difficulties may be encountered when purchasing food products from local suppliers, but four of the most common and significant challenges relate to:

- Quality issues
- Consistency concerns
- Contractual and legal issues
- Shortages or unavailability

QUALITY ISSUES To understand the quality-related difficulties that may be encountered when purchasing from a local supplier in some locations, consider the purchase of a common item such as ground beef. In the United States, a buyer could choose among numerous suppliers. When purchasing internationally, a variety of challenges arise, including

Product Inspection The price and product content (e.g., lean-to-fat ratio) may vary between suppliers. However, U.S. buyers would be ensured of receiving products that were carefully inspected prior to production, and safely handled prior to delivery, because all beef for human consumption in the United States must be federally inspected for **wholesomeness.** The handling procedures used by the supplier will also be subject to continuous inspection and monitoring. However, in some global locations, product inspection and safety monitoring, even though they are important buyer concerns, may not be required and, therefore, may not occur when a local supplier is used.

Every country has its own food inspection program; some are rigorous, others are much less so. International buyers must know about the actual product inspection program(s) that are in place where their proposed suppliers operate. They can learn this by contacting other hospitality professionals purchasing from the same suppliers, government officials responsible for food quality assurance programs, and, often, the suppliers of desired products.

Product Safety In countries with highly developed food handling standards, it is assumed that each successive member of the food service supply chain will

---

Key Terms

Tax waivers   A forgiveness of a tax that is (or normally would be) owed.

Tax credit   A reduction in the amount of a tax that is (or will be) owed.

Wholesomeness   Suitable for human consumption.

On-the-Job Challenges in Purchasing (22.2)

Latisha, the food and beverage director at the Plata Cana Resort, loved her job in the Caribbean and was committed to ensuring her guests received only the best and freshest ingredients available. She was pleased that she had identified a Dominican Republic vendor that could supply high-quality and reasonably priced domestically grown coffee. Her Canadian, European, and American guests loved the taste, especially served (in the Dominican style) with generous additions of scalded milk. However, that was the problem!

As a highly perishable commodity, quality standards were important, but it was impractical and costly to fly in fresh USDA-inspected milk from Miami on a daily or even weekly basis. Yet, she knew the majority of her guests were accustomed to being served only fresh milk products that had been graded, inspected during processing, and nutritionally labeled. Unfortunately, in her local area, available dairy suppliers could not meet all three of those requirements.

Case Study Questions

Assume that you are Latisha:

1. How would you decide whether the available local dairy vendors would be considered "acceptable?"
2. What challenges would Latisha likely encounter if she decided to purchase her beverage milk from a local dairy supplier?
3. What alternative strategies could Latisha employ if she could not use local dairy suppliers?

maintain, to the highest degree possible, the quality of items as they pass through their hands. This is especially critical for **potentially hazardous foods (PHFs).**

Regardless of whether foods have been inspected for wholesomeness before they enter the food chain, suppliers must handle the items carefully to ensure food safety. It makes little difference if the product was inspected during or immediately after processing, or if the facility in which the processing occurred was regularly inspected, if those in the distribution channel do not use storage and transportation tactics that ensure product safety when they are delivered. Buyers using local purveyors (especially for PHFs) should be familiar with their suppliers' storage and sanitation procedures.

CONSISTENCY CONCERNS When many suppliers want to sell to a hospitality buyer, competition is a strong motivation for ensuring product consistency. If a product is not delivered as ordered, the buyer can simply change suppliers. However, when few or only one supplier is available, product consistency can become a significant issue because buyers may be able to apply limited (if any) leverage. Then, a good relationship with the supplier is necessary to help ensure maximum product consistency.

CONTRACTUAL AND LEGAL ISSUES When a buyer in New York State buys a product from a New York-based vendor, contractual and legal issues involved in the purchase are fairly straightforward. The **currency** used to complete the transaction

Key Terms

Potentially hazardous foods (PHF) A food product that requires careful handling and temperature control because it is in a form capable of causing illness if not handled properly.

Currency The system of money (including bills and coins) used by a country or geographic area.

will be U.S. dollars, and if a dispute arose, it would likely be settled by a New York State court.

Alternatively, consider a U.S. company that buys seafoods from Japan that are purchased through a Singapore-based broker. The product is shipped from Tokyo on a Norwegian-owned ship that has been registered in Liberia. In this typical case, the question of the appropriate currency exchange (who receives payment, in which currency, and when the payment is received), as well as legal jurisdiction in the event of potential difficulties, can be complex.

Although there can be many contractual and legal issues related to global purchasing, three of the most important for hospitality buyers relate to currency exchange, the appropriate jurisdiction for legal disputes, and the terminology used in international trade.

Currency Exchange Currency exchanges affect how much buyers pay for goods and services. The conversion of one currency to another when paying for products purchased in another country does not, in itself, pose any great difficulties because most currencies can be readily converted.

Typically, however, the conversion involves costs because a bank or currency conversion entity will charge for making the exchange, and therefore, costs increase when one buys in a different currency.

In addition, changes in currency values affect the price buyers pay for goods and services. If the value of the buyer's currency declines between the times an order is placed and when payment is made, the buyer incurs a price increase even though the seller will not benefit from it. Alternatively, if the value of the buyer's currency increases in the same period, he or she experiences a decrease in the price paid. When currencies fluctuate significantly, purchase transaction prices based upon these exchanges can fluctuate significantly as well.

Legal Dispute Jurisdiction Where should differences of opinion about international purchase agreements be resolved? The answer should be the country

---

HI-TECH PURCHASING (22.1)

Brother Can You Spare a Dime (Or Maybe 51.7 Colones)?

In early 2009, 51.7 colones would buy you one dime. For many Americans, the words colones, kunas, dinars, guilders, and escudos may not be well known. In their own countries, however, they are critical because they identify the national currency in, respectively, Costa Rica, Croatia, Jordan, the Netherlands, and Portugal.

To illustrate the importance of understanding local currency exchange, consider the provider of a global resort hotel's fresh egg supply. In most countries, vendors price their products and collect payment in the local currency. The problem is that successful hospitality companies may operate in dozens of countries and collect (and spend) money in many of the world's more than 100 different currencies.

Fortunately, up-to-date currency converters are widely available on the Internet. To view one such tool, go to: www.xe.com

At the home page, choose a country you would like to visit, and then convert 100 U.S. dollars into that currency. Next, do some pricing research in that country to see whether your $100 will buy more or less there than in your own country. Welcome to the inherent complexity of currency exchange!

Key Term

Currency exchange A system designed to transfer equal value from one accepted form of monetary payment to another form (e.g., from U.S. dollars to Mexican pesos).

agreed upon at the time of purchase, so this jurisdiction should be clearly identified. Sometimes, the best location for dispute resolution is neither the home country of the buyer nor the seller. This might be the case when the goods purchased will pass through several owners and countries in the course of the transaction. The result: The court hearing details of a trade dispute involving a U.S. buyer may not be a U.S. court. Courts throughout the world do not operate in a manner similar to those in the United States, nor will all courts lend a sympathetic ear to the claims of a large U.S. company in a dispute with a smaller, local business entity.

There are many good reasons why U.S.-based and other companies making purchases internationally often use a buyer's agent (see Chapter 2) when securing goods. Legal dispute jurisdiction issues are one of them. Even when direct purchases are made, it is appropriate for buyers to select skilled specialists to advise them on or arrange for matters including shipment, insurance, payment, and appropriate legal jurisdiction.

International Trade Terminology   The International Chamber of Commerce has developed a publication that suggests standard business terminology that can be used to clarify the responsibilities of suppliers and sellers in international trade. The **International commercial terms (Incoterms)** provide a standardized language that, although not universally accepted, provides a point of reference from which parties can negotiate about each other's responsibilities.

The following are some examples of international Incoterms:

- *Ex-works.*   The seller's only responsibility is to make the goods available at the seller's premises. Buyers incur the costs and risks of moving goods from the seller's site to their destination.
- *Pre-carrier: named place.*   Sellers hand goods, cleared for export, to the carrier at the place named in the shipping contract. Sellers may need to pay transport from the factory to the carrier. Delivery occurs at the seller's site, and the seller is responsible for loading.
- *Free alongside ship.*   Properly used only for ocean or inland water transport, this term means that sellers are responsible for placing the goods alongside the ship. The place named in the contract "alongside" means within reach of the ship's loading peer. Sellers are responsible for clearing goods for export.
- *Free on board.*   This term is properly used only for ocean or inland water transportation modes. The seller's obligation ends when goods, cleared for export, are placed on board a ship at the port cited in the contract. In the United States, "FOB" does not mean "free on board a ship"; it means much the same as "Ex-works," which was defined above: the seller's responsibility ends at the seller's premises.
- *Cost and freight.*   Properly used only for sea or inland water transport, this term means that sellers must clear the goods for export and pay costs and freight required to move them to the named destination. However, buyers assume the risk of lost or damaged goods and any cost increases after they pass the ship's rail in the port of shipment.
- *Cost insurance and freight.*   Applicable to water transport, this term means the same as "cost and freight," except that sellers must also buy the marine insurance.

Key Term

International commercial terms (Incoterms)   Terminology developed by the International Chamber of Commerce to clarify the responsibilities of buyers and sellers in international trade.

- *Carriage paid to (named place).* Used with any form of transport, this term means that sellers must clear the goods for export, and pay the costs, including freight necessary to bring them to the named site. However, buyers assume the risk of loss or damage to the goods and any cost increases after the first carrier receives the goods.
- *Carriage insurance paid to (named place).* This term means essentially the same as "carriage paid to (named place)" (see above), except that the seller must also pay the insurance.
- *Delivered at frontier (named place).* Buyers must clear the goods through **customs** after sellers clear goods for export and make them available at the named point, which is before the destination's customs border.
- *Delivered ex-ship.* Normally used for sea shipments, with this arrangement, buyers assume risks and costs after the ship reaches the named destination, but before goods are cleared for import.
- *Delivered ex-quay.* Also used for sea shipments, buyers assume risks and costs on the quay (wharf) at the named destination. Sellers are responsible for discharge costs, and buyers are responsible for import clearance.
- *Delivered duty unpaid (named place).* This term means that sellers pay all costs required to deliver the goods to the stipulated place except customs clearance, and buyers pay duty and taxes.
- *Delivered duty paid (named place).* With this arrangement, sellers pay all costs, including customs clearance to deliver the products to the stipulated place.

A review of the above terms explains some of the legal, contractual, and financial details required for international purchasing. It is easy to see that the cost of product purchases involves significant handling and other costs that must be borne by the buyer and/or seller. It is critical that these responsibilities are identified and agreed upon during purchase negotiations.

PRODUCT SHORTAGES/UNAVAILABILITY In many cases, sufficient food and beverage products to operate a hospitality business can be secured in virtually every area of the world if operators are willing to pay the price to have them imported and or work with local sources to generate a consistent supply. However, one ongoing challenge facing hospitality buyers, especially those in **third world** countries, is the difficulty of obtaining replacement parts for equipment and machinery.

Internet Purchasing Assistant (22.2)

You've learned that the International Chamber of Commerce (ICC) publishes the International Commercial Terms (Incoterms). To review this organization's Web site and learn more about the assistance and coordination it provides in the international marketplace, review its Web site: www.iccwbo.org

Key Terms

Customs A government agency that collects fees on goods being imported into or exported from a country.

Third world (country) A general term used to identify countries that are not as industrialized or technologically advanced as "first world" countries. Many are located in Africa, Latin America, and Asia and typically are confronted with significant economic, educational, and other challenges.

Internet Purchasing Assistant (22.3)

Finding reliable service and repair for foodservice equipment is always a challenge. This is most true for operations located in less populated areas of the world where service is difficult to obtain. Fortunately, some companies offer virtually "worldwide" equipment sales and service. To view one such company's Web site, go to: www.hobartcorp.com

At the home page:

1. Under "Dealer Directory," click on "Locate Foodservice Dealer."
2. Then click on "Outside the U.S." to view a list of the international sales and service centers maintained by this foodservice equipment and consulting company.

The on-going maintenance of elevators, air conditioners, HVAC systems, computer equipment, and other electronic and mechanical equipment in many global locations is hindered by a lack of trained technicians. Parts must be special ordered, persons required to service equipment must be brought in to the business's site, and significantly increased repair costs and delays can result. In those situations, the availability of service at any quality level might be viewed as a successful purchasing activity! As a result, buyers in these situations must carefully assess and implement appropriate parts inventory levels, **preventive maintenance** programs, and training efforts for maintenance staff.

OTHER INTERNATIONAL PURCHASING CONCERNS

Those with global purchasing responsibilities must be concerned about communication challenges and international business practices, the topics of the following discussion.

Communication Challenges

English is the dominant language of international trade and commerce, and this is of obvious benefit to those working in U.S. hospitality organizations. However,

---

PURCHASING PROS NEED TO KNOW (22.2)

The supply, quality, and continuity of essential services such as water, electricity, and telephone lines is a serious problem for hotel operators in many parts of the world. Disruptions in electricity and water supply, fluctuations in voltage delivered, and storms that damage telephone and power lines are not uncommon in developing countries. As a result, hospitality managers in these locations must consider special needs such as back-up generators and the fuel required to operate them. Also, during times of power outages, property security concerns may be heightened, and security services may be required.

Essential service disruptions illustrate what experienced buyers know: They and their procurement activities are just as critical to the effective operation of an international property as are the activities of line management staff. In many international hospitality settings, operating managers are the buyers, and they can easily recognize how these two important activities must be integrated.

Key Term

Preventive maintenance Activities required to maintain a building and its contents, including equipment, in a condition that minimizes or delays the need for major repairs.

managers can still encounter many types of communication problems that create difficulties as they attempt to conduct business with persons from different countries. For example, special meanings are frequently attached to trading terminology, and the technical vocabulary (**jargon**) in different countries also varies.

Also, one person may be less familiar with the language than another. These and related problems frequently arise in domestic business transactions, and they are much more likely to be of concern in international business.

International Business Practices

The "dos and don'ts" of **business etiquette** differ significantly around the globe. Long-standing traditions, customs, and protocols establish the foundation for the conduct of business in every country. Those negotiating purchasing contracts for shipment to global locations, and expatriate purchasers seeking to maintain the most effective relationships with their local suppliers, must consistently practice business etiquette that is proper for their location.

Figure 22.2 provides examples of business etiquette guidelines applicable to purchasers in several countries. It illustrates how business customs affect common procurement tasks. Even a cursory review will note significant differences.

Country	
Brazil	*Appointments*—Business involves personal conversations with the understanding that relationships will be long-term. Appointments should be made at least two weeks in advance. Best times: 10:00 a.m. to noon, 3:00 p.m. to 5:00 p.m. Brazilian business culture does not stress punctuality.
	Titles and respect—Many persons prefer first names rather than family names. However, titles are frequently used (e.g., "Dr. John").
	Gift giving—Gifts are not necessary for the first meeting; however, one should do so in a social situation. Inexpensive electronic items such as calculators and CDs of popular U.S. entertainers are examples.
	Negotiation procedures—English is widely spoken in business; however, the dominant language is Portuguese (not Spanish). One should emphasize relationships over business "deals." Several negotiation sessions will likely be needed, and it is inappropriate to change negotiation team members between sessions. Business cards are typically exchanged (print cards in English on one side and Portuguese on the other). Interpreters may be necessary. Subjective concerns are often more influential than "facts." Avoid confrontations, and do not exhibit frustration. Negotiations will address every point in a contract; points that seem irrelevant may be discussed at length. It is courteous to visit for some time after the meeting, so one should schedule appointments to allow for this. Paperwork is signed sometime after an agreement is made; a handshake and one's personal word means acceptance. In some Brazilian subcultures, written agreements may not be binding.
Hong Kong	*Appointments*—Appointments should be made as far in advance as possible, sometimes by as much as two months. Punctuality is important. Six-day workweeks include hours from 9:00 a.m. to 5:00 p.m. on Monday–Friday and on Saturday from 9:00 a.m. to 1:00 p.m.
	Titles and respect—Most persons should be addressed with their title and family name. Many Hong Kong Chinese adopt an English first name to make it easier for Westerners to address them, and a similar courtesy is expected from Westerners. If possible, someone who speaks Chinese should help with this.
	Gift giving—Gift giving is important and, if one receives a gift, one should be given in return. Gifts should be accepted and given with both hands. Gifts are not typically unwrapped in front of the giver. Items from one's home country and illustrated books are examples of appreciated gifts.
	Negotiation procedures—Business cards should be prepared with Chinese on one side and English on the other. When receiving a card, examine it for a few moments and place in your card case or on your table if you are seated. Business discussion should begin only after light conversations. The same team should be

Key Terms

Jargon   Technical terms specific to an industry or profession.

Business etiquette   Customs, procedures, manners, and behaviors that are appropriate for the conduct of business in a specific country.

used for all negotiation sessions. Offers of tea should always be accepted, and the position of cups change to indicate how far apart the businesspersons are in reaching an agreement. The answer, "Yes," does not necessarily signal agreement and the term, "No," will not be directly used. It is typically inappropriate to direct all information to senior representatives. Negotiations can be slow with significant attention to detail. As negotiation ends, Chinese may request a large discount as a "compromise."

Indonesia

Appointments—Business hours are generally 9:00 a.m. to 5:00 p.m., Monday–Friday. Business transactions are frequently conducted in English. Punctuality is not emphasized, but business visitors are expected to be on time.

Titles and respect—Names must be treated with respect, and it is important to try to pronounce names correctly. It is best to ask Indonesian businesspersons how they should be addressed. A title and/or, perhaps, their name, will be in order.

Gift giving—A small gift during a first meeting displays interest in establishing a long-term business relationship. A small gift representative of one's country or with one's company logo is appropriate. Gifts that have been received are not opened in front of the giver. Food is often a welcomed gift, but one's religion must be considered. For example, alcohol and pork are not given to Muslims, beef or leather-containing items are not appropriate for Hindus.

Negotiation procedures—Relationships are built on respect and trust, and negotiation may evolve over several months. When introducing persons, state the name of the most important person first. Ornate business cards are appreciated, and the card should be offered with one's right hand facing the recipient. When the card is received, examine and remark about it before putting it in a card case or on a table. The card should not be placed into a pocket or wallet. When the meeting begins, focus on business only when the most important Indonesian businessperson brings up the subject. The group, not individuals, should be addressed during meetings, and superiors should be treated with deference. Speak quietly and remain in control of your emotions. Indonesians may say little during a meeting and, before answering a question, protocol requires that a respondent make a respectful pause of 10–15 seconds. To "save face," Indonesians may say "yes" when they don't mean it. A smile may not indicate amusement or approval and, if a question is deliberately ignored, this often means "no." Bribery is common and is known as "facilitating payments." "Deals" are never complete until paperwork is signed, and this may be delayed until a "lucky day" arrives.

Italy

Appointments—If necessary, try to find a third party to help arrange introductions. Punctuality is not a priority in Italian business culture. Business is not typically conducted during early-to-mid-afternoon. The best time to plan appointments is from 10:00 a.m. to 11:00 a.m. and after 3:00 p.m. Many businesses have long summer vacation periods.

Titles and respect—Titles and family names are used as a sign of respect in most Italian companies, and titles should be used if known. Personal and professional titles are used constantly in casual conversations and formal writing.

Gift giving—Do not give a business gift until one is received. They are expected at social events and are usually opened when received. Gifts should be of a reputable brand name, but not expensive (e.g., alcohol or crafts from one's country). Do not give gifts that contain one's company's logo.

Negotiation procedures—An English translator is needed in many business situations. Italians prefer dealing with the most important persons in an organization. Business cards are common and should be translated to Italian on one side. It is important to act professionally and with formality at all times. The goal of an initial meeting should be to develop mutual respect and trust. Presentation materials and packaging should be pleasing, but not overly done. New ideas and concepts are appreciated. Hierarchy is important, and there is significant respect for power and age. Italians typically speak loudly and with animation, and interruptions are likely. They are guided by their feelings and look at specifics of each situation rather than legal or policy issues. Decisions may take several months or longer. Sudden demands can be made, but this does not necessarily mean that failure to accept them will lead to an unsuccessful conclusion.

Japan

Appointments—A personal call is more effective than a letter. Punctuality is very important. Office hours are 9:00 a.m. to 5:00 p.m. The traditional workweek is 48 hours without overtime pay over a 5½-day period.

Titles and respect—First names are not frequently used in business situations. It is best to use the last name of the Japanese businessperson. Professional titles are often used in place of last names.

Gift giving—Gift giving is an important protocol. The emphasis is on the ritual rather than the gift. Gifts are often given at the end of a visit, but they should be avoided early in a relationship. For an individual, the gift should be given in private. Gifts are presented with both hands, and the same gift should not be presented to two or more persons of unequal rank. Before being accepted, it is polite to modestly refuse the gift, and it should then be opened in private. Gifts should be wrapped and carried inside a shopping bag to reduce the chance that it will be seen before being presented.

Negotiation procedures—Business cards are very important, and a "ceremony" of exchange is typical. The card should be printed in English and Japanese on opposite sides, and it should be presented after a bow or handshake. Present the card with the Japanese side facing up. When a business card is received, make an obvious examination of it for a few moments. Cards should be placed in a card case or on the table (not in

	one's wallet or pocket). Business should not be discussed during the first several minutes of a conversation. Negotiations typically begin at the executive level, and then move to the middle-management level. One must remain professional and not make accusations or direct refusals. Remain quiet, low-key, and polite. The emphasis should be on how one's business can increase the prosperity and reputation of the Japanese company. Expect that anything you say will be taken literally. Periods of silence during meetings are considered useful (not uncomfortable). During meetings, one might not know exactly what Japanese businesspersons expect. The group—not individuals—should be given compliments. Remember that the decision-making process can be very slow, and it can take several years. Oral agreements are preferred to written ones, and contracts can be renegotiated (they are not final).
Saudi Arabia	*Appointments*—Businesses are frequently open during much of the morning, closed for the afternoon, and reopen from 5:00 p.m. to 10:00 p.m. The basic workweek is from Saturday to Thursday. Appointments are made for the time of day rather than a precise hour. Saudi secretaries do not normally make appointments for their supervisors. There is typically a "coffee protocol" that precedes meetings with higher-level officials.
	Titles and respect—The use of first names denotes greater familiarity than in the West; there is no equivalent to "Mr." or "Ms." "Bin," when preceding a name, means, "son of," and "Bint" means "daughter of."
	Gift giving—Gifts are given only to close friends. It is offensive to receive gifts from a casual acquaintance.
	Negotiation procedures—A meeting formally begins as the guest stops at the entrance to the reception room, and states a greeting. Then the visitor enters after the greeting is returned. If the room is carpeted, one's shoes should be removed and left outside. The visitor should shake hands with the most senior person first, and move around the room in a counter-clockwise direction, shaking hands with each person before taking a seat. Business cards are common but not essential. Negotiations are very slow, and meetings with no progress will likely occur before the pace of business quickens. Contracts can be unilaterally voided even if they are signed.
United States	*Appointments*—Prior appointments are needed, and the workweek is from approximately 8:30 a.m. to 5:00 or 6:00 p.m. Punctuality is important.
	Titles and respect—When meeting someone for the first time, use a title or his or her last name until requested to do otherwise. Ensure that your U.S. acquaintances know your preferred name.
	Gift giving—Gift giving is thoughtful, but not expected. Gifts are usually unwrapped immediately and shown to everyone assembled. Hosting someone for a meal is a popular gift.
	Negotiation procedures—Business cards are not refused, but they may not be given. The concept that "time is money" is taken seriously. Businesspersons like to make decisions quickly. Information should be straightforward. Money is a priority and an issue and is more important than status, protocol, and "saving face." Americans do not like periods of silence during the negotiation and may continue to speak simply to avoid silence. In general, businesspersons do not hesitate to say "no," and to disagree with someone else. There is a strong work ethic, and when a "deal" is reached, it will be honored. Americans are future-oriented, and innovation is often more important than tradition. "Small talk" may precede a business meeting, and then business is conducted at a fast pace. American businesspersons often attempt to reach an oral agreement at the first meeting, with "final" contracts drawn up after first meetings with prospective clients.

FIGURE 22.2   Business Etiquette Guidelines for Global Purchasers

Some business etiquette guidelines for the United States were listed at the end of Figure 22.2. These guidelines, selected from representative countries across the globe were provided for comparative purposes and to show how business etiquette in the United States might be explained in the context of other countries.

Internet Purchasing Assistant (22.4)

To view an excellent source of information about guidelines for business etiquette, go to the Web site for Executive Planet (www.executiveplanet.com). At that site, you can review general guidelines for the conduct of business and for international travel, which many hospitality industry executives must do as part of their positions. You can also view essential business culture guides for more than 40 countries.

INTERNATIONAL PURCHASING EXAMPLES

This section includes information and anecdotes that describe broad purchasing procurement strategies, and more specific purchasing tactics, that enable hospitality organizations to obtain required products in selected global locations.

McDonald's in India

McDonald's opened its first restaurant in India in 1996. Among its special challenges was the procurement of perishable products that consistently met its quality requirements. Its menu needed to be completely revised to avoid beef (not consumed by India's Hindu majority) and pork (not permitted in Muslim diets). The ban on beef products is very specific, and it even includes a prohibition against beef-flavored seasoning applied to french fries at the manufacturer's plant. Cheeses and sauces must be vegetarian and contain no eggs. Also, vegetarian products must be separated from their nonvegetarian counterparts from the time of procurement to serving.

McDonald's operations in India are managed through two **joint ventures** that partner with the company to plan and coordinate procurement systems. The company spent several years identifying its Indian partners and then worked with them to select approved suppliers. McDonald's officials also discussed and reviewed business plans of their joint venture teams as part of their preopening efforts.

McDonald's officials recognize the importance of customers, suppliers, and its own organizational philosophies and strengths. It attempts to work in partnership arrangements with its supply chain partners to gain efficiencies that can be shared with them. Savings that accrue to McDonald's are used to develop new products and to maintain competitive prices that increase customer visits. Suppliers' savings are expected to be used to improve production processes and to enhance and improve product quality. The results of this relationship, then, are advantageous for both parties.

Many Indian suppliers in the mid-1990s used no consistent (standardized) business processes. Without these, product consistency and the optimal use of resources were not possible. McDonald's personnel worked closely with its Indian suppliers to create the business philosophy and procedures needed to enable McDonald's leadership and quality goals to be attained.

McDonald's staff provided significant technical inputs as the bakery products, chicken patties, lettuce, and dairy items needed for the menu were selected, and (sometimes) specially developed. McDonald's and members of its supply chain developed multi-temperature trucks to transport products with different temperature requirements on very long routes between locations. This tactic was necessary because production volumes were not large enough to cost-effectively produce needed items in smaller regions.

The company's "partnership" relationship with its suppliers was incorporated into its interactions with them early on. Contracts were negotiated based upon larger future volumes than when the business relationship began. Suppliers then became responsible for their losses until preestablished volumes were reached, and they were then reimbursed for their earlier losses.

Over time, McDonald's key suppliers in India have done well. They have, in some instances, expanded product lines, begun business relationships with other

---

Key Term

Joint venture   A business or project co-owned and operated for the mutual benefit of two or more business partners.

Some hospitality operations may have been waiting, literally, for weeks (or much longer!) for products in some of these shipping containers.
Jeff Greenberg/PhotoEdit Inc.

hospitality organizations, and even formed their own joint ventures with other suppliers.

Note: This section is adapted from Devangshu Dutta, "The Perishable Food Chain in India. Case Study: McDonald's: Creating an Ecosystem." *Just-Food*, September, 2005.

Restaurants in China

As recently as 1993, restaurant food in China was typically limited to five-star hotels, traditional Chinese restaurants, and street-side vendors. Now Western-style fast-food chains including Kentucky Fried Chicken (KFC), McDonald's, and a host of other chains from the United States and other countries are popular.

Purchasers of food imported from the United States into China have several challenges, including

- High prices of imported products.
- Potential for fake (counterfeit-branded) products that can damage brand image.
- Potential for government policy changes that might increase costs.
- Lack of knowledge about handling/using imported products.
- Unreliable cold-food transportation beyond major urban areas.
- Long lag-times between product order and delivery.
- High trans-Pacific shipping costs.
- Possible quarantine and custom delays.

Food distribution in China is a challenge, especially outside major metropolitan areas. The cold-food chain is unreliable. Purchasing managers at major hotels indicate that most perishables are sent by air, and then hotel staff transport them from the airport to the property.

Distributors suffer from cash flow problems: Buyers frequently don't pay for deliveries until 45–60 days after delivery, and payments for imported food are generally required 30 days after invoicing (which usually occurs at time of shipment). Also, distributors must often make purchase deposits (e.g., 30 percent on meat imports). Air shipments of meat and dairy products, as well as some fruits and vegetables, are routine because fewer customs/quarantine difficulties occur with airborne as opposed to sea imports.

Hospitality organizations typically purchase from U.S. consolidators (who order for China-based distributors and, as well, for restaurants and hotels),

---

PURCHASING PROS NEED TO KNOW (22.3)

Want to import it yourself? Customs, licensing, and numerous other procedures create significant challenges as products are imported into China. Some distributors handle these processing requirements themselves, others use specialized import agents, and few end users (even Chinese state-owned companies) try to do it themselves. Among the licenses and permits required may be a hygiene certificate from the U.S. government, a Chinese import permit, and hygiene and quarantine inspection certificates upon entry. Labels in Chinese are typically required (stick-on labels are acceptable if they are on the product at entry), and clearance for label language may take several months.

Most large, international hotel chains offer group buying for some products, but executive chefs and purchasing managers are still the primary decision makers at specific properties. Imported foods make up 30 to 60 percent of the food buy at an internationally managed five-star hotel. Their largest suppliers are multinational organizations with manufacturing facilities in China. These companies have also created their own stand-alone supply chains which overlie the domestic Chinese market.

---

secondary wholesalers, major distributors, cash and carry (grocery) stores, and directly from U.S. suppliers.

KFC is the most popular quick-service restaurant in China. It offers chicken wings, nuggets, and sandwiches in mild or spicy variations. Chicken parts are sourced locally. One downside, however, is that domestic producers meet the needs of their export accounts first when there are product shortages. This requires KFC units in China to buy from numerous domestic poultry producers to ensure a constant source of supply.

In addition to some spices, KFC imports frozen french fries and corn-on-the-cob from the United States. Product distribution centers are operated throughout the country. KFC uses competing, local importers and distributors for the majority of its product needs, and the remainder are purchased directly by KFC distribution centers. Distributors make delivery to distribution centers that, in turn, transports products to the restaurants.

Note: This section is adapted from the USDA Foreign Agricultural Service Global Agriculture Information Network, *Gain Report Ch 5407 UN*, 2005. China, Peoples Republic of. HRI Food Service Sector. Mainland China HRI Annual Report, 2005.

Hospitality Operations in the Russian Federation

Approximately 50 percent of restaurants in Russia are quick-service (street/mobile or sit-down). The remainder are "democratic" restaurants (those that are moderately priced), "boutique" operations (which are higher priced), and coffee shops. Hotels in the Moscow and Saint Petersburg markets attract 80 percent of foreign tourists and are characterized by a high level of business activity and the existence of more high-class hotels.

Large restaurants and hospitality chains purchase from larger suppliers who are typically also importers. Many restaurants purchase vegetables and fruit during the summer season from local producers, and low-to-middle price-level operations also purchase meat directly from domestic producers. Restaurants typically contact foreign producers directly for exclusive/exotic products such as sushi ingredients. Some restaurant chains import products directly through their own purchasing/distribution organizations.

Many domestically produced restaurant products are improving in quality and consistency and are increasing their market share. Reasons for continued imports include high/consistent quality, regular/secure supply sources, tourists' preferences, and better appearance of packaging.

McDONALD'S IN RUSSIA

When McDonald's Russia opened in Moscow in 1989, food shortages were common, erratic food quality was frequently the norm, and some menu ingredients, such as iceberg lettuce, didn't even exist within the country.

McDonald's Corporation constructed a large manufacturing complex in a Moscow suburb to produce what was needed for its initial 20 units, including a bakery line for buns and a liquid line for special sauces. McDonald's entered into a joint venture with the Moscow city council for the investment required by this operation.

Today, McDonald's Russia has restaurants in approximately 40 cities, and its production and distribution facilities have had to keep up with the expansion. To do so, local entrepreneurs were identified, and corporate officials worked with them to "grow their business." For example, McDonald's lettuce supplier has increased output to the extent that it now supplies the product to other brands and even exports products to Europe. This has occurred as McDonald's has invested in a strong local supply chain and educated local producers about contemporary business and agriculture methodology.

Markets in some locations are not acceptable sources of supply for hospitality buyers because of food safety concerns.

Peter Bowater/Photo Researchers, Inc.

Purchasing Resources on the Internet

In addition to the Web sites referenced in this chapter's "Internet Purchasing Assistant," the following sites provide detailed information to enhance your purchasing knowledge and skills.

Purchasing Resources on the Internet

Site	Information About
www.state.gov/s/cpr/rls/fco/	Foreign consular offices in the United States
www.ih-ra.com	International Hotel and Restaurant Association
www.foodmp.com	Food importers/exporters
www.intlhotelsupply.com	Hotel furnishings/supplies exporter
www.bizeurope.com	European hotel and restaurant importer/exporter directory
www.cyborlink.com	International business etiquette and manners
www.wto.org	World trade organization; the entity that develops ground rules for international convenience
www.mcdonalds.com	Web site for McDonald's in the countries/markets in which it operates (Click on the county(ies) in which you are interested ["I'm going to McDonald's"] when you reach the site)
www.starbucks.com/csrannualreport	Starbucks, fair trade, and coffee social responsibility

Key Terms

Think It Through

1. Assume that you manage the Food and Beverage department of a large hotel in a remote section of a small Caribbean island. Identify two distinct advantages and two potential disadvantages of purchasing your basic meat supplies locally.

2. The chapter makes the case for using the expertise of fellow hospitality professionals when buyers seek information about suppliers in areas with which they are not familiar. Would you solicit advice from a direct competitor? Why or why not?

3. Assume that you operate an International Procurement Office (IPO) in a country from which your U.S.-based company purchases significant products. One day, a local government official whom you have come to know well suggests a financial "gift" to his uncle to ensure continued goodwill among the local suppliers of products that you frequently purchase. How would you respond to the request? Would the size of the cash request affect your response?

4. Assume you are the purchasing manager for a large, first-class hotel in a rural resort location. What are some tactics you could use to encourage local farmers to grow and sell fresh produce for your food and beverage operation?

5. What, if any, types of general and specific assistance would you expect (or desire) from the central procurement headquarters if you were a purchaser for a hotel that is part of the chain organization located in a country or area with few established distributors of hospitality products?

Team Fun

For this exercise, assume that each team consists of employees of an internationally franchised restaurant chain in the QSR (quick-service restaurant) segment. Each team member works in the company's procurement department. In one South American country in which you operate, the local populace likes your products very much, but prefers less "sweet" ketchup as a condiment. Because your U.S.-based ketchup manufacturer does not produce the desired product, a local vendor was identified and has been successfully supplying the popular "local" ketchup to your units.

Volume-wise, 97 percent of your sales in that country are derived from local residents, with the remaining 3 percent coming from U.S. and other tourists to the country. Your U.S. ketchup supplier has just announced it has now affiliated with a distributor in that country, and as a result can now supply your restaurants with the original (sweeter) ketchup product.

1. The assignment of the first team is to make a case for changing ketchup suppliers and, therefore, enhancing the image of worldwide consistency important to future franchise sales and impressions of quality affiliated with U.S. brand names.

2. The assignment of the second team is to make a case for maintaining the current ("local") product (and franchisee satisfaction in that country).

3. The assignment of the third team is to examine the potential advantages and disadvantages of offering both ketchup products in these units.

Each team should be prepared to present and discuss their findings and conclusions.

Endnote

1. Readers desiring more information about the types of taxes and other fees levied against hospitality businesses are referred to: A. J. Singh, "Tax Till They Drop": India's Tourism Mantra. World Travel & Tourism Tax Policy Center, *Travel Tax News* 1, no. 1, March, 2002.

23

Evaluating and Improving Procurement Systems

In This Chapter

This book defends the premise that professional procurement is very important to the success of the hospitality organization, and numerous activities must be managed effectively to maximize its benefits. The responsibilities that must be assumed, and the significant commitment of resources required, mandate that procurement activities be evaluated. This process is more challenging than one might initially suspect. For example, there may not be a direct relationship between a property's financial success and an effective purchasing operation. A hotel or restaurant can meet its financial goals but still be able to reduce costs further without sacrificing or compromising quality standards if procurement changes are made. Alternatively, an organization might fail to meet its financial goals, even though purchasing personnel were accomplishing all they could reasonably do, because problems can occur after, not during or as a result of, procurement activities. Fortunately, numerous tactics can be used to evaluate purchasing, and they are the topic of this chapter.

One cannot evaluate purchasing (or any other function) without, first, establishing goals that clearly specify and quantify expectations. The definition of purchasing success must be in the context of the goals established for the process. Success can then be evaluated by determining the extent to which identified goals were attained. This relationship between purchasing goals and subsequent evaluation will be emphasized and illustrated throughout the chapter.

Although it should be easy to justify procurement evaluation, this task is often de-emphasized or performed incorrectly in many hospitality organizations. Why should purchasing be evaluated, and how should it be done? The most important reasons defending the need for evaluation, and details about the process to do so, are explained in the chapter.

A wide variety of financial, operational, and other factors must be considered as purchasing goals are developed. Many are explored in this chapter to, first, reinforce our emphasis about the wide range of purchasing responsibilities and, second, to suggest how each factor might be considered during a comprehensive purchasing evaluation.

The concept of the "intelligent customer" is introduced in this chapter within the context of evaluation. The premise is that the hospitality organization benefits when all of its leaders, not just those with immediate responsibility for the function, recognize the importance of procurement and broaden their roles in attaining procurement goals. Another concept, benchmarking, is introduced to explain how the organization can determine "best practices" against which to compare and improve its own purchasing processes.

Finally, the purchasing evaluation task may identify changes necessary to allow personnel to move further along on their journey toward an optimal procurement function. What concerns become important as changes are planned and implemented? What challenges are likely, and how should purchasing managers address them? These questions are answered in the last section of this chapter.

■ ■ ■

Outline

EVALUATION AND EFFECTIVE PROCUREMENT

You've learned that a significant commitment of professional talent and creativity, time, financial resources, and dedication are required to effectively procure the numerous types of products, equipment, and services required by a hospitality organization. How well are procurement responsibilities being performed? How can purchase activities be improved to more fully meet the needs of the organization? These and related questions cannot be addressed until, first, they are posed and, second, unless they are objectively considered. Evaluation of procurement is, then, just as important for this as for any other major functions of the organization. Figure 23.1 (originally presented as Figure 1.4) reviews the entire procurement process and illustrates that evaluation might be considered the final sequential step in the process. However, the feedback that it provides has a follow-up (improvement) effect on both the steps related to basic process decisions (Steps 1–4) and to those related to recurring purchasing activities (Steps 5–10).

Evaluation is an important activity that is necessary in the management of any organization. Figure 23.2 provides an overview of basic management activities, and it is shown to identify where evaluation "fits in" to the basic management process.

First, notice that evaluation is the last step in the overall management process. The reason is that comprehensive evaluation addresses, in part, how well each of the other management functions has been performed.

Let's review Figure 23.2 in the context of procurement:

- *Planning.* This activity relates to defining goals, establishing strategies to achieve them, and designing ways to get work done. You'll recall that this book has stated the goals of purchasing very simply: "To purchase the right (quality) product from the right supplier at the right price, in the right quantity, and at the right time." Although these broad statements cannot be evaluated until they are stated much more specifically, they do establish the parameters within which the purchasing activity should be performed and evaluated.
- *Organizing.* This activity relates to developing and grouping work tasks. What are the responsibilities of user and purchasing department personnel in procurement functions? Once these are known, the process to evaluate the fulfillment of responsibilities can be put in place.
- *Coordinating.* This activity involves arranging group efforts in an orderly manner. It occurs as user department personnel and those with purchasing

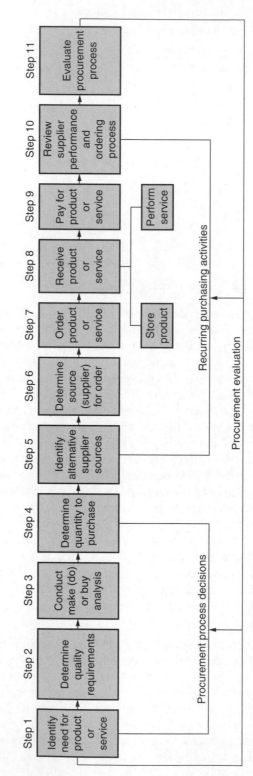

FIGURE 23.1 Steps in Procurement Process

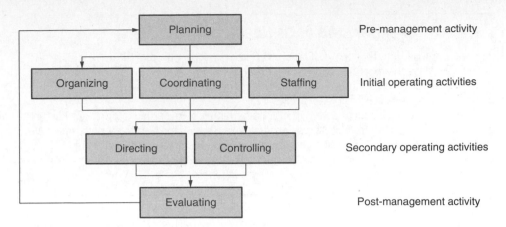

FIGURE 23.2 Overview of Basic Management Activities[1]

and accounting responsibilities work together to ensure that the operation consistently has the products and services required to serve its customers.

- *Staffing.* This activity relates to finding the right people for the job. You may recall the job description for a director of purchasing noted in Chapter 1. To be successful in this position, one must have a wide array of knowledge and skills and, as well, the attitude that purchasing can really "make a difference" in the success of the organization.

- *Directing.* This activity concerns the supervision of staff members in the purchasing department. A large purchasing department may employ several (or more) buyer specialists, and other staff members must also be needed for additional purchasing responsibilities. The extent to which purchasing managers facilitate the work of those employees has a direct effect upon their performance.

- *Controlling.* This activity helps to determine the extent to which the department "keeps on track" of achieving its goals. It relates to broad concerns such as the extent to which budget goals are attained, and to more specific concerns such as ensuring that items purchased are of agreed-upon quality and delivered to user personnel when needed.

- *Evaluating.* This activity, the subject of the chapter, involves assessing the extent to which plans are attained. Effective evaluation can identify issues (problems or challenges), which should be addressed by additional planning. Therefore, as shown in Figure 23.2, the management process is cyclical. Over time, evaluation will likely lead to other issues that should be addressed by additional planning efforts.

All hospitality managers, including those with purchasing responsibilities, are very busy. A significant amount of their time and attention must be devoted to day-to-day operating responsibilities. Do we have the employees we need? How

Purchasing staff must do everything "right" for these guests' visit to be as enjoyable as possible.
Courtesy Marriott International, Inc.

PURCHASING PROS NEED TO KNOW (23.1)

Purchasing pros know that the evaluation of purchasing is important. They recognize the need to evaluate the extent to which purchasing goals are attained. They also understand the importance of assessing how purchasing activities can be improved to enable future goals to be attained even more effectively.

Purchasing pros are also aware that evaluation may be overlooked, done quickly ("to get it over with"), and/or undertaken incorrectly (e.g., by simply rationalizing that "We can't do it any better"). They also recognize that procurement cannot evolve from "buying things" to becoming an integral part of the organization's strategic process unless an ongoing method of improving procurement activities is in place.

---

many customers will be staying (in the hotel) or served (in the restaurant)? What special events are occurring? How are we doing financially? These concerns are understandable and help to explain why the first and last management activities identified in Figure 23.2 (planning and evaluating) may not receive a priority. It is difficult to plan for tomorrow and to evaluate past performance when the many pressures of today demand immediate attention. However, experienced managers recognize the importance of these steps, know how they are interrelated, and develop and undertake an ongoing procurement evaluation activity.

As you've learned, buyers cannot evaluate purchasing without considering their purchasing goals. In effect, then, this is a never-ending process. Figure 23.3 reviews how goal setting and evaluation lead to improvements in the procurement process.

As you review Figure 23.3, you'll note that the development of purchasing goals (Step 1) leads to the development of procedures to attain them (Step 2). Once developed, these procedures must be implemented (Step 3) and, finally, the entire purchasing process can be evaluated (Step 4). The results of evaluation may lead to additional purchasing goals, or to revisions in purchasing procedures or implementation tactics. This figure illustrates that purchasing really begins with planning and ends (or, really, begins again!) with evaluating. Therefore, planning and evaluating processes are ongoing and cyclical.

REASONS TO EVALUATE PROCUREMENT

There are many reasons why it is important to evaluate procurement:

- *To recognize the function.* Busy managers are concerned about those things most important to them. They know, for example, how customers perceive the operation because they analyze revenue and customer feedback data. They know about the current financial condition of the organization from the study of income statement and balance sheet "numbers." If managers cannot or do not measure the overall performance of a function such as purchasing, their actions suggest that it is unimportant relative to other activities that are evaluated.

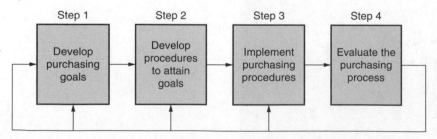

FIGURE 23.3 Planning and Evaluating Yields Purchasing Improvements

- *To measure goal attainment.* Figures 23.2 and 23.3 reviewed the relationship between procurement planning and evaluation. How, if at all, can the process be improved? Evaluation allows hospitality purchasers and managers to consider how tasks can be undertaken more effectively.
- *Improvement benchmarks can be determined.* If objective (measurable) factors are used to evaluate purchasing, they provide standards against which to assess improvement during subsequent evaluation periods. For example, if the number of stockouts is known for a previous period, a goal to reduce the number of stockouts for a subsequent time period can be established. Then the results of process improvement activities can subsequently be measured to assess the extent of stockout reduction.
- *To manage costs.* Money saved through effective purchasing reduces costs and increases profitability. Purchasing dollars must be wisely spent, and purchasers can be challenged to work with user department personnel to determine the best ways to reduce costs without sacrificing quality concerns.
- *Purchasing evaluation helps to establish procedures for measuring and rewarding the performance of purchasing personnel.* Performance appraisal for these staff members should be undertaken in the same manner as that used for their peers in the other departments. The extent to which their work outputs meet expectations should be an integral aspect of the performance evaluation process.
- *Purchasing evaluation can yield insights for improvement.* Purchasing evaluation can help purchasers and managers to learn how the functions, duties, and responsibilities of the department and its personnel should be reorganized and/or reassigned. These are important concerns as purchasers and managers attempt to more fully integrate the purchasing function with the organization's strategic direction.

PURCHASING PROS NEED TO KNOW (23.2)

Purchasing pros know that cost reduction affects the "bottom line" more than a similar volume of revenue increases. Which would you prefer, $10,000 of decreased costs or $10,000 of increased revenues? Let's consider two private clubs:

Private Club A ($10,000 Decreased Costs)		Private Club B ($10,000 Increased Revenues)	
Food revenue	$250,000	Food revenue	$260,000
Food costs (42%)	$105,000	Food costs (42%)	109,200
Less savings	($10,000)	Less savings	(0)
Net food costs	($95,000)	Net food costs	($109,200)
Contribution margin	$155,000	Contribution margin	$150,800

Private Club A reduced its food costs by $10,000 with use of more effective purchasing tactics, and it generated a contribution margin of $155,000.

Private Club B increased its food revenue by $10,000 by use of creative marketing tactics. However, it still incurred a food cost of 42 percent of revenues. Therefore, its contribution margin was $4,200 less than Private Club A ($155,000 − $150,800 = $4,200.)

Key Term

Contribution margin Food (or beverage) revenue remaining after subtracting food (or beverage) product costs.

Many complaints that these customers might have can be caused by problems stemming from improper purchasing.

Photodisc/Getty Images

OVERVIEW OF EVALUATION AND IMPROVEMENT PROCESS

Figure 23.4 illustrates a simple process that can be used to evaluate a hospitality organization's procurement process.

Figure 23.4 provides an overview of how procurement evaluation can be undertaken and, as importantly, how it can be used to yield improvements in the overall purchasing system. Hospitality organizations can have numerous purchasing goals, and many are described in the next section. However, let's use product costs to illustrate how the evaluation process noted in the figure can be implemented.

- *Step 1: Develop purchasing goals.* Efforts to reduce product costs without sacrificing quality should be a primary concern of all purchasing personnel. However, it is often difficult to determine the causes of higher-than-desired costs. For example, if product cost evaluations are based on total dollar purchases, high costs could be due to ineffective purchasing and/or ineffective handling and control procedures after products are received (and no longer within the control of purchasing staff). Also, increased total purchases may be due simply to increased product sales. If, instead, product costs are based upon purchase unit cost (the cost for a specified unit such as pound, gallon, case of specified size, or other container), the costs can be better associated with purchasing personnel; however, they still have no control over the marketplace, which significantly influences purchase unit costs. One possible "compromise": assume that the following purchasing goal is established: "Purchasing personnel shall maintain per unit purchase costs for "A" products to no more than 2 percent above the adjusted market costs for the time period covered by the evaluation. Recall that "A" items are those relatively few, most expensive products purchased by the organization. Market prices for these products are publicly available, and they can be used as a benchmark against which to compare purchase prices.

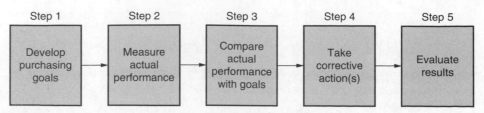

FIGURE 23.4 Overview of Procurement Evaluation Process

Internet Purchasing Assistant (23.1)

The Internet offers numerous sources of information about the current market price of many different commodities. For example, the U.S. Department of Agriculture's (USDA) Agriculture Marketing Source provides information for growers, shippers, wholesalers, and others about current demand, supplies, and prices of more than 400 fresh fruits and vegetables, and other crops. Wholesale market reports on fruits and vegetables are issued daily for fifteen major U.S. cities. To review this data, go to: http://marketnews.usda.gov/portal/fv

Wholesale beef price information is available from sources such as www.beefretail. org, which reports prices on beef subprimal cuts from the previous week. Another resource, USDA's Livestock and Seed Program (www.marketnews.usda.gov/portal/lg) provides updated statistics for cattle, meat, swine, and other products. Also, purchasers can ask their suppliers to suggest the most appropriate sources for wholesale market prices of the products they provide.

- *Step 2: Measure actual performance.* Delivery invoices adjusted as necessary for credit memos will be available for the "A" items addressed in the goal statement. These invoices can be summed for the period addressed by evaluation to yield actual per unit costs. Perhaps, for example, the average purchase unit cost can be calculated for the period (beginning purchase unit cost + ending purchase unit cost ÷ 2). This calculation will yield the average purchase unit cost for the "A" products.
- *Step 3: Compare actual performance with goals.* This actual purchase unit cost for the "A" products is known (from Step 2), and it can be compared with the benchmark average purchase unit cost available from market sources. If the actual purchase unit cost is not above the planned purchase unit cost, the purchasing staff was successful, and the stated goal was attained. By contrast, if the actual purchase unit cost was greater than the expected (planned) cost, investigation may be needed. What are the reasons for

---

PURCHASING PROS NEED TO KNOW (23.3)

Purchasing pros know that purchasing goals must be objective (measurable) to permit evaluation. Consider, for example, the following goal: "Purchasers will minimize product purchase costs during the next six months." This objective is not measurable because, even though we all know that "minimize" means to "keep as low as possible," there is no way to ensure that products were purchased at the minimal (lowest possible) cost.

A better-stated goal might, for example, assign purchasers the responsibility to "maintain product purchase costs at a level of no more than 103 percent of product costs for the previous period." This goal is measurable. For example, if product purchases were $100,000 for the previous six months, they can be no more than $103,000 for the period of evaluation given the same production or occupancy volumes. As you've learned, however, purchasers have little/no control over product usage rates after they reach the property, and it is also necessary to assume that $100,000 was a reasonable purchase cost during the previous period. In fact, if this cost were excessive, the revised purchasing goal "approves" and extends this excessive cost.

A better approach is to use a goal such as that stated earlier in the chapter ("per unit purchase costs for 'A' products should be no more than 2 percent above the adjusted market cost for the time period. . . ."). This goal can be measured, attempts to isolate the role of purchasing staff in the expenditure, and allows for cost changes that are beyond the purchaser's control.

the **variance?** Are they understandable and defensible? The answers to these and related questions are best understood in the context of whether the goal was attained in previous periods. If costs per purchase unit goals were consistently met in the past, there may be some special circumstance that should be investigated. By contrast, if the purchase unit goal has been unmet in the past, it is important to reassess whether the goal is reasonable and, if it is, to require more concerted corrective actions to move toward it.

When comparisons are undertaken, it is important to ensure that all information describing performance is arithmetically and factually accurate. Also, the activities being evaluated should be within control of purchasing personnel, and they, along with top-level managers, should be involved in the comparison process. Finally, because comparisons are being made between different time periods, it is important to ensure that the information is collected in the same way, and that it has the same meaning.

- *Step 4: Take corrective action.* When the comparison between expected and actual performance (Step 3) suggests an unacceptable variance, corrective action is required. If multiple problems are observed, it is typically best to, first, address those that are most significant unless "quick and easy" sources of minor problems can be resolved. Details about problem solving for procurement improvement will be discussed in the next section.
- *Step 5: Evaluate results.* One must determine the extent to which corrective action (Step 4) adequately addresses problems discovered during the evaluation process. In addition to ensuring that the problems are resolved, one should also confirm that "spin-off" problems were not created. For example, purchasers may determine that higher-than-necessary costs can be reduced by the use of different suppliers. Although costs might, in fact, then decrease, other problems such as untimely (late) deliveries may occur. If, by contrast, purchasers determine that corrective actions have been successful, the evaluation process was effective: Problems were identified and then corrected as a result of the evaluation. However, if a problem is not satisfactorily addressed or if additional problems now occur, it is necessary to reconsider and plan additional corrective actions (Step 4) in an ongoing effort to further improve the purchasing process.

MORE ABOUT PROCUREMENT PROBLEM SOLVING

The previous section noted that corrective actions might be necessary to improve the purchasing process when actual performance does not meet standards expressed in measurable goals. Basic problem-solving procedures can be helpful for this activity.

Figure 23.5 shows steps in the basic problem-solving process that managers can use to reduce problems identified during procurement evaluation.[1]

Let's review the process described in Figure 23.5.

- *Step 1: Define the problem.* The definition of the property's quality requirements for this product is defined in its purchase specification. Unless the same knowledgeable food production employee always prepares this product, it is possible that concerns about inferior quality may be more significant than easily noticed because other staff members may be unable or unwilling to recognize proper quality. Although a problem cannot be resolved until it is first identified, the hospitality operation is fortunate to have one or more staff members who are concerned about and who report the poultry quality problem.

Key Term

Variance The difference between a planned and actual amount of revenue or expense.

Steps	Example
Step 1: Define the problem.	• There is an increasing problem with the quality of fresh poultry products when they are issued from the storeroom.
Step 2: Generate solution alternatives.	• Poultry products are not being properly checked for quality at time of receiving, and lower-than-desired products are accepted. • The poultry supplier is substituting lower-quality poultry products at the bottom of shipping cases. (This is, in part, a function of the previous alternative.) • Poultry products are not being properly rotated to minimize storage time. • Excessive product is being purchased, resulting in excessive quantities in storage. • Products are not being stored at the proper temperature, or the property's issuing procedures may not be used.
Step 3: Evaluate solution alternatives.	• The long-term receiving and storeroom clerk has just retired; his duties are being assumed by several kitchen staff while a replacement is being recruited. • Managers have confirmed that poultry products (and all other stock) are being rotated under a "first in, first out" system. • Purchase quantities are in line with usage rates. • The chef has confirmed that poultry products are kept under ice during the relatively short time that they are in storage.
Step 4: Select the "best" solution alternative.	• Designate one production employee to be the "designated receiver" until a permanent replacement is hired. Review the training program to ensure that it addresses the recognition of quality requirements for all products (including poultry); make sure that the "designated receiver" is properly trained to perform these responsibilities.
Step 5: Implement the solution alternative.	• Train the existing staff members; request that the chef, purchaser, and kitchen manager be present on a routine but random basis during times when products are received to ensure that all receiving tasks, including those relating to quality, are implemented.
Step 6: Evaluate the effectiveness of the solution.	• Determine the extent to which problems with the inferior quality of fresh poultry products issued to the kitchen continues. This is relatively easy to do because of the restaurant's policy that no food can be discarded without approval of the chef (who maintains a record of the quantity of products that must be discarded).

FIGURE 23.5 Basics of the Procurement Problem-Solving Process

• *Step 2: Generate solution alternatives.* What can be done to address the problem? It may be caused by the purchaser (who may not have effectively communicated the specification or who has not consistently mandated that specification standards be addressed), or by staff members who perform product receiving and storing activities. An ad hoc team comprised of the purchaser, chef, and, perhaps, another kitchen employee may be able to quickly generate alternatives to resolve the problem and to evaluate which are best.

Internet Purchasing Assistant (23.2)

Hospitality purchasers must make decisions about numerous concerns throughout the procurement process in addition to occasions when evaluation occurs. To gain access to an online library of great information about decision making, go to: www.bettermanagement.com

At the home page, type "decision-making" into the search box. The basic principles of decision making discussed in many of the articles listed are applicable to hospitality purchasers, managers, and, as well, leaders in other businesses.

- *Step 3: Evaluate solution alternatives.* In this example, confirmation that effective storage practices are in use makes it possible to eliminate all alternatives except those related to improper receiving. In other situations, concerns about cost, ease of implementation, and effect upon other work processes are among those factors that can be used to evaluate and select solution alternatives.
- *Step 4: Select the "best" solution alternative.* Often, the "best" solution involves using aspects of several possible alternatives generated in Step 2. In this example, quality standards are appropriate, and the need to train existing and future receiving personnel about these standards is a "must."

On-the-Job Challenges in Purchasing (23.1)

"We've done very well for so many years, and I don't see the need for change now," said Quincy as he spoke to Aria, the general manager of the White Fence Hotel.

"Quincy, you are a great purchasing manager, and I'm not complaining at all about your performance. In fact, I think it has been exceptional. Our company's interest in initiating a formalized evaluation process for every department, including purchasing, has nothing to do with you or any other department head. Instead, we want to ensure that we are using our resources as wisely as possible to forestall inevitable price increases for our customers," said Aria.

"Aria," replied Quincy, "I understand the concept of evaluation; I think it's important for departments that generate revenues. However, a support department such as purchasing has a very tough time coming up with measurable indicators of performance. You can't go by cost, for example, because we in purchasing have no control over the products once they enter the storage areas. About all I do is select suppliers and order products. Fortunately, in our town, suppliers are very competitive, and they want to keep our business. Things like untimely deliveries, quality problems, and stockouts just don't occur. I don't understand, therefore, how you propose to evaluate my department or me. We're doing the best job that we can, and I wish you would just take my word for that. Every second I'm on the job, I'm trying to reduce costs while still recognizing the quality concerns so we can provide the best products and services for our customers."

Case Study Questions

Assume that you are Aria, the general manager:

1. How would you respond to Quincy about his concern that revenue-producing, but not support, departments should be evaluated?
2. What types of evaluation factors can you suggest that would be applicable to, and within the control of, Quincy and his purchasing department?
3. Quincy has noted that his primary job is to select suppliers and order products. What else can he and his department do to help the White Fence Hotel with its longer-term and strategic concerns?

- *Step 5: Implement the solution alternative.* Employee training and close after-training supervision, including coaching, if necessary, can ensure that proper receiving practices, including those relating to quality assurance, are consistently used to address the problem.
- *Step 6: Evaluate the effectiveness of the solution.* In this example, evaluation is relatively easy; after the alternative is implemented, there should be no further problem with the inferior quality of fresh poultry products issued to the kitchen. If, however, the problem does continue, even if on a lessened scale, further problem-solving and decision-making procedures are necessary. For example, there may be periodic malfunctioning of cooling equipment in the refrigerated storage area (are there quality-related problems with other products?). Also, perhaps some, but insufficient, quantities of ice are being placed on the poultry products during storage because ice must be "shared" since the property's ice machine cannot produce at the capacity required for the operation.

PURCHASING GOALS AFFECT PURCHASING EVALUATION

Purchasing should be evaluated to assess the extent to which the goals established for the process have been attained. The goals developed for purchasing relate to its purpose within the hospitality organization. A review of Figure 23.6 (originally shown as Figure 1.9) provides a useful foundation for this discussion.

A review of Figure 23.6 suggests the goals of, and how, the purchasing function might be evaluated in organizations with differing philosophies about its role. Evaluation concerns will differ significantly depending upon the function of purchasing within the organization as it evolves from Phase 1 to Phase 4.

As you review Figure 23.6, recall the emphasis of each phase in procurement evolution:

- *Phase 1: Price-conscious purchasing.* The emphasis is on purchasing products at the lowest possible price.
- *Phase 2: Price and quality purchasing.* Prices are of concern but the quality of purchases is also important, so there is an increasing emphasis on value (the relationship between price and quality).
- *Phase 3: Purchaser–supplier "partnerships."* Suppliers are considered a valuable resource whose expertise is an important consideration as supplier decisions are made.
- *Phase 4: Integrative procurement.* Purchasing is an integral part of the organization's competitive strategy, and value addition rather than cost reduction is viewed as the primary role of purchasing.

Now that we've reviewed the four phases of procurement evolution, let's consider how the focus of evaluation changes as the purchasing function is seen to be more important to the organization. Figure 23.7 reviews these differences.

Figure 23.7 suggests that the process of evaluating the procurement function becomes increasingly more important (because more is expected of it) as its function within the hospitality organization takes on greater importance. The evaluation

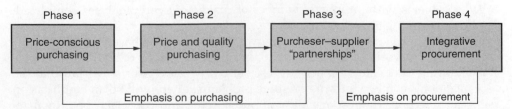

FIGURE 23.6 Evolution of Procurement within a Hospitality Organization

Phase	Function of Purchasing	Importance to Organization	Focus of Evaluation
1.	Price-Conscious Purchasing	Low	• Cost per purchase unit. • Total purchase costs. • Maintain budget.
2.	Price and Quality Purchasing	Improving	• Development of specifications. • Supplier performance (selection). • Make (do)–buy analyses. • Extent of suppliers' assistance.
3.	Purchaser–Supplier "Partnerships"	High	• Methods by which suppliers provide value. • Assistance in resolving organizational problems. • Purchaser's performance as member of top-level management team.
4.	Integrative Procurement	Exemplary	• Cross-functional training. • Emphasis on value addition (not cost reduction). • Method(s) by which the purchasing function assists customers. • Use of leading-edge concepts in supply chain management. • Contributions to strategy development.

task also becomes more challenging because of the increased difficulty of quantifying purchasing goals.

At the first phase of procurement evolution (price-conscious purchasing), purchasing is essentially reactive, and the tasks are mostly clerical: "Get products into the organization when they are needed, and do so at a low cost." Although it is always important to minimize costs, this must be done without comprising quality requirements. Unfortunately, this is frequently of lessened concern when the emphasis is only on price. It is, however, relatively easy to evaluate the attainment of this less-than-ambitious price goal. The extent to which purchasing staff keep within their budget, the assessment of costs per purchase unit, and total purchase cost statistics can be easily calculated with information that should be readily available in most hospitality operations.

The importance of the purchasing function increases with Phase 2 (price and quality) purchasing concerns. Figure 23.7 indicates that the development of specifications, selection of the "best" suppliers, conduct of make–buy analyses, and the extent to which suppliers provide value-added assistance become important. Price will still be important, but it will be evaluated in the context of these other factors. Evaluation can address, respectively, the number of specifications developed, problems with suppliers, number of make (do)–buy analyses completed, and instances of value-added assistance.

As the hospitality organization moves to Phase 3 (purchaser–supplier "partnerships"), the worth of the supplier's contributions will be of significant importance during the evaluation activity, as will be the purchaser's assistance to the organization's managers as they resolve problems. There will be an emphasis on supplier selection (the responsibility of purchasers), and concerns about total acquisition costs rather than lowest price will become more important.

THE SUPPLIER'S SIDE (23.1)

The concept of "partnership" between the purchaser and supplier suggests that both entities assist each other in mutually beneficial ways. As part of the procurement evaluation process, purchasers routinely assess the performance of their suppliers, hopefully in the context of preestablished, previously disseminated, and agreed-upon goals. Then, if the evaluation suggests discrepancies in the ideal relationship, they can be corrected.

Suppliers are also interested in ongoing improvement, and if effectively managed, they will be equally concerned about planning and evaluation efforts leading to improved performance. Their assessments will, in part, focus on relationships with their buyers ("What can we do to better serve them?"). Suppliers, then, should be just as proactive in identifying and addressing obstacles to an ideal relationship as their purchasing partners.

Moreover, purchasers can ask their suppliers about ways that they (the purchasers) can make it easier for the supplier to help them. Responses to questions such as "What can we do to make it easier for you to sell to us?" and "What requirements do we impose that hinder your ability to sell to us?" may suggest procedural changes that can make the partnership even more mutually beneficial.

At the highest level of purchasing contribution (Phase 4: integrative procurement), the success of cross-functional training that moves top-level managers into and out of procurement functions becomes important as does the evaluation of leading-edge supply chain management concepts (e.g., contemporary distribution systems such as just-in-time purchasing). Contributions made by purchasing staff to the development of the organization's strategies will also be of concern. At this level, evaluation could also emphasize:

- Commitment for strategic supplier alliances.
- Education of the supplier base.
- Improvements in the supply chain, including interaction with suppliers to assist in this effort.
- Interactions with suppliers to assist in the adoption of total quality management and zero defects efforts.

Professional purchasers know that some goals, although difficult to state in quantifiable terms, must still be considered when the activities of purchasing staff are planned and evaluated. How does one measure the contributions made by other members of the organization's team of top-level managers? Perhaps these same factors apply to the director of purchasing. Evaluation must also focus on financial measurements because these are, indeed, useful (critical), and they should be assessed. However, nonfinancial concerns will also be important evaluation factors as the role of the procurement function expands.

PROCUREMENT EVALUATION FACTORS

Numerous goals to drive procurement planning and evaluation can be developed by top-level purchasers and managers. Some, including the selection and use of the most appropriate suppliers, and the extent to which the procurement function contributes to the organization's financial success (when these can be measured), will likely be of ongoing importance. Others, such as the development of purchase specifications for new products, and the selection of service providers for one-time use, may not be important after the specific assignments are completed. These, then, are likely to be replaced with other concerns that yield evaluation factors for subsequent analysis periods.

One way to categorize purchasing evaluation factors is to consider those that relate to basic operational concerns, and those relating to other important factors.

Many aspects of procurement evaluation can occur informally when a manager talks to production personnel.

Bruce Ayres/Getty Images Inc.-Stone Allstock

Basic Operational Concerns

Basic operational concerns relate to product or service quality, quantity, timing, and price. How might the effectiveness of procurement relate to these concerns? Examples of some measures of these factors are listed in Figure 23.8.

When reviewing Figure 23.8, note that most of these evaluation factors are relatively easy to measure because, in many operations, the applicable data is already collected and used for other purposes. For example, buyers may track the number of reject shipments (quality) as part of supplier performance rating systems, and inventory turnover rates may be assessed for accounting purposes. Timing factors are also integral to supplier performance evaluation, and prices paid for products relative to market indexes are also commonly tracked by some, especially large, hospitality organizations.

Numerous other potential purchasing evaluation factors also address financial concerns. These include

- Purchase as percent of revenue: $\dfrac{\text{Total purchases (\$)}}{\text{Total revenues (\$)}}$

- Purchasing department operating expenses as percent of revenue:
$$\frac{\text{Purchasing department operating expenses (\$)}}{\text{Total revenues (\$)}}$$

- Purchasing department operating expenses as percent of total purchases:
$$\frac{\text{Purchasing department operating expenses (\$)}}{\text{Total purchases (\$)}}$$

FIGURE 23.8 Possible Operational Concerns and Evaluation Factors

Operational Concern	Evaluation Factors
Quality	Percentage of shipment rejects. Number of production problems related to product quality.
Quantity	Number of stockouts. Inventory turnover rates compared to goals. Number of expedited orders.
Timing	Suppliers' delivery performance. Time for requisition processing. Time required for remedial action.
Price	Prices paid against expected prices. Prices paid for key items compared with market indexes. Prices paid against budget.

- Revenue per purchasing employee: $\dfrac{\text{Total revenue (\$)}}{\text{Total purchasing employees}}$

(full-time equivalents)

- Purchase per total purchasing employee:

$$\frac{\text{Total purchases (\$)}}{\text{Total purchasing employees (FTE)}}$$

- Purchase per professional purchasing employee: $\dfrac{\text{Total purchases (\$)}}{\text{Total professional staff}^*}$

- Purchases per supplier: $\dfrac{\text{Total purchases (\$)}}{\text{Total number of suppliers}}$

- Percent of food, beverages, and related products as percent of

total purchases: $\dfrac{\text{Total food, beverages, and related purchases (\$)}}{\text{Total purchases (\$)}}$

- Percent of capital equipment purchases as percent of total purchases:

$$\frac{\text{Total capital equipment purchases (\$)}}{\text{Total purchases (\$)}}$$

- Percent of services purchased as a percent of total purchases dollars:

$$\frac{\text{Service purchases (\$)}}{\text{Total purchases (\$)}}$$

Note: Purchasing ratios suggested by the Center for Advanced Purchasing Studies. Purchasing Performance Benchmarking for the U.S. Foodservice Industry, Tempe, AZ.

Internet Purchasing Assistant (23.3)

The Center for Advanced Purchasing Studies (CAPS) at Arizona State University is a nonprofit research organization dedicated to supply and supply chain issues. It conducts a wide range of research and benchmarking studies that provide information useful to develop purchasing evaluation programs and, when applicable, to compare one organization's purchasing data with other comparable organizations.

To access this site, go to:www.capsresearch.org

At the home page, you can review a wide range of information applicable to research, benchmarking, and other topics. You may have to create a new user account (complementary) to view some data.

---

*Exclude clerical and other support employees in the purchasing department.

Key Term

Full-time equivalent   The number of full-time employees that would have been employed if the number of hours worked by part-time employees was worked by full-time employers. For example, 4 employees each working 20 hours weekly are the equivalent of 2 full-time (40-hour) employees (4 employees × 20 hours ÷ 40 hours); commonly abbreviated "FTE."

Purchasing managers, like their counterparts in all other departments of a hospitality organization, must help to develop and then operate within an approved departmental budget. The extent to which all expenses **allocated** to the department are within budget restraints will be an important concern as the procurement function is evaluated.

Other Evaluation Factors

In addition to basic operational and financial factors, purchasing activities can be evaluated relative to other concerns. Some examples include

- *Relationships with other departments.* This factor might be assessed by considering the number of procurement-related complaints lodged by personnel in other departments. In addition, the number of complaints made by purchasing staff regarding other department personnel can also be considered, as can the number of purchases that must be expedited. Stockouts requiring immediate replenishment typically cause stress and anxiety that can affect the relationship between purchasing and other departments. Periodic (and anonymous, if applicable) surveys may be used to generate this type of information. These surveys may also yield information about the "friendliness" of purchasing procedures, and perceived obstacles that affect purchasing from the perspectives of user department personnel.

- *Creative assistance.* These factors are typically difficult, but important, to evaluate. Have value analyses been effective? Is it possible to quantify the results of supplier price and cost analyses? Have purchasing personnel located more than one useful supplier for difficult-to-locate products? Has the department helped to improve the productivity of user department personnel? These and related questions address concerns of many user department employees and reflect services that might be provided by purchasing staff.

- *Development of effective purchasing policies.* Purchasing personnel will be asked to advise about policies relating to specification development, make (do) or buy analysis, supplier and organization reciprocity, single or multiple supply sources, and the utility of moving toward nontraditional purchasing arrangements with suppliers. What policies are needed? Are existing policies clearly stated? Are they understood and applied equitably by applicable personnel? Are policies updated as conditions warrant? These types of questions point to areas that might be addressed by planning and evaluation tactics.

- *Supplier performance.* Many problems (challenges) within the purchasing function concern the failure of suppliers to meet purchasers' expectations. Are expectations reasonable? Why, if at all, do purchasers continue to interact with "problem" suppliers? You learned in Chapter 8 that purchasers should develop and routinely use a supplier performance rating system to evaluate existing supply sources. Only suppliers that are "acceptable" should be used, and those who do not meet the purchasers' expectations should not be considered eligible for the organization's business. Therefore, it seems reasonable to evaluate purchasers about supplier performance because they (the purchasers) are typically responsible for supplier selection decisions.

Key Term

Allocation The process of distributing expenses incurred between departments on a basis that approximates each department's share of the total expenses.

PURCHASING PROS NEED TO KNOW (23.4)

There's an old saying in the hospitality industry that, "The vast majority of operating problems in a hotel or restaurant are caused by the managers." This statement is at odds with the perception of many persons who believe that employees cause most problems because they do not "do what they are supposed to do." In fact, managers are responsible for selecting, training, and supervising staff members to help ensure that performance standards are attained.

   This same reasoning applies to supplier-related problems incurred by the hospitality organization. If product or service quality is unacceptable, invoices are incorrect, deliveries are late, and delivery personnel or distributor sales representatives are disruptive, why does the organization continue to use the supplier? Perhaps, then, the statement noted above can be paraphrased: "The vast majority of supplier-related problems are caused by purchasing personnel." Hospitality organizations depend on their suppliers for an ever-increasing number of basic and value-added services in addition to the products and services that are purchased. There are few, if any, more important purchasing responsibilities than to ensure that the "best" suppliers are used. The extent to which they are successful can be an integral part of the purchasing evaluation process.

On-the-Job Purchasing Challenges (23.2)

"Well, it just happened again. I don't believe it, and this is just not a good way to manage," said Robert as he slammed the door behind him after entering the purchasing department's small office.

   "Robert, you're really fired-up, aren't you?" said Aileen, the food and beverage buyer for the organization, and the only purchasing employee present.

   "Yes, I am really upset, Aileen," replied Robert. "I'm the director of purchasing for this property, and I should know what our general manager expects of us. However, I really don't, and I think his expectations depend upon what day of the week he is talking to me. We need some consistent direction, and we're not getting it. I just don't know what to do."

   "What happened this time, Robert, if you don't mind that I ask?" questioned Aileen.

   "I don't know where to start," said Robert. "I clearly understand that it is my responsibility to select suppliers given input from the user department personnel we buy for. I would like to use the 'best' suppliers to meet their needs, but I just don't know what 'best' means."

   "About three weeks ago, the general manager was very upset about our property's budget performance. He spent more than an hour talking to all of us department heads about the need to cut costs. I remember him looking at some of our invoices, and indicating that the purchase unit costs of some products were more than what he was paying at a local grocery store for, he alleged, the same products. He questioned why our prices weren't much lower because of the greater quantity of purchases that we make. I tried to talk with him about quality, service, and other factors that are part of the purchase price. However, he just wouldn't listen to me. I went away from that meeting with the clear knowledge that he wanted me to buy cheap."

   "Now, three weeks later, the general manager is getting complaints about quality. He told me that the recent deliveries of some products didn't meet our standards, and it was my fault! When I reminded him about his cost concerns, he basically said that we did have to cut costs, but I couldn't reduce quality when I did so. This is very frustrating; I don't know what to do, and I certainly don't know where to start."

   "Well," replied Aileen, "I've heard the old phrase about buying for value, not for quality or price. I guess this is what the general manager wants, although he sure doesn't do a good job of expressing himself."

Case Study Questions

Assume that you are Robert:

1. What do you think is the real problem here?
2. What would you do if you were Robert in efforts to improve your relationship with the general manager, and to purchase products that are acceptable to user personnel and the general manager?
3. How, if at all, might existing suppliers help Robert to resolve his problem? Suppliers who are not being used?

In addition to the evaluation factors noted above, hospitality organizations can consider other categories of concerns that can be incorporated into purchasing goals. Examples of concerns that can be evaluated for successful attainment include

- Specific procedures used to address purchasing concerns. For example, identifying suppliers for difficult-to-buy products, researching all alternatives for equipment needs, and implementing procedures as electronic purchasing processes are implemented.
- Organization of the purchasing department itself. Are all positions cost-justified? Are communication and coordination channels connecting purchasing personnel to internal departments and external suppliers as helpful and error-free as they can be?
- Are purchasing policies reasonable? Do some policies need modification or elimination? Are other policies necessary? Are purchasing policies written, and are they consistently followed? If not, what, if anything, should purchasing personnel do to make them more understandable and useful?
- Are purchasing reports and records adequate for user and accounting department personnel and for top-level managers as they make decisions based upon "the numbers"?
- Are purchasing activities centralized to the extent they should be? Are there clear guidelines about what, if any, purchasing commitments can be made by nonpurchasing personnel?

Evaluation of the purchasing department should also address the personnel who work within it. Are they qualified for, and consistently able to perform effectively

---

PURCHASING PROS NEED TO KNOW (23.5)

Purchasing pros know that hospitality organizations may address their concerns for broad societal issues as the procurement function is evaluated. Companies may, for example, be actively engaged in efforts to increase business relationships with the minority- and women-owned suppliers, and simple calculations can be used for this purpose:

- Percent of purchases from minority-owner suppliers:

$$\frac{\text{Total purchases : Minority-owned suppliers (\$)}}{\text{Total purchases : All suppliers (\$)}}$$

- Percent of **supplier base** (minority-owned):

$$\frac{\text{Total number of minority-owned suppliers}}{\text{Total number of suppliers}}$$

- Percent of purchases from women-owned suppliers:

$$\frac{\text{Total purchases : Women-owned suppliers (\$)}}{\text{Total purchases : All suppliers (\$)}}$$

- Percent of supplier base (women-owned):

$$\frac{\text{Total number of women-owned suppliers}}{\text{Total number of suppliers}}$$

Hospitality organizations that establish goals such as the above should evaluate the extent to which they have been attained. If systems are in place to collect and categorize information needed for these calculations, objective assessments become possible.

Key Term

Supplier base The total number of suppliers used by a hospitality organization to purchase all products and services during a specific time period.

in, their positions? Do purchasing staff participate in organizational activities? The need for purchasing managers to be active participants in the property's organizational-wide decision-making process has been emphasized throughout the book. The basic procedures used to evaluate professional and other staff members in other departments throughout the organization should be used to assess the performance of purchasing personnel.

"INTELLIGENT CUSTOMER" EVALUATION

The concept of **"intelligent customer"** recognizes that procurement competencies should be shared throughout the organization. As this occurs, managers in other departments have a greater understanding of procurement principles, and they then address purchasing-related responsibilities more efficiently. In effect, then, the hospitality organization becomes an "intelligent customer" as it interacts with its suppliers.

As the organization's managers expand their purchasing knowledge and gain greater skills, they will better understand basic purchasing concerns and work with purchasing staff to address them. In some ways, an intelligent customer model is similar to cross-functional team processes. Needs and requirements of each department are better understood throughout the organization, and there is lessened concern that procurement needs are merely transferred from a user department to the purchasing department. The concept also enables user department personnel to have a greater role in procuring the products and services required to satisfy their customers.

The cross-functional team similarities continue as business processes are coordinated, information is shared (technology can help!), and policy and procedural changes are made after considering the effect on all departments.

Several tactics can be used to evaluate the extent to which within-organization relationships improve and move toward a more cooperative procurement process.

The director of purchasing should be a member of a hotel's top-management team and should receive feedback from all department heads about departmental performance.

Craig Lovell/Stock Connection

Key Term

Intelligent customer   The concept that managers throughout an organization should become knowledgeable about basic procurement principles and processes to enable them to assist purchasing personnel in making wise decisions.

Questions that can be posed and answered as internal relationships are evaluated include

- What is the primary objective of increased between-department cooperation?
- What is the ideal outcome of the relationship improvement effort?
- What will happen if nothing is changed?
- What tactics can be used to encourage participation in an intelligent customer model and to transfer applicable purchasing knowledge and skills to managers participating in the effort?

As the hospitality organization becomes a more intelligent customer, it realizes numerous benefits related to:

- *Products and services.*   Managers know about the wide range of alternative products and services available in the marketplace. They also learn the relative advantages and disadvantages of each, and they quickly become aware of new products, services, and likely trends.
- *Suppliers.*   Managers are aware of the range of supply sources, the reputation of each, and those who will likely be "best" for their organization.
- *Procurement requirements.*   Managers can correctly identify what the organization's customers want and need. They are then able to translate this knowledge into purchasing requirements that can be identified with purchase specifications.
- *Overall purchasing process.*   Managers work together to identify the products that are needed and to use the most efficient processes to purchase them.

The intelligent customer model provides an entirely new dimension of procurement responsibilities and the subsequent need to evaluate the extent to which they are attained. This book has emphasized the need for purchaser–supplier "partnerships" to best ensure long-term relationships and value-added assistance from preferred suppliers, and procedures to evaluate supplier performance have also been noted. At the same time, purchasers must establish more extensive relationships with their internal customers (those in user departments). The partnerships that arise will better ensure that an organized and cooperative approach to procurement is used to best obtain the products and services required to benefit customers.

BENCHMARKING PROCUREMENT PRACTICES

Hospitality organizations and the purchasing departments within them do not "stand still." They either get better (improve), or they get worse (increasingly fail to meet goals). Because the hospitality industry is highly competitive, this observation is likely to become even more correct in the future. Benchmarking involves searching for **best practices,** understanding how they are achieved, and considering how process components can be incorporated into "the way things are done" by an organization. It involves discovering how an organization is performing and learning the very best processes that should be used.

Benchmarking is not a tactic used to generate information about whether purchasing staff meet requirements or attain goals. Neither is benchmarking an effort to discover what other hospitality organizations are doing, and to then replicate their practices. Instead, it is an effort to learn about the best ways to do things and to consider how these practices might be used by the organization to improve performance.

Key Term

Best practice   An activity or procedure that has been successful in another situation, and which might be the best way to do something in one's own organization.

Purchasing processes can be benchmarked by carefully analyzing how they are currently being done in one's organization and by learning how they are presently being undertaken by other organizations. Then processes can be revised, if necessary, to make them the best possible to reduce defects. A system to measure defects is developed, and the journey away from the current number of defects toward the desired lower number of defects can begin. In other words, benchmarking involves ongoing analysis and improvement.

For example, a restaurant may have a goal of **"zero defects"** in managing inventory to eliminate stockouts. However, there may be times when inventory levels are depleted (defects occur). What are the problems that cause these stockouts? What are practical ways to measure their effect upon the organization? How can they be corrected? These and related questions can be addressed only when benchmarking of the current inventory management procedures are undertaken.

There are three common types of benchmarking; each might be useful in determining some best practices for the purchasing function:

- *Internal benchmarking.* This is used to compare (measure) similar activities within an organization. Perhaps, for example, purchasing practices are being done differently in separate units of a hotel chain, or there are differences in the way purchasing activities are performed in different departments in the same property when a decentralized system is used.
- *External benchmarking.* This process involves analysis of external organizations to address questions such as "How do our competitors do it?" "Is the way they do it better than how we do it?" "What can we learn from studying our competitors?" It is likely that some organizations use more effective procurement tactics than do others. Why do some properties seem to operate more effectively (have fewer defects)? Today, outsourcing alternatives are increasingly being considered and used. What processes do these organizations use? How effective are they?
- *Functional benchmarking.* This involves the study of a specific process or function (e.g., procedures used for e-commerce by an organization well known for being on the "cutting edge" of this business process). Purchasers and other managers may visit a specific facility using state-of-the-art processes or one known to be "best in class." What they learn can, then, be helpful in decisions to continue, implement, or modify processes within their own organization.

As noted in Figure 23.9, the benchmarking process has seven basic steps. Let's review each of these steps:

- *Step 1: Determine what should be benchmarked.* Almost any purchasing activity, or indicator of a purchasing activity, can be benchmarked. Perhaps, for example, there are recurring problems such as excessive time required for specification development or make (do)–buy analysis or, alternatively, perhaps there are concerns about receiving practices. These and other physical activities related to purchasing can be benchmarked. Recall also our earlier discussion in this chapter about purchasing evaluation factors. Purchasers may wish to compare their organization's performance (specific ratios) with those experienced by other organizations. If so, index comparisons may be possible.
- *Step 2: Plan benchmarking procedures.* Steps involved in planning for the benchmarking process include determining benchmark outputs (what is to be measured?), the organization's own best processes, whether processes

Key Term

Zero defects A goal of no deviations from standards; there are no times when reasonable goals are not attained.

FIGURE 23.9 Basic Steps in Benchmarking Process

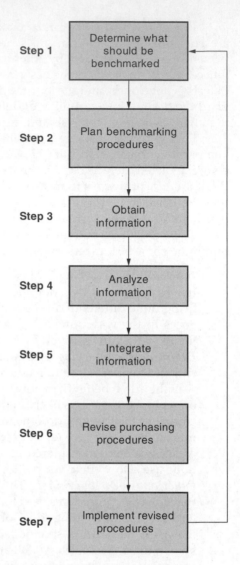

used by other organizations should be studied, and the appropriate data collection methods.

- *Step 3: Obtain information.* Purchasers will likely find much useful information in the trade press and in Internet searches applicable to the benchmarking topic. Successful managers, purchasing directors, and entire organizations may share information. Personal contacts can be helpful, and "clearing houses," such as professional associations and others interested in the discipline of procurement, may also be helpful.

- *Step 4: Analyze information.* Steps in this phase of benchmarking include determining the current competitive "gap" and projecting future performance levels. The objective is to help purchasers understand strengths of the processes used by their own organizations and by others and to assess their own performance against that of competitors. For example, purchasers might study and be well aware of their organization's product receiving procedures. These activities could be "researched" (what steps are suggested in relevant written resources?). Purchasers can also interview others and/or observe receiving procedures used by other organizations that may (or may not) be in the hospitality industry.

- *Step 5: Integrate information.* This step involves using information obtained as the basis for comparison with the processes used by the purchaser's organization.

The "numbers" tell only part of the story as the purchasing function is evaluated.

Getty Images, Inc.-Photodisc

- *Step 6: Revise purchasing procedures.*   Careful analysis and integration (Steps 4 and 5 above) may yield process improvement alternatives. If so, affected procedures should be revised accordingly.
- *Step 7: Implement revised procedures.*   Strategies and actions planned established in Step 6 should be implemented and periodically assessed to measure progress in achieving plans. This is the topic of the next section.

Figure 23.9 also indicates that the benchmarking process is cyclical. Revised procedures that are implemented as a result of the benchmarking process (Step 7) may, over time, require additional revision. Recall the point made at the beginning of this section: Hospitality organizations are on a never-ending journey of improvement. As this occurs, the need for benchmarking (Step 1) for further improvements may be necessary.

PURCHASING PROS NEED TO KNOW (23.6)

Purchasing pros know that successful benchmarking has four basic requirements:

1. A consistent commitment from top levels of management is required.
2. Purchasers must clearly understand exactly how procedures to be studied "work" in their own operation.
3. Purchasers must have a willingness to change and adapt: Benchmarking is not a process that helps to defend the status quo.
4. Purchasers should recognize that other organizations are constantly improving, and that customer requirements continually become more demanding. They recognize the need to look for leading-edge purchasing departments for their best practice studies.

Internet Purchasing Assistant (23.4)

Literally, millions of articles and other information about benchmarking are available on the Internet. Just type "benchmarking" into your favorite search engine. One excellent reference is the "Benchmarking Exchange," a network comprised of professionals in many different industries and businesses. To view this site, go to: www.benchnet.com

IMPLEMENTING PROCUREMENT IMPROVEMENT CHANGES

A primary reason to evaluate procurement is to identify how it might be improved. Failure to meet goals, decisions about operating changes to improve performance, and results of benchmarking activities may all prompt purchasing staff to revise and implement purchasing procedures. Purchasers, like other hospitality managers, must be knowledgeable about procedures to implement change.[2]

One of the obstacles that must frequently be overcome as changes are implemented relate to employee resistance to them. Staff members who are accustomed to doing something in a specific way may resist changes in standard operating procedures ("We have always done it this way!" "We have never done it that way!"). Staff members may be uncertain about how they will be affected by the change, and they may not want to take the time to learn "new ways of doing things." Also, affected staff members may be concerned about the closer coaching and supervision interactions that may be necessary as the change is implemented and evaluated. When this human nature to resist change is understood and addressed, purchasers are much more likely to be successful in their change efforts.

How can employee resistance to change be overcome? Hopefully, the purchaser has a history of involving employees in change processes and in explaining, defending, and justifying why it is necessary. If he or she has historically been "right" (the situation is "better" after the change than before it is made), the likelihood of "easy" change implementation is better ensured.

Purchasing managers may use the following tactics to reduce resistance to change:

- Involve employees in the decision-making process. A **participative management** style improves the quality of the decision-making process. It makes the implementation of corrective actions easier because the decisions made are "ours" rather than those of the purchasing manager.
- Inform affected employees in advance about changes that will impact them.
- Select an appropriate time to implement the change. Typically, "trying something new" during a busy work period or season may be counterproductive.
- Share past successes; review changes that have benefited the employees, the purchasing department, and the hospitality organization.
- Reward employees for sharing ideas in the decision-making process that benefit the department and its staff members.

PURCHASING PROS NEED TO KNOW (23.7)

Purchasing pros know that the increased use of technology has affected purchasing departments and the staff within them, perhaps more so than any other factor during the past ten years. Purchasers with many years of experience may have been initially employed without much, if any, experience with purchasing technology, and they may have since become very comfortable with manual purchasing systems. As these are replaced with their newer "high-tech" counterparts, anxieties and frustration may result. The tactics used (or not used) by those implementing system changes typically have a significant effect on the ease of implementation, and on the time required for staff members to adapt to new purchasing processes.

Key Term

Participative management   A leadership method of increasing the quality of the decision-making process by involving employees in the decision.

HIGH-TECH PURCHASING (23.1)

Answers to the question: "How successful are our procurement efforts, and how can they be improved?" can be facilitated with the use of technology. A wide range of tools that go beyond e-mail and teleconferencing are available and are increasingly used.

Chain organizations may use surveys that can be sent by e-mail or posted on an organization's intranet with subsequent electronic tabulation of survey responses. Wireless handheld devices and cell phone camcorders provide opportunities for real-time analysis that can identify potential issues applicable to purchasing goals and their evaluation.

Information about advances in procurement that can be integrated into planning activities can be generated with online electronic resources such as e-journals, e-books, and specialized databases. Individual group interviews can be conducted by e-mail, online discussions, real-time chat, and even video conferencing.

Electronic discussion forums permit evaluators to interact by grouping and storing messages in a way that encourages organized discussion. Project management software allows evaluators at different sites to schedule evaluation sessions, keep "on track" of progress, and meet required evaluation activities on time. Evaluation reports including recommendations for improvement can be electronically generated, revised, and disseminated.

Strategies for corrective action deemed necessary as a result of the evaluation can be shared electronically (and quickly) by members of groups in multiple units. Savvy purchasers know that their emphasis should be on ways to improve the evaluation process, and not to find ways to incorporate available technology that will "catch up" with their needs. However, as seen above, technology can assist with the communication and collaborative activities required for successful procurement evaluation.

Purchasing staff work with departmental processes daily, and their input to improving procedures can be very helpful. Time may be necessary after changes are implemented for minor problems to be corrected and to allow employees to gain the skills through experience that are required to perform work at required quality levels.

Purchasing professionals recognize that, regardless of how small a process revision may appear, the hospitality organization will improve as a result of any change that helps it to better meet its mission and goals. They recognize the critical importance of evaluation because they are aware of its benefits. They understand that evaluation is an ongoing process, and not one that is brought to their immediate attention only once every six or twelve months (or whenever a formalized evaluation process is required).

Purchasing managers also recognize the important role that their staff can play in helping to improve the purchasing process. For many improvement efforts, purchasing managers are really facilitators. After identifying a problem and mutually agreeing on the need for its resolution, they use a team approach when analyzing, taking corrective action, and implementing necessary changes.

Purchasing Resources on the Internet

In addition to the Web sites referenced in this chapter's "Internet Purchasing Assistant," the following sites provide detailed information to enhance your purchasing knowledge and skills.

Purchasing Resources on the Internet

Site	Information About
www.benchnet.com	Benchmarking practices and procedures
www.findarticles.com	Auditing purchasing activities (Enter "purchasing audits" in the site's search box)
www.pasba.com	Procurement and supply-chain benchmarking association

(continued)

Site	Information About
www.work911.com	Managing change (Click on "Change Management" at the home page)
www.businessballs.com	Managing organizational change (Click on "change management" on the margin's scrolling menu)
www.projectkickstart.com	Project planning—this is useful if one considers the procurement evaluation process to be an ongoing project.
www.about-goal-setting.com	Goal setting for businesses
www.mindtools.com	Problem-solving procedures that can address problems noted during purchasing evaluation (Click "problem solving" on the site's home page)
www.allbusiness.com	"Intelligent Customer" concept (Type "intelligent customer" in the site's search box)
www.q2000.com.au	Goal setting (At the home page, click on "search," and then type "goal setting" in the site's search box)

Key Terms

contribution
  margin *565*
variance *568*

full-time equivalent
  (FTE) *575*
allocation *576*

supplier base *578*
intelligent customer *579*
best practice *580*

zero defects *581*
participative
  management *584*

Think It Through

1. Assume that you are the director of purchasing for a large hotel and that the property's income statement indicates no significant problem areas. Revenues are on target for all revenue-producing departments, and their expenses along with those of support departments, including purchasing, are basically what was anticipated. In this instance, would you want to evaluate your department's activities for improvement purposes? Explain your response.

2. Assume that several financial, operational, and other goals were established for your purchasing department and, further, that subsequent evaluation indicated that these goals were not attained. How would you as the director of purchasing determine priorities for departmental improvements? Would you also consider additional goals beyond those that have yet to be addressed? Why or why not?

3. The chapter makes the statement that "Supplier-related problems are often caused by the purchasing department." Do you agree or disagree? Defend your answer.

4. The chapter introduces the concept that the hospitality organization should be an "intelligent customer." What does this mean? What role should the director of purchasing have in attempting to educate the organization's managers about purchasing responsibilities and, at the same time, to learn about the major duties of his or her peers in other departments?

5. Assume that you are responsible for purchasing in a hospitality organization that is implementing electronic systems for inventory management, ordering, and for interfacing purchasing information with the property's accounting system. Assume also that your organization had just recently (within the last several years) purchased the technology now being used that replaced manual procedures. How might you interact with department staff members who were in support of the new technology? Who are now resisting changes because "We just changed our system, and we should use it for a while?"

Team Fun

Top-level managers in a small restaurant chain believe that the organization will be improved if it practices the "basics" of a purchaser–supplier "partnership" with long-term suppliers with whom it has done business for several years. You and your team have been asked to suggest measurable goals against which purchasing activities can be evaluated. Three parameters applicable to each goal have been developed: It should be measurable, important, and attainable with a slight (stretch) effort. Goals should also address the primary relationship that the property desires with these "partner" suppliers.

Each team is assigned one task to help develop the purchasing goals:

1. The assignment of the first team is to suggest goals addressing the products provided by applicable suppliers.
2. The assignment of the second team is to suggest goals applicable to services that are desired from these suppliers.
3. The assignment of the third team is to suggest goals relevant to the information the property may require that it would like to receive from its suppliers as a value-added aspect of the relationship.

Each team should be prepared to provide an explanation about their suggested goals to the rest of the class. Suggestion: Each team might select several suppliers for specific products (e.g., meat items, restaurant operating supplies, and landscaping services).

Endnotes

1. Adapted from J. Ninemeier and J. Perdue, *Discovering Hospitality Operation: Careers in the World's Greatest Industry*, 2nd ed. Upper Saddle River, NJ: Pearson Education, Inc. 2008.

2. The remainder of this section is loosely based on J. Ninemeier and D. Hayes, *Restaurant Operations Management: Principles and Practices*. Upper Saddle River, NJ: Pearson Education, Inc. 2006. (See Chapter 16.)

INDEX